ANGER, VIOLENCE, AND POLITICS

Edited by

IVO K. FEIERABEND
ROSALIND L. FEIERABEND

San Diego State College

TED ROBERT GURR

Northwestern University

PRENTICE-HALL, INC., Englewood Cliffs, N.J.

ANGER, VIOLENCE, AND POLITICS

THEORIES AND RESEARCH

ANGER, VIOLENCE, AND POLITICS:
THEORIES AND RESEARCH

Edited by
Ivo K. Feierabend, Rosalind L. Feierabend, and Ted Robert Gurr

© 1972 by Prentice-Hall, Inc.
Englewood Cliffs, New Jersey

ISBN: C 13–036848–2   P 13–036830–X

Library of Congress Catalog Card Number: 70–152314

Printed in the United States of America

10   9   8   7   6   5   4   3   2   1

Prentice-Hall International, Inc., *London*
Prentice-Hall of Australia Pty. Ltd., *Sydney*
Prentice-Hall of Canada Ltd., *Toronto*
Prentice-Hall of India Private Limited, *New Delhi*
Prentice-Hall of Japan, Inc., *Tokyo*

CONTENTS

PREFACE

During the 1960's, studies exploring the nature, causes, and consequences of internal, civil strife assumed a new importance in the social sciences. Prior to that decade, theories of violence and aggression were generally fashioned by the psychologist to fit the individual, or were applied by the political scientist to conflicts between nations. Social theorists marveled at the intricately patterned structures and functions of orderly societies, and most seemed more inclined to describe and explain social order than to examine flux and social disarray.

In the United States, the relevance of civil strife was forcibly brought home by a violent decade. The tragic deaths of a president, a senator, and a civil rights leader, the spectacle of urban violence, the Black Revolution, antiwar protests and campus disorders—all have been responsible. In the contemporary world outside the United States, violence also seems endemic. In fact, the frequency and extent of internal violence have increased throughout the world since World War II, sharpening our awareness of the problems of civil conflict. We are not likely to forget, as students or citizens, how immediate are the sources of violence and how fateful an impact violence can have on daily life. There are seeds of violence in every man and woman, and in every society. The human bonds of which all societies are made are easily damaged but they are not easily healed. For all of these reasons, and many more, recent efforts to understand the nature of violence are not likely to be ephemeral.

Our immediate reactions to violence are personal and often intense: we may preach or pray, advocate or condemn. The approach taken by social science, however, seeks a clear, dispassionate understanding of the social and human circumstances that lead to violence, and a similar comprehension of its effects. This book suggests some ways that such understanding can be achieved. We have sought to present a consistent set of theoretical and empirical studies on civil violence, most of them recent and several of them previously unpublished. The selections show how social discontent arises and the kinds of social circumstances that determine its expression and effects. Other explanations of civil violence focus on group conflict and on the tactical effects of violence. We think these approaches are consistent with "social discontent" explanations, and some readings which make use of these theories are included in this volume, especially in the case studies of Part III. We are convinced, however, that general explanations of political violence must consider closely the social origins and nature of the collective grievances that make men willing and eager to commit violence. This conviction is reflected in our choice of articles. In their entirety, these selections should give the reader some understanding of the state of knowledge and systematic research on violence, and suggest further research.

One subject the readings do not treat is violence in the United States, since there already exist many excellent books and articles on that topic.[1] Moreover, the United States is only one of more than 100 contemporary nations, many of which show a far higher level of internal conflict than does this country. The studies selected are general and comparative, drawing

on many nations for evidence and proposing theories that should be applicable to all societies. Together they address two general questions: What are the patterns of internal conflict in the world today? and, What are the roots of these conflicts whereby some groups and some countries experience intense political violence whereas others do not? We believe that the reader who understands these issues will acquire a perspective on violence in America that he could never gain by looking only at the United States.

We do not maintain that the study of violence and revolution is the province of only one academic discipline—which is abundantly evident in our selections. The contributors represent and use the concepts and methods of political science, psychology, sociology, history, anthropology, and psychiatry. The reader whose formal academic training is restricted largely to only one of these fields will be pleasantly surprised to find how understandable and compatible are the approaches of all these disciplines when they are applied to a single issue.

The book is organized in three parts. Part I consists of theoretical analyses, Part II quantitative, comparative studies, and Part III case studies.[2] However, this tripartite structure does not imply that theory and empirical practice are divided. The empirical findings reported in Parts II and III either bear directly on the theories set out in Part I or provide qualifications of them. The last part of the book is an Appendix, which offers a manual of simple techniques of statistical analysis. These will help the student understand some of the methods used in the selections and encourage him to make his own explorations.

The studies in Part I propose theoretical frameworks, sets of propositions

---

[1] Some recent collections of studies are Hugh Davis Graham and Ted Robert Gurr, eds., *The History of Violence in America* (New York: Bantam Books and Praeger, 1969); Allen D. Grimshaw, ed., *Racial Violence in the United States* (Chicago: Aldine, 1969); Louis H. Masotti and Don R. Bowen, eds., *Riots and Rebellion: Civil Violence in the Urban Community* (Beverly Hills, Calif.: Sage Publications, 1968); and Jerome H. Skolnick, *The Politics of Protest* (New York: Ballentine, 1969).

[2] Ivo K. and Rosalind L. Feierabend bear primary responsibility for Parts I and II, and Ted Robert Gurr for Part III.

and hypotheses, and specific variables that, according to their authors, account for violent political behavior within nations. These selections are *empirical* theories, since their formulations may be tested empirically. The theoretical approaches offer explanations in terms of motivational, psychological tensions and structural, sociological processes. The different constructs are bridged, however, by the more general concept of social discontent or deprivation, which explicitly or implicitly seems common to them all. Most of the theories presented here agree that some kind of widespread psychological conflict or malaise, caused by the vagaries of social systems, provides the potential for political violence. A number of other social conditions and dynamics are said to act on this potential, either to release, channel or repress it.

Part II reports cross-national studies in which large numbers of nations are analyzed, measured, and compared on various dimensions of politically violent behavior. As many as 114 and as few as 18 nations are scrutinized in these attempts to discover global or regional patterns of internal strife in the mid twentieth century. The same nations also are measured on a variety of social, economic, psychological, and transactional characteristics. Levels and rates of socioeconomic development, literacy, urbanization, coerciveness of government, governmental legitimacy, and characteristics of political organization are among the many specific variables examined. Quantitative techniques are used to test whether and how closely the cross-national differences in political violence depend upon measured social and ecological conditions. The findings of these studies not only describe the internally violent conditions of the world in which we live, but show what kinds of conditions are most closely related to violence in what kinds of nations. In so doing, the studies provide tests of some of the theories proposed in Part I.

The contributions to Part III focus on the causes and characteristics of violence within particular nations. These case studies provide a kind of understanding that is not easily conveyed by general comparative studies. The single case best illustrates how a constellation of variables interacts to lead to a specific violent or nonviolent outcome. The case studies represent various modes of revolutionary, conspiratorial, and riotous actions in many regions of the world; and one describes a nonviolent reform movement. Some of these studies were designed to test how well the theories of Part I explain particular situations, whereas others suggest additional kinds of variables and hypotheses that ought to be considered in general theories.

The Appendix presents a manual of simple techniques of statistical analysis, which so far as we know is an innovation in collections of readings. There are far too few answers to the "what," "when," "where," and "why" questions of political violence, and we wish to encourage students to take part in the exciting business of seeking explanations. We hope the reader will use the techniques presented in the Appendix to try his hand at analyses using some of the data reported in the studies of Parts II and III, or new data, or some combination of the two. The reported studies can usefully be replicated; they are not free of errors, nor are their data fully analyzed or analyzed by alternative techniques. The student who works with these data may well make discoveries of his own.

Briefly, we have tried to present in this book a map of contemporary social science explorations of political violence, those in which theories are tested empirically in cross-national analyses and in case studies. We introduce the reader to a particular body of empirical theory, based on the concept of social discontent, and to the kinds of cross-national data and case study evidence which supports this approach. The student thus should be able to see how, through systematic exploration, social scientists can establish and add to a body of knowledge that explains the nature and occurrence of political violence. The student is also provided with some of the conceptual and statistical tools that are needed for taking part in that exploration. This formal, quantitative approach may not appeal to those who are impatient to act on immediate social issues. In a world that may be even more turbulent in the 1970's than it was a decade or two ago, however, we hope to convince the reader of the value of testing hunches and hypotheses. We also hope to persuade him that the best guide to understanding and action is theory which has some confirmation in fact.

I. K. F.
R. L. F.
T. R. G.

CONTRIBUTORS

THEODORE ABEL,
a native of Poland, taught at Columbia University from 1929 to 1951 and was Chairman of the Department of Sociology at Hunter College from 1950 to 1967. More recently he has been Visiting Professor of Sociology at Notre Dame University and the University of New Mexico. In addition to his study of *The Nazi Movement* he is the author of *Systematic Sociology in Germany* (2d ed., 1966) and *The Foundation of Sociological Theory* (1970).

DOUGLAS P. BWY
is Associate Professor of Political Science at the University of Hawaii. He received his PhD at Northwestern University and has also taught at Case Western Reserve University. His writings reflect his interest in the Latin American area and in the analysis of social conflict.

JAMES C. DAVIES
is Professor of Political Science at the University of Oregon. He is the author of *Human Nature and Politics* and the editor of *When Men Revolt and Why*, as well as of articles on the conditions which breed revolution. He received his PhD at the University of California, Berkeley.

HARRY ECKSTEIN
is Professor of Politics at Princeton University. He received his education at Harvard University. He is the author of *Division and Cohesion in Democracy* and editor of *Internal War*. He has served as editor of *World Politics* and was among the first to initiate a collection of cross-national data on political unrest.

IVO K. FEIERABEND
is Professor of Political Science at San Diego State College. He received his PhD at Yale University, and has concentrated mainly on the cross-national

analysis of political violence. He has co-authored many articles, with Rosalind L. Feierabend and Betty A. Nesvold, on the topic of political aggression and has served as consultant to the National Commission on the Causes and Prevention of Violence. He is co-director of a research project on the systemic conditions of political aggression which has collected data on world-wide incidents of political violence in the post World War II era.

ROSALIND L. FEIERABEND

is Professor of Psychology at San Diego State College. She took her PhD in social psychology at Yale University, where she was associated with the attitude change project of Carl Hovland. Together with Ivo K. Feierabend, she is engaged in the application of psychological theory to the cross-national analysis of political violence. The Feierabends' studies were awarded the Socio-Psychological Prize of the American Association for the Advancement of Science.

PAUL FRIEDRICH

is Professor of Anthropology and Linguistics at the University of Chicago. He has done extensive fieldwork in India as well as among Mexican peasants.

JOHAN GALTUNG

is Professor of Sociology at the University of Oslo and founder and editor of the *Journal of Peace Research*. He has served as director of the International Peace Research Institute, Oslo, where he is presently director of research. He is the author of numerous articles on the topic of aggression, violence and conflict.

TED ROBERT GURR

is Associate Professor of Political Science at Northwestern University. He received his B. A. in psychology from Reed College (1957) and did graduate study at the Woodrow Wilson School of Public and International Affairs at Princeton University. He holds a PhD in political science from New York University (1965). Before joining the Northwestern faculty, Professor Gurr did post-doctoral research and taught at Princeton University from 1965 to 1969. His books include *Politimetrics: An Introduction to Quantitative Macropolitics* (Prentice-Hall, 1972); *Why Men Rebel*, for which he won the Woodrow Wilson Award for the outstanding book in Political Science for 1970; and *Violence in America: Historical and Comparative Perspectives* with Hugh Davis Graham (National Commission on the Causes and Prevention of Violence, 1969).

MANUS MIDLARSKY

is Assistant Professor of Political Science at the University of Colorado. He took his PhD at Northwestern University and is the author of various articles on the topic of revolution

BETTY A. NESVOLD

is Associate Professor of Political Science at San Diego State College. She received her PhD at the University of Minnesota and has concentrated on the cross-national analysis of political violence. She is co-editor of *Macro-Quantitative Analysis* and is co-director, with the Feierabends, of the research project on political unrest.

JAMES PAYNE

is Associate Professor of Political Science at Johns Hopkins University's School of Advanced International Studies. Publications based on his fieldwork in Latin America include *Labor and Politics in Peru: The System of Political Bargaining* (1966) and *Patterns of Conflict in Colombia* (1968).

BRUCE M. RUSSETT

is Professor of Political Science at Yale University, where he also took his PhD degree. He has served as Director of the Yale Political Data Program and is first author of the *World Handbook of Political and Social Indicators*. His research interests are primarily concentrated on international politics and he has written several books in this area and on the United Nations.

ANTHONY J. RUSSO, JR.

has most recently been a senior staff member of Social Engineering Technology in Los Angeles. He received his graduate degree at the Woodrow Wilson School of Public and International Affairs, Princeton University, in 1964 and was a member of the staff of the RAND Corporation in South Vietnam and the United States until 1969. Vietnam has been one of his primary research interests.

DAVID C. SCHWARTZ

is Associate Professor of Political Science at Rutgers University. He received his PhD at Massachusetts Institute of Technology and served on the faculty at the University of Pennsylvania, where he was connected with the Foreign Policy Research Institute. He is the author of *Political Alienation and Political Behavior*, which applies psychological theories of conflict to political action.

JOHN E. SCHWARZ

is Assistant Professor of Political Science at the University of Minnesota. He did fieldwork on the Scottish nationalist movement in 1968 and his current research interests include the separatist movements of Brittany and Quebec. He has also published in the areas of coalition maintenance and legislative behavior.

RAYMOND TANTER

is Professor of Political Science at the University of Michigan. He received his PhD at Indiana University and has taught at Northwestern and Stanford Universities. He is interested in problems of international conflict and has written extensively in that area as well as on the topic of revolution and internal conflict. Together with Rudolph Rummel, he has established a collection of data on events of internal and external conflict.

CHARLES TILLY

is Professor of Sociology and History at the University of Michigan. For a number of years he has been engaged in an in-depth study of the evolution of collective violence in European countries, especially France, under the impact of the urbanization and industrialization of the nineteenth and twentieth centuries. His many books and articles include *The Vendée* (1964) and, with James Rule, *Measuring Political Upheaval* (1965).

BRYANT WEDGE,

a psychiatrist, has done extensive research on psychological aspects of politics. In 1968–69 he was Research Associate at the Edward R. Murrow Center of Public Diplomacy, Fletcher School of Law and Diplomacy, Tufts University. For a number of years he also has been head of the Institute for the Study of National Behavior.

ANN RUTH WILLNER

is Professor of Political Science at the University of Kansas. She has done extensive fieldwork in Indonesia and elsewhere and is the author of *Charismatic Political Leadership: A Theory* (1968).

ANGER,
VIOLENCE,
AND
POLITICS

THEORIES

OF

REVOLUTION

Theories of revolution, political violence, and instability span the history of Western political thought. Aristotle felt that inequalities of wealth and power were at the root of political instability; John of Salisbury justified tyrannicide; Machiavelli unhesitatingly counseled violence to his Prince; Marx, in the last century, predicted revolution, and Marxists today are still the leading advocates of violent change. Despite this lengthy tradition, the theoretical section of this volume does not deal with the breadth and depth of age-old speculations. Rather, it focuses exclusively on contributions drawn from contemporary behavioral science, and its emphasis lies with empirical theory.

The first selection, by Harry Eckstein, "On the Etiology of Internal Wars," provides a framework for examining the wide panorama of approaches to the study of revolution. It is not, in itself, a statement of comprehensive theory, although it abounds in insights and hypotheses. But it does provide an understanding of the indispensable component parts which any theory must include. It carves out relevant social domains for study, warns of irrelevancies and overemphases, and points to sets of variables that must be considered in the search for an etiology (causation) of internal war. The article orients the reader in the maze of social variables relevant to the study of revolutionary behavior.

Eckstein explores the definition of internal war and concludes that it consists of a class of distinct political behaviors. Hence it is a proper subject matter for systematic inquiry. Beyond definition, Eckstein distinguishes the domain of insurgents from that of incumbents, pointing out that both need the attention of the analyst. His distinction between the *precondi-*

tions and the *precipitants* of internal war is a crucial one, for these terms refer to distinct sets of variables. The preconditions of internal war are the deep social roots of revolution, the gathering of the revolutionary potential, whereas the precipitants of internal war are the mechanisms which trigger this energy into a revolutionary outburst.

Most of the selections in this section are concerned with the preconditions of violence, rather than with the precipitants. The J-curve hypothesis of James C. Davies stipulates a set of socioeconomic preconditions for revolutionary behavior; political alienation for David C. Schwartz, and relative deprivation for Ted Robert Gurr, indicate psychological preconditions. Social status discrepancy, in Johan Galtung's formulation, is a sociological precondition, as is inconsistency of authority patterns for Eckstein, in his second selection. Similarly, the hypotheses presented by Ivo and Rosalind Feierabend and Betty A. Nesvold generalize about a series of socioeconomic preconditions to violence. Eckstein feels that the student of internal war should concentrate on the preconditions; in his view, these preconditions are more fundamental than the precipitants, and they are generally ascertainable in social and political settings. The precipitants often have the character of fortuitous and accidental events that cannot be anticipated, and this reduces their explanatory power and predictive value.

A somewhat different but related distinction is made by Gurr in "Psychological Factors in Civil Violence." Drawing from psychological theory, Gurr speaks of the *instigating* and *mediating variables* that determine the occurrence of civil strife. Instigating variables are the social-psycho-logical preconditions that provide the energy for violence; mediating variables, the environmental and social conditions that determine the outcome of that energy by inhibiting, facilitating, or rechanneling its expression.

Another distinction drawn by Eckstein is that between structural and behavioral variables or, to give them a different name, between sociological and psychological variables. Structural variables point to objective social circumstances and processes, institutions, and economic, political, and environmental conditions. Are these of prime importance in the analysis of internal war? Or are behavioral variables—the psychological motivations of a restless people, their perceptions, collective hopes, expectations, and frustrations, and the emotional states of discontent, anxiety or anger—more important? The emphasis on one set of variables rather than the other reflects the bias of the sociologist, on the one hand, and the psychologist, on the other. Eckstein feels that no human behavior, individual or collective, can be fully understood without reference to human motivation. However, it would be erroneous to make a dichotomy or to assert a contradiction between the two. Revolutionary behavior, like any other, is motivated; hence, psychological variables are relevant. Yet the structural, objective circumstances of the social condition must not be forgotten. It is of paramount importance that the social scientist know the kinds of economic circumstances, social relationships, political regimes and policies, and international relations that create the revolutionary state of mind. These are the grounds on which to argue the relevance of both psychological and structural variables, for they complement each other in providing a fuller understanding of social reality.

In these selections, Gurr's instigating variables refer primarily to the motivational, psychological variables, and his mediating variables take into account many aspects of social structures. Schwartz is also basically concerned with human motivation. Davies, however, in postulating the J-curve of revolutionary development, stresses the consequences of changes in societal variables; and the same concern can be seen in the selections by Galtung, the Feierabends and Nesvold, and the second article by Eckstein. None of these authors are oblivious to human motivation. Rather, they point to those objective conditions and changes within political, economic, and social systems that are likely to predispose the human psyche to political violence.

Two selections owe a heavy debt to psychological theory: Gurr's article is based on the frustration-aggression hypothesis and Schwartz's on conflict theory. The authors mold these theories specifically to political violence, transforming individual psychological precepts into social concepts and settings. Gurr postulates that the most generalized social-psychological precondition of civil strife is people's perception of a discrepancy between social value expectations and value capabilities, which he calls *relative deprivation*. In simplified terms, relative deprivation is the discrepancy between what people think they are justifiably entitled to and what they think they actually can obtain. The Feierabends and Nesvold use a similar concept of *systemic frustration*, defined as the ratio of social wants to social satisfactions. In both cases the fundamental recognition is that collective aggression is the result of thwarting or arbitrarily depriving people in their attempts to satisfy their needs and aspirations.

This is the fundamental insight of the frustration-aggression hypothesis. In commonsense terms, one can say that social discontent gives rise to anger, which in turn results in the expression of political violence.

Gurr does not rest with this generalized proposition. His article is an attempt to construct a comprehensive, coherent, and parsimonious theoretical model. Its comprehensive nature may be seen in the several mediating variables introduced, conditions that either facilitate or obstruct the expression of the revolutionary potential which is generated by relative deprivation. They also determine the particular form of violence and its specific targets or victims. Among the political considerations introduced into the discussion are the use of force and repression by the government in power, the perceived legitimacy of the regime, and the political culture of the society (see the figure on p. 37).

Schwartz seemingly postulates a different, although equally psychological, approach. For him, political alienation precedes the revolutionary outburst. Political alienation itself results from a psychological conflict between an individual's own value hierarchy and the contradictory values that he perceives to be operative in the political system. In other words, psychological conflict occurs when the values that guide the behavior of the regime are perceived by the citizens as violating their own individual values. Let us note in particular that the individual in most modern societies not only values his own political beliefs but also identifies with his country. This may be illustrated by the dilemma of the true patriot who suddenly realizes that his country is in the wrong. What is he to do? Reject his country or reject his beliefs? Be a traitor to his country or a traitor to his conscience?

Certain other alternatives also present themselves. He can hope that the society will reform its ways. Or perhaps he can ignore the dilemma, at least for a while. Schwartz specifies the kinds of attitudes and reactions that characterize each of eight stages in his model of psychological alienation leading to revolutionary behavior.

Each of these psychological models may best explain a different set of violent occurrences. The model of relative deprivation, for example, is most clearly applicable today primarily to the underdeveloped countries of the world. These nations experience the revolution of rising aspirations and expectations whereby expectations consistently outstrip achievements (see pp. 117-118). The psychological conflict model, however, may better explain student unrest in the United States, where radical students qualify as a deprived stratum of society only in the sense that they perceive society as violating some of their values. And the Black Revolution may well be triggered by both mechanisms.

However, it would be a mistake to put the two psychological theories into too sharp a juxtaposition and to view them as entirely unrelated insights. The alienated person must become angry before he engages in political violence. And a prolonged sense of social discontent will surely lead to widespread political alienation within the society. More fundamentally, it is possible to say that an individual, a social stratum, or an entire society in conflict is in a state of systemic frustration, defined by the Feierabends as the thwarting of social goals, or the blocking of a drive toward social aspirations, or the withholding of social values. This blocking may be external or internal: external barriers are those restrictions imposed on the individual by his environment, such as

a low level of socioeconomic achievement within his society, whereas internal barriers are those that arise when one goal or drive or aspiration is blocked by another incompatible value or goal. An example is the psychic conflict of a patriotic pacifist who is caught between his moral convictions (the goal of nonviolence) and his sense of obligation to a nation that asks him to serve in the military (the goal of national defense). Thus, while the concepts of conflict, inconsistency, and incongruence undoubtedly add to the notion of revolutionary preconditions, they may also be fitted within the broader context of systemic frustration.

Other psychological variables related to violence also can be subsumed under the notions of deprivation and frustration. In the Feierabend and Nesvold study, for example, two such variables are briefly mentioned: uncertainty regarding value expectations and fear of the future. Both circumstances may be understood to be anxiety-provoking situations. According to this formulation, it is not only his present misfortunes which trouble man, but also his anticipation of impending disaster or, alternatively, complete uncertainty of expectations. Similarly, underlying Eckstein's discussion of authority patterns in "A Theory of Stable Democracy" is the assumption that a lack of congruence within social units gives the members feelings of strain, dissonance, or anomie. These states of mind are frustrating and thus may contribute directly to the impetus to violence.

Some of the selections put considerable emphasis on structural variables. Although it is a recent contribution to the literature, James C. Davies' work has already achieved the status of a classic statement. Davies postulates that a J-curve of social development is conducive to revolutionary violence. His hypothesis is that if within the life of a society a continuous and prolonged era of social improvement (creating high and firm expectations of continued progress) is interrupted by a sudden, sharp reversal (the J-curve), an intolerable gap between expected and actual need-satisfaction will ensue (relative deprivation or systemic frustration). Hence, a revolutionary outbreak is the likely consequence of the J-curve of development.

In the article by the Feierabends and Nesvold, a variety of patterns of social change are seen as producing systemic frustration, in the form of a discrepancy between wants and satisfactions, aspirations, expectations, and achievements. In addition to Davies' J-curve pattern of change, these authors postulate that any sudden or rapid improvement, or deterioration, in socioeconomic conditions may give an unrealistic impetus to expectations, leaving them unmatched by social achievements. The model derived from work by Victor LeVine, and referred to in this article, also fits the same general theoretical formulation. In this case, unrealistic expectations pinned to the occurrence of some future event, such as independent status for a former colony, inevitably cause disappointment. In the most generalized statement of the Feierabend and Nesvold formulation, any abrupt change in social conditions is likely to create a gap between expectations and achievements and to produce violence in its wake.

Two selections point to yet another structural source of political violence: inconsistency in social institutions. Johan Galtung, in "A Structural Theory of Aggression," identifies a particular patterning of social stratification as being responsible for aggression. The deprived, or lowest stratum in society (called the "underdogs"), and the privileged, upper stratum (called the "top dogs") are, in Galtung's view, the members of society least likely to rebel. The underdog, in his absolute deprivation, does not expect improvement, and the top dog already has attained the satisfactions which society has to offer. It is the strata in between, which in some ways resemble the underdogs and in other ways the top dogs, that are dissatisfied and provide the psychological preconditions for rebellion. In Galtung's hypothesis, the uplifting result of limited achievement in one or two social domains makes for high value expectations in all areas. If these go unmatched by equally high value capabilities, a constantly galling source of dissatisfaction plagues the individual.

A further insight, also based on inconsistency in societal institutions, is provided by Eckstein in his selection, "A Theory of Stable Democracy." The author sees conflicting and incongruent authority patterns among social institutions as providing the populace with contradictory role expectations and behavioral commands, thus creating a sense of social strain and anomie. According to Eckstein, a society with highly homogeneous authority patterns is apt to have an effective, stable government, but a political and social culture in which one institution, such as the family, is highly authoritarian and another, the government, is basically democratic, will place great strain on individual adjustment. Also, the more salient the two institutions are for the individual, the greater will be the strain produced by their incongruence. Robert LeVine (discussed briefly in the aricle by the Feierabends and Nesvold) also points to a social situation in which anxiety, ambivalence, and uncertainty of expectations are endemic. LeVine sees this as the result of conflicting policies carried out within the same political system. Thus, like Galtung, both of these authors stress structural inconsistency as a source of political turmoil. Eckstein emphasizes inconsistency of socialization patterns toward authority; LeVine, inconsistency in the use of repressive force or colonial policies by the government in power.

The final article of the section, "Social Change and Political Violence: Cross-National Patterns," seeks the sources of violence in the vast and rapid social change of the modernization process. Here a variety of change patterns are considered, each of which may breed political aggression, based either on inconsistency between competing goals or on a gap between aspirations/expectations and achievements. The Feierabends and Nesvold point to the height of the transitional process as the period most likely to generate both types of frustration.

It must be pointed out that these structural models are not in competition with one another and their basic insights are not contradictory. The social dynamics which they describe may operate simultaneously within any given society or separately in different societies. Although they are incomplete, the combined insights of these works provide a fairly coherent theoretical framework. If concerned voices sometimes decry the lack of true theory in political science, the area of political violence may be one of the first to offer a corrective. The reader may also be stimulated to the formulation of additional hypotheses regarding the genesis of violence. Since the brevity of this section prevents inclusion of many important contributions to a theory of political violence, the student is referred to additional selections below.

It must also be stressed that the frustration-aggression hypothesis is not the only explanatory concept dealing with violence. At least three additional insights also have wide currency (see Gurr, pp. 33-34). The first is the notion that violence results from the instinctual, biological nature of man. The second, quite opposite view, is that violent behavior is learned in much the same fashion as other forms of human response. The final insight argues for man's rationality: violence is seen as a calculated strategy for achieving desired ends.

These insights lead to theoretical formulations and conclusions not necessarily identical with those presented in this volume. The emphasis on frustration theories in the articles selected for this reader represents both the interests of the editors and the fact that more empirical research on political violence, especially cross-national research, has been generated by frustration theory than by any other approach.

Suggested Readings

Berkowitz, Leonard. *Aggression: A Social Psychological Analysis.* New York: McGraw-Hill Book Company, 1962.

Boulding, Kenneth E. *Conflict and Defense.* New York: Harper & Row, Publishers, 1962.

Brinton, Crane. *The Anatomy of Revolution.* New York: W. W. Norton & Company, Inc., 1938.

Coser, Lewis. *The Functions of Social Conflict.* New York: The Free Press, 1954.

Dollard, J., L. W. Doob, N. E. Miller, O. H. Mowrer, and R. R. Sears. *Frustration and Aggression.* New Haven: Yale University Press, 1939.

Eckstein, Harry, ed. *Internal War: Problems and Approaches.* New York: The Free Press, 1966.

Edwards, Lyford P. *The Natural History of Revolution.* Chicago: The University of Chicago Press, 1927.

Friedrich, Carl J., ed., *Revolution*. New York: Atherton Press, 1966.

Gurr, Ted R. *Why Men Rebel*. Princeton: Princeton University Press, 1970.

Johnson, Chalmers. *Revolution and the Social System*, Stanford: The Hoover Institute on War, Revolution, and Peace, Stanford University, 1964.

LeVine, Robert A. "Anti-European Violence in Africa: A Comparative Analysis," *Journal of Conflict Resolution,* III, No. 4 (December, 1959), 420–29.

Lorenz, Konrad. *On Aggression*. New York: Harcourt Brace Jovanovich, Inc., 1966.

Nieburg, H. L. *Political Violence: The Behavioral Process*. New York: St. Martin's Press, 1969.

Pettee, Ceorge. *The Process of Revolution*. New York: Harper, 1938.

Schelling, Thomas C. *The Strategy of Conflict*. Cambridge, Mass.: Harvard University Press, 1960.

ON THE ETIOLOGY OF INTERNAL WARS

Harry Eckstein

The term "internal war" denotes any resort to violence within a political order to change its constitution, rulers, or policies.[1] It is not a new concept; distinctions between external and internal war (*guerre extérieure* and *guerre intérieure*) were made already in the nineteenth century by writers on political violence.[2] Nor does it mean quite the same thing as certain more commonly used terms, such as revolution, civil war, revolt, rebellion, uprising, guerrilla warfare, mutiny, *jacquerie*,

[1] Elsewhere I have used more cumbersome specifications for the term, holding that internal war is "a kind of social force that is exerted in the process of political competition, deviating from previously shared social norms, 'warlike' in character (that is, conducted practically without mutually observed normative rules), and involving the serious disruption of settled institutional patterns." *Internal War: Problems and Approaches* (New York, 1964), 12. The differences between the two formulations are due to the fact that here I am defining a term, while in the other essay I was delimiting a theoretical subject. (For what I mean by delimiting a theoretical subject, see *ibid.*, 8-11).
I am grateful to the Center of International Studies at Princeton University for supporting the work that went into this study as part of a wide-ranging set of inquiries into internal war. The Center's internal war studies, in turn, have been supported by grants from the Carnegie Foundation. Another, very different, version of the paper was published in a report prepared by the Research Group in Psychology and the Social Sciences, Smithsonian Institution, Washington, D.C., *Social Science Research and National Security* (government circulation only).

[2] For example, in Pierre Kropotkin, *Paroles d'un révolté*, ed. by Elisée Reclus (Paris, not dated, but circa 1885). The term was used by Count Fersen as early as 1790 and occurs also in the writings of Sismondi and the Federalist Papers.

coup d'état, terrorism, or insurrection. It stands for the genus of which the others are species.

Using the generic concept alongside, or even in place of, the more specific terms is justifiable on several grounds. Most obviously, all cases of internal war do have common features, however much they differ in detail. All involve the use of violence to achieve purposes which can also be achieved without violence. All indicate a breakdown of some dimension in legitimate political order as well as the existence of collective frustration and aggression in a population. All presuppose certain capabilities for violence by those who make the internal war and a certain incapacity for preventing violence among those on whom it is made. All tend to scar societies deeply and to prevent the formation of consensus indefinitely. There is, consequently, at least a possibility that general theories about internal war may be discovered— general theories which may also help to solve problems posed by specific instances.

Another justification for grouping internal wars in a single universe is that actual instances of internal war often combine different types of violence, in space and time. Guerrilla warfare in one area may be combined with terrorism in another; it may be preceded by insurrections and develop into full-scale civil war, or culminate in a mere *coup d'état*. Indeed the large-scale and prolonged instances of internal war that we generally call revolutions are notable chiefly for the fact that they combine, in strikingly similar sequences, many different types of violence.[3] To focus analysis from the outset on particular species

of internal war therefore makes it necessary to abstract from actual internal wars occurrences which may not in fact be strictly separable. This may be fine for working out abstract theories, but will not do for developing theories closely relevant to historical (i.e., concrete) cases in all their complexity.

A third justification for studying internal wars generically is furnished by the very limited results so far obtained in comparative historical studies of revolutions, particularly the pre-war studies of L. P. Edwards, Crane Brinton, and George S. Pettee, and the more recent study of Hannah Arendt.[4] These studies deal only with the so-called Great Revolutions of history—conspicuous and much-studied disturbances that occurred in relatively advanced, mildly autocratic, western societies, between 1640 and 1917. Consequently, they seem to say little that is reliable about, or even relevant to, much of the political violence of our more far-flung and variegated world, or of pre-modern times, or, for that matter, of the period they cover. They draw mammoth inferences from very few cases; and they ignore not only the vast spectrum of *coups*, *Putsches*, uprisings, riots, and so forth, but also Mr. Hobsbawm's

[3] "The [French] Revolution is a series of shocks, each shock displacing power from Right to Left, from larger groups, to smaller and more determined groups, each shock taking on more and more the aspect of a *coup d'état*, less and

less that of a widespread, spontaneous outbreak of the people, until finally, in a commonplace *coup d'état* hardly worthy of a good operetta, power comes to rest in the hands of the dictator Bonaparte." Crane Brinton, *A Decade of Revolution, 1789–1799* (New York, 1934), 1. This inspired characterization of the French Revolution might well serve as a rudimentary developmental model for any internal war that begins in large-scale, mainly spontaneous, popular violence.

[4] L. P. Edwards, *The Natural History of Revolutions* (Chicago, 1927); Crane Brinton, *The Anatomy of Revolution* (New York, 1958— first published 1938); George S. Pettee, *The Process of Revolution* (New York, 1938); Hannah Arendt, *On Revolution* (New York, 1963).

hero, the "primitive rebel," once so important, and again come to the center of affairs.[5] Thus, they are neither very "scientific" nor very historical. A more extensive view of the subject should yield not only knowledge more relevant to many particular cases but generalizations more trustworthy, by sheer weight of numbers, for the cases covered in the classic comparative histories. Pettee does say that by studying the more egregious cases he intends to illuminate all the rest—but he never does, and one doubts that he can.

Finally, the terminologies presently used to distinguish types of internal war vary greatly, are generally ambiguous, often define overlapping phenomena or phenomena difficult to distinguish in practice, and rarely based on clearly discernible analytical needs. For few phenomena do social science, history, and conventional language offer so various and vague a vocabulary....

. . .

For all of these reasons it can do no harm and might do much good to consider internal wars as all of a piece at the beginning of inquiry and to introduce distinctions only as they become necessary or advisable. In this way, the possibilities of developing general theories are increased, as is the likelihood that the distinctions made will be important and precise. In any event, that is how I shall proceed here, showing at the end how a general theory about the genus "internal war" can be adapted to give an account of special cases.

The Problem of Etiology

The theoretical issues raised by internal wars can be classified according to the phases through which such wars pass. They include problems about their preconditions, the way they can be effectively waged, the courses they tend to take, the outcomes they tend to have, and their long-run effects on society.

Curiously enough, the later the phase, the less there is to read about the issues involved. Despite the protracted normative argument between pro-revolutionaries and anti-revolutionaries, initiated by Paine and Burke, almost nothing careful and systematic has been written about the long-run social effects of internal wars, least of all perhaps about some of the most poignant and practical problems they raise: how political legitimacy and social harmony may be restored after violent disruption, what makes internal wars acute or chronic, and what the comparative costs (and probabilities) are of revolutionary and evolutionary transformations. Little more is available on the determinants of success or failure in internal wars. A fair amount has been written about the dynamic processes of revolutions, above all in the comparative historical studies already mentioned and in a very few more recent books, like Crozier's *The Rebels*.[6] But in regard to etiology, to "causes," we are absolutely inundated with print.

This abundance of etiological studies is not, however, an unmixed blessing. If studying other aspects of internal wars poses the basic problem of thinking of theoretical possibilities, studying their etiology poses a difficulty equally great: how to choose among a rare abundance of hypotheses which cannot all be equally valid nor all be readily combined. This problem exists because most propositions about the causes of internal wars have

[5] E. J. Hobsbawm, *Primitive Rebels* (London, 1960).

[6] Brian Crozier, *The Rebels: A Study of Post-War Insurrections* (London, 1960), Parts III-V and Postlude.

been developed in historical studies of particular cases (or very limited numbers of cases) rather than in broadly comparative, let alone genuinely social-scientific, studies. In historical case-studies one is likely to attach significance to any aspect of prerevolutionary society that one intuits to be significant, and so long as one does not conjure up data out of nothing one's hypotheses cannot be invalidated on the basis of the case in question.

That most studied of all internal wars, the French Revolution, provides a case in point—as well as examples in abundance of the many social, personal, and environmental forces to which the occurrence of internal wars might be attributed. Scarcely anything in the French *ancien régime* has not been blamed, by one writer or another, for the revolution, and all of their interpretations, however contradictory, are based on solid facts. . . .

.   .   .

We could take other internal wars and arrive at the same result—similarly large lists of explanations, most of them factual, yet inconclusive. The more remote in time and the more intensively analyzed the internal war, the longer the list of hypotheses. Yet even so recent a case as the Chinese Communist Revolution has given rise to a fearful number of plausible hypotheses, many directly contradictory. . . .

.   .   .

How can this embarrassment of interpretative riches (one hesitates to say theoretical riches) be reduced? If the examination of any single case allows one to determine only whether an interpretation of it is based on facts, then broad comparative studies in space and/or time are needed to establish the significance of the facts on which the interpretations are based. Was a blockage in the channels of social mobility a significant precondition of the French Revolution? We can be reasonably confident that it was only if it can be shown that elite circulation and political stability are generally related. Was the Chinese population explosion really an important cause of the Chinese revolution? Surely this is unlikely if demographic pressures do not generally affect the viability of regimes.

This is the simplest conceivable methodology, and easy to indicate abstractly. But actually to find the broad general relationships on the basis of which particular interpretations can be assessed is not so easy. For this purpose we need a tremendous amount of historical work that comparative historiographers of internal wars have hardly even begun to do. There are so many possibilities to be tested against so many cases. A general etiology of internal wars, at this stage, can only be a remote end of inquiry, and neither limited comparative studies nor interpretations of particular instances of internal war should pretend otherwise.

But even prior to undertaking that work, theoretical reflection can introduce some order into the chaos that internal war studies present. Most important, it can produce useful judgments as to the more economic lines to pursue in empirical inquiry. We can in a small way approach an etiology of internal wars by classifying the theoretical possibilities available, indicating the analytical choices they require and do not require to be made, and attempting to determine what lines of analysis are most likely to prove rewarding. Where the theoretical possibilities are as varied and chaotic as in the case of internal war, such reflection, to organize and restrict inquiry, is a necessary preliminary to the more definitive work of rigorously testing well-formulated propositions.

"Preconditions" or "Precipitants"?

Perhaps the first thing that becomes apparent when one tries to classify causal explanations of the sort sketched above is that many of the explanations do not really require a choice to be made by the analyst. The propositions do not always contradict one another; often, in fact, they are complementary, differing only because they refer to different points in the time-sequence leading to revolution, or because they refer to different kinds of causality, or because they single out one factor among many of equal significance.

The most important distinction to make in this connection is between preconditions and precipitants of internal wars. A "precipitant" of internal war is an event which actually starts the war ("occasions" it), much as turning the flintwheel of a cigarette lighter ignites a flame. 'Preconditions' of internal war, on the other hand, are those circumstances which make it possible for the precipitants to bring about political violence, as the general structure of a lighter makes it possible to produce a flame by turning the flintwheel. Some of the causal explanations of the French Revolution already mentioned clearly fall into the first category, while others fall equally clearly into the second; and between explanations singling out precipitants and explanations emphasizing preconditions of internal war there obviously is no genuine contradiction. The distinction between precipitants and preconditions can therefore prevent much pointless argument between those who stress short-run setbacks and those who emphasize long-term trends in the etiology of civil strife. Clearly no internal war can occur without precipitant events to set it off; and clearly no precipitants can set off internal war unless the condition of society makes it possible for them to do so.

The greatest service that the distinction between precipitants and preconditions of internal war can render, however, is to shift attention from aspects of internal war which defy analysis to those which are amenable to systematic inquiry. Phenomena which precipitate internal war are almost always unique and ephemeral in character. A bad harvest, a stupid or careless ruler, moral indiscretion in high places, an ill-advised policy: how could such data be incorporated into general theories? They are results of the vagaries of personality, of forces external to the determinate interrelations of society, of all those unique and fortuitous aspects of concrete life which are the despair of social scientists and the meat and drink of narrative historians.

Closely related, the distinction between precipitants and preconditions of internal wars will also help one to avoid what is perhaps the most misleading theory about their causes: an unqualified conspiracy theory of internal war. To be sure, conspiracy seems to play an essential role in certain types of internal war, particularly those previously referred to as *coups* and palace revolutions. As well, one undoubtedly finds conspiratorial organizations in every internal war of any consequence—in one case Jacobins, in others fascists, in still others communists. This is precisely what tempts so many to attribute internal wars solely or mainly to conspirators, and thus to regard them, in the manner of Malaparte, essentially as matters of technique—plotting on one hand and intelligence and suppression on the other. In many cases, however, the conspirators seem to do little more than turn the flint-wheel in volatile situations, or indeed not even as much as that; sometimes they merely turn the revolutionary conflagration to their own purposes. Internal wars do not always have a clear aim, a tight organization, a distinct shape and tendency from the outset. Many seem to be characterized in their early stages by nothing so much as amorphousness. They are formless matter waiting to be shaped, and if there is an art of revolution, it involves, largely at least, not making or subduing it, but capitalizing on the unallocated political resources it provides.

This reference to techniques of revolution leads to another point. If one leaves precipitants aside and focuses solely on data the social scientist can handle, one does not even leave out of consideration anything that matters from a practical standpoint. Preconditions are the crucial concern of men of affairs, revolutionaries or anti-revolutionaries, no less than of social scientists. After all, they have an interest in the etiology of internal wars in order to anticipate such wars in good time, prevent them when they are preventable, further their actual occurrence, or otherwise prepare for them. But unique and ephemeral phenomena cannot, by their very nature, be anticipated; they simply happen. The vital knowledge to have concerns those conditions under which almost any setback or vagary, any misguided policy or indiscretion, can set society aflame.

Certain kinds of precipitants of internal war have a special importance of their own, however, in what one might call "practical etiology"—the anticipation of internal wars for policy purposes. A precipitant may be found so frequently on the eve of internal wars that its existence can be treated as a particularly urgent danger signal, particularly if its effects are delayed sufficiently to allow some adaptation to the danger. As far as we know, both of these conditions are satisfied by economic precipitants of internal war. The point deserves some elaboration, particularly in view of the persistent emphasis on economic conditions in writings on internal war.

It now seems generally agreed that persistent poverty in a society rarely leads to political violence. Quite the contrary. As Edwards points out, following an argument already developed by de Tocqueville, economic oppression, indeed all kinds of oppression, seems to wane rather than increase in prerevolutionary periods.[7] Brinton makes the same point. While not underestimating the amount of poverty in the societies he analyzes in *The Anatomy of Revolution*, he does point out that all of these societies were economically progressive rather than retrograde. He points out also that revolutionary literature, at any rate in the pre-Marxist period, hardly ever dwelt on economic misery and exploitation—one hears about economic grievances, to be sure, but not the sort of grievances which arise out of "immiseration."[8] Even some Marxists seem to share this view. Trotsky, for example, once remarked that if poverty and oppression were a precipitant of revolution the lower classes would always be in revolt, and obviously he had a point.

It is equally difficult to establish a close link between economic improve-

[7] Edwards, *The Natural History of Revolutions*, 33.
[8] Brinton, *The Anatomy of Revolution*, 29–37.

ment and internal war. Pre-revolutionary periods may often be economically progressive, but economic progress is not always (or even often) connected with internal war. From this, however, one need not conclude that economic tendencies are simply irrelevant to the occurrence of political violence. Only the long-term tendencies seem, in fact, to be irrelevant. The moment one focuses on short-term tendencies, a fairly frequently repeated pattern emerges—and one which tells us why it is that some writers adhere stubbornly to the immiseration theory of internal war and others, with just as much conviction, to the economic progress theory. It so happens that before many internal wars, one finds both economic improvement and immiseration; more precisely, many internal wars are preceded by long-term improvements followed by serious short-term setbacks.[9] The bad harvests and unfavorable weather conditions in pre-revolutionary France, the American recession of 1774–1775, the bad Russian winter of 1916–1917 (not to mention the economic impact of the war on Russia) and the marked rise of unemployment in Egypt before Naguib's *coup* are cases in point. All dealt serious short-term blows to economic life and all followed long periods of economic progress, especially for those previously "repressed."

It is this dual pattern which really seems to be lethal, and it is not difficult to see why. In times of prolonged and marked economic progress, people become accustomed to new economic standards and form new economic expectations, which previously they could scarcely imagine. Confidently

[9] See James C. Davis, "Toward a Theory of Revolution," *American Sociological Review*, 27 (1962), 5–19. This paper traces the pattern in Dorr's Rebellion, the Russian Revolution, and the Egyptian Revolution.

expecting continuous progress, they also tend to take risks (like accumulating debts) which they might not take otherwise. All this greatly exaggerates the impact of serious temporary setbacks; both psychologically and economically the costs of such setbacks are bound to be greater than if they occurred after long periods of stagnation or very gradual progress.

Occasionally, perhaps, the study of precipitants of internal war may play a minor role in "theoretical" as well as "practical etiology." It could conceivably shed some light on the preconditions themselves in that there might be a connection between revolutionary conditions and how internal wars are actually brought about. For example, someone may blame internal war on dissatisfactions in the rural population of a society; but if we find peasants playing no role in the fomenting of violence, then we have good reason to doubt the interpretation. Precipitants may not directly tell us what the preconditions of internal war are, but they can sometimes indicate what they are not—be useful for falsifying hypotheses or at least shedding doubt on them. But this does not alter the basic point: that the task of an etiology of internal wars is to discover their preconditions.

Common Hypotheses about the Preconditions of Internal War

We can profitably relegate to a secondary role most of those greatly varying, unique, and largely fortuitous events which occasion the outbreak of internal wars. But even if we do, a great variety of hypotheses remains—great enough if we confine ourselves to general treatments of internal war, and greater still if we deal with hypotheses formulated to deal with particular cases. In this connection, it might be useful to supplement the explanations of particular revolutions listed above with a sample of propositions frequently found in the more general literature on internal war. These include[10]:

a. *Hypotheses emphasizing "intellectual" factors:*
   1. Internal wars result from the failure of a regime to perform adequately the function of political socialization.
   2. Internal wars are due to the coexistence in a society of conflicting social "myths."
   3. Internal wars result from the existence in a society of unrealizable values or corrosive social philosophies.
   4. Internal wars are caused by the alienation (desertion, transfer of allegiance) of the intellectuals.

b. *Hypotheses emphasizing economic factors:*
   1. Internal wars are generated by growing poverty.
   2. Internal wars result from rapid economic progress.
   3. Internal wars are due to severe imbalances between the production and distribution of goods.
   4. Internal wars are caused by a combination of long-term economic improvement and short-term setbacks.

c. *Hypotheses emphasizing aspects of social structure:*
   1. Internal wars are due to the inadequate circulation of elites (that is, inadequate recruitment into the elite of the able and powerful members of the non-elite).
   2. Internal wars result from too much recruitment of members of the non-elite into the elite, breaking down the internal cohesion of the elite.

   3. Internal war is a reflection of *anomie* resulting from great social mobility.
   4. Internal war is a reflection of frustration arising from little general social mobility—from general social stagnation.
   5. Internal wars result from the appearance in societies of new social classes.

d. *Hypotheses emphasizing political factors:*
   1. Internal wars are due to the estrangement of rulers from the societies they rule.
   2. Internal war is simply a response to bad government (government which performs inadequately the function of goal-attainment).
   3. Internal wars are due, not to the attacks of the governed on those who govern, but to divisions among the governing classes.
   4. Internal wars are responses to oppressive government.
   5. Internal wars are due to excessive toleration of alienated groups.

e. *Hypotheses emphasizing no particular aspects of societies, but general characteristics of social process:*
   1. Political violence is generated by rapid social change.
   2. Political violence results from erratic and/or uneven rates of social change, whether rapid or not.
   3. Internal war occurs when a state is somehow "out of adjustment" to society.

From this sample of propositions, all of them at least plausible, we can get some idea of the overwhelming ambiguities that general studies of the preconditions of internal war have created to supplement those originating in case studies. These ambiguities arise most obviously from the fact that many of the propositions are manifestly contradictory; less obviously, from the sheer variety and disparity of factors included, not all of which, surely, can be equally significant, or necessary, in the etiology of internal wars. For this reason, even when precipitants are subtracted, a considerable range of

[10] The hypotheses come from a large variety of sources, including: Lasswell and Kaplan, *Power and Society* (New Haven, 1950); the works by Edwards, Pettee, and Brinton cited above; Rudé, *The Crowd in the French Revolution* (Oxford, 1959); Trotsky, *The History of the Russian Revolution* (Ann Arbor, Michigan, 1957); De Grazia, *The Political Community* (Chicago, 1948); Gaetano Mosca, *The Ruling Class* (New York, 1939); and Vilfredo Pareto, *The Mind and Society* (New York, 1935).

choices between theories remains to be made.

Insurgents or Incumbents?

One crucial choice that needs to be made is whether to put emphasis upon characteristics of the insurgents or incumbents, upon the side that rebels or the side that is rebelled against. Not surprisingly, the existing literature concentrates very largely on the rebels, treating internal war as due mainly to changes in the non-elite strata of society to which no adequate adjustment is made by the elite. This would seem to be only natural; after all, it is the rebels who rebel. At least some writings suggest, however, that characteristics of the incumbents and the classes that are usually their props must be considered jointly with characteristics of the insurgents, indeed perhaps even emphasized more strongly. Pareto, for example, while attributing revolution partly to blockages in a society's social mobility patterns, considered it equally necessary that certain internal changes should occur in an elite if revolution was to be possible; in essence, he felt that no elite which had preserved its capacity for timely and effective violence, or for effective manipulation, could be successfully assailed, or perhaps assailed at all. One must, according to this view, seek the origins of internal war not only in a gain of strength by the non-elite, but also in the loss of it on the part of the elite. Brinton makes the same point: revolutions, in his view, follow the loss of common values, of internal cohesion, of a sure sense of destiny and superiority and, not least, of political efficiency in elites, and thus must be considered results as much as causes of their disintegration. And in Edwards's and Pettee's studies as well, revolutions emerge as affairs of the elites (if not always directly of the actual rulers): the crucial roles in them are played by intellectuals, by men rich and powerful but "cramped" by their lack of status or other perquisites, and by the gross inefficiency of the ruling apparatus.

Significantly enough, this view is stated perhaps more often in the writings of actual revolutionaries than in those of students of revolution. Trotsky, for example, believed that revolution requires three elements: the political consciousness of a revolutionary class, the discontent of the "intermediate layers" of society, and, just as important, a ruling class which has "lost faith in itself," which is torn by the conflicts of groups and cliques, which has lost its capacity for practical action and rests its hopes in "miracles or miracle workers."[11]

The joint consideration of insurgent and incumbent patterns thus would seem to be the logical way to proceed in the early stages of inquiry into the causes of revolution. But one should not overlook the possibility that sufficient explanations of the occurrence of many internal wars might be found in elite characteristics alone. A ruling elite may decay, may become torn by severe conflict, may be reluctant to use power, may come to lack vital political skills—and thus make it perfectly possible for a relatively weak, even disorganized, opposition of a sort that may exist in any political system to rise against it and destroy it. Indeed, there are theories which maintain that internal wars are always caused solely or primarily by changes in elite characteristics, and that one can practically ignore the insurgents in attempting to account for the occurrence of internal wars.

One such theory is propounded in Mosca's *The Ruling Class*. If the

---

[11] Trotsky, *The Russian Revolution*, 311.

elementary needs of human life are satisfied, argued Mosca, one thing above all will cause men to rebel against their rulers, and that is their feeling that the rulers live in a totally different environment, that they are "separated" from their subjects in some profound sense. In other words, the estrangement of the elite from the non-elite is inseparable from the alienation of the latter; only the elite itself, consequently, can undermine its political position. . . .

.   .   .

It is worth noting that in the postwar period internal wars have been relatively rare in two kinds of societies: either thoroughly modernized countries or very underdeveloped countries whose elites have remained tied closely to the traditional ways and structures of life.[12] Of course, a generalization of this kind is becoming increasingly harder to test, since the number of societies without a gulf between highly modernized elites and much less modernized masses seems to be rapidly shrinking. Nevertheless the notion is given credibility by the fact that, while transitional societies seem to suffer more from internal wars than either traditional or modern societies—as one would expect upon many hypotheses—a very few seem to have strikingly low rates of violence compared to the rest. Egypt is one example, and Pakistan another. These societies seem to differ from the rest in one main respect. They have had "secondary" revolutions, so to speak, in which men of rather humble origins and popular ways (colonels' regimes) have unseated previously victorious transitional elites. All this is not meant to validate the

[12] Cases in point are the stable, highly developed democracies on the one hand, and countries like Ethiopia and Somalia on the other.

idea that elite estrangement is the main cause of internal war but only to show why it should be taken very seriously. The possible consequences of elite estrangement are not, however, the only reason for emphasizing studies of the incumbents at least as much as studies of insurgents in the etiology of internal wars. Another is the fact that internal wars are almost invariably preceded by important functional failures on the part of elites. Above all is this true of difficulties in financial administration—perhaps because finance impinges on the ability of governments to perform all their functions.[13] And finally, insurgent groups seem rarely to come even to the point of fighting without some support from alienated members of incumbent elites. On this point, agreement in the literature on internal war is practically unanimous.

Structural or Behavioral Hypotheses?

A second strategic choice to be made in constructing an etiology of internal wars is between structural and behavioral hypotheses. A structural hypothesis singles out, so to speak, "objective" social conditions as crucial for the occurrence of internal war: aspects of a society's "setting," such as economic conditions, social

[13] One of the most common conditions found before large-scale political violence is the financial bankruptcy of government, due to profligacy, over-ambitious policies, or the failure of a traditional tax structure in an inflationary situation, followed by an attack upon the financial privileges of strata which were previously the main props of the regime. R. B. Merriman, in *Six Contemporaneous Revolutions, 1640–1660* (Oxford, 1938), points out that the seventeenth-century revolutions in England, France, the Netherlands, Spain, Portugal, and Naples all had this point in common.

stratification and mobility, or geographic and demographic factors. A behavioral hypothesis, on the other hand, emphasizes attitudes and their formation—not setting, but "orientations" (such as degrees of strain and *anomie* in societies, the processes by which tension and aggression are generated, and the processes by which human beings are "socialized" into their communities). The great majority of propositions regarding the causes of internal war are, on the basis of these definitions, structural in character. But, in concentrating upon structural explanations have writers on internal war taken the more promising tack?

At first glance, there would seem to be little to choose between structural and behavioral approaches. Since most human action is motivated, not reflexive, one always wants to know, if one can, about attitudes underlying men's actions. At the same time, there can be little doubt that attitudes are always formed somehow in response to external conditions. The difference between structural and behavioral theories would therefore seem to be, at best, one of emphasis or point of view. Yet emphasis can make a difference. Certain research results do seem to be associated with one point of view or the other. Behavioral approaches, for instance, may lead to theories stressing "intellectual" and voluntaristic factors in the etiology of political violence, or to theories attributing internal war mainly to efficient revolutionary indoctrination or inadequate value-formation by the incumbents. Structural explanations may lead to theories of mechanical imbalance in society, or to theories attributing internal war mainly to specific situational conditions, attitudes being treated as mechanical responses to such conditions.

Which approach is preferable? Despite the fact that there is a danger that the behavioral approach might lead to naive conspiracy theory (the belief that internal wars are always the results of insidious indoctrination by subversive elements, and could therefore always occur or always be avoided) the arguments against a primary emphasis on structural theories are very strong.

One such argument derives from the general experience of modern social science. Purely structural theories have generally been found difficult to sustain wherever they have been applied, and one fundamental reason for this is that patterns of attitudes, while responsive to the settings in which men are placed, seem also to be, to an extent, autonomous of objective conditions, able to survive changes in these conditions or to change without clearly corresponding objective changes. This is one of the basic insights underlying the sociological theory of action, which, to be sure, assigns an important role to the situations in which human action occurs, but treats "culture" largely as a separate variable and attaches particularly great significance to agencies of socialization and acculturation. It underlies as well the relatively successful use of mediational models, rather than simple S-R models, in behavioral psychology.

No doubt this point should be much elaborated.[14] But one can make a cogent case for stressing behavioral theories of the causes of internal wars without going lengthily into the general nature and past experiences of social science.

The most obvious case for behavioral theories of internal war derives from the very fact that so many different objective social conditions seem ca-

[14] Useful summaries of action and behavior theories can be found in Roland Young, ed., *Approaches to the Study of Politics* (Evanston, Illinois, 1958), 217–243 and 285–301.

pable of generating it. We may have available many interpretative accounts of internal wars simply because an enormous variety of objective conditions can create internal-war potential. Certain internal wars do seem to have followed economic improvement, others seem to have followed closely the Marxist model of internal wars, however many more have followed some combination of the two. Some internal wars have in fact been preceded by great, others by little social mobility; some regimes have been more oppressive and others more liberal in the immediate pre-revolutionary period, some both and some neither. Is it not reasonable to conclude that one should not seek explanations of the occurrence of internal wars in specific social conditions, but rather in the ways in which social conditions may be perceived? Instead of looking for direct connections between social conditions and internal war, should one not look rather for the ways in which an existing cognitive and value system may change, so that conditions perceived as tolerable at one point are perceived as intolerable at another; or, concomitantly look for the ways in which old systems of orientation are in some cases maintained rather than adapted in the face of social change, so that changes which one society absorbs without trouble create profound difficulties in another?

The point is not that objective conditions are unrelated to internal war. Rather it is that orientations mediate between social setting and political behavior, and—because they are not simply mirrors of environment —so that different objective conditions may lead to similar political activities, or similar conditions to different activities in different contexts; that in a single context a considerable change in political activity may occur without changes in objective conditions or

changes in objective conditions without changes in activity. What should be avoided is linking aspects of social setting *directly* to internal war or *mechanically* to orientations. Internal wars are best conceived as responses to political disorientation (such as "cognitive dissonance," *anomie*, and strains in the definition of political roles), particularly in regard to a society's norms of legitimacy; and political disorientation may follow from a considerable variety of conditions, due to the variable nature of the orientations themselves and of the agencies that implant them in different societies.

One conspicuous point of agreement in comparative studies of revolution gives further credence to this argument. This is that revolutions are invariably preceded by the "transfer of allegiance" of a society's intellectuals and the development by them of a new political "myth." If intellectuals have any obvious social "functions," in the sense social scientists understand the term function, they are surely these: to socialize the members of a society outside of the domestic context, in schools and adult learning situations; to reinforce and rationalize attitudes acquired in all social contexts; and to provide meaning to life and guidelines to behavior by means of conscious doctrines where events have robbed men of their less conscious bearings. Intellectuals are particularly important in the education of adolescents and young people, and it has been shown quite definitely that political socialization occurs (or fails) mainly in the years between early childhood and full maturity.[15] It could also be shown that among revolutionaries the young tend to predominate, sometimes quite

[15] For evidence, see Herbert H. Hyman, *Political Socialization* (Glencoe, Illinois, 1959).

remarkably. Together these points go far to explain why the alienation of intellectuals is, in Edwards's language, a "master-symptom" of revolution: a condition that makes revolutionary momentum irreversible.

Another point that speaks for behavioral propositions is that internal wars can, and often do, become chronic. In some societies, the most manifest cause of internal war seems to be internal war itself, one instance following another, often without a recurrence of the conditions that led to the original event. This means that political disorientation may be followed by the formation of a new set of orientations, establishing a predisposition toward violence that is inculcated by the experience of violence itself. In such cases, internal wars result not from specifiable objective conditions, and not even from the loss of legitimacy by a particular regime, but from a general lack of receptivity to legitimacy of any kind. Violence becomes a political style that is self-perpetuating, unless itself "disoriented."

The very fact that elite estrangement so often precedes acute political unrest itself fits the case for behavioral propositions. It fits in part because the Establishment of any society includes its intellectuals, but also for a more important, rather technical, reason. Orientations, particularly as treated in action theory, are not purely internal and self-sufficient, as it were, but involve expectations from others ("alters")—mutualities or complementarities in behavior. Hence men are likely to become disoriented and alienated when those with whom they interact become aliens to them, even if the alien ways involve, from abstract moral standpoints, a change for the better. The Polish peasant probably did not positively like to be beaten, but he *expected* to be, and he himself

undoubtedly committed a good deal of institutionalized mayhem on anyone subordinated to his authority. A liberal aristocrat would appear to him not only to act strangely but arbitrarily, and, in a way, as a constant personal reproach.

To give still more support to the argument for behavioral theories there is the object lesson provided by the sad history of Marxist theory. Marxism singles out certain objective social conditions as underlying internal wars. It also singles out certain social groups as indispensable to the making of internal war. But Marxist revolutions themselves have been made neither under the social conditions nor by the groups emphasized in the theory. What is more, these revolutions have been made in a large variety of conditions, with a large variety of means, by organizations constituted in a large variety of ways. This is true even if one can show that the appeal of Marxism is greatest in transitional societies, for the term transition, in its very nature, denotes not a particular social state but a great many different points on whatever continuum social development may involve.

Particular Conditions or General Processes?

This argument has a close bearing upon a third strategic choice to be made in analyzing the causes of internal war. Even if one emphasizes behavioral characteristics in theories of internal wars, one must, as I have said, always relate these characteristics to the social setting. The question is how to do this. Should one, in the manner of most of the hypotheses listed above, develop propositions emphasizing particular social conditions or, in the manner of a few of them, select propositions about general characteristics of social process? In the first case, one would relate internal war to particular socio-economic changes, in the second to characteristics of the general phenomenon of social change itself, such as rapid change or erratic change in any sectors of society, or conditions that may result from any social change whatever, such as imbalances between social segments (e.g., between elites of wealth and elites of status) or incongruities among the authority patterns of a society.

The proper choice between these alternatives is already implied in the arguments of the previous section. If many particular social conditions may be connected with internal wars, then clearly one should stress broad propositions about social processes and balances that can comprehend a variety of such conditions. The same position results if disorientation is conceived, in large part, as a breakdown in mutualities and complementarities of behavior. Not least, there is overwhelming evidence to show that "anomie," the feeling that one lacks guidelines to behavior, is increased by rapidity of change in any direction (for example, by rapid economic betterment no less than rapid economic deterioration) and that "strain," the feeling that one's roles make inconsistent demands, is aggravated by uneven or incongruent changes in different social sectors (for example, when the economic sector of society becomes significantly modern while the political remains largely traditional).

What has been said about economic conditions preceding internal wars fits the argument particularly well. It is not just that cases can be found to support both immiseration and improvement theories of revolution, hence the view that internal wars are related to economic changes as such, not to change in any particular direction; more suggestive still is the fact that internal wars most frequently follow an irregular—an anomalous—course of economic change, long-term trends being interrupted by abrupt and short-lived reversals. Such a course exhibits at least two of the general characteristics of social processes that would, upon earlier arguments, seem to be related to the occurrence of internal wars: rapidity of change and eccentricity of change.

From this standpoint it would be most interesting to investigate whether *any* rapid and eccentric course of economic development tends to be related to internal war, perhaps even one involving long-term stagnation or deterioration followed by abrupt short-term improvement. This idea is not as farfetched as may seem; after all has not Durkheim fully documented the argument that "*fortunate crises*, the effect of which is abruptly to enhance a country's prosperity, affect suicide like *econonic disasters*"?[16]

Undoubetdly there is a danger that broad formulations concerning general social processes will turn into empty and untestable generalizations, trivialities like the much-repeated proposition that political violence tends to accompany social or economic change. But this danger is avoidable; one can, after all, be specific and informative about general social processes as well as about their substantive content.

Obstacles to Internal War

So far I have tried to make two related points. The first is that one is most likely to gain understanding of the forces impelling societies toward

---

[16] Emile Durkheim, *Suicide* (London, 1952), 243 (my italics).

internal war if one avoids preoccupation with the more visible precipitants of internal wars, including conspiracies, and directs one's efforts to the analysis of their preconditions, stressing disorientative general social processes and particularly taking into account elite behavior, performance, and cohesion. The second point is in a sense the converse of this: that existing etiologies of internal wars are chaotic and inadequate precisely because studies have so far concentrated on precipitants rather than preconditions, insurgents rather than incumbents, and particular aspects of social structure rather than the effects on orientations of general social processes.

An important point must now be added. Even if we had better knowledge of the forces which push societies toward political violence, a crucial problem relating to the etiology of internal wars would remain, one that is generally ignored in the studies available to us. This problem concerns forces that might countervail those previously discussed: "obstacles" to internal war, as against forces which propel societies toward violence.

In the real world of phenomena, events occur not only because forces leading toward them are strong, but also because forces tending to inhibit, or obstruct, them are weak or absent. An automobile may generate a great deal of force, but if driven up a steep incline is unlikely to go very fast. A government may have the desire and technical capacity for rapid industrialization, but if faced by the rapid growth of an already too great population may simply find it impossible to channel sufficient resources into capital goods to achieve a certain rate of development. So also internal wars may fail to occur solely or mainly because of certain hindrances to their occurrence.

Some of these hindrances may be absolute in character, in that wherever they exist internal war fails to materialize; hence their obverse may be considered "requisites" of internal war (necessary, but not sufficient, conditions). In the main, however, obstacles to internal war, like forces making for internal war, are better conceived as factors making such wars more or less likely, rather than either inevitable or impossible—their actual significance depending, at least in part, on the strength of forces pulling in a contrary direction. It certainly seems unlikely that we shall ever find a condition that makes internal war quite inevitable under any circumstances, and equally unlikely that we could discover conditions that always rule it out (except perhaps purely definitional ones: e.g., the absence of any perceived frustrations). In real life, internal war, like other concrete events, results from the interplay of forces and counterforces, from a balance of probabilities pulling toward internal war and internal peace.

REPRESSION

The most obvious obstacle to internal war is, of course, the incumbent regime. It goes almost without saying that by using repression the established authorities can lessen the chances of violent attack upon themselves, or even reduce them to nil. Internal wars, after all, are not made by impersonal forces working in impersonal ways, but by men acting under the stress of external forces. This much at least there is in the conspiracy theory of revolution: wholly spontaneous riots by wholly unstructured and undirected mobs may occur, but hardly very frequently or with much effect. Actual cases of internal war generally contain some element of subversion, some structure for forming political will and acting upon decisions, however primitive and changeable. On this point, if no other, the great enemies of revolution (Burke, Chateaubriand, Taine) are at one with the great revolutionaries (Lenin, Trotsky); it is also this point, rather than some more subtle idea, which underlies Pareto's and Brinton's argument that revolutions are due to elites as much as non-elites. And anything with a structure can of course be detected and repressed, though not always very easily.

The matter, however, is not quite so simple. Repression can be a two-edged sword. Unless it is based upon extremely good intelligence, and unless its application is sensible, ruthless, and continuous, its effects may be quite opposite to those intended. Incompetent repression leads to a combination of disaffection and contempt for the elite. Also, repression may only make the enemies of a regime more competent in the arts of conspiracy; certainly it tends to make them more experienced in the skills of clandestine organization and *sub rosa* communication. No wonder that botched and bungled repression is often a characteristic of pre-revolutionary societies. The French *ancien régime*, for example, had a political censorship, but it only managed to make French writers into masters of the hidden meaning, and whet the appetite of the public for their subversive books. . . . Russia, under the later Czars, was practically a model of repressive bumbledom; her policy of exile, for example, created close-knit communities of revolutionaries more than it destroyed their cohesion.

The worst situation of all seems to arise when a regime, having driven its opponents underground, inflamed their enmity, heightened their contempt, and cemented their organization,

suddenly relaxes its repression and attempts a liberal policy. The relaxation of authority is a part of the pre-revolutionary syndrome, no less than other forms of social amelioration; in that sense, repression in societies with high internal war potential is little more than a narcotic, intensifying the conditions it seeks to check and requiring ever larger doses to keep affairs in balance—if other things are equal. We can see this dynamic at work in the development of totalitarian rule, particularly if we remember that blood-letting, while certainly the ultimate in repression, is only one form that coercion can take.

From this standpoint, repression may be both an obstacle to and precipitant of internal war. Repression is of course least likely to prevent internal war in societies which, unlike totalitarian regimes, have a low capacity for coercion. In such societies, adjustive and diversionary mechanisms seem to check revolutionary potential far better. Indeed, they may in any society.[17]

DIVERSIONS AND CONCESSIONS

Diversionary mechanisms are all those social patterns and practices which channel psychic energies away from revolutionary objectives—which provide other outlets for aggressions or otherwise absorb emotional tensions. . . . English nonconformist evangelicalism, especially the Methodist movement, furnishes an excellent case in point. . . .[18] England did not have any serious revolution in the early nineteenth century, despite conditions which, on their face,

[17] "Power," says Merriam, "is not strongest where it uses violence, but weakest. It is strongest where it employs the instruments of substitution and counter-attraction, of allurement, of participation . . ." C. E. Merriam, *Political Power* (New York, 1934), 179–80.
[18] Elie Halévy, *A History of the English People*, 6 vols. (London, 1960), vol. 1.

seem to have contained very great revolutionary potential—conditions resulting from the industrial revolution and from the fact of endemic revolution throughout the Western world. . . . English evangelicalism, more than anything else, performed a series of functions which greatly lowered the revolutionary level of British politics. Among these functions were the provision of outlets for emotional expression and the inculcation of a philosophy which reconciled the lower classes to their condition, made that condition seem inevitable, and made patient submission to it a sacred obligation. . . .

England may have been spared major political violence since the seventeenth century for other reasons too: for example, because at least twice in English history, just when she seemed to be on the very brink of civil war, external war opportunely occurred, unifying the country as external wars will. . . . Indeed, diverting popular attention from domestic troubles by starting foreign wars is one of the most venerable dodges of statecraft. This too, however, is a weapon that cuts two ways. Military adventures are excellent diversions, and military successes can marvellously cement disjoined societies, but military failure, on the evidence, can hardly fail to hasten revolution in such cases. Russia may well have entered the First World War to distract domestic unrest, but, if so, the outcome was revolution rather than the contrary.

Orgiastic excitements—festivals and dances, parades and circuses, *Reichsparteitäge* and mass gymnastics—also provide diversionary outlets for popular discontent. . . .

. . .

Adjustive mechanisms reduce, or manage, tensions, rather than providing for them surrogate outlets. Conces-sions are perhaps the most obvious of such mechanisms. . . . But concessions too may work in two directions, no less than repression and certain diversionary tactics. They may only lead to further and greater demands, further and greater expectations of success, and must therefore, like repression, be continuous, and continuously greater, to succeed. . . .

FACILITIES FOR VIOLENCE

A final set of obstacles to internal war are conditions that affect the capacities of alienated groups to use violence at all, or more often in real life, to use it with fair prospects of success. These conditions do not always prevent violence. But they can prevent its success. For this very reason, they help determine the likelihood of decisions to use violence at all. What are some of these conditions?

Perhaps the first to come to mind is terrain. While practically all kinds of terrain can be used, in different ways, for purposes of rebellion, not all can be used to equal advantage. The ideal, from the viewpoint of the insurgents, seems to be an area which is relatively isolated, mountainous, overgrown, criss-crossed by natural obstacles (hedges, ditches, etc.), and near the sea or other sources of external supply—terrain which affords secure bases to the insurgents in their own territory, gives them the advantage of familiarity with local conditions, and allows ready access to them of external supporters.[19]

The communications facilities of a

[19] For examples of how such terrain benefits insurgents, see Peter Paret, *Internal War and Pacification: The Vendée, 1793–1796* (Princeton, 1961); W. E. D. Allen, *Guerrilla War in Abyssinia* (London, 1951), 19; Chalmers Johnson, "Civilian Loyalties and Guerrilla Conflict", *World Politics*, July 1962; and Ernesto Guevara, *Che Guevara on Guerrilla War* (New York, 1951)—among many others.

society are another relevant condition. Marx, among many others, seems to have realized this when he argued that urbanization increases the likelihood of revolution, if only in that it makes men accessible to one another and thus makes revolutionary organization easier to achieve. . . . In this one case, a condition which may heighten the chances of successful internal war (bad communications) may also discourage its outbreak. There may be nothing more mysterious to the celebrated peaceability of peasants, as compared to city-dwellers, than the physical difficulty in rural life, especially if fairly primitive, to form a "collective revolutionary mentality."

Terrain and communications are physical obstacles to (or facilities for) internal war. There are human obstacles as well. For example, internal wars seem rarely to occur, even if other conditions favor them, if a regime's instruments of violence remain loyal. . . . We could enlarge this point to read that internal wars are unlikely wherever the cohesion of an elite is intact, for the simple reason that insurgent formations require leadership and other skills, and are unlikely to obtain them on a large scale without some significant break in the ranks of an elite. Even if elites do not always "cause" their own downfall by becoming rigid or foreign to their people, they can certainly hasten their own demise by being internally at odds. From this standpoint, if not from that of Mosca's theory, elite cohesion is a factor which should be classified among the obstacles to internal war, as well as among their causes.

A final human obstacle to internal war—perhaps the greatest of all—is lack of wide popular support for rebellion. It seems generally accepted among modern writers on internal war, indeed it is the chief dogma of modern revolutionaries, that without great popular support the insurgents in an internal war can hardly hope to win (and with it are hardly likely to lose)—unless by means of a *coup d'état*. So vital is this factor that some writers think that the distinctive characteristic of internal war is the combination of violent techniques with psychological warfare, the latter designed, of course, to win the active support of the non-combatants; this is asserted in the much repeated pseudo-formula of the French theorists of *guerre révolutionnaire:* revolutionary warfare = partisan war + psychological warfare.[20] To be sure, psychological warfare occurs nowadays also in international wars. Its role in these, however, is not nearly so crucial as in internal war; it is incidental in one case but seems to be decisive in the other.

One reason for this is that in internal wars, unlike international wars, there is generally a great disparity in capacity for military effort between the incumbents and insurgents. The former tend to be in a much stronger position—not always, of course, for this is where the loyalties of the established instrumentalities of violence enter the picture, but more often than not. The insurgents are therefore forced, in the normal case, to supplement their capabilities by taking what advantage they can of terrain and the cooperation of the non-combatant population. Like terrain itself, a well-disposed population affords a secure base of operations to rebels, as well as providing them with indispensable logistical support. Rebels who can count on popular

[20] G. Bonnet, *Les guerres insurrectionelles* (Paris, 1958), 60. The point that in guerrilla warfare almost everything turns on popular support is argued in many sources, most strongly perhaps in C. A. Johnson, "Civilian Loyalties and Guerrilla Conflict," *World Politics,* July 1962.

support can lose themselves in the population (according to Mao "the populace is for revolutionaries what water is for fish"), count on the population for secrecy (in wars in which intelligence is practically the whole art of defense), and reconstitute their forces by easy recruitment; if they can do all of these things, they can be practically certain of victory, short of a resort to genocide by the incumbents.

Great popular support is necessary also because internal wars, precisely because the common disparity of forces rules out quick victory by the insurgents (except by *coup*), tend to be long drawn-out wars of attrition—perhaps better, either very prolonged or very quickly settled. In such wars, when victory always seems remote, when, at times, impasse is the best that can be hoped for, when the disruption of normal life is greater even than in external war, the morale of the revolutionaries, their ultimate trump card against their opponents, can hardly be sustained if they feel themselves isolated from their own people.

For all of these reasons, calculations about popular loyalties normally play a role in the decision to resort to political violence. The calculations may be mistaken but they are almost always made, sometimes, as in the case of the Algerian nationalist struggle, in ways approaching the survey research of social science.[21]

Toward an Etiology of Internal Wars

Needless to say, these arguments do not amount to anything like a finished etiology of internal wars. My concern here has been with preliminary,

[21] Interview with M. Chanderli, F. L. N. Observer at the United Nations, December, 1961.

but fundamental and neglected, questions of strategy in theory-building, no more. Nevertheless, taking it all in all, this study does imply something more than that certain lines of inquiry are more promising than others in internal-war studies. When its arguments are added up, there emerges at least a considerable clue to the *form* that an adequate etiology of internal wars should take, even if little of a very specific nature can as yet be said about content. We have arrived at a paradigm, if not a fully-fledged theory.

Two points can serve as summary, as well as to spell out the nature of the paradigm I have in mind. One is that internal-war potential (the likelihood that internal war in some form will be precipitated)[22] should be conceived formally as a ratio between positive forces making for internal war and negative forces working against it—with the *possibility* that internal war of some kind may be fomented existing no matter what the overall potential, and the *probability* of its occurrence increasing as internal-war potential rises. This is certainly elementary, but it is in fact far more usual, in both general theories and specific interpretations of internal war, to speak of revolutionary or pacifying forces alone, and to depict rebelliousness as either absolutely present or absolutely lacking in societies. The other, and more important point, is that the forces involved should be conceived in both cases as functions of four factors. The positive forces are produced by the *inefficacy of elites* (lack of cohesion

[22] I stress internal-war *potential* because this is all one can assess if the actual occurrence of internal wars depends on precipitants beyond the scope of systematic analysis or even the predictive capacities engendered by practical wisdom. Needless to say, however, the actual occurrence of internal wars gives the best assurance that the societies concerned indeed had great internal-war potential.

and of expected performance), *disorienting social processes* (delegitimization), *subversion* (attempts deliberately to activate disorientation, to form new political orientations and to impede the efficacy of elites), and the *facilities* available to potential insurgents. Countervailing these factors are four others: the *facilities* of incumbents, *effective repression* (not any kind of repression), *adjustive concessions* and *diversionary mechanisms*—the first referring to the incumbents' perceived capacity to fight if internal war occurs, the others to preventative actions.

This summation provides at least the minimum that one expects from paradigms: a formal approach to study and a checklist of factors that should be particularly considered whether one is interpreting specific cases or constructing general theory. But a minimum is not much. It is necessary to go further, particularly in the direction of determining the relative values of the factors and their relations to one another. After being stated, the variables must be ordered. Consequently, to conclude, I should like to add some suggestions that indicate how one might proceed from the mere cataloguing of promising variables toward their systematization.

In the first place, it seems, from what has been said about possible obstacles to internal war, that the negative forces vary within a much smaller range than the positive ones, so that beyond a point, internal-war potential can be reduced only with geometrically decreasing effectiveness, if at all. Take, for example, adjustive concessions. These cannot be indefinitely increased, for in the end, they would be tantamount to surrender, and long before that point, would only serve to increase the insurgents' capabilities (not to mention the probable effects on the insurgents'

demands and the incumbents' cohesion). Repression is intrinsically limited as well, among other reasons because it requires repressors and because its use will tend to intensify alienation; as in the case of concessions there may be an optimum of repression, but a maximum of it is as bad as none at all. And one can doubt the efficacy of diversions where disorientation is very widespread and goes very deep; besides, intrinsic limitations operate in the case of this factor too, for a society that lives on diversions to the extent of say, the Roman Empire is for that very reason in decay. The factors that make for internal-war potential clearly are less inherently circumscribed. More clearly still, certain of them, like the crucial facility of popular support, belong to the realm of zero-sums, so that an increase of forces on the positive side implies a concomitant decrease on the other. In this sense, the variables involved in internal-war potential have a certain hierarchical order (an order of "potency"): one set is more significant than the other.

Such an order seems to exist within each set as well. For example, no one rebels simply because he has appropriate facilities—otherwise, the military and police would be everywhere and constantly in rebellion. At the very least, internal war presupposes some degree of subversion as well as brute capabilities. Subversion in turn, however, presupposes something that can be subverted—disorientations to activate and to reshape toward new legitimizations. And much evidence suggests that, whatever forces may be at work in a society, in whatever fashion, disorientation and subversion are both unlikely where the elite performs well, is highly cohesive, and is deeply enough attuned to the general spirit of social life to provide the mutualities and complementarities that settled social orientations require—granted that certain social processes make this extremely improbable. Per contra, elite inefficacy in itself always invites challenge, from within or without, no matter what other forces may be at work in the non-elite; in one form (incohesion), it implies the likelihood of internecine elite conflict, in others the probability of alienation of the non-elite. If disorientation arising from other sources is added, the brew obviously becomes more lethal (and its explosion tends to take a different form), with or without much concerted subversion. The latter, and insurgent facilities, are essentially extra additives, the more so since insurgents can hardly lack facilities on some scale where elite inefficacy and political disorientation are great; these factors may intensify internal-war potential, but do not create it.

The factors that reduce internal-war potential can be arranged (with rather more ambiguity, to be sure) in a similar order of potency. The essential criterion that establishes their weight is the extent to which they are intrinsically limited, either because they can become self-defeating or because they are zero-sums that do not allow increases on the positive side to be balanced by increases on the other. Diversions, while certainly not unlimited, are probably the most potent of the factors, for they can apparently be carried very far before they thoroughly devitalize societies. Repression and concessions seem to have a much lower optimum point. It is difficult at present to say which of them is the less potent; in all probability, however, it is repression—if only because concessions may increase the legitimation of authority among potential dissidents (that is, serve as surrogates for other

kinds of elite "performance") while acts of repression, as well as being inherently self-denials of legitimacy, are well-tailored to cope only with the less potent factor of subversion. Incumbent facilities, finally, while being by all odds the most ambiguous factor, seem to belong somewhere between diversions on one hand and concessions on the other. The reasons for this are three: First, since the most vital of them are zero-sums, they can be, in a sense, either very weak or very potent, a decrease in them implying a corresponding increase in insurgent facilities and the reverse holding as well (a sort of inherent limitation different from that operating in the case of the other factors). Secondly, it seems, on the evidence, more difficult for incumbents to regain lost facilities (especially lost loyalties) than for insurgents to multiply their stock of them, even if "logical" reasons for this are not readily apparent. And thirdly, while an increase in incumbent facilities most clearly reduces one of the positive factors, that factor happens to be least potent of the four.

The catalogue of forces making for internal-war potentials thus takes on a certain preliminary order—even if this order is as yet far from precise.

A further element of order can be introduced into the list of variables by noting that, to an extent, they can be paired with one another, specific negative and positive forces being particularly closely related. This is manifest in the case of insurgent and incumbent facilities—clearest of all where the facilities in question are zero-sums. All else being equal, it is obviously not the absolute value of facilities on either side that matters, but the ratio of the facilities concerned. Just as obviously, as already stated, there is a special relation between subversion and repression. Disorientation or elite inefficacy can hardly be repressed; only subversion can.[23] Less manifestly, but pretty clearly still, adjustive concessions bear a particular relation to certain elite failures, particularly in performance, and diversions can, to an extent, provide gratifications that alleviate the psychic stresses of disorientation; but neither is likely to counteract anything else.

One final point that bears more indirectly upon the ordering of the variables listed above requires consideration. It is an appropriate theme on which to conclude, for it is the point with which we started. Throughout the discussion, no distinction has been made between types of internal war, and this not without reasons.[24] The fact remains, however, that internal wars, although in some ways similar, are in most respects greatly various. An adequate etiology of internal wars should therefore be able to tell one more than whether internal war in some form will occur in a society. It should also enable one to account for the specific forms internal wars take in different circumstances.

Any discussion of this matter is at present greatly handicapped by the lack of a settled, well-constructed typology of internal wars—and constructing such a typology is a task great enough to require another, and rather extensive, study. This much can be said, however, without settling on specific typological categories: Approaching the etiological study of internal wars in the manner suggested here makes it possible to deal with the many different phenomena covered by the term internal war within a single theoretical framework, yet in a way that yields quite different accounts of clearly disparate events. And this is surely desirable where phenomena that differ in many respects have also much in common. . . .

[23] To avoid misunderstanding, it should be clearly understood that repression here refers not to putting down rebels in internal wars but preventative actions by the incumbents.

[24] See above, pp. 9–11.

PSYCHOLOGICAL FACTORS IN CIVIL VIOLENCE

Ted Robert Gurr*

Until recently many political scientists tended to regard violent civil conflict as a disfigurement of the body politic, neither a significant nor a proper topic for their empirical inquiries. The attitude was in part our legacy from Thomas Hobbes's contention that violence is the negation of political order, a subject fit less for study than for admonition. Moreover, neither the legalistic nor the institutional approaches that dominated traditional political science could provide much insight into group action that was regarded by definition as illegal and the antithesis of institutionalized political life. The strong empirical bent in American political science led to ethnocentric inquiry into such recurring and salient features of American political life as voting and legislative behavior. The American Revolution and Civil War appeared as unique events, grist for exhaustive historical inquiry but unlikely subjects for systematic comparative study or empirical theory. Representative of the consequences of these attitudes is a recent judgment that political violence "by its very nature [is] beyond

* This article is a revision of a paper read to the panel on "The Psychology of Political Unrest," at the Annual Meeting of the American Psychological Association, New York, September 2–6, 1966. Harry Eckstein's careful and helpful evaluation of draft versions of this paper is gratefully acknowledged. Others who have provided useful, though not always satisfiable, criticism of the theoretical model include Leonard Berkowitz, Alfred de Grazia, Mohammed Guessous, Marion J. Levy, Jr., John T. McAlister, Jr., Mancur L. Olson, Jr., Joel Prager, Bryant Wedge, and Oran R. Young. Theoretical work was supported by an award from a National Science Foundation institutional grant to New York University and by the Center for Research on Social Systems (formerly SORO) of The American University.

Reprinted from *World Politics*, XX (January, 1968), 245–78, by permission of Princeton University Press.

any simple or reasonable laws of causation."[1]

This article proposes, first, that civil violence *is* a significant topic of political inquiry and, second, not only that it is capable of explanation, but that we know enough about the sources of human violence to specify in general, theoretical terms some of the social patterns that dispose men to collective violence.

The proposition that civil violence is important as a genus is widely but not yet universally accepted, even by scholars concerned with some of its forms, revolution in particular.[2] This is the case, one suspects, because revolutions have traditionally been regarded as the most significant form of civil strife, because the universe of such events has been defined by reference to their consequences rather than their common characteristics or preconditions, and because the older theoretical generalizations have emphasized primarily the processes of such events and categorization of their concomitants at a low level of generality.[3] But the evidence both of

recent history and of systematic attempts at specifying the incidence of civil strife suggests that revolutions are but one of an extraordinarily numerous variety of interrelated forms of strife;[4] that some of these forms, among them coups d'état, guerrilla war, and massive rioting, can alter political processes and social institutions as drastically as any of the classic revolutions; and that the forms themselves are mutable, or rather, that by reifying our arbitrary distinctions among forms of strife we have overlooked some fundamental similarities.[5] Examination of those special conditions and

[1] Arnold Forster, "Violence on the Fanatical Left and Right," *Annals of the American Academy of Political and Social Science,* CCCLXIV (March 1966), 142.

[2] For example, Lawrence Stone, "Theories of Revolution," *World Politics,* XVIII (January 1966), 159–76, advances the curious argument that collective violence generally cannot be the object of useful theorizing because it is at the same time both pervasive and somehow peripheral.

[3] The emphasis on processes is evident in the major theoretical analyses of the "classic" revolutions, including Lyford P. Edwards, *The Natural History of Revolutions* (Chicago 1927); Crane Brinton, *The Anatomy of Revolution* (New York 1938); George S. Pettee, *The Process of Revolution* (New York 1938); Louis R. Gottschalk, "Causes of Revolution," *American Journal of Sociology,* L (July 1944), 1–9; and Rex D. Hopper, "The Revolutionary Process: A Frame of Reference for the Study of Revolutionary Movements," *Social Forces,* XXVIII (March 1950), 270–79.

[4] A great many counts of the incidence of civil strife events have recently been reported. Harry Eckstein reports 1,632 "internal wars" in the period 1946–1959 in "On the Etiology of Internal Wars," *History and Theory,* IV, No. 2 (1965), 133–63 [reading 1 in this volume]. Rummel and Tanter counted more than 300 "domestic conflict events" per year during the years 1955–1960, including an annual average of 13 guerrilla wars and 21 attempted overthrows of government; see Raymond Tanter, "Dimensions of Conflict Behavior Within Nations, 1955–60: Turmoil and Internal War," *Peace Research Society Papers,* III (1965), 159–84. Most important to the argument that civil strife is a single universe of events are results of Rudolph Rummel's factor analysis of 236 socioeconomic and political variables, including nine domestic conflict measures, for a large number of nations. Eight of the conflict measures—e.g., number of riots, of revolutions, of purges, of deaths from group violence—are strongly related to a single factor but not significantly related to any others, strong empirical evidence that they comprise a distinct and interrelated set of events. See *Dimensionality of Nations Project: Orthogonally Rotated Factor Tables for 236 Variables,* Department of Political Science, Yale University (New Haven, July 1964), mimeographed.

[5] The "French Revolution" was a series of events that would now be characterized as urban demonstrations and riots, peasant uprisings, and a coup d'état. It is called a revolution in retrospect and by virtue of the Duc de Liancourt's classic remark to Louis XVI. The American Revolution began with a series of increasingly violent urban riots and small-scale terrorism that grew into a protracted guerrilla war.

processes that lead from turmoil to revolution provides a partial understanding of revolution *per se*, but for a sufficient explanation we require a more general theory, one capable of accounting for the common elements of that much larger class of events called civil strife.

The resort to illicit violence is the defining property that distinguishes these collective events from others. We can regard this as just a definitional point,[6] but it has a crucial theoretical consequence: to direct attention to psychological theories about the sources of human aggression.

Some types of psychological theories about the sources of aggressive behavior can be eliminated at the outset. There is little value in pseudopsychological speculation about revolutionaries as deviants, fools, or the maladjusted. Psychodynamic explanations of the "revolutionary personality" may be useful for microanalysis of particular events but scarcely for general theory. Aggression-prone victims of maladaptive socialization processes are found in every society, and among the actors in most outbreaks of civil violence, but they are much more likely to be mobilized by strife than to be wholly responsible for its occurrence. Nor can a general theory of civil strife rest on culturally specific theories of modal personality

traits, though it might well take account of the effects of these traits. Some cultures and subcultures produce significantly more aggression-prone than cooperative personalities, but an explanation of this order says little of the societal conditions that elicit aggression from the aggression-prone, and nothing at all of the capacity for civil violence of even the most apparently quiescent populations.

The only generally relevant psychological theories are those that deal with the sources and characteristics of aggression in all men, regardless of culture. Such psychological theories do not directly constitute a theory of civil strife. They do offer alternative motivational bases for such a theory and provide means for identifying and specifying the operation of some crucial explanatory variables. As is demonstrated in the following section, one or another of these theories is implicit in most theoretical approaches to civil strife that have no explicit motivational base, although only one of them appears highly plausible in the light of empirical evidence.

Psychological Theories of Aggression

There are three distinct psychological assumptions about the generic sources of human aggression: that aggression is solely instinctual, that it is solely learned, or that it is an innate response activated by frustration.[7] The instinct

[6] The universe of concern, civil violence, is formally defined as *all collective, nongovernmental attacks on persons or property, resulting in intentional damage to them, that occur within the boundaries of an autonomous or colonial political unit*. The terms "civil strife," "violent civil conflict," and "civil violence" are used synonymously in this article. The universe subsumes more narrowly defined sets of events such as "internal war," which Harry Eckstein defines as "any resort to violence within a political order to change its constitution, rulers, or policies" (in "On the Etiology of Internal Wars," 133), and "revolution," typically defined in terms of violently accomplished fundamental change in social institutions.

[7] Bryant Wedge argues (in a personal communication) that much human aggression, including some civil strife, may arise from a threat-fear-aggression sequence. Leonard Berkowitz, however, proposes that this mechanism can be subsumed by frustration-aggression theory, the inferred sequence being threat (anticipated frustration)-fear-anger-aggression, in *Aggression: A Social Psychological Analysis* (New York 1962), chap 2. It may be conceptually useful to distinguish the two mechanisms;

theories of aggression, represented, among others, by Freud's attribution of the impulse to destructiveness to a death instinct and by Lorenz's view of aggression as a survival-enhancing instinct, assume that most or all men have within them an autonomous source of aggressive impulses, a drive to aggress that, in Lorenz's words, exhibits "irresistible outbreaks which recur with rhythmical regularity."[8] Although there is no definitive support for this assumption, and much evidence to the contrary, its advocates, including Freud and Lorenz, have often applied it to the explanation of collective as well as individual aggression.[9] The assumption is evident in Hobbes's characterization of man in the state of nature and is perhaps implicit in Nieburg's recent concern for "the people's capability for outraged, uncontrolled, bitter, and bloody violence,"[10] but plays no significant role in contemporary theories of civil strife.

Just the opposite assumption, that aggressive behavior is solely or primarily learned, characterizes the work of some child and social psychologists, whose evidence indicates that some aggressive behaviors are learned and used strategically in the service of particular goals—aggression by children and adolescents to secure attention, by adults to express dominance strivings, by groups in competition for scarce values, by military personnel in the service of national policy.[11] The assumption that violence is a learned response, rationalistically chosen and dispassionately employed, is common to a number of recent theoretical approaches to civil strife. Johnson repeatedly, though not consistently, speaks of civil violence as "purposive," as "forms of behavior *intended* to disorient the behavior of others, thereby bringing about the demise of a hated social system."[12] Parsons attempts to fit civil violence into the framework of social interaction theory, treating the resort to force as a way of acting chosen by the actor(s) for purposes of deterrence, punishment, or symbolic demonstration of their capacity to act.[13] Schelling is representative of the conflict theorists: he explicitly assumes rational behavior and interdependence of the adversaries' decisions in all types of conflict.[14] Stone criticizes any emphasis on violence as a distinguishing or definitional property of civil strife on grounds that it is only a particular means, designed to serve political ends.[15]

The third psychological assumption about aggression is that it occurs primarily as a response to frustration. A "frustration" is an interference with goal-directed behavior; "aggression" is behavior designed to injure,

---

it nonetheless appears likely that most variables affecting the outcome of the frustration-aggression sequence also are operative in the postulated threat-aggression sequence.

[8] Konrad Lorenz, *On Aggression* (New York 1966), xii.

[9] Sigmund Freud, *Civilization and Its Discontents*, trans. Joan Riviere (London 1930); Lorenz, chaps. 13, 14. Freud's instinctual interpretation of aggression is advanced in his later works; his early view was that aggression is a response to frustration of pleasure-seeking behavior. For a review and critique of other instinct theories of aggression, see Berkowitz, chap. 1.

[10] H. L. Nieburg, "The Threat of Violence and Social Change," *American Political Science Review*, LVI (December 1962), 870.

[11] A characteristic study is Albert Bandura and Richard H. Walters, *Social Learning and Personality Development* (New York 1963). For a commentary on instrumental aggression, see Berkowitz, esp. 30–32, 182–83, 201–2.

[12] Chalmers Johnson, *Revolutionary Change* (Boston 1966), 12, 13, italics added.

[13] Talcott Parsons, "Some Reflections on the Place of Force in Social Process," in Harry Eckstein, ed., *Internal War: Problems and Approaches* (New York 1964), 34–35.

[14] Thomas C. Schelling, *The Strategy of Conflict* (Cambridge, Mass., 1960), 4.

[15] P. 161.

physically or otherwise, those toward whom it is directed. The disposition to respond aggressively when frustrated is considered part of man's biological makeup; there is an innate tendency to attack the frustrating agent. Learning can and does modify the tendency: what is perceived to be frustrating, modes of aggressive response, inhibition through fear of retaliation, and appropriate targets are all modified or defined in the learning process, typically but not solely during socialization.

Frustration-aggression theory is more systematically developed, and has substantially more empirical support, than theories that assume either that all men have a free-flowing source of destructive energy or that all aggression is imitative and instrumental. Moreover, the kinds of evidence cited in support of theories of the latter type appear to be subsumable by frustration-aggression theory, whereas the converse is not the case.

One crucial element that frustration-aggression theory contributes to the study of civil violence concerns the drive properties of anger. In the recent reformulation of the theory by Berkowitz, the perception of frustration is said to arouse anger, which functions as a drive. Aggressive responses tend not to occur unless evoked by some external cue, but their occurrence is an inherently satisfying response to that anger.[16] Similarly, Maier has amassed extensive evidence that the innate frustration-induced behaviors (including regression, fixation, and resignation, as well as aggression) are for the actor ends in themselves, unrelated to further goals and qualitatively different from goal-directed behavior.[17]

To argue that aggression is innately satisfying is not incompatible with the presence of learned or purposive components in acts of individual or collective aggression. Cues that determine the timing, forms, and objects of aggression are learned, just as habits of responding aggressively to moderate as well as severe frustration can be learned. The sense of frustration may result from quite rational analysis of the social universe. Leaders can put their followers' anger to rational or rationalized uses. If anger is sufficiently powerful and persistent it may function as an autonomous drive, leading to highly rational and effective efforts by both leaders and the led to satisfy anger aggressively. The crucial point is that rationalization and organization of illicit violence are typically subsequent to, and contingent upon, the existence of frustration-induced anger. Collective violence may be a calculated strategy of dispassionate elite aspirants, and expectations of gains to be achieved through violence may be present among many of its participants. Nonetheless the implication of frustration-aggression theory is that civil violence almost always has a strong "appetitive," emotional base and that the magnitude of its effects on the social system is

[16] The most influential and systematic statement of the theory is John Dollard and others, *Frustration and Aggression* (New Haven 1939). Two important recent syntheses of the evidence are Berkowitz, *Aggression*, and Aubrey J. Yates, *Frustration and Conflict* (New York 1962). Also see Leonard Berkowitz, "The Concept of Aggressive Drive: Some Additional Considerations," in Berkowitz, ed., *Advances in Experimental Psychology*, Vol. II (New York 1965), 307–22.

[17] Norman R. F. Maier, *Frustration: The Study of Behavior Without a Goal* (New York 1949), 92–115, 159–61. Maier postulates a frustration threshold that may open the way to any of four classes of "goal-less" behavior of which aggression is only one. His findings have not been related adequately to the body of research on the frustration-aggression relationship. One can suggest, however, that the nonaggressive responses—fixation, repression, and apparent resignation—can be treated as more or less innate responses in a response hierarchy which are resorted to in the absence of aggression-evoking cues.

substantially dependent on how widespread and intense anger is among those it mobilizes.

If anger implies the presence of frustration, there is compelling evidence that frustration is all but universally characteristic of participants in civil strife: discontent, anger, rage, hate, and their synonyms are repeatedly mentioned in studies of strife. Moreover, the frustration assumption is implicit or explicit in many theoretical analyses of the subject. Smelser's concept of "strain" as one of the major determinants of collective behavior, particularly hostile outbursts and value-oriented movements (revolutions) can be readily reformulated in terms of perceived frustration.[18] So can Willer and Zollschan's notion of "exigency" as a precursor of revolution.[19] Ridker characterizes the consequence of failure to attain economic expectations as "discontent," analogous in source and consequence to anger.[20] In Davies' theory of revolution, the reversal of a trend of socioeconomic development is said to create frustration which instigates revolution.[21] Galtung's theory of both intranational and international aggression recognizes that "the external conditions leading to aggression . . . probably have to pass through the minds of men and precipitate as perceptions with a high emotive content before they are acted out as aggression."[22]

In none of these approaches to theory, however, has frustration-aggression theory been systematically exploited nor have its variables been taken into account.[23] The primary object of this article is to demonstrate that many of the variables and relationships identified in social psychological research on the frustration-aggression relationship appear to underlie the phenomenology of civil violence. Juxtaposition of these two diverse types of material provides a basis for an interrelated set of propositions that is intended to constitute the framework of a general theory of the conditions that determine the likelihood and magnitude of civil violence. These propositions are of two types, whose proposed relationships are diagrammed in Figure 1: (1) propositions about the operation of *instigating variables*, which determine the magnitude of anger, and (2) propositions about *mediating variables*, which determine the likelihood and magnitude of overt violence as a response to anger.[24]

This approach does not deny the relevance of aspects of the social structure, which many conflict theorists have held to be crucial. The supposition is that theory about civil violence is most fruitfully based on systematic knowledge about those properties of

[18] Neil J. Smelser, *Theory of Collective Behavior* (New York 1963).

[19] David Willer and George K. Zollschan, "Prolegomenon to a Theory of Revolutions," in George K. Zollschan and Walter Hirsch, eds., *Explorations in Social Change* (Boston 1964), 125–51.

[20] Ronald G. Ridker, "Discontent and Economic Growth," *Economic Development and Cultural Change*, XI (October 1962), 1–15.

[21] James C. Davies, "Toward a Theory of Revolution," *American Sociological Review*, XXVII (February 1962), 5–19 [reading 4 in this volume].

[22] Johan Galtung, "A Structural Theory of Aggression," *Journal of Peace Research*, II, No. 2 (1964), 95 [reading 5 in this volume].

[23] Ivo K. and Rosalind L. Feierabend, in "Aggressive Behaviors within Polities, 1948–1962: A Cross-National Study," *Journal of Conflict Resolution*, X (September 1966), 249–71, have formally equated political instability with aggressive behavior and have derived and tested several hypotheses about stability from frustration-aggression theory. They have attempted no general theoretical synthesis, however.

[24] The term "instigating" is adapted from the behavioristic terminology of Dollard and others. Instigating variables determine the strength of instigation, i.e., stimulus or motivation, to a particular kind of behavior. Mediating variables refer to intervening conditions, internal or external to the actors, which modify the expression of that behavior.

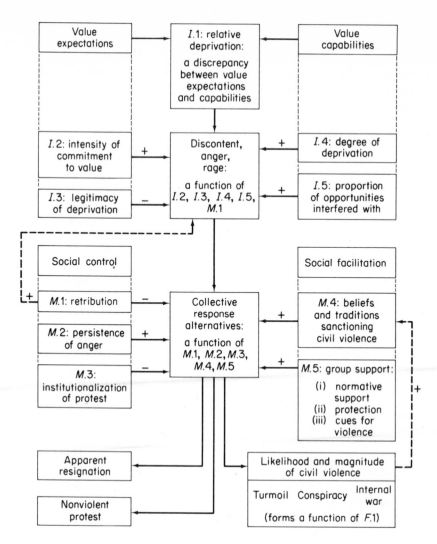

The direction(s) of proposed effects on magnitude of
civil violence are indicated by + and −.

FIGURE 1. Variables Determining the Likelihood and Magnitude
of Civil Violence.

men that determine how they react to certain characteristics of their societies.

Relative Deprivation: Variables Determining the Magnitude of Anger

My basic premise is that the necessary precondition for violent civil conflict is relative deprivation, defined as actors' perception of discrepancy between their *value expectations* and their environment's apparent *value capabilities*.[25] Value expectations are

[25] The phrase "relative deprivation" was first used systematically in Samuel A. Stouffer and others, *The American Soldier: Adjustment During Army Life*, Vol. I (Princeton 1949), to denote the violation of expectations. J.

the goods and conditions of life to which people believe they are justifiably entitled. The referents of value capabilities are to be found largely in the social and physical environment: they are the conditions that determine people's perceived chances of getting or keeping the values they legitimately expect to attain. In a comparable treatment, Aberle defines relative deprivation as "a negative discrepancy between legitimate expectation and actuality," viewing expectations as standards, not mere prophecies or hopes.[26] For purposes of general theoretical specification I assume that perceived discrepancies between expectations and capabilities with respect to any collectively sought value—economic, psychosocial, political—constitute relative deprivation. The extent to which some values may be more salient than others is a subject of theoretical and empirical inquiry not evaluated here.

Stacy Adams reviews the concept's history and some relevant evidence and suggests that feelings of injustice intervene between the condition of relative deprivation and responses to it, in "Inequity in Social Exchange," in Berkowitz, ed., *Advances in Experimental Psychology*, 267–300. The "injustice" aspect is implicit in my definition and use of relative deprivation as *perceived* discrepancy between what people think they will get and what they believe they are entitled to. The Stouffer concept has been related to levels of social satisfaction and to anomie, but has not, so far as I know, been associated with the discontent-anger-rage continuum in the frustration-aggression relationship.

[26] David F. Aberle, "A Note on Relative Deprivation Theory," in Sylvia L. Thrupp, ed., *Millennial Dreams in Action: Essays in Comparative Study* (The Hague 1962), 209–14. Bert Hoselitz and Ann Willner similarly distinguish between expectations, regarded by the individual as "what is rightfully owed to him," and aspirations, which represent "that which he would like to have but has not necessarily had or considered his due," in "Economic Development, Political Strategies, and American Aid," in Morton A. Kaplan, ed., *The Revolution in World Politics* (New York 1962), 363.

Relative deprivation can be related to the concept of frustration by extending Yates's distinction between the frustrating situation and the frustrated organism.[27] A frustrating situation is one in which an actor is, by objective standards, thwarted by some social or physical barrier in attempts to attain or continue enjoyment of a value. The actor can be said to be frustrated, however, only when he is aware of interference or thwarting. The awareness of interference is equivalent to the concept of relative deprivation as defined above.

A further distinction is necessary between two general classes of deprivation: those that are personal and those that are group or category experiences.[28] For given groups, and for some classes of societies, it is possible to identify events and patterns of conditions that are likely to be widely seen as unjust deprivation. Such events may occur abruptly—for example, the suppression of a political party or a drastic inflation—or slowly, like the decline of a group's status relative to other social classes. Such conditions can be called collective frustrations[29] to distinguish them from such unexpected personal frustrations as failure to obtain an expected promotion or the infidelity of a spouse, which may be relatively common but randomly incident in most populations.

Whether empirical research ought to focus on conditions defined as collectively frustrating or directly on perceived deprivation is an operational question whose answer depends on the researcher's interest and resources, not upon the following theoretical formulation. Survey techniques

[27] Pp. 175–78.
[28] Aberle, 210.
[29] The Feierabends use the comparable term "systemic frustration" to describe the balance between "social want satisfaction" and "social want formation."

permit more or less direct assessment of the extent and severity of relative deprivation.[30] To the extent that the researcher is prepared to make assumptions about measurable conditions that are collectively frustrating in diverse nations, cross-national aggregate data can be used in correlational studies.[31]

The basic relationship can be summarized in a proposition analogous to and assuming the same basic mechanism as the fundamental theorem of frustration-aggression theory[32]:

Proposition I.1: The occurrence of civil violence presupposes the likelihood of relative deprivation among substantial numbers of individuals in a society; concomitantly, the more severe is relative deprivation, the greater are the likelihood and intensity of civil violence.

This proposition may be truistic, although theories were noted above. which attempt to account for civil strife without reference to discontent. Moreover, relative deprivation in some degree can be found in any society. The usefulness of the basic proposition is best determined by reference to the set of propositions that qualify it. These propositions specify the conditions that determine the severity and in some cases the occurrence of deprivation, whether or not it is likely to lead to civil violence, and the magnitude

[30] Hadley Cantril's work offers examples, especially *The Pattern of Human Concerns* (New Brunswick 1965).

[31] This approach is exemplified by the Feierabends' work and by Bruce M. Russett, "Inequality and Instability: The Relation of Land Tenure to Politics," *World Politics*, XVI (April 1964), 442–54 [reading 8 in this volume].

[32] The basic postulate of Dollard and others is that "the occurrence of aggressive behavior always presupposes the existence of frustration and, contrariwise, that the existence of frustration always leads to some form of aggression" (p. 1). It is evident from context and from subsequent articles that this statement was intended in more qualified fashion.

of violence when it does occur. The fundamental question, which is susceptible to a variety of empirical tests, is whether the proposed precise relationship between severity of deprivation, as determined by variables I.2 through I.5, and magnitude of violence does hold when the effects of the mediating variables M.1 through M.5 are taken into account.

DEFINITIONS AND QUALIFICATIONS

Civil violence and relative deprivation are defined above. If relative deprivation is the perception of frustrating circumstances, the emotional response to it tends to be anger. Obviously there are degrees of anger, which can usefully be regarded as a continuum varying from mild dissatisfaction to blind rage. The severity of relative deprivation is assumed to vary directly with the modal strength of anger in the affected population; the determinants of strength of anger are specified in propositions I.2 to I.5, below.

The concept of magnitude requires elaboration. Various measures of quantity or magnitude of aggression are used in psychological research on the frustration-aggression relationship—for example, the intensity of electric shocks administered by frustrated subjects to a supposed frustrater, numbers of aggressive responses in test situations, or the length of time frustrated children play destructively with inanimate objects. A consideration of theory, however, suggests that no single measure of magnitude of aggression is *prima facie* sufficient. Assuming the validity of the basic frustration-aggression postulate that the greater the strength of anger, the greater the quantity of aggression, it seems likely that strong anger can be satisfied either by inflicting severe immediate damage on the source of frustration or by prolonged but less severe aggression, and that either of these tactics is probably more or less substitutable for the other. Which alternative is taken may very well be a function of opportunity, and while opportunities can be controlled in experimental situations, in civil violence they are situationally determined. Hence neither severity nor duration alone is likely to reflect the modal strength of collective anger or, consequently, to constitute an adequate measure of magnitude of civil violence.

Moreover, there are evidently individual differences—presumably normally distributed—in the strength of anger needed to precipitate overt aggression. Hence the proportion of a population that participates in collective violence ought to vary with the modal strength of anger: discontent will motivate few to violence, anger will push more across the threshold, rage is likely to galvanize large segments of a collectivity into action. This line of argument suggests that magnitude of civil violence has three component variables: the degree of participation within the affected population, the destructiveness of the aggressive actions, and the length of time violence persists.

Frustration-aggression theory stipulates a set of variables that determine the strength of anger or discontent in response to a given frustration. Dollard and others initially proposed that the strength of instigation to aggression (anger) varies with "(1) the strength of instigation to the frustrated response, (2) the degree of interference with the frustrated response, and (3) the number of frustrated response-sequences."[33] The first of these variables, modified in the light of empirical evidence, provides the basis for propositions about charac-

teristics of value expectations that affect the intensity of anger. The second and third variables, similarly modified, suggest several propositions about value capabilities.

Before the propositions are presented, two qualifications of the classic behaviorist conceptualization of frustration as interference with specific, goal-directed responses must be noted. First, it appears from examination of specific outbreaks of civil violence that abrupt awareness of the likelihood of frustration can be as potent a source of anger as actual interference. The Vendée counterrevolution in eighteenth-century France was triggered by the announcement of military conscription, for example.[34] A survey of twentieth-century South African history shows that waves of East Indian and Bantu rioting historically have coincided with the parliamentary discussion of restrictive legislation more than with its actual imposition. The Indian food riots in the spring of 1966 were certainly not instigated by the onset of starvation but by its anticipation.

Second, it seems evident that the sense of deprivation can arise either from interference with goal-seeking behavior or from interference with continued enjoyment of an attained condition. As an example from psychological experimentation, frustration is often operationalized by insults; it seems more likely that the insults are a threat to the subjects' perceived level of status attainment or personal esteem than they are an interference with behavior directed toward some as-yet-unattained goal. Several examples from the history of civil violence are relevant. A student of the coup d'état that overthrew the Perón regime in Argentina states that the crucial events

[33] Ibid., 28.

[34] Charles Tilly, The Vendée (Cambridge, Mass., 1964).

that precipitated the anti-Perónists into action were Perón's public insults to the Catholic hierarchy and isolated physical depredations by his supporters against Church properties—events symbolizing an attack on the moral foundations of upper-middle-class Argentine society.[35] In Soviet Central Asia, according to Massell, the most massive and violent resistance to Sovietization followed systematic attempts to break Muslim women loose from their slavish subordination to Muslim men.[36] The two kinds of interference may have differential effects on the intensity and consequences of anger; the point to be made here is that both can instigate violence.

Consequently, analysis of the sources of relative deprivation should take account of both actual and anticipated interference with human goals, as well as of interference with value positions both sought and achieved. Formulations of frustration in terms of the "want: get ratio," which refers only to a discrepancy between sought values and actual attainment, are too simplistic. Man lives mentally in the near future as much as in the present.[37] Actual or anticipated interference with what he has, and with the act of striving itself, are all volatile sources of discontent.

VALUE EXPECTATIONS

The propositions developed here concern the effects on perceived deprivation of the salience of an expecta-

tion for a group, rather than the absolute level of the expectation.[38] The first suggestion derived from psychological theory is that the more intensely people are motivated toward a goal, or committed to an attained level of values, the more sharply is interference resented and the greater is the consequent instigation to aggression. One can, for example, account for some of the efficacy of ideologies in generating civil violence by reference to this variable. The articulation of nationalistic ideologies in colonial territories evidently strengthened preexisting desires for political independence among the colonial bourgeoisie at the same time that it inspired a wholly new set of political demands among other groups. Similarly, it has been argued that the desire of the nineteenth-century European factory worker for a better economic lot was intensified as well as rationalized by Marxist teachings.

Experimental evidence has suggested qualifications of the basic proposition which are equally relevant. One is that the closer men approach a goal, the more intensely motivated toward it

[35] Reuben de Hoyos, personal communication.

[36] Gregory Massell, "The Strategy of Social Change and the Role of Women in Soviet Central Asia: A Case Study in Modernization and Control," Ph.D. diss., Harvard University, 1966.

[37] For this kind of approach, see Daniel Lerner, "Toward a Communication Theory of Modernization: A Set of Considerations," in Lucian W. Pye, ed., Communications and Political Development (Princeton 1963), 330–35.

[38] This general statement of theory is concerned with specification of variables and their effects, not with their content in specific cases; hence the conditions that determine the *levels* of expectation and changes in those levels are not treated here, nor are the conditions that affect perceptions about value capabilities. For some attempts to generalize about such conditions, see Gurr, *Why Men Rebel* (Princeton, 1970), esp. chaps. 4 and 5. For empirical evaluation or application of the theory, it is of course necessary to evaluate in some way levels of expectation in the population(s) studied. Some approaches to evaluation are illustrated in Gurr with Charles Ruttenberg, *The Conditions of Civil Violence: First Tests of a Causal Model*, Center of International Studies, Princeton University, Research Monograph No. 28 (Princeton 1967), and Gurr, "A Causal Model of Civil Strife: A Comparative Analysis Using New Indices," *American Political Science Review*, LXII (December 1968), 1104–24 [reading 10 in this volume].

they appear to be.[39] This finding has counterparts in observations about civil violence. Hoffer is representative of many theorists in noting that "discontent is likely to be highest when misery is bearable [and] when conditions have so improved that an ideal state seems almost within reach. ... The intensity of discontent seems to be in inverse proportion to the distance from the object fervently desired."[40] The intensity of motivation varies with the perceived rather than the actual closeness of the goal, of course. The event that inflicts the sense of deprivation may be the realization that a goal thought to be at hand is still remote. The mechanism is clearly relevant to the genesis of post-independence violence in tropical Africa. Failure to realize the promises of independence in the Congo had extraordinarily virulent results, as is evident in a comparison of the intensive and extensive violence of the uprisings of the "Second Independence" of 1964–1965 with the more sporadic settling of accounts that followed the "First Independence" of 1960.[41]

The proposition relates as well to the severity of discontent in societies in the full swing of socioeconomic change. The rising bourgeoisie of eighteenth-century France, for example, individually and collectively had a major commitment to their improving conditions of life, and great effort invested in them. Many felt their aspirations for political influence and high social status to be close to realization but threatened by the declining responsiveness of the state and by economic deprivations inherent in stumbling state efforts to control trade and raise taxes.[42]

Although much additional evidence could be advanced, the relationships cited above are sufficient to suggest the following proposition and its corollaries:

Proposition I.2: The strength of anger tends to vary directly with the intensity of commitment to the goal or condition with regard to which deprivation is suffered or anticipated.

I.2a: The strength of anger tends to vary directly with the degree of effort previously invested in the attainment or maintenance of the goal or condition.

I.2b: The intensity of commitment to a goal or condition tends to vary inversely with its perceived closeness.

It also has been found that, under some circumstances, anticipation or experience of frustration tends to reduce motivation toward a goal. This is particularly the case if frustration is thought to be justified and likely.[43] Pastore, for example, reports that when subjects saw frustration as reasonable or justifiable, they gave fewer aggressive responses than when they perceived it to be arbitrary. Kregarman and Worchel, however, found that the reasonableness of a frustration did not significantly reduce aggression and that anticipation of frustration tended not to reduce anger but rather to inhibit external aggressive responses.[44]

---

[39] See Berkowitz, *Aggression*, 53–54.

[40] Eric Hoffer, *The True Believer* (New York 1951), 27–28.

[41] Compare Crawford Young, *Politics in the Congo* (Princeton 1965), chap. 13, with commentaries on the Kwilu and Stanleyville rebellions, such as Renée C. Fox and others, "'The Second Independence': A Case Study of the Kwilu Rebellion in the Congo," *Comparative Studies in Society and History*, VIII (October 1965), 78–109; and Herbert Weiss, *Political Protest in the Congo* (Princeton 1967).

[42] See, among many other works, Georges Lefebvre, *The Coming of the French Revolution* (Princeton 1947), Part II.

[43] Value expectations are defined above in terms of the value positions to which men believe they are justifiably entitled; the discussion here assumes that men may also regard as justifiable some types of interference with those value positions.

[44] Nicholas Pastore, "The Role of Arbi-

The low levels of motivation and the moderate nature of interference that characterize these studies make generalization to "real," collective situations doubtful. If applied to a hypothetical example relevant to civil strife—say, the effects of increased taxation on a population under conditions of varying legitimacy attributed to the action—the experimental findings suggest three alternatives: (1) that anger varies inversely with the legitimacy attributed to interference; (2) that anger is constant, but inhibition of its expression varies directly with legitimacy; or (3) that no systematic relationship holds between the two. If the sources of legitimacy are treated in Merelman's learning-theory terms, the first of these alternatives appears most likely: if legitimacy is high, acceptance of deprivation (compliance) provides symbolic substitute rewards.[45] It may also be that the first alternative holds in circumstances in which legitimacy is high, the second in circumstances in which it is moderate. The first relationship can be formulated in propositional form, with the qualification that evidence for it is less than definitive:

Proposition I.3: The strength of anger tends to vary inversely with the extent to which deprivation is held to be legitimate.

trariness in the Frustration-Aggression Hypothesis," *Journal of Abnormal and Social Psychology*, XLVII (July 1952), 728–31; John J. Kregarman and Philip Worchel, "Arbitrariness of Frustration and Aggression," *Journal of Abnormal and Social Psychology*, LXIII (July 1961), 183–87.

[45] The argument is that people comply "to gain both the symbolic rewards of governmental action and the actual rewards with which government originally associated itself" and rationalize compliance with "the feeling that the regime is a morally appropriate agent of control ..." (Richard M. Merelman, "Learning and Legitimacy," *American Political Science Review*, LX [September 1966], 551). The argument applies equally well to compliance, including acceptance of deprivation, with the demands of other social institutions.

VALUE CAPABILITIES

The environment in which people strive toward goals has two general characteristics that, frustration-aggression theory suggests, affect the intensity of anger: the degree of interference with goal attainment and the number of opportunities provided for attainment.

Almost all the literature on civil strife assumes a causal connection between the existence of interference (or "frustration," "cramp," or "disequilibrium") and strife. "Discontent" and its synonyms are sometimes used to symbolize the condition of interference without reference to interference *per se.* A direct relationship between degree of interference and intensity of strife is usually implicit but not always demonstrated. Rostow has shown graphically that poor economic conditions—high wheat prices, high unemployment—corresponded with the severity of overt mass protest in England from 1790 to 1850.[46] Variations in bread prices and in mob violence went hand in hand in revolutionary France.[47] There is correlational evidence that the frequency of lynchings in the American South, 1882–1930, tended to vary inversely with indices of economic well-being.[48] From cross-national studies there is suggestive evidence also—for example, Kornhauser's correlations of $-.93$ between per capita income and the Communist share of the vote in sixteen Western democracies in 1949.[49]

[46] Walt W. Rostow, *British Economy of the Nineteenth Century* (Oxford 1948), chap. 5.

[47] George Rudé, "Prices, Wages, and Popular Movements in Paris During the French Revolution," *Economic History Review*, VI (1954), 246–67, and *The Crowd in History, 1730–1848* (New York 1964), chap. 7.

[48] Carl Hovland and Robert Sears, "Minor Studies in Aggression, VI: Correlation of Lynchings with Economic Indices," *Journal of Psychology*, IX (1940), 301–10.

[49] William Kornhauser, *The Politics of Mass Society* (New York 1959), 160.

The Feierabends devised "frustration" measures, based on value capability characteristics of sixty-two nations, and correlated them with a general measure of degree of political stability, obtaining a correlation coefficient of .50.[50]

As far as the precise form of the relationship between extent of interference and intensity of aggression is concerned, the experimental results of Hamblin and others are persuasive. Three hypotheses were tested: the classic formulation that instigation to aggression varies directly with the degree of interference, and the psychophysical hypotheses that aggression ought to be a log or a power function of interference. The data strongly support the last hypothesis, that aggression is a power function of degree of interference—i.e., if magnitude of aggression is plotted against degree of interference, the result is a sharply rising "J-curve." Moreover, the power exponent—the sharpness with which the J-curve rises—appears to increase with the strength of motivation toward the goal with which interference was experienced.[51] It is at least plausible that the J-curve relationship should hold for civil strife. Compatible with this inference, though not bearing directly on it, is the logarithmic distribution curve that characterizes such cross-polity measures of intensity of civil violence as deaths per 100,000 population.[52] It also may account for the impressionistic observation that moderate levels of discontent typically lead to easily quelled turmoil but that higher levels of discontent seem associated with incommensurately intense and persistent civil violence. In propositional form:

Proposition I.4: The strength of anger tends to vary as a power function of the perceived distance between the value position sought or enjoyed and the attainable or residual value position.[53]

Experimental evidence regarding the hypothesis of Dollard and others that the greater the number of frustrations the greater the instigation to aggression is somewhat ambiguous. Most people appear to have hierarchies of response to repeated frustration, a typical sequence being intensified effort, including search for alternative methods or substitute goals, followed by increasingly overt aggression as other responses are extinguished, and ultimately by resignation or apparent acceptance of frustration. Berkowitz suggests that most such evidence, however, is congruent with the interpretation that "the probability of emotional reactions is a function of the degree to which all possible nonaggressive responses are blocked, more than to the interference with any one response sequence."[54]

The societal equivalents of "all possible nonaggressive responses" can be regarded as all normative courses of action available to members of a collectivity for value attainment, plus all attainable substitute value positions. Relevant conditions are evident in the portraits of "transitional man" painted by Lerner and others. Those who are

[50] "Aggressive Behaviors within Polities."

[51] Robert L. Hamblin and others, "The Interference-Aggression Law?" *Sociometry*, XXVI (1963), 190–216.

[52] Bruce M. Russett and others, *World Handbook of Political and Social Indicators* (New Haven 1963), 97–100.

[53] There is a threshold effect with reference to physical well-being. If life itself is the value threatened and the threat is imminent, the emotional response tends to be fear or panic; once the immediate threat is past, anger against the source of threat tends to manifest itself again. See n. 7 above, and Berkowitz, *Aggression*, 42–46.

[54] Leonard Berkowitz, "Repeated Frustrations and Expectations in Hostility Arousal," *Journal of Abnormal and Social Psychology*, LX (May 1960), 422–29.

committed to improving their socioeconomic status are more likely to become bitterly discontented if they have few rather than many prospective employers, if they can get no work rather than some kind of work that provides a sense of progress, if they have few opportunities to acquire requisite literacy and technical skills, if associational means for influencing patterns of political and economic value distributions are not available, or if community life is so disrupted that hearth and kin offer no surcease from frustration for the unsuccessful worker.[55] All such conditions can be subsumed by the rubric of "opportunities for value attainment," with the qualification that perception of opportunities tends to be more crucial than actual opportunities.

Much evidence from studies of civil strife suggests that the greater are value opportunities, the less intense is civil violence. The argument appears in varying guises. Brogan attributes the comparative quiescence of mid-nineteenth-century English workers vis-à-vis their French counterparts in part to the proliferation in England of new cooperatives, friendly and building societies, and trade unions, which provided positive alternatives to violent protest.[56] The first of the American Negro urban rebellions in the 1960's occurred in a community, Watts, in which by contemporary accounts associational activity and job-training programs had been less effective than those of almost any other large Negro community. Cohn explains the high participation of unskilled workers and landless peasants in the violent millenarian frenzies of medieval Europe by reference to the lack of "the material and emotional support

afforded by traditional social groups; their kinship groups had disintegrated and they were not effectively organised in village communities or in guilds; for them there existed no regular, institutionalised methods of voicing their grievances or pressing their claims."[57] Kling attributes the chronic Latin American pattern of coup d'état to the lack of adequate alternatives facing elite aspirants with economic ambitions; political office, seized illicitly if necessary, provides opportunity for satisfying those ambitions.[58]

More general observations also are relevant. Economists suggest that government can relieve the discontents that accompany the strains of rapid economic growth by providing compensatory welfare measures—i.e., alternative means of value satisfaction.[59] Numerous scholars have shown that migration is a common response to deprivation and that high emigration rates often precede outbreaks of civil violence. In a cross-national study of correlates of civil violence for 1961–1963, I have found a rather consistent association between extensive educational opportunities, proportionally large trade union movements, and stable political party systems on the one hand and low levels of strife on the other, relationships that tend to hold among nations whatever their absolute level of economic development. Education presumably increases the apparent range of opportunity for socioeconomic advance, unionization can provide a secondary means for economic goal attainment, and parties serve as primary mechanisms for attainment of

[55] See, for example, Daniel Lerner, *The Passing of Traditional Society* (Glencoe 1958).

[56] Denis W. Brogan, *The Price of Revolution* (London 1951), 34.

[57] Norman R. C. Cohn, *The Pursuit of the Millennium*, 2d ed. rev. (New York 1961), 315.

[58] Merle Kling, "Toward a Theory of Power and Political Instability in Latin America," *Western Political Quarterly*, IX (March 1956), 21–35.

[59] Ridker, 15; Mancur Olson, Jr., "Growth as a Destabilizing Force," *Journal of Economic History*, XXIII (December 1963), 550–51.

participatory political values.[60] Hence:

Proposition I.5: The strength of anger tends to vary directly with the proportion of all available opportunities for value attainment with which interference is experienced or anticipated.

The Mediation of Anger: The Effects of Social Control and Social Facilitation

For the purpose of the theoretical model I assume that the average strength of anger in a population is a precise multiple function of the instigating variables. Whether or not civil violence actually occurs as a response to anger, and its magnitude when it does occur, are influenced by a number of mediating variables. Evidence for these variables and their effects is found both in the psychological literature and in studies of civil violence *per se*. It is useful to distinguish them according to whether they inhibit or facilitate the violent manifestation of anger.

SOCIAL CONTROL:

THE EFFECTS OF RETRIBUTION

The classic formulation is that aggression may be inhibited through fear of "such responses on the part of the social environment as physical injury, insults, ostracism, and deprivation of goods or freedom."[61] Good experimental evidence indicates that anticipation of retribution is under some circumstances an effective regulator of aggression.[62] Comparably,

a linear relationship between, on the one hand, the capacity and willingness of government to enforce its monopoly of control of the organized instrumentalities of force and, on the other, the likelihood of civil violence is widely assumed in the literature on civil strife. Strong apparent force capability on the part of the regime ought to be sufficient to deter violence, and if violence should occur, the effectiveness with which it is suppressed is closely related to the likelihood and intensity of subsequent violence. Smelser states that a major determinant of the occurrence of civil strife is declining capacity or loyalty of the police and military control apparatus.[63] Johnson says that "the success or failure of armed insurrection and ... commonly even the decision to attempt revolution rest ... upon the attitude (or the revolutionaries' estimate of that attitude) that the armed forces will adopt toward the revolution."[64] In Janos' view, the weakening of law-enforcement agencies "creates general disorder, inordinate concrete demands by various groups, and the rise of utopian aspirations."[65] Military defeat is often empirically associated with the occurrence of revolution. Race riots in the United States and elsewhere have often been associated with tacit approval of violence by authorities.[66] Paret and Shy remark that "terror was effective in Cyprus against a British government without sufficient political strength or will; it failed in Malaya against a

---

[60] Gurr with Ruttenberg.

[61] Dollard and others, 34.

[62] For summaries of findings, see Richard H. Walters, "Implications of Laboratory Studies of Aggression for the Control and Regulation of Violence," *Annals of the American Academy of Political and Social Science*, CCCLXIV (March 1966), 60–72; and Elton D. McNeil, "Psychology and Aggression," *Journal of Conflict Resolution*, III (September 1959), 225–31.

[63] Pp. 231–36, 261–68, 332, 365–79.

[64] Chalmers Johnson, *Revolution and the Social System* (Stanford 1964), 16–17.

[65] Andrew Janos, *The Seizure of Power: A Study of Force and Popular Consent*, Center of International Studies, Princeton University, Research Monograph No. 16 (Princeton 1964), 5.

[66] See, for example, H. O. Dahlke, "Race and Minority Riots: A Study in the Typology of Violence," *Social Forces*, XXX (May 1952), 419–25.

British government determined and able to resist and to wait."[67]

It also has been proposed, and demonstrated in a number of experimental settings, that if aggression is prevented by fear of retribution or by retribution itself, this interference is frustrating and increases anger. Maier, for example, found in animal studies that under conditions of severe frustration, punishment increased the intensity of aggression.[68] Walton inferred from such evidence that a curvilinear relationship ought to obtain between the degree of coerciveness of a nation and its degree of political instability, on the argument that low coerciveness is not frustrating and moderate coerciveness is more likely to frustrate than deter, while only the highest levels of coerciveness are sufficient to inhibit men from civil violence. A permissiveness-coerciveness scale for eighty-four nations, based on scope of political liberties, has been compared against the Feierabends' political stability scale, and the results strongly support the curvilinearity hypothesis.[69] Bwy, using a markedly different measure of coerciveness—one based on defense expenditures—found the same curvilinear relationship between coerciveness and "anomic violence" in Latin America.[70] Some theoretical speculation about civil strife implies the same relationship—for example, Lasswell and Kaplan's stipulation that the stability of an elite's position varies not with the actual use of violence but only with ability to use it,[71] and Parsons' more detailed "power deflation" argument that the repression of demands by force may inspire groups to resort to increasingly intransigent and aggressive modes of making those demands.[72]

One uncertainty about the curvilinear relationship between retribution and aggression is whether or not it holds whatever the extent of initial deprivation-induced anger. It is nonetheless evident that the threat or employment of force to suppress civil violence is by no means uniform in its effects, and that it tends to have a feedback effect that increases the instigation to violence. Such a relationship is diagrammed in Figure 1 and is explicit in the following proposition and its corollary:

Proposition M.1: The likelihood and magnitude of civil violence tend to vary curvilinearly with the amount of physical or social retribution anticipated as a consequence of participation in it, with likelihood and magnitude greatest at medium levels of retribution.

M.1a: Any decrease in the perceived likelihood of retribution tends to increase the likelihood and magnitude of civil violence.

These propositions and corollaries, and all subsequent propositions, hold only, of course, if deprivation-induced anger exists. If the modal level of collective discontent is negligible, a condition that holds for at least some small, although few large, collectivities, the mediating variables have no inhibiting or facilitating effects by definition.

The propositions above do not exhaust frustration-aggression evidence

[67] Peter Paret and John W. Shy, *Guerrillas in the 1960's*, rev. ed. (New York 1964), 34–35.

[68] *Frustration, passim.*

[69] Jennifer G. Walton, "Correlates of Coerciveness and Permissiveness of National Political Systems: A Cross-National Study," M.A. thesis, San Diego State College, 1965.

[70] Douglas Bwy, "Governmental Instability in Latin America: The Preliminary Test of a Causal Model of the Impulse to 'Extra-Legal' Change," paper read at the Annual Meeting of the American Psychological Association, 1966.

[71] Harold Lasswell and Abraham Kaplan, *Power and Society: A Framework for Political Inquiry* (New Haven 1950), 265–66.

[72] "Some Reflections on the Place of Force."

about effects of retribution. Experimental evidence further indicates that a delay in the expression of the aggressive response increases its intensity when it does occur.[73] Observations about civil violence also suggest that the effects of feared retribution, especially external retribution, must take account of the time variable. The abrupt relaxation of authoritarian controls is repeatedly associated with intense outbursts of civil violence, despite the likelihood that such relaxation reduces relative deprivation. Examples from recent years include the East German and Hungarian uprisings after the post-Stalin thaw, the Congo after independence, and the Dominican Republic after Trujillo's assassination.

A parsimonious way to incorporate the time dimension into frustration-aggression theory is to argue that in the short run the delay of an aggressive response increases the intensity of anger and consequently the likelihood and magnitude of aggression, but that in the long run the level and intensity of expectations decline to coincide with the impositions of reality, and anger decreases concomitantly. Cognitive dissonance theory would suggest such an outcome: men tend to reduce persistent imbalances between cognitions and actuality by changing reality, or if it proves intransigent, by changing their cognitive structures.[74] The proposed relationship is sketched in Figure 2.

One example of experimental evidence to this point is the finding of Cohen and others that once subjects became accustomed to certain kinds of frustration—withdrawal of social reinforcement in the experimental

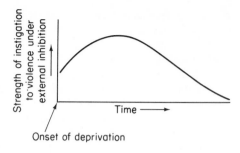

FIGURE 2. Displacement of Instigation to Violence Over Time.

situation used—they were less likely to continue to seek the desired value or condition.[75] One can, moreover, speculate that the time-scale is largely a function of the intensity of commitment to the frustrated response or condition. The effects of South Africa's apartheid policies and the means of their enforcement offer an example. These policies, which impose substantial and diverse value-deprivations on non-whites, especially those in urban areas, were put into effect principally in the 1950's. Violent protests over their implementation were repressed with increasing severity, culminating in the Sharpeville massacre of 1960 and a series of strikes and riots. By the mid-1960's, when deprivation was objectively more severe than at any time previously in the twentieth century, levels of civil strife were very low, inferentially the result of very high levels of deterrence (feared retribution). Since deprivation remains severe and has affected a wide range of values, avoidance of violence in this case probably would require the maintenance of very high and consistent deterrence levels beyond the active life-span of most of those who have personally experienced the initial value-deprivation. Any short-run decline in the

[73] J. W. Thibaut and J. Coules, "The Role of Communication in the Reduction of Interpersonal Hostility," *Journal of Abnormal and Social Psychology*, XLVII (October 1952), 770–77.

[74] See Leon Festinger, *A Theory of Cognitive Dissonance* (Evanston 1957).

[75] Arthur R. Cohen and others, "Commitment to Social Deprivation and Verbal Conditioning," *Journal of Abnormal and Social Psychology*, LXVII (November 1963), 410–21.

perceived likelihood or severity of retribution, however, is highly likely to be followed by intense violence. In propositional form:

Proposition M.2: Inhibition of civil violence by fear of external retribution tends in the short run to increase the strength of anger but in the long run to reduce it.

M.2a: The duration of increased anger under conditions of inhibition tends to vary with the intensity of commitment to the value with respect to which deprivation is suffered.

SOCIAL CONTROL: THE EFFECTS OF INSTITUTIONALIZED DISPLACEMENT

On the evidence, the effects of repression in managing discontent are complex and potentially self-defeating in the short run. Displacement theory suggests means that are considerably more effective. Several aspects of displacement theory are relevant for civil violence. Among Miller's basic propositions about object and response generalization is the formulation that the stronger the fear of retribution relative to the strength of anger, the more dissimilar will the target of aggression be from the source of interference and the more indirect will be the form of aggression.[76] With reference to object generalization, Berkowitz has proposed and demonstrated that hostility tends to generalize from a frustrater to previously disliked individuals or groups.[77] A counterpart of this thesis is that displaced aggressive responses tend to be expressed in previously used forms.

Examples of object generalization in civil violence are legion. Several

[76] Neal E. Miller, "Theory and Experiment Relating Psychoanalytic Displacement to Stimulus-Response Generalization," *Journal of Abnormal and Social Psychology*, XLIII (April 1948), 155–78.

[77] *Aggression*, chap. 6.

studies have shown positive relationships between poor economic conditions and lynchings of Negroes in the American South.[78] An initial reaction of urban white colonialists to African rural uprisings in Madagascar in 1947 and Angola in 1961 was vigilante-style execution of urban Africans who had no connections with the rebellions. English hand-weavers, when their livelihood was threatened by the introduction of new weaving machines, destroyed thousands of machines in the Luddite riots of 1811–1816, but almost never directly attacked the employers who installed the machines and discharged superfluous workers.[79]

Object generalization is a crucial variable in determining who will be attacked by the initiators of particular acts of civil violence, but is only peripheral to the primary concern of the theory, the determination of likelihood and magnitude of violence as such. Most important in this regard is the psychological evidence regarding response generalization. Experimental evidence suggests that only a narrow range of objects provides satisfying targets for men's aggressive responses, but that almost any form of aggression can be satisfying so long as the angry person believes that he has in some way injured his supposed frustrater.[80]

[78] See n. 48 above.

[79] Rudé, *The Crowd in History*, chap 5. The high levels of verbal aggression directed against the employers suggest that displacement was involved, not a perception of the machines rather than employers as sources of deprivation. In the Luddite riots, fear of retribution for direct attacks on the owners, contrasted with the frequent lack of sanctions against attacks on the machines, was the probable cause of object generalization. In the Madagascar and Angola cases structural and conceptual factors were responsible: the African rebels were not accessible to attack but local Africans were seen as like them and hence as potential or clandestine rebels.

[80] Some such evidence is summarized in Berkowitz, "The Concept of Aggressive Drive," 325–27.

By extension to the collectivity, insofar as adequate response displacement options are available, much anger may be diverted into activity short of civil violence. The evidence is diverse and extensive that participation in political activity, labor unions, and millenarian religious movements can be a response to relative deprivation which permits more or less nonviolent expression of aggression. Studies of voting in the United States show that politicians in farm states are rather consistently voted out of office after periods of low rainfall and that the occurrence of natural disasters may lead to hostility against officials.[81] Extremist voting—which may be regarded as nonviolent aggression—in nine European countries during the Depression has been shown to correlate $+.85$ with the percentage of the labor force unemployed.[82] Studies of labor movements repeatedly document the transformation of labor protest from violent to nonviolent forms as unionization increases. Comparative and case studies similarly document the development of aggressive millenarian religious movements as a response to natural disaster or political repression, in places and eras as diverse as medieval Europe, colonial Africa, and among the indigenous peoples of the Americas and the South Pacific.[83]

This is not to imply that displacement is a sole or exclusive function of such institutions. Their instrumental functions for participants (Proposition 1.5) can be crucial: peaceful political and union activism are alternative means to goals whose attainment by other means is often impaired; religious chiliasm provides hope and belief for those whose social universe has been destroyed. But insofar as men become accustomed to express discontents through such institutional mechanisms, the likelihood that anger will lead to civil violence is diminished. In propositional form:

Proposition M.3: The likelihood and magnitude of civil violence tend to vary inversely with the availability of institutional mechanisms that permit the expression of nonviolent hostility.

SOCIAL FACILITATION: COGNITIVE FACTORS

Experimental, developmental, and field studies of the effects of rewarding individual aggression demonstrate that habitual aggression may be developed and maintained through intermittent rewards and may also be generalized to situations other than those in which the habits were acquired.[84] A number of experiments indicate that the presence of cues or stimuli associated with anger instigators is necessary for most aggressive responses to occur. A summary proposition is that "a target with approporiate stimulus qualities 'pulls' (evokes) aggressive responses from a person who is ready to engage in such actions either because he is angry or because particular stimuli have acquired cue values for aggressive responses from him."[85]

---

[81] A critical and qualifying review of evidence to this effect is F. Glenn Abney and Larry B. Hill, "Natural Disasters as a Political Variable: The Effect of a Hurricane on an Urban Election," *American Political Science Review*, LX (December 1966), 974–81.

[82] Kornhauser, 161. For interview evidence on the motives of protest voting, see Hadley Cantril, *The Politics of Despair* (New York 1958).

[83] Representative studies are Cohn; James W. Fernandez, "African Religious Movements: Types and Dynamics," *Journal of Modern African Studies*, II, No. 4 (1964), 531–49; and Vittorio Lanternari, *The Religions of the Oppressed* (New York 1963).

[84] Summarized in Walters.

[85] Leonard Berkowitz, "Aggressive Cues in Aggressive Behavior and Hostility Catharsis," *Psychological Review*, LXXI (March 1964), 104–22, quotation from 106.

For members of a collectivity a variety of common experiences can contribute to the acquisition of aggressive habits and the recognition of aggression-evoking cues. Among them are socialization patterns that give normative sanction to some kinds of aggressive behavior; traditions of violent conflict; and exposure to new generalized beliefs that justify violence. The literature on civil violence suggests at least four specific modes by which such experiences facilitate violent responses to deprivation. They can (1) stimulate mutual awareness among the deprived, (2) provide explanations for deprivation of ambiguous origin, (3) specify accessible targets and appropriate forms of violence, and (4) state long-range objectives to be attained through violence.

Subcultural traditions of violent protest are well documented in European history. The frequency with which Parisian workers and shop-keepers took to the streets in the years and decades following the great *journées* of 1789 is one example. At least 275 food riots, most of them similar in form and sequence, took place in rural England between 1725 and 1800 in close correlation with harvest failures and high food prices.[86] Hobsbawm points out that in Southern Italy "every political change in the nineteenth century, irrespective from what quarter it came, automatically produced its ceremonial marches of peasants with drums and banners to occupy the land," while in Andalusia "millenarian revolutionary waves occurred at roughly ten-year intervals for some sixty or seventy years."[87] Lynching as a Southern white response to Negro transgressions and the mobbing of white policemen by Negroes are comparable expressions of subcultural traditions that facilitate civil violence.

The theoretical point is that the initial occurrences of civil violence among some homogeneous group of the deprived—those events that set the pattern—tend to be nonrational responses to extreme deprivation. If violence provides a satisfactory outlet for tensions or if it motivates authorities to remedy the sources of deprivation, civil violence tends to become a sanctioned group activity. The fact that normative support for violence thus develops does not mean that violence subsequently occurs without instigation. Deprivation remains a necessary precondition for violence; the strength of anger at which it is likely to occur is lowered.

A related source of attitudinal support for collective violence is the articulation of ideology or, more generally, what Smelser calls generalized belief among the deprived. Such beliefs, ranging from rumors to fully articulated ideologies, are said to develop in situations characterized by social strain that is unmanageable within the existing framework for social action.[88] It is evident that in many social settings relative deprivation is manifest but its sources obscure. In psychological terms, no cues associated with the anger instigator are present. The agency responsible for an unwanted tax increase is apparent to the most ignorant villager; the causes of economic depression or of the disintegration of traditional mores are often unclear even to economists and sociologists. A new ideology, folk-belief, or rumor can serve to define and explain the nature of the situation, to identify those responsible for it, and to specify appropriate courses of action.

Moreover, there usually are a number of competing generalized beliefs

[86] Rudé, *The Crowd in History*, 19–45.
[87] E. J. Hobsbawm, *Social Bandits and Primitive Rebels*, 2nd ed. (Glencoe 1959), 63–64.

[88] Chap. 5.

circulating among the deprived. Those most likely to gain acceptance tend to be those with substantial aggressive components, i.e., those that rationalize and focus the innate drive to aggression. Cohn's comparative study of the waves of chiliastic excitement that swept medieval Europe in times of plague and famine, for example, documents the fact that the heresies that most effectively mobilized the deprived were those that suited or could be molded to their states of mind: "when . . . eschatological doctrines penetrated to the uprooted and desperate masses in town and country they were re-edited and reinterpreted until in the end they were capable of inspiring revolutionary movements of a peculiarly anarchic kind."[89]

Some of these observations can be summarized in this proposition and its corollary:

Proposition M.4: The likelihood and magnitude of civil violence tend to vary directly with the availability of common experiences and beliefs that sanction violent responses to anger.

M.4a: Given the availability of alternative experiences and beliefs, the likelihood that the more aggressive of them will prevail tends to vary with the strength of anger.

SOCIAL FACILITATION: SOURCES OF GROUP SUPPORT FOR VIOLENCE

A classic subject of social psychological theory is the extent to which some social settings facilitate overt aggression. It is incontrovertible that individuals tend to behave in crowds differently from the way they act alone. The crowd psychologies of scholars such as Le Bon and Sorokin have emphasized the "unconscious" nature of crowd behavior and its "de-indivi-

duating" effects.[90] It appears more fruitful to examine experimentally identified variables that contribute to the "crowd behavior" phenomenon. From this point of departure one can distinguish at least three modes by which groups affect individuals' disposition to violence: (1) by providing normative support, (2) by providing apparent protection from retribution, and (3) by providing cues for violent behavior.

1. *Normative Support* There is good experimental evidence that individuals alone or in poorly cohesive groups are less likely to express hostility than those in highly cohesive groups. Members of highly cohesive friendship groups respond to external frustrations with greater hostility than randomly formed groups. Similarly, if individuals believe that their peers generally agree with them about a frustrater, their public display of antagonism more closely resembles their privately expressed antagonism than if they do not perceive peer agreement.[91]

Theoretical and empirical studies of civil violence repeatedly refer to the causal efficacy of comparable conditions. Social theorists describe the perception of anonymity and of universality of deprivation characteristic of riotous crowds. Hopper's classic picture of group interaction under conditions of relative deprivation in the early

[90] Gustave Le Bon, *The Psychology of Revolution* (London 1913); Pitirim Sorokin, *The Sociology of Revolutions* (Philadelphia 1925).

[91] Representative studies include J. R. P. French, Jr., "The Disruption and Cohesion of Groups," *Journal of Abnormal and Social Psychology*, XXXVI (July 1941), 361–77; A. Pepitone and G. Reichling, "Group Cohesiveness and the Expression of Hostility," *Human Relations*, VIII, No. 3 (1955), 327–37; and Ezra Stotland, "Peer Groups and Reactions to Power Figures," Dorwin Cartwright, ed., *Studies in Social Power* (Ann Arbor 1959), 53–68.

[89] P. 31.

stages of the revolutionary process is relevant: by participating in mass or shared behavior, discontented people become aware of one another; "their negative reactions to the basic factors in their situations are shared and begin to spread. . . . Discontent . . . tends to become focalized and collective."[92] Comparative studies of labor unrest show that the most strike-prone industries are those whose workers are relatively homogeneous and isolated from the general community.[93] Some of the efficacy of revolutionary brotherhoods and tightly knit bands of rebels in prosecuting civil violence can be interpreted in terms of the reinforcement of mutual perception of deprivation and the justification of violence as a response to it.

2. *Protection from Retribution*   Groups appear capable of reducing fears of external retribution for violence in at least three ways. Crowd situations in particular provide members with a shield of anonymity. In an experimental study by Meier and others, two-thirds of subjects who were prepared to join a lynching mob said, *inter alia*, that they would do so because in the crowd they could not be punished. The same relationship is apparent in the handful of studies made of riot participants: crowd members usually feel insulated from retribution.[94]

Organized groups can provide apparent protection from retribution

by acquiring sufficient force capability to prevent the agents of retribution— i.e., military and internal security forces—from effectively reaching them. Increases in the relative force capability of a deprived group may also reinforce rationalization for violence by raising hopes of success or may merely facilitate the expression of rage by providing desperate men with the means to strike at tormentors who had previously been unassailable.

A third aspect of group protectiveness is the perceived effect of hierarchical organization and the presence of highly visible leaders. Leaders of revolutionary organizations, in addition to their other manifest functions, not only foment but assume responsibility for illicit violence. Their followers tend to see such leaders as the likely objects of retaliatory efforts and hence feel less personal risk.

3. *Cues for Violence*   The transition from anger to aggression is not automatic or even abrupt. Laboratory studies of imitative behavior repeatedly document the significance of aggression-releasing cues provided by social models. The act of punishing aggression itself can serve as a model for imitation by the person punished. Aggression-releasing cues need not necessarily originate with high-status persons. Polansky and others found that when frustrations were imposed on groups of children, "impulsive" but low-status children were both initiators and ready followers of aggressive behavioral contagion. On the other hand, not any aggressive model evokes aggression from angered subjects; the models that evoke greatest aggression are those associated with the subjects' present situation or with settings in which they were previously aggressive.[95]

[92] Pp. 272–75, quotation from 273.

[93] Clark Kerr and Abraham Siegel, "The Isolated Mass and the Integrated Individual: An International Analysis of the Inter-Industry Propensity to Strike," in Arthur Kornhauser and others, eds., *Industrial Conflict* (New York 1954), 189–212.

[94] Norman C. Meier and others, "An Experimental Approach to the Study of Mob Behavior," *Journal of Abnormal and Social Psychology*, XXXVI (October 1941), 506–24. Also see George Wada and James C. Davies, "Riots and Rioters," *Western Political Quarterly*, X (December 1957) 864–74.

[95] See Walters; Norman Polansky and others, "An Investigation of Behavioral Contagion in Groups," *Human Relations*, III,

Angry crowds of men also appear to require some congruent image or model of violent action before they will seize cobblestones or rope or rifles to do violence to fellow citizens. Such models may be symbolic: invocation of a subcultural tradition of violence by a leader, or articulation of a new generalized belief that is explicit in its prescription of violence. In general, however, a "call to arms" or an appeal to a tradition of violence appears less effective by itself than when accompanied by the sight or news of violence. The calculated use of terrorism by rebels can have such an effect, and so can a soldier's random shot into a crowd of demonstrators. Many specific cases of civil violence have been set off by comparable acts of violence elsewhere. "Revolutionary contagion" is evident in the 1830 and 1848 waves of European revolutionary upheavals and in the post-Stalin uprisings in Eastern Europe and Siberia. The same phenomenon is apparent in the initiation of inumnerable cases of small-scale, unstructured violence. Series of riots in rural France and England have graphically been shown to spread outward from one or a few centers, riots occurring in the furthest villages days or weeks after the initial incident. Such patterning is evident, to mention a few cases, in the French Corn Riots of 1775, the "Plug-Plot" riots around Manchester in 1842, and the incidence of farmers' protest meetings and riots in Brittany in the summer of 1961.[96] The demonstration effect apparent in such series of events appears to have affected their form and timing more

than the likelihood of the occurrence of strife. The people who responded to the events were already angered; they probably would have erupted into violence in some form sometime in the proximate future.

These three modes of group facilitation of civil violence can be summarized in propositional form:

Proposition M.5: The likelihood and magnitude of civil violence tend to vary directly with the extent to which the deprived occupy organizational and/or ecological settings that provide (1) normative support through high levels of interaction, (2) apparent protection from retribution, and (3) congruent models for violent behavior.

The Forms of Civil Violence

The theoretical framework comprising the ten propositions is formally restricted to physically violent collective behavior. It is likely that it is as applicable to a still larger class of events, including those characterized by the threat of violence or by high levels of verbal aggression—for example bloodless coups, demonstrations, and political strikes. Violent events tend to be more salient for the political system, however, and for most operational purposes constitute a more workable and clearly defined universe.

I have not discussed the propositions with reference to specific forms of civil violence on grounds that all of the variables specified are relevant to each form specified in current typologies.[97] It is nonetheless likely that the propositions are of differential weight

No. 3 (1950), 319–48; and Leonard Berkowitz and Russell G. Geen, "Film Violence and the Cue Properties of Available Targets," *Journal of Personality and Social Psychology*, III (June 1966), 525–30.

[96] Rudé, *The Crowd in History;* Henri Mendras and Yves Tavernier, "Les Manifestations de juin 1961," *Revue française des sciences politiques*, XII (September 1962), 647–71.

[97] Representative typologies are proposed by Johnson, *Revolution and the Social System*, 26–68; Rudolph J. Rummel, "Dimensions of Conflict Behavior Within and Between Nations," *Yearbook of the Society for General Systems Research*, VIII (1963), 25-26; and Harry Eckstein, "Internal Wars: A Taxonomy," unpubl. (1960).

for different forms, and it is useful to demonstrate how variations in form may be generally accounted for in the context of the theoretical model. The first question to be asked is how detailed a listing of forms one should attempt to account for. A series of factor analytic studies provide a systematic, empirical answer to that question. In each of eleven studies, data on the incidence and characteristics of various types of strife were collected and tabulated, by country, and the "country scores" (number of riots, assassinations, deaths from civil violence, coups, mutinies, guerrilla wars, and so on, in a given time period) were factor analyzed. Whatever the typology employed, the period of reference, or the set of countries, essentially the same results were obtained. A strong *turmoil* dimension emerges, characterized by largely spontaneous strife such as riots, demonstrations, and nonpolitical clashes, quite distinct from what we may call a *revolutionary* dimension, characterized by more organized and intense strife. This revolutionary dimension has two components, appearing in some analyses as separate dimensions: *internal war*, typically including civil war, guerrilla war, and some coups; and *conspiracy*, typically including plots, purges, mutinies, and most coups.[98] Events within each of the three types tend to occur together; events within any two or all three categories are less likely to do so. The implication is that they are substantively distinct forms of strife for each

[98] Two summary articles on these factor analyses are Rudolph J. Rummel, "A Field Theory of Social Action With Application to Conflict Within Nations," *Yearbook of the Society for General Systems Research*, X (1965), 183–204; and Tanter. What I call internal war is referred to in these sources as subversion; I label conspiracy what these sources call revolution. My terminology is, I believe, less ambiguous and more in keeping with general scholarly usage.

of which separate explanation is required.

Two complementary approaches to accounting for these three basic types of civil violence can be proposed within the context of the theoretical model. The first is that the two major dimensions, turmoil and revolution, reflect the varying class incidence of deprivation among societies. The defining characteristic of "turmoil" events is mass participation, usually rather spontaneous, disorganized, and with low intensity of violence; the forms of "revolution" reflect organized, often instrumental and intense, application of violence. The ability to rationalize, plan, and put to instrumental use their own and others' discontent is likely to be most common among the more skilled, highly educated members of a society—its elite aspirants. Thus if the incidence of mass deprivation is high but elite deprivation low, the most likely form of civil violence is turmoil. But if severe discontent is common to a substantial, alienated group of elite aspirants, then organized, intensive strife is likely.

The forms of revolution differ principally in their scale and tactics: internal wars are large-scale, and their tactics are typically to neutralize the regime's military forces; conspirators, usually few in number, attempt to subvert the regime by striking at its key members.

The differences between internal war and conspiracy can be accounted for by several characteristics. If severe deprivation is restricted largely to elite aspirants, the consequence is likely to be "conspiracy" phenomena such as plots, coups d'état, and barracks revolts. If discontent is widespread among substantial numbers of both mass and elite aspirants, the more likely consequence is large-scale, organized violence—civil and guerrilla war. The strategic position of the discontented elite aspirants may be relevant as well. If they are subordinate members of the existing elite hierarchy, they are likely to attack the regime from within, hence coups, mutinies, and plots. If they are instead excluded from formal membership in the elite though they possess elite qualities—acquired, for example, through foreign education—they must organize violent resistance from without. These are essentially Seton-Watson's explanations for the relative frequency of conspiracy in underdeveloped societies compared with the frequency of massive revolutionary movements in more developed states. In summary, "it is the combination of backward masses, extremist intellectuals and despotic bureaucrats which creates the most conspiratorial movements."[99]

These observations are of course only the beginning of an accounting of the forms of civil strife. They are intended to demonstrate, however, that such a theoretical explanation not only is compatible with but can be formulated within the framework of the theoretical model by showing the loci of deprivation in a society. They can be stated thus in propositional form:

Proposition F.1: The characteristic form of civil violence tends to vary with the differential incidence of relative deprivation among elite aspirants and masses: (1) mass deprivation alone tends to be manifested in large-scale civil violence with minimal organization and low intensity; (2) elite-aspirant deprivation tends to be manifested in highly organized civil violence of high intensity.

F.1a: Whether organized and intense civil violence is large-scale or small-scale is a joint function of the extent of mass deprivation and the strategic access of deprived elite aspirants to the incumbent political elite.

[99] Hugh Seton-Watson, "Twentieth Century Revolutions," *Political Quarterly*, XXII (July 1951), 258.

Conclusion

I have advanced eleven general propositions about the variables operative in generating and structuring violent political unrest. They are based on the assumption that the frustration-aggression mechanism, however culturally modified, is the source of most men's disposition to illicit collective violence. The propositions do not consitute a theory of the revolutionary process or of the outcomes of strife, but of the conditions that determine the *likelihood* and *magnitude* of strife. On the other hand, the variables stipulated by the propositions are not irrelevant to revolutionary processes. Process models can be formulated wholly or partly in terms of changing patterns of weights on the component variables.

It is likely that most "causes" and "correlates" of the occurrence and intensity of civil strife can be subsumed by these variables, with one exception: foreign intervention. This exception is no oversight but simply recognition that decisions to intervene are external to domestic participants in civil strife. The effects of foreign intervention can be readily interpreted by reference to the model, however: intervention on behalf of the deprived is likely to strengthen group support (M.5) and may, as well, heighten and intensify value expectations (I.2). Foreign assistance to a threatened regime is most likely to raise retribution levels (M.1), but may also alter aspects of value capabilities (I.4, I.5) and strengthen justification for violence among the deprived, insofar as they identify foreigners with invaders (M.4).

The framework has not been elaborated merely to provide a satisfying theoretical reconstruction of the general causes of civil violence. It is intended primarily as a guide for empirical research using the techniques of both case and comparative studies. The framework stipulates the variables for which information should be sought in any thorough case study of the origins of an act of civil strife.[100] For purposes of comparative analysis it stipulates relationships that should hold among cultures and across time. Its most important objectives are to encourage empirical validation of its component propositions in a variety of contexts by a variety of operational means, and specification of their separate weights and interacting effects in those contexts.[101]

[100] For example, it has been used by Bryant Wedge to analyze and compare interview materials gathered in the study of two Latin American revolutions, in "Student Participation in Revolutionary Violence: Brazil, 1964, and Dominican Republic, 1965," a paper read at the Annual Meeting of the American Political Science Association, 1967.

[101] Studies based on this theoretical model and using cross-national aggregate data include Ted Gurr, *New Error-Compensated Measures for Comparing Nations: Some Correlates of Civil Strife*, Center of International Studies, Princeton University, Research Monograph No. 25 (Princeton 1966); Gurr with Ruttenberg; Gurr, "A Causal Model of Civil Strife" [reading 10 in this volume]; *idem*, "Urban Disorder: Perspectives from the Comparative Study of Civil Strife," *American Behavioral Scientist*, XI (March-April 1968), 50–55; and *idem*, "Sources of Rebellion in Western Societies: Some Quantitative Evidence," *The Annals*, CCCXCI (September 1970), 128–44.

POLITICAL ALIENATION: THE PSYCHOLOGY OF REVOLUTION'S FIRST STAGE

David C. Schwartz*

Revolutions, like all political phenomena, originate in the minds of men and, thus, it is there that at least part of the explanation of revolutionary behavior is to be sought. This, of course, has long been recognized, if not systematically treated, "the state of mind which creates revolutions" having been a subject of Aristotelian inquiry[1] and much consideration since.

Virtually all revolutionary organizations, however, are composed both of persons: (1) who have been previously socialized to accept a political system from which they became alienated; and (2) whose loyalties have never been effectively tied to the polity. This suggests the need to distinguish between at least two possibly distinct "mind states" which predispose men to make, or at least to hear, revolutionary appeals.

This paper is concerned with the first of these early revolutionary conditions: with the reasons why, and the processes whereby, men become estranged from a previously accepted polity. Herein, we state a provisional theory to explain the conditions under which political alienation occurs and the sequences in which alternative alienation forms (i.e., withdrawal vs. radicalization) manifest themselves . . . .

All analyses of collective behavior

* The research on which this paper is based was conducted at the Foreign Policy Research Institute, University of Pennsylvania with the support of the U.S. Navy Nonr-551 (60). I am pleased to acknowledge the extensive assistance of Mr. Peter Shubs.

[1] *Politics*, Book V.

Excerpted from a paper presented at the Annual Meeting of the American Psychological Association, Washington, D.C., 1967, pp. 1–28, by permission of the author. Footnotes have been renumbered.

presuppose a theory of motivation.[2] In this regard the study of revolutions has been consonant with most modern analyses of macro-social and political processes. The fundamental difficulty here has been the absence of a synthetic, general psychological theory to integrate the less complete middle-range theories which have been applied in revolution studies. Frustration-aggression-displacement,[3] the outplay of guilt,[4] the operation of cognitive consistency tendencies,[5] to name but a few—have all been recently applied to the phenomena of revolutions and all seem to suggest useful research. At present, however, there exist neither adequate experimental data to allow us to select the most revolution-relevant of these psychic processes nor a well articulated theory about the simultaneous interplay of these processes should they prove equally relevant. It seems likely that different processes will be elaborated by different personality types, but the psychological materials on this are embryonic and not yet applied (if applicable) to the analysis of revolution.[6]

Fortunately, there have been several recent efforts to integrate heretofore seemingly disparate psychological theories[7]; and we shall use these below to construct a plausible psychodynamic of alienation—moving from ambivalence, through conflict, to cognitive consistency and adjustment.

More important for our purposes is the fact that each of these middle-range theories (i.e., those concerned with frustration, guilt, conflict, or cognitive consistency) yields the same initial deduction: *revolutions begin with the attempted withdrawal from politics of individual (and especially intellectual's) attention, affection and involvement....*

The behavioral manifestations of withdrawal—or better, of passive political alienation—include: diminished affect, support and sense of legitimacy for the political system, individuation, privatization, reduction in the scope of loyalties, a sense of public-purposelessness, non-voting, decreased political action and interactions (as in membership and meetings of political organizations), and the like. Such behavior is a recurrent theme in revolution. "There is a good deal of evidence that as revolutions go on, a very large number of people just drop out of active politics, make no attempt to register their votes."[8]

The notion of a withdrawal phase in the process of alienation helps to explain the "earliest symptom of revolution which is an increase in restlessness."[9] This restlessness, as noted by Edwards and Brinton, man-

[2] Lylford P. Edwards, *The Natural History of Revolution* (Chicago: University of Chicago Press, 1962), p. 2.

[3] James C. Davies, "Toward a Theory of Revolution" *American Sociological Review*, Vol. 27, No. 1. (February 1962), pp. 15–19; Ted Gurr, *The Conditions of Civil Violence* (Princeton: Center of International Studies Monograph, 1967), *passim.*

[4] E. Victor Wolfenstein, *Violence or Nonviolence: A Psychoanalytic Exploration of the Choice of Political Means in Social Change* (Princeton: Center of International Studies Monograph, 1965).

[5] David C. Schwartz, "A Theory of Revolutionary Behavior," (unpublished manuscript, 1967), *passim.*

[6] But see Section IV of this paper for some "first cuts" at this problem.

[7] Roger Brown, "Models of Attitude Change," in Brown *et al.*, *New Directions in Psychology* (New York: Holt, Rinehart & Winston, 1962), pp. 74 ff.; Judson S. Brown, "Principles of Intrapersonal Conflict," *Journal of Conflict Resolution*, I, No. 2 (June 1957), 135 ff.; C. N. Cofer and M. H. Appley, *Motivation: Theory and Research* (New York: John Wiley & Sons, 1964), especially pp. 808 ff.

[8] Crane Brinton, *The Anatomy of Revolution* (New York: Norton, 1938), p. 160.

[9] Edwards, *op. cit.*, p. 23.

ifests itself in "aimless interactions" and "purposeless activity."[10] Hopper aptly calls this "The Milling Process" wherein individual restlessness tends to spread and become social as is evidenced, *inter alia*, by "the wandering of attention from one individual, object or line of action to another . . . ."[11]

An emphasis on withdrawal suggests that at least part of what these scholars are observing are *the normal social interactions of persons who no longer share common orientations to the political system;* that different people withdraw different degrees of attention, salience, and affection from different institutions and symbols at different rates of speed (e.g., the greater the disturbance, the more rapid and complete the withdrawal). Change in attitude sets and attention foci are posited by the very notions of privatization and withdrawal. Previously effective interactions might well become or appear aimless under these circumstances and even the fragmentary data which have sometimes been marshaled in support of the inference of restlessness[12] comports with the idea of privatization or individuation which results from political withdrawal.

The social isolation, extreme individuation and reinforced aggression which characterize political withdrawal also seem useful in explaining other phenomena which have been associated with early stages of revolution. An increase in crime, especially violent crime, observed by Edwards and others, is consonant with the properties of political withdrawal, as the direct outplay of associated rage or aggression.[13] The increased focus on the self which is the privatization aspect of political withdrawal may also account, in part, for the increase in personal "disorders" (vice, insanity, suicide) noted by Hopper[14] as an early indicator of revolution. Political withdrawal also explains the relationship between high crime and suicide rates and low voting turnout which Jack L. Walker and Robert A. Dahl have recently found of interest.[15]

Perhaps more important is the fact that political withdrawal helps to explain the "availability" of persons for revolutionary behavior. Political withdrawal effects social isolation and atomization by breaking down common orientations to the social and political system. The consequent "loss of community" (in both real and perceived terms) constitutes an essential aspect of mass society, the "high availability of a population for mobilization by elites,[16] because people who are atomized tend more readily to be mobilized."[17]

But if passive alienation is a necessary condition for the individual to be available to hear revolutionary appeals, it is still insufficient to explain the predispositions to accept such appeals. Revolutionary men may begin by withdrawing, or attempting to withdraw, from the polity; they end in the active alienation of accepting or employing political violence. Accordingly, a comprehensive theory of political alienation must move beyond withdrawal to that mode of disaffection which is radicalization. Is radicalization an alternative mode of alienation

---

[10] *Ibid.*, and Brinton, *op. cit.*, p. 72.

[11] Rex D. Hopper, "The Revolutionary Process," *Social Forces*, Vol. 28 (March 1950), 271.

[12] Edwards, *op. cit.*, pp. 23–27.

[13] See Section II, below, for an explanation of the process whereby rage and/or aggression accompanies passive alienation.

[14] *Op. cit.*, p. 271.

[15] Jack L. Walker, "A Critique of the Elitist Theory of Democracy," *American Political Science Review*, LX, No. 2 (June 1966), 290; Robert A. Dahl, "Further Reflections on 'A Critique of the Elitist Theory of Democracy,'" *Ibid.*, p. 303.

[16] William Kornhauser, *Politics of Mass Society* (Glencoe, Ill.: Free Press of Glencoe, 1959), p. 33.

[17] *Ibid.*

adopted by certain person-types who are responding to the same stimuli which, in others, induces withdrawal? Alternatively, is radicalization a function of social and psychological conditions different from those which inure toward passive alienation? Must one go through passive political alienation before radicalization can manifest itself? These questions are crucial if we are to arrive at a comprehensive and precise understanding of early revolutionary behavior .... If, as we shall show, radicalization is a process which is in part coeval with, and in part subsequent to, withdrawal—we can conclude that the frustration-aggression-displacement paradigm (useful in explaining radicalization) can and must be integrated with other psychological theories which help to explain withdrawal.

Finally, in introduction to the theory we must specify the meaning of "alienation" as employed herein. The enormous variety of meanings with which the term has been invested in psychological, sociological and popular usage has been well noted elsewhere.[18] ...
... Essentially, we are concerned with a sense of individual estrangement from the political institutions, organizations, and activities which comprise the political system. In this, we are investigating one of Seeman's[19] five dimensions of alienation—estrangement (here, estrangement from a social subsystem and not necessarily from the self). Another of Seeman's dimensions, powerlessness, was employed as an independent variable. It was subconceptualized as "perceived personal political inefficacy" in our study. We

do not include "normlessness" or "meaninglessness" because neither seems to characterize even the earliest known mental state of revolutionary men; nor do we work with "social isolation," as it is more often a consequence than a concomitant of political withdrawal in the lives of revolutionaries.

．　　．　　．

II. A Processual Theory of Political Alienation

．　　．　　．

In analyzing the general case of political alienation, it seems useful to identify at least eight separate stages. These are:

1. Allegiance: identity or balance between political values (PV) and the political system (PS)
2. Ambivalence: differentiation of PV and PS
3. An approach-approach conflict: PV vs. PS
4. Double approach-avoidance: the conditions of initial withdrawal
5. Threat and rage: the concomitants of initial withdrawal
6. Alienation from all or part of the polity: differentiation or generalization, approach-avoidance
7. Passive alienation: from differentiation to generalization
8. Active alienation: from withdrawal to radicalization

These stages constitute a partial "psycho-political space" (a partially defined matrix of possible states of a cognitive-affective system relevant to politics). The transition conditions under which the individual moves through these stages are stated below.[20]

---

[18] See Kenneth Kenniston, *The Uncommitted* (New York: Harcourt, 1966), Appendix and *passim;* Gaylord C. LeRoy, "The Concept of Alienation," in Herbert Aptheker, ed., *Marxism and Alienation* (New York: Humanities Press, 1965), pp. 1–14.

[19] Melvin Seeman, "On the Meaning of Alienation," *American Sociological Review*, XXIV, No. 6 (December 1959).

[20] Reversibility rules, if they exist, have not been identified nor has the possibility of skipping a stage (i.e., the "telescoping of alienation") been analyzed. The model does recognize that change can be discontinuous and abrupt.

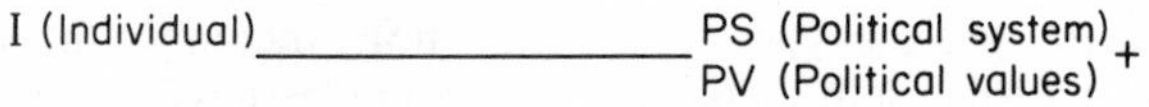

I (Individual)_____ PS (Political system) +
                                  PV (Political values)

FIGURE 1.

or

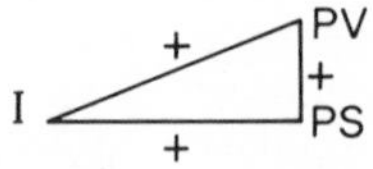

I ∠‾‾‾‾⌐ PV
   +   +
   +   PS

FIGURE 2.

If the transition conditions for movement between, say, stages 1 and 2 are not met, the system will either remain in stage 1 or move to an unspecified state. This theory, of course, does not identify every possible alternative condition (so, other alienative paths and patterns may exist). But the behavior rules within each stage (i.e., the relationships which govern behavior and interactions within each stage) may help explain changes to alternative states.

THE STAGES OF POLITICAL ALIENATION

A cognitive structure which exists in persons who have undergone effective political socialization experiences and who support an existing political system—at least by regarding themselves as citizens or participants therein—may be represented either as: (1) an identity between images of the political system and politicized values (such that typically no distinction is made between the two); or (2) a balanced cognitive set of highly positive relationships between images of the self, the polity and politicized values.[21] These cogni-

---

[21] See Gabriel A. Almond and Sidney Verba, *The Civic Culture* (Princeton: Princeton University Press, 1963), *passim*. The alienative process undergone by persons who are not politically conscious—the unincorporated groups or "pre-politicals"—is very similar to that described here and is set forth in Schwartz, *op. cit.*, pp. 50 ff. No experimental evidence concerning such persons or persontypes has been generated in our studies, however.

tive structures may be iconically represented as in Figures 1 and 2.

These two figures are balanced sets (multiply the signs, + = balance, — = imbalance), connoting that governments are deemed legitimate when they are perceived to be facilitative of, or consonant with, the significant politicized values of the population.

Such a sense of legitimacy and support for government are jeopardized when the political system comes to be viewed as inconsonant with, or non-supportive of, an individual's basic politicized values (i.e., that the political system is either discriminating against, or is unable to protect or create the conditions requisite for holding or enjoying the values). In stage 2, an ambivalence, a potentially unbalanced cognitive structure results and: (1) the political system and the set of politicized values become (more) separate and therefore potentially conflictful; and (2) a reevaluation of the polity becomes necessary. This is represented in Figure 3.

The ambivalence represented in Figure 3 has motivational implications; above a "tolerance of ambiguity" threshold, some political behavior may

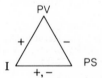

FIGURE 3.

be expected. Three gross directions which this behavior might take can be identified. First, the individual can "remain where he is," reducing the psycho-political disturbance of ambivalence by modifying some of his less salient political values. Second, he may "move toward the system," modifying his behavior to become more politically active (e.g., reformist) and thereby seeking to influence the government in ways he regards as desirable. Finally, he may "move away from the system," reducing disturbance by entering a phase of withdrawal or passive alienation from politics.

These possibilities suggest that the structure of our problem (i.e., stage 3) may be akin to basic spatial conflict forms in psychology (i.e., approach-approach, approach-avoidance, avoidance-avoidance, and double approach-avoidance situations). We can eliminate both the avoidance-avoidance and the simple approach-avoidance condition, because in our situation the polity and the politicized values have initial positive valuation. This leaves only the approach-approach and the double approach-avoidance forms.

In approach-approach conflict environments, two points of reinforcement (here, polity and politicized values) are desirable objects. Any movement toward either object tends to place the individual in a position of reinforced stimulation from that object, resulting in further movement toward the object. In periods of "early political ambivalence" (in the absence of effective stimuli from revolutionary organizations) movement is likely to be toward the system.

Under the circumstances of everyday living, however, it is doubtful whether pure approach-approach conditions . . . ever exist. In nearly every case, the choice of one goal generates an avoidance tendency due to the fact that the other goal may have to be relinquished . . . . such double approach-avoidance conflicts are not readily resolved. By and large, these . . . conflicts reduce to a kind of avoidance-avoidance paradigm . . . . (where conflict must continue unless withdrawal is feasible).[22]

Under certain circumstances (psychological conditions) psycho-political disturbances are likely to be structured as double approach-avoidance conflict and withdrawal is likely to be attempted (stage 4). These are: (1) the condition that the values at stake are basic or fundamental in character and/or many in number. These may be economic, religious, cultural, social structural or power-role related values; they may be personal aspirations, new identities, or values concerning the procedures of government. Revolutions have been made for all of these. The only relevant limitations are that they be basic and politicized[23]; (2) the political system is perceived to be inherently incapable (inefficacious) to maintain or create the significant politicized values; (3) the individual perceives himself to be incapable (inefficacious) of operating within the political system to bring about the changes he desires; but that (4) early and continuing socialization and daily life patterns establish and reinforce positive identifications with the polity so that the negative evaluations fostered by (1) through (3) above produce fundamental conflict or psychopolitical disturbance.

The perceptions of personal and systemic inefficacy posited above, operating in the salient political sphere, produce strong feelings of frustration and aggression. In addition, the disturbance is associated with significant tension or threat. There are three reasons for this: (1) a perceived negative relationship between one's basic values

[22] Judson S. Brown, op. cit., pp. 143 ff.
[23] A perceived threat to basic values, in the absence of other effective, protective mechanisms, will tend toward politicization of the values.

and one's organized society is, itself, threatening (e.g., as a separation anxiety); (2) the cognitive conflict or imbalance is itself tensionful; and (3) some free-floating anxiety is likely to become fixed on politics (i.e., on the dislocation between ego and politics). As the bonds between self and society weaken (in stage 5) latent rage tends to reinforce feelings of frustration and aggression and threat. Such rage results from the too constraining character of general socialization, when the conditions to which one has been socialized fall.

These, then, are the conditons conducive to, and associated with, the occurrence of passive alienation in the participant sectors of a polity: (1) a perceived incongruity between significant politicized values and the operations and/or structures of government; (2) a sense of personal political futility; (3) a sense of systemic political futility; and (4) a syndrome of associated, mutually reinforcing frustration, aggression, rage, threat, and tension.

By the end of stage 5, the individual has become passively alienated from all or at least a part of the political system. But the difference between a withdrawal of attention, affection and involvement from one institution or from the polity as a whole is a very important difference in assessing the likelihood that revolution will issue from alienation. It is from the latter, relatively complete estrangement from polities, that revolutionary behavior emerges. Accordingly, the two subprocesses whereby passive alienation generalizes to the political system as a whole, which are discussed here as stages 6 and 7, are crucial to an understanding of early revolutionary behavior. In addition, these are particularly illuminating sub-processes, for they show the sequential relationship of threat-reduction and *f-a-d-* and indicate how real world political occurrences "drive" the process of alienation.

Partial passive alienation (i.e., estrangement from some subset of political institutions, organizations and activities) can arise in either of two modes. First, the individual may simply have perceived only some of the system elements as incompatible with his fundamental political values and, hence, have withdrawn only from (devalued only) that element. Alternatively, he may initially withdraw from the polity as a whole (as in Figure 4) but then be

FIGURE 4.

able to psychologically differentiate the political system as a whole from some part of the system which needs to be, and can be, reformed. If he perceives that, though the actions of the system contravene his basic values, it is only some separable personnel, or process, or structure or even cultural norm that needs change (and not the fundamental character of the system), he is likely at least to remain in, not withdraw from the system (see Figure 5). An example of this is the widely prevalent and persistent notion that "the Czar would help us if only he knew our plight" which delayed any Russian revolution for some time, as it reduced peasant support for governmental overthrow. In this case the peasantry were differentiating the personnel of the system from its central authoritarian character as manifested in the Czar.

In whichever fashion the partial political alienation comes into being, it results in an approach-avoidance conflict in stage 6 (PV = approach object, devalued political system element as avoidance object). This conflict is threat-generating and threat-rein-

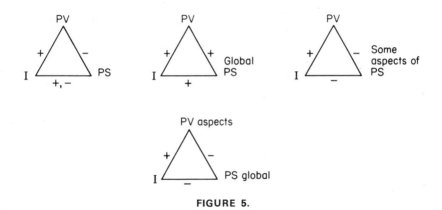

FIGURE 5.

forcing. To the extent that the devalued system element imposes negative sanctions for withdrawal, threat is generated. Far more important, this conflict reinforces the threat which is associated with disassociating oneself from one's national public life. Most modern polities are viewed as a whole and withdrawal from any major institution is tension-producing. Then too, of course, devaluing a political institution rarely suffices to attain one's basic politicized values.

In order to attain these values, in order to reduce the functional drive state of threat, the individual engages in "threat-coping" behavior; seeking to find (or influence) other institutions to foster his values. Here, the real-world experiences of the individual are of paramount importance. If he can find some alternative channel of politics in which he is efficacious, at best only partial alienation will obtain. If, however, his "threat-coping" behavior meets only a series of system-closures, threat will be reinforced and a perception of systemic inefficacy will be induced. These obtacles to value attainment and threat-reduction generate frustration and a perception of personal inefficacy. The order is important: value conflict (*VC*) yields threat from value conflict (*TVC*) and a failure to reduce *TVC* generates threat reinforce-

ment, perceived system inefficacy, frustration and perceived personal inefficacy. When all the major political institutions relevant to the attainment of the politicized values are seen as closed (both to self and self-surrogates), the threat and frustration generalizes to the system as a whole (stage 7) and passive political alienation results.

Any national political system is sufficiently complex so that this sub-process of differentiation-rationalization can go on for some time before complete withdrawal occurs, and this may explain why alienation sub-processes sometimes take place over long periods of time. As the reformer continues to eliminate differentiable elements of the system as possible causes of his value conflict, or fails to change the plausible conflictful features of the polity, it becomes increasingly difficult simultaneously to adjust his perceptions along cognitively consistent lines and still stay within the system. Accordingly, frustrations rise. The probability of passive or active alienation increases with time and the escalation of revolutionary potential builds up within the system. Therefore, criticism of the regime (including its legitimacy) becomes commonplace. This occurs first among intellectuals either before they withdraw or because they can't effectively withdraw. Here the decades of philosophical, political, and artistic criticism before both the French and Russian Revolutions are the type-cases.

Disgusted (and tired), one drops out or, ritualistically and half-withdrawn, one stays in until an appealing revolutionary organization develops. The major point to be made here is that the pool of withdrawn, passively alienated persons is made up not only of those who opt out early but also of a subset of reformers who are thoroughly familiar with the system. When the time comes for infiltration of the polity, requiring a knowledge of and contacts in the system, these men become strategically crucial.

Revolution, like political alienation, is a process; and the men who move the political system from widespread passive alienation . . . to organized revolutionary activity . . . will be among those individuals who first move from passive to active alienation . . . . As indicated, these are likely to be the most highly politicized persons for whom withdrawal creates a conflict between basic politicized values and the value of participation. These tend to be intellectuals who are tied to the modern media of communication and who, therefore, find withdrawal particularly infeasible. We expect radicalization to vary inversely with threat from system sanctions.

TOWARD A THEORY OF REVOLUTION[*]

James C. Davies

In exhorting proletarians of all nations to unite in revolution, because they had nothing to lose but their chains, Marx and Engels most succinctly presented that theory of revolution which is recognized as their brain child. But this most famed thesis, that progressive degradation of the industrial working class would finally reach the point of despair and inevitable revolt, is not the only one that Marx fathered. In at least one essay he gave life to a quite antithetical idea. He described, as a precondition of widespread unrest, not progressive degradation of the proletariat but rather an improvement in workers' economic condition which did not keep pace with the growing welfare of capitalists and therefore produced social tension.

A noticeable increase in wages presupposes a rapid growth of productive capital. The rapid growth of productive capital brings about an equally rapid growth of wealth, luxury, social wants, social enjoyments. Thus, although the enjoyments of the workers have risen, the social satisfaction that they give has fallen in comparison with the increased enjoyments of the capitalist, which are inaccessible to the worker, in comparison with the state of development of society in general. Our desires and pleasures spring from society; we measure them, therefore, by society and not by the objects which serve for their satisfaction. Because they are of a social nature, they are of a relative nature.[1]

[*] Several people have made perceptive suggestions and generous comments on an earlier version of this paper. I wish particularly to thank Seymour Martin Lipset, Lucian W. Pye, John H. Schaar, Paul Seabury, and Dwight Waldo.

[1] The *Communist Manifesto* of 1848 evidently antedates the opposing idea by about a year. See Edmund Wilson, *To the Finland Station* (Anchor Books edition), New York:

Reprinted from *American Sociological Review*. XXVII (1962), 5–18, by permission of the author and the American Sociological Association.

Marx's qualification here of his more frequent belief that degradation produces revolution is expressed as the main thesis by de Tocqueville in his study of the French Revolution. After a long review of economic and social decline in the seventeenth century and dynamic growth in the eighteenth, de Tocqueville concludes:

So it would appear that the French found their condition the more unsupportable in proportion to its improvement.... Revolutions are not always brought about by a gradual decline from bad to worse. Nations that have endured patiently and almost unconsciously the most overwhelming oppression often burst into rebellion against the yoke the moment it begins to grow lighter. The regime which is destroyed by a revolution is almost always an improvement on its immediate predecessor.... Evils which are patiently endured when they seem inevitable become intolerable when once the idea of escape from them is suggested.[2]

On the basis of de Tocqueville and Marx, we can choose one of these ideas or the other, which makes it hard to decide just when revolutions are more likely to occur—when there has been social and economic progress or when there has been regress. It appears that both ideas have explanatory and possibly predictive value, if they are juxtaposed and put in the proper time sequence.

Revolutions are most likely to occur when a prolonged period of objective economic and social development is followed by a short period of sharp reversal.[3] The all-important effect on the minds of people in a particular society is to produce, during the former period, an expectation of continued ability to satisfy needs—which continue to rise—and, during the latter, a mental state of anxiety and frustration when manifest reality breaks away from anticipated reality. The actual state of socio-economic development is less significant than the expectation that past progress, now blocked, can and must continue in the future. [See Figure 1.]

Political stability and instability are ultimately dependent on a state of mind, a mood, in a society. Satisfied or apathetic people who are poor in goods, status, and power can remain politically quiet and their opposites can revolt, just as, correlatively and more probably, dissatisfied poor can revolt and satisfied rich oppose revolution. It is the dissatisfied state of mind rather than the tangible provision of "adequate" or "inadequate" supplies of food, equality, or liberty which produces the revolution. In actuality, there must be a joining of forces between dissatisfied, frustrated people who differ in their degree of objective, tangible welfare and status. Well-fed, well-educated, high-status individuals who rebel in the face of apathy among the objectively deprived can accomplish at most a coup d'état. The objectively deprived, when faced with solid opposition of people of wealth, status, and power, will be smashed in their rebellion

Doubleday & Co. (n.d.), p. 157; Lewis S. Feuer, *Karl Marx and Friedrich Engels: Basic Writings on Politics and Philosophy*, N. Y.: Doubleday & Co., Inc., 1959, p. 1. The above quotation is from Karl Marx and Frederick Engels, "Wage Labour and Capital," *Selected Works in Two Volumes*, Moscow: Foreign Languages Publishing House, 1955, vol. 1, p. 94.

[2] A. de Tocqueville, *The Old Regime and the French Revolution* (trans. by John Bonner), N. Y.: Harper & Bros., 1856, p. 214. The Stuart Gilbert translation, Garden City: Doubleday & Co., Inc., 1955, pp. 176–177, gives a somewhat less pungent version of the same comment. *L'Ancien régime* was first published in 1856.

[3] Revolutions are here defined as violent civil disturbances that cause the displacement of one ruling group by another that has a broader popular basis for support.

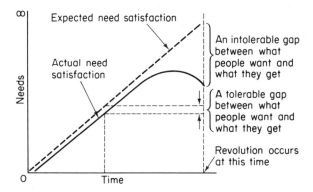

FIGURE 1.   Need Satisfaction and Revolution.

as were peasants and Anabaptists by German noblemen in 1525 and East Germans by the Communist élite in 1953.

Before appraising this general notion in light of a series of revolutions, a word is in order as to why revolutions ordinarily do not occur when a society is generally impoverished—when, as de Tocqueville put it, evils that seem inevitable are patiently endured. They are endured in the extreme case because the physical and mental energies of people are totally employed in the process of merely staying alive. The Minnesota starvation studies conducted during World War II[4] indicate clearly the constant pre-occupation of very hungry individuals with fantasies and thoughts of food. In extremis, as the Minnesota research poignantly demonstrates, the individual withdraws into a life of his own, withdraws from society, withdraws from any significant kind of activity unrelated to staying alive. Reports of behavior in Nazi concentration camps indicate the same pre-

occupation.[5] In less extreme and barbarous circumstances, where minimal survival is possible but little more, the preoccupation of individuals with staying alive is only mitigated. Social action takes place for the most part on a local, face-to-face basis. In such circumstances the family is a—perhaps the major—solidary unit[6] and even the local community exists primarily to the extent families need to act together to secure their separate survival. Such was life on the American frontier in the sixteenth through nineteenth centuries. In very much attenuated form, but with a substantial degree of social isolation persisting, such evidently is rural life even today. This is clearly related to a relatively low level of political participation in elections.[7] As Zawadzki and Lazars-

[4] The full report is Ancel Keys *et al.*, *The Biology of Human Starvation*, Minneapolis: University of Minnesota Press, 1960. See J. Brozek, "Semi-starvation and Nutritional Rehabilitation," *Journal of Clinical Nutrition*, 1 (January, 1953), pp. 107–118 for a brief analysis.

[5] E. A. Cohen, *Human Behavior in the Concentration Camp*, New York: W. W. Norton & Co., 1953, pp. 123–125, 131–140.

[6] For community life in such poverty, in Mezzogiorno Italy, see E. C. Banfield, *The Moral Basis of a Backward Society*, Glencoe, Ill.: The Free Press, 1958. The author emphasizes that the nuclear family is a solidary, sensual, moral unit (see p. 85) but even within it, consensus appears to break down, in outbreaks of pure, individual amorality—notably between parents and children (see p. 117).

[7] See Angus Campbell *et al.*, *The American Voter*, New York: John Wiley & Sons, 1960, Chap. 15, "Agrarian Political Behavior."

feld have indicated,[8] preoccupation with physical survival, even in industrial areas, is a force strongly militating against the establishment of the community-sense and consensus on joint political action which are necessary to induce a revolutionary state of mind. Far from making people into revolutionaries, enduring poverty makes for concern with one's solitary self or solitary family at best and resignation or mute despair at worst. When it is a choice between losing their chains or their lives, people will mostly choose to keep their chains, a fact which Marx seems to have overlooked.[9]

It is when the chains have been loosened somewhat, so that they can be cast off without a high probability of losing life, that people are put in a condition of proto-rebelliousness. I use the term proto-rebelliousness because the mood of discontent may be dissipated before a violent outbreak occurs. The causes for such dissipation may be natural or social (including economic and political). A bad crop year that threatens a return to chronic hunger may be succeeded by a year of natural abundance. Recovery from sharp economic dislocation may take the steam from the boiler of rebellion.[10] The slow, grudging grant of reforms, which has been the political history of England since at least the Industrial Revolution, may effectively and continuously prevent the degree of frustration that produces revolt.

A revolutionary state of mind requires the continued, even habitual but dynamic expectation of greater opportunity to satisfy basic needs, which may range from merely physical (food, clothing, shelter, health, and safety from bodily harm) to social (the affectional ties of family and friends) to the need for equal dignity and justice. But the necessary additional ingredient is a persistent, unrelenting threat to the satisfaction of these needs: not a threat which actually returns people to a state of sheer survival but which puts them in the mental state where they believe they will not be able to satisfy one or more basic needs. Although physical deprivation in some degree may be threatened on the eve of all revolutions, it need not be the prime factor, as it surely was not in the American Revolution of 1775. The crucial factor is the vague or specific fear that ground gained over a long period of time will be quickly lost. This fear does not generate if there is continued opportunity to satisfy continually emerging needs; it generates when the existing government suppresses or is blamed for suppressing such opportunity.

Three rebellions or revolutions are given considerable attention in the sections that follow: Dorr's Rebellion of 1842, the Russian Revolution of 1917, and the Egyptian Revolution of 1952. Brief mention is then made of several other major civil disturbances, all of which appear to fit the J-curve pattern.[11] After considering these

---

[8] B. Zawadzki and P. F. Lazarsfeld, "The Psychological Consequences of Unemployment," *Journal of Social Psychology*, 6 (May, 1935), pp. 224–251.

[9] A remarkable and awesome exception to this phenomenon occurred occasionally in some Nazi concentration camps, e.g., in a Buchenwald revolt against capricious rule by criminal prisoners. During this revolt, one hundred criminal prisoners were killed by political prisoners. See Cohen, *op. cit.*, p. 200.

[10] See W. W. Rostow, "Business Cycles, Harvests, and Politics: 1790–1850," *Journal of Economic History*, 1 (November, 1941), pp. 206–221 for the relation between economic fluctuation and the activities of the Chartists in the 1830s and 1840s.

[11] This curve is of course not to be confused with its prior and altogether different use by Floyd Allport in his study of social conformity. See F. H. Allport, "The J-Curve Hypothesis of Conforming Behavior," *Journal of Social Psychology*, 5 (May, 1934), pp. 141–183,

specific disturbances, some general theoretical and research problems are discussed.

No claim is made that all rebellions follow the pattern, but just that the ones here presented do. All of these are "progressive" revolutions in behalf of greater equality and liberty. The question is open whether the pattern occurs in such markedly retrogressive revolutions as Nazism in Germany or the 1861 Southern rebellion in the United States. It will surely be necessary to examine other progressive revolutions before one can judge how universal the J-curve is. And it will be necessary, in the interests of scientific validation, to examine cases of serious civil disturbance that fell short of producing profound revolution—such as the Sepoy Rebellion of 1857 in India, the Pullman Strike of 1894 in America, the Boxer Rebellion of 1900 in China, and the Great Depression of the 1920s and 1930s as it was experienced in Austria, France, Great Britain, and the United States. The explanation for such still-born rebellions—for revolutions that might have occurred—is inevitably more complicated than for those that come to term in the "normal" course of political gestation.

Dorr's Rebellion of 1842

Dorr's Rebellion[12] in nineteenth-century America was perhaps the first of many civil disturbances to occur in America as a consequence, in part, of the Industrial Revolution. It followed by three years an outbreak in England

---

reprinted in T.H. Newcomb and E.L. Hartley, *Readings in Social Psychology*, N. Y.: Henry Holt & Co., 1947, pp. 55–67.

[12] I am indebted to Beryl L. Crowe for his extensive research on Dorr's Rebellion while he was a participant in my political behavior seminar at the University of California, Berkeley, Spring 1960.

that had similar roots and a similar program—the Chartist agitation. A machine-operated textile industry was first established in Rhode Island in 1790 and grew rapidly as a consequence of domestic and international demand, notably during the Napoleonic Wars. Jefferson's Embargo Act of 1807, the War of 1812, and a high tariff in 1816 further stimulated American industry.

Rapid industrial growth meant the movement of people from farms to cities. In Massachusetts the practice developed of hiring mainly the wives and daughters of farmers, whose income was thereby supplemented but not displaced by wages. In Rhode Island whole families moved to the cities and became committed to the factory system. When times were good, industrialized families earned two or three times what they got from the soil; when the mills were idle, there was not enough money for bread.[13] From 1807 to 1815 textiles enjoyed great prosperity; from 1834 to 1842 they suffered depression, most severely from 1835 to 1840. Prosperity raised expectations and depression frustrated them, particularly when accompanied by stubborn resistance to suffrage demands that first stirred in 1790 and recurred in a wave-like pattern in 1811 and then in 1818 and 1820 following suffrage extension in Connecticut and Massachusetts. The final crest was reached in 1841, when suffrage associations met and called for a constitutional convention.[14] [See Figure 2.]

[13] Joseph Brennan, *Social Conditions in Industrial Rhode Island: 1820–1860*, Washington D.C.: Catholic University of America, 1940, p. 33.

[14] The persistent demand for suffrage may be understood in light of election data for 1828 and 1840. In the former year, only 3600 votes were cast in Rhode Island, whose total population was about 94,000. (Of these votes, 23 per cent were cast for Jackson and 77 per cent for Adams, in contrast to a total national division of 56 per cent for Jackson and 44

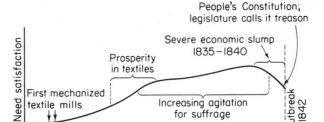

FIGURE 2.

Against the will of the government, the suffragists held an election in which all adult males were eligible to vote, held a constitutional convention composed of delegates so elected and in December 1841 submitted the People's Constitution to the same electorate, which approved it and the call for an election of state officers the following April, to form a new government under this unconstitutional constitution.[15]

These actions joined the conflict with the established government. When asked—by the dissidents—the state supreme court rendered its private judgment in March 1842 that the new constitution was "of no binding force whatever" and any act "to carry it into effect by force will be treason against the state." The legislature passed what became known as the Algerian law, making it an offense punishable by a year in jail to vote in the April election, and by life imprisonment to hold office under the People's Constitution.

The rebels went stoutly ahead with the election, and on May 3, 1842 inaugurated the new government. The next day the People's legislature met and respectfully requested the sheriff to take possession of state buildings, which he failed to do. Violence broke out on the 17th of May in an attempt to take over a state arsenal with two British cannon left over from the Revolutionary War. When the cannon misfired, the People's government resigned. Sporadic violence continued for another month, resulting in the arrest of over 500 men, mostly textile workers, mechanics, and laborers. The official legislature called for a new constitutional convention, chosen by universal manhood suffrage, and a new constitution went into effect in January, 1843. Altogether only one person was killed in this little revolution, which experienced violence, failure, and then success within the space of nine months.

It is impossible altogether to separate the experience of rising expectations among people in Rhode Island from that among Americans generally. They all shared historically the struggle against a stubborn but ultimately rewarding frontier where their self-confidence gained strength not only in the daily process of tilling the soil and harvesting the crops but also by improving their skill at self-government. Winning their war of independence, Americans continued to press for more goods and more democracy. The pursuit of economic expectations was greatly facilitated by the growth

per cent for Adams.) All votes cast in the 1828 election amount to 4 per cent of the total Rhode Island population and 11 per cent of the total U.S. population excluding slaves. In 1840, with a total population of 109,000 only 8300 votes—8 per cent—were cast in Rhode Island, in contrast to 17 per cent of the national population excluding slaves.

[15] A. M. Mowry, *The Dorr War*, Providence, R. I.: Preston & Rounds Co., 1901, p. 114.

of domestic and foreign trade and the gradual establishment of industry. Equalitarian expectations in politics were satisfied and without severe struggle—in most Northern states—by suffrage reforms.

In Rhode Island, these rising expectations—more goods, more equality, more self-rule—were countered by a series of containing forces which built up such a head of steam that the boiler cracked a little in 1842. The textile depression hit hard in 1835 and its consequences were aggravated by the Panic of 1837. In addition to the frustration of seeing their peers get the right to vote in other states, poor people in Rhode Island were now beset by industrial dislocation in which the machines that brought them prosperity they had never before enjoyed now were bringing economic disaster. The machines could not be converted to produce food and in Rhode Island the machine tenders could not go back to the farm.

When they had recovered from the preoccupation with staying alive, they turned in earnest to their demands for constitutional reform. But these were met first with indifference and then by a growing intransigence on the part of the government representing the propertied class. Hostile action by the state supreme court and then the legislature with its Algerian law proved just enough to break briefly the constitutional structure which in stable societies has the measure of power and resilience necessary to absorb social tension.

The Russian Revolution of 1917

In Russia's tangled history it is hard to decide when began the final upsurge of expectations that, when frustrated, produced the cataclysmic events of 1917. One can truly say that the real beginning was the slow modern-ization process begun by Peter the Great over two hundred years before the revolution. And surely the rationalist currents from France that slowly penetrated Russian intellectual life during the reign of Catherine the Great a hundred years before the revolution were necessary, lineal antecedents of the 1917 revolution.

Without denying that there was an accumulation of forces over at least a 200-year period,[16] we may nonetheless date the final upsurge as beginning with the 1861 emancipation of serfs and reaching a crest in the 1905 revolution.

The chronic and growing unrest of serfs before their emancipation in 1861 is an ironic commentary on the Marxian notion that human beings are what social institutions make them. Although serfdom had been shaping their personality since 1647, peasants became increasingly restive in the second quarter of the nineteenth century.[17] The continued discontent of peasants after emancipation is an equally ironic commentary on the belief that relieving one profound frustration produces enduring contentment. Peasants rather quickly got over their joy at being untied from the soil after two hundred years. Instead of declining, rural violence increased.[18] Having gained freedom but not much free land, peasants now had to rent or buy land

[16] There is an excellent summary in B. Brutzkus, "The Historical Peculiarities of the Social and Economic Development of Russia," in R. Bendix and S. M. Lipset, *Class, Status, and Power*, Glencoe, Ill.: The Free Press, 1953, pp. 517–540.

[17] Jacqueries rose from an average of 8 per year in 1826–30 to 34 per year in 1845–49. T. G. Masaryk, *The Spirit of Russia*, London: Allen and Unwin, Ltd., 1919, Vol. 1, p. 130. This long, careful, and rather neglected analysis was first published in German in 1913 under the title *Zur Russischen Geschichts- und Religionsphilosophie.*

[18] Jacqueries averaged 350 per year for the first three years after emancipation. *Ibid.*, pp. 140–141.

to survive: virtual personal slavery was exchanged for financial servitude. Land pressure grew, reflected in a doubling of land prices between 1868 and 1897.

It is hard thus to tell whether the economic plight of peasants was much lessened after emancipation. A 1903 government study indicated that even with a normal harvest, average food intake per peasant was 30 per cent below the minimum for health. The only sure contrary item of evidence is that the peasant population grew, indicating at least increased ability of the land to support life, as . . . Table [1] shows.

Table 1

POPULATION OF EUROPEAN RUSSIA (1480–1895)

	Population (in Millions)	Increase (in Millions)	Average Annual Rate of Increase* (Per cent)
1480	2.1	—	—
1580	4.3	2.2	1.05
1680	12.6	8.3	1.93
1780	26.8	14.2	1.13
1880	84.5	57.7	2.15
1895	110.0	25.5	2.02

Source (for gross population data): *Entsiklo-pedicheskii Slovar*, St. Petersburg, 1897, vol. 40, p. 631. Russia's population was about 97% rural in 1784, 91% in 1878, and 87% in 1897. See Masaryk, *op. cit.*, p. 162n.
* Computed as follows: dividing the increase by the number of years and then dividing this hypothetical annual increase by the population at the end of the preceding 100-year period.

The land-population pressure pushed people into towns and cities, where the rapid growth of industry truly afforded the chance for economic betterment. One estimate of net annual income for a peasant family of five in the rich black-earth area in the late nineteenth century was 82 rubles. In contrast, a "good" wage for a male factory worker was about 168 rubles per year. It was this difference in the degree of poverty that produced almost a doubling of

the urban population between 1878 and 1897. The number of industrial workers increased almost as rapidly. The city and the factory gave new hope. Strikes in the 1880s were met with brutal suppression but also with the beginning of factory legislation, including the requirement that wages be paid regularly and the abolition of child labor. The burgeoning proletariat remained comparatively contented until the eve of the 1905 revolution.[19]

There is additional, non-economic evidence to support the view that 1861 to 1905 was the period of rising expectations that preceded the 1917 revolution. The administration of justice before the emancipation had largely been carried out by noblemen and landowners who embodied the law for their peasants. In 1864 justice was in principle no longer delegated to such private individuals. Trials became public, the jury system was introduced, and judges got tenure. Corporal punishment was alleviated by the elimination of running the gauntlet, lashing, and branding; caning persisted until 1904. Public joy at these reforms was widespread. For the intelligentsia, there was increased opportunity to think and write and to criticize established institutions, even sacrosanct absolutism itself.

But Tsarist autocracy had not quite abandoned the scene. Having inclined but not bowed, in granting the inevitable emancipation as an act not of justice but grace, it sought to

[19] The proportion of workers who struck from 1895 through 1902 varied between 1.7 per cent and 4.0 per cent per year. In 1903 the proportion rose to 5.1 per cent but dropped a year later to 1.5 per cent. In 1905 the proportion rose to 163.8 per cent, indicating that the total working force struck, on the average, closer to twice than to once during that portentous year. In 1906 the proportion dropped to 65.8 per cent; in 1907 to 41.9 per cent; and by 1909 was down to a "normal" 3.5 per cent. *Ibid.*, p. 175n.

maintain its absolutist principle by conceding reform without accepting anything like democratic authority. Radical political and economic criticism surged higher. Some strong efforts to raise the somewhat lowered floodgates began as early as 1866, after an unsuccessful attempt was made on the life of Alexander II, in whose name serfs had just gained emancipation. When the attempt succeeded fifteen years later, there was increasing state action under Alexander III to limit constantly rising expectations. By suppression and concession, the last Alexander succeeded in dying naturally in 1894.

When it became apparent that Nicholas II shared his father's ideas but not his forcefulness, opposition of the intelligentsia to absolutism joined with the demands of peasants and workers, who remained loyal to the Tsar but demanded economic reforms. Starting in 1904, there developed a "League of Deliverance" that coordinated efforts of at least seventeen other revolutionary, proletarian, or nationalist groups within the empire. Consensus on the need for drastic reform, both political and economic, established a many ringed circus of groups sharing the same tent. These groups were geographically distributed from Finland to Armenia and ideologically from liberal constitutionalists to revolutionaries made prudent by the contrast between their own small forces and the power of Tsardom.

Events of 1904–5 mark the general downward turning point of expectations, which people increasingly saw as frustrated by the continuation of Tsardom. Two major and related occurrences made 1905 the point of no return. The first took place on the Bloody Sunday of January 22, 1905, when peaceful proletarian petitioners marched on the St. Petersburg palace and were killed by the hundreds. The myth that the Tsar was the gracious protector of his subjects, however surrounded he might be by malicious advisers, was quite shattered. The reaction was immediate, bitter, and prolonged and was not at all confined to the working class. Employers, merchants, and white-collar officials joined in the burgeoning of strikes which brought the economy to a virtual standstill in October. Some employers even continued to pay wages to strikers. University students and faculties joined the revolution. After the great October strike, the peasants ominously sided with the workers and engaged in riots and assaults on landowners. Until peasants became involved, even some landowners had sided with the revolution.

The other major occurrence was the disastrous defeat of the Russian army and navy in the 1904–5 war with Japan. Fundamentally an imperialist venture aspiring to hegemony over the people of Asia, the war was not regarded as a people's but as a Tsar's war, to save and spread absolutism. The military defeat itself probably had less portent than the return of shattered soldiers from a fight that was not for them. Hundreds of thousands, wounded or not, returned from the war as a visible, vocal, and ugly reminder to the entire populace of the weakness and selfishness of Tsarist absolutism.

The years from 1905 to 1917 formed an almost relentless procession of increasing misery and despair. Promising at last a constitutional government, the Tsar, in October, 1905, issued from on high a proclamation renouncing absolutism, granting law-making power to a duma, and guaranteeing freedom of speech, assembly, and association. The first two dumas, of 1906 and 1907, were dissolved for recalcitrance. The third was made pliant by reduced representation of workers and peasants and by the prosecution and conviction of protes-

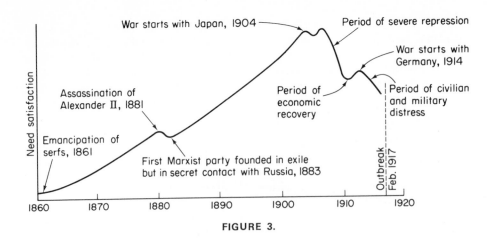

FIGURE 3.

tants in the first two. The brief period of a free press was succeeded in 1907 by a reinstatement of censorship and confiscation of prohibited publications. Trial of offenders against the Tsar was now conducted by courts martial. Whereas there had been only 26 executions of the death sentence, in the 13 years of Alexander II's firm rule (1881–94), there were 4,449 in the years 1905–10, in six years of Nicholas II's soft regimen.[20]

But this "white terror," which caused despair among the workers and intelligentsia in the cities, was not the only face of misery. For the peasants, there was a bad harvest in 1906 followed by continued crop failures in several areas in 1907. To forestall action by the dumas, Stolypin decreed a series of agrarian reforms designed to break up the power of the rural communes by individualizing land ownership. Between these acts of God and government, peasants were so preoccupied with hunger or self-aggrandizement as to be dulled in their sensitivity to the revolutionary appeals of radical organizers.

After more than five years of degrading terror and misery, in 1910 the country appeared to have reached

[20] *Ibid.*, p. 189n.

a condition of exhaustion. Political strikes had fallen off to a new low. As the economy recovered, the insouciance of hopelessness set in. Amongst the intelligentsia the mood was hedonism, or despair that often ended in suicide. Industrialists aligned themselves with the government. Workers worked. But an upturn of expectations, inadequately quashed by the police, was evidenced by a recrudescence of political strikes which, in the first half of 1914—on the eve of war—approached the peak of 1905. They sharply diminished during 1915 but grew again in 1916 and became a general strike in February 1917.[21]

Figure 3 indicates the lesser waves in the tidal wave whose first trough is at the end of serfdom in 1861 and whose second is at the end of Tsardom in 1917. This fifty-six-year period appears to constitute a single long phase in which popular gratification at the

[21] In his *History of the Russian Revolution*, Leon Trotsky presents data on political strikes from 1903 to 1917. In his *Spirit of Russia*, Masaryk presents comparable data from 1905 through 1912. The figures are not identical but the reported yearly trends are consistent. Masaryk's figures are somewhat lower, except for 1912. Cf. Trotsky, *op. cit.*, Doubleday Anchor Books ed., 1959, p. 32 and Masaryk, *op. cit. supra*, p. 197n.

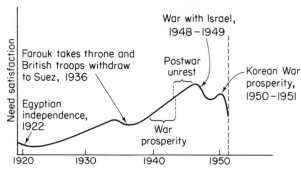

FIGURE 4.

termination of one institution (serfdom) rather quickly was replaced with rising expectations which resulted from intensified industrialization and which were incompatible with the continuation of the inequitable and capricious power structure of Tsarist society. The small trough of frustration during the repression that followed the assassination of Alexander II seems to have only briefly interrupted the rise in popular demand for more goods and more power. The trough in 1904 indicates the consequences of war with Japan. The 1905–6 trough reflects the repression of January 22, and after, and is followed by economic recovery. The final downturn, after the first year of war, was a consequence of the dislocations of the German attack on all kinds of concerted activities other than production for the prosecution of the war. Patriotism and governmental repression for a time smothered discontent. The inflation that developed in 1916 when goods, including food, became severely scarce began to made workers self-consciously discontented. The conduct of the war, including the growing brutality against reluctant, ill-provisioned troops, and the enormous loss of life, produced the same bitter frustration in the army.[22] When civilian dis-

[22] See Trotsky, *op. cit.*, pp. 18–21 for a vivid picture of rising discontent in the army.

content reached the breaking point in February, 1917, it did not take long for it to spread rapidly into the armed forces. Thus began the second phase of the revolution that really started in 1905 and ended in death to the Tsar and Tsardom—but not to absolutism—when the Bolsheviks gained ascendancy over the moderates in October. A centuries-long history of absolutism appears to have made this post-Tsarist phase of it tragically inevitable.

The Egyptian Revolution of 1952

The final slow upsurge of expectations in Egypt that culminated in the revolution began when that society became a nation in 1922, with the British grant of limited independence. [See Figure 4.] British troops remained in Egypt to protect not only the Suez Canal but also, ostensibly, to prevent foreign aggression. The presence of foreign troops served only to heighten nationalist expectations, which were excited by the Wafd, the political organization that formed public opinion on national rather than religious grounds and helped establish a fairly unified community—in striking contrast to late-nineteenth-century Russia.

But nationalist aspirations were not the only rising expectations in Egypt of the 1920s and 1930s. World War I had spurred industrialization, which opened opportunities for peasants to improve, somewhat, their way of life by working for wages in the cities and also opened great opportunities for entrepreneurs to get rich. The moderately wealthy got immoderately so in commodity market speculation, finance, and manufacture, and the uprooted peasants who were now employed, or at any rate living, in cities were relieved of at least the notion that poverty and boredom must be the will of Allah. But the incongruity of a money-based modern semi-feudality that was like a chariot with a gasoline engine evidently escaped the attention of ordinary people. The generation of the 1930s could see more rapid progress, even for themselves, than their parents had even envisioned. If conditions remained poor, they could always be blamed on the British, whose economic and military power remained visible and strong.

Economic progress continued, though unevenly, during World War II. Conventional exports, mostly cotton, actually declined, not even reaching depression levels until 1945, but direct employment by Allied military forces reached a peak of over 200,000 during the most intense part of the African war. Exports after the war rose steadily until 1948, dipped, and then rose sharply to a peak in 1951 as a consequence of the Korean war. But in 1945 over 250,000 wage earners[23]— probably over a third of the working force—became jobless. The cost of living by 1945 had risen to three times the index of 1937.[24] Manual laborers were hit by unemployment; white collar workers and professionals probably more by inflation than unemployment. Meanwhile the number of millionaires in pounds sterling had increased eight times during the war.[25]

Frustrations, exacerbated during the war by German and thereafter by Soviet propaganda, were at first deflected against the British[26] but gradually shifted closer to home. Egyptian agitators began quoting the Koran in favor of a just, equalitarian society and against great differences in individual wealth. There was an ominous series of strikes, mostly in the textile mills, from 1946–48.

At least two factors stand out in the postponement of revolution. The first was the insatiable postwar world demand for cotton and textiles and the second was the surge of solidarity with king and country that followed the 1948 invasion of the new state of Israel. Israel now supplemented England as an object of deflected frustration. The disastrous defeat a year later, by a new nation with but a fifteenth of Egypt's population, was the beginning of the end. This little war had struck the peasant at his hearth, when a storage of wheat and of oil for stoves provided a daily reminder of a weak and corrupt government. The defeat frustrated popular hopes for national glory and—with even more portent—humiliated the army and solidified it

[23] C. Issawi, *Egypt at Mid-Century: An Economic Survey*, London: Oxford University Press, 1954, p. 262. J. & S. Lacouture in their *Egypt in Transition*, New York: Criterion Books, 1958, p. 100, give a figure of over 300,000. Sir R. Bullard, editor, *The Middle East: A Political and Economic Survey*, London: Oxford University Press, 1958, p. 221 estimates total employment in industry, transport, and commerce in 1957 to have been about 750,000.

[24] International Monetary Fund, *International Financial Statistics*, Washington, D. C. See monthly issues of this report, 1950–53.

[25] J. and S. Lacouture, *op. cit.*, p. 99.

[26] England threatened to depose Farouk in February 1942, by force if necessary, if Egypt did not support the Allies. Capitulation by the government and the Wafd caused widespread popular disaffection. When Egypt finally declared war on the Axis in 1945, the prime minister was assassinated. See J. & S. Lacouture, *op. cit.*, pp. 97–98 and Issawi, *op. cit.*, p. 268.

against the bureaucracy and the palace which had profiteered at the expense of national honor. In 1950 began for the first time a direct and open propaganda attack against the king himself. A series of peasant uprisings, even on the lands of the king, took place in 1951 along with some 49 strikes in the cities. The skyrocketing demand for cotton after the start of the Korean War in June, 1950 was followed by a collapse in March, 1952. The uncontrollable or uncontrolled riots in Cairo, on January 26, 1952, marked the fiery start of the revolution. The officers' coup in the early morning of July 23 only made it official.

Other Civil Disturbances

The J-curve of rising expectations followed by their effective frustration is applicable to other revolutions and rebellions than just the three already considered. Leisler's Rebellion in the royal colony of New York in 1689 was a brief dress-rehearsal for the American Revolution eighty-six years later. In an effort to make the colony serve the crown better, duties had been raised and were being vigorously collected. The tanning of hides in the colony was forbidden, as was the distillation of liquor. An embargo was placed on unmilled grain, which hurt the farmers. After a long period of economic growth and substantial political autonomy, these new and burdensome regulations produced a popular rebellion that for a year displaced British sovereignty.[27]

The American Revolution itself fits the J-curve and deserves more than the brief mention here given. Again prolonged economic growth and political autonomy produced continually rising expectations. They became acutely frustrated when, following the French

[27] See J. R. Reich, *Leisler's Rebellion*, Chicago: University of Chicago Press, 1953.

and Indian War (which had cost England so much and the colonies so little), England began a series of largely economic regulations having the same purpose as those directed against New York in the preceding century. From the 1763 Proclamation (closing to settlement land west of the Appalachians) to the Coercive Acts of April, 1774 (which among other things, in response to the December, 1773 Boston Tea Party, closed tight the port of Boston), Americans were beset with unaccustomed manifestations of British power and began to resist forcibly in 1775, on the Lexington-Concord road. A significant decline in trade with England in 1772[28] may have hastened the maturation of colonial rebelliousness.

The curve also fits the French Revolution, which again merits more mention than space here permits. Growing rural prosperity, marked by steadily rising land values in the eighteenth century, had progressed to the point where a third of French land was owned by peasant-proprietors. There were the beginnings of large-scale manufacture in the factory system. Constant pressure by the bourgeoisie against the state for reforms was met with considerable hospitality by a government already shifting from its old landed-aristocratic and clerical base to the growing middle class. Counter to these trends, which would *per se* avoid revolution, was the feudal reaction of the mid-eighteenth century, in which the dying nobility sought in numerous nagging ways to retain and reactivate its perquisites against a resentful peasantry and importunate bourgeoisie.

But expectations apparently continued rising until the growing oppor-

[28] See U.S. Bureau of the Census, *Historical Statistics of the United States, Colonial Times to 1957*, Washington, D.C., 1960, p. 757.

tunities and prosperity rather abruptly halted, about 1787. The fiscal crisis of the government is well known, much of it a consequence of a 1.5 billion livre deficit following intervention against Britain in the American war of independence. The threat to tax the nobility severely—after its virtual tax immunity —and the bourgeoisie more severely may indeed be said to have precipitated the revolution. But less well-known is the fact that 1787 was a bad harvest year and 1788 even worse; that by July, 1789 bread prices were higher than they had been in over 70 years; that an ill-timed trade treaty with England depressed the prices of French textiles; that a concurrent bumper grape crop depressed wine prices—all with the result of making desperate the plight of the large segment of the population now dependent on other producers for food. They had little money to buy even less bread. Nobles and bourgeoisie were alienated from the government by the threat of taxation; workers and some peasants by the threat of starvation. A long period of halting but real progress for virtually all segments of the population was now abruptly ended in consequence of the government's efforts to meet its deficit and of economic crisis resulting from poor crops and poor tariff policy.[29]

The draft riots that turned the city of New York upside down for five days in July, 1863 also follow the J-curve. This severe local disturbance began when conscription threatened the lives and fortunes of workingmen whose enjoyment of wartime prosperity was now frustrated not only by military service (which could be avoided by paying $300 or furnishing a substitute—

neither means being available to poor people) but also by inflation.[30]

Even the riots in Nyasaland, in February and March, 1959, appear to follow the pattern of a period of frustration after expectations and satisfactions have risen. Nyasaland workers who had enjoyed the high wages they were paid during the construction of the Kariba dam in Rhodesia returned to their homes and to unemployment, or to jobs paying $5 per month at a time when $15 was considered a bare minimum wage.[31]

One negative case—of a revolution that did not occur—is the depression of the 1930s in the United States. It was severe enough, at least on economic grounds, to have produced a revolution. Total national private production income in 1932 reverted to what it had been in 1916. Farm income in the same year was as low as in 1900; manufacturing as low as in 1913. Construction had not been as low since 1908. Mining and quarrying was back at the 1909 level.[32] For much of the population, two decades of economic progress had been wiped out. There were more than sporadic demonstrations of unemployed, hunger marchers, and veterans. In New York City, at least 29 people died of starvation. Poor people could vividly contrast their own past condition with the present—and their own present condition with that of those who were not seriously suffering. There were clearly audible rumbles of revolt. Why, then, no revolution?

[30] The account by Irving Werstein, *July 1863*, New York: Julian Messner, Inc., 1957, is journalistic but to my knowledge the fullest yet available.

[31] E. S. Munger, "The Tragedy of Nyasaland," American Universities Field Staff Reports Service, vol. 7, no. 4 (August 1, 1959), p. 9.

[32] See U.S. Bureau of the Census, *Historical Statistics of the United States: 1789-1945*, Washington, D.C.: 1949, p. 14.

[29] See G. Lefebvre, *The Coming of the French Revolution*, Princeton: Princeton University Press, 1947, pp. 101–109, 145–148, 196. G. Le Bon, *The Psychology of Revolution*, New York: G. P. Putnam's Sons, 1913, p. 143.

Several forces worked strongly against it. Among the most depressed, the mood was one of apathy and despair, like that observed in Austria by Zawadzki and Lazarsfeld. It was not until the 1936 election that there was an increased turnout in the national election. The great majority of the public shared a set of values which since 1776 had been official dogma—not the dissident program of an alienated intelligentsia. People by and large were in agreement, whether or not they had succeeded economically, in a belief in individual hard work, self-reliance, and the promise of success. (Among workers, this non-class orientation had greatly impeded the establishment of trade unions, for example.) Those least hit by the depression—the upper-middle class businessmen, clergymen, lawyers, and intellectuals—remained rather solidly committed not only to equalitarian values and to the established economic system but also to constitutional processes. There was no such widespread or profound alienation as that which had cracked the loyalty of the nobility, clergy, bourgeoisie, armed forces, and intelligentsia in Russia. And the national political leadership that emerged had constitutionalism almost bred in its bones. The major threat to constitutionalism came in Louisiana; this leadership was unable to capture a national party organization, in part because Huey Long's arbitrariness and demagogy were mistrusted.

The major reason that revolution did not nonetheless develop probably remains the vigor with which the national government attacked the depression in 1933, when it became no longer possible to blame the government. The ambivalent popular hostility to the business community was contained by both the action of government against the depression and the government's practice of publicly and successfully eliciting the cooperation of businessmen during the crucial months of 1933. A failure then of cooperation could have intensified rather than lessened popular hostility to business. There was no longer an economic or a political class that could be the object of widespread intense hatred because of its indifference or hostility to the downtrodden. Had Roosevelt adopted a demagogic stance in the 1932 campaign and gained the loyalty to himself personally of the Army and the F. B. I., there might have been a Nazi-type "revolution," with a potpourri of equalitarian reform, nationalism, imperialism, and domestic scapegoats. Because of a conservatism in America stemming from strong and long attachment to a value system shared by all classes, an anticapitalist, leftist revolution in the 1930s is very difficult to imagine.

Some Conclusions

The notion that revolutions need both a period of rising expectations and a succeeding period in which they are frustrated qualifies substantially the main Marxian notion that revolutions occur after progressive degradation and the de Tocqueville notion that they occur when conditions are improving. By putting de Tocqueville before Marx but without abandoning either theory, we are better able to plot the antecedents of at least the disturbances here described.

Half of the general, if not common, sense of this revised notion lies in the utter improbability of a revolution occurring in a society where there is the continued unimpeded opportunity to satisfy new needs, new hopes, new expectations. Would Dorr's rebellion have become such if the established electorate and government had readily acceded to the suffrage demands of the unpropertied? Would the Russian Revolution have taken place if the Tsarist autocracy had, quite out of character, truly granted the popular demands for constitutional democracy in 1905? Would the Cairo riots of January, 1952 and the subsequent coup actually have occurred if Britain had departed from Egypt and if the Egyptian monarchy had established an equitable tax system and in other ways alleviated the poverty of urban masses and the shame of the military?

The other half of the sense of the notion has to do with the improbability of revolution taking place where there has been no hope, no period in which expectations have risen. Such a stability of expectations presupposes a static state of human aspirations that sometimes exists but is rare. Stability of expectations is not a stable social condition. Such was the case of American Indians (at least from our perspective) and perhaps Africans before white men with Bibles, guns, and other goods interrupted the stability of African society. Egypt was in such a condition, vis-à-vis modern aspirations, before Europe became interested in building a canal. Such stasis was the case in Nazi concentration camps, where conformism reached the point of inmates cooperating with guards even when the inmates were told to lie down so that they could be shot.[33] But in the latter case there was a society with externally induced complete despair, and even in these camps there were occasional rebellions of sheer desperation. It is of course true that in a society less regimented than concentration camps, the rise of expectations can be frustrated successfully, thereby defeating rebellion just as the satisfaction of expectations does. This, however, requires the uninhibited exercise

of brute force as it was used in suppressing the Hungarian rebellion of 1956. Failing the continued ability and persistent will of a ruling power to use such force, there appears to be no sure way to avoid revolution short of an effective, affirmative, and continuous response on the part of established governments to the almost continuously emerging needs of the governed.

To be predictive my notion requires the assessment of the state of mind—or more precisely, the mood—of a people. This is always difficult, even by techniques of systematic public opinion analysis. Respondents interviewed in a country with a repressive government are not likely to be responsive. But there has been considerable progress in gathering first-hand data about the state of mind of peoples in politically unstable circumstances. One instance of this involved interviewing in West Berlin, during and after the 1948 blockade, as reported by Buchanan and Cantril. They were able to ascertain however crudely, the sense of security that people in Berlin felt. There was a significant increase in security after the blockade.[34]

Another instance comes out of the Middle Eastern study conducted by the Columbia University Bureau of Applied Social Research and reported by Lerner.[35] By directly asking respondents whether they were happy or unhappy with the way things had turned out in their life, the interviewers turned up data indicating marked differences in the frequency of a sense of unhappiness between countries and between "traditional," "transitional," and "modern" individuals in these

[33] Eugen Kogon, *The Theory and Practice of Hell*, New York: Farrar, Straus & Co., 1950, pp. 284–286.

[34] W. Buchanan, "Mass Communication in Reverse," *International Social Science Bulletin*, 5 (1953), pp. 577–583, at p. 578. The full study is W. Buchanan and H. Cantril, *How Nations See Each Other*, Urbana: University of Illinois Press, 1953, esp. pp. 85–90.
[35] Daniel Lerner, *The Passing of Traditional Society*, Glencoe, Ill.: Free Press, 1958.

countries.[36] There is no technical reason why such comparisons could not be made chronologically as well as they have been geographically.

Other than interview data are available with which we can, from past experience, make reasonable inferences about the mood of a people. It was surely the sense for the relevance of such data that led Thomas Masaryk before the first World War to gather facts about peasant uprisings and industrial strikes and about the writings and actions of the intelligentsia in nineteenth-century Russia. In the present report, I have used not only such data—in the collection of which other social scientists have been less assiduous than Masaryk—but also such indexes as comparative size of vote as between Rhode Island and the United States, employment, exports, and cost of living. Some such indexes, like strikes and cost of living, may be rather closely related to the mood of a people; others, like value of exports, are much cruder indications. Lest we shy away from the gathering of crude data, we should bear in mind that Durkheim developed his remarkable insights into modern society in large part by his analysis of suicide rates. He was unable to rely on the interviewing technique. We need not always ask people whether they are grievously frustrated by their government; their actions can tell us as well and sometimes better.

In his *Anatomy of Revolution*, Crane Brinton describes "some tentative uniformities" that he discovered in the Puritan, American, French, and Russian revolutions.[37] The uniformities were: an economically advancing society, class antagonism, desertion of intellectuals, inefficient government, a ruling class that has lost self-confidence, financial failure of government, and the inept use of force against rebels. All but the last two of these are long-range phenomena that lend themselves to studies over extended time periods. The first two lend themselves to statistical analysis. If they serve the purpose, techniques of content analysis could be used to ascertain trends in alienation of intellectuals. Less rigorous methods would perhaps serve better to ascertain the effectiveness of government and the self-confidence of rulers. Because tensions and frustrations are present at all times in every society, what is most seriously needed are data that cover an extended time period in a particular society, so that one can say there is evidence that tension is greater or less than it was N years or months previously.

We need also to know how long is a long cycle of rising expectations and how long is a brief cycle of frustration. We noted a brief period of frustration in Russia after the 1881 assassination of Alexander II and a longer period after the 1904 beginning of the Russo-Japanese War. Why did not the revolution occur at either of these times rather than in 1917? Had expectations before these two times not risen high enough? Had the subsequent decline not been sufficiently sharp and deep? Measuring techniques have not yet been devised to answer these questions. But their unavailablity now does not forecast their eternal inaccessibility. Physicists devised useful temperature scales long before they came as close to absolute zero as they have recently in laboratory conditions. The far more complex problems of scaling in social science inescapably are harder to solve.

We therefore are still not at the point of being able to predict revolution, but

[36] *Ibid.*, pp. 101–103. See also F. P. Kilpatrick & H. Cantril, "Self-Anchoring Scaling, A Measure of Individuals' Unique Reality Worlds," *Journal of Individual Psychology*, 16 (November, 1960), pp. 158–173.

[37] See the revised edition of 1952 as reprinted by Vintage Books, Inc., 1957, pp. 264–275.

the closer we can get to data indicating by inference the prevailing mood in a society, the closer we will be to understanding the change from gratification to frustration in people's minds. That is the part of the anatomy, we are forever being told with truth and futility, in which wars and revolutions always start. We should eventually be able to escape the embarrassment that may have come to Lenin six weeks after he made the statement in Switzerland, in January, 1917, that he doubted whether "we, the old [will] live to see the decisive battles of the coming revolution."[38]

[38] Quoted in E. H. Carr, *A History of Soviet Russia*, vol. 1, *The Bolshevik Revolution: 1917–23*, London: Macmillan, 1950, p. 69.

A STRUCTURAL THEORY OF AGGRESSION*

Johan Galtung

This theoretical essay is concerned with the conditions of aggression. We shall define aggression somewhat vaguely as "drives towards change, even against the will of others."[1] The

* This is a revised version of a paper presented during spring and summer 1964 at the Circolo Turati, Milano, Facoltà delle scienze politiche, Università di Torino, Polemological Institute, University of Groningen, Danish Conflict Research Society in Copenhagen, the study group in conflict and peace research, Lund University, the study group under the Scandinavian Summer University in Aarhus, and at a plenary session of the Scandinavian Summer University in Bergen, here published as PRIO publication no. 1-1. Deep gratitude is expressed for all the good ideas received during these discussions—particularly to Mr. Bengt Höglund of the study group in Lund. The study is an outcome of a grant from the Aquinas Foundation, New York, and from the Norwegian Research Council for Science and the Humanities, and serves as a theoretical basis for a series of empirical investigations.

[1] This is different from standard definitions in the field, e.g., the famous definition given by Dollard that aggression is any "sequence of behavior, the goal-response to which is the injury of the person toward whom it is directed." This definition is also used in the standard work by Berkowitz, L., *Aggression: A Social Psychological Analysis* (New York: McGraw-Hill, 1962). But we agree with Klineberg when he writes (*The Human Dimension of International Relations*, New York: Holt, Rinehart and Winston, 1964, p. 11) that "The question of universality of aggression is further complicated by considerable difference in the definition of the term itself. One writer, for example, refers to the original meaning of aggression as a tendency to go forward or approach. This is regarded as instinctive, whereas the inborn or instinctive nature of *hostility* has never been demonstrated. Another describes it as the will to assert and to test our capacity to deal with external forces, and it is this, rather than hostility, that is a fundamental characteristic of all living beings" (p. 10). But universality or fundamentality still leaves us with the problem of where or for

Excerpted from *Journal of Peace Research*, II (1964), 95–119, by permission of the author and publisher. Footnotes have been renumbered.

extreme forms of this phenomenon are crimes, including homicide, between individuals; revolutions, including elimination, between groups; and wars, including genocide, between nations. These forms make aggression negative and problematic, a cause of concern and prevention. But one can also turn the coin and look at the other face: aggression as the driving force in history, as the motivational energy that moves mountains. However, we shall be mainly concerned with aggression in its extreme forms where it becomes a drive to hurt and harm others because they stand in the way of one's own self-assertion, and not look at the good causes this may serve in the aggressors' own minds. Aggression in this sense is pervasive, important and catastrophic, with modern technology as a multiplier. It should be studied at its roots, at the very points where it emerges. . . .

.   .   .

. . . This is where the minds of men enter: a theory of aggression should combine the idea of frustration with the idea of perceiving aggression as a possible way out of the frustrating situation.

We now turn to the construction of a theory of that kind.

2. The Hypothesis about Rank-Disequilibrium

Imagine that we have a system of elements that are *actors* in the traditional social science sense of having goals and being capable of directing actions towards them, and that they

---

whom aggression in this broad sense is most pronounced, and with the problem of under what conditions aggression expresses itself as hostility. We use aggression somewhat in the sense of "self-assertion," but only insofar as this self-assertion implies an effort to change social relations, i.e., no longer to comply with existing conditions.

interact with each other.[2] Concretely, we are thinking of three such types of systems: the system of *individuals* found in a group and particularly in a nation; the system of *groups* found in a nation if the groups are so homogenized and organized that they can be seen as actors; and the *nations* in an international system. However, we shall prefer to proceed with the general theory for a while without making references to these three interpretations, and only return to them at length later on.

Even under these very general conditions it seems difficult to find counter examples to the following: (1) There will be a *division of labor* in the sense that the elements will not carry out the same tasks all the time; (2) the elements will tend to be *ranked* according to a number of criteria evaluating their position in the system; and (3) the relative position of the elements according to these criteria will have a certain *stability*. All we are saying by this is that *stratification* seems to be a universal phenomenon. The distance from "high" to "low" can be reduced, the consequences of stratification can be alleviated, but it cannot be declared to be non-existent. If one wants an egalitarian society where everybody has the same rank this must be arrived at by such techniques as making an element that is low in one context high in another context (compensation) or letting individuals who have high ranks in one period have low ranks in the next period (rotation). It cannot be done by abolishing differential ranking as such. For as long as there is interaction there will tend to develop a certain cultural similarity and as soon as this is the case the element that has more of, or is closer to or is more in agreement with the values of the system

---

[2] For an analysis of the concept of interaction see Galtung, J., "Expectations and Interaction Processes," *Inquiry*, 1959, pp. 213–34.

will rise high, and the elements that have little of these values and seem to be far from realizing them—whether it is might and glory, power, intelligence, money, beauty, health—will stay low in the system.

Thus, an interaction system is a multidimensional system of stratification, where those who have and those who have not, those who have more and those who have less, find, are given, or are forced into their positions. For the sake of simplicity, let us deal with these criteria of rank in terms of two positions only—high and low. We shall refer to them as *topdog* and *underdog* positions (T and U). Thus, an element in a system with five rank criteria, will have a profile, say TUTTU the interpretation of which depends on what kind of system and what kind of dimensions we are referring to. It may, for instance, stand for "high on power, low on income, high on occupation, high on education, low on ancestry" (for individuals or groups) or "high on military power, low on income *per capita*, high on industrialization, high on educational level, low on past glory" (for nations), and one may discuss how likely the configuration is. But two configurations are beyond doubt: the complete topdog, TTTTT, and the complete underdog, UUUUU, are both well-known occurrences in any social system, individual or national. We shall refer to these two as "equilibrated positions," since the ranks of the elements in these positions are in equilibrium with each other; they are equivalents.

With five dimensions and two positions on each there are 32 possible configurations, or in general 2^n combinations when n dimensions are used in the analysis. The theoretical problem is now: *where in the system, for what social types, is aggression most likely to accumulate and express itself?* For common sense as well as social ex-perience make us doubt that aggression is randomly distributed on the configurations or social positions.

With the conceptual apparatus developed so far there are three possible answers: aggression will mainly come from the elements equilibrated at the top (the complete topdog), mainly from the elements equilibrated at the bottom (the complete underdog), or mainly from the elements in rank-disequilibrium, i.e., the elements with some positions high and some positions low. . . .

. . . . .

. . . [O]ur hypothesis . . . is very simple:

Aggression is most likely to arise in social positions in rank-disequilibrium. In a system of individuals it may take the form of crime, in a system of groups the form of revolutions, and in a system of nations the form of war. But these extreme forms of aggression are unlikely to occur unless (1) other means of equilibration towards a complete topdog configuration have been tried, and (2) the culture has some practice in violent aggression.[3]

We shall now present extensive comments on this hypothesis. . . .

3. The Theory about How Disequilibrium Works

The thesis is very simple and the theory behind it is also simple. It rests on a comparison between the social situation of, say, a TU and a UU, in our terminology. There are three such

[3] The condition of rank-disequilibrium is, of course, not a necessary condition for aggression. Aggression may arise for other reasons. And it is hardly a sufficient condition either—perfect relationships between variables are rarely if ever found in the social sciences—but we shall argue later that for high levels of disequilibrium aggression seems to be a very probable consequence.

differences that seem to be decisive in this context.

A. DISEQUILIBRIUM MEANS DIFFERENTIAL TREATMENT

We have assumed that rank matters in the sense that the elements are treated according to their rank. An element in a TU position will be constantly reminded of his objective state of disequilibrium by the differential treatment he is exposed to. . . .

In more sociological terms, the crux of the matter is the high probability that the disequilibrated TU will use TT as his reference group even if UU is his membership group, whereas a complete underdog, UU, may not even dare to think in terms of TT as a reference group; the complete topdog will be beyond his imagination. The absolute deprivation of the UU may be higher, but the TU has relative deprivation built into his position. The destabilizing effect of this discrepancy will produce a mobility pressure, and the thesis is then that if there are no open channels of mobility, rectification of the disequilibrium will be carried out by other means. In this process two other aspects of the disequilibrium situation are of major importance.

B. DISEQUILIBRIUM MEANS RESOURCES

We have commented on the effects on the TU of having one foot in either camp, for instance, of being white and poor, as nation or as individual. Obviously, the position in the top camp not only creates the motivation towards equilibration, but also some of the resources that will come in handy in the struggle. The *nouveau riche* may be green, but he is nevertheless rich and the stories about him are about his efforts to obtain balance by converting money into culture and prestige. The small, overcrowded but economically developed nation has in its economic potential the possibility for conversion into military power with subsequent territorial expansion. The member of the intellectual proletariat may be low on almost everything, and yet have in his intellectual maturity, knowledge and academic discipline, invaluable tools that can be converted into power, high-ranking occupations and income. And the "white" but "poor" nation may draw on its kinship with white and rich nations to gain influence and recognition, as is the case with many Latin-American nations.

C. DISEQUILIBRIUM MEANS SELF-RIGHTEOUSNESS

Our culture seems to be more dominated by themes of balance and adequacy than by the theme of compensation. We have no empirical backing for this, but there seem to be more cases of people and nations saying "considering our high rank on X it is right and proper that we should also have a high rank on Y, because that corresponds to what is due to us" than of people and nations saying "considering my low ranks everywhere I think I am entitled to some compensation on at least one dimension." Claims must be justified not only in the eyes of the others but also in the eyes of the claimants themselves; they must feel they are right to the point of self-righteousness. In the kind of achievement-oriented world in which we live, claims will be based on achievement rather than on lack of achievement— in the latter case they are usually made explicit by others and the Welfare State is an example of the institutionalization of rank-compensation.

.   .   .

To summarize: it is socially guaranteed, by the very structure of the system, that the disequilibrated is never left in peace with his disequilibrium unless he cuts out and closes down some interaction channels. In this unstable situation he has both the resources and the inner justification needed for acts of deviance. Nevertheless, we do not hypothesize aggression unless (1) other means of rectification have been tried and (2) the culture has some practice in aggression.

4. More about Rank-Dimensions and Disequilibria

The time has now come to be more specific about the rank-dimensions. These are concerned with the most crucial things of life, the matters for which people live and die.[4] But they differ tremendously, and should be

[4] The following list may be useful as a reference. We have presented two sets of variables for nations, depending on whether the variables are "analytic" (based on statistical information about individuals) or "global," i.e., *sui generis*.

Individual Dimensions	Nations, Analytic	Nations, Global
1. *Age* (adults *v.* adolescents and children)	population pyramid	*Age as a nation*
2. *Sex*. (men *v.* women)		
3. *Family* ("good" *v.* "bad")		*Alliances* ("good" *v.* "bad")
4. *Primogeniture* ("first born")		*Doyen* in a group of nations
5. *Race* (Caucasoid, Mongoloid, Negroid, etc.)	rates of racial composition	*Dominant culture*
6. *Ethnicity* (Gentiles *v.* Jews, emigrants *v.* immigrants)	rates of ethnical composition	*Dominant culture*
7. *Ecology* (urban *v.* rural)	*rate of urbanization*	
8. *Geography* (center *v.* periphery)		*Central v. peripheral nation*
9. *Nation* (for individuals only—all national variables relevant as context)		
10. *Education* (degree)	*rate of literacy*	*Educational structure*
11. Occupation, split into		*Occupational structure*
a. *sector* (tertiary, secondary, primary)	*1-rate in primary occupations* *1-rate of population in low*	
b. *position* (high *v.* low)	*occupations*	*Social structure*
12. *Ideology* ("right" *v.* "wrong")	*rates of believers*	*Dominant ideology*
13. *Income, property* (rich *v.* poor-"dispossessed"; bourgeoisie *v.* proletariat)	*per capita income = per capita consumption + per capita investment standard of living*	*Stage of economic growth* *GNP* (development) *natural resources* *utilization of resources* (rate of growth)
14. *Power* (rulers *v.* subjects)	*rate of popular participation*	*Political structure* *International power*
15. *Legality* (law-abiding *v.* law-breaking)	*rates of criminality*	*Legality*
16. *Health* (well *v.* ill)	*rates of morbidity etc., life expectancy*	*Medical Structure*
17. *Knowledge* (those who know *v.* those who do not know)		*Cognitive culture*
18. *Skill* (those who can *v.* those who cannot)		*Technical culture*
19. *Conviction* (the "true believers" *v.* the others)	*rates of true believers*	*Ethical culture*
20. *Taste* (artists *v.* laymen)		*Esthetic culture*

analyzed from at least three angles: (1) is it possible, both in theory and in practice, for one element to change position at all, (2) how does the change of one element affect the position of the other elements, and (3) what kinds of disequilibria are most important?

Where the first problem is concerned the traditional distinction made in sociology between ascribed and achieved dimensions is useful. The ascribed position is known at birth, the achieved position is what the individual himself makes out of his life-situation. However, this conceals the important distinction between dimensions that are *indelible* in the sense that the element cannot escape from it (age, sex, race, primogeniture, family, ethnicity) and perhaps even *visible* (age, sex, race)—and the "delible" dimensions like nationhood or ecological background which the individual can move away from—even though they are known at his birth. Achievement may also be so conditioned by the matrix of ascribed dimensions, as in most societies today (skill is not known at birth, but the possibility or impossibility of demonstrating it if it exists is known), that mobility becomes illusory except for persons with the particular mixture of good and evil that makes for mobility. The most aggression-provoking case is probably the half-open dimension of unfulfilled promises, but the completely closed channel will also serve to accumulate aggression unless *all* channels are closed.

The second problem is more interesting. Imagine a system with two elements and one dimension only: we are interested in how the position of one affects the position of the other. In principle, there are three possibilities. The *units* may be *positively coupled* in the sense that if one rises so does the other, and that they will also follow each other on the way down. Then,

again, they may be *negatively coupled:* the rise of one is the fall of the other.[5] And, thirdly, they may not be coupled at all. Different economic systems provide examples of all three. Concretely, the most dramatic example of negative coupling in the case of nations is the dimension of *area:* one nation's gain will have to be the loss of one or more other nations unless the game can be made "variable-sum" through the exploration of outer space (or as it was in the period of the great discoveries). And the same applies to property at any given point of time: one person's loss is somebody else's gain, unless the game is changed through such factors as destruction or creation of property or is stretched out in time.

Correspondingly, the *dimensions* may be coupled positively, negatively, or not at all: the rising of a unit on one dimension may imply its rising on another dimension, or its fall, or it may imply nothing at all. More age means more power—at least the power to influence elections through voting, and so on.

In general it is obvious that dimensions with negative coupling between units are the dangerous ones, . . .

.   .   .

Finally, we turn to the problem of distinguishing between disequilibria. To say that disequilibrium matters is not to say that all kinds of disequilibrium matter equally much. A typology of disequilibria is needed, and we shall discuss this from three angles, two of them formal and one of them substantive.

First of all, there is the obvious dimension of degree of disequilibrium.

[5] This corresponds to the distinction made in game theory between cooperative and competitive games. Also see Schelling, T., *The Strategy of Conflict* (Cambridge: Harvard University Press, 1960), Chs. 2, 3 and 6.

Imagine that we introduce a "middle-dog," call him M. We define "degree" of disequilibrium as internal distance between the ranks, which would make TTM less disequilibrated than TTU. Generally, the experience based on data from persons in disequilibrium tend to show that the effects of disequilibrium do not show up unless there is a considerable amount of disequilibrium present.[6] The consequence is a tendency towards J-shaped relationships: deviation tendencies stay at the base level for equilibrium and low degrees of disequilibrium, and then rise quickly for high degrees of disequilibrium.

Secondly, there is the problem of disequilibrium *profile*. The sum of internal distances in the combinations TTU, UUT and TMU are the same, viz., 4, so we would expect more of an effect than for the combination TTM where the sum is 2. But do we expect the *same* effect with this crude measure of internal distance? *A priori*, one might argue that TTU is more desperate about his low status and UUT more proud about his high status, so that the former is the more aggressive, and then one might argue just the other way round.[7] One might say that TMU is exposed to a particularly deviation-generating mixture, and one may say that his aggression will be neutralized precisely because of the complex social structure in which he finds himself. In other words, one should leave this problem to the data; their richness, provided they are good, will probably by far outdo even a good theoretical imagination.

Thirdly, there is the problem of *which* dimensions. Obviously, not all disequilibria even with the same profile will have the same deviation-generating

effect. The effect will depend on the salience of the dimensions and of the disequilibrium. There is also the important suggestion made by Jackson[8] that the *achieved v. ascribed* distinction may be used here. Let us compare these two patterns with the same internal distance, based on three dimensions:

Dimension:	ascribed	achieved	ascribed
Pattern 1	high	low	high
Pattern 2	low	high	low

Of the three mechanisms we have mentioned in the section on "how disequilibrium works" this distinction should affect the third mechanism, the norm about justice, in particular. The unit with the second pattern is an overachiever relative to his ascribed case; the unit in the first pattern is an underachiever, and the overachiever more than the underachiever will feel that he deserves a fairer deal, at least in an achievement-oriented culture.

According to Jackson one might predict extrapunitivity for the overachiever and intrapunitivity for the underachiever[9]; the overachiever will blame society for constraining him, the underachiever will blame himself for doing less than society or the system might expect from him. But the overachiever is in the difficult situation that he is low on ascribed dimensions where mobility, by definition, is impossible. Hence, he will have to fight like the educated Negro, not for white status, but for the elimination of race as a rank-dimension. Thus, outward aggression takes a form other than simple fight for mobility and scarce value; it may be a fight about the definition of value.

The underachiever, e.g., the white high-class who is low on education or income, might be more motivated to

6 See Jackson (9, p. 473) or Galtung, J., *Members of Two Worlds, A Sociological Investigation of Three Villages in Western Sicily* (Oslo: PRIO publication no. 6–2), section 4.6.
7 See Jackson, *op. cit.*

8 *Ibid.*, pp. 476 ff.
9 *Loc. cit.*

direct aggression to promote his own mobility. But just as likely is aggression due to a desire to keep what he has—perhaps precisely against the attacks of the overachiever. Thus, the two will be pitted against each other, probably with the strongest aggression potential for any possible pair of combinations. In more concrete terms, the underachiever may possibly be identified as a member of the extreme right and the overachiever as a member of the extreme left[10]; the former will keep his privileges since that is the high basis he has in the system, the latter will deny the system of privileges or change them to his own advantage. Thus, we disagree with Jackson that outwardly directed aggression should necessarily be less probable for the underachiever, only that it *may* come as a reaction to the aggression of the overachiever and be less spontaneous.

It is interesting in this connection to compare the state of the Negroes in the U.S.A. and in Brazil. Comparisons are very often to the effect that there is less discrimination or prejudice in Brazil, but statistical data do not appear to demonstrate this. Rather, the impression is that there are more Negroes in higher positions in the U.S.A. than in Brazil. We shall only suggest an interpretation in terms of the present theory. If we have a nation where race and position are equilibrated we would predict a very low level of aggression, and hence more of a tendency to express oneself in accordance with the predominant ideology of our time, the ideology of racial equality. Thus, there will be no laws prescribing segregation and little overt prejudice, for rank-equilibrium is built into the social structure.

On the other hand, imagine a nation where many Negroes are high in social position and many whites are low. In that case we would predict formal and informal barriers to secure segregation, and as a barrier against aggression resulting from the disequilibrium. In fact, the way to obtain "racial equality" will be through the suppression of race as a dimension at all—and here as elsewhere the role of ideology and perception is probably tremendous. Thus, to the extent that these models are approximations to Brazilian and U.S reality the U.S.A seems to be much further along the road towards racial equality than Brazil, only she is in a transitional period with tremendous potentials of aggression that Brazil has not yet really entered. The revolt of the Negroes in the U.S.A is like the revolt of the colonies in this age of anti-colonialism: these are both efforts to eliminate dimensions, by making all citizens "first class," or all nations "independent."

A. THE CONSEQUENCES OF ECONOMIC DEVELOPMENT

Economic development is a major issue of our times, for most people on earth probably the major issue. . . . Imagine a world with four salient rank-dimensions, (or three, or two for that matter) and that aid is given from TTTT nations to UUUU nations, developing some of them into TUUU nations. In all probability this would be a more, not a less dangerous world to live in—*ceteris paribus*. All theoretical reasons mentioned in the beginning of this article, the sense of self-righteousness, the access to resources of different kinds, the internal strains due to differential treatment in different interaction contexts would operate. As a matter of fact, the following development seems much more likely: that a group of TUUU nations join their newly gained forces and resources in making an organization for revolu-

[10] I am indebted to Tom Broch for this suggestion.

tion in the international community. Another version of this would correspond to a pattern for revolutions discussed in the following section: one or a few heavily disequilibrated nations mobilize the complete underdog nations against the complete topdog nations according to the eightpoint scheme to be presented below.[11]

In other words, and to put it bluntly: economic development *per se* will probably create more, not less rank-disequilibrium and hence be conducive to more, not less aggression. It is unnecessary to add that this does not imply that it cannot be justified on other bases, or that economic development and technical assistance in particular cannot have peace-building functions for other reasons, e.g., by contributing to international superstructure.

B. THE CONDITIONS FOR REVOLUTIONS

According to the theory presented the recipe for a revolution should be relatively clear. A revolution needs leaders and followers, and traditionally the leaders seem to come from somewhere high up in the tertiary sector of society whereas the followers come from somewhere low down in the primary and secondary sectors. Thus, what is needed is first of all a sufficient amount of built-in disequilibrium in these social positions. If the point of departure is a feudal system, for instance a newly independent, formerly colonial territory, then one way of arriving at this would be as follows[12]:

1. *Create universities* and other institutions of higher learning so as to turn out a sizeable number of intellectuals who feel they have a key—their high level of education—not only to their own well-being, but to the welfare of the whole society, e.g., economists, physicians.
2. *Make few positions available* so that the high educational status will not be translated into the kind of instrumentality that gives power. Regardless of the economic situation, this intellectual proletariat is a proletariat in the sense of not having access to the machinery they know (or think they know) how to turn. They are forced into other positions, and these positions will call for subsidiary capacities (accounting, typing, low administration) and the disequilibrium is created.

It should be noticed how easily such an intellectual proletariat is created: in the age of technical assistance and international fellowships it takes little time to turn out university graduates, but it still takes much time to tune an administration to an efficient utilization of their skills. The intellectuals will probably oversell their products precisely because they are underbought and underdemanded, and they will be feared, envied and hated by their rank opposites, the powerful non-intellectuals. Both sides will develop ideologies that make symbiosis less likely, as is so easily observed in most countries in Latin America. Thus, a climate for the emergence of revolutionary leadership is created, unless the rulers are clever enough to co-opt the intellectual proletariat by giving them something that tastes of power, e.g., by paying them for writing recommendations.

The revolutionaries may be able to sway a sufficient number of followers to do the footwork for them, but we are concerned with the structural conditions for automatic supply, not with special conditions. Thus, one simple formula is to copy what is mentioned

[11] The role of China in the follow-up of the 1955 Bandoeng conferences can probably be studied under this perspective.
[12] A study of the Cuban revolution guided by this theoretical perspective is in process at the Peace Research Institute in Oslo. The reader may find it useful to test the ideas against standard knowledge of this revolution and of the life history of Fidel Castro.

above lower down, and in the primary or secondary sectors of society:

3. *Institute mass education* with a compulsory base and easy access to educational follow-up institutions of various kinds especially so as to permit autodidactic leaders to emerge. The factor of self-righteousness will probably work more strongly for the autodidact than for the formally trained person, especially if he is high on what he has learned himself and low on formal schooling. This contributes to an explanation of the role of typographers in social revolutions: their work brings them close to a source of rank-disequilibrium through studies.
4. *Make no other changes*, which means that the recent rise in education is not accompanied by any corresponding rise in economy or power.

Again, it should be noticed how easily this is done. Mass education, like mass medication, costs little compared to building dams or irrigation schemes or the creation of a sector of heavy industry. Also, like mass medication it can bring quick results and cause disequilibria. The disequilibrium caused by raising the hygienic standard without a corresponding rise in the economic basis is well known—to this can be added the effects of a free education market without a corresponding freedom in the markets of economies (goods) and politics (power).[13]

Let us then add to these four conditions four more, and we should have a relatively good set of predictors:

[13] Thus, it is not surprising that turns towards the left have taken place where the rate of illiteracy is relatively low, as in Kerala in Southern India, Cuba or Chile, which stood a fair chance of electing into power a Marxist president, Senator Salvador Allende. The relation between the interplay of social indicators and the type of political system is probably a good deal more complicated than the famous analysis by Seymour Lipset: "Economic Development and Democracy," in *Political Man* (New York: Doubleday, 1960), pp. 45–76.

5. *A pattern of boom followed by depression or repression* as mentioned earlier—the pattern made explicit by Davies in his article.
6. *Contact* between the two (or more) disequilibrated groups, between the tertiary high and the primary or secondary low in disequilibrium. Urbanization provides the medium for such contacts, and is a rapidly increasing resource on the world level.
7. *An ideology* that does not have to explain the past or present nor to predict or prescribe the future, but has to provide a kind of semantic bridge over the social distances within the group urging change. This function of ideology, to provide a revolutionary group with emotive symbols that are easily applied and have the same reference for those who use them, is the more necessary the greater the social distance within the group.
8. *A charismatic leader.* The functions of personification and centralization are not easily satisfied without a leader. To say that he should have charisma is probably a tautology since the proof of his charisma lies in his ability to be a leader and sway people into action. But a personality with appeal across social distances is indispensable.

Any one of these conditions may serve as a spark to ignite the motivational energy stored in the disequilibrium mentioned in points 1–4—and all four together should be more than sufficient. We would, as mentioned, believe more in disequilibrated rank as a source of revolutions than in the Davies factor, for a completely balanced underdog group is so psychologically and ideologically conditioned as to absorb the vagaries of economic cycles. But it may also be argued that the two factors are rather similar. They are both themes of frustration, and more than that: a boom followed by a depression or repression is likely to create rapidly a high number of disequilibria at critical points in the social structure. But disequilibria are also created by rapid economic growth, so the arguments in the preceding section about the consequences of economic development for external war can also be turned into arguments for internal war. In other words, there is little inspiration in our theory for anyone who might want to stop "communism" nationally or internationally through a policy of technical assistance and economic aid. What is wrong with that theory is that it confuses the social situation in nations or groups equilibrated at the top with all the disequilibrium states they have to go through on their way up from a complete underdog situation.

C. ON THE NUMBER OF ELEMENTS IN A SYSTEM

All our reasoning so far has been with no reference whatsoever to the number, N, of elements in a system. This simple variable, number, is rarely used for other purposes than data analysis in social science; here we shall try to point out one theoretical implication of *number*. We choose a simple world: it is ranked according to two dimensions and in a random way so that 1/4 of the elements are TT, 1/4 are TU, 1/4 are UT and 1/4 are UU. The question is: what difference, if any, does it make if this world has 4, 40, 400, 4,000 or 4 million elements?

We expect the drastic demands for reallocations to come from the TU and UT positions. But there is a long distance between making a demand, a request and open aggression, and the probability of aggression will also depend on the number of alternatives. With increasing N the number of combinations for a given element increases very rapidly. There is no need to enter into the mathematics of the combinatorics since they reflect nothing of substantive interest except the ex-treme rapidity with which the number of subsystems that can be formed increases with N.

.   .   .

If the idea is simply that people and groups and nations like feeling superior or at least not inferior, then the implications are equally simple. A TU for N = 4 will have one other element to associate with (UU), whereas the TU will have 19 others for N 40 (10 UU and the remaining 9 TU). The UT are excluded because their profiles lie over the profile for TU at one point. The gain in sources of gratification is conspicuous and continues: 1, 19, 199, 1,999, ... On the other hand, as soon as these subsystems are formed they may serve to reduce effectively the number of elements until one has a supersystem of four elements, where the elements are complicated organizations bearing the TT, TU, UT and UU characteristics.

Thus, the higher the number of elements, the higher the probability of finding some kind of organizational insulation against the strains produced by a disequilibrium position. The world with four elements throws the elements against each other mercilessly: all comparisons involve some element of strain, there is no refuge in the relaxed atmosphere of the complete peer, the real equal. With only two elements it would be still worse, especially if they were posited against each other in TU and UT positions, one being high in power and low in culture and the other one being just the opposite. It is easy enough to see where the difficulties disappear: only at the point where all elements have coalesced into one.

If there is stability of the kind under discussion in systems consisting of one element on the one hand and systems consisting of many (hundreds, thousands, millions) on the other hand, then some conclusions can be drawn. Nations owe their stability, if they have any, to (1) a large number of individuals, and (2) a sufficiently complicated social structure in terms of all kinds of rank-dimensions to prevent a simplification to a very low number of groups. Of course, stability is enhanced by obliterating the rank-dimensions, by making them irrelevant, as during a foreign occupation—but this is a rare occasion and when it does not obtain there is strength in number alone. . . .

D. ON THE NUMBER OF DIMENSIONS

It looks as if one may use the same argument about the stability in one and many, but not in few, for the number of dimensions. Of course, the number of dimensions is a more volatile characteristic of the system than the number of elements. But it is not operationally meaningless, as indicated in the section on methodology. One will have to count the number of criteria of ranking on which there is a degree of consensus above a pre-established level.

Imagine that there is only one such dimension—for instance *per capita* income. This does not mean that conflicts and aggression will disappear, but that one source of aggressive behavior, arising from disequilibrium (e.g., with size of territory) does not exist. The "haves" will be envied by the "have-nots" but quite possibly be more safe in their topdog position than they would have been if there were some more dimensions available. For on these other dimensions the underdogs might rise and get into the web of disequilibrium. No doubt, there are exceptions to this. Topdogs have always and everywhere known the importance of stretching out a ladder of compensation to the underdogs, for instance in the form of an ideology that

promises salvation in a transcendent existence (religion) or in this world ("die orgiastische Chiliasmus"). But these ladders are not rank-dimensions in the sense that they lead to identifiable positions where one is treated differently by the whole society. Thus, to institute mass education and give knowledge to the masses with the idea that "this will satisfy them, they will think less of getting property" is both unpsychological and unsociological. Not much time will pass before the UT, high on education, starts wondering why he should be less well off than the TT, not to mention the TU— he may find comfort in his top position for a while, and then start worrying about his low position.

The question is now whether there is a limit to this kind of reasoning set by the number of dimensions. A world with a very high number of salient dimensions would permit more flexibility; the number would serve as a cushioning against the effects of disequilibrium. For each new dimension gives a possibility upwards, and hence a source of gratification, especially if different nations climb on different dimensions. . . . Our hypothesis, then, is that a U position may loom high in the national conscience if it is surrounded by one or a couple of T positions but not if it is surrounded by very many such positions. Then it may even be turned into a point of pride: look at what we have been able to do in spite of that handicap (the national ethos of the small nations in North-West Europe, Norway for instance, illustrates the case).[14] Again, if the U is surrounded by nothing because the system is seen as one-dimensional, then the hypothesis is that an attitude of

[14] Norwegians love *per capita* statistics, for the simple reason that many indicators when divided by a small population will make Norway rank relatively high.

acquiescence will be more likely, for there is no disequilibrium present to provoke restlessness.

The consequence of this is a prediction of stability in extremely monolithic and extremely pluralistic cultures —in the former there will be one criterion, in the latter many, for pluralism is precisely a multi-faceted basis for evaluation. . . .

6

A THEORY
OF STABLE
DEMOCRACY

Harry Eckstein

. . . [A] theory of stable democracy should consist of two parts, one stating the general conditions which make governmental stability probable, the other stating the particular conditions required to make democracies stable. These particular conditions should of course be special instances of the more general conditions which produce governmental stability. It may be that no general theory of governmental stability can really be developed, that every kind of government is *sui generis* in this regard; but at this stage of inquiry we have no reason whatever to think that this is the case. Hence the first proposition of the present theory is in fact a proposition about the stability or instability of any governmental order, whatever its special character. This proposition concerns the nature of, and the relations among, the different authority patterns in a society.

In every society we can discover numerous authority patterns, both attitudes regarding authority and, to use Lasswell's terminology, authority "practices." Certainly this is so if we use the term "authority" in its broadest and most conventional sense, to denote relationships of superordination and subordination among individuals in social formations, relationships in which some members of the formation take decisions and others treat the decisions as binding. In this simple sense of a hierarchy of wills, the state certainly has no monopoly upon authority. It may be quite possible, and even useful, to distinguish between the authority of the state and other kinds of authority; and it is easy enough to define authority in a way that will confine it arbitrarily to the state. But as

Excerpted from *Research Monograph No. 10*, Center of International Studies, Princeton University (1961), by permission of the author and Princeton University. Footnotes have been renumbered.

the term is used here, authority in some form is a characteristic of practically any persistent social aggregate, at least in that certain actual practices of subordination and superordination will be found in such aggregates, and probably also in that there will exist in the society as a whole and in its subunits certain dominant notions as to how such practices *should* be conducted. Authority exists not only in the state itself, but in parties and pressure groups, in economic organizations, in various kinds of associations, in schools and families, and even in friendships, bands, clubs, and the like. We can discover it in any set of social relations which, in the not too happy jargon of social psychology, is "cooperatively interdependent" (2, pp. 129–152)— that is, very simply, not competitive. The only persistent social relations in which we are pretty certain not to find it are "competitively interdependent" relations, like the bargaining relations which take place in a free economic market or in international politics— granted that a certain amount of bargaining can be an aspect of authority relations as well, and a certain amount of authority sets limits to the scope and content of bargaining.

I assert this universality of authority patterns in noncompetitive social relations, not because it is absolutely necessary to my theory to assert it, but because it is a palpable fact. All that is necessary to the present theory, however, is that authority should exist in *some* social relations other than those of formal government, particularly in those social relations, like the family or economic organizations, which one finds in any society; and this assertion will surely not be disputed by anyone without some sort of redefinition of authority.

Stated very briefly, the first proposition of the theory I would suggest is that *a government will tend to be stable if its authority pattern is congruent with the other authority patterns of the society of which it is a part.* The crucial term in this proposition is of course "congruence," and it needs to be defined, particularly since, as used here, the term is not at all self-explanatory.

Authority patterns are congruent, in the first place (but only in the first place), if they are identical (that is to say, since we are dealing not with an abstract geometric universe but real life, if they very closely resemble each other). An example of congruence in this sense is furnished by the authority patterns in British government and British political parties, at any rate if we accept the standard analyses of the latter by Beer and McKenzie (1, 4). Both patterns consist of a curious and very similar mixture of democratic, authoritarian, and, so to speak, constitutional elements; this despite the fact that British government can be traced back to the eras of medieval constitutionalism and royal absolutism, while political parties are, in almost every respect, creatures of a much later period, the era of the mandate; and this also despite the fact that the formal constitution of the Labour Party makes it seem very different from both the Conservative Party and the British governmental structure.[1] . . .

·   ·   ·

[1] We can treat this breakdown of authority patterns into democratic, authoritarian, and constitutionalist patterns at least as a first approximation toward a useful typology of authority patterns, although by no means the only one available. *Democracy* in this case refers to the rule of numbers, hence its equation with the idea of the mandate; in other words, it denotes a high degree of participation in

The essential patterns of cabinet government, and the essential attitudes on which it is based, . . . all have their counterparts in the major British parties. In fact, it has been argued, cogently I think, that cabinet government on the British model compels a certain correspondence between party structure and governmental structure, certainly while a party is in power, and therefore also perhaps while it is in opposition and presumably aspiring to power. Cabinet government could not otherwise work at all on a party basis; hence the anxieties of many Englishmen when the Labour Party strays, as it infrequently does, from the model of the cabinet system and acts as if it really believed in its formal consitution. But this argument should not be taken to mean that British parties cannot help but have a structure similar to that of British government. "Compel" does not in this case mean "cause." The argument means merely that British government can work smoothly only if such a congruence of governmental and party structures exists, not that things could not actually be otherwise. There are plenty of parliamentary systems in which the same logic holds, but few in which the same congruence can be found.

decision making, regularized choice between competing political elites, and the transmission, usually not very precisely, of instructions from the political "mass" to the political "elite." *Authoritarianism* refers to limited participation in decisions by the mass and to a high degree of autonomy and a low degree of formal precariousness of position on the part of the elite. *Constitutionalism* refers to the subjection of the elite to a broad and highly explicit impersonal framework of rules, procedural and substantive, where this framework of rules operates as the principal limitation on the autonomy of the elite. We might say that democracy involves the rule of a dependent elite, authoritarianism the rule of an autonomous elite, and constitutionalism the rule of law; but this is such a great oversimplification that it can only serve as a shorthand to help one keep the vital distinctions in mind.

The most extreme and plainest form of congruence, then, is identity. Mixing metaphors, we might speak in this case of isomorphic authority patterns. But identity cannot exhaust the meaning of congruence when applied to social phenomena, for it is difficult even to imagine a society in which all authority patterns closely resemble each other. Certainly such a state of affairs is impossible in a democracy. Some social relations simply cannot be conducted in a democratic manner, or can be so conducted only with the gravest dysfunctional consequences. Take, for example, those social units which link different generations—families and schools. An infant cannot be cared for democratically, or a child brought up and schooled democratically. Families and schools can be permissive, but this is merely to say that they can be authoritarian in a lax and lenient manner. Families and schools can also carry on a certain amount of democratic pretense, and indeed more than pretense, and when they do so on a large scale, that fact is not without significance; but by and large they cannot carry such simulation and imitation of democracy to very great lengths, if they are not to produce warped and ineffectual human beings. One of the most basic and indispensable functions in any social system, the socialization function, must therefore always be to some extent out of tune with democratic patterns, and potentially at odds with them. The same point applies, almost as obviously, to certain relations among adults. We have every reason to think that economic organizations cannot be organized in a truly democratic manner, at any rate not without consequences that no one wants; and we certainly know that capitalist economic organization and even certain kinds of public ownership (like the nationalization in Britain of industries absolutely vital to the health of the whole economy) militate against a democratization of economic relations. The case of military organizations is even plainer in this regard, and the case of public bureaucracy just as clear. Again, there can be some simulation and imitation of democracy in firms, or public offices, or military units, but only within rather narrow limits. Precisely those social relations in which most individuals are engaged most of the time—family life, schools, and jobs (most kinds of jobs)—are the least capable of being democratically organized. To expect all authority relations in a democracy to be identical would therefore be unreasonable, and we could probably demonstrate the same thing, in other ways, for other kinds of governmental structures. In any complex society but above all in democracies, we must expect some heterogeneity in authority patterns, even if we deal only with fundamental patterns and not circumstantial details.

In that case, however, one can still speak meaningfully of a congruence of authority patterns if the patterns have a certain "fit" with one another—if they dovetail with, or support, the governmental pattern, however indirectly. One way in which they can do this is by the partial imitation of the govenmental authority patterns in other social structures. Democratic (or other) pretenses, if taken seriously and carried far, may have important consequences for the operation of the governmental structure, even though they are pretenses. Furthermore, structures like economic or military organizations may, in some cases, willingly incur certain functional disadvantages for the sake of acting out norms associated with governments in their substantive decision-making processes. For instance, capitalistic economic organizations which play a great deal at democracy and permit certain deviations from the logic of the double-entry ledger in order actually to carry on

certain democratic practices may be said to be more congruent with democratic government than those which stick closely, both in ritual and process, to the economically most rational practices.

In view of this, we might be tempted to say that authority patterns are congruent if they have, not everything, but something in common. But if the equation of congruence with identity makes demands which are too great, its equation with mere resemblance, however slight, does not demand enough. On the first basis, we shall almost never find a society in which authority patterns are really congruent; on the second, we shall assuredly not find any in which authority patterns are incongruent. However, by congruence I do not mean any resemblance at all among authority patterns. Where authority relations are not all highly similar, the term refers rather to a particular pattern of resemblance among them, one which makes stringent reuirements, but not requirements impossible to fulfill—a pattern of *graduated resemblances*, so to speak.

To grasp the concept of graduated resemblances, one must think of societies as being composed of segments which are more or less distant from government [see the figure]. Governments themselves are adult structures, and for this reason families, for example, are more "vertically" distant from them, in terms of age levels, than schools, and schools more distant from them than purely adult structures. In the same way, adult structures may be "horizontally" segmented, so that some appear close to, others distant from, government. Parties, for example, ordinarily are situated closer to government than pressure groups; among pressure groups certain types may be particularly closely involved in government or parties; and all pressure groups are located more closely to

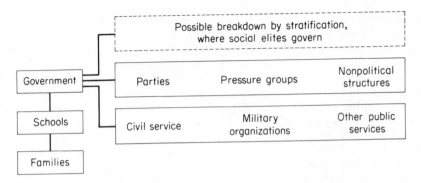

government than nonpolitical organizations. These are very rough breakdowns; in some concrete cases, moreover, it may be difficult to make unambiguous distinctions, and the same social structures will not always fall into the same positions in every society. But none of this affects the definition: that social authority patterns are congruent, either if they are very similar, or if similarity to the governmental pattern increases significantly as one approaches the governmental segment itself.[2]

On the basis of these explications of the term "congruence," we can now restate the first proposition of the theory. *Government will be stable, (1) if social authority patterns are identical with the governmental pattern, or (2) if they consitute a graduated pattern in a proper segmentation of*

[2] The illustration below (and it is only an illustration, of course) should help to clarify this definition, if it is not clear enough already. Assume the following segmentation of society:

$$A^1 - A^2 - A^3 - A^4 - A^5$$

Let d_n stand for democratic pattern, so that d_5 equals complete democracy and d_4, d_3, d_2, and d_1 correspondingly smaller degrees of democracy. Let a_n similarly stand for authoritarian pattern. Now society (1) and (2) have congruent authority patterns, society (3) incongruent ones:

$$A^1d_5a_1 - A^2d_4a_2 - A^3d_3a_3$$
$$- A^4d_2a_4 - A^5d_1a_5 \quad (1)$$
$$A^1d_5a_1 - A^2d_4a_2 - A^3d_4a_2$$
$$- A^4d_3a_3 - A^5d_3a_3 \quad (2)$$
$$A^1d_5a_1 - A^2d_1a_5 - A^3d_3a_3$$
$$- A^4d_5a_3 - A^5d_1a_5 \quad (3)$$

society, or (3) *if a high degree of resemblance exists in patterns adjacent to government and one finds throughout the more distant segments a marked departure from functionally appropriate patterns for the sake of imitating the govenmental pattern or extensive imitation of the governmental pattern in ritual practices.* Conditions (2) and (3) are both, of course, looser and less demanding versions of condition (1); all refer to a basic need for considerable resemblance in authority patterns if government is to be stable, particularly in those segments of society which impinge directly on government. Condition (3) may be regarded, in this way, as the minimum required for governmental stability (and the minimum meaning of congruence), but perhaps the most that can be realized in relation to some particular pattern of government. By the same token, *governments will be unstable* (and the authority patterns of a society incongruent) *if the governmental authority pattern is isolated* (that is, substantially different) *from those of other social segments, or if a very abrupt change in authority pattern occurs in any adjacent segments of society, or if several different authority patterns exist in social strata furnishing a large proportion of the political elite* (in the sense of active political participants). In the last case, congruence with the authority patterns of a particular part of the elite—say, a particular social class—may be quite possible, but congruence with the overall authority patterns of a society is logically out of the question.

.   .   .

Motivational Basis of the Theory

In addition to the fact that it seems to fit the most unambiguous cases of stability and instability, the theory of congruence has, prior to any concerted testing, one other important point to recommend it: it leads one immediately to the motivational (or psychological) links between the variables it relates. This is important. Any generalization about human behavior obviously lacks an important element of plausibility if it makes no sense in terms of what we know about human motivations. Conceivably societies may involve certain purely mechanical relations which require no motivational explanation at all, but follow simply from the fact of interaction, whatever may underlie it; but even theories about competitive interdependence seem always to proceed from particular views of probable human conduct. In any event, to ask *why* certain relations exist in social life is always to ask what there is about one state of society that induces behavior leading to another.

Such motivational connections between different aspects of social life are by no means easy to see whenever one finds a positive correlation between social variables. . . .

.   .   .

The motivational basis of the theory of congruence, however, is quite readily apparent. This is due to the fact that the conditions described by the term "incongruity" are very similar to the conditions denoted by two other concepts of social science, two concepts, which, appropriately enough, denote both certain social conditions

and certain psychological states, or propensities to act: the closely related concepts of anomie and strain.

Anomie exists, in its purest form, whenever there is a complete breakdown of a normative order governing action, when individuals lack clear and commanding guidelines to behavior, do not know what is expected of them, and are thus compelled to rely solely upon their egos, their "rational" calculations, to inform their conduct (3, pp. xi ff.; 5, p. 39). Anomie, in this sense, may be more or less acute and more or less widespread in a society; it may extend to few or many, important or unimportant, phases of life, and it may be found in society generally or only in certain of its members. It is always disturbing, but becomes, in its more acute form, unbearable; the actual responses to it depend, however, not only upon its acuteness but also upon the extent of its diffusion throughout a society. At its less acute levels, it manifests itself in merely annoying, possibly even constructive, anxieties, and the resort to perfectly innocuous means of relieving them. But in its more acute forms it has been linked, on the individual level, with serious functional disorders (even suicide), and, on the social level, with mass movements in general, particularly movements of religious fanaticism and political movements of a chiliastic and highly ideological character—in general, with movements which provide men with a sense of orientation, a sense of belonging to a bearable social order, or merely with the opportunity for escaping from the dilemmas of everyday life or submerging themselves in some comforting collectivity.

Anomie may result from many conditions. In individuals, it may be the result of inadequate socialization, or rapid mobility from one stratum of society to another, or transplantation from one culture to another, or indeed any important change in one's condition in life. In societies it may result from any social change (especially rapid change) requiring important adjustments in conduct, or from a widely successful attack upon traditional norms, or from large-scale mobility.

Among these many conditions which can give rise to anomie, the condition "strain" is perhaps the most common in any complex society. "Strain" is used here in a technical sense; it refers, not to the utter lack of settled guides to behavior, or to ambiguous norms, but to *ambivalent* expectations—that is, the coexistence of different, perhaps even contradictory, norms of conduct in regard to a particular set of actions or an individual's actions in general (5, p. 253). We may speak of strain whenever men are expected to conform to different, but equally legitimized, norms of conduct—as, for example, when a man simultaneously performs some roles involving universalistic norms and others involving particularistic norms, or some roles permitting affective responses and others demanding affective neutrality; and strains are of course particularly acute if a single role makes contradictory normative demands. Strain exists between the role of a man who is given access to the female body as a doctor and who seeks access to the female body as a lover, and strain will be particularly great in that case if patient and lover are one and the same person.

Incongruity between the authority patterns of a society, like any other incongruity among social patterns, is an obvious source of strain, and through strain of anomie, and through anomie of behavior potentially destructive to the stability of any pattern of government. This seems obvious; yet one cannot let the argument go at that. Conflicting expectations inevitably exist in any highly differentiated society, and are perhaps given in the very nature of

the human condition, for human beings are inherently multifaceted. One can no more imagine a bearable existence which is utterly devoid of affect than one which consists only of emotional responses; pure and complete universalism is unattainable, men being what they are, and pure and complete particularism leads to chaos and gross inefficiency in any kind of social life. It is not, therefore, the simple absence of strains which distinguishes an integrated and stable society from one which is unintegrated and unstable, but rather the successful reduction and management of strains which can never be eliminated. How then can strains be "managed," in order to prevent them from leading to acute anomie?

Perhaps the only reliable way is through the institutionalized segregation of roles—through preventing one role as much as possible from impinging upon, or even being mentally associated with, another, if the other makes conflicting normative demands. Such segregation of roles is in fact a feature of any society which is functionally differentiated to a high degree; it may be physical (note, for example, the fact that the doctor's office is generally separated from his domicile) or "psychological"—that is, achieved only through the widespread mental disjunction of particular roles. Why then should not incongruities in authority patterns be similarly "manageable" through segregation? Why should it matter, for example, that authority is strong in one context and weak in another?

A number of things need to be said about this issue. First of all, the theory here sketched does not assert that *any* disparity among authority patterns is disastrous; it only asserts that disparities of a particular kind and degree have fatal consequences. After all, I have already argued that the very notion of congruence encompasses certain kinds of disparities. Some disparate authority patterns can be tolerated well enough—anyway, without serious anomic consequences; the argument here is merely that *incongruent* patterns cannot be tolerated, partly because they are, by definition, patterns in which disparities are particularly stark and great, and partly because strains arising from incongruent authority patterns are not alleviated by "intermediate" patterns which help to reconcile the starkly disparate patterns in relatively distant segments of society. In any case, no one would argue that all strains can be "managed" equally well; and, obviously, the greater the strain, the more unlikely it is to be successfully managed.

Another point to bear in mind is that "managing" a strain is not the same thing as abolishing it; when we manage strains, we merely reduce them to a tolerable level, or, without reducing them, in some way accommodate ourselves to their existence. The strains, however, persist, and may at any time lead to behavior modifying the social relations which give rise to them. What is more, certain kinds of strains are hard to reduce or tolerate and strains among authority patterns, in my view, are of this type. The reason is precisely that authority relations are nearly universal in social relations, aspects of almost every social role, a fact which makes it inherently difficult to "segregate" authority patterns from one another. Whether a man is acting the role of father, teacher, boss, or politician, he is almost always in some context involving authority; the operation of authority is one of the more inescapable facets of life. Not so for a man playing both the affective husband and affectively neutral professional, or both the particularistic father and universalistic boss. In these cases, not only the structures but the functions also are different. There is, in other words, a crucial difference between performing different

functions in different ways and performing the same function in different ways; conflicts of the latter sort obviously impose incomparably the greater psychological burden. Imagine, on one hand, a doctor who is expected to take a coldly scientific attitude toward his female patients and a warmly unscientific attitude toward his wife; imagine, on the other, a doctor who is expected to administer only to his wealthy patients but wash his hands of others, or who is supposed to help friends and kin but let strangers suffer, or to alleviate the pains of adults but not those of children. In the latter cases strain is bound to be the more severe, whatever grotesque value system might be used to legitimize such behavior—and functioning in incongruent authority relations is like the latter cases rather than the former.

This is not to say that a single man cannot rule in one context and be ruled in another. Although such a duality of positions does create strains which, apparently, are unmanageable by some people, most of us do just that most of the time. The question here is one of operating in conflicting authority patterns, not of occupying different positions in similar authority patterns. When one is subordinated in one pattern of authority, one may in fact learn very well how properly to be dominant in a similar pattern of authority, but being tossed back and forth among radically different authority patterns is another matter.

·　　·　　·

But my purpose here is not to show that strains arising from incongruent authority patterns cannot be managed or tolerated under any circumstances. Rather it is to show that, among the manifold strains of life in a complex society, such strains are unusually, perhaps incomparably, difficult to manage, so that it seems logical for men to try and cope with them by reducing them at the source, that is, ordinarily, by changing the governmental patterns under which they live. Even if this is not granted, however, one fact is surely beyond doubt: societies possessing congruent authority patterns possess an enormous "economic" advantage over those that do not. In the more extreme cases, like Great Britain, individuals are in effect socialized into almost all authority patterns simultaneously (even if they belong to the nonelite strata), while in highly incongruent societies men must repeatedly be resocialized for participation in various parts of social life. For society, then, congruence in regard to authority patterns, at the very least, saves much effort; for individuals, it saves much psychological wear and tear resulting from uncertainty and ambivalence. In that basic and indisputable sense, the congruent society starts with a great advantage over the incongruent society; and we have many reasons to think that it enjoys greater advantages still.

References

1. Beer, S. H. "Great Britain: From Governing Elite to Organized Mass Parties," in S. Neumann, ed., *Modern Political Parties*. Chicago: University of Chicago Press, 1956, pp. 9–57.
2. Deutsch, M. "A Theory of Cooperation and Competition," *Human Relations*, II (1949), 129–152.
3. De Grazia, Sebastian. *The Political Community: A Study of Anomie*, Chicago, University of Chicago Press, 1948.
4. McKenzie, R. T. *British Political Parties*. New York: St. Martin's Press, 1955.
5. Parsons, Talcott. *The Social System*. Glencoe, Ill.: The Free Press of Glencoe, 1951.

SOCIAL CHANGE AND POLITICAL VIOLENCE : CROSS-NATIONAL PATTERNS[1]

Ivo K. Feierabend
Rosalind L. Feierabend
Betty A. Nesvold

The assumption of a relationship between change and violence is based on arguments which are intuitively persuasive. Change, especially extensive, rapid, and abrupt change, is an unsettling and bewildering human experience. It is likely to create strain in the psyche of the individual and crisis in the social order. Old ways, familiar environments, deep-seated habits, and social roles become obsolescent, while at the same time a new way of life and a new routine are not yet clearly established. Social change is perhaps analogous to the experience of the individual who moves suddenly from one community to another. He lives in a new dwelling, interacts with a new set of individuals, and faces new and strange situations which require an inordinate amount of difficult adjustment.

To project this example to a broader social base, one might argue that massive change which moves people physically into new environments, exposes their minds to new ideas, and casts them in new and unfamiliar roles is very likely to create collective bewilderment. This bewilderment may find its expression in turmoil and social violence. However, there are other, conflicting theoretical speculations that are equally persuasive. These suggest that change has beneficial and pacifying social consequences. If social change is

[1] We are grateful for the support of the National Science Foundation (Grant No. GS–1781), which made it possible to collect and analyze the data on internal political aggression as well as the underlying conditions of political instability.

Reprinted from H. D. Graham and T. R. Gurr, eds., *Violence in America*, Vol. II. A Report to the National Commission on the Causes and Prevention of Violence (Washington, D.C.: U.S. Government Printing Office, 1969), pp. 498–509. Footnotes have been renumbered.

perceived as bringing gratification, if it fulfills aspirations, there is no reason to expect social crisis in its wake. On the contrary, obstructing such change, or slowing its pace, should result in social discontent registered in protest movements and violence.

Given these contradictory insights, the idea of change alone is not sufficient to explain the occurrence of violent political behavior. It is only when change brings with it social circumstances which breed discontent and strain that such change may be assumed to be responsible for social turmoil. Other modes of change will not so qualify, for they may have a stabilizing, rather than unsettling, effect on the political order. The blanket assertion that change breeds violence is too simplistic.

Our theoretical assumption linking change to violence begins with the notion that political turmoil is the consequence of social discontent. This commonsense assumption is predicated on a motivational rather than a structural orientation. And it reaffirms the often-repeated insight that political protest and revolution begin in the minds of men. Nevertheless, structural and processual variables are intimately a part of the wider view, since men's experience of change in the ecological, social, or political universe may create the revolutionary state of mind. In other words, although our assumptions are based on psychological, motivational factors, we are nevertheless interested in analyzing change in environmental, structural circumstances of political systems. What is required is some refinement of the idea of discontent and strain. Also needed is an effort to identify those modes of change and development that can be presumed to lead to the discontent that is the necessary precondition of political instability and violence.

Change, Systemic Frustration, and Aggression

Although the concept of aggression has received extensive elaboration within psychology, the frustration-aggression hypothesis seems the most useful for our purposes.[2] In its most basic and fundamental formulation, this hypothesis maintains that aggression (as well as some other specified behaviors) is the result of frustration. Frustration itself is defined as the thwarting of or interference with the attainment of goals, aspirations, or expectations. On the basis of frustration-aggression theory, it is postulated that frustration induced by the social system creates the social strain and discontent that in turn are the indispensable preconditions of violence. The common-sense assertion that revolutionary behavior has its roots in discontent, and the more technical postulate that frustration precedes aggression, are parallel statements indicating a common insight.

The concept of frustration is often thought to be more appropriate to individual than to social circumstances. We believe, however, that the notion of *systemic frustration* makes the concept applicable to the analysis of aggregate, violent political behavior within social systems.[3] We define systemic frustration

[2] For the classic theoretical statement of the frustration-aggression hypothesis see John Dollard, et al., *Frustration and Aggression* (New Haven: Yale University Press, 1939). There are also several more recent general restatements, including Leonard Berkowitz, *Aggression: A Social Psychological Analysis* (New York: McGraw-Hill Book Company, 1962); and Arnold H. Buss, *The Psychology of Aggression* (New York: John Wiley & Sons, Inc., 1961).

[3] In the literature of political science, Ted Gurr systematically applies the frustration hypothesis and modifies its terms to develop a coherent empirical and multivariate theory of political violence. His use of the concept of

in reference to three criteria: (1) as frustration interfering with the attainment and maintenance of social goals, aspirations, and values; (2) as frustration simultaneously experienced by members of social aggregates and hence also complex social systems; and (3) as frustration or strain that is produced within the structures and processes of social systems. Systemic frustration is thus characterized as frustration that is experienced collectively within societies.

Guided by this definition, we may adopt two basic propositions from the frustration-aggression hypothesis and restate them with reference to social systems. (1) Violent political behavior is instigated by systemic frustration. (2) Systemic frustration may stem, among other circumstances of the social system, from specific characteristics of social change.

Four general hypotheses further qualify the notion of systemic frustration. (1) Systemic frustration at any given time is a function of the discrepancy between present social aspirations and expectations on the one hand, and social achievements on the other. (2) In addition, present estimates or expectations of future frustrations (or satisfactions) are also responsible for the level of present frustration (or satisfaction). (3) Uncertainties in social expectations in themselves increase the sense of systemic frustration. (4) Conflicting aspirations and conflicting expectations provide yet another source of systemic frustration.

---

relative deprivation comes very close to our use of systemic frustration. Also, we believe that the broad insights, hypotheses, and models presented here would generally be sustained by his theoretical constructs, although they might be couched in different terminology. See Ted Robert Gurr, *Why Men Rebel* (Princeton: Princeton University Press, 1970), and "Psychological Factors in Civil Violence," *World Politics*, XX (January, 1968), 245–78.

The first hypothesis focuses on the discrepancy between aspirations, expectations, and attainments within the present situation. This discrepancy is a result of the interplay between these factors in the present, and level of frustration is postulated to be a function of the number of aspirations involved, their level of valuation, their frequency of occurrence within various population strata, their expected level of attainment, and the degree of certainty with which these expectations are held. Similar criteria apply to the notion of social attainment. It should also be pointed out that perceived, rather than actual, social attainment is most important.

The distinction between aspirations and expectations needs clarification. In simplest definition, aspirations are the goals which people wish to attain. Also included in the definition are presently valued possessions which people desire to maintain. Expectations, on the other hand, include only that portion of aspirations which we realistically expect to achieve. Strictly speaking, expectations always refer to the future, yet they are disappointed—or fulfilled—in the context of the present. And this is the measure of systemic frustration as formulated in the first hypothesis.

The expectation of future frustration or satisfaction may also intensify or counteract present predicaments. The second hypothesis recognizes this possibility. Hence this hypothesis uses the term expectation in a somewhat different sense. It does not refer to expectations regarding the present situation, but to present expectations of future occurrences. The third hypothesis singles out uncertainty as yet another source of frustration. Uncertainty is a special quality of expectation; ambiguity as to whether the future will bring disaster or salvation should be considered a distressful experience, adding to the present sense of frustration. Only when disaster strikes is certainty likely to be judged as more frustrating than uncertainty. Finally, the fourth hypothesis sees conflict as a systematically frustrating circumstance. Conflict is considered a specific case of frustration in which an individual's alternative motives, aspirations, and expectations work at cross-purposes, blocking one another.[4] The notions of intensity, scope, and distribution of aspirations are as relevant in this context as in the previous one.

Patterns of Social Change and Discontent

These theoretical propositions refine the general notion of systemic frustration and social discontent, but the important question still remains: What modes of change and development may we assume lead toward systemic frustration? Let us point to a few studies in the recent literature of political violence, in order to identify objective social situations that are presumed to create a sense of systemic frustration.

Davies, in his analysis of several revolutions, concludes that, contrary to Marxian expectations, revolutions do not occur during periods of prolonged abject or worsening situations of social

[4] In the most recent literature on revolution, David Schwartz uses the notion of conflict, as well as of cognitive dissonance, to build a processual model of revolution. See his "Political Alienation: A Preliminary Experiment on the Psychology of Revolution's First Stage," paper presented at the Annual Meeting of the American Psychological Association, Washington, D.C., 1967. The psychological literature on which these applications are based may be found in F. Heider, "Social Perception and Phenomenal Causality," *Psychological Review*, LI (1944), 358–74; Theodore Newcomb, "An Approach to the Study of Communicative Acts," *Psychological Review*, LX (1953), 393–404; and Leon Festinger, *The Theory of Cognitive Dissonance* (New York: Harper & Row, Publishers, 1957).

deprivation.[5] Neither does the evidence sustain the insight of de Tocqueville and others that revolutions are perpetrated during periods of relative prosperity and improvement. Instead, Davies postulates a J-curve of socioeconomic development, whereby revolution occurs in social systems in which social well-being has been continually raised for an extended period of time, followed by an abrupt and sharp setback. His explanation is in accord with our notion of discontent and systemic frustration. We suggest that certainty of social expectations is reinforced during the period of continued socioeconomic development. The sharp reversal in social fortunes creates an intolerable discrepancy between achievement and expectation. It is also possible that the unexpected reversal in attainment creates an alarmist expectation of continued severe decreases in levels of achievement. Such a fear for the future, possibly exaggerated, motivates present actions as much as do actual present conditions.

Figure 1 graphically portrays Davies' hypothesis of the J-curve pattern of change. Furthermore it takes into account not only the sense of frustration that is created by disappointed expectations in the present, but also depicts estimates of the future. If men still anticipate future gratifications (depicted by line A in Figure 1), political violence is less likely to occur in the present. If, on the other hand, men anticipate intensified frustration (depicted by line B), the likelihood of violence is strengthened. In the latter case, the sense of frustration resulting from disappointed expectations in the present is intensified by the gap between present level of achievement and an even more pessimistic estimate of the future.

[5] See James C. Davies, "Toward a Theory of Revolution," *American Sociological Review*, XXVII (January, 1962), 5–19.

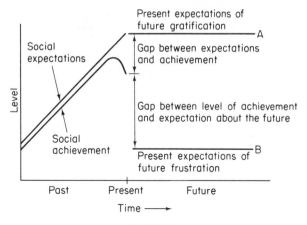

J-curve change model
Deterioration pattern

Present expectations of future gratification — A

Social expectations

Gap between expectations and achievement

Level

Gap between level of achievement and expectation about the future

Social achievement

Present expectations of future frustration — B

Past   Present   Future

Time ⟶

FIGURE 1.

Another type of J-curve may be equally productive of social discontent. A sudden and unexpected improvement in social circumstances may give rise to hopes of better things to come. If actual improvement is not sufficiently high to meet the newly aroused expectations, an intolerable gap between expectation and attainment will ensue, constituting systemic frustration. Again the argument is based on a contrast effect, one that gives impetus to expectations. The novelty of gratification following a long history of deprivation may give the aspect of reality to long-suppressed aspirations. It is exaggerated hope for the future, in this case, which inevitably breeds disappointment.[6]

Figure 2 illustrates this situation.

[6] The notion of a marked contrast among sets of ecological conditions having a greater effect on expectations and behavior than would a continuous series can be viewed as an application of adaptation level theory. See Harry Helson, *Adaptation-Level Theory: An Experimental and Systematic Approach to Behavior* (New York: Harper & Row, Publishers, 1964). According to Helson's view, a cohesive set or series of stimulus conditions creates adaptation; a contrast within the stimulus conditions triggers response.

As shown, the social achievement line intersects the line of expectations at time t_1, or shortly after achievement exceeds expectations. Hence this is the point of social satisfaction. Yet at t_2, where achievement does not keep pace with soaring, newly awakened expectations, a gap occurs comparable to that in Davies' J-curve model. Expectations regarding the future in this model also may either detract or add to the present sense of systemic frustration.

These models of social change indicate the dynamics of motivational factors stipulated in the first two hypotheses. There are also social circumstances that can be judged as unlikely to stimulate social discontent such as situations in which objective achievement remains constant, no matter what that level may be, and situations in which acceleration or deceleration of change is either consistent or slight. Situations in which a minimal, gradual, or constant amount of change is experienced are the least likely to produce striking discrepancies between present social expectations and present levels of achievement. Also, by avoiding contrast effects in achievement, ex-

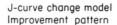

J-curve change model
Improvement pattern

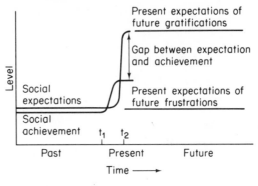

FIGURE 2.

pectations about the future are held fairly realistically in line with attainments. These social situations are represented in Figure 3.

As shown in Figure 3c, it should be noted that even deteriorating social circumstances may not in themselves be stimulants to violent behavior, provided the deterioration is gradual and constant. However, very rapid social deterioration should have the consequences postulated in the J-curve of Davies: a discrepancy between expectations and achievements is created by rapid decline in social attainments. It is also conceivable that a rapidly improving situation could follow the pattern of the J-curve in Figure 2.

This impact of rapid and consistent change is illustrated in Figures 4 and 5. The model in Figure 4 assumes that a rapidly deteriorating level of attainment not only creates an increasing gap between presently disappointed expectations and achievement, but also a very pessimistic outlook for the future. As shown in Figure 5, which may seem less persuasive as a model for the outburst of civil violence, the rise in social achievement is outstripped by an even steeper curve of rising expectations. Moreover, if social achievement were growing as a power function

rather than as a straight line, the gap between expectations and achievement could be eliminated.

The dynamics of the systemic frustration situations shown in the figures reflect the sudden onset of improvement or deterioration, as well as rapid rates of growth or decline. Levels of social expectation depend very much on past performance of the social system. Men who experience a constant history of either frustration or satisfaction will develop learned expectations consistent with their experience. Abrupt change in objective circumstance, especially a reversal of direction but also, at least at the outset, a very rapid rise or decline, will have a sharp and sometimes unrealistic impact on expectations. The consequent lack of alignment between expectations and attainments creates an intolerable discrepancy which is postulated as the motivational antecedent to political violence.

Unrealistic expectations regarding the future may also be a result of a major change in circumstance which is clearly certain to occur at a particular time. Such expectations are unrealistic because a variety of other changes are also anticipated concomitant with the single, clearly stated event.

There are situations in the present

century wherein exaggerated expectations regarding some future event are likely to bring an immediate sense of sharp systemic frustration. Speaking of the trauma of independence in West Africa, Victor LeVine points out that the advent of independence is often counted upon as a panacea for all the social ills besetting a country.[7] When independence does occur, however, it falls far short of a perfect solution to all problems. This experience proves a shattering frustration if, in fact, such high expectations were held (see Figure 6). As a result, the extent of revolutionary behavior in Africa increased sharply after independence was granted: the expectation of momentous nonrevolutionary change proved illusory.

In Figure 7, flux in social and economic performance or policy is postulated as creating social discontent and political violence. Flux is likely to create ambiguity and uncertainty of expectations, as suggested in the third hypothesis. Discontinuous economic growth, that is, alternating periods of relative prosperity and economic slump in quick succession, or conflicting policies simultaneously pursued or sequentially administered, as well as other inconsistencies within the domain of social change, exemplify another set of circumstances that increases the impulse toward political violence.[8]

[7] Victor LeVine, "The Trauma of Independence in French-Speaking Africa," paper presented at the Midwest Conference of Political Scientists, Lafayette, Indiana, 1967.

[8] Robert LeVine observes that, in sub-Saharian Africa, those colonial powers which over the decades consistently denied self-rule to the indigenous populace, or those which consistently fostered such a goal, experienced the lowest incidence of anti-European violence. Those regimes which vacillated between the two policies of permissiveness and coerciveness were often subject to intense outbreaks of violence. See LeVine's "Anti-European Violence in Africa: A Comparative Analysis," *Journal of Conflict Resolution*, III (December, 1959).

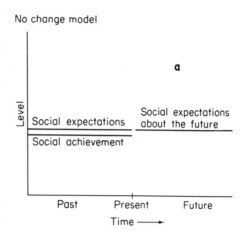

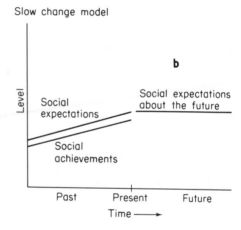

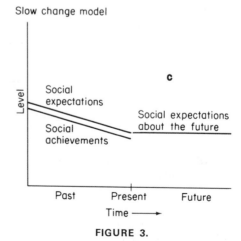

FIGURE 3.

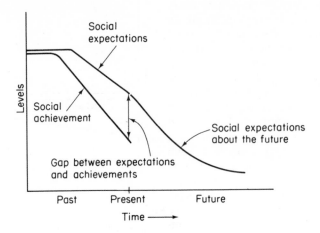

Rapid change model
Deterioration pattern

Social
expectations

Levels

Social
achievement

Social expectations
about the future

Gap between expectations
and achievements

Past   Present   Future

Time ———→

FIGURE 4.

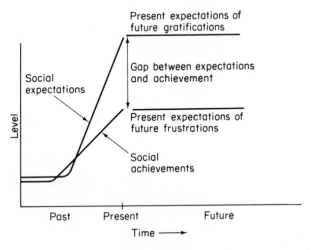

Rapid change model
Improvement pattern

Present expectations of
future gratifications

Gap between expectations
and achievement

Social
expectations

Level

Present expectations of
future frustrations

Social
achievements

Past   Present   Future

Time ———→

FIGURE 5.

Conflict between the Traditional and Modern

All of these change models—and more could be generated[9]—suggest

[9] These models are given fuller elaboration in I. K. Feierabend, R. L. Feierabend, and B. A. Nesvold, "Political Violence and Social Discontent," in David C. Schwartz, ed., *Revolution Studies*, forthcoming.

situations that give rise to a sense of systemic frustration, as postulated in the first three propositions. The fourth proposition introduces the idea of systemic conflict and may best be traced to the process of transition. Here, social change is conceptualized as transforming the social order from one form, or stage of development, to another. Since these forms may differ

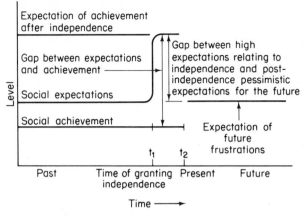

Disappointed expectations tied to future event

FIGURE 6.

radically in social structure, economic achievement, culture, or other respects, and since one form is receding and another only slowly gaining ground, a large area of struggle and conflict between the new and the old is likely to exist. Indeed, conflict may be seen to be indispensable to the very notion of transition and transformation. If the new and the old were similar and harmonious, if little or no change were required, it would be superfluous to speak of transition.

The notions of development, stages, and transition are familiar themes, as is the idea that political violence is associated with the transitional process. In different periods of history, the process of transition has been conceptualized in different ways; for example, as a change from religious to secular society or from small principalities to nation-states. The dominant contemporary view stresses the process of modernization which is seen as engulfing the less developed nations of today's world. In this view, nations may be classified into three groups: modern

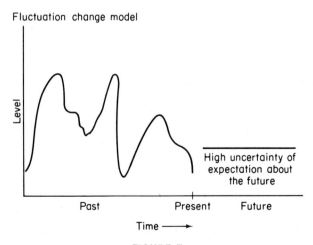

FIGURE 7.

Ivo K. Feierabend / Rosalind L. Feierabend / Betty A. Nesvold   115

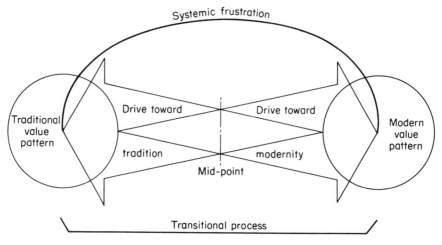

Systemic conflict model of transition

Systemic frustration

Traditional value pattern

Drive toward tradition

Drive toward modernity

Mid-point

Modern value pattern

Transitional process

FIGURE 8.

societies, traditional societies, and modernizing societies. The latter are passing through the transitional stage from traditional society to modernity. Generally, this period of transition is regarded as one that entails an inordinate amount of strain, tension, and crisis.[10]

On the evidence, members of transitional societies aspire to the benefits of modernity, yet modern goals may be blocked by the values inherent in traditional society.[11] Any modicum of

[10] See, for example, Lucian W. Pye, *Aspects of Political Development* (Boston: Little, Brown & Company, 1966). Pye identifies six such crises that hamper smooth political processes: the identity crisis, the legitimacy crisis, the penetration crisis, the participation crisis, the integration crisis, and the distribution crisis.

[11] David E. Apter, *The Politics of Modernization* (Chicago: The University of Chicago Press, 1965), describes these more or less intense conflicts, especially in the African context and on the Gold Coast. Destruction of traditional culture may ensue if the indigenous culture is entirely hostile to innovation and the acceptance of modernity. However, if the traditional culture is more instrumentally oriented, the conflict may be less intense. Apter also speaks of the appropriate political systems that may follow from these situations.

modernity introduced into traditional society will conflict with its traditions. The further the process of transition progresses, the more likely and the more intense the conflicts between modern and established patterns. The situation may be depicted as a massive conflict, reflected in myriad individual psyches of different strata of the population and infecting different domains of the social process. It may lead to intergroup conflict between more traditional and more modern strata with conflicting social roles, structures, and expectations.

Figure 8 schematizes the pattern. If we assume that many traditional patterns are in fact incompatible with modernity, then the midpoint of the transitional process is the point of highest intensity of conflict and hence the point of highest systemic frustration. The stage of transition is also the one most likely to be characterized by a high incidence of violent activity. It is at this midpoint that the accomplishments of modernity equal those of tradition, and the drive toward modernity is offset by the contradictory and equal attraction of traditional ways.

This should be the stage of the most intense struggle between the traditional and the modern. Figure 8 symbolizes this systemic conflict situation with two intersecting arrows representing traditional and modern drives. The closer the transitional process to the stage of modernity (tradition), the stronger the modern (traditional) drive, and the weaker the traditional (modern) drive. (This strengthening and weakening of drives is depicted by the varying width of the two arrows.) The forces determining the strength and weakness of the two drives are specified by the psychological hypothesis which postulates a strengthening of drive with proximity to the goal.[12] Hence the closer the transitional country to either modernity or tradition, the less intense the systemic conflict. As a country approaches either end of the transition continuum, the attraction toward the closest value pattern overcomes the drive in the opposite direction.

The Processes of Modernization

It can be argued that all of the conditions conducive to systemic frustration are produced by the modernization process, in addition to the occurrence of systemic conflict. Modernization, especially since World War II, affects an uneven array of nations at different levels of development. The less developed nations, even those which are quite traditional, are exposed to the modern ways of the more advanced nations. This exposure alone may create new aspirations and expectations which are left unmatched by social achievements.

Modernity itself denotes very specific modes of culture and social organization. It includes a society's ability and desire to produce and consume a wide range and quantity of goods and services. It includes advanced development in science, technology, and education, and widespread attainment of numerous specialized skills. It includes, moreover, a secular culture, new structures of social organization and more specialized and differentiated participation in these structures, and new sets of aspirations, attitudes, and ideologies. Modern affluent nations, with their complex economic, political, and social systems, serve best as models of modernity to nations emerging from traditional society.

The adoption of modern goals, although an integral aspect of modernity, is hardly synonymous with their attainment. The arousal of an underdeveloped society to awareness of complex modern patterns of behavior and organization brings with it a desire to emulate and achieve the same high level of satisfaction. But there is an inevitable lag between aspiration and achievement. The more a country is exposed to modernity and the lower its level of development, the greater the discrepancy between achievement and social aspirations. It is postulated that the peak discrepancy between systemic goals and their satisfaction, and hence maximum systemic frustration, is likely to occur during the transitional phase. Highly modern and truly traditional nations should experience less systemic

[12] This is the goal-gradient hypothesis which derives from psychological learning theory and which has wide applicability to both animal and human behavior. It maintains that the impulse to action, or the strength of attraction, varies as a function of the distance (spatial or temporal) between the organism and the goal. The closer the individual comes to attaining a desired goal, the stronger the level of attraction and the greater the impulse to action. The further the individual is from a goal, the less the attraction and the weaker the impulse to action. See N. E. Miller, "Experimental Studies of Conflict Behavior," in J. McV. Hunt, ed., *Personality and the Behavior Disorders* (New York: Ronald Press, 1944); and C. L. Hull, *Principles of Behavior* (New York: Appleton-Century-Crofts, 1943).

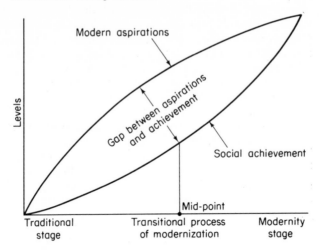

Model of uneven growth of modern aspirations and achievement during transition

FIGURE 9.

frustration—in the modern nations, because of their ability to provide a high level of attainment commensurate with modern aspirations; in the traditional nations, unexposed to modernity, because modern aspirations are still lacking. Figure 9 depicts the increasing and decreasing gap between modern aspirations and modern achievements.

A similar logic is applicable not only to social aspirations but also to social expectations. Furthermore, there may also be a feedback effect stemming from modern social attainment. It could be argued that the satisfaction of modern wants and aspirations reinforces the expectation of further satisfaction. As modern aspirations are formed through the process of exposure to modernity, if even a few aspirations are satisfied, they may create the drive and expectation for more, thus adding to the sense of systemic frustration. If so, it could be assumed that the faster the rate of modern achievement, the

greater the feedback effect and the more thorough the "revolution of rising expectations." It is in this sense that rapid rates of change, as opposed to gradual change toward modernity, could lead to more rather than less frustration, the situation postulated in the model in Figure 5. At the same time, rapid achievement could reduce the gap between aspirations and attainment and hence reduce the sense of frustration. Rapid rate of change in the establishment of modernity in this estimation then could have contradictory effects.

The aura of uncertainty also hangs over the entire process of social change, a consequence of its conflicts and confusions. There is ambivalence of attitude to old ways now on the wane, as well as toward the modern future. Ambiguity epitomizes the transitional process, and ambiguity is postulated to increase frustration.

CROSS-

NATIONAL

ANALYSES

OF

POLITICAL

VIOLENCE

In contrast to Part I, in which the selections are almost entirely theoretical, those included here are empirical in emphasis. Rather than speculate on violence, the authors explore the actual situations and circumstances that prevail. These studies are ambitious attempts to assess cross-national, global patterns of violence. Ted Robert Gurr examines violence in 114 nations; Ivo and Rosalind Feierabend in 84; Bruce M. Russett in 47; and Manus Midlarsky and Raymond Tanter, and Douglas P. Bwy focus on the republics of Latin America.

This comparative, cross-national approach has its merits. The examination of many nations and myriad instances of political strife, violence, crisis, and turmoil can reveal overall patterns that may otherwise go unnoticed in the unique circumstances of a specific episode. To generalize from a wealth of information is less hazardous than from only one episode, or from a few case studies. However, the cross-national method also has its shortcomings. Important depth and detail are lost in the panoramic overview, which would be more thoroughly preserved in intensive explorations of a single country or a single violent incident. Part III of this reader contains such case studies. Therefore, what may be lost or distorted in the macro assessments of conflict which follow is in part supplemented by the individual studies of Part III.

An additional merit of the cross-national approach must be emphasized. This method need not be purely descriptive but may also be used to test hypotheses and theories—which is the essence of a mature strategy of empirical science. It is also the most difficult strategy to follow, combining descriptive, empirical exploration with nonempirical, theoretical analysis. Testing takes place in the experiential arena of observations and data wherein all terms refer to concrete observations such as assassinations, strikes, imprisonments, executions, the Gross National Product, or the percentage of the population that is literate. It is with reference to the empirical world that we may say that the United States is a country with a Gross National Product per capita of $2,577 in 1957, 98.0 percent literate, and experiencing sixteen assassination events (including plots and attempts) since 1948. These are specific, concrete descriptive statements.

What is tested in this empirical arena of data are hypotheses and theories, formed from interrelated sets of tentative propositions of relationship. Theories do not rely on observational terms—quite the opposite. They are couched in a highly abstract, generalized language employing terms such as *political aggression, coerciveness, social facilitation, relative deprivation,* or the *J-curve of social development.* These terms are then tied together in tentative statements of relationship: political aggression is the result of relative deprivation, or, midlevels of political coerciveness lead to high levels of political aggression.

The testing of hypotheses thus combines theoretical and empirical endeavors. Those hypotheses that find support (or that "test out") are retained and those that do not are rejected, or reformulated, refined, and retested. Theorizing alone cannot provide a reliable understanding of reality since theories must remain tentative until, and if, the relative validity of their hypotheses is assessed. Nor can description alone suffice. The more meticulously detailed the description of specific phenomena, the further removed from general explanation, which must always be couched in abstract terms.

It is the merit of the cross-national studies which follow that they strive to test hypotheses, many of which were formulated in the previous section. Each investigator is concerned with exploring a different relationship, although there is much conceptual overlap among these studies. For Russett, the primary question is the impact of inequality upon the level of political instability within a society. The Feierabends assess the relationship to political instability of systemic frustration, modernity, and rates of socioeconomic change, measured by means of ecological variables, as well as of coerciveness of regime and international conflict. Gurr predicts level of civil strife from political and ecological variables assessing deprivation, coercive potential, legitimacy of political regime, institutionalization, and facilitation of violence. Bwy explores deprivation, coerciveness, and legitimacy as predictors of violence in Latin America. And Midlarsky and Tanter, in an analysis that is also limited to Latin America, bring in an additional international variable—the United States' economic presence in these countries. Together these studies offer an array of political, ecological, socioeconomic, and international variables in their efforts to explain the internal violence besetting nations.

The student must grasp the manner in which each author translates theoretical constructs into observable terms, the types of data which he gathers, how numerical values are assigned to the data, and the techniques for assessing relationships between measured dimensions. Only then can he evaluate the findings for himself and determine the validity of the theoretical propositions. Also, only by following these steps will he understand and appreciate the research endeavor which the various authors have undertaken. It was noted above that cross-national study, macroscopic as it must be, cannot do justice to the intricacies and complexities of the problems of violence. As a result the findings may be grossly over-simplified due to the aggregation of data into one score for an entire nation, which cannot fully reflect the variety of patterns and conditions within each national unit. This is undoubtedly the case, and yet the reader may well be struck, not by the simplicity of these cross-national analyses, but by their tremendous complexity. Take, for example, the range of possibilities for measuring the theoretical notion of internal political conflict, political aggression, or civil strife, as it is called by the various authors. Bwy operationalizes this notion by reference to nine specific categories of events, which were originally identified in previous studies by Rummel (1963, 1966) and Tanter (1966). The Feierabends, however, distinguish 29 different kinds of events. Furthermore, Midlarsky and Tanter rely on the number of people killed in domestic violence and the number of revolutions, whereas Russett uses three types of measures: the turnover ratio in top office-holders, the number of people killed in domestic violence, and thirteen types of violent events previously specified by Eckstein (1962). Nor is this all. The measurements of aggressive profiles show equal variety. A simple frequency count of violent acts may be the basis for ascertaining national instability profiles. Or scales may be constructed that take into account the intensity of the violent act (see the Feierabends and Gurr). Here the type of violence, its persistence, and its pervasiveness are all considered and weighted. Furthermore, various dimensions of conflict may be used as distinct measures. This is best demonstrated in Bwy's work, and also in Gurr's, although the latter uses a combined Total Magnitude of Civil Strife score in addition to separate scalings of distinct types of conflict.

Given this variety, obviously each measure will be different, since different methods tap different aspects or observational meanings of violence. Furthermore, these different measures do not refer to identical time periods. Since there are very few fixed points within social processes, even identical measurements taken at different points in time should yield different national profiles. Last, to add to all of these complexities, it must be remembered that the different authors use different source materials that may be more or less comprehensive, and more or less guilty of imprecision and omissions. These, too, will color descriptive findings regarding the global patterns of violence in the twentieth century.

The complexities of the empirical domain are equally and perhaps even more strikingly illustrated in the treatment of the independent variables. The most direct way of measuring the elusive state of mind that motivates strife, be it called dissatisfaction, frustration, or relative deprivation, is through the use of questionnaires and interviews. A scale for this purpose has been designed and applied in many nations of the world (see Cantril and Free, 1962). All the selections reported here, however, resort to an indirect method of measuring psychological variables, employing structural and ecological indicators. Bwy regards annual percentage rate of growth in GNP per capita as an aggregated measure of psychological satisfaction within a society, whereas Russett measures inequality of land distribution. Midlarsky and Tanter view the level of GNP per capita as an index of development, and U.S. investments in and trade with Latin America as an index of economic presence. The Feierabends, guided by the theoretical ratio of want formation to want satisfaction, select the level of literacy and the degree of urbanization to assess the formation of wants in a society, and GNP per capita, caloric intake, and number of radios, newspapers, telephones, and physicians to indicate the level of satisfactions. Gurr, in the most elaborate combination of indices, seeks to operationalize relative deprivation in the various forms of discrimination practiced within nations. Economic discrimination, political discrimination, potential separatism, religious cleavages, lack of educational opportunities, and dependence on foreign capital all serve to index persisting relative deprivation. To this, Gurr adds five measures of short-term economic deprivation based on trends in national economic conditions such as foreign trade and inflation, and two measures of short-term political deprivation—new restrictions on political participation and new value-depriving policies of government.

The various studies also differ in their interpretations of mediating variables. *Coerciveness of regime* is explored by Bwy, Gurr, and the Feierabends, but by each in a different manner. For the Feierabends, permissiveness-coerciveness is a structural dimension of political regimes, including openness of elections, tolerance of opposition parties, and protection of civil rights. For Bwy and Gurr, coerciveness is estimated in terms of the relative size of the army. Bwy assesses defense expenditures and Gurr, manpower resources supplemented by two indices of the loyalty of coercive forces. A second mediating variable, *legitimacy*, is introduced by both Bwy and Gurr. For the former, legitimacy is ascertained in terms of changes toward greater popular participation in politics. For the latter, it is a function of the autochthonous character of political institutions and their durability.

In addition, Gurr has two further mediating variables: *institutionalization* and *facilitation*. Institutionalization is determined by the strength of labor union membership, the relative size of central government budget expenditure, and the stability of the political party system. Facilitation is viewed as a function of past levels of civil strife ("violent culture"); "inaccessibility" (transportation networks, area, population density, and type of terrain); communist party strength; and degree of external support for rebels.

A final variable, *internation hostility* —as manifested in economic sanctions, for example—is used by Midlarsky and Tanter and by the Feierabends. Based on the same data, this variable indexes hostility for the former authors and an alternative form of political violence for the latter.

In this mass of specific operationalizations, a number of points may be noted. The same concept may be indexed in quite different ways by different authors. Also, the same specific measure may be used by more than one author but interpreted differently. Furthermore, the student must pay particular attention to the variety of techniques employed for measuring specific indicators. Some indicators are quantified by their very nature, for example, GNP per capita in U.S. dollars. Others, such as the Feierabends' measure of coerciveness or Gurr's assessment of political deprivation, represent a series of judgmental ratings by the authors. And somewhere between these two extremes lie a variety of more or less complex techniques for weighting and scaling the different dimensions.

Finally, there is a variety of techniques of analysis employed in these studies. Although all the studies use a correlational approach, the authors are not satisfied with the simple correlation of two variables. Given the multivariate nature of the studies, multiple correlations are used to assess the degree of prediction attained when all explanatory variables are combined. The technique of step-wise multiple regression further allows the investigator to assess the relative degree of influence of each independent and mediating variable on the final level of political violence. Scatter plots and complex contingency tables allow the reader to see the shape of the relationship and to determine whether it is curvilinear rather than linear. Finally, the use of partial correlations enables the authors to assess the degree of relationship between two variables when the influence of a third variable (or a set of other variables) is removed from the equation. The use of partial correlations to test the direction or path of influence among a set of variables is especially stressed in the studies by Gurr and by Midlarsky and Tanter. (The student who has no prior knowledge of statistics should consult the Appendix to this volume.)

What picture emerges from these macro assessments of violence based on aggregate data? It would seem that certain findings are consistently supported. For example, psychological dissatisfaction, measured largely in socioeconomic terms, or relative deprivation, measured in economic and political terms, always are found in these studies to be related to the level of internal political violence within societies. Level of development, inequality of land distribution, and modernization all have some bearing on strife. Furthermore, all three of the studies which explore the concept of coerciveness of government find a curvilinear relationship between force and the level of overt violence within society: the highest levels of violence are likely to occur in societies with mid-levels of force.

In fact, in view of the success claimed by each of these studies in explaining the sources of political instability in the contemporary world, the student may well wonder how to reconcile these claims. Are all studies overlapping? Do all aspects of the ecology interrelate, such that inequality of land distribution, economic and political discrimination, level of development, and U.S. economic presence co-vary? It is entirely possible. An effort to interrelate all the ecological indicators employed in these studies would help to clarify the

picture. Such efforts are under way in various cross-national research projects, but it is suggested that the student also explore these relationships for himself, using the data supplied in these studies and, if desired, some of the simple techniques described in the Appendix.

A final qualification which should be placed on the results of these studies stems from the fact that all of them are limited to an analysis of the contemporary world. Since they are based on data collected primarily in the era following World War II, the relationships or patterns discovered may not represent the constellation of factors in some other era. For example, the principle that psychological dissatisfaction is at the root of the impulse to violence may be a valid generalization which knows no limitations of time. But the sources of dissatisfaction can be quite different from one era to another. The process of socioeconomic development has been a major focus of attention for scholars concerned with the sources of strife in the mid-twentieth century. As a prognosis of the future, we may be observing new social and political sources of dissatisfaction in the most highly developed societies. If our focus were on an earlier historical period, we would surely pinpoint yet another set of tension-producing societal conditions. Although the cross-national studies presented in this section are global in the number of nation-units examined, they are case studies of single historical epochs. The directions for future research include both cross-national and cross-era assessments, with formidable requirements for gathering and analyzing data and great prospects for testing and refining theory.

Suggested Readings

Banks, Arthur S., and Robert B. Textor. *A Cross-Polity Survey*. Cambridge, Mass.: The M. I. T. Press, 1963.

Cantril, Hadley, and Lloyd A. Free. "Hopes and Fears for Self and Country," *American Behavioral Scientist*, VI, No. 2 (October, 1962), 3–30.

Cutright, Phillips. "National Political Development: Measurement and Analysis," *American Sociological Review*, XXVIII (April, 1963), 253–64.

Eckstein, Harry. "The Incidence of Internal Wars, 1946–59," Appendix I of *Internal War: The Problem of Anticipation*, report submitted to Research Group in Psychology and the Social Sciences, Smithsonian Institution, January 15, 1962.

Feierabend, Ivo K., and Betty A. Nesvold, with Rosalind L. Feierabend. "Political Coerciveness and Turmoil: A Cross-National Inquiry," *Law and Society Review* (August, 1970), 93–118.

Fossum, Egil. "Factors Influencing the Occurrence of Military Coups d'Etat in Latin America," *Journal of Peace Research*, III (1967), 228–51.

Graham, Hugh Davis, and Ted R. Gurr, eds. *Violence in America: Historical and Comparative Perspectives*, Vols. 1 and 2. A Report to the National Commission on the Causes and Prevention of Violence. Washington, D.C.: Government Printing Office, 1969.

Gurr, Ted R. "Sources of Rebellion in Western Societies: Some Quantitative Evidence," *The Annals of the American Academy of Political and Social Science* (September, 1970), 128–45.

Hernes, Gudmund. "On Rank Disequilibrium and Military Coups d'État," *Journal of Peace Research*, I (1969), 65–72.

Kirkham, James F., Sheldon G. Levy, and William J. Crotty. *Assassination and Political Violence*, Vol. 8. A Report to the National Commission on the Causes and Prevention of Violence. Washington, D.C.: Government Printing Office, 1969.

Lipset, Seymour H. "Some Social Requisites of Democracy," *American Political Science Review*, LIII (March, 1959), 69–105.

Ridker, Ronald. "Discontent and Economic Growth," *Economic Development and Cultural Change*, XI, No. 18 (October, 1962), 1–15.

Rummel, Rudolph J. "Dimensions of Conflict Behavior Within and Between Nations," *General Systems Yearbook*, VIII (1963), 1–50.

————. "Dimensions of Conflict Behavior within Nations, 1946–59," *Journal of Conflict Resolution*, X, No. 1 (March, 1966), 65–74.

Russett, Bruce M., Hayward R. Alker, Jr., Karl W. Deutsch, and Harold D. Lasswell. *World Handbook of Political and Social Indicators*. New Haven: Yale University Press, 1964.

Tanter, Raymond. "Dimensions of Conflict Behavior within and between Nations, 1958–60," *Journal of Conflict Resolution*, X, No. 1 (March, 1966), 41–64.

Wilkenfeld, Jonathan. "Domestic and Foreign Conflict Behavior of Nations," *Journal of Peace Research*, I (1968), 56–69.

Winslow, Robert W. *Society in Transition*. New York: The Free Press, 1970.

INEQUALITY AND INSTABILITY: THE RELATION OF LAND TENURE TO POLITICS

Bruce M. Russett*

At least since the ancient Greeks many thinkers have regarded great diversity of wealth as incompatible with stable government. According to Euripides:

> In a nation there be orders three:—
> The useless rich, that ever crave
>   for more;
> The have-nots, straitened even for
>   sustenance,
> A dangerous folk, of envy overfull,
> Which shoot out baleful stings at
>   such as have,
> Beguiled by tongues of evil men,
>   their "champions":
> But of the three the midmost saveth
>   states;
> They keep the order which the state
>   ordains. [1]

Alexis de Tocqueville, writing many centuries later, declared:

Remove the secondary causes that have produced the great convulsions of the world and you will almost always find the principle of inequality at the bottom. Either the poor have attempted to plunder the rich, or the rich to enslave the poor. If, then, a state of society can ever be founded in which every man shall have something to keep and little to take from others, much will have been done for the peace of the world. [2]

* This article is part of the research of the Yale Political Data Program, supported by a grant from the National Science Foundation. I am grateful to John Shingler and Seth Singleton for research assistance. An earlier version was presented at the Annual Meeting of the American Political Science Association, September 1963.

[1] "The Suppliants," *The Tragedies of Euripides*, trans. by Arthur S. Way (London 1894), 373.

[2] Alexis de Tocqueville, *Democracy in America* (Vintage edn., New York 1954), 266.

Reprinted from *World Politics*, XVI, No. 3 (April, 1964), 442–54, by permission of the author and Princeton University Press.

Many modern writers echo the same thought. Merle Kling, for example, blames political instability in Latin America on the extreme concentration of economic bases of power in what he terms "colonial economies." Land ownership, he says, is so heavily concentrated that no individual not already possessing great tracts of agricultural land can reasonably hope to achieve wealth through farming. Foreign exploitation of mineral resources effectively blocks the ambitious native from that source of wealth. Industry remains rudimentary. Of the possible sources of enrichment, only government is open to competition. Political office provides such a unique source of gain that "large segments of the population are prepared to take the ultimate risk of life, in a revolt, in a *coup d'état*, to perpetuate a characteristic feature of Latin American politics—chronic political instability."[3]

Both Plato and Karl Marx so despaired of the pernicious effects of wealth that they saw no way to abolish the evil except to abolish private property itself. Tocqueville, on the other hand, thought that he found in America a society which had been able to reach another solution:

Between these two extremes [very few rich men and few poor ones] of democratic communities stands an innumerable multitude of men almost alike, who, without being exactly either rich or poor, possess sufficient property to desire the maintenance of order, yet not enough to excite envy. Such men are the natural enemies of violent commotions; their lack of agitation keeps all beneath them and above them still and secures the balance of the fabric of society.[4]

[3] Merle Kling, "Toward a Theory of Power and Political Instability in Latin America," *Western Political Quarterly*, IX (March 1956), 21–35. Note that land distribution is only one element of the "colonial economy" defined by Kling.

[4] Tocqueville, 266.

Yet if we check the matter empirically with present-day polities the answer is not so clear-cut. Wealth is everywhere distributed unequally; even in the most egalitarian societies the income of the rich is many times that of the poor. And one can readily point to a number of instances—such as Spain—where, despite an impressionistic judgment that goods are distributed highly unequally, the polity is seemingly stable under the rule of a dictator.

Part of the difficulty stems from a conceptual problem, a lack of clarity about just what is the dependent variable. Is economic inequality incompatible with *stable* government, or merely with *democratic* or "*good*" government? If we mean stable government, do we mean regimes in which the rulers maintain themselves in power for long periods despite the chronic outbreak of violence (Colombia and South Vietnam), or simply the avoidance of significant violence even though governments may topple annually (France throughout most of the Third and Fourth Republics)? Or must "stable" government be both peaceful and reasonably long-term? Finally, what do we mean by the government? A particular individual (Spain), a particular party (Uruguay), the essential maintenance of a particular coalition (France under the system of "replastering"), or the continued dominance of a particular social stratum (Jordan)?

Another part of the difficulty stems from the absence of comparative study. Numerous authors have examined the distribution of agricultural land in particular countries or areas, and its contribution to a particular political situation. Several books have drawn together studies giving attention to many different nations.[5] But none of

[5] See, for example, Kenneth Parsons, *et al.*,

these has been based on the same concepts or have presented data for the same variables in a manner necessary for true comparative analysis. Case studies are essential for providing depth and insight, but generalization requires eventual attention to many cases.

Comparative analysis is dependent on the provision of comparable data. For instance, one may know that in contemporary England the upper 5 per cent of income earners receive over 15 per cent of all current income, even after taxes.[6] Is this high or low compared with other nations? All too often the necessary data simply are not available or, if they are, they are not in comparable form. For another country one may, for instance, know the proportion of income going to the top 10 per cent and top 1 percent of earners, but not to the top 5 per cent, as in England.

In this article we shall attempt to clarify the problem conceptually, present for the first time a large body of distribution data, and test some hypotheses about the relation between economic inequality and politics. First, the data. We shall be concerned with information on the degree to which agricultural land is concentrated in the hands of a few large landholders. Information on land tenure is more readily available, and is of more dependable comparability, than are data on the distribution of other economic assets like current income or total wealth.[7] Material on land dis-

tribution is available for many countries about which we know nothing precise or reliable in regard to income distribution. In addition, land distribution is intrinsically of major interest. Kling's theory of Latin American political instability was built in large part on land inequality; the United States government has long warned its allies in poorer nations about the need for land reform. In Japan, and to a lesser extent in South Korea, the American military government took upon itself a major redistribution of land with the intention of providing the necessary bases for political democracy.

II

I have discussed elsewhere the uses of various summary statistical measures designed to indicate the degree of inequality in a distribution.[8] Here we shall employ three separate indices, each of which measures somewhat different aspects of land distribution. The first two are directed to the relative size of farms, the last to tenancy.

1. The *percentage of landholders who collectively occupy one-half of all the agricultural land* (starting with the farmers with the *smallest* plots of land and working toward the *largest*).

any case it cannot indicate the quality of the land in question. Nevertheless, while these caveats may be important with regard to a few distributions, they do not fundamentally alter the character of the data shown.

Although a few of the data presented were compiled some time ago, patterns of land tenure normally change but little over the years. Only for Bolivia, Taiwan and, to a lesser degree, Italy is there evidence of a significant change between the year given and 1960.

[8] Hayward R. Alker, Jr., and Bruce M. Russett, "Indices for Comparing Inequality," in *Comparing Nations: The Use of Quantitative Data in Cross-National Research*, ed. by R. L. Merritt and Stein Rokkan (New Haven 1966).

eds., *Land Tenure* (Madison 1958), and Walter Froelich, *Land Tenure, Industralization, and Social Stability* (Milwaukee 1961).

[6] Robert M. Solow, "Income Inequality Since the War," in *Postwar Economic Trends in the United States*, ed. by Ralph Freeman (New York 1960).

[7] One must always introduce comparative data, particularly on land tenure, with certain caveats. The quality of data collection is not uniform from one country to the next, and in

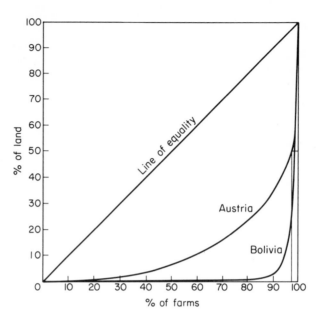

FIGURE 1. Lorenz Curves of Land Distribution: Austria
and Bolivia

2. *The Gini index of concentration.*
We begin with a Lorenz curve (Figure
1) drawn by connecting the points
given in a cumulative distribution
(e.g., the proportion of land held by
each decile of farmers). All farms are
ranked in order from the smallest to
the largest, so that one can say what
proportion of the total *number* of
farms accounts for a given proportion
of the total *area* of agricultural land.
In Figure 1 the cumulated percentage
of farms is given along the horizontal
axis, and the cumulated percentage
of the area along the vertical axis. The
45° line represents the condition of
perfect equality, wherein each percentile
of farmers would make an equal contribution to the cumulated total of
agricultural land. Thus, under complete equality each 10 per cent of the
population would have exactly 10
per cent of the land; any two-thirds of
the population would have exactly
two-thirds of the land. How far in
fact the curve for a particular distribution departs from the "line of equality"

gives us a visual measure of the inequality involved.

The Lorenz curve provides an extremely useful way of showing the
complete pattern of a distribution,
but it is impractical to try to compare
whole Lorenz curves for any substantial
number of countries. But if we measure
the *area* between the cumulated distribution and the line of equality we
have the Gini index, a simple summary measure of the total inequality of
a distribution.[9] The Gini index cal-

[9] The Gini number for a Lorenz curve is
actually twice the area mentioned divided by
the area (10,000 for 100 by 100 axes) of the
whole square. Formula:

$$G = \frac{2\int_0^{100} (x - f(x))\, dx}{10{,}000}$$

where: x = the cumulated population per-
    centage and
  f(x) = the height of the Lorenz curve.

Cf. Mary Jean Bowman, "A Graphical
Analysis of Personal Income Distribution in
the United States," *American Economic Review*,
XXXV (September 1945), 607–28. In Table 1
below, the Gini index is multiplied by 100.

culates over the whole population the difference between an "ideal" cumulative distribution of land (where all farms are the same size) and the actual distribution. The higher the Gini index, the greater the inequality.

Though the percentage of farmers with one-half the land is simple and useful, the more comprehensive Gini index, by examining the whole distribution, is in many ways superior. The curves for the two countries in Figure 1, for example, both show virtually the same percentage of farmers with half the land. But below the 50 per cent mark, the distribution for Bolivia is much more unequal than is that for Austria. In Bolivia the top 10 per cent of all farmers owned nearly 95 per cent of the land; in Austria the top 10 per cent of farmers owned only about 65 per cent of the land. The implications for a theory of political stability are obvious. (The Bolivian figures actually apply to 1950. Since that date Bolivia has experienced a social revolution.)

3. Probably less important than the relative size of farms, but still relevant, is the question of *ownership*. If a farmer tills a substantial piece of land but nevertheless must pay much of the produce to a landlord, the effect may be much the same as if he actually owned a much smaller plot. Therefore we also present data, where available, on *farm households that rent all their land as a percentage of the total number of farms*.

It is even more difficult to find a satisfactory operational definition of stability than to measure inequality. In our effort to account for different aspects of "stability," we shall use several quite different indices.

a. *Instability of Personnel*. One measure of stability is simply the term of office of the chief executive. As the numerator of our index, we have used the number of years during the period 1945–1961 in which a country was independent; and, as the denominator, the number of individuals who held the post of chief executive during the same period. By subtracting this figure from 17 (the number of years in the period) we obtain what we shall term the index of "personnel instability." It may vary from 0 to 17; in fact, the highest figure in our sample is 16.32 for France.[10]

b. *Internal Group Violence*. Rudolph Rummel, in his Dimensionality of Nations Project, collected data on the number of people killed as a result of internal group violence—i.e., civil wars, revolutions, and riots—during the years 1955–1957. We have extended the time period to 1950–1962, and have modified the data to allow for the size of the total population in question, making the index deaths per 1,000,000 people.[11]

[10] With this definition, most of the indices fall between 11 and 17. Our use of logarithmic transformations in the correlations below compensates for this bunching.

In some ways it might have been more desirable to measure the average tenure of a party or coalition, but that solution raises other problems. When a government in the French Fourth Republic fell and was replaced by a new cabinet composed basically of the same parties, was this a new coalition or just the old one under a new Premier? The first answer immediately involves one in difficulties of comparability with other countries' experiences; the second answer would cause France to appear much more stable than any observer would agree was correct.

Measuring the tenure of the chief executive tells nothing about the *form* of government, nor about what Kling (p. 25) describes as concealed instability. A government may appear stable only as long as its repressive techniques succeed; when they fail, it may be violently and suddenly overthrown. Thus Trujillo's Dominican Republic was "stable" for several decades. Nevertheless it is difficult to see how "hidden instability" can be allowed for other than through some definition of a democratic-dictatorial continuum, which we attempt in index d below [see original source].

[11] Cf. Rudolph J. Rummel, "Dimensions of Conflict Behavior Within and Between Nations," in *General Systems*, Yearbook of the Society for the Advancement of General

Table 1

LAND DISTRIBUTION AND POLITICAL STABILITY, 47 COUNTRIES

	Land Data			Political Data			Economic Data	
Country	*Gini Index*	*% of Farms with ½ Land*	*% of Farms Rented*	*Personnel Instability*	*Eckstein Internal War*	*Deaths from Civil Group Violence per 1,000,000*	*GNP per Capita ($-1955)*	*% Labor Force in Agriculture*
Yugoslavia	43.7	79.8	0*	0	9	0	297	67
Poland	45.0	77.7	0*	8.5	19	5.0	468	57
Denmark	45.8	79.3	3.5	14.6	0	0	913	23
Japan	47.0	81.5	2.9	15.7	22	0.1	240	40
Canada	49.7	82.9	7.2	11.3	22*	0	1667	12
Switzerland	49.8	81.5	18.9	8.5	0	0	1229	10
India	52.2	86.9	53.0	3.0	83	14.0	72	71
Philippines	56.4	88.2	37.3	14.0	15	292.0	201	59
Sweden	57.7	87.2	18.9	8.5	0	0	1165	13
France	58.3	86.1	26.0	16.3	46	0.3	1046	26
Belgium	58.7	85.8	62.3	15.5	8	0.9	1015	10
Ireland	59.8	85.9	2.5†	14.2	9	0	509	40
Finland	59.9	86.3	2.4	15.6	4	0	941	46
Netherlands	60.5	86.2	53.3	13.6	2	0	708	11
Luxembourg	63.8	87.7	18.8	12.8	0	0	1194	23
Taiwan	65.2	94.1	40.0	0	3	0	102	50
Norway	66.9	87.5	7.5	12.8	1	0	969	26
South Vietnam	67.1	94.6	20.0*	10.0	50*	1000*	133	65
West Germany	67.4	93.0	5.7	3.0	4	0	762	14
Libya	70.0	93.0	8.5	14.8	8	0*	90	75
United States	70.5	95.4	20.4	12.8	22*	0	2343	10
United Kingdom	71.0	93.4	44.5	13.6	12	0	998	5

Country								
Panama	73.7	95.0	12.3	15.6	29	25.0	350	54
Austria	74.0	97.4	10.7	12.8	4	0	532	32
Egypt	74.0	98.1	11.6	15.8	45	1.6	133	64
Greece	74.7	99.4	17.7	15.8	9	2.0	239	48
Honduras	75.7	97.4	16.7	13.6	45	111.0	137	66
Nicaragua	75.7	96.4	n.a.	12.8	16	16.0	254	68
New Zealand	77.3	95.5	22.3	12.8	0	0	1249	16
Spain	78.0	99.5	43.7	0	22	0.2	254	50
Cuba	79.2	97.8	53.8	13.6	100	2900.0*	361	42
Dominican Rep.	79.5	98.5	20.8	11.3	6	31.0	205	56
Italy	80.3	98.0	23.8	15.5	51	0.2	442	29
Uruguay	81.7	96.6	34.7	14.6	1	0.3	569	37
El Salvador	82.8	98.8	15.1	15.1	9	2.0	244	63
Brazil	83.7	98.5	9.1	15.5	49	1.0	262	61
Colombia	84.9	98.1	12.1	14.6	47	316.0	330	55
Guatemala	86.0	99.7	17.0	14.9	45	57.0	179	68
Argentina	86.3	98.2	32.8	13.6	57	217.0	374	25
Ecuador	86.4	99.3	14.6	15.1	41	18.0	204	53
Peru	87.5	96.9	n.a.	14.6	23	26.0	140	60
Iraq	88.1	99.3	75.0*	16.2	24	344.0	195	81
Costa Rica	89.1	99.1	5.4	14.6	19	24.0	307	55
Venezuela	90.9	99.3	20.6	14.9	36	111.0	762	42
Australia	92.9	99.6	n.a.	11.3	0	0.0	1215	14
Chile	93.8	99.7	13.4	14.2	21	2.0	180	30
Bolivia	93.8	97.7	20.0	15.3	53	663.0	66	72

SOURCES: GNP: Norton Ginsburg, *Atlas of Economic Development* (Chicago 1962), 22; Land, Personnel Instability, Violent Deaths, and Percentage of Labor Force in Agriculture: Russett, *et al.*, *World Handbook of Political and Social Indicators* (New Haven 1964); Internal War: Eckstein, Appendix I.

* Yale Data Program estimate—very approximate.

† % Area (not farms) rented.

c. *Internal War*. As an alternative to the violent-death material, we shall use Harry Eckstein's data on internal war for the period 1946–1961.[12] These data include the total number of violent incidents, from plots to protracted guerrilla warfare.

d. Quite a different problem is the *Stability of Democracy*. With a few adaptations we shall use the distinctions employed by Seymour Martin Lipset. "Stable democracies" will be defined as states that have been characterized by the uninterrupted continuation of political democracy since World War I, *and* the absence over the past thirty years of a totalitarian movement, either Fascist or Communist, which at any point received as much as 20 per cent of the vote. "Unstable democracies," again following Lipset, are countries which, although unable to meet the first criteria, nevertheless have a "history of more or less free elections for most of the post-World War I period."[13] "Dictatorships" are those countries in which, perhaps despite some democratic interludes, free elections have been generally absent. These judgments are impressionistic and do not permit precise rankings from most to least democratic; nevertheless they generally agree with those of other scholars and with widely accepted standards.[14]

Note again that our political dependent variables measure distinctly different aspects—stability of executive personnel, the incidence of violence, and "democracy." No one is by itself an adequate measure of all the conditions to which land distribution has been thought relevant.

Table 1 indicates the rankings of 47 countries (all those for which distribution data are available) on the first six of these indices. It also gives 1955 *GNP per capita*, in U. S. dollars, and the *percentage of the labor force employed in agriculture* in the most recent year for which we have data. The possible relevance of these additional variables will be discussed below.

III

Land is everywhere distributed unequally. In even the most egalitarian states, about four-fifths of the farmers are concentrated on only half the land. Still, the degree of inequality varies widely from state to state. Table 2 presents the correlation coefficients (r) indicating the degree of association between each of the three measures of land distribution and each of the first three indices of instability.[15]

For the three indices of inequality there is in each case a positive relationship to instability, though in two instances the correlation is extremely slight. The highest correlation is between violent deaths and the Gini index. Judged by the standards of

---

Systems Theory (Ann Arbor 1963). The nature and limitations of the data used in this article will be discussed in Bruce M. Russett *et al.*, *World Handbook of Political and Social Indicators* (New Haven 1964).

[12] Harry Eckstein, *Internal War: The Problem of Anticipation*, a report submitted to the Research Group in Psychology and the Social Sciences, Smithsonian Institution (Washington 1962), Appendix I.

[13] Seymour Martin Lipset, "Some Social Requisites of Democracy," *American Political Science Review*, LIII (March 1959), 73–74.

[14] For a similar classification of regimes in the underdeveloped countries, see Gabriel A. Almond and James S. Coleman, eds., *The Politics of the Developing Areas* (Princeton 1960), 579–81.

Lipset's categorization is of course crude and subject to a number of criticisms. For example, cf. Phillips Cutright, "National Political Development: Measurement and Analysis," *American Sociological Review*, XXVIII (April 1963), 253–64. The alternative index that Cutright suggests, however, really deals with the complexity of political institutions—quite a different matter.

[15] For the three political variables, I used logarithmic transformations instead of the raw data.

Table 2

CORRELATION COEFFICIENTS (r) FOR MEASURES OF LAND EQUALITY
WITH MEASURES OF POLITICAL INSTABILITY FOR 47 COUNTRIES

	Personnel Instability	Violent Political Deaths (per 1,000,000)	Eckstein Internal War Data
% of farms with ½ land	.24	.45	.35
Gini index	.33	.46	.29
% of farms rented (44 countries only)	.01	.27	.11

most social science this is a fairly high correlation, with a significance level of .001 (i.e., unless there really were a positive relationship between land distribution and instability, this high a correlation would not occur, purely by chance, as often as one time in a thousand). Nevertheless, these correlations indicate that much remains unexplained. Even the highest (.46) gives an r^2 of only .21. (The squared product moment coefficient—r^2—can be interpreted as the percentage of the total variation in one index that can be explained by another.) Inequality of land distribution does bear a relation to political instability, but that relationship is not a strong one, and many other factors must be considered in any attempted explanation.[16] The

degree to which farmland is rented is not a factor of great explanatory power, given the low level of the correlations of rental with all the stability indices.

A more complex hypothesis, closely related to Kling's, might read as follows: extreme inequality of land distribution leads to political instability only in those poor, predominantly agricultural societies where limitation to a small plot of land almost unavoidably condemns one to poverty. In a rich country, the modest income a farmer can produce from even a small holding may satisfy him. Or, if that is not the case, at least in wealthy countries there are, besides agriculture, many alternative sources of wealth.[17] Finally, one might assert that the *combination* of inequality *and* a high rate of tenancy would cause instability. While neither by itself would necessarily lead to violence or frequent change of government, the combination almost inevitably would.

To test these hypotheses we examined simultaneously the effect of GNP per capita, percentage of labor force in

[16] Nor is great concentration of farmland always a prelude to violent revolution in predominantly agricultural societies. Even according to figures cited by the Communists, inequality in Czarist Russia and interwar China was less than in most of the countries listed in Table 1. Cf. V. I. Lenin, *The Agrarian Program of Social Democracy*, in *Selected Works*, III (New York, n.d.), 164–65; and Yuan-li Wu, *An Economic Survey of Communist China* (New York 1956), 119. Wu lists several estimates, the most extreme of which was the report of the Hankow Land Commission, which he alleges was Communist-dominated. The Gini indices for Russia and China were, respectively, approximately 73.0 and 64.6. According to George Pavlovsky, in *Agricultural Russia on the Eve of the Revolution* (London 1930), chap. 4, the difficulty in Russia stemmed less from the *relative* size of farm plots than from the fact that the *absolute* size of

most holdings was too small to produce more than bare subsistence. Given the technological backwardness of the Russian peasant, this may well be true.

[17] "Rich" countries and "societies where there are many alternative sources of wealth" are to some degree synonymous. Denmark and Australia, two rich nations often thought of as "agricultural," actually have only 23 and 14 per cent, respectively, of their labor forces in agriculture.

Table 3

STABLE DEMOCRACIES, UNSTABLE DEMOCRACIES, AND DICTATORSHIPS BY DEGREE OF INEQUALITY IN LAND DISTRIBUTION

Gini Index	Stable Democracies	Unstable Democracies	Dictatorships
Greater than median equality	Denmark	Japan	Yugoslavia
	Canada	France	Poland
	Switzerland	Finland	Taiwan
	India	West Germany	South Vietnam
	Philippines		Libya
	Sweden		Panama
	Belgium		
	Ireland		
	Netherlands		
	Luxembourg		
	Norway		
	United States		
	United Kingdom		
Median equality or less	New Zealand	Austria	Egypt
	Uruguay	Greece	Honduras
	Australia	Italy	Nicaragua
		Brazil	Spain
		Colombia	Cuba
		Argentina	Dominican Rep.
		Costa Rica	El Salvador
		Chile	Guatemala
			Ecuador
			Peru
			Iraq
			Venezuela
			Bolivia

agriculture, tenancy, and land distribution on our various indices of political stability.[18] These refinements improved our explanation rather strikingly in some cases. The strongest relationship was between the Gini index and violent deaths; r^2 was raised to .50. By far the most important variables in the equations for "predicting" instability were first the Gini index and then the percentage of the

population in agriculture, as suggested by our first hypothesis. The percentage of farms rented again added little explanatory power. Qualifications of this sort help to explain the stability of a country like Australia, despite a highly unequal distribution of agricultural land. Venezuela's land distribution is also very unequal (but no more so than Australia's), yet Venezuela is somewhat poorer and has three times as many people (proportionately) employed in agriculture.[19] All the

[18] The technique used was multiple regression. For a description and application of this method, see Donald Stokes, Angus Campbell, and Warren Miller, "Components of Electoral Decision," *American Political Science Review*, LII (June 1958), 367–87. This procedure also allows us to test for the independent "explanatory" power of each variable with the other variables *controlled*.

[19] This points up rather sharply the flaw in any attempt to use land distribution as an indicator of the degree of inequality in all wealth for *advanced* economies. Australia is widely acknowledged to be a highly egalitarian society.

indices of instability are quite high for Venezuela. Nevertheless, even the strongest relationship found among these variables leaves over half the variance "unexplained"—as the sophisticated student of politics might expect. The old saws about equality can be accepted only with caution.

There remains one other possibility yet to be explored—that equality may be related to the stability of a *democratic regime*. That is, there may or may not be sporadic outbreaks of violence; there may or may not be frequent changes of personnel at the highest level; but it is highly unlikely that a nation with a grossly unequal pattern of distribution of a major source of wealth, like agricultural land, will have a consistently democratic government. Table 3 presents a sixfold table showing each of the countries in our sample classified, after Lipset, as a "stable democracy," an "unstable democracy," or a "dictatorship,"[20] and also listed as

above or below the median for the Gini index of land inequality.

The results are again quite striking. Of the 23 states with the more equal pattern of land distribution, 13 are stable democracies, whereas only three of 24 more unequal countries can be classified as stable democracies. And of these three, each is a fairly rich state where agriculture is no longer the principal source of wealth. Tocqueville's basic observation would therefore appear correct: no state can long maintain a democratic form of government if the major sources of economic gain are divided very unequally among its citizens. American policy in urging the governments of underdeveloped nations to undertake massive land reform programs seems essentially well-founded. A "sturdy yeomanry" may be a virtual *sine qua non* for democratic government in an underdeveloped land. Nevertheless there are many instances where relative equality of land tenure is not associated with stable democracy; it is no *guarantee* of democratic development. Land reform may provide the soil to nourish free institutions, but the seed must first be planted.

[20] Note that these definitions of stability say nothing about the rate of turnover among government personnel, but only about the stability of democratic forms of government. We have included India and the Philippines in the category "stable democracy" because, though independent only since the end of World War II, they met the above test. Nevertheless this decision is open to some question, as political conditions in these countries clearly are *not* the same as in Western Europe.

If they instead were classified as "unstable democracies" it would, however, only very moderately change the pattern of the following table.

SYSTEMIC CONDITIONS OF POLITICAL AGGRESSION: AN APPLICATION OF FRUSTRATION-AGGRESSION THEORY[1]

Ivo K. Feierabend
Rosalind L. Feierabend

Although political instability is a concept that can be explicated in more than one way, the definition used in this analysis limits its meaning to aggressive, politically relevant behaviors. Specifically, it is defined as the degree or the amount of aggression directed by individuals or groups within the political system against other groups or against the complex of officeholders and individuals and groups associated with them. Or, conversely, it is the amount of aggression directed by these officeholders against other individuals, groups, or officeholders within the polity.

Once this meaning is ascribed, the theoretical insights and elaborations of frustration-aggression theory become available (Berkowitz, 1962, 1965; Buss, 1961; Dollard et al., 1939; McNeil, 1959; Maier, 1949). Perhaps the most basic and generalized postulate of the theory maintains that "aggression is always the result of frustration" (Dollard et al., 1939, p. 3), while frustration may lead to other modes of behavior, such as constructive solutions to problems. Furthermore, aggression is not likely to occur if aggressive behavior is inhibited through devices associated with the notion of punishment. Or it may be displaced onto objects other than those perceived as the frustrating agents.

[1] The authors gratefully acknowledge support from the San Diego State College Foundation and from the National Science Foundation (Grant No. 1781).

These studies represent a revised and abridged version of a manuscript awarded the 1966 Socio-Psychological Prize of the American Association for the Advancement of Science. The first three studies are reprinted From *The Journal of Conflict Resolution*, X, No. 3 (September, 1966), 249–71, by permission of the publisher. Footnotes have been renumbered.

The utility of these few concepts is obvious. Political instability is identified as aggressive behavior. It should then result from situations of unrelieved, socially experienced frustration. Such situations may be typified as those in which levels of social expectations, aspirations, and needs are raised for many people for significant periods of time, and yet remain unmatched by equivalent levels of satisfactions. The notation:

$$\frac{\text{social want satisfaction}}{\text{social want formation}} = \frac{\text{systemic}}{\text{frustration}}$$

indicates this relationship.

In applying the frustration-aggression framework to the political sphere, the concept of punishment may be identified with the notion of coerciveness of political regimes. And the constructive solution of problems is related to the political as well as the administrative, entrepreneurial, and other capabilities available in the environment of politics. The notion of displacement may furthermore be associated with the occurrence of scapegoating against minority groups or aggression in the international sphere or in individual behaviors.

The following general hypotheses are yielded by applying frustration-aggression theory to the problem of political stability:

1. Under a situation of relative lack of systemic frustration, political stability is to be expected.
2. If systemic frustration is present, political stability still may be predicted, given the following considerations:
   a. It is a nonparticipant society. Politically relevant strata capable of action are largely lacking.
   b. It is a participant society in which constructive solutions to frustrating situations are available or anticipated. (The effectiveness of government and also the legitimacy of regimes will be relevant factors.)

c. If a sufficiently coercive government is capable of preventing overt acts of hostility against itself, then a relatively stable polity may be anticipated.
d. If as a result of the coerciveness of government, the aggressive impulse is vented or displaced in aggression against minority groups and/or
e. against other nations, then stability can be predicted.
f. If individual acts of aggression are sufficiently abundant to provide an outlet, stability may occur in the face of systemic frustration.
3. However, in the relative absence of these qualifying conditions, aggressive behavior in the form of political instability is predicted to be the consequence of systemic frustration.

Methodology

The methodology of the studies is indicated by the scope of the problem. Concern is not with the dynamics underlying stability in any one particular country but with the determinants of stability within all national political systems. As many cases as possible, or at least an appropriate sample of cases, must be analyzed. Thus the present studies are cross-national endeavors in which data are collected and analyzed for as many as 84 polities. (The 84 nations are listed in Table 1.) The cross-national method is here conceived in similar terms as the cross-cultural studies of anthropology (Feierabend, 1962; Murdock, 1957; Whiting and Child, 1953).

In order to carry out the research, data on internal conflict behaviors were collected for 84 nations for a fifteen-year period, 1948–1962. The data derive from two sources: *Deadline Data on World Affairs* and the *Encyclopaedia Britannica Yearbooks*. They are organized into a particular format in which each instability event is characterized,

Table 1

FREQUENCY DISTRIBUTION OF COUNTRIES IN TERMS OF THEIR DEGREE OF RELATIVE POLITICAL STABILITY, 1955–1961 (STABILITY SCORE SHOWN FOR EACH COUNTRY)

0 STABILITY	1	2	3	4	5	6
N. Zea. 000	Norway 104	W. Germany 217	Tunisia 328	France 499	India 599	Indonesia 699
	Netherlands 104	Czech. 212	Gr. Britain 325	U. of S. Africa 495	Argentina 599	Cuba 699
	Cambodia 104	Finland 211	Portugal 323	Haiti 478	Korea 596	Colombia 681
	Sweden 103	Romania 206	Uruguay 318	Poland 465	Venezuela 584	Laos 652
	Saudi Ar. 103	Ireland 202	Israel 317	Spain 463	Turkey 583	Hungary 652
	Iceland 103	Costa Rica 202	Canada 317	Dom. Rep. 463	Lebanon 581	
	Philippines 101		U.S. 316	Iran 459	Iraq 579	
	Luxembourg 101		Taiwan 314	Ceylon 454	Bolivia 556	
			Libya 309	Japan 453	Syria 554	
			Austria 309	Thailand 451	Peru 552	
			E. Germany 307	Mexico 451	Guatemala 546	
			Ethiopia 307	Ghana 451	Brazil 541	
			Denmark 306	Jordan 448	Honduras 535	
			Australia 306	Sudan 445	Cyprus 526	
			Switzer. 303	Morocco 443		
				Egypt 438		
				Pakistan 437		
				Italy 433		
				Belgium 432		
				Paraguay 431		
				U.S.S.R. 430		
				Nicaragua 430		
				Chile 427		
				Burma 427		
				Yugoslavia 422		
				Panama 422		
				Ecuador 422		
				China 422		
				El Salvador 421		
				Liberia 415		
				Malaya 413		
				Albania 412		
				Greece 409		
				Bulgaria 407		
				Afghanistan 404		

STABILITY ⟶ ⟶ INSTABILITY

according to country in which it occurs, date, persons involved, presence or absence of violence, and other pertinent characteristics (Feierabend and Feierabend, 1965b). The data are on IBM cards, creating a storage bank of some 5,000 events.[2]

Study 1: The Analysis of the Dependent Variable: Political Stability

WITH BETTY A. NESVOLD, FRANCIS W. HOOLE, AND NORMAN G. LITELL

In order to evaluate the political stability-instability continuum, data collected on internal conflict behavior were scaled. The ordering of specific instability events into a scale was approached from the viewpoint of both construct validity and consensual validation (Nesvold, 1964).

A seven-point instrument was devised, ranging from 0 (denoting extreme stability) through 6 (denoting extreme instability). Each point of the scale was observationally defined in terms of specific events representing differing degrees of stability or instability. An illustration may be given of one item typical of each position on the scale. Thus, for example, a general election is an item associated with a 0 position on the rating instructions. Resignation of a cabinet official falls into the 1 position on the scale; peaceful demonstrations into the 2 position; assassination of a significant political figure into the 3 position; mass arrests into the 4 position; *coups d'état* into the 5 position; and civil war into the 6 position.

Consensual validation for this intensity scale was obtained by asking judges to sort the same events along the same

continuum. The level of agreement among judges on the distribution of the items was fairly high (Pearson $r = .87$). Other checks performed on the reliability of the method were a comparison of the assignment of items to positions on the scale by two independent raters. Their level of agreement for the task, involving data from 84 countries for a seven-year time period, was very high (Pearson $r = .935$).

Using this scaling instrument, stability profiles for the sample of 84 nations were ascertained for the seven-year period, 1955–1961. Countries were assigned to groups on the basis of the most unstable event which they experienced during this seven-year period. Thus countries which experienced a civil war were placed in group 6; countries which were prey to a *coup d'état* were placed in group 5; countries with mass arrests were assigned to group 4, and so on. The purpose of this assignment was to weight intensity (or quality) of instability events equally with the frequency (or quantity) of events.

Following the allotment to groups, a sum total of each country's stability ratings was calculated. Countries were then rank-ordered within groups on the basis of this frequency sum total. The results of the ratings are given in Table 1.

In this table, it may be seen first of all that the distribution is skewed. Instability is more prevalent than stability within the sample of nations, and the largest proportion of countries are those experiencing an instability event with a scale weighting of 4. Furthermore, there is an interesting combination of countries at each scale position. The most stable scale positions, by and large, include modern nations but also a sprinkling of markedly underdeveloped polities and some nations from the Communist bloc. Again, the small group of extremely unstable countries at scale position 6 comprise nations from Latin

[2] The data bank of political instability events, including the *Code Index* to the bank, instructions to raters, etc., is available through the Inter-University Consortium for Political Research, Box 1248, Ann Arbor, Michigan.

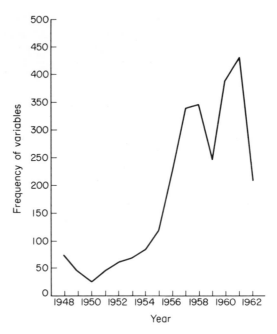

FIGURE 1. Frequency of Variables by Year,
1948–1962.

America, Asia, and the Communist bloc. The United States, contrary perhaps to ethnocentric expectations, is not at scale position 1 although it is on the stable side of the scale.

Another approach to the ordering of internal conflict behavior was based upon frequency alone (Hoole, 1964).[3] The frequency of occurrence of 30 types of internal conflict behaviors was determined for the 84 countries for the time period, 1948–1962. Analysis in terms of frequency was used in three different ways:

1. A global instability profile for all types of events, for all countries, was drawn to show changes in world level of instability during the time period under study. As may be seen in Figure 1,

[3] The data used in Hoole's 1964 study were gathered from a single source, *Deadline Data on World Affairs*. The data bank as presently constituted comprises two sources, *Deadline Data on World Affairs* and *The Encyclopaedia Britannica Yearbooks*.

instability has been on the increase in recent years, reaching one peak in the late 1950's and an even higher level in the early 1960's.

2. Frequencies of particular types of instability behaviors were compared for the entire sample of countries. The range of frequencies was from 18 (execution of significant persons) to 403 (acquisition of office). When the events were rank-ordered in terms of frequency of occurrence and the rank-ordering divided into quartiles, the first quartile, with the highest frequency of occurrence (1,555 occurrences) included events denoting routine governmental change (such as acquisition of office, vacation of office, elections, and significant changes of laws). The second quartile (704 occurrences) appeared to be one of unrest, including such events as large-scale demonstrations, general strikes, arrests, and martial law. The third quartile (333 occurrences) indicated serious societal

disturbance, in the form of *coups d'état*, terrorism and sabotage, guerrilla warfare, and exile. And the fourth quartile (150 occurrences) consisted primarily of events connoting violence: executions, severe riots, civil war. Thus an inverse relationship was revealed between the frequency of occurrence of an event and the intensity of violence which it denotes.

3. Finally, countries were compared for the relative frequency of occurrence of all thirty instability behaviors during this time period. The range was from 136 events (France) to one event (Switzerland). The median of this distribution was represented by Laos and Burma, with 28 and 26 events, respectively.

An additional refinement in the understanding of political instability is achieved by factor analysis, which reduces the large number of observed variables to a smaller number of underlying dimensions. Four previous factor analyses of internal conflict behaviors have been performed. Rummel (1963), factor-analyzing nine types of internal conflict behaviors for a three-year time period (1955–1957), emerged with three underlying dimensions: turmoil, revolution, and subversion. Tanter (1964, 1966), replicating the Rummel variables for the years 1958–1960, found a two-factor solution: turmoil and internal war. Recently, Rummel (1966) factor-analyzed thirteen variables obtained from Eckstein's collection of internal conflict behaviors (Eckstein, 1962) for the time period 1946–1950. This factor analysis again yielded three dimensions, which Rummel identifies with the three dimensions of the 1963 factor solution, namely, revolution, subversion, and turmoil. Hoole (1964) factor-analyzed 30 variables collected over a fifteen-year time span, 1948–1962, from a single source (see footnote 2), and emerged with five major and five minor

factors. The five major factors were labeled: demonstrations, change of officeholder, riots, guerrilla warfare, and strikes.

Most recently, Feierabend, Feierabend, and Litell (1966), using Hoole's 30 variables for the fifteen-year period 1948–1962 and the complete data bank derived from two sources, performed a factor analysis with a principal components solution and an orthogonal Varimax rotation. (See Table 2 for the rotated factor matrix.) Nine factors emerged. The first three of these, ranked according to importance in terms of the amount of variance accounted for after rotation, were labeled, first, a turmoil dimension (characterized by violence and mass participation); second, a palace-revolution–revolt dimension (distinguished by a marked lack of mass support); and, third, a power-struggle–purge dimension (connoting violent upheavals and changes of office within regimes). It will be noted that there is definite correspondence between the first two factors revealed in this analysis and the factors discovered by both Rummel and Tanter.

Looking at the variables with the highest loadings on each factor, we see that the first factor comprises strikes of all types; demonstrations and riots, large and small, violent and severe; and also mass arrests and terrorism. One could say that it denotes serious, widespread disturbance, anomie, popular mass participation, and some governmental retaliation.

The second factor presents a sharp contrast to this mass turmoil dimension. It encompasses revolts, *coups d'état*, martial law, arrests of politically prominent leaders, and governmental action against specific groups. These events do not connote mass participation but rather extreme instability created by highly organized and conspiratorial elites and cliques. And the third factor presents yet another

Table 2

ROTATED FACTOR MATRIX OF DOMESTIC CONFLICT MEASURES

Factors*

Variables	Mass Participation—Turmoil	Palace Revolution—Revolt	Power Struggle—Purge	Riot	Election	Demonstration	Imprisonment	Civil War	Guerrilla Warfare
1. Elections	29	-02	09	-18	70*	-10	-17	-05	-23
2. Vacation of office	38	08	74*	-14	20	-11	-15	-25	09
3. Significant change of laws	38	41	41	-01	31	15	-16	-23	-11
4. Acquisition of office	29	06	75*	-19	15	-04	-25	-19	22
5. Crisis within a nongovernmental organization	40	13	12	-21	04	-09	62*	07	-23
6. Organization of opposition party	08	10	-02	02	56*	36	19	-39	-10
7. Repressive action against specific groups	46	61*	27	01	-03	16	12	04	12
8. Micro strikes	67*	00	-15	-26	-16	05	12	03	23
9. General strikes	73*	13	04	-42	09	-06	03	08	-18
10. Macro strikes	43	-22	-11	-35	15	-17	-33	-12	-19
11. Micro demonstrations	61*	19	-02	02	20	59*	10	03	02
12. Macro demonstrations	73*	-01	00	26	06	19	18	-21	03
13. Micro riots	46	11	-06	68*	27	-03	-03	-15	11
14. Macro riots	69*	28	-04	33	20	02	04	-08	-05
15. Severe macro riots	64*	-03	-04	53*	11	-19	-02	-20	14
16. Arrests of significant persons	09	64*	54*	07	-14	-06	23	-10	-01
17. Imprisonment of significant persons	-14	12	49	17	-05	16	38	-33	-22
18. Arrests of few insignificant persons	42	09	05	-08	07	75*	07	07	21
19. Mass arrests of insignificant persons	52*	33	14	54*	-12	-02	-01	05	01
20. Imprisonment of insignificant persons	26	-08	09	08	-12	34	64*	-03	-14
21. Assassination	17	40	23	06	24	23	-07	-10	56*
22. Martial law	11	71*	03	03	15	09	-27	-06	-08
23. Execution of significant persons	-08	01	54*	31	-26	14	-04	31	05
24. Execution of insignificant persons	01	-10	63*	32	-07	12	-02	47	-02
25. Terrorism and sabotage	62*	28	12	-21	13	-01	10	07	38
26. Guerrilla warfare	04	42	07	-19	19	-35	25	21	55*
27. Civil war	-14	25	31	14	45	08	-08	60*	02
28. Coup d'état	03	69*	07	01	-02	12	-40	07	-32
29. Revolts	06	75*	-01	11	07	-01	-10	32	16
30. Exile	-09	40	00	03	-36	32	-19	-13	04
Percentage of common variance	23.37	16.30	13.20	9.67	8.33	8.00	7.99	6.76	6.40 = 100.0
Percentage of total variance	23.33	11.11	7.52	6.77	5.89	5.32	4.18	3.82	3.62 = 71.46

divergent pattern, including acquisition and loss of office, arrests and executions of politically significant figures, and some punitive action. Mass turmoil is not evident, as on the first factor; neither is the situation one of revolt and *coup d'état*. This is an instability dimension of violent internal power struggles, purges, depositions, and changes within ruling parties and cliques, which nevertheless remain in power.

The nine factors in combination account for 71.5 percent of the total variance. After rotation the three first factors combined account for over half of the common variance (53 percent). The remaining six factors, accounting in combination for less than half of the common variance, seem to reveal the following patterns: a specific riot dimension; an election dimension; two factors connoting mild, limited unrest; and, finally, two separate dimensions of civil war and guerrilla warfare, respectively, the extreme forms of political instability.

Study 2: The Relation of Social Frustration and Modernity to Political Stability

WITH BETTY A. NESVOLD

Once the data for the dependent variable, political stability, were collected, factor-analyzed, and scaled, the major step of seeking correlates of instability became feasible. In this attempt, two generalized and related hypotheses were investigated. (1) *The higher (lower) the social want formation in any given society and the lower (higher) the social want satisfaction, the greater (the less) the systemic frustration and the greater (the less) the impulse to political instability.* (2) *The highest and the lowest points of the modernity continuum in any given society will tend to produce maximum stability in the political order, while a medium position on the continuum will produce maximum instability* (Nesvold, 1964).

These hypotheses embody the basic propositions of the frustration-aggression theory, as well as insights gained from the literature on processes of modernization (Cutright, 1963; Deutsch, 1961; Lerner, 1958). In the first hypothesis, the discrepancy between social wants and social satisfactions is postulated to be the index of systemic frustration. The relationship is represented as follows:

$$\frac{\text{want satisfaction low}}{\text{want formation high}} = \text{high frustration}$$

$$\frac{\text{want satisfaction low}}{\text{want formation low}} = \text{low frustration}$$

$$\frac{\text{want satisfaction high}}{\text{want formation high}} = \text{low frustration}$$

A variety of social conditions may satisfy or leave unsatisfied the social wants of different strata of the population within social systems. In our present century the process of modernization is certain to create new wants and aspirations, as well as to lead to their satisfaction.

The notion of modernity denotes a very complex set of social phenomena. It includes the aspiration and capacity in a society to produce and consume a wide range and quantity of goods and services. It includes high development in science, technology, and education, and high attainment in scores of specialized skills. It includes, moreover, new structures of social organization and participation, new sets of aspirations, attitudes, and ideologies. Modern affluent nations, with their complex of economic, political, and social systems, serve best as models of modernity to nations emerging from traditional society. In these transitional nations, the growing, politically relevant strata of the population are all participants in modern life. Lerner (1957), for one, states categorically that once traditional societies are exposed to the modern way of life, without exception they desire benefits associated with modernity.

The acquisition of modern goals, although an integral aspect of modernity, is hardly synonymous with their attainment. The notion of "the revolution of rising expectations" (Lerner, 1958), also termed "the revolution of rising frustrations," points to the essentially frustrating nature of the modernization process. The arousal of an underdeveloped society to awareness of complex modern patterns of behavior and organization brings with it a desire to emulate and achieve the same high level of satisfaction. But there is an inevitable lag between aspiration and achievement which varies in length with the specific condition of the country. Furthermore, it may be postulated that the peak discrepancy between systemic goals and their satisfaction, and hence the maximum frustration, should come somewhere in the middle of the transitional phase between traditional society and the achievement of modernity. It is at this middle stage that awareness of modernity and exposure to modern patterns should be complete, that is, at a theoretical ceiling, whereas achievement levels would still be lagging far behind. Prior to this theoretical middle stage, exposure and achievement would both be lower. After the middle stage, exposure can no longer increase, since it already amounts to complete awareness, but achievement will continue to progress, thus carrying the nation eventually into the stage of modernity. Thus, in contrast to transitional societies, it may be postulated that traditional and modern societies will be less frustrated and therefore will tend to be more stable than transitional societies.

The most direct way to ascertain systemic frustration is through field work in the many countries, administering questionnaires (See Almond and Verba, 1963; Cantril, 1963, 1965; Doob, 1960; Inkeles, 1960). For the purpose of this study, an inexpensive and very indirect method was adopted.

The highly theoretical notions of want satisfaction and want formation were translated into observable definitions. For this purpose, available collections of cross-national statistical data were consulted and a few statistical items were chosen as appropriate indicators. The following selection of indicators was made. GNP and caloric intake per capita, physicians and telephones per unit of population were singled out as indices of satisfaction. Newspapers and radios per unit of population were also included. Many other indicators denoting material or other satisfactions could have served the purpose. The selection was guided by parsimony as well as availability of data.

The indicators, of course, have different significance in referring to the satisfaction of different wants. Furthermore, their significance may vary at different levels of relative abundance or scarcity. A great deal of theorizing is necessary to select and use the indicators wisely. For example, it is possible that in a country with many physicians and telephones people may still be starving. Or, beyond a certain point, caloric intake cannot measure the satisfaction of some other less basic needs than hunger, while GNP per capita may do so.

For want formation, literacy and urbanization were chosen as indicators. This selection was influenced by the notion of exposure to modernity (Deutsch, 1961; Lerner, 1958). Exposure to modernity was judged a good mechanism for the formation of new wants, and literacy and city life were taken as the two agents most likely to bring about such exposure.

These eight indices (GNP, caloric intake, telephones, physicians, newspapers, radios, literacy, and urbanization) were used to construct both a frustration index and a modernity index. The modernity index was formed by combining scores on all of the eight indicators. Raw scores were first transformed into standard scores and then a mean standard score was calculated for each of the 84 countries on the basis of the available data. The frustration index was a ratio. A country's combined coded score on the six satisfaction indices (GNP, caloric intake, telephones, physicians, newspapers, and radios) was divided by either the country's coded literacy or coded urbanization score, whichever was higher.[4]

The data on the independent variables were collected for the years 1948–1955 whereas the stability ratings were made for the years 1955–1961. It was assumed that some lag would occur before social frustrations would make themselves felt in political aggressions, that is, political instability. (Country scores on the frustration and modernity indexes are given in the Appendix.)

Results

The main finding of the study is that the higher the level of systemic frustration, as measured by the indices selected, the greater the political instability. The results are shown in Table 3. The stable countries are those which experience

[4] The difficulty of dividing these highly correlated indicators should be noted. Each contains some error component due to the unreliable reporting of cross-national data. For an estimate of error in cross-national data, see Russett (1964) and Rummel (1963).

the least amount of measured systemic frustration. Conversely, the countries beset by political instability also suffer a high level of systemic frustration, although certain interesting exceptions occur.

Each indicator of want formation and satisfaction is also significantly related to political stability. The relationships between each indicator and stability are presented in Table 4. Another finding of interest in this table is that all eight indicators do not predict degree of stability with equal efficiency. Level of literacy is the best single predictor, as seen by the .90 degree of relationship (Yule's Q) between literacy and stability. Comparatively, GNP is one of the weaker predictors, along with percent of urbanization, population per physician, and caloric intake per capita per day.

These data on the predictors of political stability also determine empirical threshold values for each indicator. Above these values, countries are predominantly stable; below them, countries are predominantly unstable. The cutting point for each of the indicators was selected so as to reveal the maximum difference between stable and unstable countries.

From these empirical thresholds, a composite picture of the stable country emerges. It is a society which is 90 percent or more literate; with 65 or more radios and 120 or more newspapers per 1,000 population; with two percent or more of the population having telephones; with 2,525 or more calories per day per person; with not more than 1,900 persons per physician; with a GNP of $300 or more per person per year; and with 45 percent or more of the population living in urban centers. If all of these threshold values are attained by a society, there is an extremely high probability that the country will achieve relative political

Table 3

RELATIONSHIP BETWEEN LEVEL OF SYSTEMIC FRUSTRATION AND DEGREE OF POLITICAL STABILITY*

Degree of Political Stability	Index of Systemic Frustration			
	Ratio of Want Formation to Want Satisfaction			
	High Systemic Frustration		*Low Systemic Frustration*	*Total*
Unstable	Bolivia	Iran	Argentina	
	Brazil	Iraq	Belgium	
	Bulgaria	Italy	France	
	Ceylon	Japan	Lebanon	
	Chile	Korea	Morocco	
	Colombia	Mexico	Union of South Africa	
	Cuba	Nicaragua		
	Cyprus	Pakistan		
	Dom. Republic	Panama		
	Ecuador	Paraguay		
	Egypt	Peru		
	El Salvador	Spain		
	Greece	Syria		
	Guatemala	Thailand		
	Haiti	Turkey		
	India	Venezuela		
	Indonesia	Yugoslavia		
		34	6	40
Stable	Philippines		Australia New Zealand	
	Tunisia		Austria Norway	
			Canada Portugal	
			Costa Rica Sweden	
			Czech. Switzerland	
			Denmark United States	
			Finland Uruguay	
			West Germany	
			Great Britain	
			Iceland	
			Ireland	
			Israel	
		2	Netherlands 20	22
Grand Total		36	26	62

Chi square** = 30.5, p = <.001   Yule's Q = .9653
* The number of cases in this and the following tables varies with the data available in the UN statistical sources. This table includes only those countries with data on all eight indices.
** All chi squares in this and the following tables are corrected for continuity in view of the small frequencies in the nonconfirming cells.

stability. Conversely, if gratifications are less than these threshold values, the more they fail to meet these levels, the greater the likelihood of political instability.

In order to investigate the relationship between modernity and stability, countries were rank-ordered on the modernity index and the distribution was broken into three groups representing modern countries, transitional countries, and traditional countries. The cutting points for these three groups were to some extent arbitrary: the 24 countries which were highest on the modernity index were selected as the

Table 4

RELATIONSHIPS BETWEEN THE EIGHT INDICATORS OF SYSTEMIC FRUSTRATION AND DEGREE OF POLITICAL STABILITY

A. LITERACY

	% Literate		
	Low (below 90%)	High (above 90%)	Total
Unstable	48	5	53
Stable	10	19	29
Total	58	24	82

Chi square = 25.83; p = <.001
Yule's Q = .90

B. RADIOS

	Per 1,000 Population		
	Low (below 65)	High (above 65)	Total
Unstable	45	6	51
Stable	9	20	29
Total	54	26	80

Chi square = 25.02; p = <.001
Yule's Q = .887

C. NEWSPAPERS

	Per 1,000 Population		
	Low (below 120)	High (above 120)	Total
Unstable	48	5	53
Stable	6	10	16
Total	54	15	69

Chi square = 17.34; p = <.001
Yule's Q = .88

D. TELEPHONES

	% of Population Owning Telephones		
	Low (below 2%)	High (above 2%)	Total
Unstable	35	6	41
Stable	7	18	25
Total	42	24	66

Chi square = 19.68; p = <.001
Yule's Q = .875

E. CALORIES

	Per Capita Per Day		
	Low (below 2,525)	High (above 2,525)	Total
Unstable	39	10	49
Stable	8	20	28
Total	47	30	77

Chi square = 17.42; p = <.001
Yule's Q = .81

F. PHYSICIANS

	People per Physician		
	Low (above 1,900)	High (below 1,900)	Total
Unstable	40	13	53
Stable	6	19	25
Total	46	32	78

Chi square = 11.41; p = <.001
Yule's Q = .81

G. GNP

	Per Capita (in U.S. Dollars)		
	Low (below 300)	High (above 300)	Total
Unstable	36	8	44
Stable	9	18	27
Total	45	26	71

Chi square = 14.92; p = <.001
Yule's Q = .80

H. URBANIZATION

	% of Population Living in Urban Centers		
	Low (below 45%)	High (above 45%)	Total
Unstable	38	6	44
Stable	11	15	26
Total	49	21	70

Chi square = 13.08; p = <.001
Yule's Q = .79

Table 5

RELATIONSHIP BETWEEN MODERNITY AND STABILITY

Modernity Level	N	Mean Stability Score	t	p*	t	p*
Modern countries	24	268 ⎫				
			6.18	<.001 ⎫		
Transitional countries	37	472 ⎬			3.71	<.01
			1.53	>.05 ⎭		
Traditional countries	23	420 ⎭				

* Probability levels are two-tailed.

modern group. The traditional group was chosen to be equal in size to the modern group, while ranking at the opposite end of the modernity continuum. The remaining countries, falling between the modern and traditional groups, were designated transitional. The difficulty in determining the true state of the countries lies not so much in finding the cutting point for the modern group as in selecting the traditional one. Truly traditional countries do not report data and hence have no way of being included in the study. The countries designated traditional are simply less modern than those classed as transitional, but they have nonetheless been exposed to modernity.[5]

A mean stability score was calculated for each group of countries. The differences between the mean stability scores for the three groups were then estimated. According to the hypothesis, the difference in mean stability score should be greatest between the transitional group and either of the other two groups. The difference in mean stability score between modern and traditional countries should not be significant. The results are given in Table 5.

As may be seen in the table, the predicted difference between the stability level of modern and of transitional countries emerges as highly significant. The difference between modern and traditional countries is less but nonetheless also significant. And the difference between traditional and transitional countries does not reach significance. The difficulty in obtaining data on truly traditional countries undoubtedly contributes to the lack of significant difference between countries labeled in this sample as transitional and traditional.

In view of the lack of support in these 84 nations for the hypothesized curvilinear relationship between modernity and stability, the assumption may be made that all of the countries have been exposed to modernity. Hence want formation should be at a relatively high level throughout the sample. One might hypothesize that want formation reaches an early maximum with exposure to modernity, after which further awareness of the modern world can no longer increase desire for modernity. Under these conditions, the modernity index is also in fact a frustration index, indicating the extent to which these measured economic satisfactions are present within a society which may be presumed to have already been exposed to modernity.

To compare the relative efficacy of these two frustration indices, product-moment correlations were calculated between each index and stability. The results show that while both indices are

[5] This modernity ranking, based on eight indices, is highly comparable to that of Russett *et al.* (1964) based on GNP alone. A Spearman *r* calculated between the two rank-orderings is .92.

significantly correlated with stability, the correlation between the so-called modernity index and stability is the higher of the two. The product-moment correlation between modernity and stability is .625; the correlation between the so-called frustration index and stability is .499. An *eta* calculated between the modernity index and the stability index, to show curvilinearity of relationship, is $\eta = .667$, which is not significantly different from the Pearson *r* of .625. Thus again the hypothesis of curvilinearity between modernity and stability is not supported.

Study 3: The Prediction of Changes in Political Stability over Time

WITH WALLACE R. CONROE

In the previous study, stability, modernity, and the frustration index were all calculated as static measures. Each variable was represented by a single score, indicating an overall estimate of the level of the variable during the time period under study. The question raised in this study concerns the effect of relative rates of change over time in the ecological variables. It seeks to uncover dynamic relationships which would supplement the static ones.

The assumptions made in this study of dynamic trends are based on a view of change as essentially disruptive in character. The process of transition toward modernity, discussed in the previous study, is one during which, almost inevitably, goals and demands will exceed achievements. It is also a process during which former patterns of behavior, outdated technologies, established roles, statuses and norms must all give way to new, unfamiliar patterns. The transitional personality is frustrated by his breakoff from the past and the uncertainty of the present.

To this picture of a society in ferment is now added the notion of the relevance of time. Insofar as the transitional process is a gradual one, there is a possibility that new patterns may be adopted and adjusted to before old ones are completely abandoned. There is also the further possibility that achievements may begin to approximate the level at which aspirations are set, before aspirations move even further ahead. Where the transitional process is rapid, however, the effect will be to decrease the possibility of adaptation, thus increasing the probability of disruption, chaos, and feelings of personal discontent. Furthermore, the more rapid the process of change, the greater the likelihood of opening new perspectives of modernity, that is, of creating higher and higher levels of aspiration, thus inevitably increasing the gap between aspiration and achievement, at least in the early stages.

Thus the hypothesis promulgated in this study is that: *the faster (the slower) the rate of change in the modernization process within any given society, the higher (the lower) the level of political instability within that society* (Conroe, 1965).

As a first step in investigating this hypothesis, yearly changes in instability pattern for each of the 84 countries were calculated for the time period under study, 1948–1962. From the evidence accumulated on the global frequency of occurrence of instability events (Figure 1), it was clear that the world instability level increased sharply during the fifteen years, reaching its highest peak in the last six years. In order to compare countries as to their relative position on the instability continuum over time, the period was split in half and country instability scores were calculated for each seven-year period separately. The country scores for the second period tended to be higher than for the first one. A rank-order correlation between stability levels in the two seven-year periods for the 84 countries showed a moderate degree of relationship (Spearman $r = .43$). Not only was the instability level generally on the increase, but there was a tendency for countries to maintain their relatively stable or unstable positions over time.

As a further, more refined method of analyzing the stability–instability continuum over time, stability scores for the 84 nations were calculated on a year-by-year basis and plotted as a function of time. To characterize the time function, at least two measures were necessary: the slope of a best-fit line, indicating the average instability trend, over the fifteen-year period; and amplitude of change from year to year, as estimated by variance.

A calculation of the relationship between these two measures showed them to be independent and unrelated dimensions (Spearman $r = .06$). Of the two, only amplitude was related to static stability level as measured by the intensity scale (Spearman $r = .64$). This indicates that the meaning of instability as empirically ascertained in these studies is identified with the fluctuation of instability rather than with the average trend over time. Furthermore, it is the measure of amplitude and not the average trend over time which is directly related to rate of change in the independent variables. The average instability trend over time (increases or decreases) is related to the ecological variables only when combined with the data on yearly fluctuations in stability levels.

Turning to the predictors of instability, interest was in the effect of changes in levels of ecological variables upon changes in stability. The general hypothesis of this study was that rapid change will be experienced as an unsettling, frustrating societal condition and hence will be associated with a high level of internal conflict. To test the hypothesis, nine predictor indices were selected for study: caloric intake, literacy, primary and postprimary education, national income, cost of living, infant mortality, urbanization, and radios per thousand population. Data for these indices were collected for a 28-year period from 1935 through 1962. Plotting of the data revealed a consistent trend for substantially all countries in the sample to improve their position on all indices over time. Hence a yearly percent rate of change was calculated for each indicator.[6] These indicators are not identical to those of the previous study, although there is overlap. The new choice was determined by the availability of data for as many years as possible and for a maximum number of countries in the sample.

To summarize the results of the interrelationship between rates of change in the independent indices and rate of change in stability, it may be said that the higher the rate of change on the indices, the greater the increase in instability. A contingency table showing the relationship between mean rate of change on six or more of the nine indices and instability, as measured only by variation in pattern (amplitude), is given in Table 6.

As may be seen from the table, the countries experiencing a highly erratic instability pattern are those also undergoing a rapid rate of change in the ecological variables selected for study. On the other hand, countries experiencing political stability in the sense of a steady pattern are the static countries in which ecological change proceeds at a slower pace.

Furthermore, the rate at which modernization occurred from 1935 to

[6] The yearly percent rate of change on the ecological variables was calculated by subtracting the lowest value of the variable in the 28-year period from the highest value attained, dividing by the lowest value to convert to a percentage change, and then dividing by the number of years spanned to obtain the yearly percentage change.

Table 6

RELATIONSHIP BETWEEN MEAN RATE OF CHANGE ON ECOLOGICAL VARIABLES AND RATE OF CHANGE IN STABILITY

Mean Rate of Change on Ecological Variables (%)	*Change in Stability:*		
	Amplitude of Fluctuations in Yearly Stability Scores		
	Low Change (Amplitude)	*High Change (Amplitude)*	*Total*
Low change	Argentina Mexico Australia Netherlands Austria New Zealand Bulgaria Norway Canada Pakistan Chile Philippines Denmark Spain Ecuador Sweden Finland Switzerland France Taiwan Guatemala Union of S. Africa Iceland United Kingdom Ireland United States Israel Uruguay Italy West Germany Luxembourg 31	Belgium Cuba Greece Hungary Paraguay 5	36
High change	Ceylon Ghana India Syria Turkey 5	Bolivia Japan Brazil Korea Burma Malaya Cambodia Morocco Colombia Panama Costa Rica Peru Dom. Republic Poland Egypt Portugal El Salvador Thailand Haiti Tunisia Honduras USSR Indonesia Venezuela Iraq Yugoslavia 26	31
Total	36	31	67*

Chi square = 30.0; p = <.001.
* The N on this and some of the following tables is reduced to include only those countries with data on six or more indices, from which to calculate the mean rate of change score.

1962 is correlated with static stability level in the 1955–1961 time period (as measured in Study 1). A Pearson r of .647 was found between rate of change (calculated as a combined measure on six or more of the nine indices) and static stability score. Relationships were also calculated between rates of change on each of the nine independent indices taken separately and instability level, measured both as a static score and as a dynamic fluctuation (variance measure) for the 1948–1962 period (see Table 7).

The pattern is somewhat the same for both sets of calculations, indicating

Table 7

**RANK-ORDER CORRELATIONS (RHO)
BETWEEN RATE OF CHANGE ON
ECOLOGICAL VARIABLES AND
TWO MEASURES OF STABILITY, 1948–1962**

	N	*Static Stability*	*Dynamic Stability (Amplitude)*
Primary education	70	.61	.57
Calories per capita per day	39	.49	.35
Postprimary education	30	.36	.41
Cost of living	72	.36	.21
Radios	82	.34	.31
Infant mortality rate	60	.33	.36
Urbanization	69	.17	.14
Literacy	82	.03	.01
National income	70	−.34	−.45

Table 8

**RELATIONSHIP BETWEEN MODERNITY LEVEL AND MEAN RATE OF CHANGE
ON ECOLOGICAL VARIABLES**

Mean Rate of Change (%)	*Traditional Countries*	*Transitional Countries*		*Modern Countries*		*Total*
Low change	Pakistan Philippines Taiwan	Bulgaria Chile Cuba Guatemala Hungary Italy Mexico Paraguay Spain Union of South Africa		Argentina Australia Austria Belgium Canada Denmark Finland France Iceland Ireland Israel	Luxembourg Netherlands New Zealand Norway Sweden Switzerland United Kingdom United States Uruguay W. Germany	
	3	10		21		34
High change	Bolivia Burma Cambodia Ghana Haiti India Indonesia Iraq Malaya Morocco	Brazil Ceylon Colombia Costa Rica Dom. Rep. Ecuador Egypt El Salvador Greece Honduras Japan	Korea Panama Peru Poland Portugal Syria Thailand Tunisia Turkey Venezuela Yugoslavia	USSR		
	10	22		1		33
Total	13	32		22		67

Chi square = 31.0; $p = <.001$.

Table 9

RELATIONSHIP BETWEEN MODERNITY LEVEL AND RATE OF CHANGE IN NATIONAL INCOME

Rate of Change in National Income (%)	*Modernity Level*					*Total*
	Traditional Countries		*Transitional Countries*		*Modern Countries*	
Low change	Burma	Indonesia	Bulgaria	Honduras	E. Germany	
	Cambodia	Malaya	Colombia	Lebanon	Ireland	
	China	Morocco	Costa Rica	Panama	Switzerland	
	Ghana	Pakistan	Dom. Rep.	Poland	USSR	
	Haiti	Philippines	Ecuador	Portugal	United Kingdom	
	India	Sudan	Egypt	Syria		
	Iraq		El Salvador	Tunisia		
	Jordan		Guatemala	Venezuela		
	14		16		5	35
High change	Taiwan		Brazil	Mexico	Argentina	Luxembourg
			Chile	Paraguay	Australia	Netherlands
			Ceylon	Peru	Austria	New Zealand
			Cuba	Spain	Belgium	Norway
			Greece	Thailand	Canada	Sweden
			Hungary	Turkey	Denmark	United States
			Italy	Un. of So.	Finland	W. Germany
			Japan	Africa	France	
			Korea	Yugoslavia	Iceland	
					Israel	
	1		17		17	35
Total	15		33		22	70

Chi square $= 17.8$; $p = <.001$.

primary education to be the best single predictor of instability and literacy the worst.[7] The most interesting finding is the inverse relationship revealed between rate of change in national income and instability. In the case of this indicator, the higher the rate of change, the greater the likelihood of stability. This finding may be understood when one contrasts the pattern of rate of change on national income to that for the nine indices taken together (see Tables 8 and 9).

From Table 8 it is clear that all countries except the modern show a

high rate of change on ecological variables. (This again confirms the point made earlier that no truly traditional countries are included in the sample. By definition, a traditional country should be characterized by lack of change.) The modern countries are those undergoing the least amount of change. They are also those experiencing the least amount of instability.

In Table 9, however, we find the situation reversed for growth in national income. On this indicator, it is the modern countries which show the highest rate of change over time. National income may be viewed as a variable with no intrinsic ceiling and one on which marked improvement will not occur until a country is well advanced toward modernity and has achieved a relatively high standard on

[7] This finding is in contrast to the high level of relationship obtained between literacy and static stability level reported in Study 1. The explanation may lie in the observed inconsistency in the literacy data reported over the longer time period in various sources.

other ecological variables, such as literacy, education, caloric intake, and infant mortality. Thus again it is the modern countries which are the most stable and which show the greatest growth rate in national income.

A final comparison between rate of change in modernization and instability level was made by grouping countries on instability in terms of both amplitude of yearly fluctuations and general trend in instability over time (variance and slope). Three groups of countries were distinguished: stable countries (in which yearly fluctuations are low and the trend over time is either stationary or improving); unstable countries (in which yearly fluctuations are high and the trend over time is either stationary or worsening); and indeterminate countries which represent conflicting combinations of trend and fluctuation. Four levels of rate of change were also distinguished. With these refinements, the relationship between rate of modernization and instability level over time appears more clearly (see Table 10).

The countries with the lowest rate of change are predominantly stable, as measured both by a low level of yearly fluctuations in instability and by a lack of any worsening trend toward instability over time. Conversely, the countries with the highest rate of change on the ecological variables are beset by instability, as measured both by yearly fluctuations in instability levels and the absence of evidence of any improvement in trend toward stability over time. Furthermore, countries experiencing intermediate rates of change toward modernization are also intermediate in instability, showing some conflicting combination of fluctuation and trend over time.

In conclusion, one might speak of a syndrome which is exemplified by the modern group of nations. With interesting exceptions, they are relatively satisfied economically and relatively stable politically, no longer changing rapidly on many economic dimensions, although making sizable gains in national income. In contrast are the transitional nations, some moving more rapidly toward modernity than others but, by and large, all characterized by relative economic deprivation, a high rate of change on many economic dimensions but a low rate of growth on national income, and a strong tendency to political instability, finding overt expression in many diverse events such as strikes, demonstrations, riots, *coups d'état*, and even civil war.

On the basis of these findings, it may be suggested that one compelling reason for the greater stability of modern countries lies in their greater ability to satisfy the wants of their citizens. The less advanced countries are characterized by greater instability because of the aggressive responses to systemic frustration evoked in the populace. It could be argued simply that the increase in instability resulting from a change in ecological conditions is due to the disruptive effect of change. But it is also possible that the satisfaction of wants has a feedback effect, adding to the strength of the drive for more satisfactions. As wants start to be satisfied, the few satisfactions which are achieved increase the drive for more satisfactions, thus in effect adding to the sense of systemic frustration. It is only when a high enough level of satisfaction has been reached that a country will tend toward stability rather than instability.

Study 4: The Relationship between Political Instability and the Coerciveness and Permissiveness of National Political Systems

WITH JENNIFER G. WALTON

Conflict and frustration are bound to occur in the context of social action, yet aggression is not the uniform

Table 10
RELATIONSHIP BETWEEN MEAN RATE OF CHANGE ON ECOLOGICAL VARIABLES AND CHANGE IN STABILITY AS MEASURED BY VARIANCE AND SLOPE

Mean Rate of Change on Ecological Variables	Stable — Low variance and either negative or zero slope	Indeterminate — Low variance/positive slope or high variance/negative slope	Unstable — High variance and either positive or zero slope	Total
Low change	Norway, New Zealand, W. Germany, Australia, Denmark, Iceland, Israel, United States, Canada, Sweden, Switzerland, Netherlands, Luxembourg — 13	Great Britain, Austria — 2	Belgium — 1	16
Moderately low change	Ireland, Guatemala, Bulgaria, Taiwan, Finland, Italy, Chile, Philippines — 8	France, Un. S. Africa, Mexico, Pakistan, Greece, Argentina, Uruguay, Spain, Ecuador — 9	Cuba, Paraguay, Hungary — 3	20
Moderately high change	0	Thailand, Colombia, Egypt, Ceylon, Poland, Costa Rica, Ghana, Turkey, India — 9	Peru, Portugal, Panama, Brazil, Haiti, Iraq, Japan, Yugoslavia, Tunisia, Burma, U.S.S.R. — 11	20
High change	Syria — 1	Korea, Malaya — 2	El Salvador, Bolivia, Venezuela, Dom. Rep., Cambodia, Morocco, Honduras, Indonesia — 8	11
Totals	22	22	23	67

response. Other variables, in particular restraints or inhibitions to aggression, must also be taken into account. In the original formulation of the frustration-aggression hypothesis, Dollard *et al.* (1939, p. 33) postulated that "the inhibition of any act of aggression varies directly with the strength of the punishment anticipated for its expression." Punishment was seen to play a dual role. On the one hand, as already stated, it could serve to inhibit the aggressive response. On the other hand, interference with aggressive behavior in the form of punishment also served to heighten frustration and thus acted as a further instigation to aggression. Punishment itself, then, was seen as acting both as a "negative sanction" and as a source of frustration. The authors suggested that the strength of the anticipated punishment determined whether or not it functioned successfully as an inhibitor of aggression. Maier (1949), however, has emphasized the importance of the level of frustration experienced rather than simply the adequacy of the penalties imposed. Certain aggressive behaviors are likely to occur during periods of intense stress regardless of the penalties entailed.

The relationship of strength of punishment to instigation to aggression is, in fact, curvilinear. Low levels of punishment do not serve as inhibitors; it is only high levels of punishment which are likely to result in anxiety and withdrawal. Punishment at mid-levels of intensity acts as a frustrator and elicits further aggression, maintaining an aggression-punishment-aggression sequence (Buss, 1961, p. 58).

In order to fit the notion of punishment into the systemic frustration-political instability sequence, it must be described in politically relevant terms. Punishment is equated with patterns of permissiveness and coerciveness of political regimes. Thus a permissive system, commonly identified with free,

democratic states, will show greater tolerance for demonstrations of political unrest than will coercive systems, typically identified with tyrannous states.

The addition of the permissiveness-coerciveness variable to the systemic frustration-systemic aggression sequence leads to the following set of hypotheses:

1. *In the case of polities with permissive political regimes, there is a greater likelihood of political stability, the higher the level of socioeconomic systemic satisfaction. Conversely, there is a greater likelihood of political instability, the higher the level of socioeconomic systemic frustration.*
2. *In the case of polities with coercive political regimes, there is a greater likelihood of political stability if coerciveness is sufficiently high to act as a deterrent to aggression. Conversely, there is a greater likelihood of political instability if coerciveness is at mid-level, not sufficient to act as a deterrent to aggression but sufficient to be a source of systemic frustration.*
3. *Combining the variables of coerciveness of political regimes and socioeconomic systemic frustration yields the following predictions:*
   a. *The threshold level of coercion necessary to act as a deterrent to systemic aggression will be a function of the level of socioeconomic systemic frustration. The greater the socioeconomic systemic frustration, the higher the level of coerciveness necessary to act as a deterrent to aggression.*
   b. *The greatest tendency to political instability will result from a high level of socioeconomic systemic frustration in combination with mid-level coerciveness of political regime.* This combination, in fact, pools two sources of systemic frustration, one socioeconomic, the other political.
4. Finally, the coerciveness level of political regimes may be a function of, and possibly a response to, the level of socioeconomic systemic frustration. *The higher the level of systemic frustration,*

the higher the level of political coerciveness.

A curvilinear relationship is thus postulated between coercion and stability. Highly permissive and highly coercive governments are also those with relatively high levels of socio-economic systemic satisfaction. When coercion is not sufficiently strong, as in the authoritarian systems of transitional states, it will not be capable of preventing overt aggression and will further stimulate frustration. Political instability should then be greatest in these states at mid-levels of coerciveness.

In order to test these hypotheses, some method was needed to reduce the permissiveness-coerciveness variable to an empirical, measurable dimension. In defining political coerciveness, various authors and approaches were considered (Almond and Coleman, 1960; Deutsch, 1963; Easton, 1958; Lasswell and Kaplan, 1950). The most useful definition was felt to result from taking both Bay (1958) and Oppenheim (1961) as a point of departure. The following questions were asked as guidelines to assessing the political and social freedom present within a society:

1. To what degree are civil rights present and protected?
2. To what extent is political opposition tolerated and effective?
3. How democratic is the polity?

These three questions might seem to be redundant, in that they refer to three aspects of political regimes in which a common policy is pursued in most modern western democracies. Conceptually, however, they are three distinct domains and, in less developed societies at least, or in nineteenth-century European political history, the three are not necessarily characterized by concomitance of policy.

The task of assigning a value to permissiveness-coerciveness was pur-

sued by constructing an ordinal, six-point scale which rated countries from most permissive (scale position *1*) to most coercive (scale position *6*). The indicators appropriate to each rank position are given below (Walton, 1965):

Rating	Description of polity
1	*Most permissive:*

Civil rights present and protected; rights of political opposition protected, i.e., in press, parliament, party formation, etc.;

Government elected at regularized intervals in fair, free elections;

Public opinion effective in policy formation;

Significant heads of government limited in power and duration of office;

Legislative bodies effective participants in decision process;

Judicial bodies independent and have regularized procedures;

Tradition of structures mediating between individual and central government, e.g., strong local government, states' rights, etc.;

Constitution representative of sectors and interests within population, respected yet not impossible to amend.

| 2 | *Moderately permissive:* |

Civil rights protected by law with perhaps occasional attempts at infringement;

Rights of political opposition usually protected, e.g., press occasionally reprimanded, or certain parties illegal;

Government elected at periodic intervals in usually fair, free elections;

Public opinion usually effective in policy formation;

Significant head of government responsible to public or popular legislature yet may be more powerful or have greater ability to perpetuate his tenure in office;

Legislative bodies usually participate in decision process;

Judicial bodies adequately independent and regularized;

Structures mediating between individual and central government moderately strong;

Constitution representative, respected and procedures for amendment adequate.

3 *Slightly permissive:*

Intermittent interference with protection of civil rights, e.g., press occasionally suspended or censored, states of seige occasional;

Political opposition tolerated but generally ineffective, e.g., only one party effectively participates in decisions;

Government elected at more or less periodic intervals in elections which are usually free;

Public opinion occasionally effective in policy formation;

Significant head of government not very responsible, e.g., is hereditary office, or appointive from within nonpopular legislative branch;

Significant head of government may possess rather extraordinary powers within an otherwise democratic polity, or has been able to perpetuate tenure in office by changing the constitution, etc.;

Legislative bodies occasionally participate in decision-making process;

Judicial bodies adequately independent but may not have entirely fixed procedures, e.g., existence of ad hoc bodies or "drumhead courts" or military tribunals;

Structures mediating between individual and central government relatively weak;

Constitution rather easily altered, or, the converse, is rather difficult to amend.

4 *Slightly coercive:*

Regular infringement of civil rights, e.g., press regularly suspended or censored, or frequent states of seige;

Political opposition severely limited or harassed, e.g., occasional suspension of all parties, or opposition leaders arrested;

Government changes at arbitrary intervals set by party in power; elections often interfered with or manipulated;

Alternation of civilian and military government;

Significant head of government irresponsible or perpetual, i.e., unlimited by constitution, tradition, etc.;

Judicial bodies often interfered with by executive or legislature;

Few, and very weak, structures mediate between individual and central government;

Constitution unrepresentative of society, occasionally suspended or disregarded.

5 *Moderately coercive:*

Civil rights respected in arbitrary fashion, e.g., trade unions illegal or press severely censored;

Political opposition unlikely but not impossible, e.g., parties outlawed most of the time;

Government perpetual, elections usually serve no democratic function;

Public opinion usually disregarded in policy formation;

Significant head of government irresponsible, unlimited in powers or tenure of office;

Legislative bodies ineffective in policy formation;

Judicial bodies dependent on executive or legislature;

Constitution often suspended or extremely difficult to amend.

6 *Most coercive:*

Civil rights nonexistent, i.e., entirely dependent on whim of government;

Political opposition impossible, e.g., no parties or autonomous associational groups exist, government penetrates all institutions of society;

Government perpetual, elections serve only showcase function;

Public opinion disregarded in policy formation;

Significant head of government has dictatorial and absolute powers;

Legislative bodies serve only to reiterate executive decisions, have no powers of their own;

Judicial bodies completely dependent;

No intermediary structures or institutions exist between the individual and central government;

Constitution completely disregarded in practice, impossible to amend.

These criteria were applied to the sample of 84 nations used in the three previous studies, in order to arrive at a judgmental rating of these polities on the six-point, permissiveness-coerciveness scale. Approximately five separate works on each nation were consulted[8] before an overall judgment was made. A reliability check on the judgmental procedure consisted of a second rater judging a sample of the polities independently, using the same rating criteria and source materials. Agreement between the two raters was satisfactorily high.[9]

The resultant country profiles on the permissiveness-coerciveness dimension are given in Table 11. The equating of high permissiveness with democracy and high coercion with totalitarianism is obvious from the table. Almost all of the modern democracies fall at scale positions *1* and *2* (with the exception of Austria and France) and all of the totalitarian regimes of the communist bloc, without exception, may be found

at scale position *6*. Between these two extremes lie polities which experience varying degrees of coerciveness or permissiveness within the three aspects of political life considered in making the ratings.

This coerciveness-permissiveness profile finds considerable support in works by other authors interested in analyzing similar aspects of political regimes. Thus Almond and Coleman's (1960) distinction between Competitive, Semi-Competitive. and Authoritarian systems, although it excludes the modern democracies, yields a very similar rating of those nations which it has in common with our sample of 84. Similarly, Lipset's (1960) distinctions between European and English-speaking stable democracies and European and English-speaking unstable democracies plus dictatorships, on the one hand, and Latin American democracies and unstable dictatorships plus Latin American stable dictatorships, on the other, also bears a strong relationship to the ratings given in Table 11 for the 49 nations in common to the two studies. Finally, the factor analysis of cross-national political variables by Gregg and Banks (1965) also lends some support both to the criteria used in determining permissiveness-coerciveness level and to the ranks assigned the nations. Thus Factor I in the Gregg and Banks analysis, labeled the "Access" factor, shows high loadings on such aspects of democratic regimes as electoral system, constitutional regime, and group opposition. The regional group labeled "Advanced Western Area Group" also shows high loadings on this factor. The components of Factor I seem very similar to the criteria used in determining coerciveness scale positions *1* and *2*.[10] Furthermore,

---

[8] The complete bibliography may be found in Walton (1965), Appendix B.

[9] The correlation between the two sets of ratings for a small sample of nine countries chosen from all scale positions (in the estimation of the first rater) was $r = .88$. Projection onto the sample of 84 nations, using the Spearman-Brown formula, yields a corrected correlation of .985.

[10] Specifically, the variables with the high loadings on Factor I are the following, with their loadings indicated in parentheses: Electoral System (.94); Constitutional Regime (.93); Group Opposition (.92); Status of

Table 11

**COERCIVE-PERMISSIVE SCALING
OF NATIONAL POLITICAL SYSTEMS***

Country	Rank	Country	Rank	Country	Rank
Australia	1	Greece	3	Afghanistan	5
Canada	1	India	3	Argentina	5
Denmark	1	Japan	3	Cuba	5
Netherlands	1	Malaya	3	Egypt	5
Norway	1	Pakistan	3	Ethiopia	5
Sweden	1	Panama	3	Haiti	5
Switzerland	1	Philippines	3	Korea	5
United Kingdom	1	Turkey	3	Morocco	5
United States	1			Nicaragua	5
		Bolivia	4	Paraguay	5
Belgium	2	Colombia	4	Portugal	5
Costa Rica	2	Cyprus	4	Saudi Arabia	5
Finland	2	Ecuador	4	Spain	5
Iceland	2	El Salvador	4	Union of South Africa	5
Ireland	2	Ghana	4	Venezuela	5
Israel	2	Guatemala	4		
Italy	2	Honduras	4	Albania	6
Luxembourg	2	Indonesia	4	Bulgaria	6
Mexico	2	Iran	4	China	6
New Zealand	2	Iraq	4	Czechoslovakia	6
West Germany	2	Jordan	4	Dominican Republic	6
Uruguay	2·	Laos	4	East Germany	6
		Lebanon	4	Hungary	6
Austria	3	Liberia	4	Poland	6
Brazil	3	Libya	4	Romania	6
Burma	3	Peru	4	Taiwan	6
Cambodia	3	Sudan	4	U.S.S.R.	6
Ceylon	3	Syria	4	Yugoslavia	6
Chile	3	Thailand	4		
France	3	Tunisia	4		

* Based on data collected for the years 1948–1960.

totalitarian regimes have a very high negative loading on Factor I, and they also place at the opposite end of the coerciveness scale, at scale position 6.

Thus the permissiveness-coerciveness profiles, based on the six-point rating scale, appear to have construct validity in terms of the criteria used to deter-

---

Legislature (.87); Horizontal Power Distribution (.86); Representativeness of Regime (.85); Press Freedom (.80); Aggregation by Legislature (.73); Military Neutral (.73); Articulation by Parties (.68); Articulation by Associational Groups (.63); Modern Bureaucracy (.52).

mine each scale position, to have some consensual validation and corroboration in related studies by other authors, and to be based on some degree of interrater reliability. What, then, is the result of introducing the permissiveness-coerciveness variable to the predictive systemic frustration-systemic aggression equation?

The first comparison was made between political stability level and coerciveness level for the sample of 84 nations. Ratings of stability, it will be remembered, are based on the years 1955–1961, and coerciveness ratings are

Table 12

RELATIONSHIP BETWEEN LEVEL OF COERCION AND DEGREE OF POLITICAL STABILITY, 1955–1961

Degree of Political Stability	*Level of Coercion*			*Total*
	Permissive (1–2)	*Mid-level Coercive (3–4)*	*Coercive (5–6)*	
Stability (000–328)	Australia, Canada, Costa Rica, Denmark, Finland, Iceland, Ireland, Israel, Luxembourg, Netherland, New Zealand, Norway, Sweden, Switzerland, United Kingdom, United States, Uruguay, W. Germany — 18	Austria, Cambodia, Libya, Philippines, Tunisia — 5	Czechoslovakia, East Germany, Ethiopia, Portugal, Romania, Saudi Arabia, Taiwan — 7	30
Mid-level instability (329–499)	Belgium, Italy, Mexico — 3	Burma, Ceylon, Chile, Ecuador, El Salvador, France, Ghana, Greece, Iran, Japan, Liberia, Malaya, Pakistan, Panama, Jordan, Sudan, Thailand — 17	Afghanistan, Albania, Bulgaria, China, Dominican Rep., Egypt, Haiti, Morocco, Nicaragua, Paraguay, Poland, Spain, U. of So. Africa, U.S.S.R., Yugoslavia — 15	35
Instability (500–699)	0	Bolivia, Brazil, Colombia, Cyprus, Guatemala, Honduras, Indonesia, India, Iraq, Laos, Lebanon, Peru, Syria, Turkey — 14	Argentina, Cuba, Hungary, Korea, Venezuela — 5	19
Total	21	36	27	84

Chi square = 38.37   p < .001

based on the time period 1948–1960. The results of this comparison are given in Table 12.

The first finding which emerges is the strong relationship between stability and coerciveness. The permissive countries are overwhelmingly stable, whereas the coercive countries tend toward mid-levels and high levels of political instability. The Chi square calculated from this contingency table is 38.37, which is highly significant at less than the .001 level of probability. A product-moment correlation calculated between the variables of coercion and political instability is .41.

Examining the table in more detail, it may be seen that all countries ranked *1* on the coercion index are stable and that the three permissive countries which are moderately unstable all received a *2* coerciveness rating. This finding, that there are no permissive, unstable countries in the sample may be explained by the fact that the countries falling at scale position *1* (and, to some extent, at scale position *2*) on the coerciveness scale are also the modern democracies that are relatively satisfied in socio-economic terms on the frustration index calculated in a previous study. Thus permissiveness of regime appears to be another component of this particular stability pattern.

Looking at the coercive countries, the question arises, does the predicted curvilinearity of relationship obtain, such that the more highly coercive nations tend to be more stable politically than the nations at mid-levels of coercion? There is evidence in the table that highly coercive regimes show less tendency to extreme political instability, and somewhat more of a tendency to political stability, than do regimes at mid-level coerciveness. Also, countries at mid-level values of coerciveness tend to aggregate at both mid-level instability and extreme instability positions. Only five of 36 polities at mid-coerciveness level are politically stable.

This curvilinear tendency is brought out more clearly in Table 13, which gives the number and proportion of countries which are politically stable and those which are politically unstable at each level of coerciveness. It may be seen in Table 13, that two-thirds of the countries at coercion level *6* tend to be stable and only one-third are unstable. For the countries at position *5*, however, these proportions are reversed: two-thirds of these countries are unstable and only one-third are stable. Furthermore, at scale position *4*, three-quarters of the countries are politically unstable. An *eta* calculated to assess the degree of curvilinearity in these data yields a relationship of .72, which is a significant improvement over the *r* of .41 ($F = 14.02$, $p < .001$). Thus, the curvilinear hypothesis is

Table 13

RELATIONSHIP BETWEEN LEVEL OF COERCION AND DEGREE OF POLITICAL STABILITY, 1955–1961

	Level of Coercion						
	1 *p* N	*2* *p* N	*3* *p* N	*4* *p* N	*5* *p* N	*6* *p* N	*Total* N
Stable (000–422)	1.00 9	.75 9	.40 6	.24 5	.33 5	.67 8	42
Unstable (423–699)	.00 0	.25 3	.60 9	.76 16	.67 10	.33 4	42
Total	1.00 9	1.00 12	1.00 15	1.00 21	1.00 15	1.00 12	84

supported by the data, with countries at mid-coerciveness levels showing a greater tendency to political instability than countries with highly coercive regimes.

These data, taken in combination, would seem to reveal another finding of this study—that level 5 coerciveness is not sufficient to act as an inhibitor to aggression. It may be suggested that the coerciveness exhibited by authoritarian regimes classed at ordinal position 5 may serve as much as a source of frustration to the populace, thus promoting political aggression, as it serves to deter these acts of political instability. The finding may be indicative of a threshold level of political coerciveness necessary to achieve some degree of political stability in the face of systemic frustration. Nothing less than a full-fledged totalitarian regime seems sufficient, over time, to keep the populace from expressing dissatisfaction; then only if totalitarianism is unambiguously pursued will it be successful. Hungary serves as an example of what may ensue from a temporary relaxation of totalitarian policy. However, it is also true that level 4 countries show an even greater tendency toward high levels of political instability than do countries at level 5. Hence the conclusion should perhaps be modified to say that interference with liberties without the imposition of an authoritarian regime simply adds to the level of frustration and hence also of aggression within the country, without imposing any apparent inhibition upon the expression of that aggression. Countries with authoritarian regimes (level 5) do curb the expression of political aggression somewhat, although certainly not sufficiently to eliminate high levels of such expression entirely.

The second relationship of interest to this study is that between the coerciveness level of political regimes and the degree of systemic frustration calculated

in terms of socioeconomic components. It was hypothesized above that level of coerciveness would co-vary with systemic frustration in such a way that the higher the frustration level, the greater the coerciveness of the political regime. Table 14 shows the relationship between these two variables for the sample of 62 nations for which data are available on both indexes.

Again, the pattern is very much the same as in Table 12. The permissive countries, in large measure, experience relative socioeconomic satisfaction, as was anticipated in view of their high level of political stability. Frustrated countries, on the other hand, tend toward both mid-levels and high levels of coerciveness of regime. The Chi square for this contingency table is again very high: 36.12, with a probability level of less than .001. The product-moment correlation between the two variables of coercion and systemic frustration is .57. Thus, in fact, the data support the notion that more coercive regimes tend to occur in countries experiencing socioeconomic frustration.

It is interesting to note, however, contrary to our hypothesis, that there is also a tendency toward a high level of coerciveness of political regime in systemically satisfied countries. This reversal of tendency in the highly coercive countries suggests that some factor other than systemic frustration, measured in terms of ecological indicators, is also related to coerciveness of political regime. Thus, while it seems quite clear that permissiveness of a regime does not occur unless the country experiences socioeconomic satisfaction and is also politically stable, a high level of coerciveness may occur in relatively satisfied countries.

A look at the relationship between modernity level and coerciveness of regime completes the picture. As in study 2, the sample of 84 nations was divided into three groups, designated

Table 14

RELATIONSHIP BETWEEN LEVEL OF COERCION AND DEGREE OF SOCIOECONOMIC FRUSTRATION

Level of Social Frustration	Level of Coercion			Total
	Permissive (1-2)	Mid-level Coercive (3-4)	Coercive (5-6)	
Satisfaction (4.00-4.75)	Australia, Belgium, Canada, Denmark, Finland, Iceland, Ireland, Netherlands, New Zealand, Norway, Sweden, Switzerland, United Kingdom, United States, Uruguay, W. Germany — 16	France — 1	Argentina, Czechoslovakia, Morocco, Portugal, So. Africa — 5	22
Mid-level frustration (3.00-3.75)	Costa Rica, Israel, Italy, Mexico — 4	Austria, Brazil, Chile, Colombia, Cyprus, India, Indonesia, Iran, Japan, Lebanon, Pakistan, Panama, Tunisia, Turkey — 14	Bulgaria, Cuba, Haiti, Spain, Venezuela — 5	23
Frustration (1.50-2.75)	0	Bolivia, Ceylon, Ecuador, El Salvador, Greece, Guatemala, Iraq, Peru, Philippines, Syria, Thailand — 11	Dominican Rep., Egypt, Korea, Nicaragua, Paraguay, Yugoslavia — 6	17
Total	20	26	16	62

Chi square = 36.12 $p < .001$

modern, transitional, and traditional, and compared with regard to permissiveness and coerciveness of political regime. These results are given in Table 15.

Again, we find a clear-cut pattern combining modernity with permissiveness of regime. Furthermore, the table gives striking evidence, in corroboration of works on economic development (Almond and Coleman, 1960; Cutright, 1963; de Schweinitz, 1964; Hagen, 1962) that coerciveness of regime is the norm in nonmodern countries. The Chi square for this contingency table is 53.9, well beyond the .001 level of probability, and the product-moment correlation measuring the degree of relationship between these two variables is −.699. While both traditional and transitional countries tend toward coerciveness of regime, it is evident from Table 15 that the least modern countries (designated traditional) are more apt to fall at mid-levels of coerciveness than in the highly coercive category. Transitional states, however, which are also the most unstable group of countries in the sample, are almost evenly divided between mid-levels and high levels of political coerciveness.

As a final analysis of the relationship between the three variables, political stability, systemic frustration, and coerciveness of regime, an expanded table was constructed dividing the 62 nations for which scores were available on all indexes into those experiencing high, those experiencing medium, and those subject to low levels of all three variables. Since the present study indicated that coerciveness level is curvilinearly related to level of political instability, countries are ordered in the table in such a way that those at mid-levels of coerciveness appear at the end of the coerciveness distribution (see Table 16).

Two syndromes appear in this table. The first indicates the strong relationship among high levels of ecological systematic satisfaction, permissiveness of political regime and political stability, typified in the modern industrial nations of the world. Of 22 stable polities, 15, or 68 percent, fit this pattern. The opposite syndrome, of the politically unstable polity, emerges more clearly in this expanded table than in the previous tables based on single indices. Of 16 countries forming the most unstable group of nations, 12, or 75 percent, experience a combination of two sources of systemic frustration: mid-level coerciveness of political regime and some degree of frustration having its source in socioeconomic deprivations. No country in this highly unstable group is among the permissive countries of the world and only one nation, Argentina, is rated as satisfied in socioeconomic terms.

The third group of countries, exhibiting mid-levels of political instability, also show some combination of frustrations. Seventy-five percent of this mid-instability group show some combination of mid-level coerciveness and socioeconomic frustration. Finally, it should be pointed out that the largest number of exceptions occurs in the case of the satisfied, permissive, politically stable syndrome. As may be seen in the table, there are stable countries in the world stemming from many other combinations of coerciveness and frustration levels, although they are certainly not as frequent as the permissive, satisfied combination.

What may be concluded from this exploration of systemic variables? At the simplest level, it affords an empirical mapping of the state of the world in terms of variables of considerable interest to political and social scientists. The map which emerges is, in large measure, a corroboration of insights which have often been stated. The combination of modernity, permissiveness, socioeconomic satisfaction and

Table 15

RELATIONSHIP BETWEEN LEVEL OF COERCION AND LEVEL OF MODERNITY

Level of Modernity	Level of Coercion			Total
	Permissive (1–2)	*Mid-level Coercive (3–4)*	*Coercive (5–6)*	
Modern (.34–2.54)	Australia Canada Belgium Denmark Finland Iceland Ireland Israel Luxembourg Netherlands New Zealand Norway Sweden Switzerland United Kingdom United States Uruguay W. Germany 18	Austria France 2	Argentina Czechoslovakia East Germany U.S.S.R. 4	24
Transitional (−.49–.24)	Costa Rica Italy Mexico 3	Brazil Ceylon Chile Colombia Cyprus Ecuador El Salvador Guatemala Greece Honduras Japan Lebanon Panama Peru Syria Thailand Turkey Tunisia 18	Albania Bulgaria Cuba Dominican Rep. Egypt Korea Nicaragua Paraguay Poland Portugal Romania So. Africa Venezuela Yugoslavia 16	37
Traditional (−1.62– −.50)	0	Bolivia Burma Cambodia Ghana Indonesia India Iraq Jordan Laos Liberia Libya Malaya Pakistan Philippines Sudan 16	Afghanistan China Ethiopia Haiti Morocco Saudi Arabia Taiwan 7	23
Total	21	36	27	84

Chi square = 53.91 $p < .001$

Table 16

RELATIONSHIP BETWEEN LEVEL OF COERCION, LEVEL OF SOCIOECONOMIC FRUSTRATION, AND DEGREE OF POLITICAL STABILITY

Level of Coercion, Socioeconomic Frustration

	Permissive, Satisfied	Permissive, Mid-level Frustrated	Permissive, Frustrated	Coercive, Satisfied	Coercive, Mid-level Frustrated	Coercive, Frustrated	Mid-level Coercive, Satisfied	Mid-level Coercive, Mid-level Frustrated	Mid-level Coercive, Frustrated	Total
Stability	Australia Canada Denmark Finland Iceland Ireland Netherlands New Zealand Norway Sweden Switzerland U.K. U.S.A. Uruguay W. Germany	Israel Costa Rica		Czechoslovakia Portugal				Austria Tunisia	Philippines	
	15	2	0	2	0	0	0	2	1	22
Mid-level instability	Belgium	Mexico Italy		Morocco U. of S. Africa	Bulgaria Haiti Spain	Egypt Dominican Rep. Nicaragua Paraguay Yugoslavia	France	Chile Iran Japan Pakistan Panama	Ceylon Greece Ecuador El Salvador Thailand	
	1	2	0	2	3	5	1	5	5	24
Instability				Argentina	Cuba Venezuela	Korea		Brazil Colombia Cyprus India Indonesia Lebanon Turkey	Bolivia Guatemala Iraq Peru Syria	
	0	0	0	1	2	1	0	7	5	16
Total	16	4	0	5	5	6	1	14	11	62

political stability, on the one hand, and low modernity, coerciveness, socio-economic frustration and political instability, on the other, entails the gross division between "have" and "have-not" nations of the globe. To this may be added the variable of rates of change explored in a previous study, which, when calculated in percentage terms, also correlates with modernity so that modern nations are low changers on ecological variables and nonmodern nations are high changers.

The scaling techniques used in these empirical analyses, however, allow for more than a gross division among countries. By placing each country in its relative position on all scales, a more refined set of groupings and sub-groupings, exceptions and confirmations, are revealed. Also, it must be emphasized as a methodological point of considerable import that the scaling of each systemic variable was approached independently. Only after scaling was completed were patterns sought between systemic variables. Thus the map which emerges offers independent empirical support for many current notions regarding the interrelationships among democracy, economic development, and political stability.

Study 5: The Relation between Sources of Systemic Frustration, International Conflict, and Political Instability

WITH FRANK W. SCANLAND, III

The fifth study broaches the topic of international conflict, introducing the variable of level of international hostility into the analysis. The intention is to combine the data on external and internal conflict, yielding an estimate of the overall conflict level experienced by each nation in the sample. The rationale behind this procedure is to include international hostility and conflict within the concept of systemic aggression. *International hostility* is specifically defined, for the purposes of this study, as any hostile act perpetrated by members of one polity against another in the international system. Used in this way, the term *external aggression* has a more general meaning than is normally ascribed to it in the field of international relations. First, a variety of behaviors are covered in the definition, including acts of international antagonism short of the use of force, such as embargoes or severance of diplomatic relations. Verbal behavior in the form of diplomatic notes of protest and accusations, and even negative attitudes and unfavorable national stereotypes would qualify, according to this definition, as mild forms of external aggression. Second, the term is not meant to designate the initiation of conflict, but simply participation in a conflict. No distinction is drawn between the party which initiates hostilities and the party which responds to provocation. Each nation is scored for the acts which it performs.

With this view of external aggression as a diverse set of behaviors of varying levels of hostility, an attempt may be made to seek the correlates of external systemic aggression in some of the sources of systemic frustration explored in previous studies. Adding the variable of external systemic aggression to the systemic frustration-systemic aggression framework generates the following set of hypotheses:

1. *The higher the level of systemic frustration within a polity, the higher the consequent level of systemic aggression, which may be expressed either in the form of internal political instability or in external conflict and hostility, or in both forms of aggression.*

2. *Sources of systemic frustration within a society identified in previous studies consist of: (a) the discrepancy between socioeconomic wants and socioeconomic satisfaction; (b) a high rate of change on socioeconomic indicators, and (c) coerciveness level of political regime.*
3. *Thus, the greater these three sources of systemic frustration, the higher the level of external as well as of internal aggression.*

In order to determine empirically the relationship between systemic frustration and externally directed systemic aggression, some means was needed to assess the external aggression dimension. As a first step, a data collection of the external aggression behaviors of a large sample of nations for a specified time period was needed. Thus, we hoped to analyze and scale the external conflict dimension in the same manner as the political instability dimension, so that countries could be scored comparatively for level of external hostility.

In approaching this problem, we decided to utilize the available collection of external conflict data amassed by Rummel (1963) and Tanter (1964). These data include overt manifestations of external conflict for a sample of nations for a six-year period, 1955–1960, inclusive. The format for the data collection comprises twelve categories of events.[11] (Event names and definitions are given in the Appendix to this volume at the end of Table 13—see pp. 412–414.) Using the collection of data as a basis, an external aggression index was designed to score the sample of nations. Each event was assigned a position on the following four-point ordinal sclale:

[11] The data were collected from five sources: *The New York Times Index, New International Yearbook, Keesing's Contemporary Archives, Facts on File*, and *Britannica Book of the Year*.

Scale Position	Intensity Range	Indicators Included
1	Low intensity	Protests, accusations, threats
2	Low-medium intensity	Anti-foreign demonstrations, diplomatic officials of lesser than ambassador's rank expelled or recalled, mobilizations
3	High-medium intensity	Negative sanctions, ambassadors expelled or recalled, troop movements
4	High intensity	Diplomatic relations severed, presence of military action, war

In constructing the external aggression index, a procedure was followed similar to that adopted for the scaling of political instability. The frequency of occurrence of each indicator was multiplied by the scale value assigned to the indicator. These figures were then summed, yielding three of the four digits of the external aggression score. To these three, an initial digit was added, representing the scale position of the most severe act of external aggression perpetrated by the country during the time period. A country-by-country external aggression profile was then drawn. The profiles appear in Table 17.

A number of interesting observations may be made from this table. The most aggressive country of the sample is the U.S.S.R. A close second is the United States. Finland did not perpetrate a single aggressive act in the international arena during the six-year period, which may well be explained by that country's precarious geographical position. Relatively new nations are predominantly found in the high aggression portion of the profile. And most of the polities occupying the extreme lower range of the distribution are either geographically isolated from the main-

Table 17

EXTERNAL AGGRESSION PROFILE, 1955–1960*

Country	Score	Country	Score	Country	Score
U.S.S.R.	4516	Yugoslavia	4036	Netherlands	3035
U.S.A.	4505	Haiti	4035	Afghanistan	3033
U.A.R.	4353	Iran	4035	Thailand	3021
Israel	4245	Cambodia	4030	Canada	3020
China	4204	Honduras	4030	Brazil	3016
India	4185	Chile	4025	Bolivia	3015
France	4180	N. Korea	4022	El Salvador	3014
Jordan	4174	Paraguay	4022	Belgium	3012
U.K.	4156	U. of S. Africa	4022	Nepal	3011
Indonesia	4099	Costa Rica	4021	Philippines	3011
Cuba	4096	Albania	4019	Japan	2064
Pakistan	4087	Burma	4017	Czechoslovakia	2029
S. Korea	4079	Australia	4015	Sweden	2023
Lebanon	4076	Colombia	4014	Switzerland	2018
Iraq	4068	Ecuador	4014	Panama	2016
Argentina	4067	Peru	4013	Rumania	2016
Hungary	4065	Uruguay	4011	Norway	2012
Formosa	4063	Spain	4011	Denmark	2011
Turkey	4054	Ethiopia	4009	Bulgaria	2009
E. Germany	4051	Irish Republic	3137	Portugal	1006
Nicaragua	4050	Poland	3073	New Zealand	1003
Guatemala	4049	Italy	3043	O. Mongolia	1002
Venezuela	4045	Saudi Arabia	3042	Liberia	1002
W. Germany	4043	Dom. Republic	3041	Ceylon	1002
Mexico	4040	Greece	3039	Finland	0000

* Based on data collected by Rudolph J. Rummel and Raymond Tanter. The scaling is the responsibility of the authors.

stream of international discourse or are noted for the relative weakness of their military establishments.

This distribution, in which the U.S.S.R. is first, the U.S. is second, China is fifth, France, seventh, and the United Kingdom is ninth in rank-order position, suggests that beyond systemic frustration, power prominence in international relations is a primary factor underlying involvement in external conflict. This circumstance would appear to transcend the confines of the frustration-aggression sequence in the case of the five "super" powers. On the basis of this reasoning, these five nations were omitted from the test sample.

In order to investigate the hypotheses underlying this study, that level of external aggression co-varies with level of systemic frustration, a comparison was made between these two variables in a sample of 53 nations for which data were available on all indicators (excluding the five major world powers). Frustration level was ascertained in terms of each country's position on four separate indexes: the index based on relative socioeconomic deprivation, the index of modernity, the index of rate of change on selected socioeconomic indicators, and the index of coerciveness-permissiveness of political regime.

Table 18 reports the product-moment correlations between each of these measures of systemic frustration and both external aggression and political instability. As may be seen, relatively low correlations were found between systemic frustration and external aggres-

Table 18

PRODUCT-MOMENT CORRELATIONS AMONG SYSTEMIC FRUSTRATION AND SYSTEMIC AGGRESSION INDEXES (N = 53)

	Political Instability	External Aggression
Socioeconomic Frustration	$r = .48$	$r = .33$
Socioeconomic Rate of Change	$r = .67$	$r = .30$
Permissiveness-Coerciveness of Political Regime	$r = .54$	$r = .27$
Level of Modernity	$r = -.66$	$r = -.46$
Level of Political Instability		$r = .52$

sion. Level of development shows the highest relationship to external aggression, $r = -.46$, and level of coerciveness shows the lowest, $r = .27$. This is in contrast to the moderately strong correlations found between sources of systemic frustration and internal aggression, or political instability (which range from $r = .48$ to $r = .67$). From these findings it must be concluded that the instigation to internal systemic aggression in the face of systemic frustration appears far more important than the impulse to external aggression.

The strongest single correlate of external aggression among the variables measured is level of political instability. Thus, internal and external aggression appear to co-vary and to complement one another. The product-moment correlation between political instability and external aggression is $r = .52$. This strength of relationship is also indicated in Table 19. As may be seen in this table, of 32 stable countries, 23, that is, almost three-quarters, are peaceful and only 9 are externally aggressive. And of 35 unstable countries, 23 are externally aggressive whereas the remainder, 12, are peaceful. The results of these computations identify political instability as a far better indicator of external aggression than is systemic frustration.

This finding is of particular interest since it has been both denied and asserted by different researchers. Rummel (1963), for example, as a result of his factor analysis of internal and external conflict, asserts that the two dimensions are unrelated. Denton (1966), however, again using factor analysis, finds some relationship between level of civil strife and the occurrence of large-scale war. And Haas (1964) finds that levels of domestic violence first increase and then decrease, several years before the onset of external conflict.

The moderately high correlation between political instability and external aggression, as well as the moderately strong relationship between systemic frustration and political instability, suggested yet another treatment of the data. An expanded table was constructed employing 16 possible dichotomized combinations of the independent variable and four possible combinations of the two forms of systemic aggression. As may be noticed in Table 20, satisfaction-frustration, high change-low change, permissiveness-coerciveness, and modern-nonmodern in the columns, and stability-instability and peacefulness-aggression in the rows, are arranged in all possible combinations. The columns are ordered from highest satisfaction to highest frustration levels. Between these two extremes are countries either satisfied or frustrated on two of the three indexes. The center of the table separates the four satisfaction from the four frustration categories. Similarly, the rows of the table are ordered from the peaceful-

Table 19

RELATIONSHIP BETWEEN POLITICAL STABILITY AND EXTERNAL AGGRESSION

Level of External Aggression	Level of Political Instability					Totals
	Stability (000–422)			Instability (423–699)		
Peaceful (0000–4014)	Afghanistan	Netherlands		Belgium		
	Bulgaria	New Zealand		Bolivia		
	Canada	Norway		Brazil		
	Czechoslovakia	Panama		Ceylon		
	Denmark	Philippines		Colombia		
	Ecuador	Portugal		Dom. Republic		
	El Salvador	Romania		Italy		
	Ethiopia	Saudi Arabia		Japan		
	Finland	Sweden		Peru		
	Greece	Switzerland		Poland		
	Ireland	Uruguay		Spain		
	Liberia		23	Thailand	12	35
Aggressive (4015–4516)	Albania			Argentina	Iraq	
	Australia			Burma	Jordan	
	Cambodia			Chile	Lebanon	
	Costa Rica			Cuba	Mexico	
	East Germany			Egypt	Nicaragua	
	Israel			Guatemala	Pakistan	
	Taiwan			Haiti	Paraguay	
	West Germany			Honduras	S. Korea	
	Yugoslavia			Hungary	Turkey	
				India	U. of S. Africa	
				Indonesia	Venezuela	
			9	Iran	23	32
Totals			32		35	67

Chi square = 7.10 $p = <.01$

stable category to the aggressive-unstable one.

The grouping of countries in the table supports the notion that syndromes may be identified in the present-day international arena. It had been the original intent of this study to attempt to locate and describe conditions conducive to external aggression, perhaps viewed as an "aggression syndrome," and to determine whether the absence of such conditions was also conducive to the absence of external aggression, perhaps constituting a "non-aggression syndrome." In the upper left-hand cell of the table a poten-tial nonaggression syndrome may be identified. Here are ten countries (Canada, Denmark, Finland, Ireland, Netherlands, New Zealand, Norway, Sweden, Switzerland, and Uruguay) which are satisfied on three measures of possible systemic frustration and which are also relatively peaceful and stable. These countries enjoy permissive political regimes, experience low rates of change on ecological variables, and have a small discrepancy between social want formation and social want satisfaction. As may be seen, this is the most populated cell in the table.

At the other extreme, in the lower

Table 20

RELATIONSHIP BETWEEN THE SOURCES OF SYSTEMIC FRUSTRATION, POLITICAL STABILITY, AND EXTERNAL AGGRESSION

	Satisfied Permissive Modern High Change (2.54–.34)(3.25–4.75)	Satisfied Permissive Low Change (1.22–2.57)(1–3)	Satisfied Permissive Nonmodern Low Change (.24–1.16)	Satisfied Permissive Modern High Change (2.60+)	Satisfied Permissive Nonmodern High Change	Satisfied Coercive Modern Low Change (4–5)	Satisfied Coercive Nonmodern Low Change	Frustrated Permissive Modern Low Change (1.5–3.0)	Frustrated Permissive Nonmodern Low Change	Satisfied Coercive Modern High Change	Satisfied Coercive Nonmodern High Change	Frustrated Permissive Modern High Change	Frustrated Permissive Nonmodern High Change	Frustrated Coercive Modern Low Change	Frustrated Coercive Nonmodern Low Change	Frustrated Coercive Modern High Change	Frustrated Coercive Nonmodern High Change	Totals
Peaceful Stable (0000–4014)(000–422)	Canada, Denmark, Finland, Ireland, Nether., Norway, Sweden, Switzerland, Uruguay, New Zealand — 10					Czechoslovakia	Greece, Philippines		Bulgaria		Portugal		Panama		Ecuador		El Salvador	18
Aggressive Stable (4015–4516)	Australia, Israel, West Germany — 3				Costa Rica												Yugoslavia	5
Peaceful Unstable (423–699)	Belgium — 1		Italy		Brazil				Spain		Colombia		Ceylon, Japan — 2				Bolivia, Dom. Republic, Peru, Thailand — 4	11
Aggressive Unstable			Mexico, Pakistan — 2			Argentina	Chile		U. of S. Africa, Cuba — 2		Indonesia, Iran, Lebanon — 3		India, Turkey — 2		Guatemala, Paraguay — 2		Egypt, Haiti, Iraq, Nicaragua, S. Korea, Venezuela — 6	19
Totals	14	0	3	0	2	2	3	0	4	0	5	0	5	0	3	0	12	53

right-hand cell of the table are countries illustrative of a possible external aggression syndrome. Of the twelve countries in the extreme right-hand column, six or 50 percent, are collected in this cell: Egypt, Haiti, Iraq, Nicaragua, South Korea, and Venezuela. They register as frustrated on the same four measures of systemic frustration and are both unstable and externally aggressive. Again, as may be seen, this is the second most populated cell in the table.

The fact that other patterns of frustration-aggression are also in evidence, however, points up the fact that there is less than perfect predictability of either external aggression or nonaggression. Nevertheless, the possibility for prediction of a nation's behavior in the international sphere is improved by knowing its level both of systemic frustration and of political instability.

On the basis of these findings, one might characterize the external aggression syndrome by saying that the country which is sufficiently frustrated to be politically unstable has the strongest probability of also being externally aggressive. Conversely, the nonaggression syndrome seems to indicate that the satisfied country has the greatest probability of being both internally stable and externally nonaggressive. This finding is qualified, however, by the overriding demands of international relations for the major powers, which were excluded from the sample under investigation.

Study 6: A Multiple-Factor Explanation of Political Instability and External Conflict

Given these findings, we may ask how successfully the levels of internal political unrest and external conflict experienced by a society may be es-timated from all of these socioeconomic and political conditions in combination, rather than individually. The technique suited for this purpose is multiple regression. By the use of multiple correlational techniques, we may discover the degree of prediction yielded by a set of variables and also the relative weight each carries in the prediction equation.

For this analysis, four ecological indexes were used: socioeconomic frustration (social wants/social satisfactions); modernity; rate of socioeconomic change; and level of permissiveness-coerciveness of political regime. The sample of nations is reduced to 53 countries with complete data on all indexes, omitting the five major world powers, the U.S.S.R., the U.S., the United Kingdom, France, and China.[12]

The interrelationships among the ecological indexes and the conflict behaviors are given in Table 21. Two profiles of political instability are included, one based on fifteen years, 1948–1962, and the other on the seven-year period, 1955–1961, which almost exactly matches the years scored for

[12] Complete ecological data are not available for the U.S.S.R. and China; hence these countries must be dropped from the multiple regression analysis on these grounds as well. Analyses were carried out including the other three major powers, the U.S., the United Kingdom, and France, yielding a sample of 56 nations. Although the multiple correlation coefficients are somewhat lower, the results are not significantly altered, as shown in the following table.

	R	R²
Political instability, 1948–1962	.76	.58
Political instability, 1955–1961	.68	.46
External conflict, 1955–1960	.32	.10
External conflict (using political instability, 1955–1961, in the prediction equation)	.57	.32

These values may be compared to those given in Table 22, below, for the sample of 53 nations.

Table 21

INTERCORRELATION MATRIX AMONG MEASURES OF POLITICAL INSTABILITY, EXTERNAL CONFLICT, AND ECOLOGICAL INDEXES (PRODUCT-MOMENT COEFFICIENTS) (N = 53 COUNTRIES)

	1	*2*	*3*	*4*	*5*	*6*	*7*
1. Political Instability 1948–1962		.80	.43	.56	−.71	.68	.70
2. Political Instability 1955–1961			.52	.48	−.66	.67	.54
3. External Conflict 1955–1960				.33	−.46	.30	.27
4. Systemic Frustration 1948–1955					−.80	.71	.58
5. Modernity 1948–1955						−.85	−.65
6. Rate of Change 1935–1962							.62
7. Permissiveness-Coerciveness 1948–1960							

external conflict (1955–1960). It may be noted that all of the ecological indexes show a higher degree of relationship to the fifteen-year measure of political unrest than to the seven-year measure. This is encouraging, since one may expect increased reliability of measurement with increased data. Furthermore, considerable relationship is shown between instability and the economic and political environment. The correlation coefficients range from $r = .56$, in the case of systemic frustration, to $r = .70$ and $r = −.71$ with coerciveness of regime and level of modernity.[13] Only external conflict shows more relationship to the seven-year measure of political unrest. Since these two forms of aggressive behavior appear to be

[13] The permissiveness-coerciveness dimension of political regime shows a considerable increase in relationship to political instability in comparison to the result obtained with the entire sample of 84 countries (Study 4). The relationship between this index and the fifteen-year measure of political instability is $r = .70$; with the seven-year instability score it is now $r = .54$, whereas in the earlier study, using 84 countries, it was $r = .41$. This increase requires some explanation. Permis-

more highly related when they are more nearly coincident in time, some support is provided for the claim that they represent two responses to the same underlying set of conditions.

A high degree of interrelationship among the three socioeconomic indexes is also apparent in the table. Coefficients range from $r = .71$ between systemic frustration and rate of socioeconomic change, to $r = −.85$ between level of modernity and rate of change. Both frustration and rate of change are inverse functions of modernity; the

siveness-coerciveness of regime was shown to have a nonlinear relationship to political instability in the larger sample of 84 nations. Highly permissive and highly coercive regimes both tended to be stable. In reducing the sample of states from 84 to 53 because of a lack of reported ecological data, we exercised systematic bias in excluding states. The group of nations lowest in development and the group highest in coerciveness (the communist bloc) tended to have the least complete reporting of ecological data to the United Nations. With these states largely omitted from the analysis, a strong linear tendency emerges in the data, representing primarily the difference between permissive regimes and regimes at mid-levels of coercion.

higher the level of modernity, the lower the level of systemic frustration and the slower the annual percentage rate of socioeconomic change. The political dimension of permissiveness-coerciveness shows less overlap with the economic dimensions. Correlation values range from $r = .58$ between systemic frustration and permissiveness-coerciveness, to $r = -.65$ between permissiveness-coerciveness and modernity.

Having examined the intercorrelations among variables, we may ask to what extent internal and external conflict may be explained by these indicators in combination. Table 22

Table 22

POLITICAL INSTABILITY AND EXTERNAL CONFLICT PREDICTED FROM FOUR ECOLOGICAL INDEXES: SYSTEMIC FRUSTRATION, MODERNITY, RATE OF SOCIOECONOMIC CHANGE, AND COERCIVENESS OF REGIME (N = 53 COUNTRIES)

	Multiple R	Multiple R^2
Political Instability, 1948–1962	.78	.61
Political Instability, 1955–1961	.71	.51
External Conflict, 1955–1960	.49	.24
External Conflict (including political instability, 1955–1961, in the prediction equation)	.61	.37

shows the multiple correlation coefficients for fifteen-year and seven-year ratings of political instability predicted from the ecological indexes. Coefficients are also shown for external conflict, in one case using the same four indexes and, in the second case, adding seven-year level of political unrest to the prediction equation. The squared values of the multiple correlation coefficient are given, indicating the amount

of variance in the dependent variable which may be explained from the ecological indexes.

The highest level of prediction is found for the longer assessment of political unrest. With a multiple correlation coefficient of $R = .78$, 61 percent of the variance in fifteen-year political instability levels among this sample of nations may be explained from a knowledge of their levels of modernity, systemic frustration, and permissiveness-coerciveness of political regime, as well as their rates of socioeconomic change. This represents an improvement of 11 percent in the level of explanation obtained using the single best predictor, level of modernity. As indicated in the table, the level of explanation is somewhat lower for the seven-year assessment of political unrest. Fifty-one percent of the variance in this measure may be explained in terms of the same four ecological indexes. We thus find a 6 percent improvement in prediction using the four indexes in combination, as compared to using the single best predictor, rate of socioeconomic change.

In the case of external conflict, the level of relationship indicated is considerably lower. A multiple correlation coefficient of $R = .49$ is obtained using the four ecological indexes, indicating that 24 percent of the variance in level of external conflict among these nations may be due to their broad socioeconomic conditions and levels of permissiveness-coerciveness of political regime. This represents a gain of only 3 percent in level of explanatory power over the efficiency of the single best predictor, level of modernity. If we add internal political unrest to the prediction equation, however, the degree of relationship is increased. The multiple correlation coefficient is now $R = .61$, yielding 37 percent of explained variance in external conflict. This is a 10 percent increase over the efficiency of the single best predictor, political unrest.

It seems apparent that level of internal political unrest, especially when assessed over a sufficient period of time to yield a fair sample of behavior, can be predicted to a considerable degree from a gross knowledge of the economic and political conditions prevailing within societies. This is less true for the prediction of external conflict. Only when the level of internal political unrest is included among the predictors do we obtain an equation which can account for close to 40 percent of the variance in internation conflict behavior.

We may also ask whether each of the independent indexes is equally efficient in predicting systemic aggression or whether, in fact, some indexes could be omitted from the analysis. The statistical technique suited to answering this question is a step-wise multiple regression, which assesses the contribution of each index to the overall level of prediction. Table 23 shows the results of the step-wise multiple regression analysis.

By and large, the outcome of the analysis may be anticipated in terms of the correlational patterns shown in Table 21. For example, level of modernity and permissiveness-coerciveness of political regime are the indexes with the single highest relationships to the fifteen-year assessment of political instability. In the step-wise multiple regression analysis, these two indexes in combination yield a squared multiple correlation coefficient of .60. This represents a loss of only 1 percent in predictive power as compared to the $R^2 = .61$ obtained when all four indexes are combined.

If we look at the seven-year assessment of political unrest, we find a different outcome. Omitting systemic frustration from the equation represents a loss of 2 percent in predictive power, and omitting coerciveness rep-resents a loss of another 1 percent. If modernity is omitted, an additional 3 percent of predictive explanation is lost, leaving rate of socioeconomic change as the single best predictor, explaining 45 percent of the variance in political unrest.

Finally, we may look at the results of the step-wise analysis of level of external conflict. This shows that both systemic frustration and coerciveness of regime may be omitted from the equation with no consequent loss in prediction. Level of modernity, rate of socioeconomic change, and level of internal political unrest, in combination, account for 37 percent of the variance in external conflict. Surprisingly, the direction of relationship involving rate of change was found to be reversed. The partial correlation coefficients and beta weights for this indicator are now negative, indicating that a slower rate of change is associated with a higher level of external conflict when all the other variables are removed (partialled) from the equation.

From this step-wise multiple regression analysis, we must conclude that the most efficient set of predictors varies with the time span of political instability, as well as between internal and external aggression. Given a certain amount of error in all these cross-national assessments, and a certain amount of trial and error in the devising of indexes, it is perhaps premature to expect complete accuracy in the picture which emerges. At this stage, the broad mapping of interrelationships yields a more consistent pattern.

We wished finally to know the relationship of the four ecological indexes to a combined index of internal and external conflict. A canonical correlation finds the best solution between two sets of variables which will maximize the correlation between the dependent variables, taken as a combined index,

Table 23

STEP-WISE MULTIPLE REGRESSION ANALYSIS

	Systemic Frustration			Modernity			Rate of Change			Coerciveness of Regime			Political Instability, 1955–1961			R	R^2
	Partial r	Beta	t	Partial r	Beta	t	Partial r	Beta	t	Partial r	Beta	t	Partial r	Beta	t		
Political Instability, 1948–1962	.10	.10	.69	−.26	−.38	−1.87	.15	.19	1.07	.42	.39	3.24	Not used			.78	.61
Step 1	—	—		—	−.24	−.31	−1.76	.14	.17	1.02	.42	.38	3.20			.78	.61
Step 2	—	—	⌐	−.47	−.45	−3.81	—	—	—	.43	.40	3.40				.77	.60
Political Instability, 1955–1961	.17	.20	1.19	−.23	−.38	−1.64	.27	.38	1.96	.19	.18	1.31	Not used			.71	.51
Step 1	—	—	—	−.17	−.24	−1.20	.26	.36	1.85	.17	.16	1.19				.70	.49
Step 2	—	—	—	−.23	−.32	−1.65	.28	.40	2.05	—	—	—				.69	.48
Step 3	—	—	—	—	—	—	.67	.67	6.42	—	—	—				.67	.45
External Conflict, 1955–1960	−.02	−.03	−.14	−.30	−.58	−2.16	−.30	−.51	−2.19	−.09	−.09	−.59	.42	.52	3.15	.61	.37
Step 1	—	—	—	−.35	−.60	−2.62	−.30	−.50	−2.22	−.08	−.09	−.59	.42	.51	3.20	.61	.37
Step 2	—	—	—	−.34	−.57	−2.57	−.31	−.52	−2.31	—	—	—	.41	.50	3.17	.61	.37

and an index formed from the independent variables.[14] In this case, fifteen-year level of political instability was combined with the seven-year assessment of external conflict. The complete analysis is given in Table 24.

Table 24

CANONICAL CORRELATION ANALYSIS

	Equations	
	1	*2*
Canonical R	.78	.33
Canonical R²	.615	.11
Dependent Variables		
Political Instability, 1948–1962	0.995	0.454
External Conflict, 1955–1960	0.096	−0.891
Independent Variables		
Systemic Frustration	0.178	−0.033
Rate of Change	0.246	0.546
Permissiveness-Coerciveness	0.618	0.272
Modernity	−0.725	0.792

One significant solution emerged, a canonical R of .78, which may be compared to the same value yielded by the multiple regression analysis of fifteen-year level of internal political conflict. Also, the relative weightings of the ecological indexes in the canonical correlation are very much the same as in the multiple regression. We could then conclude that our ability to predict level of internal unrest is the same as to predict to a combined index of internal and external conflict. In both cases, there is strong evidence of relationship

[14] The canonical analysis yields more than one solution, or more than one factor, relating the independent to the dependent variables. The number of possible solutions is equal to the number of independent or dependent variables, whichever is smaller. In our case, there are two dependent variables and four independent ones; hence there are two solutions to the canonical analysis. Only one of these is significant, however (see Table 24).

between the ecological indicators and the conflict behaviors.

Summary and Conclusions

In summary, we may draw together the findings from all the studies into a global picture. At least three broad principles emerge from this cross-national research:

1. First, political turmoil and violence comprise a structured and patterned universe of events. The factor analysis reported in Study 1 reveals independent clusters of aggressive behaviors. Also, the scaling and measurement of aggression imply an ordered rather than a random universe. A similar assertion can be made regarding the other two modes of aggressive behavior: external conflict and coerciveness of regime.

2. Second, political violence has many correlates in the socioeconomic environment of political systems. A definite pattern of ecological trait associations, perhaps the underlying conditions of political instability, can be identified in the cross-national sample of contemporary nations.

3. Considerable evidence was found for the principle of social discontent and systemic frustration as the genesis of political turmoil. Socioeconomic conditions that thwart the aspirations and expectations of large segments of the population were seen as the condition leading to political aggressiveness. The political variable of coerciveness was postulated as an additional systemic frustration, an instigator to violence, while at the same time it was also regarded as analogous to punishment, inhibiting the overt expression of violence.

4. The cross-national analyses yielded specific findings of relationship, some indicating considerable associa-

tion, others more moderate relationships.

a. Socioeconomic frustration (the discrepancy between want formation and satisfaction, measured by ecological indicators) was positively and linearly related to political instability and turmoil.

b. Level of modernity, measured in terms of ecological indicators, also showed a linear but negative relationship to violence. It should be noted that this was not anticipated. A curvilinear pattern was predicted between modernity and political stability.

c. Socioeconomic change, as measured by percentage increase in ecological variables over time, was also linearly and positively related to political instability. Yet it also appears that some of the measures of change, for example, national income, do not follow this pattern but are negatively related to violence. Change undoubtedly belongs among the most complex theoretical concepts and is the most difficult to measure.

d. Coerciveness of regime is curvilinearly related to overt violence within society. Permissive as well as highly coercive nations seem predominantly stable, whereas countries at mid-levels of coerciveness show the greatest amount of civil strife.

e. These independent variables—socioeconomic frustration, rate of change, and coerciveness—are only negligibly related to external conflict. This would seem to indicate that the systemic frustration-political aggression hypothesis as applied in these studies provides a less adequate explanation of the international scene than it does of internal conflict. Perhaps we need to tap other sources of frustration, or perhaps theoretical constructs other than frustration-aggression could provide more adequate explanatory schemes.

f. Among our variables, there is one significant predictor that provides the linkage between external and internal aggression—internal political unrest. External violence and internal political instability are positively and linearly related.

From these findings, two prototypes emerge in the world scene today. One type includes highly developed, modern, satisfied nations, in the socioeconomic sense. These nations exhibit low change in their socioeconomic conditions and are internally stable. In their stance in the international arena they are relatively peaceful, if we may discount the major powers. We may also include as borderline to this pattern the few nations which qualify in all respects except that they are highly coercive.

The second prototype is the exact opposite of the first. The traits of systemic frustration, low modernity, rapid change, and mid-level of coerciveness are combined with internal political turmoil. It seems that this group of nations has an almost equal probability of being involved or not involved in international conflict. The remaining nations, for the most part, approximate one of the two prototypes, although they may violate some of the traits of the syndrome. There are very few complete exceptions to this patterning, however.

The results of these studies provide an encouraging indication that cross-national, correlational, and scaling methods can profitably be applied to complex areas such as the analysis of internal conflict behaviors. The scalings, as well as the identification of the dimensions of internal conflict behavior, show that these events can be classified and disentangled. The findings are sufficiently striking and persuasive to argue for continuing with additional designs. A large-scale series of studies using additional sets of hypotheses, and a wider scope of ecological, psychological, and political variables for longer time periods, with more varied and refined measurement techniques, should lead to more reliable results.

References

Almond, Gabriel A., and James S. Coleman, eds. *The Politics of the Developing Areas*. Princeton: Princeton University Press, 1960.

———, and Sidney Verba. *The Civic Culture*. Princeton: Princeton University Press, 1963.

Banks, Arthur S., and Robert B. Textor. *A Cross-Polity Survey*. Cambridge, Mass.: The M. I. T. Press, 1963.

Bay, Christian. *The Structure of Freedom*. Stanford: Stanford University Press, 1958.

Berkowitz, Leonard. *Aggression: A Social Psychological Analysis*. New York: McGraw-Hill Book Company, 1962.

———. "The Concept of Aggressive Drive: Some Additional Considerations," in L. Berkowitz, ed., *Advances in Experimental Social Psychology*, Vol. 2. New York: Academic Press, 1965.

Buss, Arnold H. *The Psychology of Aggression*. New York: John Wiley & Sons, Inc., 1961.

Cantril, Hadley. "A Study of Aspirations," *Scientific American* (February 1963), 41–45.

———. *The Pattern of Human Concerns*. New Brunswick, N.J.: Rutgers University Press, 1965.

———, and Lloyd A. Free. "Hopes and Fears for Self and Country," *American Behavioral Scientist*, VI, No. 2 (October, 1962), 3–30.

Cattell, Raymond, H. Breul, and H. Parker Hartman. "The Dimensions of Culture Patterns of Factorization of National Characters," *Journal of Abnormal and Social Psychology* (1949), 443–69.

———. "The Principal Culture Patterns Discoverable in the Syntal Dimensions of Existing Nations," *Journal of Social Psychology* (1950), 215–53.

———. "An Attempt at More Refined Definition of the Cultural Dimensions of Syntality in Modern Nations," *American Sociological Review*, XVI (1951), 408–21.

Conroe, Wallace W. *A Cross-National Analysis of the Impact of Modernization Upon Political Stability*. Master's Thesis, San Diego State College, 1965.

Cutright, Phillips. "National Political Development: Measurement and Analysis," *American Sociological Review*, XXVIII (April, 1963), 253–64.

Davies, James C. "Toward a Theory of Revolution," *American Sociological Review*, XXVII (January, 1962), 5–19.

Denton, F. H. "Some Regularities in International Conflict, 1820–1949," *Background*, IX (1966).

De Schweinitz, K. *Industrialization and Democracy*. New York: The Free Press, 1964.

Deutsch, Karl W. "Toward an Inventory of Basic Trends and Patterns in Comparative and International Politics," *American Political Science Review*, LIV (March, 1960), 34–57.

———. "Social Mobilization and Political Development," *American Political Science Review*, LV (September, 1961), 493–514.

———. *The Nerves of Government*. New York: The Free Press, 1963.

Dollard, John, *et al. Frustration and Aggression*. New Haven: Yale University Press, 1939.

Doob, Leonard W. *Becoming More Civilized: A Psychological Exploration*. New Haven: Yale University Press, 1960.

Easton, David B. *The Political System: An Inquiry Into the State of Political Science*. New York: Alfred A. Knopf, 1958.

———. *A Framework for Political Analysis*. Englewood Cliffs, N.J.: Prentice-Hall, Inc., 1965a.

———. *A Systems Analysis of Political Life*. New York: John Wiley & Sons, Inc., 1965b.

Eckstein, Harry. *Internal War: The Problem of Anticipation*. A Report submitted to the Research Group in Psychology and the Social Sciences, Smithsonian Institution, Washington, D.C., January 15, 1962.

———, ed. *Internal War*. New York: The Free Press, 1964.

Feierabend, Ivo K. "Exploring Political Stability: A Note on the Comparative Method," *Western Political Quarterly* (Supplement), XV, No. 3 (September, 1962), 18–19.

———, and Rosalind L. Feierabend. "Aggressive Behavior within Polities: A Cross-National Study." Paper delivered at the Annual Meeting of the American Psychological Association, Chicago, September, 1965a.

———. *Cross-National Data Bank of Political Instability Events (Code Index)*. Public Affairs Research Institute, San Diego State College, January, 1965b.

———. "The Relationship of Systemic Frustration, Political Coerciveness, International Tension and Political Instability: A Cross-National Study." Paper prepared for presentation at the Annual Meeting of the American Psychological Association, New York, September, 1966.

———, and Norman G. Litell. "Dimensions of Political Unrest: A Factor Analysis of Cross-National Data." Paper delivered at the annual meeting of the Western Political Science Association, Reno, Nevada, March, 1966.

Feierabend, Ivo K., Rosalind L. Feierabend, and Betty A. Nesvold. "Correlates of Political Stability." Paper delivered at the annual meeting of the American Political Science Association, New York, September, 1963.

Fitzgibbon, R. H., and Kenneth Johnson. "Measurement of Latin American Political Change," *American Political Science Review*, LV (September, 1961).

Gregg, Philip M., and Arthur S. Banks. "Dimensions of Political Systems: Factor Analysis of a Cross-Polity Survey," *American Political Science Review*, LIX (September, 1965), 602–14.

Gurr, Ted. *The Genesis of Violence: A Multivariate Theory of the Preconditions of Civil Strife*. Ph.D. dissertation, New York University, 1965.

———, and Charles Ruttenberg. *The Conditions of Civil Violence: First Tests of a Causal Model*. Research Mono-

graph No. 28, Center of International Studies, Princeton University, April 1967.

Haas, Michael. *Some Societal Correlates of International Political Behavior*. Stanford: Studies in International Conflict and Integration, Stanford University, 1964.

Hagen, Everett E. *On the Theory of Social Change*. Homewood, Ill.: Dorsey Press, 1962.

Hoole, Francis W. *Political Stability and Instability within Nations: A Cross-National Study*. Master's Thesis, San Diego State College, August, 1964.

Inkeles, Alex. "Industrial Man: The Relation of Status to Experience, Perception and Value," *American Journal of Sociology* (July, 1960), 1–31.

Kling, Merle. "Taxes on the 'External' Sector: An Index of Political Behavior in Latin America," *Midwest Journal of Political Science* (May, 1959), 127–50.

Lasswell, Harold D. *The Political Writings of Harold D. Lasswell*. New York: The Free Press, 1951.

———, and Abraham Kaplan. *Power and Society: A Framework for Political Inquiry*. New Haven: Yale University Press, 1950.

Lerner, Daniel. "Communication Systems and Social Systems: A Statistical Exploration in History and Policy," *Behavioral Science*, II, No. 4 (October, 1957), 266–75.

———. *The Passing of Traditional Society*. New York: The Free Press, 1958.

LeVine, Robert A. "Anti-European Violence in Africa: A Comparative Analysis," *Journal of Conflict Resolution*, III, No. 4 (December, 1959), 420–29.

Lipset, Seymour. *Political Man*. Garden City, N.Y.: Doubleday & Company, Inc., 1960.

McClelland, David. *The Achieving Society*. New York: Van Nostrand Reinhold, 1961.

McGuire, William J. "Some Impending Reorientations in Social Psychology: Some Thoughts Provoked by Kenneth Ring," *Journal of Experimental Social Psychology*, III, No. 2 (April, 1967).

McNeil, Elton B. "Psychology and Aggression," *Journal of Conflict Resolution*, III, No. 3 (September, 1959), 195–293.

Maier, Norman R. F. *Frustration: The Study of Behavior Without a Goal.* New York: McGraw-Hill Book Company, 1949.

Merritt, Richard L., and Stein Rokkan. *Comparing Nations: The Uses of Quantitative Data in Cross-National Research.* New Haven: Yale University Press, 1966.

Merton, R. K. *Social Theory and Social Structure.* New York: The Free Press, 1949.

Murdock, George P. "Anthropology as a Comparative Science," *Behavioral Science*, II, No. 4 (October, 1957), 249–54.

Nesvold, Betty A. *Modernity, Social Frustration, and the Stability of Political Systems: A Cross-National Study.* Master's Thesis, San Diego State College, June 1964.

Oppenheim, Felix E. *Dimensions of Freedom.* New York: St. Martin's Press, 1921.

Parsons, Talcott, and Edward A. Shils. *Toward a General Theory of Action.* Cambridge, Mass.: Harvard Univeristy Press, 1951.

——, K. Naegele, and J. Pitts. *Theories of Society.* New York: The Free Press, 1961.

Ring, Kenneth. "Experimental Social Psychology: Some Sober Questions about Some Frivolous Values," *Journal of Experimental Social Psychology*, III, No. 2 (April, 1967).

Rokkan, Stein. "Comparative Cross-National Research: II. Bibilography," *International Social Science Bulletin* (1955), 622–41.

Rostow, Walt W. *The Process of Economic Growth.* New York: W. W. Norton & Company, 1952.

Rummel, Rudolph J. "Dimensions of Conflict Behavior Within and Between Nations," *General Systems Yearbook*, VIII (1963), 1–50.

——. "A Field Theory of Social Action with Application to Conflict Within Nations," *General Systems Yearbook*, X (1965), 183–211.

——. "Dimensions of Conflict Behavior within Nations, 1946–59," *Journal of Conflict Resolution*, X, No. 1 (March, 1966), 65–74.

Russett, Bruce M. "Inequality and Instability: The Relation of Land Tenure and Politics," *World Politics*, XVI, No. 3 (April, 1964), 442–54.

——, et al. *World Handbook of Social and Economic Indicators.* New Haven: Yale University Press, 1964.

Singer, J. David, and Melvin Small. "The Composition and Status Ordering of the International System: 1815–1940," *World Politics*, XVIII, No. 2 (January, 1966), 236–82.

Tanter, Raymond. *Dimensions of Conflict Behavior Within and Between Nations, 1958–60.* Monograph prepared in connection with research supported by National Science Foundation Contract NSF-GS224, 1964.

——. "Dimensions of Conflict Behavior Within and Between Nations, 1958–60," *Journal of Conflict Resolution*, X, No. 1 (March, 1966), 41–65.

Walton, Jennifer C. *Correlates of Coerciveness and Permissiveness of National Political Systems: A Cross-National Study.* Master's Thesis, San Diego State College, 1965.

Whiting, John W., and Irvin L. Child. *Child Training and Personality: A Cross-Cultural Study.* New Haven: Yale University Press, 1953.

A CAUSAL MODEL OF CIVIL STRIFE: A COMPARATIVE ANALYSIS USING NEW INDICES[1]

Ted Robert Gurr

This article describes some results of a successful attempt to assess and refine a causal model of the general conditions of several forms of civil strife, using cross-sectional analyses of data collected for 114 polities. The theoretical argument, which is discussed in detail elsewhere, stipulates a set of variables said to determine the likelihood and magnitude of civil strife.[2] Considerable effort was given here to devising indices that represent the theoretical variables more closely than the readily available aggregate indices often used in quantitative cross-national research. One consequence is an unusually high degree of statistical explanation: measures of five independent variables jointly account for two-thirds of the variance among nations in magnitude of civil strife ($R = .80$, $R^2 = .64$).

It should be noted at the outset that this study does not attempt to isolate

[1] This is a revised version of a paper read at the 1967 Annual Meeting of the American Political Science Association, Chicago, September 5–9. The research was supported in part by the Center for Research in Social Systems (formerly SORO), The American University, and by the Advanced Research Projects Agency of the Department of Defense. This support implies neither sponsor approval of this article and its conclusions nor the author's approval of policies of the U.S. government toward civil strife. The assistance of Charles Ruttenberg throughout the process of research design, data collection, and analysis is gratefully acknowledged. Substantial portions of the data were collected by Joel Prager and Lois Wasserspring. The author owes special thanks to Harry Eckstein for his advice and encouragement. Bruce M. Russett and Raymond Tanter provided useful criticisms of the paper in draft form. Research was carried out at the Center of International Studies, Princeton University.

[2] Ted Gurr, "Psychological Factors in Civil Violence," *World Politics*, 20 (January 1968), 245–278.

Reprinted from *The American Political Science Review*, LXII (December, 1968), 1104–24, by permission of The American Political Science Association. The Appendix has been added to the original article.

the set of conditions that leads specifically to "revolution," nor to assess the social or political impact of any given act of strife except as that impact is reflected in measures of "magnitude" of strife. The relevance of this kind of research to the classic concern of political scholarship with revolution is its attempt at identification and systematic analysis of conditions that dispose men to strife generally, revolution included.

I. Theoretical Considerations

The basic theoretical proposition is that a psychological variable, relative deprivation, is the basic precondition for civil strife of any kind, and that the more widespread and intense deprivation is among members of a population, the greater is the magnitude of strife in one or another form. Relative deprivation is defined as actors' perceptions of discrepancy between their value expectations (the goods and conditions of the life to which they believe they are justifiably entitled) and their value capabilities (the amounts of those goods and conditions that they think they are able to get and keep). The underlying causal mechanism is derived from psychological theory and evidence to the effect that one innate response to perceived deprivation is discontent or anger, and that anger is a motivating state for which aggression is an inherently satisfying response. The term relative deprivation is used below to denote the perceived discrepancy, discontent to denote the motivating state which is the postulated response to it. The relationship between discontent and participation in strife is however mediated by a number of intervening social conditions. The initial theoretical model stipulated three such societal variables that are explored here, namely coercive potential, institutionalization,

and social facilitation.[3] Results of a previous attempt to operationalize some of these variables and relate them to strife suggested that a fourth variable whose effects should be controlled is the legitimacy of the political regime in which strife occurs.[4]

The initial model, sketched in simplified form in Figure 1, specified no hierarchical or causal interactions among the mediating variables. Each was assumed to have an independent effect on the fundamental relationship between deprivation and strife. The theoretical arguments with reference to each variable are briefly stated here.

Great importance is attributed in psychological theory and equally, in theoretical and empirical studies of revolutionary behavior, to the inhibiting effects of punishment or coercion, actual or threatened, on the outcome

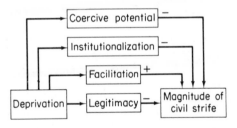

FIGURE 1.

[3] Coercive potential is labelled "retribution" in *ibid*. The theoretical model also stipulates a set of variables that determines the intensity of deprivation. In the research reported in the present article, deprivation was operationalized directly rather than by reference to its component variables. The causal mechanism of the theory is the frustration-aggression relationship, which the author has attempted to modify and apply to collective strife in the light of recent empirical and theoretical work, e.g., Leonard Berkowitz, *Aggression: A Social Psychological Analysis* (New York: McGraw-Hill, 1962), and Aubrey J. Yates, *Frustration and Conflict* (New York: Wiley, 1962).

[4] Ted Gurr with Charles Ruttenberg, *The Conditions of Civil Violence: First Tests of a Causal Model* (Princeton: Center of International Studies, Princeton Univeristy, Research Monograph No. 28, April 1967).

of deprivation. The relationship is not necessarily a linear one whereby increasing levels of coercion are associated with declining levels of violence. Psychological evidence suggests that if an aggressive response to deprivation is thwarted by fear of punishment, this interference is itself a deprivation and increases the instigation to aggression. Comparative studies of civil strife suggest a curvilinear relationship whereby medium levels of coercion, indexed for example by military participation ratios or ratings of regime repressiveness, are associated with the highest magnitudes of strife. Only very high levels of coercion appear to limit effectively the extent of strife.[5] No systematic comparative study has examined whether the curvilinear relationship also holds for levels of coercion actually applied. Comparative studies have, however, emphasized the importance of the loyalty of coercive forces to the regime as a factor of equal or greater importance than the size of those forces in deterring strife, and this relationship is almost certainly linear, i.e., the greater the loyalty of coercive forces, the more effective they are, *ceteris paribus*, in deterring strife.[6] Two measures of coercion are used in this study: *coercive force size*, which is hypothesized to vary curvilinearly with levels of strife, and coercive force size weighted for the degree of loyalty of coercive forces to the regime, referred to throughout as *coercive potential*, which is expected to have a linear relationship with strife.

The second intervening variable is *institutionalization*, i.e., the extent to which societal structures beyond the primary level are broad in scope, command substantial resources and/or personnel, and are stable and persisting. Representative of the diverse arguments about the role of associational structures in minimizing strife are Huntington on the necessity of political institutionalization for political stability, Kornhauser on the need for structures intervening between mass and elite to minimize mass movements, and a variety of authors on the long-range tendencies of labor organizations to minimize violent economically-based conflict.[7] Two underlying psychological processes are likely to affect the intensity of and responses to discontent. One is that the existence of such structures increases men's value opportunities, i.e., their repertory of alternative ways to attain value satisfaction. A complementary function is that of displacement: labor unions, political parties, and a range of other associations may provide the discontented with routinized and typically non-violent means for expressing their discontents.[8] The proposed relationship is linear: the greater the institutionalization, the lower the magnitude of strife is likely to be.

Given the existence of widespread discontent in a population, a great number of social and environmental conditions may be present that facilitate the outbreak and persistence of strife.

[5] See Douglas Bwy, "Governmental Instability in Latin America: The Preliminary Test of a Causal Model of the Impulse to 'Extra-Legal' Change," paper read at the American Psychological Association Annual Convention, New York, September 2–6, 1966; Jennifer Walton, "Correlates of Coerciveness and Permissiveness of National Political Systems: A Cross-National Study," (M.A. thesis, San Diego State College, 1965); Gurr and Ruttenberg, *The Conditions of Civil Violence* . . . , 81–84.

[6] See, for example, Chalmers Johnson, *Revolution and the Social System* (Stanford: The Hoover Institution on War, Revolution and Peace, 1964), pp. 14–22.

[7] Samuel P. Huntington, "Political Development and Political Decay," *World Politics*, 17 (April 1965), 386–430; William Kornhauser, *The Politics of Mass Society* (New York: The Free Press, 1959); and Arthur M. Ross and George W. Hartmann, *Changing Patterns of Industrial Conflict* (New York: Wiley, 1960), among others.

[8] Gurr, "Psychological Factors . . ."

They may be categorized according to their inferred psychological effects, for example, according to whether they facilitate interaction among the discontented, or provide the discontented with a sense that violent responses to deprivation are justified, or give them the means to make such responses with maximum effect, or shelter them from retribution.[9] Two aspects of facilitation are treated separately in this study: *past levels of civil strife* and *social and structural facilitation* per se. The theoretical basis for the first of these variables is that populations in which strife is chronic tend to develop, by an interaction process, a set of beliefs justfying violent responses to deprivation; the French tradition of urban "revolution" is a striking example. Social and structural facilitation (referred to below as "facilitation") comprises aspects of organizational and environmental facilitation of strife, and the provision of external assistance. The operational hypotheses are that the greater the levels of past strife, and of social and structural facilitation, the greater is the magnitude of strife.

Two considerations suggested the incorporation of the fourth intervening variable examined in this study, *legitimacy of the regime*. A study of strife for the years 1961–1963 identified a number of nations that had less strife than might be expected on the basis of characteristics they shared with more strife-ridden polities.[10] One apparent common denominator among them was a high degree of popular support for the regime. This appeared consistent with Merelman's recently proposed learning-theory rationale for legitimacy, to the effect that people comply with directives of the regime in order to gain both the symbolic rewards of governmental action and the actual

rewards with which government first associated itself, an argument that applies equally well to acceptance of deprivation and is compatible with experimental findings, in work on the frustration-aggression relationship, that people are less aggressive when they perceive frustration to be reasonable or justifiable.[11] The proposed relationship of legitimacy as an intervening variable is linear: the greater is regime legitimacy at a given level of deprivation, the less the magnitude of consequent strife.

II. Operational Measures

The universe of analysis chosen for evaluating the model comprised 114 distinct national and colonial political entities, each of which had a population of one million or more in 1962.[12] Data on civil strife were collected for 1961 through 1965. Cross-sectional multiple and partial correlation techniques were used. The use of product-moment correlation coefficients was justified on grounds of their necessity for multiple regression, although not all the indicators formally meet the order-of-measurement requirements of the techniques used.

Because of the very considerable difficulties of operationalizing a number of the variables, and the fact that most of the indicators constructed are new,

[9] *Ibid.*

[10] Gurr and Ruttenberg, *The Conditions of Civil Violence . . .* , 100–106.

[11] Richard M. Merelman, "Learning and Legitimacy," *The American Political Science Review*, 60 (September 1966); see also the work of Pastore and of Kregarman and Worchel, reviewed in Berkowitz, *op. cit.*, *passim.*

[12] Five polities meeting these criteria were excluded: Laos on grounds that at no time in the 1960's did it have even the forms of a unified regime, and Albania, Mongolia, North Korea, and North Vietnam for lack of sufficient reliable data. The universe nonetheless includes polities with more than 98 percent of the world's population.

this article gives relatively close attention to the data collection and scaling procedures.

With the exception of magnitude of strife and its components, the underlying variables examined in this study are unmeasured and must be inferred from indicators. In most instances they are in fact unmeasureable by aggregate data, since they relate in the instance of deprivation-induced discontent to a state of mind, and in the case of the intervening variables to conditions that have their effect only insofar as the discontented perceive them, and moreover perceive them as relevant to their response to deprivation. Following Blalock's recommendation that "when dealing with unmeasured variables it will usually be advisable to make use of more than one indicator for each underlying variable," each of the summary measures used in this study is derived by combining two to seven indicators of the underlying variable. This procedure has not only the advantage Blalock attributes to it, namely of minimizing the effects of confounding variables, but also facilitates incorporation of various empirically-discrete conditions that have theoretically-identical effects.[13]

MAGNITUDE OF CIVIL STRIFE

The dependent variable of the theoretical model is magnitude of civil strife. Civil strife is defined as all collective, nongovernmental attacks on persons or property that occur within the boundaries of an autonomous or colonial political unit. By "nongovernmental" is meant acts by subjects and citizens who are not employees or agents of the regime, as well as acts of such employees or agents contrary to

[13] Hubert M. Blalock, Jr., *Causal Inferences in Nonexperimental Research* (Chapel Hill: University of North Carolina Press, 1964), pp. 166–167, italicized in original.

role norms, such as mutinies and coups d'état. Operationally the definition is qualified by the inclusion of symbolic demonstrative attacks on political persons or policies, e.g., political demonstrations, and by the exclusion of turmoil and internal war events in which less than 100 persons take part.

A three-fold typology of civil strife is also employed, based on an empirical typology of civil strife events identified by Rummel, Tanter, and others in a series of factor analyses. The general categories, and representative subcategories, are

1. *Turmoil:* relatively spontaneous, unstructured mass strife, including demonstrations, political strikes, riots, political clashes, and localized rebellions.
2. *Conspiracy:* intensively organized, relatively small-scale civil strife, including political assassinations, small-scale terrorism, small-scale guerrilla wars, coups, mutinies, and plots and purges, the last two on grounds that they are evidence of planned strive.
3. *Internal war:* large-scale, organized, focused civil strife, almost always accompanied by extensive violence, including large-scale revolts.[14]

[14] In each of a number of analyses by Rummel and others a set of "domestic conflict" measures was factor analyzed. Turmoil, indexed by riots and demonstrations, is found to be a distinct dimension in all the analyses; two other factors, labelled by Rummel "revolution" and "subversion," are in some cases separate and in others combined. Principal components of the "revolution" dimension are coups, palace revolutions, plots, and purges; the category is labelled here conspiracy. Guerrilla war and terrorism are major components of the "subversion" dimension, here labelled internal war. See Rudolph J. Rummel, "A Field Theory of Social Action with Application to Conflict within Nations," *Yearbook of the Society for General Systems Research*, X (1965), 189–195; and Raymond Tanter, "Dimensions of Conflict Behavior Within Nations, 1955–1960: Turmoil and Internal War," *Peace Research Society Papers*, III (1965), 159–183. The subcategories used here are adapted, with their operational definitions, from Rummel, "Dimensions of Conflict

Various measures of the relative extent of civil strife have been used in recent literature, among them counts by country of number of strife events of various types, factor scores derived from such typologies, number of deaths from violent strife, man-days of participation in strife, and scaling procedures that take account of both number of events and their severity.[15] One can infer from frustration-aggression theory that no single measure of magnitude of aggression, individual or collective, is likely to be sufficient. It is likely that high levels of discontent may be expressed either in intense, short-lived violence or in more protracted but less severe strife. Moreover, the proportion of a collectivity that participates in civil strife ought to vary with the modal intensity of discontent: mild discontent will motivate few to participate, whereas rage is likely to galvanize large segments of a collectivity into action.

Three aspects of civil strife thus ought to be taken into account in specifying its magnitude:

1. *Pervasiveness:* the extent of participation by the affected population, operationally defined for this study as the sum of the estimated number of participants in all acts of strife as a proportion of the total population of each polity, expressed in terms of participants per 100,000 population.
2. *Duration:* the persistence of strife, in-

dexed here by the sum of the spans of time of all strife events in each polity, whatever the relative scale of the events, expressed in days.
3. *Intensity:* the human cost of strife, indexed here by the total estimated casualties, dead and injured, in all strife events in each polity as a proportion of the total population, expressed as casualties per 10,000,000 population.

To approximate these requirements an extensive data-collection and -estimation effort was undertaken. Coding sheets and a coding manual were devised for recording a variety of information about any strife event, and a large number of sources scanned and coded to get as full as possible a representation of the strife events that occurred in the 114 polities in the 1961–1965 period. Three sources were systematically searched for data: *The New York Times* (via its *Index*), *Newsyear* (the annual volumes of *Facts on File*), and *Africa Digest*. This information was supplemented from a variety of other sources, among them *The Annual Register of World Events, Africa Diary: Weekly Record of Events in Africa, Hispanic-American Report,* and country and case studies. Some 1100 strife events were thus identified, coded, and the data punched onto IBM cards.[16]

[16] Information coded, in addition to that required for the three measures specified, included the socio-economic class(es) of the initiators, the social context in which they acted, the category of events, the targets and apparent motives of action, the number and role of coercive forces, and the extent and types of external support for initiators and regime, if any. Although no formal reliability tests were undertaken, the four coders did extensive practice coding on the same set of materials prior to coding and reviewed points of disagreement, and the author reviewed all coding sheets for internal consistency and, where necessary, recoding or search for additional information. It should be noted that the 1100 "events" include many cumulated reports, e.g., civil rights demonstrations in the U.S. were treated as a single set of events, all European-OAS terrorism in Algeria as a single event, etc.

Behavior Within and Between Nations," *Yearbook of the Society for General Systems Research*, VIII (1963), 25–26.

[15] See, for example, Rummel, *op. cit.;* Tanter, *op. cit.;* Bruce M. Russett, "Inequality and Instability: The Relation of Land Tenure to Politics," *World Politics*, 16 (April 1964), 442–454; Charles Tilly and James Rule, *Measuring Political Upheaval* (Princeton: Center of International Studies, Princeton University, 1965); and Ivo K. and Rosalind L. Feierabend, "Aggressive Behaviors within Polities, 1948–1962: A Cross-National Study," *Journal of Conflict Resolution*, 10 (September 1966), 249–271.

Many small-scale strife events, and some larger ones, probably went unreported in these sources and hence are not included in this civil strife data bank. Moreover, much reported and estimated data is in varying degrees inaccurate. However, neither random nor systematic error seem sufficient to affect in any substantial way the analyses or conclusions reported here; the data are adequate for the purposes to which they are put.[17]

Data estimation procedures were used to circumvent the substantial missing-data problem. Methods for determining number of initiators serve as examples. The coding sheet itself contained two "number of initiators" scales. The first was a modified geometric progression of two used to record proximate estimates of initiators, its first interval being 1 to 40, its highest 55,001 to 110,000; for purposes of summing such estimates to obtain total number of initiators, the midpoint of each interval was used. The second scale was used for recording rough estimates, sometimes coder estimates, of number of initiators, ranging from "less than 100" (set equal to 40 for purposes of computing totals) to "10,001 to 100,000" (set equal to 40,000). Data for events

for which no estimate could be made were supplied by calculating and inserting means for the appropriate subcategory of event, e.g., if a riot was coded "no basis for judging" for number of initiators, it was assigned the average number of initiators of all riots for which estimates were available.

"Duration" posed little difficulty, being coded on a geometric progression whose first two intervals were "one-half day or less" and "one-half to one day," and whose upper intervals were four to nine months, nine to fifteen months, etc. No event was assigned a duration of more than five years, though some began before and/or persisted after the 1961–1965 period.

Casualties were coded similarly to number of initiators, the principal missing-data component being estimates of injuries. The ratio of injuries to deaths was calculated for all events of each subcategory for which both data were available—the general ratio for all well-reported strife being 12: 1—and was used to estimate injuries for all such events for which "deaths" but not injuries estimates were given.[18]

Strife events occurred in 104 of the 114 polities during the 1961–65 period. Pervasiveness, Duration, and Intensity scores were calculated separately, following the guidelines specified above, for turmoil, conspiracy, and internal war for each country, and for all strife taken together for each polity. All the distributions were highly skewed, hence were subjected to a $\log (X + 1)$ transformation. To obtain combined magnitude scores for turmoil, conspiracy, internal war, and all strife, the three component logged scores were

[17] It has been suggested that strife in countries with press restrictions is underreported. As a check on this type of systematic error a nine-point measure of press freedom was incorporated in initial analyses; the measure is from Raymond B. Nixon, "Freedom in the World's Press: A Fresh Appraisal With New Data," *Journalism Quarterly* (Winter 1965), 3–14. The correlations of this measure, in which high scores reflect low press freedom, with some measures of strife are: Duration, +19; Intensity, +17; Pervasiveness, −16; Total magnitude of strife, +11. The first two are significant at the .05 level, the third at .10. In effect, *more* strife tends to be reported from polities with low press freedom, not less, as might be expected. The results almost certainly reflect the association of high levels of economic development and press freedom in the Western nations, which tend to have less strife than the developing nations.

[18] The missing-data procedures gave implausibly-high estimates for initiators and casualties for a number of events. In subsequent and comparable analysis it seems advisable to rely on estimates of deaths alone, rather than casualties, and to insert means derived from comparable events *in comparable countries* rather than such events in all countries.

added, divided by eight to obtain their eighth root, and the anti-log used as the polity magnitude-of-strife score. The distributions remained skewed, but substantially so only in the case of internal war, which by our definitions occurred in only 25 of the 114 polities.[19]

MEASURES OF DEPRIVATION

A very large number of conditions are likely to impose some degree of relative deprivation on some proportion of a nation's citizens. Similarly, all men are likely to be discontented about some of their conditions of life at some point in time. On the basis of prior theoretical and empirical work, however, it was possible to construct, and subsequently to combine, a set of cross-nationally comparable indices of conditions that by inference cause pervasive and intense types of deprivation, relying in part on aggregate data and in part on indices constructed by coding narrative and historical material. In the initial stages of data collection a large number of measures were constructed, some of them representing short-term and some persisting conditions, some of each relating to economic, political, and sociocultural deprivation. Whenever possible, separate measures were included of the intensity of inferred deprivation and of its pervasiveness, i.e., of the proportion of population presumably affected, plus a third measure combining the two elements. A correlation matrix for 48 such measures and a variety of strife measures was generated, and 13 representative deprivation measures selected for combination.[20] The general rationale for the two general types of measure, short-term and persisting deprivation, and the measures finally selected, are summarized [in the list below].

1. *Economic discrimination* is defined as systematic exclusion of social groups from higher economic value positions on ascriptive bases. For each polity the proportion of population so discriminated against, if any, was specified to the nearest .05, and the intensity of deprivation coded on a four-point scale (see below). The proportion and the intensity score were multiplied to obtain a polity score.
2. *Political discrimination* is similarly defined in terms of systematic limitation in form, norm, or practice of social groups' opportunities to participate in political activities or to attain elite positions on the basis of ascribed characteristics. Proportionality and intensity scores were determined and combined in the same manner as economic discrimination scores. The "intensity" scales were defined as follows:

Intensity Score	Economic Discrimination	Political Discrimination
1	Most higher economic value positions, *or* some specific classes of economic activity, are closed to the group.	Some significant political elite positions are closed to the group, *or* some participatory activities (party membership, voting, etc.).

[19] Tables are available on request from the author listing the 114 countries, their strife scores, the summary measures of deprivation and mediating conditions discussed below, and the data sources.

[20] The 48 deprivation measures, with only one statistically significant exception, were positively associated with strife, most of them at a relatively low level. The thirteen were selected with regard to their representativeness, relatively high correlations with the dependent variables, and low intercorrelations.

2	Most higher and some medium economic value positions are closed, *or* many specific classes of economic activity.	Most or all political elite positions are closed *or* most participatory activities, *or* some of both.
3	Most higher and most medium economic value positions are closed.	Most or all political elite positions and some participatory activities are closed.
4	Almost all higher, medium, and some lower economic value positions are closed.	Most or all political elite positions and most or all participatory activities are closed.

3. *Potential separatism* was indexed by multiplying the proportional size of historically-separatist regional or ethnic groups by a four-point intensity measure.[21] The intensity of separatist deprivation was scored as follows:

Intensity Score	*Type of Inferred Separatism*
1	The separatist region or group was incorporated in the polity by its own request or mutual agreement.
2	The separatist region or group was assigned to the polity by international agreement or by fiat of a former colonial or governing power, except when (3) or (4) below holds.
3	The separatist region or group was forcibly assimilated into the polity prior to the twentieth century, *or* was forcibly conquered by a former colonial power prior to the twentieth century.
4	The separatist region or group was forcibly assimilated into the polity during the twentieth century, *or* was forcibly reassimilated in the twentieth century after a period of autonomy due to rebellion or other circumstance.

4. *Dependence on private foreign capital*, indexed by negative net factor payments abroad as a percentage of Gross Domestic Product in the late 1950's, is assumed to be a chronic source of dissatisfaction in an era characterized by economic nationalism. The greater the proportion of national product that accrues to foreign suppliers of goods or capital, the greater the inferred intensity of deprivation; the extent of such deprivation was assumed equal to the proportion of population engaged in the monetary economy. The polity score is the extent score × the intensity score.[22]

5. *Religious cleavages* are a chronic source of deprivation-inducing conflict. The scale for intensity of religious cleavage takes account both of number of organized religious groups with two percent or more of total population (the major Christian and Muslim subdivisions are counted as separate groups) and of the duration of their coexistence, the greater that duration the less the inferred intensity. The extent measure is the proportion of the population belonging to any organized religious group. The polity score is the product of the two scores.

[21] Coding judgments for both discrimination indices and for separatism were made on the basis of country studies. The proportionality measures are versions of indices reported in Ted Gurr, *New Error-Compensated Measures for Comparing Nations* (Princeton: Center of International Studies, Princeton University, 1966), 67–90.

[22] A crude measure of the proportion of each polity's population engaged in the monetary economy, to the nearest .10, was constructed for the purpose of weighting this and some other measures. The measure was based primarily on labor census data.

6. *Lack of educational opportunity* was indexed, in proportionality terms only, by subtracting primary plus secondary school enrollment ratios ca. 1960 from 100. Education is so widely regarded as an essential first step for individual socioeconomic advancement that one can infer deprivation among the uneducated, and among the parents of children who cannot attend school if not yet among the children themselves.

Persisting Deprivation In the very long run men's expectations about the goods and conditions of life to which they are entitled tend to adjust to what they are capable of attaining. In the shorter span, however, some groups may persistently demand and expect values, such as greater economic opportunity, political autonomy, or freedom of religious expression, that their societies will not or cannot provide. Six indicators of persisting deprivation were combined to obtain a single long-run deprivation measure.

These six measures all had distributions approaching normality, and correlations with several strife measures ranging from .09 to .27. To combine them they were weighted to bring their means into approximate correspondence, and each polity's scores added and then averaged to circumvent the missing data problem.

Short-Term Deprivation Any sharp increase in peoples' expectations that is unaccompanied by the perception of an increase in value capabilities, or any abrupt limitation on what they have or can hope to obtain, constitute relative deprivation. We inferred that short-term, relative declines in system economic and political performance were likely to be perceived as increased deprivation for substantial numbers of people. Indices were devised of five kinds of short-term economic deprivation and two of political deprivation.

1. *Short-term trends in trade value, 1957–60 compared with 1950–57:* The percentage change of trade value, exports + imports, for 1957–60 was compared with the rate for 1950–1957, and any relative decrease in the later period was treated as an indicator of short-term economic deprivation. Decreases were scaled so that polities with lower rates of increase in the earlier period received greater deprivation scores than those with high rates.
2. *Short-term trends in trade value, 1960–63 compared with 1950–60:* Procedures identical with 1 above, were used. Both measures were incorporated in the final analysis because both were markedly correlated with strife measures but had a relatively low intercorrelation of .18.[23]
3. *Inflation 1960–63 compared with 1958–61:* Data on cost-of-living indices were scaled and combined in such a way that the highest deprivation scores were assigned to polities with substantial and worsening inflation in the 1958–63 period, the lowest scores (0) to polities with stable or declining costs-of-living throughout the period.
4. *1960–63 GNP growth rates compared with 1950's growth rate:* Economic growth rate data were scaled so that polities having low rates in the 1950's and even lower rates in the early 1960's received the highest deprivation scores; those with moderate rates in the 1950's but substantial relative decline in the

[23] The two measures will be used in subsequent analyses to examine time-lag relationships between short-term economic deprivation and strife. The trade data, obtained primarily from United Nations sources, was converted to U.S. currency when necessary to maintain comparability over time.

early 1960's received somewhat lower deprivation scores; and those with steadily high, or moderate but steadily increasing, rates received zero deprivation scores.

5. *Adverse economic conditions 1960–63:* To supplement aggregate data indicators of economic deprivation, several summary news sources were searched for evaluative statements about adverse internal economic conditions such as crop failures, unemployment, export market slumps, drought, etc. Each such description was coded on the following intensity and extent scales:

"Severity" (Intensity) Scores		*"Proportion Affected" (Extent) Scores*	
Moderate	= 1	One region or city, *or* a small economic sector	= 0.2
Substantial, *or* moderate and persisting for more than one year	= 2	Several regions or cities, *or* several economic sectors	= 0.5
Severe, *or* substantial and persisting for more than one year	= 3	Much of country, *or* several major or one dominant economic sector	= 0.7
Severe *and* persisting for more than one year	= 4	Whole country, *or* all economic sectors	= 1.0

The score for each such condition is the product of the extent and intensity scores; the score for each polity for each year is the sum of the "condition" scores; and the score used for the summary index is the sum of annual scores for 1960 through 1963. The sources used were *Hispanic-American Report* for Latin America and the *Annual Register* for other polities.[24]

6. *New restrictions on political participation and representation by the regime* were coded from the same sources for the same years. Seventeen types of action were defined on *a priori* grounds as value-depriving political restrictions, including harassment and banning of parties of various sizes, banning of political activity, and improper dismissal of elected assemblies and executives. These were ranked on a nine-point intensity scale.[25] The extent measure was the

[24] The *Hispanic-American Report* is much more comprehensive a source, hence the mean deprivation scores for Latin America were much higher than those for other polities. As a crude adjustment, the Latin American polity scores were divided by a constant so that their mean approximated that of other polities. The same procedure was followed for indices 6 and 7, below. Analyses of regional clusters of polities, not reported here, provide a check on the adequacy of the procedure.

[25] Types of restrictive actions, and their scale values, are as follows:

1 Amalgamation of splinter party with larger party
1 Restriction or harassment of splinter party
2 Banning of splinter party
2 Amalgamation of minority party with larger party
2 Restriction or harassment of minority party
3 Banning of minority party
3 Amalgamation of a major party with

another major party
3 Restriction or harassment of major party
4 Banning of major party
4 Improper dismissal of regional representative body
4 Improper dismissal of elected regional executive
5 Ban on party activities, parties allowed to continue their organizational existence
5 Improper dismissal of national legislature, with provision for calling new one within a year
5 Improper dismissal of elected chief executive, with provision for replacement within a year
6 Dissolution of all parties, ban on all political activity
6 Improper dismissal of national legislature, no short-term provision for reestablishment
6 Improper dismissal of elected chief executive, no short term provision for reelection

politically-participatory proportion of the population, crudely estimated to the nearest .10 on the basis of voting participation levels and, in lieu of voting data, on the basis of urbanization and literacy levels. The score for each action identified is the product of the intensity and extent scores; the annual polity score the sum of "action" scores; and the summary index the sum of annual scores for 1960–63.

7. *New value-depriving policies of governments 1960–63* were defined as any new programs or actions that appeared to take away some significant proportion of attained values from a numerically or socially significant group, for example land reform, tax increases, restrictions on trade, limitations of civil liberties, restrictive actions against ethnic, religious, or economic groups, and so forth. Two aspects of such policies were taken into account in scaling for intensity: the degree of deprivation imposed, and their equality of application. The "degree of deprivation" scale values are: small = 1, moderate = 2, substantial = 3, most or all = 4. The "equality of application" scale values are: uniform = 1, discriminatory = 2. The intensity score is the product of values on these two scales. The most intensely depriving policies are assumed to be those intentionally discriminatory and designed to deprive the affected group of most or all the relevant value, e.g., seizure of all property of absentee landlords without compensation (score = 8). Deprivation is inferred to be least intense if the policy is uniformly applicable to all the affected class of citizens and deprives them of only a small part of the value, e.g., a 5 percent increase in corporation tax rates (score = 1). The extent measure is a crude estimate of the proportion of the adult population likely to be directly affected, the permissible values being .01, .02, .05, .10, .20, .40, .60, .80 and 1.00. The score for each policy identified is the product of the intensity and extent scores; the annual polity score the sum of "policy" scores; and the summary index the sum of annual scores for 1960–63. The sources are the same as for (6) and (7).[26]

Three summary short-term deprivation scores were calculated for each polity from these seven indices. The five economic variables were multiplied by constants so that their means were approximately equal and averaged to circumvent the missing-data problem. This is the "short-term economic deprivation" index referred to below. The summary measures of politically-related deprivation were similarly combined to obtain a summary "short-term political deprivation" measure. The two measures were then added to comprise a single "short-term deprivation" measure for the purposes of some subsequent analyses.

[26] The annual scores for (5), (6), and (7) are being used in a series of time-lagged and cross-panel correlation analyses, not reported here, in further tests of causal relationships.

MEASURES OF
THE MEDIATING VARIABLES

Coercive Potential and Size of Coercive Forces A composite index was constructed to take into account four aspects of the regime's apparent potential for controlling strife. Two of the component indices represent the man-power resources available to the regime, namely military and internal security forces participation ratios, i.e., military personnel per 10,000 adults ca. 1960 (n = 112), and internal security forces per 10,000 adults (n = 102). The two distributions were normalized and their means brought into correspondence by rescaling them using 10-interval geometric progressions. The other two component indices deal respectively with the degree of *past loyalty of coercive forces to the regime,* and the extent of *illicit coercive-force participation in strife in the 1960–65 period.*

The rationale for the five-point coercive-force loyalty scale, below, is that the more recently coercive forces had attacked the regime, the less efficacious they would be perceived to be by those who might initiate strife—and the more likely they might be to do so again themselves. Countries were scored on the basis of information from a variety of historical sources.

Loyalty Score	Regime States and Military Attempts to Seize Control of the Regime
5	As of 1960 the polity or its metropolitan power had been autonomous for 25 years or more and had experienced no military intervention since 1910.
4	As of 1960 the polity or its metropolitan power had been autonomous for 5 to 24 years and had experienced no military intervention during that period; *or* had been autonomous for a longer period but experienced military intervention between 1910 and 1934.
3	The polity last experienced military intervention between 1935 and 1950, inclusive.
2	The polity last experienced military intervention between 1951 and 1957, inclusive.
1	The polity last experienced military intervention between 1958 and 1960, inclusive.

For 28 polities that became independent after 1957 no "loyalty" score was assigned unless the military or police did in fact intervene between independence and the end of 1960. For purposes of calculating the summary score, below, a military loyalty score for these polities was derived from the "legitimacy" score.

Insofar as the military or police themselves illicitly initiated strife in the 1961–65 period, they lost all deterrrent effect. To quantify the extent of such involvement, all military or police participation in strife was determined from the data bank of 1100 events and for each polity a "coercive forces strife participation" score calculated, by weighting each involvement in a mutiny or a turmoil event as one and each involvement in any other event (typically coups and civil wars) as two, and summing for each country.

All four of the "coercive potential" measures were correlated in the predicted direction with several preliminary measures of strife levels. The participation ratios had low but consistently negative correlations with strife; the "loyalty" and "strife participation" indices had correlations of the order of -40 and $+40$ with strife respectively.[27] The composite "coercive potential" score was calculated by the following formula:

Coercive potential

$$= 10 \cdot \sqrt{\frac{L[2(\text{HiR}) + 1(\text{loR})]}{1 + P}}$$

where: L = "loyalty" score;
HiR = the higher of the scaled military and security forces participation ratios;[28]

[27] These are product-moment correlation coefficients, the strife measures including measures of duration, pervasiveness, intensity, and total magnitude of strife for 1961–65. The last two strife measures are defined differently from those employed in the present analysis, but are derived from the same 1100-event data bank.

[28] If one or the other ratio was missing, it was assumed equal to the known ratio. Internal security force ratios for 94 polities are reported in Gurr, *New Error-Compensated Measures for Comparing Nations,* 111–126.

loR = the lower of the participation ratios; and

P = "coercive forces strife participation" score.

The effect of the formula is to give the highest coercive potential scores to countries with large coercive forces characterized by both historical and concurrent loyalty to the regime. The more recently and extensively such forces have been involved in strife, however, the lower their coercive potential score.

A second coercion measure was included in the final analysis to permit a further test of the curvilinearity hypothesis. The measure used is the expression in brackets in the coercive potential formula above, i.e., a weighted measure of the relative sizes of military and internal security forces (*coercive force size*).

Institutionalization Indices of institutional strength and stability which I found in previous analyses to be negatively associated with strife are the *ratio of labor union membership to nonagricultural employment, central government budgeted expenditure as a percentage of Gross Domestic Product*, ca. *1962*, and the *stability of the political party system*.[29] A ten-interval geometric progression was used to normalize the first of these indices, the second was multiplied by 100 and rounded to the nearest 10. To index characteristics of party systems two scales were used, one relating to the number of parties, the other to party system stability per se:

No. of parties score	Characteristics
0	no parties, or all parties illegal or ineffective
1	one or several parties, membership sharply restricted on ascriptive bases (typically along ethnic lines) to less than 20 percent of the population
2	one party with no formal or substantial informal restrictions on memberships
3	one party dominant
4	two-party (reasonable expectation of party rotation)
5	multi-party

Party system stability score	Party System Characteristics
0	no parties, or membership restricted on ascriptive bases to less than 20 percent of population
1	unstable
2	all parties relatively new (founded after 1945), long-range stability not yet ascertainable
3	moderately stable
4	stable

Scores on these two scales were combined on an 8-point scale using party stability as the primary indicator of institutionalization but giving highest scores at each stability level to systems with larger numbers of party structures.

The summary institutionalization measure was constructed using this formula:

Institutionalization
$$= 3(hiI) + 2(midI) + loI,$$

where: hiI = the highest of the three institutionalization scores, etc.

This procedure gives greatest weight to the most institutionalized sector of society on the assumption that high institutionalization in one sector com-

[29] The first two indices are reported in *ibid.*, 33–66, 91–110. Correlations among all three and strife measures are reported in Gurr and Ruttenberg, *The Conditions of Civil Violence*, *passim*. The party characteristics are recoded from Arthur S. Banks and Robert B. Textor, *A Cross-Polity Survey* (Cambridge: M.I.T. Press, 1963), raw characteristics 41 and 43.

pensates for lower levels in others. The highest scores are attained by the Eastern European Communist states while the scores of the Western European democracies are slightly lower. The lowest-scoring polities are Ethiopia, Haiti, Nepal, and Yemen.

Facilitation Two aspects of facilitation were indexed separately: *past levels of civil strife* and "*social and structural facilitation*" per se. The "past levels of strife" measure was derived from the Eckstein data on frequency of internal wars of various types in the period 1946–59; although its reliability is only moderate it covers a longer period and a larger number of polities than other available data.[30] Data were collected for those of the 114 polities not included in the Eckstein tabulation, using the same procedure, a *New York Times Index* count, and recollected for a few others. Weights were assigned to events in various categories, e.g., riots = 1, coups = 5, and a summary score for each polity calculated. The distribution was normalized with a $\log (X + 1)$ transformation.

The terrain and transportation network of a country constitute a basic structural limitation on the capabilities of insurgents for maintaining a durable insurrection. A complex "inaccessibility" index was constructed taking account of the extent of transportation networks related to area, population density, and the extent of waste, forest, and mountainous terrain; the highest inaccessibility scores were received by polities like Bolivia, Sudan, and Yemen, which have limited transportation networks and large portions of rugged terrain.[31]

[30] Harry Eckstein, "Internal War: The Problem of Anticipation," in Ithiel de Sola Pool *et al.*, *Social Science Research and National Security* (Washington, D.C.: Smithsonian Institution, March 5, 1963).
[31] Inaccessibility appears to be an almost-

A crucial "social" variable that facilitates strife is the extent to which the discontented can and do organize for collective action. The relative strength of Communist Party organizations was used as a partial index, taking into account both the number of party members per 10,000 population and the status of the party. Unfortunately no comparable data could be obtained for extremist parties of the right. Party-membership ratios were rescaled to an 11-point scale based on a geometric progression of 2. The party status scale, below, is based on the premise that illegal parties are more facilitative of strife because their membership is likely, because of the exigencies of repression, to be more dedicated, better organized, and committed to the more violent forms of conflict. Factionalized parties are assumed to be more facilitative because they offer more numerous organizational foci for action.

Communist party status
Score *and characteristics*

0 In power *or* nonexistent.
1 Out of power; no serious factionalization or multiple organization; party permitted to participate in electoral activities.
2 Out of power; multiple factions or organizations; party permitted to participate in electoral activities.
3 Out of power; party excluded from electoral activities but other party activities tolerated.
4 Out of power; no serious factionalization or multiple organization; party illegal and/or actively suppressed.
5 Out of power; multiple factions or organizations; party illegal and/or actively suppressed.

The score for each polity is the scaled

but-not-quite necessary condition for protracted internal wars. With one exception all such internal wars in the post-1945 period occurred in polities with high or very high scores on this index; the exception, a notable one, is Cuba.

membership ratio times the party status score.

The third measure of facilitation is the extent of external support for initiators of strife in the 1961–65 period. Each strife event in the 1100-event data bank was coded for the degree of support for initiators (if any) and for the number of nations supporting the initiators in any of these ways. The scale points for "degree of support" are provision of arms and supplies ($= 1$), refuge ($= 2$), facilities and training ($= 3$), military advisors and mercenaries ($= 4$), and large ($1,000 +$) military units ($= 5$). The event support score is the "degree" score times the "number of nations" score, these scores then being summed for all events for each polity to obtain a polity score. This measure alone has a relatively high correlation with strife level measures, ranging from .3 to .4; its two extreme outliers, South Vietnam and the Congo, are also among the three extreme outliers on the total magnitude of strife distribution.

The three social and structural facilitation measures were weighted to bring their means into approximate correspondence, several missing-data items estimated, and the weighted measures added to obtain the composite index.

Legitimacy The legitimacy of a regime can be defined behaviorally in terms of popular compliance, and psychologically by reference to the extent to which its directives are regarded by its citizens as properly made and worthy of obedience. In lieu of evidence on compliance or allegiance necessary to operationalize the concept directly, I combined one indicator of an inferred cause of legitimacy, the circumstances under which the regime attained its present form, with an indicator of an inferred effect, the durability of the regime. The "character" of the regime was scored on a seven-point scale:

Character Score	*Origins of national political institutions*
7	Institutions are wholly or primarily accretive and autochthonous; reformations, if any, had indigenous roots (although limited foreign elements may have been assimilated into indigenous institutions).
6	Institutions are a mixture of substantial autochthonous and foreign elements, e.g., polities with externally-derived parliamentary and/or bureaucratic systems grafted to a traditional monarchy.
5	Institutions are primarily foreign in origin, were deliberately chosen by indigenous leaders, and have been adapted over time to indigenous political conditions. (By adaptation is meant either the modification of regime institutions themselves or development of intermediate institutions to incorporate politically the bulk of the population.)
4	Institutions are primarily foreign in origin, have been adapted over time to indigenous political conditions, but were inculcated under the tutelage of a foreign power rather than chosen by indigenous leaders of their own volition.
3	Institutions are primarily foreign in origin, were deliberately chosen by indigenous leaders, but have *not* been adapted over time to indigenous political conditions.

| 2 | Institutions are primarily foreign in origin, were inculcated under the tutelage of a foreign power, and have not been adapted to indigenous political conditions. |
| 1 | Institutions are imposed by, and maintained under threat of sanctions by, foreign powers (including polities under colonial rule as of 1965). |

A similar scale, based on the number of generations the regime had persisted as of 1960 without substantial, abrupt reformation, was constructed for durability:

Durability Score	Last major reformation of institutions before 1960
7	More than eight generations before 1960 (before 1800).
6	Four to eight generations (1801–1880).
5	Two to four generations (1881–1920).
4	One to two generations (1921–1940).
3	One-half to one generation (1941–1950).
2	One-quarter to one-half generation (1951–1955).
1	Institutions originated between 1956 and 1960, or were in 1960 in the process of transition.

Examples of coding decisions about "major reformations" are that France experienced such a change in 1957; that most French tropical African polities date their basic institutional structures from the 1946 reforms, not the year of formal independence; that the Canadian regime dates from 1867, when dominion status was attained; and that many Latin American regimes, despite performance of musical chairs at the executive level, attained their basic institutional structures at various (historically specified and coded) points in the mid- or late nineteenth century.

The summary legitimacy index was constructed by summing and rescaling the "character" and "durability" scores.[32]

III. Results of Correlation and Regression Analysis

The results of four multiple regression analyses are discussed in this paper, one of them in detail. The dependent variables in the four analyses are, respectively, total magnitude of civil strife, magnitude of conspiracy, magnitude of internal war, and magnitude of turmoil. The correlations between the ten summary independent variables and these four strife measures are given in Table 1. The independent variables all correlate with the dependent variables in the predicted direction, with the exception of coercive force size. The r's for the remaining nine independent variables are significant at the .01 level except for four correlates of internal war, three of which are significant at the .05 level.

The hypothetical curvilinear relationship between coercive force size and total magnitude of strife (TMCS) is examined graphically in Figures 2 and 3, each of which is a smoothed curve of deciles of the independent variable plotted against TMCS. Figure 2, based on all 114 polities, suggests an apparent tendency, among countries with relatively small forces, for strife to increase with the size of those forces, and also a slight increase in TMCS at very high

[32] The following rescaling was used, the sum of the "durability" and "character" scores being given on the upper line, the final legitimacy score on the lower:

Sum:	3,4	5	6	7	8	9	10	11	12	13,14
Legitimacy:	0	1	2	3	4	5	6	7	8	9

Table 1

CORRELATES OF CIVIL STRIFE[a]

Variable[b]	1	2	3	4	5	6	7	8	9	10	11	12	13	14
1. Economic deprivation (+)		48	83	−02	−17	−16	−36	−09	26	32	34	31	25	44
2. Political deprivation (+)			88	08	−18	03	−37	−20	33	27	44	18	30	38
3. Short-term deprivation (+)[c]				04	−20	−07	−42	−17	34	34	46	28	32	48
4. Persisting deprivation (+)					−04	−21	−14	−37	−04	17	29	26	27	36
5. Legitimacy (−)						25	48	02	−05	−15	−29	−23	−29	−37
6. Coercive force size (±)							53	27	31	04	−23	−11	−01	−14
7. Coercive potential (−)								41	−14	−37	−44	−39	−35	−51
8. Institutionalization (−)									−19	−40	−35	−23	−26	−33
9. Past strife levels (+)										41	24	16	30	30
10. Facilitation (+)											42	57	30	67
11. Magnitude of conspiracy												30	32	59
12. Magnitude of internal war													17	79
13. Magnitude of turmoil														61
14. Total magnitude of strife														

[a] Product moment correlation coefficients, multiplied by 100. Underlined r's are significant, for $n = 114$, at the .01 level. Correlations between 18 and 23, inclusive, are significant at the .05 level.

[b] The proposed relationships between the independent variables, nos. 1 to 10, and the strife measures are shown in parentheses, the ± for coercive force size signifying a proposed curvilinear relationship. Examination of the r's between the independent and dependent variables, in the box, shows that all are in the predicted direction with the anticipated exception of coercive force size, and that all but one are significant at the .05 level.

[c] Short-term deprivation is the sum of scores on the short-term economic and short-term political deprivation measures. The separate short-term deprivation measures were used in the regression analyses reported below; the summary measure was used in the causal inference analysis.

levels of coercive forces.[33] It is quite likely that countries with protracted political violence expand their coercive forces to meet it. It also seems likely that armies in countries facing foreign threats cause less dissatisfaction—by their presence or actions—than armies in states not significantly involved in international conflict. Both factors might contaminate the proposed curvilinear relationship, so countries with either or both characteristics were removed and the relationship plotted for the remaining 69 countries; the results, in Figure 3, show curvilinearity

[33] The S-shape of this relationship is considerably more pronounced when coercive-force size is related to total magnitude of turmoil; see Ted Gurr, "Urban Disorder: Perspectives from the Comparative Study of Civil Strife," *American Behavioral Scientist*, 10 (March-April 1968).

even more distinctly. Figure 4 indicates that the measure of coercive force potential, in which size is weighted for military loyalty to the regime, is essentially linear, as predicted. The latter measure is used in the multiple regression analyses, below.[34]

[34] Note: The vertical axes in Figures 2, 3 and 4 give the average magnitude of civil strife scores for deciles of countries with coercive forces of increasing size (Figures 2 and 3) and for deciles of countries with increasingly large coercive forces relative to their loyalty. The range of TMCS scores for the 114 polities is 0.0 to 48.7, their mean 9.0, and their standard deviation 7.7. Units on the horizontal axes represent numbers of cases, not proportional increases in force size/loyalty; the figures represent the scores of the extreme cases. Eleven rather than ten groupings of cases were used in computations for Figures 2 and 4; the curves of all three figures were smoothed by averaging successive pairs of decile scores.

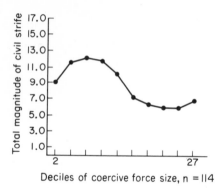

FIGURE 2. Magnitude of civil strife and coercive force size, 114 polities.

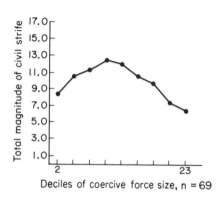

FIGURE 3. Magnitude of civil strife and coercive force size, 69 low-conflict polities.

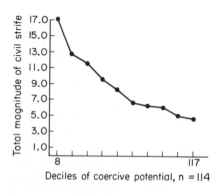

FIGURE 4. Magnitude of civil strife and coercive potential.

Eight of the ten independent variables (excluding coercive force size and short-term deprivation, the sum of the two specific short-term deprivation measures) are included in the multiple regression analyses summarized in Table 2. The variables yield considerable and significant multiple correlation coefficients (R), including a high R of .806 for total magnitude of strife (R² = .650); a moderately high R for conspiracy of .630 (R² = .397); a similar R for internal war of .648 (R² = .420); and a somewhat lower R for turmoil of .533 (R² = .284).[35] There are several possible explanations for the finding that total magnitude of strife is accounted for nearly twice as well as the several forms of strife. One technical factor is that all the class-of-strife measures have greater distributional irregularities than does TMCS, hence TMCS should be somewhat better explained. It is also possible that the categorization employed has less empirical merit than other work has suggested, i.e., that conspiracy, internal war, and turmoil are not sharply distinct forms of civil strife. To qualify this possibility, the correlation matrix in Table 1

[35] Significant computational errors in internal war and TMCS scores of several countries were identified and corrected after completion of the analyses reported here. Robert van den Helm of Princeton University has analyzed the corrected data, using the combined short-term deprivation measure in lieu of the two separate measures, with these multiple regression results: for TMCS, R² = .638; conspiracy, R² = .391; internal war, R² = .472; and turmoil, R² = .284. The significant increase in the degree of explanation for internal war is the result of increased correlations between magnitude of internal war and short-term deprivation (from .28 in Table 1 to .34); facilitation (from .57 to .61); and legitimacy (from −.23 to −.26). The r between magnitudes of turmoil and internal war increases from .17 to .23, the r between TMCS and internal war from .79 to .86. No other results of the analyses reported here are significantly affected by the reanalysis. The actual TMCS scores shown in Table 3 are corrected ones.

Table 2

MULTIPLE LINEAR REGRESSION RESULTS: SIMPLE CORRELATIONS, PARTIAL CORRELATIONS, AND STANDARD WEIGHTS[a]

Dependent Variables	Independent Variables								R, R²
	Econ. Dep.	Pol. Dep.	Per. Dep.	Coerce.	Instit.	Past CS	SS Facil.	Legit.	
Total Magnitude of Strife:									
Simple r's	44	38	36	−51	−33	30	67	−37	
Partial r's	24	(09)	39	−17	(07)	(04)	55	−26	
Constant	−3.11								
Weights	.177	.066	.271	−.140	.056	.024	.481	−.184	R = .806 R² = .650
Magnitude of Conspiracy:									
Simple r's	34	44	29	−44	−35	24	42	−29	
Partial r's	(10)	24	22	(−11)	(−09)	(03)	19	(−15)	
Constant	1.10								
Weights	.094	.238	.194	−.120	−.088	.026	.181	−.135	R = .630 R² = .397
Magnitude of Internal War:									
Simple r's	31	18	26	−39	−23	16	57	−23	
Partial r's	(14)	(−08)	22	−17	(11)	(−07)	48	(−07)	
Constant	−3.66								
Weights	.128	−.073	.186	−.179	.102	−.066	.513	.063	R = .648 R² = .420
Magnitude of Turmoil:									
Simple r's	25	30	27	−35	−26	30	30	−29	
Partial r's	(07)	(08)	23	(−09)	(−05)	21	(04)	−19	
Constant	1.37								
Weights	.072	.085	.223	−.102	−.056	.205	.043	.192	R = .533 R² = .284

[a] Simple correlations from Table 1 are repeated here to facilitate comparisons. Partial correlations in parentheses have standard (beta) weights that are significant at less than the .05 level, using the one-tailed *t* test *within* = 114. Since this analysis is concerned with what is, effectively, the entire universe of polities, all the correlations are in one sense "significant," but those in parentheses are of substantially less consequence than the others. The weights are reported to facilitate comparisons of the relative importance of the independent variables; because of the use of a variety of scaling and combination procedures for both independent and dependent variables, the weights do not permit direct interpretations, for example, of the effect of a one-unit decrease in intensity of economic discrimination on extent of turmoil.

suggests that the forms of strife are only weakly related in magnitude—the highest r among the three is .32—but it may still be that they are more strongly related in likelihood, and hence that the universe of strife is more homogenous than the typology suggests. The least-predicted class of strife—turmoil—might be better accounted for if turmoil events in the context of internal wars, e.g., riots and localized rebellions in such polities as the Congo and South Vietnam, were categorized as aspects of the internal wars in these countries rather than turmoil per se. The most likely substantive interpretation of the relatively low predictability of turmoil, however, is that much turmoil is a response to a variety of locally-incident deprivations and social conditions of a sort not represented in the indices used in this study.

The multiple regression equation for total magnitude of strife was used to calculate predicted magnitude of strife scores. Only ten polities have predicted scores that differ from their actual scores by more than one standard deviation (7.70 units of TMCS). These polities, and three others that have discrepancies approaching one standard deviation, are listed in Table 3.

In five of the thirteen polities—the Congo, Indonesia, Zambia, Rwanda, and Yemen—there is probably systematic error from data-estimation procedures. All of these countries had intense but inadequately-reported civil violence for which only rough and quite possibly exaggerated estimates of deaths were available. When estimates of "wounded" were added to deaths estimates, using a ratio of about twelve to one based on better-reported but smaller-scale events (see above), the result was almost certainly a gross inflation of actual casualties, and hence inflation of TMCS scores. The high actual TMCS score for Israel is the result of a questionable

Table 3

POLITIES WITH LEAST-PREDICTED TOTAL MAGNITUDE OF CIVIL STRIFE[a]

Polity	Predicted TMCS	Actual TMCS[b]	Residual
Congo-Kinshasa	31.6	48.7	+17.1
Rwanda	12.7	28.2	+15.5
Yemen	9.4	23.6	+14.2
Indonesia	23.8	33.7	+ 9.9
Dominican Republic	12.1	21.9	+ 9.8
Italy	3.1	12.3	+ 9.2
Belgium	2.4	10.5	+ 8.1
Zambia	8.1	15.5	+ 7.4
Israel	6.9	14.0	+ 7.1
Argentina	20.5	13.2	− 7.3
Ecuador	18.6	10.1	− 8.5
Volta	9.3	0.0	− 9.3
Paraguay	17.2	5.0	−12.2

[a] See text. A negative residual indicates that a polity had less strife than would be predicted on the basis of the characteristics it shares with other polities; a positive residual indicates more than predicted strife.
[b] Corrected scores. See footnote 35.

coding judgment about the extent and duration of extremist Orthodox religious conflict. More substantive questions are raised by some of the countries. Paraguay, Argentina, Ecuador, and Volta all could be argued to have had an unrealized potential for strife: in fact both Argentina and Ecuador experienced coups in the mid-1960's that according to their initiators were preventive or protective in nature, and early in 1966 the government of Volta succumbed to rioting followed by a coup. In the Dominican Republic, the Congo, and Rwanda the unexpectedly high levels of violence followed the collapse of rigid, authoritarian regimes; one can infer a time-lag effect from the deprivation incurred under the old regimes. These are special explanations rather than general ones however. The lack of apparent substantive similarities among the thirteen poorly-predicted polities suggests that the analysis has included measures of most if not all the general determinants of magnitudes of civil strife.

IV. A Revised Causal Model

One striking result of the regression analyses is that the partial correlations of several of the variables tend to disappear when the other variables are introduced (see Table 2). The short-term deprivation measures consistently decline in consequence, in most instances falling below the .05 level of significance. Institutionalization is in all analyses controlled for by the other variables. One or the other of the two facilitation variables declines to zero in each analysis, "past levels of strife" vanishing in three of the four. Coercive potential and legitimacy also decline in their relation to strife rather sharply. The only variable that is consistently unaffected by the introduction of the control variables specified by the model is persisting deprivation. A preliminary analysis of the behavior of first- and second-order partials suggests what causal interactions and sequences may be involved in these results. The causal path analysis is concerned principally with the sources of the total magnitude of strife, examining the causal sequences of the specific forms of strife only when they appear to deviate from that of all strife.

A basic supposition for the evaluation of causal models is that, if X_1 is an indirect cause of X_3 whose effects are mediated by an intervening variable X_2, then if X_2's effects are controlled the resulting partial correlation between X_1 and X_3 should be aproximately zero. Similarly, if several intervening variables are specified, controlling for all of them or for the last in a causal chain should, if the causal model is not to be falsified, result in a partial correlation

not significantly different from zero.[36]

The initial model of the causes of civil strife (Figure 1) postulated that all the mediating variables intervened separately and simultaneously between deprivation and strife. The results indicate that this supposition is only partly correct: none of the mediating variables appear to affect the relationship between *persisting deprivation* and strife, i.e., there is a certain inevitability about the association between such deprivation and strife. Persisting deprivation is moreover equally potent as a source of conspiracy, internal war, and turmoil. With the partial and weak exception of institutionalization, no patterns of societal arrangements nor coercive potential that are included in the model have any consistent effect on its impact.

The effects of short-term deprivation on strife are substantially different—and, it should be added, uncorrelated with persisting deprivation. The intervening variables do tend to control for short-term deprivation's effects. To determine which one or ones exercise primary control, first-order partials were calculated for the several postulated intervening variables, with these results.

1. The simple r between short-term deprivation and strife = .48[37]

[36] These and other fundamental arguments about causal inference are well summarized in Blalock, *Causal Inferences* . . . , Chapters 2 and 3. A partial correlation coefficient can be most easily regarded as the correlation between X and Z after the portions of X and Z that are accounted for by Y are removed, or held constant. The results discussed below are based on the use of only one of a variety of related causal inference techniques and are open to further, more refined analysis and interpretation. For other applicable approaches see, for example, Hayward R. Alker, Jr., *Mathematics and Politics* (New York: Macmillan, 1965), Chapters 5 and 6.
[37] To simplify evaluation of the effects of the control variables, the summary short-term deprivation variable was employed rather

2. The partial r between short term deprivation and strife is: when the control variable is:

.46	Institutionalization
.45	Legitimacy
.42	Past strife
.36	Facilitation
.34	Coercive potential

Only the last two constitute a significant reduction, and moreover when they are combined, the second-order partial, $r_{d}s \cdot {}_{fc}$, $= .27$, i.e., *coercive potential* and *facilitation* are the only consequential intervening variables affecting the outcome of short-term deprivation. Short-term deprivation taken alone accounts for $(.48)^2 = .23$ of the magnitude of strife; controlling for coercive potential and facilitation reduces the proportion of strife directly accounted for to $(.27)^2 = .07$, a relatively small but still significant amount.

The same controlling effects of coercive potential and facilitation on short-term deprivation occur among the three generic forms of strife. It is worth noting that when the mediating variables are controlled, short-term economic deprivation still accounts directly for a portion of strife, internal war in particular, while political deprivation contributes significantly to conspiracy. These relationships may reflect contamination of the independent and dependent variables because of their partial temporal overlap. Some short-term economic deprivation in the early 1960's may be attributable to protracted internal wars, and successful conspirators may impose politically-depriving policies once they are in power. The relationship between short-term deprivation of both types and the magnitude of turmoil, however, is effectively mediated or controlled by characteristics of the society and its response to strife.

than its economic and political components separately.

The relationships among the mediating variables remain to be examined. Institutionalization has no significant relation to any measure of strife when the other variables are controlled, and in the case of magnitude of total strife and of internal war a weak *positive* relationship emerges, i.e., there is a slight though not statistically significant tendency for high institutionalization to be associated with higher levels of strife. A computation of partials between institutionalization and the other three mediating variables indicates that institutionalization has a preceding or causal relationship both to coercive potential and to the facilitation variables, as shown in the revised model in Figure 3. Polities with high levels of institutionalization tend to have high coercive potential and to have few of the conditions that facilitate strife.

Legitimacy apparently has a causal relationship with strife independent either of deprivation or the other intervening variables. About half of the initial correlation between legitimacy and strife is accounted for by the apparent causal relation between legitimacy and coercive potential, i.e., legitimate regimes tend to have large and, most importantly, loyal military and police establishments. Separately from this, however, high legitimacy is significantly associated with low levels of strife, a finding consistent with the postulate that political legitimacy itself is a desired value, one whose absence constitutes a deprivation that incites men to take violent action against their regimes. The relationship is relatively strongest for total magnitude of strife, less so for turmoil and conspiracy, and inconsequential for internal war.

Coercive potential appears in several respects to be a crucial variable in the revised causal model: it is evidently attributable in part to both levels of institutionalization and of legitimacy, and has a major mediating effect on short-term deprivation. Nonetheless, when all variables are controlled (see Table 2), the partial r between coercive potential and strife is sharply reduced, in two instances below the .05 level of significance. This is in part due to the effects of legitimacy, which is causally linked to both strife and coercive potential.[38] The other major intervening variable is facilitation

$$r_{cs} = -.52;$$
$$r_{cs \cdot f} = -.40,$$

where: c = coercive potential,
s = strife, and
f = social and structural facilitation),

i.e., whether or not facilitative conditions exist for civil strife is partly dependent upon the coercive potential of the regime, and thus indirectly dependent upon legitimacy as well. (The relationship is evidently between coercive potential on the one hand and the "Communist party status" and the "external support for initiators" components of facilitation on the other; coercive potential cannot have any consequential effects on "physical inaccessibility.")

This completes the revision of the causal model with the exception of the second component of facilitation, *past strife levels*. This variable has a consistently lower relationship with strife than other variables, with the exception

of the turmoil analysis. Moreover its partial correlation is reduced to zero in these analyses, with the same exception, the sole significant controlling variable being *social and structural facilitation*. Among the causes of turmoil, however, social and structural facilitation is controlled for by several variables—principally past strife, coercive potential, and institutionalization—whereas past strife remains significant when other effects are partialled out. Both findings support the theoretical argument that suggested the "past strife" measure: a history of chronic strife apparently reflects, and contributes to, attitudes that directly facilitate future turmoil, and indirectly acts to facilitate general levels of strife.

The revised model, with proportional weights inserted, is sketched in Figure 5. The most proximate and potent variable is social and structural facilitation, which accounts for nearly half the explained variance. The deprivation variables account directly for over one-third the magnitude of strife, legitimacy and institutionalization for one-eighth. But these proportions refer only to direct effects, and in the case of both coercive potential and facilitation part of that direct effect, i.e., the illicit participation of the military in strife and the provision of foreign support for initiators, can be determined only from the characteristics of strife itself.[39] The more remote causes of strife, namely deprivation, institutionalization, legitimacy, and prior strife, are the more

[38] Analysis of the correlation coefficients does not indicate definitively that legitimacy contributes to coercive potential rather than vice versa; nor would it be impossible to argue, on the basis of the partial r's alone, that short-term deprivation is a weak intervening variable between coercive potential and facilitation, on the one hand, and strife on the other. It is the plausibility of the theoretical arguments, in each case, that gives deciding force to the interpretation proposed. For a comparable argument see Hugh Donald Forbes and Edward R. Tufte, "A Note of Caution in Causal Modelling," *American Political Science Review*, LXII (December 1968), 1258–64.

[39] Tanter has examined time-lag effects between a number of measures of foreign economic and military assistance for the regime and magnitude of civil violence in 1961–63 for Latin American nations and finds generally weak relationships. The only consequential positive relationship, an indirect one, is between levels of U.S. military assistance and subsequent strife. Raymond Tanter, "Toward A Theory of Conflict Behavior in Latin America." (Paper read to the International Political Science Association, Brussels, September, 1967).

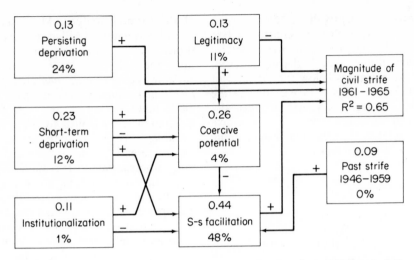

FIGURE 5. Revised causal model of the determinants of magnitude of civil strife. The proportion at the top of each cell is the simple r^2 between the variable and civil strife, i.e., the proportion of strife accounted for by each variable separately. The percentages are the proportion of explained variance accounted for by each variable when the effects of all others are controlled, determined by squaring each partial r, summing the squares and expressing each as a percentage of the sum. The explained variance, R^2, is .65.

fundamental and persisting ones. Some additional regression analyses provide some comparisons. Four of the independent variables relate to inferred states of mind: the two short-term deprivation measures, persisting deprivation, and legitimacy. The R based on these variables is .65, compared with .81 when the remaining four variables are added. The R based on the three deprivation variables alone is .60. These analyses show that all "states-of-mind" conditions contribute significantly to magnitude of strife, but that long-term deprivation has a partial controlling effect on political deprivation. The inference is that short-term political deprivation, as indexed in this study, is most likely to lead to strife if it summates with conditions of persisting deprivation.

We can also ask, and answer, the question, To what extent do the remaining four mediating conditions alone account for magnitude of strife? The variables coercive potential, facilitation, institutionalization, and past strife give

a multiple R of .73, with almost all the explained variance accounted for by the first two variables. This result should provide aid and comfort to those concerned with "levels of analysis" problems: research of this sort can focus on aggregative, societal characteristics—which the mediating variables represent—and the (inferred) psychological level can be ignored with relatively little loss of statistical explanatory power. Why these variables are strongly operative and others, like levels of development and type of political system, are relatively weak still needs answering; the answer may be to treat psychological variables as unoperationalized assumptions, or to replace them with variables whose rationale is strictly in terms of effects of social structure or processes on stability.

A further problem is identification of the set of variables that provides the most parsimonious account of magnitude of civil strife. As one approach to the answer, Figure 5 implies that three variables can be eliminated: coercive potential, institutionalization, and past strife, all of which have no consequential direct effects on TMCS. The remaining five variables—the "state of mind" variables and facilitation—give an R of .80 and R^2 of .64, results almost identical to those obtained when all eight variables are included.[40] Four of the five variables included contribute substantially to the regression equation; as expected, the effects of short-term deprivation, political deprivation in particular, are partially controlled. One important observation is that *social and structural facilitation*, though it is substantially the strongest explanatory variable,[41] has here, as in Figure 5, only a moderate direct controlling effect on short-term deprivation. One interpretation is that some of the effects of facilitation on TMCS are independent of deprivation. Two of its three component measures, Communist Party status and external support for initiators, have in common a "tactical" element, i.e., one can infer that underlying them are calculations about gains to be achieved through the employment of strife. This tactical element is not wholly independent of deprivation, inasmuch as three of the four correlations between facilitation and deprivation measures are significant, ranging from .17 to .34 (see Table 1). The basic proposition of this study, that relative deprivation is a necessary precondition for strife, is not challenged by these observations. They do, however, suggest that tactical motives for civil strife are of sufficient importance that they deserve separate operational attention comparable to the conceptual attention given them by conflict theorists.[42]

A number of additional causal inference analyses can be made which might lead to modifications of these conclusions, and of the causal model in Figure 5. Other articles will report the results of causal analyses of various subsets of the universe of polities, and of the causal sequences that can be identified for the several forms of strife.[43]

V. Summary and Conclusion

Quantitative comparative research cannot flourish in a theoretical vacuum, even if it makes use of an armamentarium of techniques of causal inference. This article may not be proof of that assertion, but it should suggest the usefulness of beginning with a theoretical model based on previous substantive work. The theoretical model of the causes of civil strife employed here dictated the construction of a number of aggregate indicators of not-easily-operationalized variables for 114 polities. Eight summary indicators proved to account jointly for two-thirds the variance among nations in relative magnitudes of civil strife during 1961–65 ($R^2 = .65$). Of greater theoretical consequence, the initial analysis of partial correlation coefficients makes possible a number of more precise statements about the causal interactions among the theoretical variables.

---

[40] In a reanalysis using corrected data (see footnote 34), four variables—the combined short-term deprivation measure, persisting deprivation, legitimacy, and facilitation—give an R^2 of .629.

[41] The partial r's for these five variables are: economic deprivation, .27; political deprivation, .13; persisting deprivation, .39; legitimacy, .36; facilitation, .61.

[42] For example Kenneth E. Boulding, *Conflict and Defense: A General Theory* (New York: Harper and Row, 1962); Lewis Coser, *The Functions of Social Conflict* (New York: The Free Press, 1956); and Thomas C. Schelling, *The Strategy of Conflict* (Cambridge, Mass.: Harvard University Press, 1960).

[43] See Gurr, "Urban Disorder," for a causal inference analysis of the sources of turmoil. The turmoil model differs principally in that "past strife levels" has the primary mediating role that facilitation has in the TMCS model.

The fundamental proposition that strife varies directly in magnitude with the intensity of relative deprivation is strongly supported; the three deprivation variables alone provide an R of .60 ($R^2 = .36$), and when a fourth state-of-mind variable, legitimacy, is added the R^2 increases to .43. One criticism of this research, and of other cross-national studies of strife that make inferences about collective manifestations of psychological variables, is that the results are not a "direct" test of the relevance of such variables, since the indices of psychological variables are derived from aggregate data rather than being obtained, for example, from cross-national surveys. It is unquestionably necessary to test all hypotheses, including psychological ones, in a variety of ways, for example to determine whether the inferentially-deprived groups are those most likely to engage in strife, and to ask highly frustrated individuals whether they would, or have, taken part in collective violence. No scientific proposition is ever *directly* confirmed or disconfirmed, but some tests are less indirect than others. However, there is only one scientifically acceptable alternative to regarding the results reported here as strong indirect evidence for the psychological propositions relating deprivation and legitimacy to civil violence. That is to provide some reasonably parsimonious, alternative explanations (substantive or technical) of the fact that indices of inferred collective states of mind account for two-thirds of the explained variance (43 percent compared with 65 percent for all variables) in total magnitude of strife.

The effects of the intervening or mediating variables on the disposition to civil violence proved considerably more complex than those of the deprivation variables. Regime legitimacy apparently has no consequential mediating effect on deprivation but acts much as deprivation itself does:

low levels of legitimacy, or by inference feelings of illegitimacy, apparently motivate men to collective violence. Levels of institutionalization, as reflected in high levels of unionization, party system stability, and large public sectors, have no direct mediating effect on deprivation; they are however important determinants of coercive potential and of social facilitation, variables which in turn crucially affect the outcome of short-term deprivation. Social and structural facilitation is the most potent of the intervening variables and appears to have some independent effect on magnitudes of strife. One inference is that the index of this variable reflects tactical decisions to engage in strife as a means of goal attainment. The measure of past levels of strife, 1946–1959, provides a partial test of what might be called the null hypotheses of human conflict, that the best predictor of future conflict is the level of past conflct.[44] The measure has relatively weak relationships with magnitude of strife measures for 1961–65 and is an important mediating variable only among the causes of turmoil.

One striking finding is that nations' levels of persisting deprivation are consistently and directly related to their levels of strife. Deprivation attributable to such conditions as discrimination, political separatism, economic dependence, and religious cleavages tends to contribute at a relatively moderate but constant rate to civil strife whatever may be done to encourage, deter, or divert it, short only of removing its underlying conditions. One other result has important implications for theory, and also for policy, if it is supported by further research.

[44] The test is less than precise because the measures are not comparable; the past strife measure is based on an arbitrary weighting of counts of number of events, whereas the magnitude of strife measures reflect levels of participation, duration, and intensity.

The relation between coercive force size (the relative size of military and internal security forces) and the magnitude of civil violence is distinctly curvilinear: as the level of resources devoted to coercive forces increases, the magnitude of violence also tends to increase up to a certain point, and only at relatively high levels of coercive force does strife tend to decline. Moreover at the outer limit the relationship again tends to change direction: countries with the very largest coercive forces tend to have more strife than those with somewhat smaller forces. When one eliminates from analysis the countries that have experienced protracted internal or external conflict, the basic curvilinear relationship remains. The adage that force solves nothing seems supported; in fact force may make things worse.

Appendix:
Indices for 114 Polities

**MAGNITUDE OF CONSPIRACY,
INTERNAL WAR, TURMOIL, AND TOTAL STRIFE, 1961–1965[a]**

	Magnitude of Conspiracy	*Magnitude of Internal War*	*Magnitude of Turmoil*	*Total Magnitude of Civil Strife*	
				Actual	*Predicted*[b]
Congo-Kinshasa	9.7	47.0[d]	14.3	48.7	31.6
Indonesia	4.6	32.7	4.3	33.7	23.8
South Vietnam	2.6	32.8	6.4	32.8	35.5
Rwanda	9.0	26.9	7.0	28.2	12.7
Yemen	3.7	23.4	4.0	23.6	9.4
Angola	3.2	21.8	4.9	22.1	21.2
Dominican Republic	4.8	18.2	12.2	21.9[f]	12.1
Iraq	9.9	18.3	4.3	20.5	22.2
Venezuela	6.9[c]	12.2[d]	7.7	20.3[f]	18.9
Sudan	1.6	15.3	8.7	20.2	16.9
Algeria	8.8	13.1[d]	11.4	19.5[f]	21.6
Syria	8.7	0.0	15.7	17.8	16.9
Colombia	3.6	12.3[d]	6.0	16.9[f]	14.1
Rhodesia	9.5	0.0	11.2	16.4	14.5
Uganda	1.5	0.0	15.6	15.6	11.2
Zambia	1.5	6.3	14.2	15.5	8.1
Bolivia	7.2	0.0	13.3	15.2	16.4
Cuba	7.4	11.9	3.6	15.2	9.8
Kenya	5.7	9.0	10.9	15.0	12.9
Guatemala	10.1	0.0	7.8[e]	14.5[f]	15.3
Israel	0.0	0.0	13.9	14.0	6.0
Burma	3.5	11.4	3.4	13.9	18.7
Nigeria	2.1	5.7	10.1	13.8	9.5
Argentina	3.2	0.0	12.1	13.2	20.5
Ethiopia	2.1	10.2	8.3	13.2	8.5
Camerouns	13.1	0.0	0.0	13.1	13.7
Italy	4.9	0.0	7.3	12.3	3.1
Peru	2.7	8.6	5.4	12.3	13.1
France	2.3	5.8	6.9	12.1	9.5
Tunisia	2.5	0.0	5.2	11.8	9.1
Greece	2.1	0.0	8.6	11.6	5.6
Malawi	5.0	0.0	9.2	11.6	9.2
Singapore	0.0	0.0	11.5	11.5	10.1
Papua-New Guinea	3.3	0.0	10.6	11.3	12.0
India	2.0	3.8	7.7	11.0	8.2
Burundi	7.0	0.0	6.2	10.9	8.1
Belgium	1.8	0.0	10.3	10.5	2.4
Nepal	6.8	0.0	7.0	10.3	11.1
Thailand	0.0	10.3	0.0	10.3	9.1
South Korea	5.5	0.0	9.2	10.2	9.1
U.S.A.	1.0	0.0	10.2	10.2	3.7
Ecuador	4.7	0.0	8.9	10.1[f]	18.6
South Africa	4.6	0.0	6.3	10.0	13.5
Mozambique	7.2	0.0	4.4	9.8	15.5
Guinea	2.7	0.0	6.0	9.5	8.6
Panama	3.0	0.0	7.9	9.5	12.3

	Magnitude of Conspiracy	Magnitude of Internal War	Magnitude of Turmoil	Total Magnitude of Civil Strife	
				Actual	Predicted[b]
Nicaragua	5.2	0.0	6.0	9.4	9.6
Portugal	3.0	0.0	6.9	9.3	7.4
Iran	2.1	0.0	7.8	8.4	11.6
Honduras	4.7	6.2	1.9	8.3	7.6
Mali	2.0	8.1	2.4	8.3	6.9
Philippines	4.2	5.4	4.1	8.3	9.6
Ceylon	1.5	0.0	8.2	8.2	10.9
Jordan	1.7	0.0	7.0	8.1	5.9
Ghana	3.6	0.0	5.2	7.9	12.0
Somalia	2.2	0.0	7.8	7.9	4.3
Haiti	6.2	0.0	3.8	7.8	12.9
Dahomey	1.8	0.0	6.8	7.7	8.7
Brazil	2.5	0.0	6.4	7.4	14.1
Chad	2.8	0.0	4.8	7.2	11.5
Morocco	2.2	0.0	5.6	6.7	9.7
Liberia	1.9	0.0	5.3	6.6	5.6
Sierra Leone	1.9	0.0	4.4	6.5	4.0
Libya	1.2	0.0	6.3	6.3	4.2
Pakistan	1.5	0.0	6.0	6.3	8.8
Tanganyika	4.5	0.0	3.6	6.2	8.1
Uruguay	1.6	0.0	5.3	6.2	9.1
Japan	1.6	0.0	5.0	5.9	5.9
Lebanon	4.2	0.0	3.4	5.8	10.1
Niger	5.8	0.0	0.0	5.8	9.4
China	3.0	0.0	4.0	5.7[f]	10.6
East Germany	5.4	0.0	1.1[e]	5.5	4.8
El Salvador	3.8	0.0	1.8	5.4	8.1
United Kingdom	3.2	0.0	4.4	5.4	4.7
Czechoslovakia	0.0	0.0	5.3	5.3	5.6
Spain	4.1	0.0	1.7	5.2	5.1
Senegal	1.7	0.0	3.8	5.1	7.7
Paraguay	2.1	0.0	3.0	5.0[f]	17.2
Turkey	2.5	0.0	3.9	5.0	7.9
Canada	3.1	0.0	2.7	4.9	4.1
Chile	1.6	0.0	4.1	4.9	7.5
Mexico	2.0[c]	0.0	4.3	4.7[f]	6.9
West Germany	0.0	0.0	4.6	4.6	2.0
Malaya	0.0	0.0	4.5	4.5	6.3
Togo	4.1	0.0	0.0	4.1	9.0
Bulgaria	1.8	0.0	2.8	3.9	5.0
U.A.R.	1.5	0.0	2.9	3.9	2.4
Cambodia	1.6	0.0	2.6	3.8	2.8
U.S.S.R.	0.0	0.0	3.6	3.6	5.3
Poland	0.0	0.0	3.3	3.3	2.3
Yugoslavia	0.0	0.0	3.3	3.3	6.5
Austria	2.3	0.0	2.5	3.1	5.1
Puerto Rico	1.7	0.0	2.8	2.9	2.6
Hungary	2.8	0.0	0.0	2.8	4.1
Costa Rica	2.7	0.0	0.0	2.7	8.7
Australia	0.0	0.0	2.6	2.6	2.4

	Magnitude of Conspiracy	Magnitude of Internal War	Magnitude of Turmoil	Total Magnitude of Civil Strife	
				Actual	Predicted[b]
Ireland	1.2	0.0	2.3	2.3	1.1
Finland	0.0	0.0	2.1	2.1	1.3
Afghanistan	0.0	0.0	2.0	2.0	6.7
Ivory Coast	1.8	0.0	0.0	1.8	4.2
Jamaica	0.0	0.0	1.5	1.5	4.9
C.A.R.	1.3	0.0	0.0	1.3	5.6
Switzerland	1.2	0.0	0.0	1.2	1.4
Saudi Arabia	1.1	0.0	0.0	1.1	2.6
China-Taiwan	0.0	0.0	0.0	0.0	3.5
Denmark	0.0	0.0	0.0	0.0	1.6
Hong Kong	0.0	0.0	0.0	0.0	3.5
Malagasy	0.0	0.0	0.0	0.0	6.4
Netherlands	0.0	0.0	0.0	0.0	3.8
New Zealand	0.0	0.0	0.0	0.0	2.0
Norway	0.0	0.0	0.0	0.0	1.4
Rumania	0.0	0.0	0.0	0.0	2.4
Sweden	0.0	0.0	0.0	0.0	0.4
Volta	0.0	0.0	0.0	0.0	9.2
Mean	2.99	3.30	5.16	9.08	—
Standard Deviation	2.75	8.37	3.96	7.70	—

[a] Three characteristics of strife were measured for each polity: Pervasiveness, Duration, and Intensity. Separate measures of these three characteristics were made for each of the three basic forms of strife, conspiracy, internal war, and turmoil (see text), and for all types of strife taken together (TMCS). *Pervasiveness* was operationally defined as the estimated total number of initiators in all strife events (of each form separately and all forms together) in a polity per 100,000 population. *Duration* was defined as the estimated total number of days of strife (of each form) in a polity, each strife event's duration being counted separately. *Intensity* was defined as the estimated total number of deaths and injuries in all strife events (of each form) in a polity per 10,000,000 population. The distribution of each set of scores was highly skewed and therefore subjected to a $\log (X + 1)$ transformation. (The constant 1 was added because the logarithm of 1 is 0; adding the constant gives polities with no strife a logged score of 0.0.) To obtain combined magnitude scores for turmoil, conspiracy, internal war, and TMCS, the logged scores of the three characteristics of each were added and divided by 8. The anti-log was used as the summary score for each type of strife. This is equivalent to multiplying each polity's scores on the three "characteristics" measures and calculating their fourth root. The effect of the transformations is to give scores that, except for internal war, are approximately normal in distribution. Note that TMCS is not the numerical sum of the conspiracy, internal war, and turmoil measures; it is separately calculated as specified above, but is by definition equal to or greater than the magnitude of any one type of strife. South Vietnam is an example of an anomaly: the TMCS score is equal to the internal war score, although both turmoil and conspiracy scores are shown. This is the result of rounding and of the transformations: the raw score of magnitude of internal war is so great relative to that of other forms of strife that the increment provided by them is too small to be reflected in the TMCS score. The polities are listed in order of decreasing actual TMCS. See also footnotes c through f, below.

[b] The predicted magnitude of strife scores were calculated by applying the multiple regression equation in Table 5 to the data on eight of the independent variables listed in Tables 2 and 3. Only nine polities have predicted scores that deviate by more than one standard deviation (7.70 units of TMCS) from their actual scores, a degree of correspondence reflected in the high R of .806. Four polities have negative predicted TMCS scores, a result that is statistically but not empirically possible. One possible interpretation is that these polities' social patterns—as indexed by the mediating variables—are such that higher levels of deprivation could be tolerated without any consequential increase in strife. See also footnote f, below.

[c] Corrected scores for magnitude of conspiracy. Scores used in the analyses reported in the text were Venezuela, 9.1; Mexico, 2.6.

[d] Corrected scores for magnitude of internal war. Scores used in the analyses reported in the text were Congo, 26.4; Venezuela, 16.3; Algeria, 0.0; Colombia, 10.7.

[e] Corrected scores for magnitude of turmoil. Scores used in the analyses reported in the text were Guatemala, 8.7; East Germany, 0.3.

[f] Corrected scores for total magnitude of civil strife. Scores used in the analyses reported in the text, including calculation of the regression equations to obtain the "predicted" scores, were Dominican Republic, 13.6; Venezuela, 26.9; Algeria, 20.5; Colombia, 15.0; Guatemala, 13.0; Ecuador, 11.2; China, 6.1; Paraguay, 4.7; Mexico, 5.2.

Table A-2

MEASURES OF DEPRIVATION[a]

	Persisting Deprivation[b]	Short-Term Deprivation				Persisting Deprivation[b]	Short-Term Deprivation		
		Economic[c]	Political[d]	Total[e]			Economic[c]	Political[d]	Total[e]
South Africa	151	56	138	194	United States	30	76	40	116
Angola	177	73	22	95	Costa Rica	16	116	32	148
Rhodesia	128	100	133	233	Israel	45	48	10	58
Mozambique	161	47	4	51	Pakistan	45	20	34	54
Argentina	34	163	245	408	China-Taiwan	21	78	47	125
Congo-Kinshasa	47	190	172	362	El Salvador	20	66	60	126
Burundi	107	80	67	147	Canada	36	74	2	76
Indonesia	55	196	74	270	Paraguay	17	70	59	129
Venezuela	40	124	142	266	Singapore	23	84	27	111
Papua-New Guinea	116	33	0	33	Czechoslovakia	24	58	49	107
Burma	65	78	106	184	Malagasy	21	78	30	108
Algeria	38	124	136	260	Saudi Arabia	39	50	3	53
Iraq	89	24	74	98	Mexico	13	70	48	118
Yemen	91	30	42	72	New Zealand	19	78	22	100
Ecuador	67	96	37	133	Tunisia	27	58	10	68
Iran	56	52	98	150	Niger	40	16	17	33
Chad	47	100	75	175	Malawi	18	80	20	100
Cuba	7	170	123	293	Mali	36	30	13	43
Morocco	40	84	109	193	Philippines	27	68	0	68
Turkey	19	70	186	256	Netherlands	14	94	10	104
Bolivia	43	118	64	182	Panama	26	40	26	66
Ghana	41	98	85	183	Honduras	21	50	29	79
Liberia	90	7	18	25	C.A.R.	23	15	54	69
France	7	58	208	266	Guinea	15	70	21	91
India	44	93	61	154	Libya	35	0	31	31
Afghanistan	79	0	47	47	Australia	17	66	18	84
South Vietnam	39	108	55	163	Tanganyika	23	39	26	65
Camerouns	26	70	131	201	Belgium	11	44	39	83
China	20	185	31	216	Spain	17	56	26	82

Polity				
Syria	42	61	86	147
Brazil	30	142	40	182
United Kingdom	18	84	130	214
Colombia	26	145	48	193
Sudan	65	48	22	70
Uganda	63	54	21	75
Togo	17	82	130	212
Guatemala	44	66	63	129
Dahomey	23	97	94	191
Lebanon	67	46	12	58
Ceylon	30	92	74	166
South Korea	14	86	127	213
Kenya	59	68	8	76
Zambia	48	76	31	107
Dominican Republic	24	66	101	167
Ethiopia	65	28	14	42
Yugoslavia	51	76	4	80
Volta	41	70	38	108
Nepal	27	70	76	146
Rwanda	33	93	35	128
U.S.S.R.	39	54	56	110
Chile	25	114	32	146
Senegal	24	82	65	147
Nigeria	45	23	59	82
Nicaragua	36	46	61	107
Haiti	24	122	40	162
Peru	37	45	56	101
Uruguay	7	164	24	188
Malaya	53	24	24	48
East Germany	13	50	40	90
Jamaica	18	63	8	71
Jordan	36	15	2	17
Poland	6	36	70	106
U.A.R.	20	25	39	64
Somalia	33	22	2	24
Hong Kong	32	20	3	23
Ivory Coast	26	18	14	32
Sierra Leone	22	30	8	38
Bulgaria	14	42	18	60
Finland	5	58	26	84
Portugal	19	40	2	42
Puerto Rico	16	24	26	50
Cambodia	23	16	3	19
Thailand	17	30	6	36
Austria	10	40	6	46
Norway	12	40	0	40
Hungary	10	26	18	44
Switzerland	12	32	2	34
Rumania	22	0	0	0
Japan	11	30	0	30
Denmark	4	32	16	48
Greece	8	10	25	35
Italy	8	28	2	30
Sweden	5	34	0	34
West Germany	7	14	10	24
Ireland	4	16	15	31
Mean	36.3	64.3	47.5	111.8
Standard deviation	31.5	41.6	48.0	76.9

a Polities are listed in rank order of estimated total deprivation. A "total deprivation" score, not reported or used in the analyses discussed here, was calculated by adding the total short-term deprivation score to 3 × the persisting deprivation score, the weighting being designed to bring their means into correspondence.

b A weighted average of six separate measures of conditions defined on *a priori* grounds as common and relatively unchanging sources of deprivation.
1. *Economic discrimination*, n = 114, the proportion of each polity's population affected (if any) times the intensity of discrimination, rated on a four-point scale.
2. *Political discrimination*, n = 114, scored as above.
3. *Potential separatism*, n = 114, the proportion of the population politically separatist (if any) times the inferred intensity of separatist sentiment, rated on a four-point scale.
4. *Dependence on foreign capital*, n = 76, negative net factor payments abroad as a percentage of Gross Domestic Product in the late 1950's (if any) times the proportion of population estimated to be in the monetary economy.

5. *Religious cleavages*, n = 114, the number of organized, disparate religious groups in each polity times the duration of their coexistence (rated on a three-point scale, the shorter their coexistence the greater the deprivation) times the proportion of population belonging to organized religious bodies.

6. *Lack of educational opportunities*, n = 114, the proportion of children and youth aged 5–19 not in school ca. 1960.

The six separate indices were weighted and averaged, so that each component index had approximately equal weight in the summary measure.

SOURCES: Data on proportions of population subject to discrimination, and politically separatist, are reported in Ted Gurr, *New Error-Compensated Measures for Comparing Nations* (Princeton: Center of International Studies, Princeton University Research Monograph No. 25, 1966). Factor payments data are from *Yearbook of National Account Statistics 1965* (New York: United Nations, 1966), Tables 1 and 2. Primary sources of religious data are *The Europa Yearbook 1964*, Vols. I and II (London: Europa Publications, 1964); *The Statesman's Yearbook 1965–66* (New York: St. Martin's Press, 1965); and Bruce M. Russett *et al.*, *World Handbook of Political and Social Indicators* (New Haven: Yale University Press, 1964), Tables 73–75. Educational data are from *ibid.*, Table 63.

ᶜ A weighted average of five separate measures of conditions defined on *a priori* grounds as common sources of discontent, relatively susceptible to short-run change compared with those comprised under persisting deprivation, (a) above. The component measures are:

1. *Short-term relative declines in total value of foreign trade, 1957–60 compared with the 1950–57 base*, n = 110.
2. *Short-term relative declines in total value of foreign trade, 1960–65 compared with the 1950–60 base*, n = 110.
3. *Relative increases in inflation rates, 1960–63 compared with 1958–61*, n = 96.
4. *Relative decreases in GNP growth rates, 1960–63 change compared with a 1950's base period*, n = 95.
5. *Economic adversity 1960–63*, n = 112, estimates of the extent and intensity of specified types of adverse internal economic conditions.

The five indices were weighted so that their means were approximately equal, and averaged to circumvent the missing data problem.

SOURCES: The primary source of trade data is the *Yearbook of International Trade Statistics 1964* (New York: United Nations, 1966). The primary source of inflation data is the *Yearbook of Labour Statistics 1965* (Geneva: International Labour Organization, 1966), Table 25. Principal sources of GNP data are *Yearbook of National Account Statistics*, various editions (New York: United Nations), and "Gross National Product: Growth Rates and Trend Data by Region and Country" (Washington, D.C.: Statistics and Reports Division, U.S. Agency for International Development, June 15, 1966). Conditions of economic adversity were coded from *The Annual Register of World Events* (London: *The Times of London*, annual editions for 1960 through 1963), for all countries except those of Latin America, which was coded from *Hispanic-American Report* (Stanford: Institute of Hispanic American and Luso-Brazilian Studies, monthly editions for the 1960–63 period). For tropical African polities *Africa Digest* (London: Africa Publications Trust, bimonthly editions for the 1960–63 period), was used to supplement the *Annual Register*.

ᵈ A weighted total of two measures of short-term political deprivation:

1. *New restrictions on political participation and representation 1960–63*, n = 114, estimates of the seriousness (intensity) and extent of effects of various actions, e.g., banning of parties.
2. *New value-depriving policies of governments 1960–63*, n = 114, incorporating estimates of the intensity of deprivation and extent of effects of new programs.

SOURCES: As listed for economic adversity; footnote (c), above.

ᵉ The sum of the short-term economic and short-term political deprivation scores.

218

MEASURES OF MEDIATING VARIABLES[a]

	Legitimacy[b]	Coercive Potential[c]	Coercive Force Size[d]	Institution-alization[e]	Past Strife Levels[f]	Facili-tation[g]
South Vietnam	0	11	19	24	2.05	106
Congo-Kinshasa	0	3	10	13	1.34	73
Iraq	2	14	21	21	1.59	54
Paraguay	3	28	20	17	2.03	52
Algeria	2	18	20	26	1.36	49
Indonesia	2	12	13	31	2.00	44
Venezuela	5	8	12	28	1.85	42
Ecuador	5	23	14	15	1.91	46
Argentina	4	17	15	21	2.14	40
Burma	3	20	12	16	1.92	41
Guatemala	4	17	10	9	2.09	39
Sudan	0	10	9	9	1.86	34
Syria	0	17	18	14	1.67	36
Bolivia	4	18	12	21	2.02	35
Peru	5	36	13	20	1.62	39
Panama	3	35	12	12	1.76	37
Haiti	5	22	17	5	2.00	32
Colombia	4	23	13	21	1.96	28
Camerouns	3	45	10	24	1.26	34
Thailand	5	58	17	12	1.61	37
Ethiopia	9	24	12	0	1.18	28
Dominican Republic	3	30	18	22	1.26	28
Honduras	7	27	11	12	1.38	26
Iran	7	55	18	13	2.25	33
Brazil	2	24	14	21	1.93	23
El Salvador	6	15	9	12	1.37	21
Rwanda	0	22	5	9	0.60	22
Angola	4	72	13	22	0.30	36
Portugal	6	43	14	31	1.46	25
Ceylon	4	30	7	28	1.52	20
Costa Rica	7	42	6	21	1.86	23
Yemen	8	32	15	0	1.26	22
Kenya	0	23	11	18	1.23	18
France	3	18	22	27	1.80	15
Nicaragua	5	69	16	17	1.72	30
Nepal	4	95	13	5	1.79	38
Philippines	4	63	8	24	2.02	27
Pakistan	3	35	12	11	1.56	20
Lebanon	5	48	17	11	1.89	23
Nigeria	2	24	4	23	1.00	16
Ghana	2	18	11	33	1.20	13
Tanganyika	1	11	4	24	0.30	12
Guinea	3	40	8	37	0.30	19
Uruguay	6	45	12	26	0.48	20
Turkey	6	35	24	20	1.32	16
Papua-New Guinea	5	35	12	29	0.90	16
Niger	1	45	6	32	0.00	20

	Legitimacy[b]	Coercive Potential[c]	Coercive Force Size[d]	Institution-alization[e]	Past Strife Levels[f]	Facili-tation[g]
Uganda	0	19	7	14	0.78	12
Greece	5	81	22	21	1.41	29
Malawi	1	32	10	26	1.32	14
Singapore	1	46	21	21	0.00	20
Japan	3	40	12	31	1.58	15
South Korea	2	31	22	18	1.90	12
Togo	1	11	6	15	0.60	8
Chad	1	26	7	17	0.60	12
Mali	4	35	5	35	0.30	14
Volta	1	14	2	22	0.00	8
C.A.R.	3	30	9	20	0.00	12
Tunisia	2	77	15	28	1.68	23
Spain	7	79	21	15	1.73	23
Mexico	6	92	21	30	1.54	26
Austria	4	49	12	36	0.70	14
Dahomey	1	16	8	18	0.48	5
Chile	7	82	17	18	1.54	23
Mozambique	4	69	12	26	0.00	20
Morocco	4	75	14	24	1.73	19
Malagasy	5	57	11	32	1.02	14
Senegal	3	49	12	33	0.48	11
China	4	72	13	31	1.85	16
Afghanistan	7	84	14	12	1.40	21
United Kingdom	9	95	18	33	1.11	8
Somalia	3	30	14	14	1.18	5
U.S.S.R.	8	63	20	40	1.98	12
U.S.A.	9	46	21	29	1.61	8
India	5	66	11	23	2.40	13
Burundi	9	29	5	11	0.60	5
Cuba	2	35	18	35	2.14	3
Malaya	5	73	18	24	1.36	16
Jordan	5	117	27	24	1.23	28
Ivory Coast	3	42	9	38	0.30	5
Liberia	7	47	13	24	0.48	7
Zambia	1	35	12	23	0.78	3
Sierra Leone	2	35	8	27	0.00	3
Italy	5	89	20	30	2.09	16
Hungary	1	35	18	43	1.40	0
Jamaica	3	49	12	36	1.00	5
Bulgaria	1	56	23	36	1.34	5
Libya	5	96	23	35	1.11	17
Belgium	8	95	18	39	1.20	16
Netherlands	8	95	18	35	0.48	7
Israel	4	96	23	44	1.77	15
Cambodia	5	89	20	23	1.64	14
Rhodesia	2	63	10	19	0.70	7
Canada	7	81	13	27	0.60	12
Norway	8	95	18	37	0.48	15
Yugoslavia	4	79	21	33	1.40	8
South Africa	4	89	16	10	2.11	11

	Legitimacy[b]	Coercive Potential[c]	Coercive Force Size[d]	Institution-alization[e]	Past Strife Levels[f]	Facili-tation[g]
West Germany	3	82	17	29	0.70	9
Hong Kong	3	89	16	13	0.60	12
Sweden	9	95	18	38	0.00	13
Saudi Arabia	7	88	15	15	0.00	12
Puerto Rico	5	110	21	34	0.95	15
Australia	6	84	14	34	0.00	8
Czechoslovakia	1	79	21	46	1.67	3
Ireland	7	77	15	38	1.32	3
New Zealand	7	87	15	29	0.48	7
U.A.R.	4	62	19	23	1.96	13
Rumania	3	77	20	43	1.51	5
Switzerland	9	89	16	32	0.00	7
Denmark	9	95	18	35	0.30	8
China-Taiwan	5	96	23	27	0.85	8
Poland	3	85	18	43	1.67	2
East Germany	0	85	18	48	1.43	2
Finland	6	110	21	36	0.85	10
Mean	4.1	52.0	14.5	24.4	1.22	20.1
Standard deviation	2.5	29.8	5.2	10.2	0.66	15.5

[a] Polities are ranked according to their decreasing structural potential for strife, which was inferred by calculating predicted magnitude of strife scores based on a multiple regression equation that included Coercive potential, Institutionalization, Past strife levels, and Facilitation. The first polity on the list has the greatest *predicted* TMCS, using these four mediating variables, the second polity the second greatest TMCS, etc.

[b] The higher the score, the higher the inferred legitimacy of the political regime, determined by combining scores on two scales (see text) relating, respectively, to the extent to which the regime is an indigenous development and its durability. Data are from a variety of historical sources.

[c] "Coercive potential" is an estimate of the relative size of military and security forces, weighted for their loyalty to the regime. Four component measures were used:

1. *Military personnel per 10,000 adults, ca. 1961*, n = 111, reduced to a ten-interval scale based on a geometric progression.
2. *Internal security forces per 10,000 adults, ca. 1962*, n = 101, reduced to a ten-interval scale based on a geometric progression.
3. *Coercive-force loyalty, 1960*, n = 86. A five-point scale was used (see text); countries with the most recent military intervention in civilian politics as of 1960 received the lowest scores. For 28 polities that became independent between 1957 and 1965, loyalty was inferred from legitimacy using the equation

$$\text{Loyalty} = \frac{\text{Legitimacy} + 1}{2}$$

4. *Coercive forces strife participation 1961–65*, n = 114. Actual military or police participation in civil strife was counted and weighted on an event-by-event basis (see text).

The composite "coercive potential" score was calculated by the following equation:

$$\text{Coercive potential} = \sqrt{\frac{L[2(\text{hi}R) + 1(\text{lo}R)]}{1 + P}} \times 10$$

where: L = "loyalty" score;
$\quad$ $\text{hi}R$ = the higher of the scaled military and security forces participation ratios;
$\quad$ $\text{lo}R$ = the lower of the participation ratios; and
$\quad$ P = "coercive forces strife participation" score.

SOURCES: Military participation ratios are primarily from Russett *et al.*, *World Handbook*, Table 22, and David Wood, "The Armed Forces of African States," *Adelphi Papers*, No. 27 (London: Institute for Strategic Studies, April 1966). Internal security force data are reported in Gurr, *New Error-Compensated Measures*. Past military intervention was determined from historical sources. Military participation in strife, 1961–65, was determined from the 1200-event civil strife data bank.

[d] Coercive force size is the expression in brackets in the Coercive Potential equation, above, i.e., a weighted estimate of the relative sizes of military and internal security forces.

[e] "Institutionalization" is a weighted summary of three indices of institutional strength and stability:

1. *Ratio of labor union membership to nonagricultural employment ca. 1962*, n = 111, normalized by use of a ten-interval scale based on a geometric progression.
2. *Central government budgeted expenditure as a percentage of Gross Domestic Product, ca. 1962*, n = 112, multiplied by 100 and rounded to the nearest 10.9

3. *Political party System stability*, n = 114, based on an eight-point ordinal scale in which the highest scores are assigned to polities with stable multi-party systems, the lowest to polities with no organized parties.

The summary Institutionalization variable was constructed using this equation:

$$\text{Institutionalization} = 3(\text{hiI}) + 2(\text{midI}) + 1(\text{loI}),$$

where: hiI = the highest of the three component scores (above),
midI = the second highest of the three scores, etc.

Sources: Union membership ratios and government budget percentages are reported in Gurr, *New Error-Compensated Measures*. Party system data are primarily from Arthur S. Banks and Robert B. Textor, *A Cross-Polity Survey* (Cambridge: The M.I.T. Press, 1963), raw characteristics 41 and 43.

f "Past strife levels" were calculated from data on frequency of internal wars of various types in the period 1946–1959, as reported in Harry Eckstein, "Internal War: The Problem of Anticipation," in Ithiel de Sola Pool *et al.*, *Social Science Research and National Security* (Washington: Smithsonian Institution, March 5, 1963). Data were collected for those of our 114 polities not included in the Eckstein tabulation, using the same procedure, a *New York Times Index* count, and recollected for a few others. Weights were assigned to events in various categories, and a summary score for each polity calculated. The distribution was normalized with a log $(X + 1)$ trnasformation.

g Three measures of "Social and structural facilitation" were constructed and combined:

1. *Physical inaccessibility*, n = 114, a complex measure that takes account of the extent of transportation networks related to area, population density, and the extent of waste, forest, and mountainous terrain.
2. *Relative strength and status of Communist party organizations*, n = 109. Number of party members per 10,000 population and the status of the party were separately scaled (see text), and the "number" and "status" scores multiplied to obtain a combined score.
3. *External support for initiators of strife 1961–65*, n = 114. Each strife event was coded for the degree of reported foreign support for initiators and the number of nations providing support (see text), if any. The support score for each event is the "degree" score times the number of nations providing support, these scores being summed for events for each polity to obtain a polity score.

The summary Facilitation measure was constructed by weighting the component indices to equalize their means, and then averaging them.

Sources: The component indices of physical inaccessibility were obtained from a variety of sources including *Statesman's Yearbook* and *The Europa Yearbook*, various editions, for transportation data; *Production Yearbook 1965* (Rome: Food and Agricultural Organization, 1966), Table 1, for data on land area and use; and *Good's World Atlas*, 12th edition (Chicago: Rand McNally, 1964), for assessment of terrain. Communist Party data are from *World Strength of the Communist Party Organizations*, 16th Annual Report (Washington, D.C.: Bureau of Intelligence and Research, U.S. Department of State, January 1964). External support levels were calculated from the 1200-event civil strife data bank.

POLITICAL INSTABILITY IN LATIN AMERICA: THE CROSS-CULTURAL TEST OF A CAUSAL MODEL

Douglas P. Bwy*

I. The Preconditions of Political Instability: Toward a Synthesis of Theory and Research on Systemic Dissatisfaction, Legitimacy, and Retribution

PSYCHO-SOCIAL DISSATISFACTION AND POLITICAL INSTABILITY

Although at times quite thin, there does appear to be a common thread of agreement running through most of the classic and contemporary literature on theories of revolution—this being the simple proposition that the majority of the participants engaging in such activity are dissatisfied, discontented, and often disaffected individuals. If we can think of "revolution" for the moment in its most general terms—to subsume under such a conceptual label both the simplest manifestation of civil disorder to the most grandiose occurrence of what might be called basic social change—then, it seems, we are in a position to illustrate the emergence of this basic proposition throughout the literature.

. . .

. . . It appears, [however,] that the causes of political instability are numerous, and that the relationship

* Acknowledgments are due to the National Science Foundation, which partially supported (GS-789) the research for the paper. Special thanks are also due to Professors R. J. Rummel and Raymond Tanter for the use of their (1955–64) conflict data; to Professor Russell Fitzgibbon for the use of his "democratic attainment" ratings across the 20 Latin American republics for 5 time periods since 1945; to Professor Phillips Cutright for making available his individual data (1940–61) from which he composed the "Political Representativeness Index;" and to Professor George Blanksten for guidance and encouragement.

Excerpted from the *Latin American Research Review*, III, No. 2 (Spring, 1968), 17–66, by permission of the author and the Latin American Studies Association. Footnotes have been renumbered.

is indeed complex. We will want, therefore, to take a look at another predictor variable—legitimacy . . . .

LEGITIMACY AND POLITICAL INSTABILITY

Perhaps the most often quoted definition of legitimacy, or political allegiance, has been that offered by S. M. Lipset, who noted that it involved the capacity of a political system to engender and maintain the belief that existing political institutions were the most appropriate or proper ones for the society. The strength of this variable in predicting instability is emphasized by Lipset, who claims that the political stability of any given nation depends more on this factor than on its effectiveness in satisfying wants (the first variable we considered).[1]

.   .   .

Despite their separate treatment here, certainly the model's first two variables —*discontent* and *political legitimacy*— cannot be considered independent. Actually, psychosocial satisfactions and notions of positive affect are closely interrelated sub-systems of phenomena, which can only be separated for analytic purposes . . . .

.   .   .

A number of indirect indicators of legitimacy . . . are available. One such measure is that constructed by Phillips Cutright,[2] in which he used what was

[1] Seymour Martin Lipset, "Some Social Requisites of Democracy: Economic Development and Political Legitimacy," *American Political Science Review*, 53 (March 1959), pp. 90–91

[2] Phillips Cutright, "National Political Development: Measurement and Analysis," *American Sociological Review*, 28 (April 1963). . . . The PRI index was also in: "Urbanization and Change in National Political Structures: 1928–1961," paper prepared for the Carnegie IDRC Joint Study Group on Measurement Problems, Indiana University, October 1964.

termed a "Political Representativeness Index" (PRI). Cutright rated 76 nations over the years 1940 to 1961 according to criteria of: (i) representativeness of the legislative function of government, (ii) quality of the opposition within this legislative function, and (iii) open and competitive election of the central decision-maker. He summed these yearly ratings (thereby obtaining a cumulative, continuous measure for the 22-year period) and T-scored (standardized) the distribution. Since a measure for the 22-year period was not desired for the present paper, Cutright's data were obtained and 5-year raw scores calculated.

Another measure of legitimacy, and one that is also tapping such notions as national cohesion, affective feelings of political dignity, and to some extent even governmental outputs (especially in terms of social welfare legislation), is the "democratic attainment index" constructed by Russell Fitzgibbon. Every five years, since 1945, Fitzgibbon has been sampling the opinions of Latin American experts on 15 criteria[3]

[3] For the most recent publication of the results of these surveys, see: Russell H. Fitzgibbon, "Measuring Democratic Change in Latin America," *The Journal of Politics*, 29 (February 1967), pp. 129–166.

The 15 criteria were: (1) An educational level sufficient to give the political process some substance and vitality. (2) A fairly adequate standard of living. (3) A sense of internal unity and national cohesion. (4) Belief by the people in their individual political dignity and maturity. (5) Absence of foreign domination. (6) Freedom of the press, speech, assembly, radio, etc. (7) Free and competitive elections— honestly counted votes. (8) Freedom of party organization; genuine and effective party opposition in the legislature; legislative scrutiny of the executive branch. (9) An independent judiciary—respect for its decisions. (10) Public awareness of accountability for the collection and expenditure of public funds. (11) Intelligent attitude toward social legislation —the vitality of such legislation as applied. (12) Civilian supremacy over the military. (13) Reasonable freedom of political life from the

he hypothesized were measuring democratic attainment. These specialists fitted the criteria to a series of Likert-type scales, which were then summed for each nation. Since Fitzgibbon also "weighted" these scores in terms of importance (*e.g.*, "open and competitive elections" (access) was weighted twice that of most of the other indices), the adjusted (or weighted) scores were used in the present study.

Following the Almond and Verba premise that feelings of legitimacy are indeed formed during periods of rising participation, a *change* measure was calculated between each of the Fitzgibbon 5-year measures. The same type of transformation was done to the PRI indices. In one test of the model, then, the legitimacy index which measures changes in the "openness" of the regime in the five years (1950–55) just prior to the time period during which the instability data will be recorded (1958–

60), shall be used as an indicator of the formation of legitimacy.

RETRIBUTION: THE CORRELATES OF FORCE

While the distinctions between psycho-social satisfactions and positive affect or political legitimacy were difficult to maintain when discussing the first two variables in the political instability model, this does not appear to be a problem associated with the third variable: perceptions of force or punishment for "extra-legal" behavior. Some notions freely translated from psychology, and particularly those of Arnold Buss, indicate the relationship between force (punishment) and aggression (extra-legal, usually violent, behavior) to be curvilinear. Therefore, very little instability is hypothesized to be found at the two extremes of a permissive-coercive continuum, but great quantities of instability should be found in the center. Buss notes, for example, that low levels of punishment do not serve as inhibitors; it is only high levels which are likely to result in anxiety or flight. Punishment in the mid-levels of intensity acts as a frustrator and elicits further aggression, maintaining an aggression-punishment-aggression sequence.[4]

.   .   .

Theoretically, at least, the study of force in Latin America offers a particularly complex mixture of: (i) the force factor itself, that is, the military and police (which can usually be analytically segregated from other social instruments[5]), and (ii) what might be considered as the loyalty-to-the-regime of these forces. The most significant thing

---

impact of ecclesiastical controls. (14) Attitude toward and development of technical, scientific and honest governmental administration. (15) Intelligent and sympathetic administration of whatever local self-government prevails.

As Charles Wolf of RAND has observed, "there are many shortcomings in the Fitzgibbon method and data, including the ambiguity and heterogeneity of the criteria, the weights applied to the criteria . . , and the qualifications and prejudices of the respondents (nearly all of the respondents were from the United States)." See: Wolf, "The Political Effects of Military Programs: Some Indications from Latin America," *Orbis*, 8 (Winter 1965), pp. 878–879.

Wolf suggests, however, that some of these difficulties could be overcome by independent work with the original data. Among other things, he mentions: (i) the use of only responses to the more distinctly relevant and unambiguous criteria, (ii) the separation of the responses of the more qualified respondents, and (iii) reliability tests, comparing the subjective estimates of the respondents with objective data relating to education, press circulation, the frequency and character of elections, and so on. Fitzgibbon has attempted some of these tests, and the results are reported in the February 1967 issue of the *Journal of Politics*, cited above.

[4] Arnold H. Buss, *The Psychology of Aggression* (New York: John Wiley & Sons, 1961), p. 58.

[5] The budget for ordinary police forces is usually included in the total military outlay.

about tools of repression available for possible use by the regime is, of course, their commitment. Such commitment at any one point in time within any republic, is a tenuous assumption, at best. It has been noted that the fact the president is himself commander-in-chief of these forces, is not necessarily a factor in his maintaining their support.[6]

.   .   .

The ability of the central decision-making components of the government to apply force, then, is clearly tempered by the intervening variable of the loyalty-to-the-government of such force contingents. And thus, in measuring force, one cannot be content with just ratio measures of, say, the number of troops and equipment deployed within the units of analysis over a measure of the population of those units, but must ultimately take into consideration a measure of the loyalty of such forces. A systematic way to approach the problem would be to attempt to ascertain at least an indirect measure of loyalty, and to then take this into consideration when assessing more overt indices of force.[7]

From the foregoing discussion, then, it is not surprising to conclude that a realistic calibration of force within Latin America can become quite complex. Two aggregate measures were selected to assess the notion of force. Although on the face of it, neither one seems to satisfy the measurement problems with respect to (i) independence among variables, and (ii) the loyalty of the force, these considerations shall be discussed in the following section. Military Personnel as a Percentage of the Total Population (1959)[8] was the first aggregate measure. Since this variable has been reported to correlate .99 with what were originally thought to be more sophisticated measures,[9] it was selected, so that it might be more readily comparable to change measures (which take total population into consideration). A second set of data comes from sources searched by the statistical team of the Yale Data Library,[10] and from sources searched by John Powell[11]: and is the Budget Expenditure Allocated to Defense as a Percentage of GNP. The sensitivity of this statistic can be appreciated when one looks at Venezuela (with the highest GNP per capita of all of the republics in 1957, $648) which in 1959 allots only 2.2 percent of its national budget to defense. On the other hand, nations such as Haiti or Paraguay, with the lowest GNP per capita's in 1957 (Haiti = $105; Paraguay = $114), allotted for defense considerably more than

[6] R. A. Gomez, "Revolution, Violence, Political Morality," in: Gomez, *Government and Politics in Latin America* (New York: Random House, 1963), p. 59.

[7] Wyckoff has presented a systematic scheme for analyzing the quality of loyalty. He notes that in states in which the military always intervenes, that the greater the proportion of junior officers to middle and senior officers, the greater the loyalty of the armed forces. In states where the military occasionally intervenes, loyalty is best gauged by the greater proportion of junior plus middle rank officers, as opposed to senior officers. See: Theodore Wyckoff, "The Role of the Military in Latin American Politics," *Western Political Quarterly*, 13 (September 1960), pp. 749–760.

[8] John Powell searched the following source for what he considered to be dependable comparative data: Sandberg, Bengt, and others, *Comparative Data on Latin American Countries*, International Bank for Reconstruction and Development (Washington, D.C., January, 1962). See: John D. Powell, "Military Assistance and Militarism in Latin America," *Western Political Quarterly*, 18 (June 1965), pp. 382–392.

[9] For a discussion of these measures, see: Bruce M. Russett, "Measures of Military Effort," *American Behaviorial Scientist*, 7 (February 1964), pp. 26–29.

[10] Bruce Russett, *et al.*, *World Handbook of Political and Social Indicators* (New Haven: Yale University Press, 1964), pp. 79–80.

[11] Powell, *op. cit.*, p. 384.

Table I

CORRELATION COEFFICIENTS FOR NINE INDICES
OF DOMESTIC VIOLENCE (1958–60)

	1	*2*	*3*	*4*	*5*	*6*	*7*	*8*	*9*
1. Assassinations	1.000	—	—	—	—	—	—	—	—
2. Strikes	−.053	1.000	—	—	—	—	—	—	—
3. Guerrilla War	.218	.225	1.000	—	—	—	—	—	—
4. Government Crises	.226	.399	.602	1.000	—	—	—	—	—
5. Purges	.213	.159	.522	.619	1.000	—	—	—	—
6. Riots	.181	.275	.154	.070	.299	1.000	—	—	—
7. Demonstrations	.354	.401	.097	.189	.310	.582	1.000	—	—
8. Revolutions	−.133	.366	.611	.559	.430	.364	.211	1.000	—
9. Domestic Killed	.167	.141	.417	.567	.928	.122	.209	.330	1.000

[1] Any politically-motivated murder or attempted murder of a high government official or politician.

[2] Any strike of 1,000 or more industrial or service workers that involves more than one employer and that is aimed at national government policies or authority.

[3] Any armed activity, sabotage, or bombings carried on by independent bands or citizens or regular forces aimed at the overthrow of the present regime.

[4] All rapidly-developing situations that threaten to bring the downfall of the present regime, excluding situations of revolt aimed at such overthrow.

[5] Systematic elimination by jailing or execution of political opposition within the ranks of the regime or the opposition.

[6] Any violent demonstration or clash of more than 100 citizens, involving the use of physical force.

[7] All peaceful, public gatherings of at least 100 people for the primary purpose of displaying or voicing their opposition to government policies or authority, excluding those demonstrations of a distinctly anti-foreign nature.

[8] Any illegal or forced change in the top government elite; any attempt at such change; or any successful armed rebellion whose aim is independence from the central government.

[9] Deaths resulting directly from violence of an inter-group nature, thus excluding deaths by murder and execution.

Venezuela: Haiti's defense allocation was 3.0 percent of its GNP, and Paraguay's was 2.8 percent.

II. Political Instability: Defining the Domain and Systematically Measuring It

Political instability has meant many things to many researchers . . . . [T]he primary purpose of this section will not only be to define the concept, but to indicate how political instability might best be systematically measured among the twenty republics of Latin America.

.   .   .

Nine indices were selected[12] to measure different types of domes-

[12] The nine basic variables used in this part of the analysis were those selected and used in a study of conflict behavior within and between nations, conducted by R. J. Rummel in 1963, and published in the *General Systems*

tic aggressive actions against Latin American governments. The definitions of these indicators, and the results from correlating them with each other, appear in Table I. Note that although one can begin to get a notion of the clustering

Yearbook, 8 (1963), pp. 1–50. See also: Rummel, *Dimensions of Conflict Behavior Within and Between Nations*, paper prepared in connection with research supported by the National Science Foundation, under Contract G24827. June 1963, 108 pp.

The Rummel data (gathered for the years 1955–57, for 78 nations) were richly supplemented by Raymond Tanter, when he replicated the Rummel study after gathering similar data for the following three-year period (1958–60) across 83 nations. It is the Tanter data which were factor analyzed, and are presented in Tables I and II.

See: Raymond Tanter, *Dimensions of Conflict Behavior Within and Between Nations, 1958–60*, monograph prepared in connection with research supported by the National Science Foundation, Contract GS224. See also: *Journal of Conflict Resolution*, 10 (March 1966), pp. 41–64.

Table II

ROTATED FACTOR MATRIX

	Factor			
	I	II	III	h²
1. Number of Assassinations	.202	.291	−.759	.702
2. Number of General Strikes	.213	.580	.476	.609
3. Presence or Absence of Guerrilla Warfare	.761	.096	.160	.613
4. Number of Major Governmental Crises	.829	.130	.124	.720
5. Number of Purges	[.878]	.174	−.215	.847
6. Number of Riots	.081	.827	−.025	.691
7. Number of Anti-Government Demonstrations	.113	.865	−.225	.812
8. Number of Revolutions	.606	.321	.547	.770
9. Number of People Killed in Domestic Violence	.849	.029	−.233	.776
Percent of Common Variance	56.8	23.6	19.7	100.0

effect among these nine indices, the pattern is not entirely obvious. The higher coefficients (those at the .50 and above level) seem to show that guerrilla activity is moderately associated with governmental crises (.60), purges (.52), and revolutions (.61). Governmental crises, as well, seem to be correlated with revolutions (.59) and with the number of persons killed in domestic violence (.56). On the other hand, events of a more sporadic nature, such as demonstrations and riots, seem to correlate among themselves more highly than among the other indices (.58).

In order to determine whether or not the clustering effect among these indices would warrant the use of a smaller set of conceptual variables, the matrix of correlation coefficients in Table I was factor analyzed.[13] To obtain that set

[13] The computer program which monitored these calculations was MESA 1, a 95 × 95 Factor Analytic Program with Varimax Rotation. Special thanks are due Northwestern University's Vogelback Computing Center for their generous allowance of computing time.

The lower limit for eigenvalues (i.e., a proportion of variance which may vary from near zero to *n*, where *n* is the number of variables entering a factor matrix) to be included in rotation was 1.00. Rotation is carried out in order to obtain a solution which is not entirely dependent upon each particular

of factors maximizing high and low loadings, the extracted factors were then rotated and a new set of factors obtained, which are presented in Table II.

The values within the table are the correlation coefficients between the original nine indices and the three rotated factors—what were referred to as "factor loadings" previously. By looking at the highest factor loadings, the clustering effects suggested by the correlation matrix are now considerably clarified. The first of the rotated factors, then, is related to five of the indices, namely: guerrilla war, governmental crises, purges, revolutions, and deaths from domestic violence, and unrelated to the rest. The second factor is related to strikes, riots, and demonstrations, but not to the remaining indices. With the exception of two factor loadings with any weight, the third factor appears quite weak in terms of "defining" aggressive activity, and seems to be defined more by high negative loadings,

variable in the analysis. Orthogonal rotation is the fitting of factors to clusters of variables with the restriction that the correlation between factors is zero. The *varimax* criterion is used to rotate orthogonally to "simple structure," that is, the maximization of high and low loadings. Thus, this form of rotation continues to maintain independence among the factors.

and might, therefore, be interpreted as a "lack of conflict" dimension.[14]

The communalities (h^2) indicate the proportion of variation in each index explained by the three factors. The variance of each coefficient can be computed simply by squaring it, and since the factors are independent of each other, the communality of the index represents nothing more than the sum of these squared coefficients. In terms of the fifth index, for example, the three factors explain over 84 percent of the variance about the occurrence of purges. Furthermore, the three rotated factors explain a very high percentage of the variation in all of the indices. ...[A] word about the factors themselves. Demonstrations and riots, and to a certain extent, strikes, represent a kind of sporadic, unorganized conflict dimension in Latin America. To Almond and Coleman, "spontaneous breakthroughs into the political system, such as riots and demonstrations,"[15] were conceptualized as interest articulation by Anomic Groups. To use their name for such a cluster, Factor 2 reflects the degree of *Anomic violence* among the nation-units. The first factor, on the other hand, displays high loadings on guerrilla warfare, revolutions, governmental crises, and deaths from domestic violence—most of which seem to represent illustrations of aggressive actions defined more by an underlying organization and planning. This dimension, therefore, appears to be referencing an *Organized violence* factor, and will be identified as such. The last index

(deaths from domestic group violence), in associating more strongly with Organized violence, indicates that this dimension (at the nation-unit level of analysis) is by far the more violent.

. . .

In addition to the substantive discovery of the two basic dimensions of conflict in Latin America, the factors themselves may be used as criteria for the construction of indices of Organized and Anomic violence. The factor solution, therefore, goes beyond just providing an empirical assessment of the clusterings of original indices on basic underlying variables. Through factor loading, it allows the analyst to "weight" each of the variables composing the index. The indices of Organized and Anomic conflict, therefore, can be weighted according to their loadings, or correlations, with the Organized violence factor, and then with the Anomic violence factor. In this manner, the resulting indices are in effect weighted according to the strength of their intercorrelations with the other indices, rather than arbitrarily. And since the new indices are based on orthogonal factors, they too remain independent.[16]

Four of the original nine indicators of domestic conflict behavior were used

---

[14] One possible way to test this assumption, would be to compute the factor scores for each of the 20 republics on this third dimension. If the assumption is accurate, nations experiencing *low* levels of conflict (e.g., Uruguay and Costa Rica) should come out *high* on such a distribution.

[15] . . . Gabriel Almond and James Coleman (eds.), *The Politics of the Developing Areas* (Princeton: Princeton University Press, 1960), p. 34.

[16] A common term for indices which take all loadings into account is "factor scores," which represent the country's overall score (in standard score form) weighted by the factor loadings for each of the indices in the analysis. Such scores are automatically computed for both unrotated and rotated factor solutions by Mesal, but were not used here because a more discriminating index was desired. For a description of some formulas for calculating these "factor" or "component" scores, see the following sources: Benjamin Fruchter and Earl Jennings, "Factor Analysis," in: Harold Borko (ed.), *Computer Applications in the Behavioral Sciences* (Englewood Cliffs, N.J.: Prentice-Hall, Inc., 1962), pp. 260–262; Henry Kaiser, "Formulas for Component Scores," *Psychometrika*, 27 (1962), pp. 83–88.

to form an index of the first, or Organized violence, factor. Although the variable "the number of purges," came out on this dimension, the decision was made to exclude it from the index on the basis that such occurrences represent more a governmental activity—often, for example, a governmental response to aggressive activity on the part of the populace—and therefore, should not appear among variables ultimately destined for the dependent side of the model.[17] . . . [I]t is not an unwarranted assumption that guerrilla warfare, governmental crises, revolutions, and people killed in domestic group violence, are best measuring in combination Organized violence. And likewise, that strikes, riots, and demonstrations are measuring Anomic violence best in combination. In discussing the construction of indices of this type, Hagood and Price noted that it has been demonstrated that if we wish to use these items to form an index of each factor, we should weight the items (in standard score form) in proportion to their correlations with each factor.[18] The items, then, most highly correlated with Organized violence should receive the higher weights on this index, and those more highly correlated with Anomic violence should receive the higher weights on this index. With these criteria in mind, a formula for computation of the two basic indices to be used in

this study was followed, and is footnoted below. It appears first in basic form, using the Anomic Violence Index as an example, and then in converted form for both the Organized as well as the Anomic Violence Index.[19]

Indices were calculated for the 20 Latin American republics for the three time periods for which data were available: 1955–57 (3 years),[20] 1958–60 (3 years),[21] and 1962–64 (2 years).[22] Since these indices, as computed, did

[19] The computation formulas for both the Organized and Anomic Violence Indices are:

$$\text{Anomic Index} = .508\left[\frac{X_1 - \overline{X}_1}{s_1}\right]$$
$$+ .827\left[\frac{X_2 - \overline{X}_2}{s_2}\right] + .865\left[\frac{X_3 - \overline{X}_3}{s_3}\right]$$

$$\begin{aligned}\text{Anomic Index}\\ \text{Computation Formula}\end{aligned} = \frac{508}{s_1}X_1 + \frac{.827}{s_2}X_2$$
$$+ \frac{.865}{s_3}X_3 - \left[\frac{.508}{s_1}\overline{X}_1 + \frac{.827}{s_2}\overline{X}_2 + \frac{.865}{s_3}\overline{X}_3\right]$$
$$\frac{.761(\text{GU-WAR})}{1.164} + \frac{.829(\text{GVTCRS})}{1.446}$$
$$+ \frac{.606(\text{REVOLU})}{1.905} + \frac{.849(\text{D-KILL})}{995.901}$$
$$- \left[\frac{.761}{1.164}(1.250) + \frac{.829}{1.446}(1.750)\right.$$
$$\left. + \frac{.606}{1.905}(2.050) + \frac{.849}{995.901}(311.400)\right]$$

$$\text{Organized Violence} = \frac{\text{GU-WAR}}{.6537X_1} + \frac{\text{GVTCRS}}{.5733X_2}$$
$$+ \frac{\text{REVOLU}}{.3181X_3} + \frac{\text{D-KILL}}{.0008X_4} - 2.7216$$
$$\frac{.508(\text{STRIKE})}{2.762} + \frac{.827(\text{RIOTS})}{6.018}$$
$$+ \frac{.865(\text{DEMONS})}{1.638} - \left[\frac{.508}{2.762}(1.450)\right.$$
$$\left. + \frac{.827}{6.018}(5.700) + \frac{.865}{1.638}(1.500)\right]$$

$$\text{Anomic Violence} = \frac{\text{STRIKE}}{.1839Y_1} + \frac{\text{RIOTS}}{.1374Y_2}$$
$$+ \frac{\text{DEMONS}}{.5280Y_3} - 1.8419$$

[17] Purges, for example, might be one of the component parts of a factor which allows a population to perceive a government as repressive, and therefore, should appear as an intervening variable (perhaps helping "cause" potential aggressors to temper feelings of hostility with notions of possible reprisal for "deviant" behavior).

[18] S. S. Wilks, "Weighting Systems for Linear Functions of Correlated Variables When There Is No Independent Variable," *Psychometrika*, 3 (March 1938), pp. 24–43; Harold Hotelling, "Analysis of a Complex of Statistical Variables into Principal Components," *Journal of Educational Psychology*, 24 (1933), pp. 417–441, 498–520.

[20] Rummel, *Dimensions of Conflict Behavior . . .*, 1963, op. cit., Appendix II: Raw and Transformed Data, pp. 77–80.

[21] Tanter, *Dimensions of Conflict Behavior . . .*, 1964, op. cit., Appendix II: Raw Data and List of Nations, pp. 71–74.

[22] Rummel, "A Field Theory of Social Action with Application To Conflict within Nations, Appendix II: Data Tables and Definitions," *General Systems Yearbook*, X (1965), 183–211.

Table III

**Z-SCORES OF ORGANIZED AND ANOMIC VIOLENCE
ACROSS THREE TIME PERIODS**

	1955–57		*1958–60*		*1962–64*	
	Organized	*Anomic*	*Organized*	*Anomic*	*Organized*	*Anomic*
Argentina	+3.832	+2.664	+ .934	+1.455	+1.585	+ .212
Bolivia	− .167	− .472	+ .542	− .405	− .119	+ .309
Brazil	+ .539	− .381	−1.027	− .405	+ .884	+2.713
Chile	− .021	− .218	− .919	− .538	− .711	+ .021
Colombia	+ .140	+ .582	+ .251	− .672	+2.192	+1.236
Costa Rica	− .113	− .716	− .886	−1.072	− .998	− .874
Cuba	+ .708	+2.559	+2.994	+ .731	+2.046	− .139
Dominican Republic	− .685	− .716	+ .320	− .525	− .034	+1.745
Ecuador	− .500	− .333	− .904	+ .262	− .197	+1.171
El Salvador	− .685	− .716	− .784	− .605	− .998	− .874
Guatemala	+ .357	+ .705	− .122	+ .022	− .404	− .874
Haiti	+ .741	+1.065	+ .419	− .378	+ .453	− .874
Honduras	− .115	− .520	− .053	− .912	− .328	− .874
Mexico	− .672	− .569	−1.158	+2.533	− .990	− .139
Nicaragua	− .685	− .528	+ .482	− .725	− .996	− .683
Panama	− .685	− .618	− .477	+ .277	− .998	− .683
Paraguay	− .128	− .667	+ .457	+ .170	− .415	− .874
Peru	− .501	− .308	− .292	− .525	+ .629	+ .468
Uruguay	− .685	− .716	−1.167	− .965	− .998	− .874
Venezuela	− .675	− .096	+1.391	+2.278	+ .395	− .109

not allow comparisons across the three time periods (the last period resulting from a coding of conflict only for a two-year period), and since the value for any one country on any index told nothing about its position in relation to the other Latin American republics, the indices were standardized. These standard, or z-scores, appear in Table III.

．　　　．　　　．

III. Testing the Causal Model

The linkages between the three independent variables and each of the dependent variables of Anomic and Organized violence, will be tested through the use of zero-order correlational analysis. In addition, whenever the strengths of the coefficients warrant it, the scatter plots will be presented, thereby allowing us to identify the exact position of any of the twenty republics

in comparison to any of the others. But high correlations between phenomena do not give conclusive evidence about causation. Such evidence is more closely approximated from the results of the systematic application of "cross-lagged panel correlations." This design model is based on the premise that the "effect" should correlate higher with a prior "cause" than with subsequent "cause," i.e., $r_{C_1E_2} < r_{C_2E_1}$.[23] Campbell, and others, have used this design in an effort to discover causation by noticing the direction of the temporal lag which maximizes the correlation.[24] The

[23] See: Donald T. Campbell and Julian C. Stanley, "Experimental and Quasi-Experimental Designs for Research on Teaching," in: N. L. Gage, *Handbook of Research on Teaching* (New York: Rand McNally & Company, 1963), p. 239.

[24] Donald T. Campbell, "From description to Experimentation: Interpreting Trends as Quasi-Experiments," in: C. W. Harris (ed.),

Table IV

RELATIONSHIP OF LEGITIMACY
TO VIOLENCE

Legitimacy	*1955–57 Organized Violence (Z-scored)*	*1955–57 Anomic Violence (Z-scored)*	*1958–60 Organized Violence (Z-scored)*	*1958–60 Anomic Violence (Z-scored)*	*1962–64 Organized Violence (Z-scored)*	*1962–64 Anomic Violence (Z-scored)*
Change in PRI (1955–1950)	−.245	−.442	−.453	−.219	−.615	−.213
Change in PRI (1960–1955)	.111	.003	.073	−.074	.385	.190
Change in FITZ (1955–1950)			−.714	−.138		
Change in FITZ (1960–1955)	.230	.176				
Fitzgibbon Index (1955)			−.504	−.065		
Fitzgibbon Index (1960)	.114	.004				
Legitimacy (1955)[25]			−.384	−.041		
Legitimacy (1960)[26]	.085	−.067				

coefficients calculated for a number of different operationalizations of the variable "legitimacy," and presented in Table IV, offer empirical evidence of the validity of the direction of the relationship postulated in the earlier theoretical discussion of the model. In illustration, the 1955 Fitzgibbon rating of system "openness" correlates −.504 with the occurrence of Organized violence in 1958–60. That is, as the openness (or legitimacy) of the system (in 1955) goes up, instances of Organized violence go down. Ratings of system "openness" in 1960, however, have little or no relationship (.14) to organized violence taking place four to five years

Problems in Measuring Change (Madison: University of Wisconsin Press, 1963), pp. 212–242.

The *panel* correlation, originally designed for use with survey research data, where the same respondent was interviewed at more than one point in time, seems directly applicable here, where data for the same nation is analyzed, also at more than one point in time.

[25] 1950 + 1955 Fitzgibbon ratings.

[26] 1960 + 1965 Fitzgibbon ratings.

Note: Although coefficients were available for all of the data points within the matrix (as, for example, those appearing in all the cells of the first variable, "Change in PRI"), correlations only appear which test the causal model:
$r_{C_1 E_2} < r_{C_2 E_1}$

earlier. Summarizing these findings according to the causal model, we have:
$-.51_{C_1 E_2} > .14_{C_2 E_1}$.

With reasonable assurance that the correct time sequence had indeed been specified among the variables in the model, each of the explanatory variables were correlated with each of the effect variables. The first of these appears in a scatter plot (Figure I[27]) of the relationship between Satisfaction and Organized violence, where Satisfaction is measured by the Annual Growth of GNP per capita.

[27] Satisfaction: "Annual Growth of G.N.P. per Capita," data for 13 of the Latin American republics from the *World Handbook of Political and Social Indicators*, pp. 160–161; data for the remaining (including the corrected calculation for Venezuela) were computed from GNP per capita statistics from the following sources: 1952 GNP per capita: Harold Davis, *Government and Politics in Latin America*, p. 64 (most of these figures came from the *1955 Statistical Abstract of Latin America*). 1957(58) GNP per capita: figures here came from two sources: *The World Handbook of Political and Social Indicators*, pp. 155–157, and the *1960 Statistical Abstract of Latin America*, p. 30; the difference between the 1952 and 1957(58) figures was taken, and divided by the number of years involved, to obtain the annual growth figure.

Pearson Product Moment Correlation = −.63.

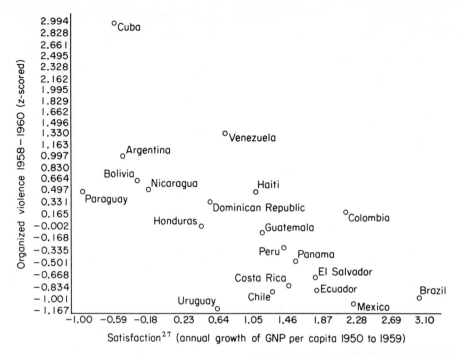

FIGURE I. Satisfaction and organized violence.

The association between satisfaction and Organized violence clearly emerges as both linear and negative (−.63) in the scatter plot displayed in Figure I. Satisfaction doesn't, however, appear to yield the same strong inverse relationship when correlated with Anomic violence. Here the coefficient drops to −.33. As a check on these findings, a separate correlation was run between another index of satisfaction (the Per Cent of the Central Government's Expenditures on Public Health and Welfare in 1958) and Organized violence, which yielded a negative correlation of −.51. Here too, the coefficient between Anomic violence and governmental inputs into public welfare seems to be somewhat lower: −.30. From Figure I, note the apparent explanatory power the change concept of increase or decrease in GNP per capita has over its static counterpart. For example, although Argentina was still the country

with the third highest GNP per capita in 1957, this seems of little consequence in explaining the high incidence of planned violence during this time period. Over the years, prior to the violence (recorded in Figure I), it seems particularly significant to note that Argentinians were steadily getting smaller shares than they had before, of the total goods and services produced by their economy.

It is of special significance that *both* the Organized and Anomic violence measures do yield negative relationships when correlated with the variable "change in GNP per capita." And, although satisfaction has a stronger impact on Organized than on Anomic violence, violence in general goes down as satisfaction goes up. . . .

The form of the relationship between "force" and "aggressive acts against government" was specified as curvilinear. Given the continuing problem of "militarism" in Latin America, however, "force" (as measured by "expenditures on defense," "number of military personnel as a percentage of the population," and so on) cannot be analyzed in the role of inhibiting aggression, simply because the inhibiting agent itself may, and often does, aggress against the government. In short, no independence can be maintained between the present operationalizations at the nation-unit level. Certainly the military often contributes to "governmental crises" (rapidly developing situations that threaten to bring the downfall of the regime) as well as to "revolutions" (extra-legal or forced change in the top government elite, or any successful armed rebellion whose aim is independence from the central government). Such contributions are being picked up by the Organized violence dimension (in Table II), and are often witnessed in the form of golpes militares, military coups, cuartelazos, and so on. To be sure, in some cases the opposition, usually being without the necessary tools for toppling a government, goads the military into performing this function. . . . The point to be made, therefore, is that no adequate test of the relationship between "force" and "violence" (as generally conceived and when measured at the nation-unit level) can be made. On the other hand, this does not appear to be the case when Anomic violence is being considered. Here the population can be reasonably sure that the military force will most likely be brought to bear on anomic breakthroughs, regardless of their origin. . . .

As hypothesized, the scatter diagram displayed as Figure II,[28] reveals the rather strong curvilinear relationship which emerges from an association of Force with Anomic Violence. Countries which input high levels of force (and it might be added, most of those on the right side of this continuum consistently do so) are: the Dominican Republic (in this 1958–60 time period, still under the rule of Trujillo), Haiti (under Duvalier), and Paraguay (under Stroessner). These same countries maintained low levels of Anomic violence during the same time period. Peru is not normally thought of as falling within the same category as the nations just mentioned—and to be sure, if any long-term analysis were being displayed, Peru would undoubtedly move toward the middle of the Force continuum. During the years in question, however, it should be recalled that Peru was ruled by a most conservative member of the "Forty-family" elite, General Manuel Prado.[29]

At the other end of the continuum, such countries as Costa Rica, Uruguay, and Chile consistently maintain open systems, and during the years in question, force inputs also continued to be minimal. The Army in Bolivia, following the 1952 National Revolution, was abolished. The period in question in Figure II saw it reorganized, but along very reduced as well as achievement-oriented lines (many Indians, for example, were recruited into its ranks). Although Nicaragua, El Salvador, and Honduras seem to be strange bedfellows for this

American Behavioral Scientist, 7 (February 1964), pp. 26, 28.

Data presented in raw form; when Y variable transformed to $\log_{10}$, the curve is smoother and more accentuated; kept in raw score form, here, for comparative purposes.

[29] The high value of 3.5 percent of GNP allocated to defense expenditures during 1959–60 does not appear to be a data-quality error. When checked against similar data gathered by Bruce Russett for the 1959 period, the Peruvian statistics is placed at 3.0 percent.

[28] Force: data directly from John D. Powell, "Military Assistance and Militarism in Latin America," *Western Political Quarterly*, 18 (June 1965), p. 384. Supplemental data for Uruguay and Cuba taken from: Bruce M. Russett, "Measures of Military Effort,"

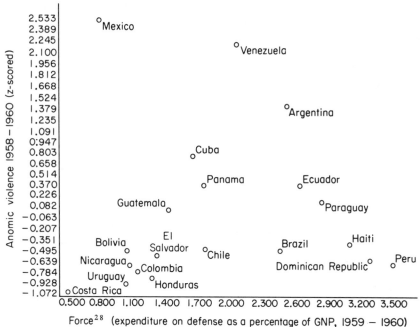

FIGURE II. The curvilinear relationship between force and anomic violence.

end of the Force continuum, the "force index" is plotting them accurately in terms of defense expenditures.

It is clear from the plot, that it is the middle-range internal force countries which are the ones experiencing most of the anomic breakthroughs. Mexico, in many respects, is a very explainable deviant case. During the end of the Ruiz Cortines and beginning of the López Mateos administrations, Mexico was fraught with demonstrations, strikes, and riots, not at all typical of other periods, which tended to be more negative than not on Anomic violence (see Table III). These data are suggestive of the fact that Mexico (like Costa Rica, Uruguay, and the other "open" systems) does not counter anomic breakthroughs with only force. Venezuela, Argentina, Ecuador, Cuba, Panama, and Guatemala, however, appear to have also sustained high amounts of anomic violence; and, as hypothesized,

lie toward the center of the Force continuum. The case of Cuba offers what seems to be the perfectly ambivalent situation[30]: with Batista's efforts at force being countered by guerrilla efforts, the perceptions of force would indeed be anything but clear. To be sure, a more sensitive interpretation of defense figures for this period would be to assume that defense allocations were more a function of the amount of Organized violence being waged by Castro guerrillas. For the same period, the z-score for Cuba's Organized Violence Index was +2.994 (against the Anomic violence z-score of +.731 presently under consideration).

[30] It should be recalled that it was ambivalence, in terms of a permissive and then a coercive colonial policy, which LeVine postulated gave rise to anti-European conflict in Africa. Robert A. LeVine, "Anti-European Violence in Africa: A Comparative Analysis," *Journal of Conflict Resolution*, 3 (1959), pp. 420–429.

The most evident manifestations of Anomic violence, of course, are Venezuela and Argentina. As was noted in the earlier discussion of Venezuela's z-score, the population has tended to remain relatively uninvolved and apathetic (which would appear to account for the middle-range input into defense), and that with the overthrow of Pérez Jiménez in 1958, the ensuing years were particularly volatile. Although Juan Perón was ousted from Argentina in 1955, it seems a reasonable assumption that the Frondizi government (whose position with respect to the Peronistas was at times unclear) internal force capability was not sufficient to contain the anomic breakthroughs which occurred throughout succeeding years.

When the same Force data (Expenditure on Defense as a Percentage of GNP) was plotted against Organized violence for the same 1958–60 time period, as hypothesized, no relationship emerged, and the data points distributed themselves randomly about the plot area. Organized violence was, however, hypothesized to be both linear and positive, when related to Force in an inverted time sequence; in other words, when Organized violence was the independent variable. Simply stated, high incidences of planned violence should bring about comparable inputs of force on the part of the government. When the 1958–60 Organized violence data was correlated with a *change*-in-defense measure[31] from 1958 to 1963, the cor-

relation coefficient was $+.416$; the same calculations for Anomic violence yielded a coefficient of .005, indicating no relationship.

Political Legitimacy was conceived in both static as well as dynamic terms. Although several measures were selected to represent this concept, the "weighted" Fitzgibbon ratings were used in the scatter plot for Figure III.[32] When a change in Legitimacy (from 1950 to 1955) was correlated with Organized violence taking place in the following three years, the form of the relationship was discovered to be linear, and the strength of the Pearson coefficient was a high, negative $-.71$. The same negative, linear relationship emerged from a cross tabulation of the static Fitzgibbon ratings for the 20 republics in 1955 with the same Organized violence data for 1958–60.[33]

While high, negative associations emerged from the relationship between measures of Legitimacy and Organized violence, no such negative associations were discovered among these measures and Anomic Violence. Furthermore, these findings do not seem to be a function of the 1958–60 conflict data represented in the plot in Figure III. Reference to Table IV will reveal that, with but one exception, all measures of Legitimacy (PRI as well as Fitzgibbon;

---

[31] The resulting coefficient, while in the same direction as hypothesized, can only be considered a suggestive test of the relationship. For various reasons, it was felt that the strength of the coefficient would be considerably boosted with more sensitive data. For example, if the change-in-defense data were available between 1960 to 1963, the period immediately following the 1958–60 Organized violence data.

Data for the calculation of the change measure was gathered from the following sources: "1958–59 per cent of central government expenditure on defense," *1960 Statistical*

Abstract of Latin America, p. 32; *1961 Statistical Abstract of Latin America*, p. 35. "1962–63 per cent of central government expenditure on defense," *1962 Statistical Abstract of Latin America*, p. 66; *1963 Statistical Abstract*, p. 76; *1964 Statistical Abstract*, p. 104.

[32] Legitimacy: Change scores calculated from data published by Russell Fitzgibbon and Kenneth Johnson, "Measurement of Latin American Political Change," *American Political Science Review*, 55 (September 1961), p. 518.

Data presented in raw form; when Y variable is transformed to $\log_{10}$, the negative correlation coefficient of $-.71$ (for the relationship in Figure II) is strengthened.

[33] The $\log_{10}$ transformation was used, which increased the $-.50$ relationship found among the raw data to $-.67$.

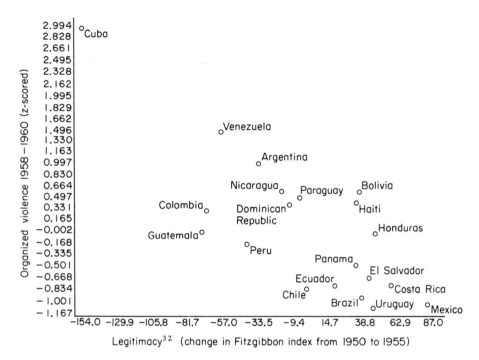

FIGURE III. The negative linear relationship between legitimacy and organized violence.

static as well as dynamic) show little or no association with Anomic violence. The impact of such a finding is obvious. Aggressive activities defined more by an underlying planning and organization (such as guerrilla activities—those most heavily emphasized by the Organized Violence Index[34]) appear to be challenging the legitimacy of the political system; whereas no such challenges exist among aggressive activities of an anomic nature (such as demonstrations, strikes, and riots). To be sure, anomic breakthroughs may be more an indica-

[34] It will be recalled that the Organized Violence Index, constructed on the basis of the empirical evidence from the factor analysis of conflict activity, weights guerrilla activities .65, governmental crisis .57, and revolutions .31. It is not surprising, therefore, that Cuba and Venezuela, which have experienced considerable guerrilla-type activity during the period 1958–60, should come out highest on Organized violence in the scatter plot in Figures I and III.

tion of "political development," than not. The fact that no strong *negative* associations were found between Legitimacy and Anomic violence seems highly suggestive of Lipset's remark that ". . . the existence of a moderate state of conflict [and it would be reasonable to interpret his reference to "conflict" as including such things as demonstrations, strikes, and riots] is an inherent aspect of a legitimate democratic system, and is in fact another way of defining it. . . ."[35]

The same negative, linear relationship emerged when Organized violence was correlated with the static Fitzgibbon ratings for 1955. In fact, with but few exceptions, the countries which were high on Legitimacy in 1955 (Uruguay, Mexico, Costa Rica, Chile, and Brazil) tended to be the same countries

[35] Lipset, "Some Social Requisites of Democracy . . . ," *op. cit.*, p. 92.

increasing on Legitimacy from 1950 to 1955 (see Figure III). In both instances, they fell at the negative end of the Organized violence axis. This finding seems to also hold for nations on the low end of the Legitimacy continuum; and it was Cuba, Venezuela, Argentina, Nicaragua, Paraguay, and Guatemala in 1955 which also made the lowest gains in Legitimacy from 1950 to 1955. These were the countries plagued with the largest amounts of Organized violence during 1958 to 1960. With respect to Cuba, the country experiencing the highest Organized violence, the Legitimacy measure cannot be considered deviant. Ratings for the change measure took place in 1950 and 1955. As has been pointed out, Fidel Castro's revolutionary invasion didn't take place until 1956 (the attack on the Moncada barracks, however, did take place in 1953). In the case of the latter, it should be remembered that it wasn't until after the consummation of the revolution, that this "symbolic" gesture of defiance gained in stature. While one must always be wary of subjectivity in judgmental codings such as those involved in the Fitzgibbon Index, it seems clear that the high rating of "illegitimacy" fell to Batista's last regime (1952–58), rather than to Castro's.

IV. Summary and Conclusions

In pointing to the preconditions of political instability, both in Latin America and elsewhere, much of the recent theory and research on domestic conflict appears to have concentrated on three basic independent variables: (i) systemic discontent, (ii) political legitimacy, and (iii) anticipated retribution (Section I).

But if it is generally agreed that these "causal" variables may lead to the presence or absence of political instability, there is no such agreement on the type of political instability they may bring about. Indeed, since it is quite conceivable that different styles of violent activity may each have its own set of correlates, the decision as to how political instability is conceived and operationalized becomes crucial. In Section II ("Political Instability: Defining the Domain and Systematically Measuring It"), the many individual types of domestic conflict were discussed. Treating each of these various types of political aggression separately, however, places one in the burdensome position of creating classification schemes of impossible proportions. While the Rummel-Tanter data operationally reduced the Latin American conflict domain to a series of basic indices (assassinations, strikes, guerrilla warfare, governmental crises, purges, riots, anti-government demonstrations, revolutions, and the number of people killed in domestic group violence), it still left us essentially with nine dependent variables. The statistical technique of Factor Analysis provided the means for reducing these nine operational indices to a smaller set of conceptual variables. The results of the factor analysis revealed (i) that political instability in Latin America is highly structured in terms of independent clusters of activities, and (ii) reduces to two basic dimensions of conflict behavior, (iii) a non-organized (or disorganized), spontaneous, or Anomic factor (indexed by such things as riots, strikes, and demonstrations), which is independent of (iv) an Organized factor (indexing, among other things, guerrilla warfare, governmental crises, revolutions, armed rebellions), defined more by an underlying planning and organization.

Factor scores, the value each nation has on each of the two basic conflict dimensions, were computed by taking each country's individual conflict score (in standard score form) and weighting it by the factor loadings participating on each of the conflict dimensions (Table II). Upon standardizing these, six distributions of Anomic and Organized violence scores for the twenty Latin American republics were available across three separate time periods (Table III). By placing each of the three independent or "causal" variables (systemic discontent, political legitimacy, and anticipated retribution) in the proper time sequence, separate tests of their impact on each of the two dependent or "effect" variables (Anomic and Organized Violence) were made, and the following general conclusions emerged:

1. Systemic Satisfaction (as measured by *change* in gross national product per capita) is negatively associated with political instability. Both the theoretical orientation and empirical findings discussed in the opening section of the paper suggested that societies past a "traditional-transitional threshold" should experience a decrease in domestic conflict as they experience an increase in wealth. This was decidedly the case with respect to Latin America, and the finding does not appear to be a function of the measures used. When Satisfaction was operationalized differently (*i.e.*, the per cent of the central government's expenditure on public health and welfare), the same negative, linear association emerged. When the dimensions of political instability were controlled for, however, the stronger correlate of discontent was discovered to be Organized violence activity (see Figure I).

2. The form of the relationship between the inhibition of political aggression through the use of force, was specified to be curvilinear. Under this model, the application of both extreme amounts of force (*e.g.*, restrictive systems), as well as little or no force (permissive systems), was predicted to yield similar results—low levels of political instability. Intermediate levels of force, on the other hand, neither sufficient to inhibit political aggression and in many cases acting as an additional frustration, would be accompanied by high levels of political instability. Arguing from the premise that (military) force can almost always be counted on to disperse demonstrations and riots of serious proportions (that is, support of this nature is given, often irrespective of the loyalty of such force to the regime in power), a test of the inhibitive effects of the use of Force (as measured by expenditures on defense as a percent of gross national product) on Anomic violence revealed that the curvilinear model does indeed apply to Latin America (see Figure II).

Correlating the same Force data with Organized violence, on the other hand, yielded no association. Two suggestive interpretations can be offered. The first involves two critical conditions not met by these data: (i) independence between the measures of Force (military expenditures) and the measures of Organized violence (primarily the variable "revolutions," which may involve military coups) cannot be maintained, and (ii) the allegiance of the forces (a condition of their impact as inhibitors of political aggression) has not been measured. The first conclusion, therefore, would be that no reasonable interpretation can be given to the correlation (in this case, lack of correlation) between Force and Organized violence. If it can be assumed that the contamination is negligible and that the punitive forces are generally allegiant, however, the lack of relationship between the extent of Force and Organized violence would lead to conclusions that guerrilla warfare, terrorism, and sabotage (the highest loading variables in the Organized violence factor score formula), as well as armed rebellions, occur and continue irrespective of the extent and quality of governmental force. That is, they may break out just as readily among militarily strong as militarily weak regimes; and they may continue in the face of what would appear to be overwhelmingly adverse inhibiting power. Knowing the Force level, then, doesn't appear to help in explaining the occurrence of Organized violent activity, but it is decidedly a factor in understanding the strength and form of Anomic violence.

3. Political legitimacy was conceived of as the amount of positive affect toward the political system (and the government) held by the populace. It was recognized that (i) feelings of allegiance can and are ascribed to non-competitive (unitary, hierarchically organized) as well as competitive (polyarchic, participant) structures, (ii) that such feelings are the products of, among other things, "politicization," or socialization over time, and (iii) that while feelings of legitimacy toward a political system can be separated analytically from those feelings developed as a result of the system's ability in satisfying demands, the two are most likely closely interrelated sub-systems of phenomena. It was equally clear, however, that people like political systems (legitimacy) not only because "this is the way it has always been" (traditional legitimacy), and because of gratifications received from the system, but also because they had a hand in making it the way it is. In short, the ability to participate in a system leads directly to the building of positive affect toward it. While this mechanism is not at work in all political systems (there is evidence, for example, to indicate that it may not function at all in semi-authoritarian structures—which may lead to serious reservations about applying it to some of the Latin American nations), Almond and Verba did find that participation led to positive affect in Mexico, Great Britain, and the United States.

On the assumption that systems mov-ing toward higher "democratic attainment" over time would be providing greater opportunities to participate, legitimacy was operationalized as the amount of change from one period to the next measured by the Fitzgibbon Index (see Figure III). In this, and the many other operationalizations of the concept (see Table IV), legitimacy proved to be the strong negative correlate of Organized violence. In all cases, as political legitimacy decreased Organized violence increased. When the effect of political legitimacy on Anomic violence was tested, however, in every case, the association was proved to be very weak or non-existent. That is, systems that were high on political legitimacy were just as likely to experience Anomic activity as those which were low on political legitimacy. Once again, by referring to the formulas for the computation of the factor scores used to distribute nations on Organized violence, one can see that activities such as guerrilla warfare, terrorism, sabotage, armed rebellion, and so on, break out in far greater proportions at times of low political legitimacy (*e.g.*, when the Fitzgibbon index of "democratic attainment" is negative—lower at t_2 than it was at t_1). In short (if we can dismiss the pitfalls of ecological correlations for the moment), the participants in Organized violent activity seem to be challenging the legitimacy of the political systems involved, while no such connection can be drawn from the roles of participants in Anomic violence.

In summary, then, what can be said of these two styles of political instability in Latin America? Anomic violence finds its strongest correlate (curvilinear) in forces of retribution. When force (punishment) is both very permissive as well as very restrictive, Anomic violence is negligible. Punishment in the mid-levels of intensity (apparently acting as a frustrator) elicits high levels of Anomic violence. Positive affect, or the amount of legitimacy ascribed to a political system, however, cannot be used in any way to determine the occurrence and intensity of riots, strikes, and demonstrations—they break out just as frequently in highly legitimate as poorly legitimate systems. Systemic discontent, on the other hand, is linearly correlated to the outbreak of Anomic violence, but at a much lower level than with Organized violence. When systemic dissatisfaction is measured in terms of negative or positive changes in per capita gross national product, one can more accurately predict the occurrence of (i) guerrilla warfare, governmental crises, and armed rebellions, than (ii) riots and demonstrations. Guerrilla insurrections and armed rebellions, on the other hand, cannot be predicted on the basis of knowing the amount of punishment (force) the government might be able to apply—that is, Organized violent activity that breaks out in Latin America at the system-level, appears to have little or nothing to do with the fear of retribution for such action. It does, however, appear to be strongly related to the open or closed nature of the system, and if systems are slipping into more closed patterns (*i.e.*, losing Fitzgibbon points on "democratic attainment"), the mechanism of participation feeding positive affect closes off this avenue of legitimacy formations. And, as legitimacy formations decrease, Organized violent activity can be observed to increase in a strong, linear pattern.

TOWARD A THEORY OF POLITICAL INSTABILITY IN LATIN AMERICA*

Manus Midlarsky
Raymond Tanter

1. Introduction

Too often it is assumed that national systems are completely autonomous political units, and that phenomena such as political instability may be explained solely with reference to factors internal to the nation-state.[1] Given the universal existence of national boundaries, it is not surprising that the assumption of autonomy, defined as self-determination, finds acceptance among social scientists. Yet numerous instances may be cited where this notion would be insufficient as an explanatory principle. To cite one contemporary example, the autonomy of the East European nations is apparently limited by the Soviet presence in that region. In addition, the presence of the German community in the Sudetenland prior to the Second World War eventually compromised Czech political autonomy.

An alternative to the assumption of autonomy is provided by the concepts of penetration and linkage. Penetration

* This is a revised version of a paper delivered at the Operations Research Society of America meeting, October 17–19, 1966, Durham, North Carolina. The data have undergone refinement in this version, so that the results differ somewhat from those of the earlier paper. Acknowledgements are due to Richard Brody, Harold Guetzkow, Ole Holsti, Kenneth Janda, and Robert North for comments and suggestions. The Carnegie-supported International Relations Program and the National Science Foundation-funded Comparative International Processes project at Northwestern University provided facilities and financial support for this study.

[1] Two of the better known works which are based largely on the assumption of autonomy are Gabriel A. Almond and James S. Coleman (eds.), *The Politics of the Developing Areas* (Princeton: Princeton University Press, 1960), and David E. Apter, *The Politics of Modernization* (Chicago: University of Chicago Press, 1965).

Reprinted from *Journal of Peace Research*, No. 3 (1967), 209–27, by permission of the authors and publisher. Textual and footnote emendations have been made by the authors.

is the inverse of autonomy, in that a complete penetration of the political system is equivalent to a total loss of autonomy. Linkage refers to the *means* through which the external environment penetrates the national system. Certain high government officials in the East European nations may comprise a linkage between these nations and the Soviet Union, whereas the Sudeten Germans in 1938 consisted of a linkage which sought a larger national identity in its affiliation with Germany. Although the linkage may often consist of a common group identity, from a broader perspective, linkages may consist of policies, psychological identifications, and national traditions as well. Linkage viewed as a process, rather than as an entity, has been defined by James N. Rosenau as "any relevant sequence of behaviors that originates in one system and is reacted to in another."[2] Applied to the Latin American context, a variety of reactions may be viewed as products of the continuous interaction between the United States and the Latin American countries. Reactions by the latter serve as the subject of investigation in this paper.

In the following sections, a framework of analysis is presented in which it is suggested that a linkage between the United States and the Latin American nations may culminate in political instability. Threat and legitimacy systems are differentiated, and both correlational and causal inference analyses are employed to transform the framework into a tentative theory of political instability in Latin America.

2. A Framework of Analysis

Perhaps the most persistent manifestation of the recurrent interaction between the U.S. and the Latin Ameri-

[2] James N. Rosenau, "Toward the Study of National-International Linkages," paper

can nations is the U.S. economic presence in that region. The enunciation of the Monroe Doctrine initiated not only a concern for the security of the entire Western Hemisphere, but also an economic interest which began to take the form of economic investment. As the U.S. economy underwent a rapid rate of development in the contemporary period, investments in Latin America also increased to the point of significant participation in local economic affairs.

It can be argued that an important effect of the U.S. economic presence may be resentment at seeing the resources of one's nation apparently developed for the benefit of a large industrial power, rather than for the material welfare of the local population.[3] The physical presence of plant facilities, foreign entrepreneurs and technicians, as well as the products of the business enterprise, may serve to heighten awareness that the local economy is indeed dependent on the initiative of an external power. The foreign entrepreneur hires labor from the local population, chooses sites for plant facilities, and often decides for himself the market practices of his business enterprise. At times, he may act without restrictions imposed by the local government and may be *perceived* as a master unto himself without consideration for the welfare of the local residents. Thus, the U.S. economic presence in Latin America may be significantly associated with hostility toward the U.S.

In theory, two possible sequential reactions to the U.S. economic presence may exist. The first suggests that the U.S. economic presence may lead to

delivered at the American Political Science Association meeting, September 6–10, 1966, New York City, p. 11.
[3] Robert H. Alexander, *A Primer of Economic Development* (New York: Macmillan, 1962), *passim*.

hostility directed at the U.S., which in turn may result in domestic violence.[4] The second sequence derives from theories of the revolutionary process which indicate that the increased level of economic development resulting from this economic presence may lead to the occurrence of revolution.[5] Since the Latin American revolution has traditionally assumed the form of a non-violent coup d'état, it is assumed, for the moment, that violence and revolution are distinct from one another.[6] This framework may be illustrated as in the figure.

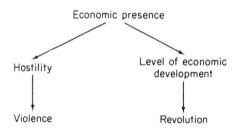

[4] See Merle Kling, "Towards a Theory of Power and Political Instability in Latin America," *Western Political Quarterly*, 9 (March 1956), 21–35. Also see Leland L. Johnson, "U.S. Business Interests and the Rise of Castro," *World Politics*, 17 (April 1965), 440–459.

[5] See Alexis de Tocqueville, *The Old Regime and the French Revolution* (Garden City, N.Y.: Doubleday Anchor, 1955), pp. 37 and 264. Also, Crane Brinton, *The Anatomy of Revolution* (New York: Vintage, 1952), pp. 3–4. For a slightly different perspective see James C. Davies, "Toward a Theory of Revolution," *American Sociological Review*, 27 (February 1962), 5–19.

[6] George I. Blanksten, for example, criticizes the failure to distinguish between the palace revolution—a frequently recurring phenomenon in Latin America—and major revolutions such as the Mexican experience, which initiated a period of intense change on all levels of society. One of the papers in which he discusses this distinction is "Revolutions," in H. E. Davis (ed.), *Government and Politics in Latin America* (New York: The Ronald Press, 1958), pp. 119–146. Also cf. "Latin American Revolutions," in *The 1962 Carolina Symposium: Today's Revolutions* (Chapel Hill: University of North Carolina Press, 1962), pp. 71–79.

With regard to the left branch of the framework, Merle Kling has pointed to the relationship between chronic political instability in Latin America and the domination of the local economy by foreign economic interests.[7] Leland L. Johnson, in his case study of the recent Cuban revolution, has indicated that one effect of the U.S. economic presence in Cuba was an increase in hostility toward the U.S., which in turn led to an increase in popular support for the revolution and facilitated Castro's expropriation of privately owned U.S. property.[8]

The Cuban case study provides a partial illustration of processes outlined in the left branch of the framework. As noted by Johnson, U.S. investments in public utilities were over ten times larger than in any other Latin American country.[9] Moreover, Cuba's agricultural economy was largely controlled by American interests. Seven of the ten largest *latifundia* were owned by American enterprises, and as of 1955 the sales of American-owned agricultural enterprises amounted to almost half the total sales of U.S. agricultural interests in Latin America. A large proportion of American-dominated agriculture lay in the cultivation and refinement of sugar. This is a seasonal crop, and the Cuban laborers were subject to the seasonal and market fluctuations of a sporadic employment. The resentment and frustration of an economic depen-

For a penetrating comparison of the Mexican and Cuban revolutions, see his "Modernization and Revolution in Latin America," in H. R. Barringer, G. I. Blanksten, and R. W. Mack (eds.), *Social Change in Developing Areas* (Cambridge, Mass.: Schenkman, 1965), pp. 225–242.

[7] Kling, *op. cit.*

[8] Johnson, *op. cit.*

[9] *Ibid.*, pp. 441 and 451–454. Also cf. George I. Blanksten, "Fidel Castro and Latin America," in M. Kaplan (ed.), *The Revolution in World Politics* (New York: Wiley, 1962), pp. 113–136.

dence on a product which was largely controlled by American interests was harnessed by Castro in his war against Batista. When Castro called for land reforms and a concomitant nationalization of privately owned enterprise, he was appealing to an already developed enmity against all things economic which were associated with the Cuban *ancien regime.*[10]

Another example is provided by instances of violence in Peru. In 1958, a popular controversy had developed over the issue of foreign domination of Peru's natural resources because the International Petroleum Company, an American subsidiary, had gained control of the vast majority of Peru's petroleum resources. Subsequent rises in the price of gasoline led to a strike by the Taxi Drivers' Union; the strike was broken by the police only after violence had erupted. This incident, coupled with demonstrations by Peruvian students against Vice President Nixon, illustrates the association between violence and hostility toward foreign-dominated enterprise.[11]

Turning now to the right branch of the framework, the sequence of reactions is treated at a different level of analysis.[12] While in the left branch political reactions are viewed at the level of the individual or group, those in the right branch are examined from the perspective of responses by the nation, and specifically by the national economy. In contrast to the Marxian argument that revolutions occur when populations are economically depressed, a number of theorists have suggested that revolutions occur when the level of economic development is comparatively high. De Tocqueville, for example, concluded that France prior to 1789 enjoyed a relatively higher level of economic development than did neighboring countries such as the German principalities.[13] Crane Brinton, in his analysis of four major revolutions, also found that each of the societies under investigation enjoyed a relative prosperity before the revolution took place.[14] Among the Latin American countries, Cuba and Venezuela were enjoying a relatively high level of prosperity before the rise of Castro in Cuba and the outbreak of guerilla warfare in Venezuela.

Perhaps a demonstration effect is operative, in which the majority of the population sees the more obvious manifestations of economic development without direct participation in that development.[15] New factories, roads, and municipal institutions become visible to the population; but if the people do not directly benefit from this economic development, then these manifestations of growth may serve to aggravate an already existent sense of deprivation.

Thus, a framework of analysis is constructed using various theories of both violence and revolution. The importance of certain variables and the relationships between them are suggested, but it should be emphasized that this framework is more in the nature of an heuristic device than a statement of theory. Before a definite theoretical formulation can be stated, the framework must be subjected to a systematic empirical evaluation which will allow for the choice of the best correspondence between observation and prediction.

[10] Johnson, *loc. cit.*

[11] See James C. Carey, *Peru and the United States, 1900–1962* (Notre Dame: University of Notre Dame Press, 1964), pp. 170–190.

[12] For a comprehensive treatment of the question of levels of analysis in social science research, see J. David Singer, "The Level of Analysis Problem," *World Politics*, 14 (October 1961), 77–91.

[13] De Tocqueville, *loc. cit.*

[14] Brinton, *loc. cit.*

[15] For a discussion of the demonstration effect, see Karl de Schweinitz, Jr., *Industrialization and Democracy* (New York: The Free Press, 1964), p. 68.

Table I

INVESTMENT PER CAPITA, PERCENTAGE TRADE WITH THE UNITED STATES,
AND THE U.S. ECONOMIC PRESENCE IN LATIN AMERICA, 1956;
PER CAPITA GROSS NATIONAL PRODUCT, 1957

Country[a]	Investment Per Capita[b]	Percentage Trade[c]	Economic Presence/10[d]	GNP/CAP[e]
Argentina	22.02	16.80	36.99	490
Brazil	19.10	40.12	76.63	293
Chile	98.21	45.11	443.03	379
Colombia	28.67	66.07	189.42	263
Costa Rica	62.75	52.82	331.45	357
Cuba	121.57	69.84	849.05	431
Dominican Republic	51.76	55.56	287.58	239
Ecuador	8.96	56.04	50.21	189
El Salvador	11.02	48.47	53.43	219
Guatemala	34.05	69.25	235.80	189
Haiti	9.87	47.88	47.26	105
Honduras	68.38	66.75	456.44	194
Mexico	21.84	76.38	166.81	262
Nicaragua	10.87	50.19	54.55	160
Panama	168.09	66.40	1,116.12	329
Peru	34.40	43.75	150.50	179
Uruguay	27.93	13.77	38.46	478
Venezuela	281.54	45.62	1,284.39	648

[a] Two countries, Bolivia and Paraguay, were omitted from the analysis since none of the data sources included investment values for these countries.

[b] In U.S. dollars per million population. With the exception of the values for El Salvador and Nicaragua, the book value of investments in Latin American countries is listed in the U.S. Department of Commerce, *Balance of Payments: Statistical Supplement* (Washington, D.C.: U.S. Government Printing Office, 1961), p. 209. The values for El Salvador and Nicaragua are estimates—investments of 25 and 14 million, respectively. These estimates are based on data in the U.S. Department of Commerce, *Investment in Central America* (Washington, D.C.: U.S. Government Printing Office, 1956) and the U.S. Department of Commerce, International Commerce Bureau, *Overseas Business Reports*. The population values are the United Nations' mid-year estimates for 1956 and are reported in the *United Nations Statistical Yearbook* 1957. The value for Cuba was estimated from data on Cuban population as well as its rate of increase. These values are found in the 1958 Yearbook.

[c] The percentage trade data were calculated from values for imports and exports for the year 1956, reported in the Alker *United Nations Yearbook of International Trade Statistics*, 1959. This later yearbook was chosen because earlier yearbooks often contain incomplete data.

[d] Although in some instances the data do not warrant it, all calculated data are reported to two decimal places for the sake of completeness and verifiability.

[e] In U.S. dollars. The source is Bruce M. Russett, Hayward R. Alker, Jr., Karl W. Deutsch, and Harold Lasswell, *World Handbook of Political and Social Indicators* (New Haven: Yale University Press, 1964), pp. 155–157.

3. Operational Referents

In order to carry out an empirical test of the framework, operational measures of the variables must be provided. Table I presents the data employed in the construction of the measure of economic presence, as well as the per capita gross national product of the Latin American countries. This latter variable acts as a measure of economic development. The first data column consists of the dollar values of private U.S. investments[16] divided by the population for each country. It is a measure of the *density* of investment in a particular country or region.[17]

[16] U.S. investment is defined as "the flow of equity and loan investments from U.S. residents to foreign firms contolled by U.S. interests," Johnson, *op. cit.* p. 441n. For the composition of these investments, see U.S. Department of Commerce, *U.S. Business Investments in Foreign Countries* (Washington, D.C.: U.S. Government Printing Office, 1960), p. 76.

[17] Another measure of investment concentration might be the value of investments

The values in the column labeled "Percentage trade" are constructed by dividing the currency value of trade with the U.S. by the total value of that country's trade, and then multiplying the result by 100. This is a measure of the extent to which a Latin American nation's trade is dependent on trade with the U.S.

Neither of these two variables taken alone, however, is an exact measure of the degree of benefit derived by the U.S. from its economic relationship with Latin America. Consider for the moment a high concentration of American investment in a Latin American country combined with a negligible percentage of trade with that country. Despite the presence of a high concentration of investment, the U.S. may not in itself be deriving much economic benefit in the form of indirect returns from the relationship.[18] With the exception of the profit on investment, a small percentage of trade with the U.S. may signify that the products of the business enterprise are being employed for the direct benefit of the local population or are being traded elsewhere. In any event, the investment can be considered more beneficial to the local economy than to the external investor power. Similar reasoning may be offered in the instance of a high percentage of trade with the U.S. and a low concentration of American investment.

A more exact measure of the economic benefit derived by the investor nation is the multiplicative product of the values in the two columns. This is a procedure which controls for the effect of an additional variable. If either of the two variables taken alone is an inadequate measure of benefit to the U.S. economy, then multiplication of the two, in effect, chooses that sector of both trade and investment which is directly beneficial to the U.S.[19] These values are presented in data column three, labeled "Economic presence."

Table II presents the measures of political instability and hostility toward the U.S. The first data column lists deaths as a result of domestic group violence divided by the population for each country. This is a measure of the density of domestic violence.[20] The second data column presents the number of successful and unsuccessful revolutions initiated in each country during this time period.[21] Data column

divided by Gross National Product. This is similar to Deutsch and Eckstein's use of the variable—foreign trade/GNP. See Karl W. Deutsch and Alexander Eckstein, "National Industrialization and the Declining Share of the International Economic Sector, 1890–1959," *World Politics*, 13 (January 1961), 267–299. Investment per capita is, however, an adequate measure of concentration and has been employed in prior research. See Johnson, *op. cit.*

[18] Direct returns may be interpreted solely as Latin American exports to the U.S. However, imports from the U.S. serve the function of providing direct monetary gain to trading sectors of the U.S. economy. Both imports and exports are therefore included as beneficial to the U.S. economy.

[19] The multiplication of the two quantities may be analogous to choosing the intersection between two sets. The area of the intersection includes only those investments which are directly beneficial to the U.S. in the form of a monetary return to the U.S. economy (by means of trade) and excludes those which may be beneficial to the local economy.

[20] One might also use the absolute magnitude of deaths rather than the density measure employed in this paper. However, utility of a per capita measure of violence has been indicated in Bruce M. Russett, Hayward R. Alker, Jr., Karl W. Deutsch, and Harold Lasswell, *World Handbook of Political and Social Indicators* (New Haven: Yale University Press, 1964), pp. 97–100.

[21] "A revolution may be said to exist when a group of insurgents illegally and/or forcefully challenges the governmental elite for the occupancy of roles in the structure of political authority. A successful revolution occurs when, as a result of a challenge to the governmental elite, insurgents are eventually able to occupy principal roles within the structure of the political authority"—Raymond Tanter and Manus Midlarsky, "A Theory of Revolution,"

Table II

MEASURES OF POLITICAL INSTABILITY AND HOSTILITY TOWARD THE UNITED STATES, 1958–60

Country	Deaths as a Result of Domestic Group Violence[a]	Number of Revolutions[b]	Hostility Towards the U.S.[b]
Argentina	1.75	4	4
Brazil	.14	1	2
Chile	.67	0	0
Colombia	12.44	2	4
Costa Rica	.00	0	0
Cuba	683.13	4	39
Dominican Republic	53.21	1	9
Ecuador	11.51	0	2
El Salvador	.40	1	3
Guatemala	.27	2	4
Haiti	12.99	2	9
Honduras	107.05	2	2
Mexico	.75	0	2
Nicaragua	80.06	2	2
Panama	11.72	3	10
Peru	.19	1	1
Uruguay	.00	0	1
Venezuela	72.48	6	3

[a] Per million population. The number of deaths are taken from the initial data matrices prepared for Raymond Tanter, "Dimensions of Conflict Behavior Within and Between Nations, 1958–60," *Journal of Conflict Resolution*, 10 (March 1966), 41–64. The population values are the United Nations' mid-year estimates for 1959 and are found in the *United Nations Statistical Yearbook*, 1960. The value for Uruguay was estimated from data on the population of Uruguay in 1960 as well as from its rate of increase, as reported in the 1961 Yearbook.

[b] The values for the number of revolutions and hostility were obtained from Tanter, *ibid*, and were originally drawn from the *New York Times Index* and cross-referenced with *Deadline Data on World Affairs*, *Britannica Book of the Year*, and *Facts on File*.

three consists of a summation of both official and unofficial acts of hostility directed at the U.S.[22] A list of the vari-

Journal of Conflict Resolution, 11 (September 1967), p. 267.

[22] Although empirically distinct, official and unofficial hostility toward the U.S. may be manifestations of a similar underlying phenomenon. Official Cuban hostility after the rise of Castro, for example, may be comparable to unofficial hostility of Marxist-oriented revolutionary movements in other Latin American countries. In other instances,

ables used in the construction of this measure as well as the definitions of these variables is found in Appendix I.

The investment, percentage trade, and economic presence data are for the year 1956, whereas the data for domestic violence, number of revolutions, and hostility are for the time period 1958–60. The relationship between independent and dependent variables is therefore a three-year "time lag" correlation (1956–59—the mean year of the time period 1958–60) and may be justified as follows.[23] Investment in an economy includes the construction of either industrial or agricultural facilities, the hiring of foreign labor, and the diffusion of information by means of advertising and word of mouth of interaction. None of these processes is instantaneous, and all require a period of

official hostility toward the U.S. may also have its roots in popular sentiment. If popular unrest exists, the government may perceive that this unrest is generated by hostility toward the U.S. The authorities may attempt to dampen the hostility of the population and at the same time increase their own security by directly engaging in anti-American diplomatic activity. It should be noted, however, that in other regions, the distinction between official and unofficial hostility may be meaningful. In an analysis of conflict behavior between the U.S., on the one hand, and Southeast Asian and Far Eastern countries, on the other, it was found that unofficial hostility toward the U.S. in 1959–61 correlated positively ($r = .56$, $N = 12$) with trade with the U.S., whereas official hostility correlated negatively ($r = -.22$, $N = 12$) with U.S. trade. See Kenneth Eldred and Tyler Marshall, "A Study in Internal-External Interaction," unpublished paper, Stanford University, 1966.

[23] The use of time lag regressions in the analysis of the relationship between domestic and foreign conflict is found in Raymond Tanter, "Dimensions of Conflict Behavior Within and Between Nations, 1958–60", *Journal of Conflict Resolution*, 10 (March 1966), 41–64. For a general discussion of the use of time lags in research designs see Otis D. Duncan, Ray P. Cuzzort, and Beverly Duncan, *Statistical Geography: Problems in Analyzing Areal Data* (New York: The Free Press, 1961).

time to mature. If the economic presence of an external power is to cause resentment within the government and among the local residents, then this resentment would probably occur after a period of time had elapsed from the point of initial investment. The choice of a three-year time lag, although somewhat arbitrary, has an empirical basis in prior research.[24]

4. Threat and Legitimacy Systems

Before proceeding to an empirical test of the data, it may be useful to introduce a distinction between the countries under investigation. Kenneth Boulding has posited two categories of political system.[25] The first, the threat system, is one which relies essentially on coercive means for the attainment of its goals. The military occupation of a conquered territory, martial law imposed on a dissident locality, or the authoritarian and totalitarian forms of dictatorship are examples of this type. The second category is a system of legitimation. Here, the goals of a decision-making unit are achieved primarily by established means for obtaining the consent of those affected by the decisions. The institution of

monarchy, for example, was legitimized by the theory of the divine rights of kings, as well as by symbols of authority sanctioned by centuries of tradition. Similarly, the presence of a constitutional system and the mandate of an electorate act to provide a legitimate basis for a democratic form of government.

The distinction between threat and legitimacy systems may be critical for an analysis of the effects of the U.S. economic presence. With regard to the left branch of the framework, if the local government is sanctioned by a legitimizing agency such as a consitution and free elections, then a high degree of economic dependence may not be resented.[26] The suspicion of a collusion between the non-democratic government and foreign business interests might be absent, and there would exist a rationale that the government had received a legitimate mandate. If the government chooses to allow foreign business enterprise to invest heavily in the economy and capture a large share of external trade, then it would have the right to do so because of its legitimation by the people. In a less democratic setting, the suspicion of collusion might indeed be present, and the rationale of a legitimate mandate would be non-existent.[27]

---

[24] For example, J. David Singer and Melvin Small employed a three-year time lag in their analysis of the relationship between alliance configurations and the frequency, magnitude, and severity of international warfare. For a more complete account, see J. David Singer and Melvin Small, "Formal Alliances, 1815–1939: A quantitative description," *Journal of Peace Research*, No. 1 (1966), p. 18. In addition, the inclusion of a time lag satisfies one of the necessary conditions for the inference of casuality.

[25] Kenneth E. Boulding, "The Nature of Political Conflict," paper delivered at the American Political Science Association meeting, Sept. 8–11, 1965, Washington, D.C. See also "The Relations of Economic, Political, and Social Systems," *Social and Economic Studies*, 11 (December 1962), 351–362.

[26] It is conceivable that even the legitimation of a monarchy might serve to decrease resentment at an economic dependence on a foreign industrial power. In this respect, the degrees of legitimacy conferred by a monarchy and by a constitutional democracy may not differ significantly from each other.

[27] An example of possible collaboration between a non-democratic Latin American country and U.S. business interests occurred in Peru after a military junta had deposed President Prado in July, 1962. Soon after the coup, the members of the junta arranged a meeting with bankers and businessmen to gain their cooperation. The U.S. business community in Peru was ready to support the junta, and Robert Koenig, the American president of a Peruvian-based mining concern,

As for the right branch of the framework, the demonstration effect referred to earlier in the paper may be more pronounced in a non-democratic setting. This effect may vary directly with the degree of inequality in the distribution of land or income,[28] and the higher the degree of inequality, the greater the resentment at seeing an economic development without an equal distribution of land or income.[29]

In the subsequent analysis, the significance of relationships is tested first for all cases under consideration (N = 18).[30] This set is divided into (1) countries which are generally acknowledged to have enjoyed a recent history of democratic government (Chile, Costa Rica, Mexico, Uruguay); and (2) the remaining countries in this set—those which are considered to be non-democratic. The democratic countries were chosen on the basis of ratings by Latin American specialists.[31]

---

sent a telegram to the junta in which he announced the company's plans for expansion in Peru and his support of the junta. See the *New York Times* (July 24, 1962) 11:1.

[28] A measure of inequality is the Gini Index of either land or income. As an index of land inequalities, it has been employed by Tanter and Midlarsky, *op. cit.*, and significant differences were obtained between Gini Indices for those nations which experienced successful revolutions in the time period 1955–60 and those which did not.

[29] A possible relationship may exist between the Gini Index and the extent to which the government may be considered democratic. This relationship might serve as a subject for future research. Tanter and Midlarsky, *op. cit.*, also investigated the relationship between the *rate* of change of economic development and the intensity of revolution. It was found that for Latin American countries there was no significant relationship between the two variables (r = −.12, N = 7). For Asian and Middle Eastern countries the relationships were significant (r = .94, N = 6, and r = .96, N = 4, respectively). In the present study, however, a significant relationship is found between the level of economic development and the number of revolutions for Latin American countries. This apparent contradiction may be resolved by noting the differences between the two studies with respect to sample selection and variables. In Tanter and Midlarsky, the sample included only successful revolutions which occurred during the time period under investigation. In the present study, the sample consists of all Latin American countries—those which experienced both successful and unsuccessful revolutions as well as those countries which experienced no revolutions. Moreover, the former study was concerned with the explanation of the intensity of revolution whereas the present one deals with the frequency of revolution. Apparently, the *rate* of change of economic development is not significantly related to the *intensity* of

revolution in Latin America, but the *level* of economic development is associated with the *occurrence* of revolution in that area.

[30] Two countries—Bolivia and Paraguay—were omitted from the analysis, since values for U.S. investments in these countries were not available.

[31] For 1955, these countries occupied the first four ranks on ratings of democracy by Latin American specialists. See Russell H. Fitzgibbon and Kenneth F. Johnson, "Measurement of Latin American Political Change," *American Political Science Review*, 44 (September 1961), 515–526. For other evaluations of Latin American democracy, see Seymour M. Lipset, "Some Social Requisites of Democracy," *American Political Science Review*, 53 (March 1959), 69–105. See also Arthur P. Whittaker, "The Pathology of Democracy in Latin America: A Historian's Point of View," *American Political Science Review*, 44 (March 1950), 101–118. In choosing these countries, the concept of democracy has been rigorously applied. Although these writers recognize that the variable democracy may be more accurately perceived as lying on a continuum, nevertheless for the purposes of this study, the distinction between democratic and non-democratic is a useful first approximation. Two additional problems are raised by the choice of these four countries. The first concerns the statistical problem of an increased standard error of a mean when one is working with very small samples. However, the concept of a standard error of the mean is not strictly applicable here because we are dealing with (by definition) the universe of democratic Latin American countries. Moreover, the choice of the countries is theoretically determined and one should not alter the theory to satisfy statistical requirements. The second problem concerns the concept of legitimacy as applied to Latin American countries. Although it may be said that Latin American governments may require a strong

Table III

CORRELATION MATRIX FOR THE TOTAL NUMBER OF CASES (N = 18),
NONDEMOCRATIC (N = 14) AND DEMOCRATIC CASES (N = 4)

		Economic Presence	Hostility	Violence	GNP/CAP	Revolution
Economic presence	Total					
	Non-democratic					
	Democratic					
Hostility	Total	(.40)				
	Non-democratic	(.45)				
	Democratic	−.86				
Violence	Total	(.45)	(.65)**			
	Non-democratic	(.51)	(.54)			
	Democratic	.46	.37			
GNP/CAP	Total	(.56)*	.15	−.05		
	Non-democratic	(.67)**	.26	.25		
	Democratic	−.55	−.41	−.68		
Revolution	Total	(.65)**	.67**	.63*	(.50)*	
	Non-democratic	(.73)**	.41	.43	(.85)**	
	Democratic	—a	—	—	—	

* p ≤ .05
** p ≤ .01
a None of the democratic countries experienced revolutions in this time period; hence, the correlation between these variables could not be calculated for this category.

5. Correlational Analysis

The product-moment correlation coefficient is a measure of the degree of association between variables, and thus provides a preliminary test of the framework. Values for this statistic, which are listed in Table III, are either for transformed or untransformed data depending on the frequency distributions and plots of the variables.[32] A

discussion of transformation analysis and the transformations employed is included in Appendix II. Since we are dealing with a statistical universe rather than a random sample, the accepted concepts of statistical significance are not directly applicable. However, they may be stated for purposes of comparison and to provide some criterion, albeit an imperfect one, for the accep-

authoritarian component to be considered legitimate by the people, we would rather opt for the definition of legitimacy embodied in this paper—that of established processes for obtaining consent of the governed. The existence of an authoritarian component within a political authority and the requirement of consent for the legitimation of that authority, are not mutually exclusive.

[32] In a number of instances the untransformed data gave higher values for the correlations between variables than did the transformed data. The relationship between hostility and violence for both the total number of cases and the non-democratic cases

was $r = .93$ before transformation. However, plots of the relationship between hostility and violence indicated that the value for Cuba was an outlying case, and since the product-moment correlation coefficient is sensitive to extreme values, it was decided to employ transformations for the sake of greater generalizability. It should be noted that with Cuba omitted from the total number of cases, the relationship between violence and hostility toward the U.S. was curvilinear, and with a double logarithmic [log(log)] transformation of violence and a single logarithmic transformation of hostility, the degree of association between the two variables was $r = .60$, a significant value.

tance or rejection of hypothesized relationships. Those relationships for which the framework predicts significance are in Table 3 included in parentheses, while empirical findings of significance are indicated by asterisks.[33]

With two major exceptions, the relationships suggested in the framework are significant for the total number of cases. The exceptions are the relationships between economic presence and both hostility and violence. In addition, two relationships which the framework suggested might not be significant are indeed significant. These are the degrees of association between revolution on the one hand, and both violence and hostility on the other.

The relationship between violence and revolution suggests that perhaps the traditional non-violent coup in Latin America may be in the process of transition to more violent forms of social change.[34] The second finding—that of a significant relationship between hostility and revolution—indicates that hostility toward the U.S. may be a motivating force in those successful and unsuccessful revolutions which do not conform to the classic model of the coup d'état. The Cuban revolution as well as guerrilla warfare in Venezuela may illustrate both of these relationships. It should be noted that even with Cuba omitted from the sample, the correlation between violence and revolution is significant.[35]

As initially suggested by the distinction between threat and legitimacy systems, none of the relationships for the democratic countries are significant. Indeed, four out of the six values are negative in sign and the relatively high value for the negative relationship between economic presence and hostility indicates that the U.S. economic presence in the Latin American democracies may help generate a cooperative attitude towards the U.S. On the other hand, certain of the relationships for the non-democratic societies are non-significant, and are actually lower in value than some coefficients for the total number of cases.

6. Causal Inference Analysis

Although we have established the statistical significance of certain relationships, we have not yet inferred the existence of causal sequences of events which culminate in domestic violence and the occurrence of revolution as forms of Latin American political instability. Nor have we determined which set of causal relationships provides the best fit between theory and empirical observation. However, there exists a mode of analysis, which, given certain assumptions, allows for the inference of causality. Recent studies by Hayward Alker, Jr. and Raymond Tanter, among others, have fruitfully employed causal inference analyses.[36]

---

[33] The calculation of the correlation coefficients was carried out on a CDC 3400 computer using the BMD 02D computer program. Levels of significance for these coefficients were obtained from Andrew R. Baggaley, *Intermediate Correlational Methods* (New York: Wiley, 1964), p. 189.

[34] For a classification of various forms of revolution, see Tanter and Midlarsky, *op. cit.*

[35] Violence during the Cuban revolution accounts for a sizable percentage of violence experienced by all the Latin American nations during this time period. Yet, even with Cuba omitted from the total number of cases, the

correlation between violence and revolution is $r = .57$, a significant value, with violence logarithmically transformed and revolution treated by a square root transformation.

[36] Hayward R. Alker, Jr., *Mathematics and Politics* (New York: Macmillan, 1965); and Raymond Tanter, "Toward a Theory of Political Development," *Midwest Journal of Political Science*, 11 (May 1967), 145–172. Other applications of causal inference analysis to political science concerns include Thad Beyle, "Contested Elections and Voter Turnout in a Local Community: A Problem in Spurious Correlations," *American Political Science*

Without entering into a detailed discussion of the mathematics of this mode of analysis, a brief description can be offered.

First, it is assumed that the variables are arranged in a hierarchial order. This assumption is most easily met by assuring that the variables are arranged in a temporal sequence. Thus, a dependent variable which occurs last in the temporal sequence theoretically cannot lead to the existence of an earlier independent variable, and the hierarchy is preserved.[37] Second, it is assumed that there is no prior variable significantly affecting the variables under consideration; that is, the effects of all other variables are assumed to be ran-

dom.[38] Mathematically, this assumption is embodied in the statement that residual error terms are not correlated with one other.

Given these assumptions, the mathematics of causal inference analysis may be translated into statistical language. A hierarchical order which embodies these assumptions may be represented by a set of simultaneous linear equations whose coefficients can be estimated by least square statistics. The regression coefficient is a least square estimator of these coefficients, and should be equal to zero if all other variables of preceding order within the hierarchy are held constant. When the regression coefficient is equal to zero, the corresponding partial correlation is also equal to zero, and in this fashion the deductions from the mathematical analysis can be transformed into predictions.

The hierarchial analysis can determine whether the inference of causality applies to each branch individually. A second mode of causal inference analysis, known as the double effect analysis, allows us to determine whether a single variable results in two independent simultaneous occurrences, and, by implication, whether a combination of the two hierarchial branches is valid. A third form of analysis is employed to determine whether a combination of certain elements of the two branches may be causally inferred. The succeeding analysis consists of an attempt to determine which set of relationships provides the best correspondence between theoretical prediction and empirical observation.

Table IV presents the outcome of the causal inference analysis applied to our original framework. All significant relationships are represented by arrows and apply to the total number of cases under consideration. While the framework did not predict a relationship between hostility and violence, the

Review, 59 (March 1965), 11–116; and Charles F. Cnudde and Donald J. McCrone, "The Linkage Between Constituency Attitudes and Congressional Voting Behavior: A Causal Model," *American Political Science Review*, 60 (March 1966), 66–72. For a detailed treatment of causal inference analysis, see Herbert A. Simon, *Models of Man* (New York: Wiley, 1957), and Hubert M. Blalock, Jr., *Causal Inferences in Nonexperimental Research* (Chapel Hill: University of North Carolina Press, 1964). Some of Blalock's numerous articles are "Four Variable Causal Models and Partial Correlations," *American Journal of Sociology*, 68 (September 1962), 182–194; "Correlation and Causality: The Multivariate Case," *Social Forces*, 39 (March 1961), 246–251; "Evaluating the Relative Importance of Variables," *American Sociological Review*, 26 (December 1961), 866–874; and "Theory Building and the Concept of Interaction," *American Sociological Review*, 30 (June 1965), 374–380. An interesting three-way discussion which highlights some of the criticisms of causal inference analysis is found in Kenneth Polk, Hubert M. Blalock, Jr., and W. S. Robinson, "Asymmetric Causal Models: A Three-Way Discussion," *American Sociological Review*, 27 (August 1962), 539–547.

[37] With one exception, the variables in the hierarchical branches of the framework are arranged in temporal sequence. The exception is hostility toward the U.S. which is not temporally prior to domestic violence. Both variables are for the time period 1958–60. It can be argued, however, that hostility may be prior to violence since violence is most often a manifestation of hostility. It seems likely that the converse of this proposition is less valid.

[38] The majority of verbal or quantitative studies make the implicit assumption that all other variables have a random effect on the phenomenon under investigation. The advantage of causal inference analysis is that it forces the investigator to make this assumption explicit.

Table IV

A CAUSAL INFERENCE ANALYSIS

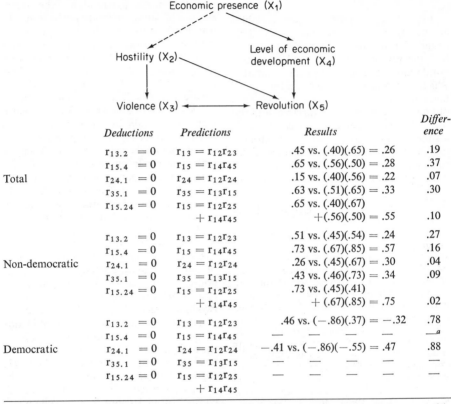

	Deductions	Predictions	Results	Difference
	$r_{13.2} = 0$	$r_{13} = r_{12}r_{23}$	.45 vs. (.40)(.65) = .26	.19
	$r_{15.4} = 0$	$r_{15} = r_{14}r_{45}$	.65 vs. (.56)(.50) = .28	.37
Total	$r_{24.1} = 0$	$r_{24} = r_{12}r_{24}$	.15 vs. (.40)(.56) = .22	.07
	$r_{35.1} = 0$	$r_{35} = r_{13}r_{15}$	.63 vs. (.51)(.65) = .33	.30
	$r_{15.24} = 0$	$r_{15} = r_{12}r_{25}$	.65 vs. (.40)(.67)	
		$+ r_{14}r_{45}$	$+(.56)(.50) = .55$	.10
	$r_{13.2} = 0$	$r_{13} = r_{12}r_{23}$	.51 vs. (.45)(.54) = .24	.27
	$r_{15.4} = 0$	$r_{15} = r_{14}r_{45}$	.73 vs. (.67)(.85) = .57	.16
Non-democratic	$r_{24.1} = 0$	$r_{24} = r_{12}r_{24}$	.26 vs. (.45)(.67) = .30	.04
	$r_{35.1} = 0$	$r_{35} = r_{13}r_{15}$	.43 vs. (.46)(.73) = .34	.09
	$r_{15.24} = 0$	$r_{15} = r_{12}r_{25}$	.73 vs. (.45)(.41)	
		$+ r_{14}r_{45}$	$+ (.67)(.85) = .75$	.02
	$r_{13.2} = 0$	$r_{13} = r_{12}r_{23}$	.46 vs. (−.86)(.37) = −.32	.78
	$r_{15.4} = 0$	$r_{15} = r_{14}r_{45}$	— — — —	—[a]
Democratic	$r_{24.1} = 0$	$r_{24} = r_{12}r_{24}$	−.41 vs. (−.86)(−.55) = .47	.88
	$r_{35.1} = 0$	$r_{35} = r_{13}r_{15}$	— — — —	—
	$r_{15.24} = 0$	$r_{15} = r_{12}r_{25}$	— — — —	—
		$+ r_{14}r_{45}$		

[a] None of the democratic countries experienced revolutions in this time period, and a causal inference test of the theory requires that the variables assume some non-zero values. Therefore, this analysis could not be applied to any of the components of the framework which included revolution as a variable for the democratic countries.

presence of such a relationship in the correlational analysis has led to its inclusion in the revised figure. In addition, the significant relationship between violence and revolution is represented by the two headed double arrow between the two variables, and indicates that each implies the existence of the other.[39]

[39] This finding for Latin American countries is in agreement with the finding of a general relationship between violence and revolution for a sample of 83 cases. See Tanter, 1966, *op. cit.* In addition, a causal inference test could have been employed to determine which of the two was the cause of the other. However, much

The dotted line between the variables economic presence and hostility indicates that the relationship between the two is not significant.[40]

of the violence in Latin America during this time period was concurrent with revolution, and a causal inference test between the two would therefore have had little meaning. However, if one can distinguish between violent acts that are associated with revolution and those which are not, then it might be possible to determine whether non-revolutionary violence is antecedent or consequent to revolution.

[40] The issue of significance in causal inference analysis as yet has not been satisfactorily

The values are presented first for the total number of cases, then for the non-democratic and democratic countries. Within each of these categories, there are five rows, each of which presents a test of a different aspect of the framework. The first row tests the validity of the left hierarchical branch, the second row tests the right hierarchical branch, and the third row (double effect) tests the validity of the proposition that the U.S. economic presence leads to both hostility and an increase in the level of economic development. The fourth row tests the extension of the double effect to include both violence and revolution, and thus tests the validity of combining both hierarchical branches into a single theory. The last row tests a four-variable theory in which economic presence leads to both hostility and level of economic development, which then together lead to the occurrence of revolution. All of the preceding possibilities are tested because of the differences in levels of significance between the three categories leading to the construction of different theoretical models.[41]

The deductions and predictions are presented respectively in the first and second columns. The first deduction in each of the categories (total, non-democratic, democratic) applies to the left branch and states that the correlation between economic presence and domestic violence, holding hostility constant is equal to zero ($r_{13.2} = 0$). From this result, it is now predicted algebraically that $r_{13} = r_{12}r_{23}$.[42] The second deduction refers to the right branch, and the algebraic predictions are similarly derived. The third deduction is applied to a test of the first double effect model, and states that the correlation between level of economic development and hostility, holding the U.S. economic presence constant, is equal to zero ($r_{24.1} = 0$). The attendant prediction is that $r_{24} = r_{12}r_{14}$.[43] The fourth set of deductions and predictions is derived in a similar fashion. The last deduction tests the four variable theory and states that the correlation between economic presence and revolution, holding both hostility and GNP/CAP constant, is equal to zero ($r_{15.24} = 0$). The prediction in this case is that $r_{15} = r_{12}r_{25} + r_{14}r_{45}$.[44]

---

resolved. Given a small enough N, even relatively high values of the correlation coefficient might still be nonsignificant. Yet, a causal inference analysis could provide a high degree of correspondence between observation and prediction. This argument may be applied to the nonsignificant correlation between economic presence and hostility.

[41] The correlational analysis for the non-democratic cases implies a somewhat different theoretical model than the one outlined in Table 4. Therefore, all of the possible components of the framework and theoretically meaningful combinations of variables are tested to account for the possibilities which would best fit the non-democratic as well as the total number of cases. The correlational analysis for the democratic cases implies that none of the components of the framework world apply to this category, and this finding is substantiated by the causal inference analysis applied to all possible components of the framework.

[42] In this instance, the equation for the first-order partial correlation coefficient is

$$r_{13.2} = \frac{r_{13} - r_{12}r_{23}}{\sqrt{(1 - r_{12}^2)(1 - r_{23}^2)}}$$

Since $r_{13.2}$ has been set equal to zero,

$$r_{13} - r_{12}r_{23} = 0, \quad \text{and}$$
$$r_{13} = r_{12}r_{23}$$

[43] The first-order partial correlation for the double effect model is

$$r_{24.1} = \frac{r_{24} - r_{12}r_{14}}{\sqrt{(1 - r_{12}^2)(1 - r_{14}^2)}}$$

By the same reasoning as in note 42:

$$r_{24} = r_{12}r_{14}$$

[44] The equation for the second-order partial correlation in this instance is

$$r_{15.24} = \frac{r_{15.2} - r_{14.2}r_{45.2}}{\sqrt{(1 - r_{14.2}^2)(1 - r_{45.2}^2)}}$$

In the third column, the *observed* values are contrasted with the *predicted* values. The fourth column presents the extent of correspondence between observation and prediction. This value consists of the algebraic difference, in absolute value, between observation and prediction, and constitutes a summary measure of the validity of the separate components. A difference of 0 represents a perfect correspondence between the observed and predicted values, whereas a difference equal to 2 is interpreted as a complete lack of theoretical correspondence to empirical reality.

A reading of the fourth column reveals that the best degrees of correspondence between observed and predicted values are found for the first of the double effect models (economic presence leads to the level of economic development and hostility) and the four variable models (economic presence leads to the level of economic development and hostility, and both lead to revolution). The two findings reinforce each other since the former is a component of the four variable model. Moreover, these results primarily apply

to the non-democratic countries, although these models also supply the best correspondence between observation and prediction for the total number of cases as well. The democratic countries yield by far the worst degrees of correspondence between theory and observation, indicating that none of the testable components of the framework, either individually or together, apply to the Latin American democracies.

7. Conclusions

The theoretical model which provides the best correspondence between observation and prediction is as follows[45]:

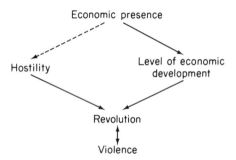

An additional finding of this study is that violent forms of revolution may be replacing the bloodless coup d'état in Latin America. Thus, the Latin American countries may be penetrated societies, and violence and revolution may be explained, in part, by the U.S. economic presence as a linkage to the external environment.

The distinction between threat and legitimacy systems is useful in differentiating between the democratic and nondemocratic countries. This model is most applicable to the non-democratic

---

If $r_{15.24} = 0$, then $r_{15.2} = r_{14.2}r_{45.2}$. Substituting the equations for the appropriate partials, this expression becomes:

$$\frac{r_{15} - r_{12}r_{25}}{\sqrt{(1 - r_{12}^2)(1 - r_{25}^2)}}$$
$$= \frac{r_{14} - r_{12}r_{24}}{\sqrt{(1 - r_{12}^2)(1 - r_{24}^2)}}$$
$$\cdot \frac{r_{45} - r_{24}r_{25}}{\sqrt{(1 - r_{24}^2)(1 - r_{25}^2)}}$$

Since $1/\sqrt{(1 - r_{12}^2)}$ and $1/\sqrt{(1 - r_{25}^2)}$ appear on both sides of the equation, this expression reduces to

$$r_{15} - r_{12}r_{25} = \frac{(r_{14} - r_{12}r_{24})(r_{45} - r_{24}r_{25})}{1 - r_{24}^2}$$

But according to the theory outlined in Table 4, $r_{24} = 0$, or is sufficiently close to zero to make a negligible contribution to both numerator and denominator. Thus,

$$r_{15} - r_{12}r_{25} = r_{14}r_{45}$$

and

$$r_{15} = r_{12}r_{25} + r_{14}r_{45}$$

[45] The first double effect model also provided a high correspondence between observed and predicted values. This model is, of course, a part of the four variable theory.

societies but also provides a moderate degree of correspondence between observation and prediction for the total number of cases. None of the possibilities derived from our initial framework were applicable to the Latin American democracies.

The weakest link in the theory is that between economic presence and hostility, and is indicated by a dotted arrow between the two. The degree of association between these variables was neither significant for the total number of cases, nor was it significant for the non-democratic countries. Moreover, certain other relationships were not significant for the non-democratic nations. Therefore, these results must be accepted with caution. The fact that certain of the relationships among variables were contrary to prediction, combined with the limited time period under investigation (1956–60), suggests that future research into other time periods is needed.

8. Policy Implications

Despite the preceding *caveat*, certain policy implications may be derived concerning relationships between the United States and the Latin American nations. The first of these concerns the distinction between the democratic and non-democratic countries in this region. The high negative relationship between the U.S. economic presence and hostility toward the U.S. for the democratic Latin American nations indicates perhaps that investment and trade with the Latin American democracies may induce a cooperative attitude toward the U.S. Thus, the U.S. may wish to augment its economic presence in the Latin American democracies.[46] As for the non-

[46] On the other hand, a threshold value may exist beyond which investment and trade, even with the Latin American democracies, might lead to hostility toward the U.S.

democratic countries, it appears that the goals of U.S. policy in this region and the stability of these societies are affected by the U.S. economic presence.

The second policy-area touched upon by this analysis is that of investment and trade with developing countries. The findings of this study present a paradox. On the one hand, developing nations such as many of the non-democratic Latin American countries may require the economic increment that investment and trade can provide. On the other hand, the inadvertent results of such an economic presence may be an hostility to the investor nation as well as local political instability. U.S. policy makers, in particular, may be caught on the horns of a somewhat different dilemma. They cannot control the external practices of American business by fiat, and to do so might constitute a violation of those freedoms of movement which are the legitimate right of the American entrepreneur. Yet, the findings of this study indicate that U.S. relations with Latin America may be affected by American business practices with perhaps grave consequences for hemispheric unity.

Appendix I

DEFINITIONS OF VARIABLES INCLUDED IN THE HOSTILITY MEASURE

"1. *Number of threats:* any official diplomatic communication or governmental statement asserting that if a particular country does or does not do a particular thing it will incur negative sanctions.
2. *Number of protests:* any official diplomatic communication or governmental statement, the purpose of which is to complain about or object to the policies of another country.
3. *Number of accusations:* any official or governmental statement involving charges and allegations of a derogatory nature against another country.

4. *Number of negative sanctions:* any nonviolent act against another country —such as boycott, withdrawal of aid— the purpose of which is to punish or threaten that country.
5. *Number of ambassadors expelled or recalled:* any expelling of an ambassador from, or recalling for other than administrative reasons an ambassador to, a particular country . . . .
6. *Number of diplomatic officials of less than ambassador's rank expelled or recalled:* replace 'ambassador' by 'officials of lesser . . . rank' in above definition.
7. *Presence . . . of military action:* any military clash of a particular country with another and involving gunfire, but short of war . . .
8. *Number of troop movements:* any rapid movement of large bodies of troops, naval units, or air squadrons to a particular area for the purpose of deterring the military action of another country, gaining concessions, or as a show of strength.
9. Number of anti-foreign demonstrations: any demonstration or riot by more than 100 people directed at a particular foreign country . . . or its policies."

Cf. Raymond Tanter, "Dimensions of Conflict: Behavior Within and Between Nations, 1958–60," *Journal of Conflict Resolution,* 10 (March 1966), 63.

Appendix II

TRANSFORMATION ANALYSIS

The product-moment correlation coefficient is a measure of linear relationships. It is also sensitive to extreme values, and requires that the frequency distributions of variables be moderately normal (no severe skewness). Thus, for purposes of statistical analysis, there may be at least three uses for transformation analysis applied to the correlation coefficient: (a) to transform a curvilinear relationship into a linear one; (b) to bring an extreme value to within an accepted number of standard deviations from the mean; and (c) to correct for the extreme skewness of a distribution.

The transformations listed in Table A represent an effort to carry out these functions of transformation analysis. Each of the variables was plotted against all of the others, and the appropriate transformations were chosen to maximize the linearity of

Table A

TRANSFORMATIONS

		Economic Presence		Hostility	Violence	GNP/CAP	Revolution
Economic presence	Total						
	Non-democratic						
	Democratic						
Hostility	Total						
	Non-democratic	$\sqrt{H}$	$\sqrt{E}$				
	Democratic	Log H	None				
Violence	Total	Log V	None	Log V	$\sqrt{H}$		
	Non-democratic	Log V	$\sqrt{E}$	Log V	$\sqrt{H}$		
	Democratic	Log V	Log E	None	None		
GNP/CAP	Total	None	None	None	None	None	Log V
	Non-democratic	None	None	None	$\sqrt{H}$	None	Log V
	Democratic	None	Log E	None	None	$\sqrt{G}$	None
Revolution	Total	None	None	$\sqrt{R}$	Log H	$\sqrt{R}$	Log V	None	None
	Non-democratic	None	None	$\sqrt{R}$	Log H	None	Log V	None	None
	Democratic	—		—		—		—	

the plots. Extreme values were brought to within an accepted number of standard deviations from the mean. In addition, the frequency distributions of the variables were plotted and chi-square goodness of fit tests were administered to assess the skewness of both transformed and untransformed data. It should be noted that if a transformation is performed, say for the purpose of correcting for an extreme value in one variable, then the nature of the relationships of this variable with others may be changed from linearity to curvilinearity. This effect is undesirable, since the correlation coefficient is a statistical measure of linear relationships. Therefore, each individual set of bivariate relationships may require a different set of transformations so that the linearity of each plot is maximized.

The relationship between violence and hostility provides an illustration of the effect of an extreme value on the correlation coefficient. An r = .93 for the total number of cases was calculated using the untransformed data. However, a plot of these variables, and chi-square goodness of fit tests revealed that the value for Cuba was an extreme outlier and apparently had affected the value of the coefficient. An r = .65 was calculated for the transformed data and a plot of the variables was uniformly linear.

Table A lists the sets of transformations which were used in the calculation of the correlation coefficients in Table 3. Each of the variables is symbolized by its first letter; thus, E = Economic Presence, H = Hostility, V = Violence, G = Gross National Product per Capita, and R = Revolution. The transformations are listed first for the variables in the rows, and then for those in the columns. The word "None" indicates that no transformation was performed.

CASE

AND

COUNTRY

STUDIES

OF

POLITICAL

VIOLENCE

Studies of specific outbreaks of revolutionary violence and characteristic patterns of violence in a country or region provide a kind of understanding that is not easily conveyed by theoretical and general comparative analyses. The case study best illustrates both how a constellation of variables interact to produce a specific, violent outcome and the place of that action in the political process.

The eight studies in this section were chosen to represent different approaches to the case study of collective protest and various types of violence in different regions of the world. The first selection, by anthropologist Paul Friedrich, illustrates how assassinations and other forms of violence have become an intrinsic part of political competition in a Mexican Indian village, and how that pattern of behavior is justified and supported by the beliefs of the villagers. The next two selections deal with modern or modernizing sectors of societies in which political violence is usually regarded as an aberration, caused by intense but transient social tensions and discontents. Theodore Abel's study of autobiographies of Nazi party members and Bryant Wedge's interviews with Brazilian and Dominican students who had been in revolutionary situations reveal how politically potent discontent can be when it is both intensely felt and given organizational expression. These two studies explicitly include both the states of mind of revolutionary actors and the settings in which they operate as causes of violence.

Anthony J. Russo's study of poverty and insurgency in South Vietnam relies on aggregate data for provinces and compares the results of its analysis with aggregate and interview data for a sample of hamlets. Like the Abel and Wedge studies, it assumes that violence has multiple causes and attempts to measure several of them. John Schwarz's study of the Scottish National Party is distinctive in several respects. Schwarz relies on interviews with Party leaders and a variety of aggregate data and other information to show what kinds of tensions give rise to separatist movements—which are increasingly common in western nations—and to determine why the Scottish separatist movement is almost wholly nonviolent.

The last three selections share two common themes: (1) that nonrevolutionary protest and violence can be and have become routinized in modernizing and modern societies; and (2) that such collective action is often used with calculation and to considerable effect in the political process. Charles Tilly draws from his enormous collection of systematic data on collective violence in French history to illustrate how such violence has shifted from primitive to reactionary to modern forms. He argues that urbanization, industrialization, and the growth of the modern state neither created nor minimized collective violence, but were responsible for its transformation and particularly for its politicization. These changes are reflected not only in Europe but elsewhere. Ann Ruth Willner's study of Indonesia draws on a number of cases to show that a politically useful and influential kind of group protest has become "an institutionalized and even ritualized tactic of the game of politics" in one of the world's most populous developing nations. James Payne describes a common Latin American variation of such developments: a political system in Peru the stability of which depends upon an insecure balance between interest groups that employ token violence to make demands and a presidency that is uniquely empowered to provide concessions—and is obliged to do so on pain of a military coup d'état if violent protest becomes too intense.

One special value of the case study is that it provides information about what kinds of people take part in political violence, and what the specific circumstances are that impel these people to go into the streets or hills. Several of the selections in this part deal specifically with these questions. Abel's study of the origins of the Nazi movement is unique in its method, for it analyzes 600 life histories of Nazi Party members which were written as a response to an essay contest organized in 1934 with the cooperation of the Nazi Party. Although the respondents may not have been representative, and their essays are often self-serving, their essays provide a dramatic portrait of the personal and nationalistic grievances of Germans in the 1920's and illustrate how the Party capitalized on those grievances.

Another approach to the study of participants in group protest and violence is to look at the social characteristics of those who participate. Some scholars, of whom Tilly is representative, make detailed studies of newspapers and court records to determine the socioeconomic classes and types of social groupings that are involved in violent clashes. Tilly's data for France, for example, show a long-term increase in specialization and organization in collective violence.

With a few exceptions we know more about the characteristics, motivations, and behavior of participants in protest and violence in western European nations than we do about participants in strife elsewhere in the world. Wedge's interviews with revolutionary student leaders in Brazil and the Dominican Republic provide a major addition to our understanding of "rebel psychology"—interviews that are that much more valuable because they were conducted and analyzed by a psychiatrist. Friedrich's fieldwork with Tarascan peasants provides invaluable knowledge, not of "rebel psychology" per se, but of the cultural frame of reference and motivations of men for whom violent politics is an accepted way of life and death. Violence in Tarascan political competition does not occur without tension. But the Tarascan peasant holds a complex set of beliefs about the inherently violent nature of man, the necessity for violent means to maintain highly valued kinds of social relationships, and the justifiability of violence in the cause of political ideals that have made political homicide an extraordinarily common means for responding to those tensions.

Another major value of case studies is that they can provide a means for assessing and improving theory. Comprehensive studies like those included in Part II of this volume test how well theories explain general patterns of conflict and violence; case studies can show how well general theories explain the dynamics and details of particular events. Schwarz uses his study of Scottish separatism to determine the extent to which several theories of the origins of violent political action also account for a nonviolent protest movement. Whereas Eckstein's congruence theory of stability suggests that dissident leaders ought to be characterized by intrapersonal tension, the Scottish nationalists that Schwarz interviewed showed few such tendencies. Other theories emphasize organizational discontinuities and consequent feelings of anomie or hopelessness as underlying causes of mass behavior. Some economic discontinuity between Scotland and England is apparent from aggregate data, but anomie and hopelessness are scarcely evident. Schwarz also assesses the extent of relative deprivation in terms of aggregate and perceived discrepancies between Scotland and England, finding that perceived though not objective deprivation is pervasive, but also that such depriva-

tion is only mild to moderate in intensity. Scotland largely lacks the distinctive, flourishing regional culture that still other theories associate with separatism. Consequently, Schwarz concludes that discontinuity and deprivation among Scots have been sufficient to stimulate an upsurge of separatist protest, but not severe enough to cause much violence.

Tilly draws upon data about the sizes and types of groups involved in group violence in different decades of French history to demonstrate his thesis that the nature—but not the extent—of violence has changed markedly over time. And whereas Tilly uses changes in patterns of violence over time to test a hypothesis, Russo uses quantitative data on provinces and hamlets within South Vietnam to determine the relationship among poverty, inequality, and degree of insurgency. Some earlier theoretical speculation about the Vietnam revolution, along with quantitative evidence, had suggested that support for the National Liberation Front (NLF) was greatest in the most economically progressive areas, but Russo's evidence suggests that this is false: the poorest provinces and poorest hamlets are most likely to support the NLF, whether poverty is measured in terms of per capita income or according to the amount of land farmers have relative to what they need for subsistence. Russo speculates that a combination of economic deprivation, revolutionary agitation, and lack of congruence between Saigon authority patterns and those of the villagers—contrasted with similarity between village and NLF authority patterns—provide a very durable basis of support for NLF insurgency that seems little affected by military efforts.

Most of the case studies in this section either test, use, or lead to theoretical generalizations. In addition to the theoretical interests of Schwarz, Tilly, and Russo, described above, we include Wedge's study of rebellious Brazilian and Dominican students, which tests how well Gurr's theory of relative deprivation and social balance explains the different outcomes of two revolutionary situations. Other case studies are designed not to evaluate general propositions but to provide case-specific descriptions, explanations, and interpretations. Friedrich's study of Mexican political homicide is a good example. Implicitly or explicitly such case studies can lead to the formulation of more general relationships. If nothing else, Friedrich's Mexican case study should persuade the reader that any general analysis of the causes of violence must take into account variations among cultures and subcultures in beliefs about violence—variations that are substantially greater than we might think. Payne's study of Peru provides another example of case-specific analysis that has considerably wider implications. Along with Willner's study of protest in Indonesia, it provides a crucial qualification to the conventional western assumption that group protest and violence represent the breakdown of politics. In Peru, in Indonesia, and in more of European past and present than we sometimes recognize, violence has been at the heart of the political process, not merely as a last resort but as a frequently used and often influential tactic of regimes and their opponents.

The selections included in Part III consider four quite different kinds of political protest and violence. Some selections in Parts I and II make use of a three-fold distinction among turmoil, conspiracy, and internal war. *Turmoil* is characterized by popular participation, a relatively low degree of organization, and objectives that are either limited or unformulated. But the case studies suggest that there are two rather dif-ferent types of turmoil, different at least in the motivations of their participants and their place in the political process One can be called *anomic turmoil*, typically spontaneous, episodic, and unstructured outpourings of anger such as ghetto riots, communal clashes, and many of the events Tilly calls "primitive violence" in European history. Although these events may have drastic local consequences they seldom have much impact on the political system.

The second type of turmoil is *tactical turmoil*, which includes demonstrations, general strikes, and some antigovernment riots, that evidence a degree of organization and specific, tactical objectives, and that are usually violent only in proportion to the severity of police or military response. Tactical turmoil seems always to be based on considerable popular discontent among its participants, but it represents a functional, specifically political response to those discontents. Tactical turmoil often seems to the social scientist to be an alternative to more violent manifestations of discontent by providing a potentially constructive expression of demands that, if left unsatisfied and unexpressed, might lead to explosions of episodic rioting or revolutionary movements. Tilly's evidence shows quite clearly that anomic turmoil was supplanted by tactical turmoil in France; the turning point, he suggests elsewhere, came in the 1840's and 1850's. Contemporary Indonesia and many other former colonies seem to have experienced just such a transition in their recent past, or are undergoing one at present.

The transition of group protest and violence from anomic to tactical forms may be a relative social good, but it can also be dysfunctional for a political system. The clearest danger, evident in the case study of Peru, is that governments may become responsive only to demands expressed with the threat or actuality of violence. In Indonesia, Willner suggests, institutionalized public protest has various functions: to exert pressure to change policies; to test the extent of popular support for various political figures, in and out of office; and to keep administrators and politicians "in line." In the later years of Sukarno's regime and after his downfall in 1967, the military tacitly encouraged some kinds of public protest in the hope that they could utilize discontent to increase their control over some of the policies and personnel of government that were the objects of this discontent, including some of their own nominal subordinates. Such patterns represent at least partial failures of conventional political processes. A so-called competitive democracy such as Peru works poorly if it is incapable of responding adequately to popular grievances when they are expressed through established mechanisms of participation and representation. An authoritarian or quasi-authoritarian state such as Indonesia functions no better, by its own standards, if members of its elites regularly challenge one another in street demonstrations and expect public protests to serve as instruments of governance.

Conspiracy is a generic term for small-scale, clandestine uses of force for specifically political purposes, usually to seize or enhance political power. The classic type of conspiracy is the coup d'état. Two examples in the selections in Part III are the coup by the Brazilian armed forces in March 1964, and the recurrent military coups of Peru, exemplified by that of July 1962. In both instances the military acted preventively, although one cannot entirely discount the intrinsic desire for power of the leaders of the coups. In Brazil coups have been very rare, that of 1964 being justified by the

desire of the military—and many civilians—to maintain the political and economic order that was seemingly threatened by the "revolutionary reforms" of President Goulart. In Peru the military coup seems essential to the functioning of the political system. The July 1962 coup occurred after a chaotic month during which three presidential candidates were totally unable to agree on a course of political action. The electoral outcome that led to this situation was unique, but the situation—political paralysis in the face of growing popular violence—was archtypical of those in which the Peruvian military has intervened. In October 1968 yet another coup occurred in Peru, when the military overthrew the elected President Fernando Belaunde Terry at a time of increasing economic crisis and widespread civil unrest.

A second type of conspiracy is the *terroristic* movement, the members of which typically lack the resources to overthrow a regime and rely instead on dramatic acts of violence to demonstrate their capacity to act hoping to stimulate others to join them or at least refrain from supporting the regime in power. Examples of such movements in the contemporary world have ranged from the revolutionary terrorists of urban Uruguay and rural Bolivia to the irredentist terrorists of the Irish Republican Army and the separatists of the Italian Tyrol. The Scottish National Party (S. N. P.) draws its strength from the same kinds of separatist sentiments and discontents that inspired terrorism in Northern Ireland and the Tyrol. Violence by Scottish separatists has been infinitesimal by comparison, however, and as a tactic was roundly condemned by the S.N.P. leaders in Schwarz's interviews. Two factors help account for the nonviolent commitments of the S.N.P.: the generally moderate level of deprivation among the Scots and the relative political effectiveness of the S.N.P. as a party. Under less favorable conditions one might expect Scottish protest to take more virulent forms.

The political homicides of Tarascan villages represent a third type of conspiracy, one in which competing political factions selectively use violence to maintain or increase their power or revenge political affronts. It is noteworthy that the leaders of the factions in the village studied were seldom the targets of this violence; most of the killers and victims were their lieutenants and followers. In this respect Tarascan political assassinations differ from the pattern intermittently seen in Slavic Europe, the United States, and elsewhere: the expression of grievances by attempts on the lives of political leaders. The Tarascan pattern does have European parallels in twentieth-century Germany and Spain—and, curiously enough, among Anglo politicians in late nineteenth-century New Mexico—where for brief periods cycles of assassination and counter-assassination became part of the style of political competition. The Tarascan pattern remains unusual in that it has persisted for two generations after its origins in the agrarian reforms of the Mexican Revolution.

Internal wars such as civil and guerrilla wars resemble turmoil because their partisans include a variety of ordinary citizens. The revolutionary or secessionist movements that precipitate such wars also tend to be well organized and both their leaders and rank-and-file participants usually hope to impose drastic changes on the social and political systems. Three examples of revolutionary movements are represented in the selections in Part III, each a different type: Vietnam, the Dominican Republic, and Germany in the 1930's. Vietnam has been the site of the most protracted, bloody

internal wars of the twentieth century. Much of the writing on revolution in Vietnam has emphasized the importance of factors of nationalist and communist ideology, of governmental incompetence and cupidity, of insurgent civilian and military organization, and of foreign intervention as determinants of those wars. The underlying social conditions by which these factors operated, however, have been given much less attention. One of them is the subject of Russo's comparative statistical study, which suggests that insurgency has been most successful in the poorest provinces. Vietnam provides an example of a revolutionary movement based primarily on rural discontent.

Cities, as well as the countryside, can be the breeding ground for internal war, as the 1965 revolution in Santo Domingo demonstrates. Young military officers attempted a coup d'état to forestall a suspected effort by senior officers to reestablish a regime of the Trujillo type. The rebel officers were joined spontaneously by tens of thousands of young men and women, many of them middle class, to precipitate a civil war that was halted only by the military intervention of the United States. This "revolution," which might be compared with those of Hungary in 1956 and Egypt in 1952, was a manifestation of popular revulsion with those in power; few of those who went into the streets planned a revolution, but once they were there they found they had made one, if not for themselves, then for those who could capitalize on the situation.

The Nazi movement provides an example of a mass response to widespread deprivation among all social sectors and across urban and rural segments of a modern society. One interpretation of the Nazi movement, as we view it, is that it was an internal war that did not take place. The Nazi

Party made such effective use of demonstrations, street fights, and small-scale terrorism, in addition to more conventional political activity, that by 1933 the leaders of the Weimar Republic had few doubts about the will and capacity of the Party to initiate a full-scale civil war to achieve power. Faced with that prospect they abdicated to Hitler, and the Nazi revolution was carried out under the auspices of the state.

Suggested Readings

These are collections of case studies of various kinds of political violence. There are also innumerable individual studies of particular events and movements.

Anderson, Charles W., Fred R. von der Mehden, and Crawford Young. *Issues of Political Development.* Englewood Cliffs, N.J.: Prentice-Hall, Inc., 1967, Part Two: "The Maintenance of Political Order."

Andrews, William G., and Uri Ra'anan. *The Politics of the Coup d'état: Five Case Studies.* New York: Van Nostrand Reinhold, 1969.

Havens, Murray Clark, Carl Leiden, and Karl M. Schmitt. *The Politics of Assassination.* Englewood Cliffs, N.J.: Prentice-Hall, Inc., 1970.

Hobsbawm, E. J. *Primitive Rebels: Studies in Archaic Forms of Social Movement in the 19th and 20th Centuries.* New York: W. W. Norton & Company, Inc., 1959.

Leiden, Carl, and Karl M. Schmitt. *The Politics of Violence: Revolution in the Modern World.* Englewood Cliffs, N.J.: Prentice-Hall, Inc., 1968, Part Two: "Case Studies in Revolution."

Lieuwen, Edwin. *Generals vs. Presidents: Neo-militarism in Latin America.* New York: Frederick A. Praeger, Inc., 1964.

Rotberg, Robert I., ed. *Rebellion in Black Africa.* New York: Oxford University Press, Inc., 1971.

Rude, George. *The Crowd in History, 1730-1848: A Study of Popular Disturbances in France and England, 1730-1848.* New York: John Wiley & Sons, Inc., 1964.

Wolf, Eric R. *Peasant Wars of the Twentieth Century.* New York: Harper & Row, Publishers, 1969.

POLITICAL
HOMICIDE IN
RURAL MEXICO[*]

Paul Friedrich

At five-thirty on a Sunday morning in June, 1955, a peasant named Manuel was shot dead while walking along a road outside his village in the Tarascan area of Mexico. Subsequent investigations revealed that he had been a member of the opposition party. He himself had taken part in such ambushes. Seventy-seven homicides, over a hundred woundings, and hundreds of small-arms exchanges without issue had taken place during the past 35 years even though the village, here called Acan, has at no time contained more than fifteen hundred persons.[1]

[*] Earlier versions of this paper were read to the Philadelphia Anthropological Society (1960) and the Columbia General Seminar (1961); gratitude is here expressed to the discussants. I stand permanently indebted to many Aceños who helped me try to understand their way of life. I am obligated to Sidney Mintz, to Carl Friedrich, to Mildred January, and, most particularly, to my wife, Lore Friedrich, for their valuable criticisms of the contents of this paper.

[1] The village of Acan is part of Tarascan society, a group of some seventy thousand Indian peasants living in the cool, green mountains of southwestern Mexico. Salient features of the village culture include general Spanish-Tarascan bilingualism, plow-and-hoe agriculture, maize as a big cash crop, a diet primarily of maize, beans, and chili, two- to four-room adobe dwellings, an almost total disappearance of native handicrafts, and, finally, the recent introduction of modern improvements, such as limited electrification. Most of the best land is administered communally as ejido and worked in plots inalienably attached to immediate or slightly extended families.

The area's recent history may be divided into four periods: (1) The period of indigenous culture, as of about 1885. (2) A socially troubled time, 1885–1921, following the desiccation by Spanish capitalists of an adjacent marshy lake that had been the principal source of a

Acan has been one of the local end-points in an informal system of caciques —leaders—and political factionalism with much attenant homicide that is today regarded as one of Mexico's serious social problems.

The peasant who kills another in the course of such politics sees himself as performing a partly justified or even obligatory act, for the culture to which both killer and victim belong often justifies or enjoins political homicide. The theory for this paper is that people's actions are based on a system of assumptions and that crisis behavior, such as homicide, indexes them with great sensitivity. What are the Tarascan assumptions?

---

livelihood based heavily on fishing and mat-weaving. During these years the region was controlled by a combination of Spanish land-lords, clergy, and mestizos (here meaning Mexican nationals who speak Spanish and are not Indian in culture). (3) The period from 1921 to 1926, when the peasants struggled for the rich, black soil of the former marsh, and a cacical system crystallized in the village. (4) 1926 until the present.

The methods used to obtain ethnographic and historical depth on the sensitive materials included: (1) Residence in the field from February, 1955, until June, 1956. (2) General ethnography following the *Outline of Cultural Materials* (George P. Murdock and others; New Haven, Human Relations Area Files Publication, 1950). (3) Hundreds of hours of informal conversation about politics with scores of persons, and 10 to 30 hours each with 15 closer individuals. (4) Rorschachs and projective tests given to nine leaders. (5) Participation in one and one-half years of fiestas, political functions, and town meetings. (6) Sociometric description of kinship, friendship, and compadre ties in both factions. (7) Study of legal records in the county seat and state capital, a 2,400-page dossier of reports and accusations in Mexico City, and the homicide accounts kept by two local chroniclers. (8) Field work in four contiguous pueblos and interviewing of many political refugees in other parts of Mexico. I would stress that people's memory for politics is a good deal sharper than for many other aspects of culture. Interviews were in Spanish and, to a very limited extent, Tarascan.

Human Nature[2]

Various ideas and feelings about human nature itself underlie the acts of political homicide. Man is thought of as basically passionate, a creature whose strong emotions, necessarily present, may at times be justifiably expressed. Such passion often breaks out in a form called "rage," a frenzy to which most men can be provoked.[3] Interestingly enough, those most susceptible to rage are normally soft-spoken and polite, but when they are enraged, their eyes go out of focus and they may sway on their feet. Let me cite just one example of the phenomenon.

"Bones" Gonzalez, a political "fighter," has always been a reasonably popular member of the community, despite numerous killings and adulterous exploits.

[2] The point of view taken here is primarily that of the politically interested adult male.

[3] Of the premeditated forms, killing by ambush (*de traición*) is more frequent, but face-to-face assault (*de asalto*) continues because it enhances the killer's reputation for valor. The victim either runs or resigns himself, sometimes saying, "Kill me." But sometimes the victim successfully counterattacks. In 1924, the most valiant agrarian fighter tried to shoot a member of the landlord party, but was himself grappled by his intended victim and eventually dispatched by allies of his victim, who had come running up with ox-goads.

A certain number of men also die because of immediate, efficient causes. All three of the principal killers have at some time been heavy drinkers, and one has suffered from delirium tremens. As long as he is operating within the framework of assumptions outlined in this paper, an intoxicated killer is less criticized by the public because "the vice seized him." On the other hand, a purely wanton murder by a drunken man arouses tremendous anger, especially if the victim had children. Theft, also, may trigger off homicidal rage, especially if a cow or horse is involved. Finally, a man's passion for a woman, and intrigues between women, may precipitate violence. Thus the "bad time" of 1937 is blamed on "a question of skirts." But these efficient causes must be related to the ultimate assumptions; a man does not kill his brother, no matter how drunk he becomes.

The news that he had been ambushed and seriously wounded on the main plaza touched off rage in his two closest ceremonial relatives. Within two hours one of the assailants had been hunted down and riddled in the cornfields whence he had fled. The other was shot dead by compadre José in a face-to-face encounter in broad daylight on one of the side alleys known as "The Street of the Dead."

A second quality of human nature, as these villagers see it, is what might be called necessary social interdependency. It is felt that every man strongly needs a certain number of intimates, many of whom are usually his ceremonial coparents, or compadres—the fathers of his godchildren and the godfathers of his children.[4] These intimates are part of the self as it has developed through time; loyalty to them is as much an act of self-help as self-defense would be; the death of a compadre is really the death of a part of oneself. A man who betrays one of these intimates may stand in greater danger from his former compadre than from someone who has always been a foe. Disloyalty to an intimate arouses the most fundamental anxieties. The typical reaction of an Aceño—an inhabitant of Acan—is: "How can you in America live without compadres?"

Politics is geared to these wheels. Political homicide always conduces to blood vengeance, and killings because of vengeance always provoke political reactions. Here is another recent example:

Remi, the father of ten children and one of the fastest field workers, was, like most active political fighters, a typical peasant. But a combination of alertness, greed, ambition, courage, and physical coordination had made him an outstanding leader.

[4] A compadre is picked shortly before the birth of a child. See Sidney Mintz and Eric Wolf, "An Analysis of Ritual Co-Parenthood (Compadrazgo)," *Southwestern J. Anthropology* (1950), 6: 341–369.

In the fall of 1959 he was killed from ambush by eight members of the opposition, his body pierced by over twenty bullets. One month later his two eldest sons shot and killed a member of the opposition and his father. This short-term interlacing of blood vengeance and political retaliation seemed logical to the Aceños. "So the sons avenged their father. What else could they do?"

Such tenacious obligations may be met after a lapse of as much as ten or twenty years, especially if the killer had departed for a while to let matters cool off.[5]

The third assumption is connected with social interdependency. The people assume that human relations are necessarily ambivalent; a man may love and be loyal and at the same time hate and feel envy; these feelings tend to be combined in any relationship, even though the proportions may vary greatly. This is poignantly illustrated

[5] The Tarascan attitudes toward death are a contributing but not sufficient cause for the acceptance of homicide as a means of settling accounts. The Aceños share some attitudes that might seem fatalistic or callous. With an infant mortality of over 50 percent until quite recently, the growing Indian has seen little friends and siblings die and has participated in the ambiguous gaiety of the wake and the stoical expressions at the funeral, as in the beautiful song, "Life is worth nothing. No worth has life." The cemetery remains small because plots are only visited for five years or so before being reused. Some Aceños think that no great divide separates the living from the dead, who live on as active spirits in this world; others think life ends with *rigor mortis*. Some men are in danger of their lives, but seem serene, and the caution of those few who hardly ever leave their houses springs from sensible calculation rather than generalized anxiety. Many enjoy, almost gratefully, the borrowed time on which they live (a realistic attitude: by March, 1960, of the formerly dominant faction, two were dead, three in jail, and three had moved to distant towns).

But this casualness is significantly qualified. Homicide is classed as a crime in national law and a sin in the religion. Most men are in fact desperately self-preserving. And there has been only one sucide in over 70 years.

by the relationship between father and son, which may combine coldness with intense loyalty. "Bones" Gonzalez has a son who hardly ever speaks to him although he provides unflinching political support. Moreover, the same man who is extemely affectionate toward his family and friends may feel intense hatred toward some other person for apparently trivial reasons. The Aceños are intuitively aware of their own ambivalence and acknowledge and tolerate much apparently contradictory behavior—for example, the same man can be a loving nephew toward his uncle and a relentless retaliator in politics—saying, "We are very good, and very bad"; "We are the most friendly, and the most aggressive"; or, finally, "We are very reserved, and very sentimental." Such ambivalence often underlies the implacable hatred that may arise between two people. Irrational hatred itself, therefore, may partially justify a killing, as reflected in the conclusion, "He killed him because of envy. That's politics."

A fourth assumption about human nature, related to the third, is that all men share a strain of egoism (*egoismo*), and that politically active persons, such as a cacique, are endowed with an undue amount. An egoist is, in the first place, a man who advances his own interest at the expense of others to a degree that is offensive and detrimental. More particularly, egoism here generates a sort of *libido dominandi* in the Italian Renaissance style, in which a fascination with the game of power is conjoined with a passionate urge to control the land and people of one's village. "Everyone has his passion. For one it is women, and for another, politics." Clearly, this is a two-sided affair; a leader may be criticized by friend and foe alike for his egoism. But egoism and its most frequently mentioned product, "envy," are also recognized as a part of the human condition and are reckoned in terms of a larger emotional complex. And individuals differ greatly. The ideal leader reveals comparatively little egoism in its objectionable forms, remaining "dedicated to progress," and "ready to explain everything."

Fifth, it is assumed that man is to some extent brave, and that all men must sometimes demonstrate their "valor," often admired when it erupts in drastic shape. A man is therefore not entirely responsible when he kills to express his courage, especially when he is also motivated by personal loyalty to someone else. On the other hand, to a limited degree the streak of cowardice that many men are recognized to share is also tolerated.

Another assumption is that man is always motivated in part by ideals. While these may be economic or social, in the sense of fighting for a just share of the land, the most widely cited ideals are more specifically political, especially those connected with left-wing, agrarian politics. Homicide tends to be justified by political ideology; Manuel was said to have "betrayed the agrarian cause." The constant reference to ideology suggests that the Aceño assumes that people act on the basis of ultimate assumptions.

An additional assumption, which throws light less on the occurrence of homicides than on their nature, is that man is not sadistic beyond very short limits. It is true that some men beat their wives, and the manner of slaughtering pigs or laughing at injured dogs might seem sadistic. But the behavior of the Aceños over the past forty years when locked in political contentions indicates both a lack of any deep-seated sadism and strong sanctions against any expression of it. Feelings against sadism contrast strongly with the frequency of violence; men must die in consequence of factionalism, but the victim should be dispatched quickly, in the spirit of an execution, almost apologetically. The extremely rare incidents to the contrary are described with phrases of horror. . . .

.   .   .

Social Organization

Political life is but one aspect of a more comprehensive social system, involving kinds of human relations which have become part of the Aceño's developing personality and which are almost impossible to dissociate from him; many values underlying Tarascan social organization motivate homicidal acts.

First, Acan is pervaded by a remarkably egalitarian ethos. All members of the community regard themselves as "indigenous peasants" (except for a few mestizos not covered here). Even the cacique describes himself in this way and dresses in the accepted fashion —khaki pants, Michoacán sombrero, and so forth—despite his various contacts at upper levels. The egalitarian ethos derives in part from the Indian past but is largely a consequence— especially in its explicit features—of the agrarian reform which resulted in the expulsion of the mestizo upper class and in a redistribution of the land so that most villagers now do have enough for subsistence. Property is distributed with comparative equality, and houses are of about the same dimensions. Agrarianism contributed an ideology of equality and fraternity. The politically active men are scattered throughout the rather fuzzy socioeconomic layers, and all control one to three ejido plots of five acres each. Killings have not followed class lines since the agrarian reform.

The one-class ethos has, on the other hand, often motivated Aceño leaders to oppose persons in higher echelons of the political system. At critical moments the caciques of Acan may adamantly block the move of some politico in the capital, reasoning as follows: "We are the indigenous revolutionaries. We have suffered. You are just one of the mestizos trying to use us." The appearance of indigenous status should be maintained within the village, and class oppression from above should be struggled against by all means, including homicide.

However, these Indian peasants do differ from one another in purely political status. At one extreme, some 30 percent of the community is largely inactive, has never held political office, and is not apt to commit political homicide. The remainder, however, are at least peripherally entangled in factional disputes. About half of the villagers are involved politically in the sense that they discuss and brood over politics; they are eligible for office on local committees and may get embroiled in homicide.

At the top stands a smaller group of about a quarter of the adult male population, some fifty to seventy men who are either actually or potentially very active. One assumes that these men display such personal qualities as idealism and fast reflexes. Their political status is partly achieved and partly inherited; most leaders and fighters emerge as a result of their involvement at birth in a preexistng network of loyalties, and political astuteness may be acquired along with the other knowledge and skills of a politically active extended family.

But "leader" and "fighter" do not necessarily mean the same thing. Several men, for example, have left the village permanently because they lacked the toughness to play their designated role. Others are sensitive and educated enough to make excellent leaders, but lack the valor or the flair for intrigue that mark the fighter.

Some with the valor and the vengeance obligations to be fighters lack the leadership ability to be "princes," as the Aceño chiefs facetiously call themselves. "Panchí the Squirrel," for example, killer of three and local expert in Tarascan songs, was never even considered for office. Some outstandingly intelligent and courageous fighters are denied a leadership role because of envy and other factors. Such conflicting standards can engender severe frustrations and resentment.

A second assumption in the social organization involves the sharp segregation of men from women; sex differences automatically channel homicide. Women may be deceived or abducted, but the death of a woman through politics is bad and ugly. In the entire period for which records were obtained, the only woman killed through political violence was accidentally shot in 1923 by a man struggling with her husband. The same taboo also accounts in part for the passionate abandon with which women throw themselves between their fighting men. In 1956 the mayor in a neighboring town came to blows with his envious cousin. The mayor's mother separated the two while his older sister snatched away his pistol. His wife and younger sister were also in the melee.

. . .

The inviolability of women has deeper roots. One is the sacredness of a man's relationship to his mother. One of the five major automatic causes for killing someone, on a par with blood vengeance, is his calling you, "Son of the fucked one." The murder of a mother—and almost all women do become mothers—arouses deep anxieties in the community at large. The affection of men toward their sisters is similarly ramified. Therefore to kill a woman defending her son or brother would be fearsome and somehow even perverse.

Within the cultural domain of politics children and adolescents are also set off as a distinct category. Injury to either is evil. Numerous verbal injunctions and many less tangible signs indicate the strength of feeling here, especially striking because it conflicts with a potential extension of the blood vengeance that actually exists in many other cultures. The only child injured in the whole period was a three-year-old boy, seriously wounded when he and his father, a nephew of the opposition leader, were gunned down from a donkey in 1947. The act was deplored by many. People are far less upset when old men get killed; old men are regarded with a peculiar combination of affection and slight condescension. . . .

Homicide is also motivated by several rather concrete assumptions related to "social interdependency." Each person is bound and needs to be bound to approximately thirty other persons, with whom he stands in what could be called an intimate relationship. The most important of these persons are immediate family members. Homicide between parents and children or between siblings is as taboo as sex relations between them, and I do not have a single case on record; interestingly enough, the range of the incest taboo on a female relative is close to isomorphic with that of blood vengeance obligations to the corresponding male relative. Blood vengeance is obligatory within the block of father, sons, and brothers in the sense that any one of these persons feels impelled to completely avenge the other and that the community will strongly support such an act. One or more of these kinsmen will leave town or retire from active political life if the block has been pulled apart through political factionalism.

The relationship of a man to his baptismal compadre has a sacred, emotional quality that places it between that to his own brother and that to a first cousin. . . . One assumes that every man wants and needs three to eight or more compadres and that his political behavior will be partly determined by these alignments. On the other hand the choice of a compadre is itself adjusted to political arrangements. As the factional lines shift through the years compadres may be pulled apart and thrown against each other in tragic conflict. One man was even shot dead by his baptismal compadre in 1945. Informants reported the event with regret and condemnation, and the killer has never been seen in Acan since that morning. The obligation to vengeance is less binding upon compadres than upon brothers, individual factors often swaying the case; the loyalty of brothers tends to be reciprocal, whereas a man may be far more loyal to his compadre than vice versa. The compadre tie changes more through time, whereas a brother is always a brother.

An intimate friend, a friend "of confidence," resembles a sibling or a ritual coparent. Friendship is largely created during the early years and may constitute a deep, lifelong tie. But friendship does not require formalized respect, as do the other two relationships. Friends are sometimes ashamed of their mutual interests, such as political extortion, adulterous affairs, or obscene language used to each other when drunk. Some friends drift apart and may even become leaders in rival factions. And friendship vengeance is more optional than either of the other two primary relationships. However, it is clear and definite; every informant could quickly name his friends "of confidence," seldom with a second thought.

A man can normally count on being surrounded by a large network of bilateral relatives; a person planning a homicide must reckon with the potential hostility of this larger core. Thus,

the first agrarian cacique had no father, brothers, or sons active in the struggle, but he was loyally supported during the period from 1920 to 1926 by six first and second cousins and several nephews. The agrarian revolt would have failed without this solid nucleus. The political framework of the immediate family tends ideally to be supplemented in this way by secondary and tertiary relatives who are close because of economic interdependence, residential proximity, personal affinity, or shared political interests, as well as family ties. Such supplementary recruitment is intensified when the individuals involved increase their political commitments or are exposed to greater danger. Success in Mexican village politics often depends on killing or expelling the extended group that forms the nucleus of a faction. A group of leaders and fighters tends to include many such relatives and friends and—although to a far lesser extent— compadres. Paradoxically, the top two caciques are "sociometric isolates," in the sense that they have almost no close friends or compadres within the village (though each has stalwart relatives).

Tarascans assume that political action is reciprocated between groups. Therefore, one hesitates to endanger one's own group by attacking a strong leader. Much of the actual killing is carried out at the middle and lower echelons between persons with comparatively small bilateral kindreds. The more notable fighters are seldom killed, both because of their quick reflexes in rapidly developing situations and because of the potential retaliation by their intimates. Only three caciques have died violently in forty years: The first was a pro-landlord mestizo whose faction was demolished two years later; the second was an agrarian hero captured by surprise and lynched by government troops from outside the community; the third was killed by members of the large Caso faction in 1928, which was driven from Acan en masse only six years later. Both of the rival caciques today are in their sixties and the more renowned fighters are in their forties, whereas dozens of less important men have been the agents and victims of reprisal. As Otón said in a moment of candor, "It is the generals who command, and the privates who get killed."

Another social assumption is that the Tarascan community will be divided into two or more large, loose kinship groups or "political families." These are groups of persons sharing the same last name as patronymic or matronymic, or who have some common ancestors and feel that they are related, and share a tradition of political cooperation. Political families also include many persons allied by marriage; Manuel, mentioned above, had married the sister of the leader of the opposition.

The importance of familial traditions is recognized: "The Aguilars are the ones who can dominate in Acan, and who should dominate." Such family ethos does not depend largely on economic circumstances. Thus Otón and some of his kindred were once at the bottom of the subsistence ladder, whereas other politically active Aguilars have been fairly well off. The membership is "loose," since it is not determined by some one, simple principle, but "tight" in that most adults know just where they belong at any given time. Acan has usually had about five political families, although at times only two of them have been prominent in the factional contention. During periods of intensified conflict family membership largely defines the political status that channels homicide; almost any member of an enemy family can at times be used to avenge a death in one's own. Thus, no legal action was taken against a gunman who

fired almost point blank at three young men of the dominant faction on one Sunday evening in 1956; he had been trying to retaliate for the killing of Manuel. Also, the dominant cacique, who was running for state congressman, wanted to avoid the fresh stains on his character that might have resulted from a too vigorous prosecution.

A political faction is a face-to-face group controlled by mutual observation, discussion, and gossip; only two factions are generally effective, but there will always be two. Thus, attempts to form a third faction in 1945 and 1954 met with ridicule and swift absorption or repression by one of the two already in existence. On the other hand, a single, "united" faction tends to split within a year. This binary principle derives from the attitudes of the leaders: Apparently there will always be some mature leaders who cannot tolerate the single cacique, whereas two caciques with their intimates are adequate to focus the loyalty of the politically active males of the village.

The members of a faction can assume for the most part that they are safe from attack by any other member. But homicide within a faction does at times occur. In earlier years an outstanding agrarian fighter, with a reputation for magical powers, was reported to have been accidentally shot when his rifle discharged while he was riding home through the mountains with some companions. Many people now say that he was shot by Boniface, a nephew of the cacique, who was jealous of the fighter and envious of his rising popularity. Murders within a nuclear family would not and could not be avenged, perhaps one result of the concerned, effective inculcation of the values of brotherly and filial loyalty. For analogous reasons, homicides within a faction are not normally avenged, since the potential avengers are somehow related to the guilty persons they might feel compelled to kill. A man must leave his faction before he can carry out some vengeance obligations.

Strong feelings for village autonomy also pattern homicide. Over 95 percent of all homicides against Aceños have been by Aceños. Outside Indian gunmen have seldom been brought into Acan, because Acan has plenty of its own. The use of outside help would have the doubly deleterious effect of indicating the cacique's weakness within the pueblo, and of making him seem a threat to its unitedness and autonomy. Indeed, few Indians have moved into Acan during the past forty years because of "the politics."

For the same reasons, government inspectors are apt to deal superficially with local problems, and not to interfere with the prevailing balance of power. In 1937, for example, a federal inspector visited Acan as a result of eleven homicides in that year. During the stormy town meetings the dominant faction brought heavy charges against the already defeated opposition, the victims for the most part, making federal intervention virtually useless. Some government investigators were in danger during the 1930's. The several confrontations of federal investigators and local Indians which could be witnessed in the field during 1956 involved a high degree of dramatic irony because the federal inspectors were so ignorant of the factual and emotional background which was motivating the village speakers and their Indian audience.

Mestizo gunmen provoke energetic responses, especially since they are brought in for tasks that no Aceño would care to attempt, such as the assassination of a cacique. In 1945 Otón was walking home from the town hall in the twilight when a group of mestizos from a neighboring hamlet opened fire, wounding him in several places, including the indispensable right wrist. Falling to the ground, he just managed to crawl into the home of a nephew, Mauro. At the same time another nephew, José, came out of his house a bit farther down the street and fired on the assailants, who fled into the darkness. Later that evening a third nephew, in a state of rage, nearly knifed one of the leaders of the rival faction. This illustrates the local saying, "When the politics get tough, it is the nephews who stand behind Otón." Several mestizos from the hamlet were subsequently killed, their families driven away, and their miserable stone huts leveled. In 1954 José and his son tried to organize a third faction and were ambushed in turn by mestizos sent in by Otón. Thus mestizos may be used to kill a traitorous relative whom no other relative would agree to dispatch. The few mestizos who are accepted in Acan politics grew up there and have adapted to its mores.

But Acan violence in external affairs is seen by Aceños as justified in intervillage disputes, especially over land boundaries. And there are egregious cases of Aceños killing "on the outside." During the agrarian reform period (1920–26) Acan was involved in many homicides in Tarascan and mestizo villages and the pueblo acquired its reputation as a breeding ground for assassins. In 1936, 1937, and 1941, Otón's men eliminated brave and respected agrarian leaders in other Tarascan towns. All three died because they were opposing Aceños who were in the race for nomination of a candidate for state representative within the dominant national party. Such killings were widely condemned; their only justification, even in Aceño eyes, is the passion engendered by the struggle of the leaders for power at a higher level.

The Tarascans have a strong sense of ethnic identity, articulated in terms of race, language, diagnostic customs—such as certain wedding dances and the ... "Dance of the Little Old Men"—and, finally, the "indigenous" social image and self-image of individuals and villages[6]; "I am an Indian and I will never forget that," is often repeated. Even before 1920 Acan stood out within this context; the intense, ethnocentric suspicion felt toward mestizos sometimes led to killings by drunken Aceños. The earliest agrarian violence occurred in 1912 when an Acan mob attacked a party of mestizo peons, killing six with slings and bird spears. During the agrarian revolution ethnic affiliation to some extent justified homicide, since the agrarians conceived of themselves as indigenes fighting under Indian leaders against the mestizo peons, hired men, and priests, who were siding with the hated Spanish landlords—the "gachupins." After 1925 the struggle for power itself came to take precedence over considerations of ethnic homogeneity; both of the Indian factions in Acan allied themselves with mestizo factions in neighboring settlements. This was criticized by many informants, and the excessive death rate sometimes attributed to it. "Before we were one family, one race. Then came pure politics and bad times."

In nearby Tacamba ethnic assumptions justified homicides until the 1930's. The cacique's party was entirely Tarascan, monolingually so in many cases; in 1934 the Christian mestizos were suppressed because "they wanted the land although they had fought with the Spaniards." In 1928 and again in 1941, sizable factions of mestizos—forty to one hundred families—tried to obtain land in adjacent Tarejo through litigation in the state and national capitals. Both times the Indian

[6] Alfonso Caso, "Definición del indio y de lo indio," *América Indígena* [Mexico] (1948) T. 8., 4: 226–234.

agrarians "dressed themselves in the blood of man," to quote the gory phrase of their cacique, and drove out the mestizos, man, woman, and child, after smallscale battles with considerable loss of life. The physical ruins of their homes were still visible in 1956, and the mayor stressed the ethnic factor during a conversation: "They were mestizos, from the outside, who were trying to get the land and control the pueblo." The mestizos will probably remain weaker in the region because the Indians firmly control the best land and their leaders are the products of local and familial traditions of Machiavellian violence and astuteness that enable them to outplay their vastly more numerous rivals in the many mestizo communities of the Zacapu valley.[7]

.   .   .

Political Ideology

The foregoing discussion may have conveyed a false impression because of the small role assigned "higher" ideals. But all Aceños cite these ideals at some point, demonstrating their subscription to the same system—although adherence to political ideals is modified according to the other interests of the speaker.

One of the loftiest ideals of Acan and many Mexican pueblos is "community solidarity"[8]; The villagers should live together in peace, guided by a unified, informal government. This actually occurs under the gerontocratic, representative political framework in some of the conservative villages. But once initiated, a cacical system undermines solidarity because

[7] Mestizo money lenders and mestizo roles in other purely economic situations will be treated in a separate paper.
[8] Ralph Beals, *Cherán: A Sierra Tarascan Village;* Washington, Smithsonian Institution, 1946.

the hunger for land and the envy bred of egoism lead to the rise of a rival party with its leaders and fighters.

Thus the pueblo was "united" from 1924 to 1926 only because of the brilliant leadership of its cacique, the persuasive power of the agrarian creed and the expulsion of over one-third of the population "for not supporting the agrarian cause." The remaining Aceños had just wrested the land from the Spaniards and felt like the "newly arrived." But within a few days after the assassination of the cacique the town started to split between two of the "political families," the Aguilars and the Casos.[9] During the last forty years both factions have justified homicide in the interest of reuniting the pueblo. Similarly, one of the most bitter accusations is that someone "is trying to divide the pueblo," as in the case of the peasant Manuel.

A second political ideal includes the assumption that it is justifiable to kill a tyrant. The opposition and many of the apolitical villagers frequently accuse the ruling cacique of authoritarian habits: "For thirty years he has dictated to the pueblo at his will" (albedrío, or wilfullness); "Why do we have to suffer such an interminable cacique?" Such speakers never admit that their own chief might try to domineer in his turn. Often the Acan masses are depicted as "poor, timid, and humble"; the opposition leaders conceive of themselves as principled liberators just as the dominant rulers conceive of themselves as the maintainers of peace and unity. In either case the feeling of moral justification is high. Actually, neither cacique is a tyrant in anything approximating the classical sense; the power has been divided between two or more factions, each using persuasion, public works, and ideology, as well as violence, to win support. If one regards competition between interest groups in accordance with certain ground rules as a kind of freedom, then Acan is fairly free. The explicit resentment at "intolerable caciques" thus acquires special significance, leading one to believe that the idealistic expression has other roots.

In the Acan region the dominant ideology has long been radically agrarian. I shall outline its four salient aspects, because they often function as ultimate assumptions.

First, the land should be worked by those who need its fruits and with whom it is traditionally associated. Land should be considered in terms of its social function and as part of the Indian heritage, rather than in terms of absolute property rights.[10] All Aceños live or have lived in a subsistence economy where a minimum of corn and beans means survival, and where it is difficult to earn much more. In this context land becomes the most meaningful symbol of life and control over land the most convincing symbol of power.[11] . . .

·   ·   ·

A curious sidelight on the sanctity of land is the strong feeling against shooting a man while at work, or on his way to or from the fields. And the agrarian struggle of the 1920's is now regarded as a sort of holy war where the means justified the ends; the "original fighters" enjoy a priority to land, and resentment or reprisals may be touched off by allocations of land to persons not somehow connected with these founding fathers. Manuel had belonged to this prestigious group.

[9] Through most of its past Acan may have been divided into two factions; one third of the community is known to have split off in the 1860's and migrated to a distant mountain town where the descendants live today in a special barrio.

[10] Lucio Mendieta y Nuñez, *El Problema Agrario de México;* Mexico, Editorial Porrúa, 1946.

[11] Susanne Langer, *Philosophy in a New Key;* New York, Penguin, 1942; pp. 117–138.

The second agrarian plank is that village and regional politics should be largely controlled by local peasants of agrarian persuasion. A climactic point in the long and determined regional struggle between the Indian agrarians, mainly centered in Acan, and the mestizo conservatives, concentrated in the county seat, occurred in the later 1920's when about twenty of the latter lost their lives during a gun battle. In 1952, assassins hired by the county merchants stopped a bus in which an agrarian leader was riding to the state capital, shot the leader, and sped away in a waiting car. This gangster-like murder differed in character from the intravillage killings and illustrates the influence of urban patterns.

Third, it is assumed that the taxes from the land should be used for public works within the community. Most improvements since 1925 have actually been carried out by the state government in return for the community's political services, while the bulk of the pueblo funds were pocketed by the leaders. But at no time has the civic claim been dropped. From 1935 to 1939, for example, the village looked with pride on its extraordinarily large staff of eight primary school teachers. The roads, maize storehouse, water system, electrification, and, above all, the winning of the ejido lands, are frequently cited, defensively. . . .

According to the fourth agrarian plank, the Catholic clergy is seen as an exploiting force that must be kept out of the village. Village priests have narrowly escaped death in the region. The so-called "Christian" party has been quiescent since 1924, when a large contingent of agrarians entered and captured a neighboring town, and after a full morning of street fighting, forced the "Christians" to surrender their position in the tower of the church. Eight of them were shot down in cold blood, leaving a legacy of hostility between the two communities. Yet all but one of the Acan caciques have permitted some church services and the numerous dances and festivities of the "folk religion."[12] . . .

In addition to the political assumptions involved in adherence to community solidarity, tyrannicide, and the four agrarian planks, a fourth such higher principle is loyalty to certain outside organizations, included here rather than under social organization because the social relationship of local factions to levels above that of the region is often inconsistent or contradictory. The ongoing, blood-and-soil issues of the village factions will at any given time be linked upwards somehow, in partial independence of the ideology of either level. Thus, before the agrarian reform one Acan faction sincerely espoused conservative values and killed in defense of the landlords and "Catholic principles." But the same factional alignments continued to generate homicides long after the upper-level conservatives had been driven from the region and all hope was lost for the "Christian" cause. Later, when Acan was torn apart by the feud between two cousins, the moral justification on both sides was that they wanted to carry on the agrarian struggle in the true spirit of Lázaro Cárdenas, the ex-president of Mexico. But Cárdenas knows and likes both Otón and his rival, Antonio, and made them confer in 1947 and promise to stop the killings. Two Cárdenas factions fighting each other in the name of the same principles is a case of *reductio ad absurdum*, demonstrating both the deep grain of factional dynamics, and the importance to the politically active of justifying their activities in terms of an allegiance to higher units. The near identity of ideology in the factions for over thirty

[12] Pedro Carrasco, *Tarascan Folk Religion;* New Orleans, Middle American Research Institute, Tulane Univ., 1955.

years partially accounts for the unusual explicitness with which it is conceived.

A fifth end toward which homicide is directed is a peaceful pueblo, an ultimate desideratum that is constantly prevented by "politics, egoism, envy," and the like. "Peace," when conceived of as a vague ideal, or the result of total victory by one faction, is partly a rationalization in the cynical sense. But the passionate way in which many Aceños speak of the subject can leave little doubt as to their sincerity. Widows and orphans, partly provided for through the kinship and compadre systems, still suffer most from the homicides; making tortillas for others can be a desperate way to eke out a living. Most women hate the homicide patterns and yearn for peace because the struggle threatens the stability of their homes. Neverthless, they are bound by loyalty, and when interrogated more deeply reveal that they too harbor animosities and desire peace under the faction to which their men belong.

Libido Dominandi

Finally, as a result of Acan's history, the struggle to dominate others—the *libido dominandi*—that characterizes some individuals, has evolved as a community-wide pattern. "Some make music, some make mats. Acan makes politics."

Articulate political individualism was stimulated by the personal example of the first agrarian cacique and the success of his ideological activities. Since then leaders have emerged who depend heavily upon violence and outside connections. The struggle for power has become a hallmark of village life, constantly gossiped about by both sexes and heard about by children from their earliest years. The choice of compadre, spouse, and friend by the growing individual is seriously influenced by political alignments. And the day-to-day political activities are more intense in Acan than in most other Tarascan pueblos. Elsewhere the town hall may be quiet for days. In Acan it is almost always open and ten to thirty men may drop by during the evening; those who never do are regarded with suspicion. Both civil and ejidal governments meet more often than is required by the usual Mexican standards. Acan leaders and fighters frequently visit the country seat, or even the state and national capitals. The exigencies of the agrarian struggle have led the pueblo sharply away from the "folk culture" of the 1880's to a comparatively discrete and articulated political system.[13] From one point of view, politics has become the dominant orientation in the same way that diet, kinship relation, religious ritual, or exploitative economics may emerge as the areas of greatest concern in other cultures. Perhaps Acan could be said to have a Machiavellian orientation.[14]

Some ideals certainly condemn homicide springing from the *libido dominandi*. As one notorious fighter said of the period after 1926, "That was no longer the struggle for the soil. That was pure politics. We entered a time that was bad,

[13] Robert Redfield, *The Folk Culture of Yucatan;* Chicago, Univ. of Chicago Press, 1951.

[14] Ralph Linton, *The Study of Man;* New York, Appleton-Century, 1936; pp. 422–463. Nicolo Machiavelli, *The Prince and Discourses,* translated by Luigi Ricci and revised by E. R. P. Vincent; New York, Modern Library, 1940. The psychological dimensions of such a thesis surely merit investigation; the present study, of course, deals almost entirely with the "cultural level." See also Paul Friedrich, "Cacique. The Recent History and Present Structure of Politics in a Tarascan Village," unpublished Ph.D. thesis, Yale, 1957; and "A Tarascan Cacicazgo: Structure and Function," pp. 23–29, in *Systems of Political Control and Bureaucracy,* American Ethnological Society, edited by Verne F. Ray; Seattle, Univ. of Washington Press, 1958.

bad!" But as part of the hypertrophy of politics in Acan, an acceptance of the inevitability of struggle and homicide has developed to a degree unusual even for Mexican villages. As another leader put it, "So we enter politics, we kill, and so forth. What else can you do?" Or, "They want to command in everything around here, but, if we lose, three or four of them will go to the graveyard, so what's the difference?" Or, finally, "They divided the pueblo and in this my compadre lost his life. . . . But that is politics." This last phrase is frequent. The struggle for power over land and men may itself justify the killing of a dangerous opponent.

.   .   .

A . . . simple . . . conclusion is perhaps the main contribution of this study to a cross-cultural understanding of the political aspect of human nature: It is widely taken for granted in Acan that individuals and groups will succumb to the homicidal impulse once tensions have passed a certain threshold. Homicide figures similarly in other cultures, such as Renaissance Rome, rural Albania, and parts of contemporary Negro Africa. The same assumptions are foreign to and indeed fundamentally at variance with those held by other cultural groups, such as many Indian castes, and, tragically, the middle- and upper-class liberals of Weimar Germany.

On the other hand, homicide in Acan, while accepted as a means, is never accepted as an end (as has happened elsewhere). Any death in the political competition results from the interaction of a complex set of motivations deriving from Aceño beliefs about human nature, social organization, and political ideology. Thus, the superficially unintelligible political homicide record of two men per year per thousand of population does become intelligible when considered in the context of the system of assumptions shared and transmitted by the members of this particular society.[15]

[15] The word "homicide" has been used throughout this paper to avoid both the technical legal meaning and the pejorative connotations of the term "murder." The theory of culture and values used throughout is largely drawn from E. Adamson Hoebel, *The Law of Primitive Man;* Cambridge, Harvard Univ. Press, 1954; and the writings of Clyde Kluckhohn, as in "The Philosophy of the Navaho Indians," pp. 356–383, in *Ideological Differences and the World Order*, edited by F. S. C. Northrop; New Haven, Yale Univ. Press, 1949.

14

... Four general factors ... may be said to have molded the character, and thus have a bearing on the ultimate success, of National Socialism:

1. The prevalence of discontent with the existing social order.
2. The particular ideology and program for social transformation adopted by the Nazis.
3. The National Socialist organizational and promotional technique.
4. The presence of charismatic leadership.

The adequacy and relative importance of these explanations will be examined in this chapter.

THE WHY OF THE HITLER MOVEMENT

Theodore Abel

1. The Function of Discontent

The social unrest which was prevalent in post-war Germany had its source in many and divergent events. The outcome of the war deeply affected two groups of the population: first, those who were in power before and during the war—the military, the conservatives, the big land owners and industrialists, and all those who indirectly drew sustenance from the exalted position which these groups occupied in the social structure of Germany; and second, nationalists. The revolution following the armistice brought about far-reaching changes in the alignment of power. Even so it had its source in despair and confusion rather than in a genuine desire for a radical transformation of the social order. The adherents of the old regime were suddenly and precipitously thrown down from their seats of power, while the socialists, the workers' and soldiers' councils, and the trade unions dominated the stage.

Reprinted from *Why Hitler Came into Power: An Answer Based on the Original Life Stories of Six Hundred of His Followers* (New York: Prentice-Hall, Inc., 1938), pp. 166–86, by permission of Prentice-Hall, Inc., Englewood Cliffs, New Jersey. Copyright 1938, © renewed 1966.

The deposed groups went into hiding but did not resign themselves to their fate. Their vital interests were affected and they were determined to stage a comeback, by force if necessary. Thus they were actively opposed to the republic not only because they harbored a grievance against the perpetrators of the revolution, but also because they realized that the continuation of the regime was an obstacle to return to power.

The second group included those whose national pride was deeply affected by the peace conditions imposed upon Germany by the Allies. The republican regime committed the grievous mistake of deluding itself and the German people with the hope that the establishment of a democratic government would enable them to obtain a "just peace." The patriots blamed the government for failure to negotiate a better peace and for putting its signature upon the Versailles Treaty. A strong social motive for opposition to the republican order was thus added to the private motives of the dispossessed. Discontent ceased to be an issue merely of the formerly privileged class and became an attitude shared by members of all classes of the German population.

The passage of time, the return to the routine of daily living after the hectic post-war days, failed to develop a conciliatory attitude and a resignation to the inevitable. On the contrary, the number of people who opposed the government was constantly increasing as post-war developments in the political and economic life of Germany were experienced by many, as threats to their personal and social values, and brought forth new grounds for discontent. Among the added reasons for opposition was ineptitude in the handling of affairs of government by a parliamentary system that lacked democratic traditions. There was a hopeless deadlock owing to the multiplicity of parties which alternately warred with each other and engaged in horse-trading, apparently more interested in self-maintenance than in the nation's welfare. Furthermore, the inability of the government to maintain the order and discipline which Germans have learned to regard as the *sine qua non* of government, and its ineptitude in the handling of foreign affairs, which kept the issue of German humiliation constantly in the foreground, were noted and resented. Finally, the government was held responsible for economic chaos—first, the disastrous inflation, later, from 1929 on, the stagnation of business enterprise, the mounting rate of unemployment, and the hopelessness of the outlook for improvement under existing conditions. The businessman who suffered deficits, the worker who lacked security of employment, the youth who saw little to encourage his hope for a career in the future, all augmented the army of the discontented.

The social unrest that was prevalent in Germany had two important features which made it a potential basis of a social movement. First, it was persistent and continuous. The passage of time did not assuage it but intensified it. While the causes of the discontent varied in the course of time, they followed each other in close succession and prevented a relaxation of the persistent tension. Secondly, discontent was focused upon a single object: the post-war political and social system. Despite the fact that the reasons for dissatisfaction varied for different individuals and different groups, almost all blamed the government for their troubles and turned their attacks against it. The existence of a common focus for many oppositions was a potential rallying point which made concerted action on a large scale possible.

Attempts to organize the discontented for collective action against the government began shortly after the end of the World War. Mainly through the initiative of disgruntled officers, small groups were formed all over Germany which were animated by a desire for a speedy counter-revolution that would restore the old regime. Political developments gave these groups a chance for action sooner than they expected. The government was hard pressed by Communist uprisings in the cities and had to appeal to the military for help. The makeshift alliance ended with the defeat of the common foe. The adherents of the old regime had regained a foothold in Germany and felt sufficiently encouraged to go ahead with their plans. They soon launched a concerted campaign against the government by instigating *Putsch*es, assassinating republican leaders and organizing subversive and secret military units. They drew their supporters mainly from the former military caste, the upper class, and those members of the middle class who, motivated by patriotic feelings, were willing to compromise with their opposition to a restoration of the old order, hoping that a defeat of the republican government might start a campaign for regaining the losses which the nation suffered as a result of the Versailles Treaty.

But the counter-revolutionary efforts were unsuccessful. They lacked the support of the masses, which the counterrevolutionists, counting upon a *coup d'état* as a short cut to success, did not endeavor to win. In the course of time the hot-heads pressing for immediate military action were replaced by the politicians, who decided to pursue different tactics. They instituted a long-range plan of propaganda and agitation aiming to defeat the government by a majority vote of the German population. Furthermore, they turned their backs on the unpopular issue of the restoration of the old regime and in its stead advocated a new social order, anti-republican as well as anti-monarchical in character. A number of political parties were formed on that basis. Among them was the National Socialist German Workers' party, which became the promotion group of the Hitler movement.

At first the party represented the counter-revolutionary sentiment, inasmuch as it drew its main support from the groups that were interested in the restoration of the old regime. It even went as far as to instigate a *coup d'état* of its own, the socalled Hitler *Putsch* of 1923, which failed. But from the very beginning the National Socialist party pursued a definite plan of winning the support of the masses by developing an ideology of its own that was broad enough to appeal to all classes, and in particular to the German workers. It was ultimately the advocacy of a new social order which saved the Hitler movement from the fate that befell other counter-revolutionary groups. A defeat like that of 1923 would have been a death blow to any other group. Such a blow was averted, however, because counter-revolution was not the only aim of the Hitler movement and because its other aims had the support of the discontented among *all* classes of the population. It was able to perpetuate itself by breaking counter-revolutionary ties after the *Putsch* and by shifting its emphasis to the single-minded advocacy of a new social order. It not only retained most of its following, but gained new adherents in ever-increasing numbers by proclaiming solutions for all the issues that had become a source of widespread discontent throughout the post-war history of Germany.[1]

The evidence points to the fact that discontent was of fundamental impor-

[1] The life histories show that dissatisfaction with the regime was a constant factor in relation to the year of joining the movement. Thus we find that for every year between 1920 and 1933 the percentage of those who gave dissatisfaction with the regime as the main reason for joining is practically the same (40 to 42 per cent of the total number of cases for each year).

tance in the development of the Hitler movement. The main items of this evidence are, first, the fact of a prevailing dissatisfaction with existing conditions and the consequent opposition to the government, which led people to seek an outlet in concerted action, [and] secondly, the fact shown by the life-history data that discontent on the part of individuals had a direct effect upon their subsequent joining of the Hitler movement. General considera-tion, furthermore, supports the con-tention as to the vital importance of discontent in accounting for the move-ment. All observations of human behavior point to the significance of problem experiences as a source of action. We also know that when indi-viduals realize that they are unable to solve a problem through their own effort, they seek the help and support of others in order to accomplish a solution through concerted action. Insofar, then, as the basic conditions for the kind of concerted action repre-sented by the Hitler movement were like problem experiences of many in-dividuals caused by factors which no individual alone could control, dis-content must be regarded as a necessary factor in the origin as well as the growth of the movement. Without it the move-ment would not have been possible. In fact, it is difficult to see how any movement can arise without a basis of widespread discontent. We should add, however, that in order to become an effective source of a movement, dis-content must be persistent and con-tinuous and capable of being focused upon a common object of opposition.

Although the evidence leads us to the recognition of discontent as a necessary factor in the Hitler movement, it would be fallacious to regard it as a sufficient explanation of what happened in Ger-many. Discontent accounts for the origin and the growth of a movement insofar as it explains why people were impelled to join groups and support collective efforts directed toward a change of the existing order. It does not, however, account for the reasons why a movement of a particular kind devel-oped and why it, rather than another, based upon the same discontent, suc-ceeded in realizing its aim. The function of discontent in regard to a social move-ment is, therefore, limited. It sets the conditions which make a movement possible, but it does not at the same time determine its special features, nor does it by itself determine its success.

2. The Functions of Ideology

The special features which distinguish the Hitler movement from other move-ments are expressed in its ideology. We have seen that the ideology of the Hitler movement comprised, in the main, three ideas: first, the idea of National Socialism with its implications of national unity and the abolition of classes, and the reintegration of national life into a *Gemeinschaft*; second, the principle of leadership, the idea of an hierarchical organization of society according to accomplishment which was to be the means for the realization of the *Gemeinschaft*; third, the racial doctrine, the idea that common blood binds individuals into a *Gemeinschaft* and that racial intermixture is the cause of disunity as well as the deterioration of the native stock. Other aspects of the ideology are merely corollaries of these three basic ideas. The anti-liberal-ism of the Hitler movement, for ex-ample, derives from the National Socialist idea that common interest comes before self-interest, which is dominant in a parliamentary system where many parties compete for ascend-ancy. The anti-intellectual attitude of the Hitler movement is conditioned by its romantic conception of the mysti-cal qualities of "Blood and Soil." The idea of the totalitarian state is derived from the principle of leadership, and so forth.

Trends that were current in German history as well as the creative imagination of its founders wrought the pattern of the ideology of the Hitler movement. But in the last analysis the acid test of public approval determined its special features, since those doctrines which appealed most were selected for emphasis. We have seen that the ideology of the movement attracted people because it was in accord with prevalent sentiments. It appealed to a strong national feeling and reinforced this appeal by linking it with another powerful sentiment directed against class and caste privilege. The synthesis of what were in Germany opposites— nationalism, on the one hand, regarded as the monopoly of the conservative-aristocratic party, and socialism, on the other, as the doctrine of the internationally minded Marxist—was a stroke of genius. It gave to the Hitler movement the broadest possible basis of appeal to the German public, which was composed, for the most part, of nationalists who for social reasons refused to identify themselves with the privilege-seeking conservative party, and of socialists who for national reasons were opposed to the international doctrine of the Marxists.

In turn, the principle of leadership appealed to a strong sentiment for the disciplinarian Prussian state ideal which most Germans considered the epitome of law and order. The mores of the majority of the German people favored submission to a supreme commander in charge of the affairs of the nation as against a parliamentary form of government.

The racial doctrine appealed to a prevalent feeling of anti-Semitism which . . . was a common popular reaction in Germany in times of crises since the period of the Crusades.

The force of the combined appeal to different sentiments that were shared by many enabled the National Socialist party to far outdistance the other promotion groups which were competing with it for public support. The support that it gained was ultimately due to the fact that, among the many programs of change advocated in Germany at the time, the Nazi program promised the realization of the sentiments that were most vital and, at the same time, threatened the least number of personal and social values held by the German people. It was in accord with traditions, although radical in nature. Near the end of the struggle for power, only the Communist party was left as a serious challenger. The Communists also appealed strongly to the idealism of youth and found many adherents to their cause. But they were handicapped by their subservience to Moscow and by their emphasis upon internationalism and the curtailment of private property. These aspects of Communism run counter to deeply rooted traditions and, in consequence, failed to attract the masses of the German people. The National Socialists were quick to turn the handicaps of the Communists to their advantage. They made the challenge of Communism to their own aspirations a challenge to the nation as a whole by presenting it as a threat to national integrity. The civil war which dominated the German scene in the years 1930 to 1933 helped materially to sustain this claim.

Our analysis of the role played by the ideology of the Hitler movement points to the fact that its importance as a determinant is at least equal to that of the general discontent which existed at the time. The National Socialist party voiced in a determined fashion the prevailing dissatisfaction with the existing order and thus appealed for the support of the discontented. It was not this appeal by itself, but the ideology which induced the decision on the part of the discontented to throw in their lot with the Hitler movement. The function of the ideology, therefore, was to provide an incentive to join the movement. To fulfill this function adequately, it had to appeal to prevalent sentiments and be sufficiently diversified to encompass divergent interests and individual predilections without involving itself in contradictions. As we have seen, the ideology of the Hitler movement met these conditions. It appealed to nationalists and socialists, to workers and employers, to the idealizers of the Prussian state and to the youths who were in favor of radical changes. In consequence, it found supporters among all classes and all age groups of the population. Those who were repelled by this or that feature of the ideology found sufficient compensation in other features to induce them to join the movement. At the same time, all the elements of the Nazi ideology were in some fashion or other related to the idea of *Gemeinschaft*. Thus, built around a central concept, the features of the ideology, in spite of their diversity, were sufficiently integrated to give the appearance of logical consistency to the ideology as a whole.

In spite of the great importance which, in view of the evidence we must assign to the ideology as a factor in determining the success of the National Socialist movement, it cannot be regarded as the sole cause. While it served many as the *justification* for joining the movement, there were others who joined although they were indifferent to the ideology, or even objected to it on intellectual grounds.

But the main reason why the ideology has only a limited causal significance is the fact that it represents only a declaration of faith and intention. A declaration of that sort by itself is ineffective unless it is backed up by adequate

promotion activities and by a belief in the possibility of victory. It is for this reason that tactics and strategy were important factors in determining the growth of the Hitler movement.

3. The Function of Tactics and Strategy

Given favorable external conditions and receptivity on the part of the masses to the proposals advocated by its leaders, the spread of the Nazi movement depended largely upon adequate promotion. The task confronting the promotion group of a movement is twofold: it must win adherents and supporters, and it must hold the allegiance of those who have been won over.

The winning of adherents is largely a matter of propaganda. We had occasion, in the historical section of this study, to describe the kind of propaganda that was carried on by the local groups of the Party. The Nazi propaganda machine was notable for its shrewd and daring use of modern advertising psychology and for its mass effect. Even more remarkable, however, was the sheer bulk of its effort. Proselytizing went on unceasingly, regardless of physical or man-made obstacles. Moreover, the Party "covered" Germany with a thoroughness that made its doctrines known in almost every home, in city and countryside alike.[2]

In the propaganda of all other German parties, these features were either totally lacking or insufficiently developed. For this reason, the National Socialist party had a decided advantage over the other parties in reaching the attention of the German public.

Adherents, however, cannot be won for a promotion scheme by effective propaganda methods alone. Many people might succumb temporarily to al-

[2] *Cf.* R. B. Nelson, "Hitler's Propaganda Machine," *Current History*, June 1933, Vol. XXXIII, pp. 287–300.

luring promises or to a persuasive sales talk for a cause. But in the long run even the best-directed verbal barrage cannot have a lasting effect unless backed up by more substantial assurances. The individual who joins a movement must first be convinced of its probable success as well as of the desirability of its objectives. Expectation of success is predicated upon *confidence* in the ability of the leaders of the movement to get what they want eventually. The people who supported Hitler, although animated by sentiment, were primarily influenced by the belief that they were backing a winning contender. The life histories show that this confidence was engendered by several tangible factors, chief of which was the superiority of the National Socialist organization over that of other parties. Its ramifications were more detailed and its sphere of influence more extensive than that of any other party. It also was better coordinated and disciplined and showed greater vitality and driving power. Its military, aggressive nature appealed to many.

[4.5.4.] I attended the meetings, and I always felt happy to see the little groups of brown-clad soldiers march through the city with rhythmic strides and straightforward mien, unlike the Communists, who shambled through the city streets like so many robbers. As an old soldier, I was pleased to see Hitler's fighters march in this disciplined fashion.[3]

[4.6.4.] The more I saw of these strong battle-hardened men, the more I came to believe that some day Hitler would take over the power of government for the good of our nation.

[3.7.3.] The Communists were the only ones who had the energy and the strength

[3] [*Editor's note:* This and following quotations are from autobiographical essays of Nazi Party members collected by the author. The numbers in brackets before each quotation are a code indicating the age, status, and date of Party membership of the respondent quoted.]

to back up their demands with the proper show of power, in that they got out on the streets and asserted themselves through brute force whenever necessary. On the other side was no one but the National Socialist party, ready to fight the Marxists with their own weapons.

[3.0.3.] Throughout 1928 I followed the work of the Nazis through the press, and it became evident to me that even the sympathizers with the movement were ready to die for Hitler's ideas. Consequently it wasn't difficult for me to make up my mind.

Many others were impressed by the aggressive character of the National Socialist organization in the pursuit of its goal, the fearless way it handled its opponents, its policy of no compromise with other parties. All these factors impressed the follower of the movement as indicating the kind of strength and endurance which carries with it the promise of success.

The dynamic nature of the movement also inspired confidence. Its very growth helped the Party to gather greater momentum by attracting people to whom evidence of growth was a prognosis of ultimate success. This was true particularly in the period after the election of 1930. Once the Party had shown its ability to get votes, its spectacular gain in voting strength became an incentive for many to throw in their lot with the movement.

In consequence of this fact, a certain portion of the support that was given to the movement came from people who were acting from the familiar motive of "getting on the band wagon." They wanted a change and even favored the social order which the National Socialists advocated. But they were motivated by expediency rather than by fanatical belief in and devotion to the cause and willingness for sacrifice which animated many adherents of the movement who joined before the 1930 election. The existence of these two kinds of membership is stated clearly in some life histories. The following two quotations illustrate the point.

[3.8.2.] At the beginning of November 1930 I became the leader of my cell. I still like to think of the party comrades who paid their dues promptly and were ready for any service on behalf of the leader. The lukewarm ones who looked on without doing a thing and only paid their dues after repeated reminders considerably added to the difficulties of my work. The curious thing is that these party members are the very ones who now act as if *they* and no others had borne the Fuehrer's colors to victory, and seem greatly offended whenever their "services" are not sufficiently honored. On the other hand, I have discovered that the most loyal fighters who made the greatest sacrifices in those days are modestly withdrawing at this time, at a loss to understand the others' mad hunt for advancement. They were and are idealists, while the others have looked upon National Socialism merely as a stepping stone. These people are a standing threat to the movement and our people. If they succeed in satisfying their materialism and thirst for power, they'll never distinguish between the cause and their own benefit, and so continue to injure the cause of our Leader.

[5.0.3.] Great rejoicing and a deluge of new members followed the election of 1930. Our own "Mommsen" local also received a number of new recruits. On the whole these new members were very decent comrades of all walks of life who promptly became valued collaborators; there were, however, those whom district leader Dr. Goebbels aptly dubbed "Septemberlings." It soon became evident that the latter had joined only to secure a certain amount of attention for their sacred egos. They made it appear as though the National Socialist movement had only achieved standing through their delayed support, and held lengthy and decidedly inferior discourses at the meetings of local groups. These giddy comrades, however, soon became less noisy at the prospect of jobs on behalf of the Party, offered them by their local group leaders, which demanded self-sacrifice.

The party congress was the foremost device by which the interest and loyalty of the members was maintained. These congresses were large annual assemblies attended since 1927 by many thousands of party members. Every local group of the Party either attended in full or sent its representatives, so that, in the course of time, the bulk of the membership attended at least one of these annual rallies. Designed to impress the members with the strength and unity of the Party and to show the confidence and determination of the leaders, the party congresses were an important agency in maintaining the evangelistic fervor of the movement and in enhancing the morale of the members. This point is frequently emphasized in the life histories.

[2.1.2.] We returned from the party meeting in Nürnberg strengthened in our belief in the Leader and his mission and determined to redouble our efforts for the movement. Position, family, every other consideration must be forgotten for the sake of our cause.

A strong feeling of comradeship was induced by the "frontline" character of the National Socialist party, especially in the storm troop units.

[2.7.2] In those days the *S.A.* represented a unity of purpose such as has never been achieved, nor shall be hereafter. We were united by the terrorism raging around us every hour of the day. It was natural for everyone to take the part of his comrade, and the fellowship thus cultivated was in itself a great experience. Yet the ideal we defended rose above our fellowship. Day by day we covered the environs and each of us became a bearer of its tidings.

[1.0.5.] We had to be careful at that, as the police were hard on us if we did anything forbidden. Nevertheless we managed to put a thing or two over on them. We had to pay for all the expenses thus incurred out of our own pockets, as the movement had no money. My apprenticeship, over the economic crisis precipitated me into the ranks of the unemployed. From that time on I lived solely for the movement. Day after day, night after night, we were on the go, enlightening the people about the corruption of the red-black governments since 1918. At the same time, we steeled our bodies through exercise and cultivated comradely relations. We were reared in a spirit of constructive social thought: our last piece of bread, our sole remaining cigarette were always shared with our fellows. This comradeship was indeed a condition of survival in the face of Red mobs that ruled the streets, as well as other opponents. Unlike other factions, however, we did not look upon our opponents as scoundrels, but rather as misled fellow Germans.

[2.3.1] During my training for *S.A.* service in 1929, I was shot in the abdomen by a Communist. As a result, I was laid up for six months. During my illness many of my comrades came to see me, and brought me all manner of little presents. One day I received something like forty bouquets of roses which were distributed throughout the hospital. In the same ward with me were some Communists who marveled at our cordial comraderie. Indeed it was this very comraderie that attracted many members, particularly among young men. I was particularly pleased when the erstwhile Berlin district leader (at this time Propaganda Minister) Dr. Goebbels came to see me and stayed about an hour at my bedside.

[4.2.5.] In the Nazi party I recovered the exhilarating sense of comraderie I had known in the army. There were fine, battle-hardened human beings here, united in their love for race and Fatherland, stubbornly holding out for an overwhelming ideal, unswerving in their faith in the future of Germany.

[2.0.2.] During my *S.A.* service I was in Storm Troop Thirty-three. Our storm leaders, Fritz Hahn, Maiko, and Appelt, were the right men to usher us into the new age. Our storm headquarters in the Hebbelstrasse near Reisig *became our second home.* The hours I passed there were too beautiful, and perhaps too difficult, to be described here.

4. The Function of Charismatic Leadership

The knowledge which we gained from our study of National Socialism gives convincing evidence of the influence which Hitler has had on the movement. His function was a twofold one. On the one hand, he was the chief executive, the planner and organizer. On the other hand, he played the role of the prophet of the movement. Recognized as such by most of the members and supporters, he commanded their unquestioned allegiance to his person and through this personal allegiance inspired them with loyalty and devotion to the movement itself. The combination of these two functions of chief executive and prophet is found among all the leaders of the past who have captained the actions of the masses. They are interdependent to a high degree, for the position of chief executive depends largely upon the ability to command personal allegiance. And in turn, the recognition of leadership depends upon superior executive ability and extraordinary accomplishments of planning and organization.

Hitler was a strong-willed, dauntless executive. LeBon has found that an indomitable will "to which everything succumbs and which nothing can resist, which asserts itself in spite of insurmountable obstacles" characterized the founders of religious and political movements and pioneers like Columbus and DeLesseps, the builder of the Suez Canal. Such rare determination is usually associated with an unshakable belief in oneself or one's mission, a quality which Hilter showed to a marked degree. Like other leaders of the masses, Hitler had the qualifications which make a good executive: organizing ability, a realistic sense for the implications of the conditions with which he was confronted, and authority in dealing with his associates. Hitler himself was the driving power and the directing genius of the movement.

The second function which Hitler fulfilled is revealed in the attitudes of our contributors toward him. Many of them were followers in the true sense of the word, submitting themselves to him willingly and unquestionably. To them he was a prophet whose pronouncements were taken as oracles. In their eyes he was a hero whom they naïvely trusted to perform the impossible if it were necessary. He was endowed by them with that highest degree of prestige which emanates not merely from the recognition of one's own inability to imitate or compete with such a person, but from the belief that he possesses an out-of-the-ordinary, superhuman power, that a special star is guiding his destiny. In all cases of mass leadership, this belief has been present to a greater or lesser degree. It is the basis of what Max Weber has called charismatic leadership.

What induces this worship of a person as a prophet and a hero? A satisfactory answer to this question would have to account for the peculiar influence which Peter of Amiens, Luther, Napoleon, Lenin, and scores of others have exercised upon masses of people. No scientific explanation of the phenomenon of charismatic leadership has been given so far. A discussion which could do justice to this problem is beyond the scope of this book. I will answer the question merely by restating the clues, with regard to Hitler's charismatic leadership, which we obtained from the life histories, without entertaining any claims that the example of Hitler is commensurate with that of other charismatic leaders.

These clues are: (1) A widespread, abject desire on the part of the people of Germany for a leader—an attitude often observed in a period of crisis when people who are seeking a way out realize that only collective action can solve their individual problems. (2) The impression which Hitler's performance and personality produced upon the people—the spell which he cast as an orator, the contagion of the faith which he had in himself, the "fascination" which he was able to evoke in many people who came into face-to-face contact with him, the success of his undertakings. (3) The legend which was built around him, often deliberately fostered by his associates, which perpetuated and rekindled a feeling of the unusual and made Hitler a man of mystery by emphasizing his "prophetic insight," "asceticism," "prodigious power of endurance," and so forth.

From the role which Hitler played in National Socialism, we can infer the function which charismatic leadership fulfills in a movement. Personal allegiance to Hitler was the common bond which united the supporters of National Socialism and counteracted the disruptive effect of divergent opinions and aims. Charismatic leadership may be said, therefore, to be an integrating factor of great importance. Furthermore, Hitler was to his followers the symbol of the movement.

[4.6.3.] Hitler alone is the true nationalist. The rest of us must try to emulate him as far as possible. Our young men and women will one day be the better for it! The first step toward becoming a National Socialist is to cease believing that one already is one.

[3.0.4.] I felt that Hitler personified all my desires for a new Germany.

[4.6.4.] A high political leader of the Nazi party once said of the oath of allegiance: "Anyone who takes the oath to Adolf Hitler can call nothing his own."

Because of his Messiah-like role, Hitler was sedulously imitated. His fanaticism and his belief in ultimate victory were incorporated into the personality patterns of many of his followers. Charismatic leadership may thus act to stabilize a social movement.

In view of the evident importance of

charismatic leadership as a determining factor in the Hitler movement, the conclusion can be drawn that it represents probably an indispensable factor in the success of any movement. A movement which possesses charismatic leadership has a decided advantage over a collective effort under diffused leadership or one that is run in the main by a bureaucratic organization. It would follow, therefore, that between two movements operating upon the same basis of discontent, whose ideologies have mass appeal, and who employ similar tactics, the one which, in addition, has a charismatic leader will win out against the other. In the period between 1930 and 1933 in Germany there was no other political leader who in any way approximated the exalted position which Hitler occupied in the eyes of his followers. If there had been no other reason, this fact alone would account for the inability of Communism to compete with National Socialism.

5. Conclusion

In short, the Nazi movement may be explained as follows. Various events simultaneously threatened the personal and social values of many individuals, resulting in discontent and attempts to find methods of collective action. The solution offered by Hitler's group appealed to many because the flexible ideology of that group embodied a large number of popular views. Finally, the energy and resourcefulness of the party organization, buttressed by popular trust in Hitler's charismatic leadership, led large numbers of people to enroll as National Socialists, confident in the ultimate success of their cause.

This conclusion is valid only if the qualifying conditions incident to any summary are kept in mind. "Discontent," "ideology," "tactics," and "charisma" are abstractions that have meaning only with reference to the concrete instances of behavior which constitute the "Hitler movement," typical illustrations of which have been already reported.

Therefore, the first qualifying condition is that the account of the origin as well as of the success of the Hitler movement be contained in the study *taken as a whole.*[4]

Another condition is equally important. We can not understand the function of the four factors which we have stressed as determinants unless we view them with reference to the milieu in which they operated. This milieu is the realistic background of the movement: the economic and political conditions in Germany, the traditions and habits of thought of its population, the international situation. These factors are determinants of the success of the movement only insofar as they operated in close interaction with the milieu and derived their specific character and content through adaptation to existing conditions.

A final qualification must be made with regard to the causal character of the factors mentioned. They may be considered as causes which explain the Hitler movement only if we realize that they are not in themselves agents, but are general terms which give us the clues to the forces that made and sustained the movement. These forces are the specific motives, the concrete actions, and the personal experiences and decisions of individuals.

These are the only *real* causes of the Hitler movement. The general terms employed in our analysis are merely reductions of the multiplicity and diversity of these causes to the meaning and characteristic features that they have in common.

[4] By "Success" I mean here not the gaining of political power but the maintenance of a "going concern," which was able to attract and hold the allegiance of thousands of followers and to outdistance its competitors.

With these three qualifying conditions in mind, we can now discuss briefly the question of the relative significance of the four factors as determinants of the movement. The result of our analysis points to the unavoidable conclusion that the growth and success of the Hitler movement was an outcome of their *combined* effect in such manner that none of the factors considered separately can be said to have played a greater or lesser role. Discontent created the condition which made large-scale collective action possible. The winning of adherents by a promotion group operating on the basis of this discontent depended upon the appeal of its ideology. In turn, the continued support of the movement by its adherents was conditioned upon the strategy and tactics by which the affairs of the movement were conducted. Charismatic leadership provided the needed integration and stabilization of the movement and conditioned the devotion of its followers and their confidence. The four factors were dependent upon and supported each other in such fashion that the absence or deficiency of any one factor would have fatally disabled the movement. For this reason, its growth and success never could be accounted for in terms of a single factor. Thus, it would be futile to see the Hitler movement merely as the result of the dissatisfaction of a class, or of economic adversity, or of the Versailles Treaty, and so forth. Equally futile would be the attempt to account for it in terms of the content of its propaganda or the methods of promotion. Nor can the movement be attributed solely to the presence of charismatic leadership.

The Hitler movement must be viewed as the resultant of factors which operated not as independent "forces" but functioned as a pattern in which none of the component parts was more significant than the others. Without the full development of this pattern, the Hitler movement as we know it would not have been possible. On the other hand, the development of the movement was inevitable once a pattern had developed in which widespread and persistent discontent, purposes that appealed to prevalent sentiments, efficient organization and propaganda, and charismatic leadership had made their appearance and had become coordinate in their effect.[5]

[5] *Cf.* T. Abel, "The Pattern of a Successful Political Movement," *American Sociological Review*, Vol. II, 1937.

STUDENTS AND POLITICAL VIOLENCE : BRAZIL, 1964, AND THE DOMINICAN REPUBLIC, 1965*

Bryant Wedge

When violent political uprisings are anticipated by potential participants, politically responsible decision-makers, and scholarly observers, and do not occur, and when violent revolutionary uprisings suddenly erupt that no one, including most of the participants, expected, serious questions are raised as to the adequacy with which the conditions of spontaneous political violence are understood and analyzed by scholar and policy-maker alike—at least in particular cases. The problem is compounded when other cases are correctly predicted, as sometimes happens.

The task of social science is to develop explanations for significant social phenomena, preferably explanations that have predictive value. If social science is to contribute to a policy science it must be united with social problem-solving; that is, it must be useful in anticipating, directing, and meliorating the problems of social change.[1] Violent uprisings represent a profound challenge to social science, particularly to political science, in

* This article has been revised from a paper presented at the 1967 Annual Meeting of the American Political Science Association in Chicago. The field studies from which the interview data are drawn were conducted by the writer under the auspices of the Institute for the Study of National Behavior of West Medford, Mass., with the support of the United States Information Agency in Brazil and the Agency for International Development in the Dominican Republic. The findings and conclusions are the writer's responsibility and do not necessarily represent the views of these agencies or of the United States government. The author is grateful to Ted Gurr for his helpful criticism.

[1] Leonard Goodwin, "The Historical-Philosophical Basis for Uniting Social Science with Social Problem-Solving," *Philosophy of Science*, XXIX (October 1964), 377–92.

Reprinted from "The Case Study of Student Political Violence: Brazil, 1964, and Dominican Republic, 1965," *World Politics*, XXI (January, 1969), 183–206, by permission of the author and Princeton University Press.

terms of both scientific explanation and social problem-solving.

The apparently simple question of under what conditions violence is likely to erupt has proved difficult to answer. Montesquieu, for example, in *The Persian Letters*, wrote, "In these States great events are not necessarily preceded by great causes; on the contrary, the least accident produces a great revolution, often as unforeseen by those who cause it, as by those who suffer from it."[2] Tocqueville considered the French Revolution "a convulsive and painful process, without transition, without precaution, without prior calculation."[3] And Arnold Forster probably represents contemporary political scholarship when he considers political violence "by its very nature beyond any simple or reasonable laws of causation."[4]

In response to this problem of explanation, Ted Gurr has proposed a theoretical model of "social patterns that dispose men to collective violence" that encompasses both the complexity of variables tending toward behavioral outcomes and the nonrational nature of human response to social circumstances.[5] Studies using cross-national aggregate data have been based on the model and generally tend to validate its component propositions.[6] This article represents a quite different approach to the phenomenon: the application of the model to the analysis and organization of case studies based primarily on the reports of participants in political events in which violent uprising was perceived as a possible outcome. I undertook the study with the conviction that progress in political analysis requires bridge-building between theory and case study, and study of the behavior of individual political actors in relation to social systems.[7]

Violent behavior is in the final analysis the action of individuals, as indeed is all political behavior. Hadley Cantril pointed out some time ago that the idea of a collective mind is not tenable: "Whatever characteristics the crowd or the mob exhibit must be owing solely to the mental processes and reactions of congregate individuals."[8] This is to say, not that social circumstances do not affect individual behavior, but that explanations for behavior must be sought in individual reactions to circumstances as well as in the circumstances themselves. So the first complexity to which this discussion is addressed is that of the interface between political systems and the individual psychology of participants in political action; this may be termed the psycho-political interface. Consideration of this arena of transaction has been rather neglected by social science, not only because it is difficult, but also because the boundaries of academic disciplines

---

[2] Montesquieu, *The Persian Letters*, as quoted by David C. Rapaport, "*Coup d'état*: The View of the Men Firing Pistols," in Carl J. Friedrich, ed., *Revolution* (New York 1966), 58.

[3] Alexis de Tòcqueville, *L'Ancien Régime et la Revolution*, as quoted by Melvin Richter, "Tocqueville's Contributions to the Theory of Revolution," *ibid.*, 2, 81.

[4] "Violence on the Fanatical Left and Right," *Annals of the American Academy of Political and Social Science*, CCCLXIV (March 1966), 142. Quotation courtesy of Ted Gurr.

[5] "Psychological Factors in Civil Violence," *World Politics*, XX (January 1968), 245–78 [reading 2 in this volume].

[6] *Ibid.*, 278; see also "A Causal Model of Civil Strife; A Comparative Analysis Using New Indices," *American Political Science Review*, LII (December 1968), and Gurr and C. Ruttenberg, "The Conditions of Civil Violence: First Tests of a Causal Model," *Research Monograph 28*. Center of International Studies, Princeton University, 1967.

[7] This argument is in accord with Michael Haas, "Bridge-Building in International Relations: A Neotraditional Plea," *International Studies Quarterly*, XI (December 1967), 320–38.

[8] *The Psychology of Social Movements* (New York 1941), 118.

restrain scientists from considering both sides of the transaction simultaneously.

The second problem in scientific explanation is that of reconciling theoretical and experimental approaches with empirical observations of actual cases in all their ambiguous complexity. Obviously, the development of explanations for complex, multifactorial phenomena requires the combined enterprise of several approaches, especially those involved in the interplay between theory and case study. I suggest that the acid test for social science comes when the actual case is examined in terms of theory, and the reverse. This, incidentally, is the way medicine has developed such competence as it has; I suggest that a professional social science will have to follow a similar path.

The Arena of Case Study

On March 21, 1964, the armed forces of Brazil intervened in the government in the name of legality and order. The intervention directly frustrated the aspirations of the dominant student political organization, the National Union of Students, whose voice had been consistently and loudly raised in support of the "revolutionary reforms" of President Goulart, especially in the preceding months. The students were prepared for this "reactionary" coup attempt; indeed, there had been many demonstrations in support of the government in the preceding weeks, and plans had been laid for a massive march on the state capitols and offices of government. The United States Embassy was fully alert to the dangerous circumstances and every man was at his post to render what service he could. The president begged students, workers, and loyal military units to

rise in his support; his plea was echoed by student leaders throughout the country. Mass violence seemed certain, the outcome in doubt.

As everyone interested in these matters knows, the anticipated violent resistance to the Brazilian coup did not materialize. Students in Rio de Janeiro staged rallies and threw rocks, the demonstrations were broken up by troop units with few shots fired and few persons killed; in Recife, two students were killed by a hard-pressed officer trying to stop the throwing of coconuts and bottles. Student leaders were rounded up and jailed, the president left the country, and a general took office as interim president.

On April 24, 1965, a group of young military officers in the Dominican Republic attempted a coup d'état in favor of "constitutionalism" and against a suspected effort to impose military-oligarchic rule; the coup was opposed by senior officers in control of the regular military forces. Dominican students who, after the assassination of the dictator, Trujillo, four years before, had been deeply frustrated in their aspirations for reform, revolution, and a better life, did not expect the coup attempt; they were unprepared and had no program of action. The United States Embassy had little hint of special circumstances and certainly did not expect a violent outbreak in a country that had undergone seven changes of government and many minor coup attempts in the previous four years without popular explosion. (In fairness to the Embassy it must be added that the *possibility* of a blow-up was thoroughly recognized; indeed, Ambassador W. Tapley Bennett, Jr., had constantly warned both Dominican leaders and his own government that the blood-bath which had been anticipated with the fall of Trujillo could still occur.) The ambassador was visiting the United

States and most military attachés were attending a routine conference in Panama. At the crucial moment the provisional president pleaded for order and the young officers called on youth and workers for support on radio and television—as was quite routine. To the very last moment it seemed that the coup would probably fail but that, at most, it might result in just another fairly orderly change in government.

But, as is now history, massive violence unexpectedly erupted in Santo Domingo as large numbers of citizens, especially youths, rallied in majestic outrage to support the "Revolution." The regular military forces were brought to a stop by an armed and angry mob that rapidly became organized in the city; at least 700 people were killed in four days, the provisional president fled into hiding, and the country, virtually leaderless, was verging on a massive civil war. The United States intervened and troops were interposed between the warring parties, but hostilities continued for some time and about 3,000 people were eventually killed. Continued interposition and heroic diplomatic efforts by the Organization of American States and others ultimately brought order from the chaos and, over a year after the outbreak, supervised elections brought a return to constitutional government.

The observations in this article are drawn from dialogic interviews with students in their normal surroundings after the revolutionary events. I conducted dialogues with Brazilian students seven months after the coup, recording 132 individual interviews and 32 group interviews involving 653 students. In the Dominican Republic, five months after the violent outbreak, I interviewed 33 students individually and 248 in eighteen groups. In the cases of both groups and individuals the sample was weighted toward politically active reformist students.

The data from such interviews are necessarily qualitative and certainly involve some retrospective revision of memory. Nevertheless, techniques of active participation in dialogue and debate, multiple sampling, and reports of observers, coupled with the emotive intensity with which the subjects express their memories of feeling and action— the phenomenon of emotional catharsis —provide the basis for a high level of confidence in the findings. Most important, subjects report on events *as they perceived them*; the actions of individuals are necessarily in terms of their particular outlooks.

Recognition of the anchoring of action in the perceptions of participants is perhaps the strongest argument for case study of participation in political acts; only in this way can the political analyst hope to avoid errors of mythologizing from his particular assumptions. This source of error is clearly present in prevalent views of the two crises examined here. For example, the impression that Communists and Castro-Communists played little role in organizing the Dominican street fighting[9] is belied by the almost universal

[9] See, for example, Theodore Draper, "The Dominican Intervention," *Commentary* (December 1965) and Tad Szulc, *Dominican Diary* (New York 1965). Firsthand observations and reports of participants concerning Communist roles in organizing the revolt at the levels of direct violent engagement indicate a very active participation, although participation at higher levels of the political structure was reported by these observers to be minimal. My direct observations agree with reports of John Bartlow Martin in *Overtaken by Events* (New York 1966) and statements of U.S. government spokesmen at the time of the uprising. I think this discrepancy arises from differences in the levels of political observation and, almost certainly, from the biases of the observers. At the outset of my studies I shared the views of Draper and Szulc, on the basis of my readings of reports and judgments as to the credibility of sources, but the method of participant dialogue led me to the different conclusions reported here.

statement of non-Communist participants who, after vehemently disclaiming any Communist character for the "revolution," would explain that "of course we needed all the help we could get and that included using the military guidance of Dominican Communists although not their political guidance"; besides this, I personally interviewed several self-proclaimed Communist youths who proudly referred to their Cuban training and whom I observed openly dispatching volunteer police forces to trouble spots.

The impression that deposed Dominican President Bosch exercised charismatic influence on the young people was similarly not supported; it is true that his return was sought as the symbol of legality, but he personally was the object of careful critical judgment by revolutionary youth throughout the Dominican Republic, as I observed in the comments of "constitutionalist" youths with whom I was conversing at the time of Bosch's speeches on his return to the country. Similarly, President Goulart of Brazil was ideologically popular until he violated ideologic standards; his personal shortcomings were regarded indulgently. In short, the identification of personalism as politically crucial by many North American scholars did not accord with the pragmatism of Dominican youth or the ideologic idealism of Brazilians as a principal and *culturally dominant* factor determining perception and action.

The Gurr model provides a sufficient degree of isomorphism with the observed phenomena of political violence to offer a systematic framework for the organization of the data, although the propositions are interpreted here in terms of the kinds of judgment the data allow. The use of such models permits comparative systematization of observations and suggests relationships that might not be observed otherwise;

moreover, the model is sufficiently flexible to accommodate observed relationships not explicitly stated—it is by such processes that heuristic models become the forerunners of established theory in empirical inductive approaches to complex realities.

The essence of Gurr's model is that discrepancies between value expectations and perceived value capabilities of societies result in relative deprivation, and the consequent response tendency of frustration-aggression is channelled into collective response alternatives by available facilities and habits of social control and social facilitation. The reader is referred to Gurr's description; the variables are interpreted below in terms of the data available.[10] The data-gathering process can be refined and the propositions sharpened in further case study, but it is necessary to begin the process in ways that do not violate the fullness of reality or impose on analysis methods that blind the observer to what Whitehead calls a "complete experience."[11]

Psychological Preconditions for Violent Uprising

One of the most firmly established, experimentally and clinically validated propositions in the psychological study of behavior is the frustration-aggression hypothesis.[12] Experimental animals and men become angry when their goal-seeking purposes are interfered with; aggressive behavior appears to be an innate response to such frustration. Among men, common social purposes may be more or less widely shared in societies; interference with the realization of these purposes constitutes collective frustration and results in

[10] P. 252.
[11] Alfred North Whitehead, *The Function of Reason* (Princeton 1929), 11.
[12] Gurr, 249 ff.

angry affects that are expressed in aggression toward the frustrating agent or surrogate agents. When the frustrating agent is perceived as political authority, aggression is directed toward aspects of the political system and the outcome is psychological predisposition toward political violence.

Central to this argument is the recognition, thoroughly adumbrated in Gurr's study, that the sense of frustration among men in society depends on shared *perceptions* of what is desirable and possible in the society. It follows from this that a basic reference point in the estimation of the degree of frustration that disposes people toward political violence must lie in the shared perceptions of individuals of what they want and deserve from their political authorities; the measurement of frustration-levels must always be based on an appreciation of the perceptual frame of reference of the individuals in given societies. We can now examine the variables contributing to relative deprivation among students in Brazil and the Dominican Republic in terms of Gurr's model.

Relative deprivation is the sense of unjustifiable frustration of expectations from the environment. How deprived did students in Brazil and the Dominican Republic perceive themselves to be and how angry were they?

Brazilian students, in 1964, were sharply aware of the discrepancy between the potential and the performance of their society. They shared the view, almost to a man, that their country held great potential wealth and capability for industrialization, self-sufficiency, and importance in the world. They unanimously subscribed to ideals of social justice, the need for extension of education and opportunity, and the right to social protection for all Brazilians from economic exploitation and hunger. But when they looked around, they saw poverty and illiteracy, under-

development of resources, instability of government, inequality of opportunity, and great economic strain. At the level of recognition and aspiration, then, the relative deprivation of social values was intense and universal: something was wrong with Brazilian society. Moreover, this view was loudly articulated by the leadership of the dominant student organization, by respected scholars and foreign experts, and by the president of the country.

Here, however, we must pause to note that the personal aspirations of Brazilian students were less frustrated than were their aspirations for society. Students in Brazil were privileged and recognized, the student voice was widely respected, the personal future of students was assured by the insatiable need of the society for educated manpower. Major subventions were made to the National Union of Students by the government and private corporations; the president asked for student support and, in turn, offered his government's help for student programs. Not only that, but the social expectations of student radicalism were well established, going back at least to the time when Brazilian students at the University of Montpellier approached Thomas Jefferson, then Ambassador to France, for advice on conducting a revolution for independence. We may fairly judge that relative deprivation was perceived as severe in the realm of social aspirations and minimal in frustration of personal expectations.[13]

Dominican students, in the months before the event, were equally disappointed in their hopes for their country. The downfall of Trujillo after thirty years of oppressive dictatorship had brought a surge of great expectations. There was very little illusion about

[13] Irving L. Horowitz, *Revolution in Brazil: Politics and Society in a Developing Nation* (New York 1964), gives substantial evidence of social frustration before the crisis.

the wealth of natural resources but there were great hopes for the benefits of liberty. Indeed, those benefits had been widely experienced—wages had risen unrestrainedly, foreign travel and imports had been extensive, political freedom was noisily exercised. There were excited plans for industrialization and land reform, for the expansion of education, and for social protection of the disadvantaged. A constitution was written and a president, Juan Bosch, was elected under OAS supervision. With this election, hopes for improvement in social conditions rose even higher among the majority of progressive-minded youth.

While hopes were high, however, material and political conditions in the nation were deteriorating. Disorder arose in many sections of society, especially as the limited resources of experienced managerial manpower were depleted by the exodus of Trujillo's associates, so that few competent personnel were left in executive positions. The economy deteriorated rapidly because of commodity price declines in the international markets—especially for sugar, on which the economy was greatly dependent. Unemployment rose, family institutions deteriorated (about a third of the university students came from broken families), and political life was in chaos as radical minority parties were formed on the right and left. Presient Bosch failed to stem these tides and, after seven months in office, he was overthrown by a military coup and sent into exile. Frustration of social aspirations was universal.

The personal expectations of most students were also frustrated. Not only were the personal circumstances of the majority, who had originated in the lower middle class, strained by economic dislocation, but their hopes for improvement of student life were disappointed. The Autonomous University of Santo Domingo expanded rapidly but conditions there deteriorated. Classes were crowded and irregular, teaching was very uneven. Student political organizations sought "reform" in terms of the criteria that had been enunciated in 1918 at Cordoba University in Argentina—autonomy of the university from political interference, extraterritoriality of university grounds from police invasion (*fuero*), and student representation on governing boards. All of these were established and all were violated, especially after the fall of Bosch. And a deep split between generations took place as most students broke politically with their parents, whom they saw as discredited by their acquiescence in Trujillo's rule (this differed from the Brazilian situation, in which family ties were maintained as radicalism was indulged). Students were frustrated to the point of desperation.

The *intensity of commitment to value* refers to the strength of motivation to seek realization of aspirations. The more seriously a goal is sought, the greater is the anger when something interferes with its attainment. To this, Gurr adds two sub-propositions: that commitment varies directly with the amount of effort previously invested in its attainment, and that the closer realization of attainment seems to be, the stronger is the motivation. In other words, the more people want something, the angrier they are when they are prevented from getting it.

Estimating the magnitude of motivation involves finding out two main facts—the distribution of commitment to a particular goal in a population, and the motivational strength of commitment in its proponents. How many people seek the goal and how much does this purpose move them to action?

Despite the fact that the dominant student voice in Brazil advocated radical reform, the voice of revolution was that of a radical minority: it represented the position of an estimated 5 percent of the student population, those occupying an active revolutionary political position. I estimated that the distribution of political orientation approximated [that shown in Table 1].

Table 1

POLITICAL POSITION AMONG BRAZILIAN STUDENTS

	Active	Passive
Conservative	3%	15%
Moderate reformist	7%	60%
Revolutionary	5%	10%

The strength of motive cannot be estimated apart from the specifics of the culture. It is true that the active revolutionary students of Brazil worked very hard to advance their programs and to arouse public support for them. But it is also true that there is a long tradition in that culture of student radicalism and that there was substantial political and economic support for their activity. In fact, the importance of the movement, the fun of speech-making and conventioneering, and the moral satisfaction of espousing ideal and intellectually satisfying causes attracted a considerable fringe of opportunists. If a few splendid souls took the commitment completely seriously and were deeply motivated to action by it, many more went along for the ride. In the Brazilian case, neither of the sub-propositions is supported; the apparent effort toward the goals had been great and the goals had been close to attainment; in fact, some of them had already been achieved, but this appeared to diminish rather than encourage motivation.

Circumstances in the Dominican Republic were considerably different. Dissent, in the Trujillo period, had been a life-and-death matter; indeed this has been true throughout Dominican history. One measure of value-commitment is willingness to risk one's life for the goal, and this willingness had been well demonstrated by Dominican youth. The downfall of Trujillo followed the landing of young Dominican guerrillas on the 14th of June 1959; they were all killed, as were many dissident youths in the following years. After the fall of Bosch in 1964, another group—mostly Castroites and Communists, and all members of the "14th of June Movement"—took to the hills and were wiped out. Ideology was weak but motive was strong. To go a step further, Dominican students were not always certain what they were for, but they knew what they were against— military oppression. Instigation to violence is greater when motivated by negative rather than by positive values, by the presence of a hated object rather than by frustration of value expectations alone. The generality of this proposition requires study as a possible added variable that would significantly modify the model; for the present it must be offered as a suggestion.

The distribution of strong sentiment for valued purpose among Dominican students was quite broad. I was able to estimate the political position of these students as [shown in Table 2].

Table 2

POLITICAL POSITION AMONG DOMINICAN STUDENTS

	Active	Passive	
Conservative	1%	14%	
Neutral	—	30%	(includes most women)
Revolutionary	20%	35%	

It appears from these cases that desperation rather than hopefulness precipitates violence, that smouldering resentment is more potent than previous effort. Overall assessment of intensity of commitment leads to the judgment that the Dominican students were strongly motivated toward anger, while the Brazilian students were only modestly motivated.

Legitimacy of deprivation refers to the perception of the interfering agent as reasonable, justified, or simply helpless to alter circumstances. If the frustration is seen as arbitrary or self-seeking there is greater anger than if it is seen as unavoidable and "just one of those things."

It will be recalled that the ultimate frustrating agent in both cases was military force directed against valued "reforms." Here, however, the similarity ends. In Brazil, the military role in government had been historically reasonable and supportive of democratic values; there was no sharp resentment of the military as such. Furthermore, the president had undermined his own legitimacy in the eyes of the student constituency by acting unconstitutionally in the weeks before the coup—and constitutionalism holds high value for most Brazilian students. The value for form, in this case, weighed against the value for substance; relatively few students wanted to achieve their goals at the price of destruction of highly valued institutions. Therefore, the military intervention was perceived as being about as justified as was the action of the government that espoused these values; neither was palatable but there wasn't much to choose between them in terms of legitimacy.

From the viewpoint of Dominican students there was no such ambivalence. The history of military oppression was 450 years old; Trujillo had ruled with a military iron fist and the constitutional president had been deposed by military coup. The senior officers, moreover, were notorious for their self-seeking; corruption and privilege had long attended their office, and they were strongly linked with the economic oligarchy in the practice of social

exploitation. The line was clearly drawn by the revolting officers who adopted the slogan of "Constitutionalism." The depriving agent had no legitimacy whatever in the minds of students.

The *degree of deprivation* represents the perceived distance between aspirations considered justified and those enjoyed. Anger is assumed to vary directly with the degree of discrepancy.

I have outlined something of student hopes in Brazil and the Dominican Republic and some of the beliefs as to attainability. Instead of extending this description here, I will refer to measurements of public judgments using a self-anchoring scale made by Lloyd Free.[14] In both countries a probability sample of the population had been asked to indicate, on an eleven-point scale, their judgment of where they stood and where their country stood with respect to their self-defined aspirations for self and country. The judgment was made for a point five years in the past, for the present, and for five years in the future [see Table 3].

These judgments fairly reflect the degree of deprivation perceived by stu-

Table 3

AVERAGE RATINGS OF JUDGMENT FOR POSITION OF SELF AND COUNTRY WITH RESPECT TO ASPIRATIONS[a]

	Brazil (1960)		Dominican Republic (1962)	
	Self	*Country*	*Self*	*Country*
Past	4.1	4.9	1.6	1.7
Present	4.8	5.1	1.6	2.7
Future	7.4	7.6	5.8	7.0

[a] Derived from L. Free; on scale running from zero at the bottom to ten at the top.

[14] "Some International Implications of the Political Psychology of Brazilians" (July 1961) and "Attitudes, Hopes, and Fears of the Dominican People" (June 1962), *Institute for International Social Research Publications* (Princeton 1962).

dents in the two countries; it is probable that at a later time Dominican students would have rated their personal positions somewhat higher and their country's position somewhat lower, and it is certain that by 1965 they would have been less hopeful for the future. Free's measurements illustrate the use of a variety of data in the assessment process that are entirely apt to the purpose; finer analysis of the data would be possible in a more elaborate study.

Brazilians thought that things were getting better, both for themselves and their country. They were optimistic about the future; Free judged that "their frustrations are not apt to build up into a feeling that the present basic system in Brazil must be smashed or radically changed."[15] Dominicans, by contrast, were exceedingly gloomy about their own positions although, in 1962, they thought that their country had improved. Their aspirations for the future, both personally and nationally, were very high—the discrepancy was greater than that measured anywhere else. By 1965, however, these hopes were already substantially disappointed. Using this measurement, Free concluded that "an extremely serious situation of popular discontent and frustration, fraught with a dangerous potential for upheaval, exists in the Dominican Republic."[16] The degree of deprivation was moderate in Brazil; it was exceedingly severe in the Dominican Republic.

The *proportion of opportunities interfered with* suggests that anger is greater as there are fewer nonviolent means to seek valued goals; the extreme case is when all channels of response are blocked, when the frustrated and angry man's back is to the wall. The likelihood of violent response is hypothesized to rise when the opportunities for value-forwarding action are narrowed.

Few students in Brazil imagined that opportunities for forwarding their values would be completely interfered with, even by a military government. Not only had the military been mild in its domestic interventions, but the traditions of freedom of the press and speech were deeply established; beyond that, the capacity for extensive underground activity was quite well developed. This is to say, not that students liked the intervention, but that the whole political culture informed them that it would not be permanent nor its consequences total and that opportunities for value-forwarding activities would remain. They were correct. After the event many, but by no means all, public opportunities were suppressed; some students spent some time in jail and a few went into exile, but the deep trends toward social transformation that they advocated have continued, although haltingly. The proportion of value opportunities interfered with was so small as to represent a negative quality as an instigator of anger-violence among the student population as a whole.

Circumstances in the Dominican Republic were quite different. University youth had enjoyed a brief period of liberty to pursue political and social ends although there were some fairly serious restrictions after the fall of Bosch. But, in the event that a military-oligarchic regime should become established, there were no illusions about the outcome; liberty would be radically suppressed. Such was the history of the country and such was the memory of Trujillo. Students were quite certain that those who had taken an active part, especially after the outbreak of violence, would be hunted down and jailed or killed unless they could escape the country. The value deprivation was extreme and very vivid, not only of the purposes espoused, but of life itself. The violence, when it came, was in good part "the revolt of the damned."

Here, I must add a variable to the Gurr model that I consider crucial

---

[15] *Ibid.*, Brazil, 66.
[16] *Ibid.*, Dominican Republic, 16.

to the *precipitation* of many "spontaneous" violent outbursts. It is hypothesized that the likelihood of violent response varies directly with perceived threat to life. The evidence for this is almost entirely clinical and observational, as the conditions are difficult to reproduce experimentally, but the "cornered-rat response" differs in psychological quality from frustration of goal-seeking purposes. When the value directly at stake is life, violent response occurs as a reaction to fear rather than as an expression of anger. This distinction is exceedingly important in the consideration of the role of police actions in precipitating and maintaining violence. Indeed, violent men and groups are sometimes disarmed by the removal of threatening forces. This threat-aggression response is often met in psychiatric work and may be distinguished also from the expectation of retribution, which is not necessarily immediate in quality.[17]

In the Dominican Republic the direct action of military forces in shooting and later bombing concentrations of "rebels" clearly precipitated violent response. Faced with a direct threat, students who had not anticipated participation in violence suddenly sought and accepted weapons. Frustration had brought them to protest, fear ensured its violent form. (It is true that the revolting young officers and their followers were armed, as were some conspiratorial groups committed to violent means to gain their ends, but this circumstance also obtained in Brazil; the difference in response lay in the character of the confrontation as well as the levels of frustration.)

Students in Brazil relied strongly on

the well-established tradition of military restraint. Students in Recife were shocked, for example, by the shooting of two of their number and actually made excuses for the officer responsible —he was "confused" and hadn't counted on ricochet. Although the military moved swiftly and with a substantial show of force, it is unlikely that fear suppressed violence or greatly increased anger.

The *psychological preconditions* for violence may now be summarized in tabular form; I have recorded judgments on a five-point scale from $--$ to $++$ in terms of the factors disposing to violence [see Table 4].

Table 4

STRENGTH INSTIGATING VARIABLES DISPOSING TO VIOLENCE

	Brazil	Dominican Republic
Relative deprivation	+	++
Intensity of commitment	+	++
Legitimacy of deprivation	0	++
Degree of deprivation	+	++
Interference with opportunity	0	++
Threat	+	++
Total Value of Instigation	+4	+12

It appears from this tabulation that students of Brazil were experiencing moderate degrees of frustration and reacted with modest anger. In the Dominican Republic every variable disposing to frustrated anger was at a very high level; moreover, conditions of threat were extreme and conducive to aggressive response.

Social Preconditions of Violent Uprising

Whether angry men turn to violence depends in large part on the effectiveness of social control balanced against the sources of social support for violent

[17] While Leonard Berkowitz considers that threat-aggression is a special case of frustration-aggression, in *Aggression: A Social Psychological Analysis* (New York 1962), 38–49, Jerome Frank clearly distinguishes the two, in *Sanity and Survival: Psychological Aspects of War and Peace* (New York 1968), 75.

behavior. Under Trujillo, for example, the controls were so effective that collective violence was virtually impossible; when frustrated men and small groups did turn to violence they were sure to be wiped out—indeed, many persons turned their anger against themselves and committed suicide. Many more went into exile. On the other hand, absolute control generates its own destruction; sooner or later, in the contemporary world, such systems prove too brittle to survive; they are temporary and transitional and often fall in violence. The likelihood of violence in any political system, in Gurr's model, depends on social mediation, on the balance between factors that control the violent expression of anger and those that facilitate violent manifestations. I will sketchily review these factors in both Brazil and the Dominican Republic.

Before entering into the analysis of social preconditions as experienced by the student segments of the populations, it is necessary to review some aspects of the authoritative structure of the governments. It is obvious that authority structures encompass the principal institutions of social control and they also permit the existence of institutionalized channels for protest. Governments, moreover, can provide social facilitation for nonviolent response alternatives. Questions of social control and social facilitation cannot be analyzed apart from consideration of political authority in case study although, conversely, political analysis alone cannot lead to estimation of the likelihood of violence within the system; this likelihood, rather, turns on the adequacy of government in relation to social conditions and social culture. This consideration in no way reflects on the validity of the Gurr propositions as general theory.

The government of Brazil derived its formal authority from constitutional processes; the elected president administered a federal authority with legislative powers resting in a bicameral legislature. And, theoretically, presidential power was restricted by legal constraints. In fact, informal agreements, sometimes amounting to conspiracy, dominated the governing process; this had long involved the consent of an elitist oligarchy and, ultimately, the military forces. The incumbent president, Goulart, had come to office somewhat irregularly from the vice-presidency when his predecessor, the quixotic Janio Quadros, had resigned after seven months in office. Still, the forms of constitutionalism were observed even as the president's influence on the directions of policy grew and as he attempted to build a new political base on the support of labor, students, and some elements of the middle class. So long as these forms were observed, the governing authority was respected—with the exception of some rebellious state governors who usually wrung compromises from the president—and the instruments of order, the police, military, and bureaucracy continued to function.

But Goulart was unquestionably a demagogic leftist and as his calls for "reforms" became more radical, so did his appeals for popular demonstration in his support become more strident, while strikes, protests, and other manifestations of civil disorder grew. Finally the president's bypassing of constitutional processes, in his attempts to promulgate law by decree, became so flagrant that the military leadership intervened in the name of preserving the constitution.

The Dominican government had much less legal justification than did the Brazilian; it was frankly the instrument of an even narrower oligarchy in league with a military junta that had overthrown constitutionally elected President Juan Bosch after seven months in office in 1963. Authority was ostensibly centralized in the office of the provisional president, Donald Reid Cabral, himself a member of the conservative oligarchy, but in fact was largely exercised by the police and military forces. Disorder, conspiracy, and small episodes of violence continued to break out in the country while efforts to stem the tide, especially by direct employment of workers by the government and by wage and other concessions to popular discontent, were only partly successful. Elections were promised for later in the year, but the former president was still in exile. The coup attempt that precipitated revolt was mounted to forestall a suspected effort by the provisional president to succeed himself in office with military support. In short, the government of the Dominican Republic based its real authority in military force and sanction, and maintained social order by force or the threat of force combined with promises of a return to democracy and concessions to public demands that had become vocal since Trujillo's downfall had weakened authoritarian control.

The *expectation of retribution* by physical or social punishment deters violent outbreaks by already angry men when the expected retribution is severe and certain. When only moderate retribution is anticipated, however, the likelihood of violence may be increased by raising the level of frustrated anger. In other words, if punishment is seen as swift and absolute, men are not so likely to act violently as when punishment is doubtful. Low levels of expectation may actually diminish the likelihood of violence, but a decreasing fear of retribution tends to increase the probability of violence. In short, violence is suppressed by sufficient fear but increased when fear is moderate or decreasing.

Fear of retribution was never very great among Brazilian students; the tradition of moderate response to political protest, by the government and even the military, was very strong and actually the object of civic pride. Dissidents might be jailed for a while or have problems obtaining jobs, but torture and killing were scarcely thinkable. Certainly there was no expectation of retribution from the government in power, which had tended to encourage and reward demonstrations on behalf of its programs. But, even should the government fall—and all but the most committed student radicals had begun to suspect and even hope it would—it was expected that any succeeding regime, even a military dictatorship, would be fairly mild in its punishments, especially of students, who constituted a privileged and rather indulged segment of the population. Although, in the event, the military moved swiftly and with a substantial show of force, there is little evidence that expectation of retribution exercised notable suppressive effect or greatly increased anger. Rather, a feeling of disappointment in Goulart and in the outcome of their cause was reported by those students most active in opposition to the military.

The Dominican situation was much more complicated and in fact varied from hour to hour. No great retribution was expected from the shaky provisional government. Should the senior officers and the regular military prevail, no one doubted that retribution would be swift and complete against the participants—the memory of military ruthlessness and torture during Trujillo's dictatorship was strong and was being reinforced by continuing experience. But the military was split—it will be remembered that junior officers and some military units had precipitated the coup attempt—and it was by no means certain which side would prevail. There is no doubt that uncertainty as to outcome both diminished the fear of immediate retribution and increased the fear of ultimate retribution should the outbreak be crushed; this uncertainty greatly increased the level of violence. Furthermore, the likelihood of retribution had decreased since the fall of Trujillo and in so doing had diminished this source of inhibition of violent action.

The *persistence of anger* occurs when violence is inhibited by fear of retribution, but the likelihood of violence diminishes as the inhibiting force is maintained over time. Furthermore, the greater the commitment to the value being suppressed, the longer anger endures. In short, people give up when they can't possibly win but they remain angry when what they lose is very important to them.

In Brazil, as I have indicated, the fear of retribution was modest in the first place; furthermore, it appears that in absolute numbers more students were relieved by the restoration of order than were distressed by the downfall of Goulart. It was only among the minority of active revolutionaries that anger persisted and since they were unable to mount any effective response this anger soon evaporated into resignation and discouragement.

Dominican students, by contrast, had stored their anger at military rule over a very long time. Many a man in his forties had suffered the insults of Trujilloist suppression and had delayed violent response; a considerable number of these men appeared side by side with youth when violence broke out. There is little doubt that much of the force of violence in 1965 sprang from persisting anger displaced from the years of Trujillo's police. To this anger was added the insult of the military coup against President Bosch; again the outbreak of violence had been delayed. The question in the minds of most Dominicans was why the outbreak of violence was delayed so long; it appears to me that the anticipation of ruthless

retribution had been so deeply established in the culture that it took some time and much testing before the fear of it was overcome. In fact, most of the Dominican population, especially in the countryside, was still cowed by fear even after the revolt; it is not surprising that youth, which had been less conditioned to fear, led the outbreak of violence.

Similarly, the values to which Brazilian students were committed were held with less intensity since they were ideal and intellectual in their primary qualities; the Dominican value for liberty, which was the principal value at stake, is held with deep emotional intensity. This is to suggest, not that Brazilians are any less sincere and serious, but only that their entire system is milder than that of the harsh tyrannies which have marked Dominican history.

Institutionalization of protest, which allows the discharge of anger by nonviolent aggression, tends to diminish the likelihood of civil violence. When established forms for the expression of anger are available, and when targets for the expression of hostility have been previously identified, the chances are that the aggression of angry men will be expressed through those channels. This is the familiar dynamic of the man who hates his boss but nightly berates his wife and kicks the dog.

Brazilian students enjoyed a vast array of channels for the expression of displeasure. I have mentioned the activities of the Student Union; these went on in every university and on the national level. Speeches, demonstrations, student strikes, and petitions constantly took place, often in connection with national issues such as the nationalization of petroleum resources. In the early months of 1964, these activities became so frenzied that university life was seriously disrupted.

There seemed little likelihood that all of these institutional channels for protest could be suppressed by any government.

It has been demonstrated by Leonard Berkowitz that hostility is generalized from the frustrator to previously disliked objects.[18] Brazilian students had a good deal of difficulty identifying the frustrating agent, and tended to speak in terms of the oligarchy or international imperialists. Some political figures were considered to be aligned with these forces but scarcely as primary agents. The further to the left the student, the more apt he was to blame "United States imperialism" for his frustration and to satisfy his hostility with savage cartoons and editorials and with an occasional demonstration in front of an embassy. But this alleged force was not directly reachable. Moreover, geography interposed itself: Brazil is a vast country and the capital quite inaccessible—in city after city it was some other place that was to blame. Thus the United States and the oligarchs, equally unreachable, provided well-established objects for displaced anger.

After the fall of Trujillo, Dominican students developed a number of institutions of protest, especially student political groupings within the university. Incorporated in the whole climate, however, was a high component of institutionalized violence. The 14th of June Movement, which was born of violence, provided a popular focal point—even after it became dominated by young Dominican Communists in 1963, this organization kept its loosely organized constituency of non-Communist adherents and never relinquished the idea of guerrilla action. The university itself was the site of intense political struggles that faithfully reflected the Dominican macrocosm; strikes, lock-outs, and demonstrations were constant. These institutions were not strongly established; Dominican students did not expect that the institutions could survive military repression.

Even less, in the Dominican situation, was there any pattern for displacement of anger from the frustrating agent. Dominican students identified, without any serious dissent, the frustrator—the Dominican police and military. Even the young Communists did not very seriously maintain that United States imperialism was a principal problem; as Lloyd Free's study also showed, the United States enjoyed great popularity among the Dominican people at large. The military were not distant and unreachable, but directly and physically confronted the citizens of Santo Domingo. There were almost no established channels of institutionalized displacement of hostility.

Beliefs and traditions sanctioning civil violence increase the likelihood of violent action when men are angry. The suggestion here is that habits and patterns of violent expression of anger tend to be self-perpetuating and that these tendencies are reinforced by the existence of beliefs and ideologies holding that violence is an effective means to achieve social purposes. There is little doubt that violent behavior tends to be contagious: once a model or pattern of violent uprising has been established it is apt to be imitated, even across national boundaries.

As I have suggested, the political culture of Brazil incorporates a long and proud tradition of resolving political conflict with minimal violence and loss of life. While this tradition is historically faulty—there have been periods of serious political bloodshed in various Brazilian crises—it is very generally subscribed to. The tradition is reinforced, moreover, by at least two other aspects of Brazilian national culture: paternalism and universalism of reason-

[18] *Ibid.*, chap. 2.

ing. The paternalistic family is still a very strong institution in Brazil and, with respect to youth, astonishingly flexible; young men are indulged during their periods of political radicalism, but family ties still exercise some restraining force. Edmund Glenn and I have noted that the extreme universalism or globalism of cognitive forms characterizing the social communication culture of educated Brazilians permits the existence of profound discrepancies between idea and action.[19] The consequences of beliefs and traditions for action are, it is clear, profoundly dependent on this aspect of civic culture.

The concepts of political violence were well represented in Brazil and quite constantly articulated on the radical left, especially among the more radical Communists. There was much talk and threat of violent mass mobilizations and of guerrilla action. But this talk had a theoretical quality—it was ideological rather than practical in its effect. Student leaders were quite well organized and prepared to agitate and lead the outraged masses of the populace; they were scarcely concerned with the conditions for violent revolution, but assumed on the basis of theory that such conditions existed. These discrepancies between tradition and ideology and between theory and practice greatly diminished the effects of belief in violence in Brazil.

Both tradition and belief supported the resort to violence in the Dominican Republic. The violent activity of a repressive police formed a model for violent response. Time and time again in Dominican history, tyrants had been

[19] Glenn, "A Cognitive Approach to the Analysis of Cultures and Cultural Evolution," *General Systems*, XI (1966), 115–31. Wedge, "Communication Analysis and Comprehensive Diplomacy," in A. Hoffman, ed., *International Communication and the New Diplomacy* (Bloomington, Ind. 1968), 24–47.

overthrown by violent civil uprisings. The 14th of June Movement explicitly subscribed to techniques of violence and guerrilla war; and the political consciousness of an entire generation had been awakened by the landings of 1959, so that the fundamental model for combating oppression was one of violent response. There was little theory —the great majority of youths who participated in the uprising had never considered violence as a strategy and most had not considered personal participation—but there were constant practical examples.

With the fall of Trujillo, as I have mentioned, there was a profound split between generations. Families rapidly lost influence with their young people and, in large degree, accepted this loss. The generation of youth became remarkably free from parental or social restraint. The reasoning patterns characteristic of Dominican society were pragmatic and case-particularistic in the extreme. In a culture where survival has depended on having one's particular facts correct —as is always true in a police state— there can be little indulgence in theory. As a consequence, ideology played little role in mobilizing violent response, although the combination of ideas and practical organization for their realization in the 14th of June Movement played a significant role in the organization of the uprising; these ideas and techniques were very largely of Communist origin and young Dominican Communists were the most effective organizers, but the ideas scarcely penetrated the consciousness of the fiercely libertarian political culture of Dominican youth.

Finally, in the Gurr model, *group support* facilitates the likelihood of violent civil action. When there is a high level of interaction among participants and agreement among them as to the frustrating agent, when there is organized support for violent action and precedents for violent action, violent outcomes are likely.

I have indicated that the tradition of noisy but nonviolent political action was strong in Brazil, while violence on the part of authorities and their opponents alike was the norm in the political culture of the Dominican Republic. This was reflected in the organization of youth for political action: although the Brazilian student organizations developed very strong propaganda activites they had almost no military plans or theory, while virtually every Dominican student knew of the quite well developed Military Bureau of the 14th of June Movement and of its smuggling and concealing of arms. Even those who did not approve of this activity relied on the organization when violence appeared inevitable: however surprised they felt, their minds had been prepared for the action.

These preconditions certainly influenced the "spontaneous" violence in the Dominican Republic and the "spontaneous" resignation in Brazil but it is certain that crowd phenomena played a critical part in the respective outcomes.

Despite all the planning in Brazil, a number of factors diluted the development of massive crowd phenomena. Typically, students gathered in university centers and organized demonstrative marches on administrative offices. But the turnout, for reasons I have mentioned, was smaller than the organizers had expected; most citizens and students stayed at home and waited to see what would happen. In no case were they attacked in defensive positions; on the contrary, the initiative of marching up to police and military lines lay with the crowd—violence appears much more likely when men are defending themselves against threat than when they are taking the initiative. There were few firearms in the crowds; stones, bottles, and coconuts were more usual weapons. Students who participated

in marches reported great uncertainty and uneasiness; they did not feel strong support from the crowd nor strong leadership from those who urged them on. While some observers have judged that a principal crowd-dampening force was exerted by the efficiency of the military coup-makers in organizing support and that "lack of support, or even a long delay, could have resulted in bloodshed or perhaps even a civil war . . . ,"[20] very few of the participants whom I interviewed shared that judgment; they felt that the crowds might have held demonstrations and dissipated rapidly in almost any event. Finally, although the uprisings were planned to take place in a number of cities simultaneously, there was poor communication among them.

Crowd conditions in the Dominican Republic were very sharply defined. The revolt centered in downtown Santo Domingo. There had been little preparation, but when the coup attempt was precipitated the nuclear forces were armed military units following the leadership of the rebelling young officers. Bands of people came spontaneously from other parts of the city and from the countryside in response to rebel calls on Radio Santo Domingo. Almost from the first it was apparent that the police could not maintain control, and most police left the area. Defensive positions were established and quantities of additional arms, from caches and from a captured arsenal, were passed out to civilians. Armed bands of civilians began to roam the streets.

Both participants and observers reported striking and unanticipated behavior. The majority of students who answered the call to support the "Constitutionalists" did so without forethought and with a vague intention

[20] Araken Tavora, *How Brazil Stopped Communism* (Rio de Janeiro, 1964), 85.

of demonstrating moral backing. Almost as soon as they encountered the crowds in the city, they recall, they were caught up in a frenzy of rage, especially after the air attacks. They sought and accepted arms, they sought and accepted assignments from the apparent leaders; their overriding thought was to resist and strike back at the military forces. They experienced the very strong feelings of solidarity with one another in a desperate cause, and of group support for their actions.

Judgments of the effects of social mediating factors on the likelihood of violence are summarized in . . . Table [5].

Table 5

STRENGTH OF MEDIATING VARIABLES DISPOSING TO VIOLENCE

	Brazil	Dominican Republic
Retribution	0	+
Persistence of anger	0	+ +
Institutionalization of protest	−	+
Beliefs and traditions	−	+ +
Group support	0	+ +
Total Mediating Factors	2−	8+

Each of the . . . judgments is made, as nearly as possible, in the context of the respective political culture; each judgment is complex and involves overlapping and feedback loops among the variables. But, once again, the arithmetical product is striking and suggests that social forces in Brazil were fairly evenly balanced in terms of contribution to the likelihood of violence, while in the Dominican Republic these forces tended strongly toward a violent outcome, at least in the perception of student participants.

Insofar as the qualitative judgments that have been made are sustainable and insofar as the Gurr model is adequate, it appears that moderate

psychological predisposition and minimal social mediation made for a low probability of the outbreak of civil violence in Brazil. With the same qualifications, both the psychological predisposition and social mediation making for violent civil uprising were at a very high level in the Dominican Republic prior to the outbreak of civil war.

It is beyond the scope of this discussion to consider the conditions of actual outbreak and the subsequent organization of violent revolutionary uprisings. Suffice it to say that a considerable number of factors, some of them quite accidental, appear to enter into the actual outbreak of violence. Factors of leadership, of specific personalities, of who is at home when the police come, of the season of the year and the weather of the day, of a single trigger-happy soldier may influence the precipitation of violence. But the case of Brazil suggests that where the preconditions for violence have only moderate force there is considerable tolerance for provocative incidents. The Dominican case—especially the behavior of persons who were mobilized from distant parts of the countryside—suggests that when the preconditions have great strength, even relatively minor provocation may precipitate violent response.

Conclusion

Exploration of the applicability of a general theoretical explanation for the likelihood of civil violence has suggested some of the possibilities and illustrated some of the difficulties in bridging the gap between theory and empirical case study of the psychology of participants. At this point, it can be said that the model succeeds in providing a guide to the assessment of specific cases and that the case-material provides suggestive empirical validation of the principal propositions. It must also be said that the evidence suggests that fairly extensive modification of the propositional statements will be necessary in order to evolve procedures for case study, and that some of the lesser propositions may not prove valid in empirical circumstances—a question that can be answered only by accumulated case studies. Finally, it appears to me that, although we are very far from possessing a reliable capability for predicting the likelihood of civil violence in specific societies, there is an encouraging possibility for developing such a capability by utilizing the Gurr model as the basis for a series of case studies.

ECONOMIC AND SOCIAL CORRELATES OF GOVERNMENT CONTROL IN SOUTH VIETNAM

Anthony J. Russo, Jr.

The purpose of this study is to explore the relationship between human welfare and resistance in rural South Vietnam using quantitative empirical data.

When I undertook this study I held the view that the war in Vietnam was a class war—between the rich and the poor, the peasants and the city-bred. This is not to say that I felt that ambitions of the men in Hanoi were not important, or that communist ideology was not a factor; I felt, though, that these things were secondary and that the forces which sustained hostilities and increasing levels of violence were a direct result of the enormous economic and social cleavages within Vietnamese society and the fact that these cleavages were highly related to the usual differences between urban and rural cultures. The government in Saigon was comprised of men who were wealthy, urban, formally educated, and strongly influenced by the French colonial presence (most had fought with the French against the Viet Minh). The Viet Cong were peasants, had a strong Vietnamese identity, and had inherited the legacy of the Viet Minh.

This view is not a universal one. In fact, a study by E. J. Mitchell claims to show that quite the opposite is true—the richer peasants tend to support the Viet Cong, but the poorer do not.[1] Mitchell presents a detailed statistical model to support his contention, showing a positive relationship between government control and a measure of inequality in the sizes of farms. He sees the results of his study as being something of a challenge to U.S. policy in Vietnam which emphasizes economic reform. This is actually not true: the U.S. has paid unprecedented lip service to the role of economic development and reform, but in practice

[1] E. J. Mitchell, "Inequality and Insurgency: A Statistical Study of South Vietnam," *World Politics*, XX (April 1968), 421–438.

has done little to promote it, probably because U.S. policy-makers cannot agree on the importance of development and reform,[2] and their persistence in viewing the conflict as one in which conventional military strategies (e.g., "search and destroy" operations and heavy reliance upon artillery and air power) are the only ones likely to provide substantial payoffs. In South Vietnam there has been no major effort to promote economic or social reform.

This study finds that geographic variations in rural income, farm sizes, and religion are highly correlated with geographic variations in the extent of control by the Saigon Government (Saigon control is relatively high where rural income is relatively high). The Mitchell paper is referred to frequently throughout because the findings presented here are in substantial conflict with its findings.

Standard multiple regression techniques comprise the principal statistical tools I employ in two approaches: the analysis of variations in province aggregates of data (using 1960 province boundaries) and the analysis of variations in data on the hamlet level. Unfortunately, it was necessary to exclude the Central Highlands from the study because complete data were not available for that region; the analyses include the Central Lowlands (referred to hereafter as the *Central Region*) and the areas designated by the U.S. Government as III and IV Corps (referred to hereafter as the *Southern Region*).

[2] "Land Reform in Vietnam," *20th Report by the Committee on Government Operations, House Report No. 1142*, March 5, 1968. This report draws attention to differences among U.S. officials which have impeded progress in agrarian reform (p. 15). Generally, the report is critical of the lack of progress, but an anti-reform statement is appended to the report by dissenting members of the committee who use the Mitchell study to support their position (p. 19).

Province Analysis

There are many ways to view inequality in distributions of welfare and more than a few indices available for quantifying the concept. Once we select a welfare measure, or measures, we can study the differences in the means of cases, or the differences in the differences (the *between-group variance* or the *within-group variances*). There are 26 provinces in the principal areas of South Vietnam—the Central and Southern Regions—and data are available for each. We have analyzed variations in the Saigon Government's control from province to province with regard to measures of welfare, and the degree to which control and welfare are related. We also consider the effects of religion and pure regional differences. The Hoa Hao religion is important because the Hoa Hao people, whose principal strength lies in Five southern provinces (see Table 1), exert a degree of local autonomy not practiced in any other part of the country. Regional differences are important because the Central Region (from and including Binh Thuan Province northward to the 17th parallel) and the Southern Region represent different levels of homogeneity; the two areas could almost be two different countries. The Central Region was settled long before the Southern Region, experienced less French influence, and has maintained strong ties with traditional Vietnamese culture, customs, and habits. The Southern Region, however, was settled more recently when the Vietnamese drove out the Cambodians (the Southern Region was once part of the Khmer Kingdom) and later French influence was more profound, the French figuring heavily in shaping the economy of the region and its land tenure characteristics. Religious practices in the two regions are also quite different; the

Table 1

PROVINCE DATA MATRIX

Province	I Per Capita Income (Thousands of Piastres)[a]	L/Ls Ratio of Mean of Subsistence Land Holding[b]	HH Percentage Population in Hoa Hao Religion[c]	g Gini Index of Inequality in Size of Land Holdings[b]	D_s Southern Dummy Variable	D_c Central Dummy Variable	C Percentage Hamlets Under Saigon Control (1965)[d]
An Giang	3.94	10.5	75	.62	1	0	75
An Xuyen	4.38	14.3	0	.44	1	0	27
Ba Xuyen	3.90	13.7	1	.60	1	0	24
Bien Hoa	4.75	4.6	0	.67	1	0	31
Binh Dinh	2.36	2.3	0	.38	0	1	9
Binh Duong	4.31	3.9	0	.54	1	0	18
Binh Thuan	2.90	4.6	0	.66	0	1	32
Dinh Tuong	6.33	7.6	0	.49	1	0	31
Khanh Hoa	3.34	4.2	0	.62	0	1	43
Kien Giang	4.40	9.6	1	.69	1	0	22
Kien Hoa	4.80	4.6	0	.57	1	0	24
Kien Phong	4.02	10.1	28	.60	1	0	42
Kien Tuong	5.17	14.3	26	.48	1	0	45
Long An	4.71	9.4	0	.42	1	0	32
Long Khanh	5.59	4.8	0	.55	1	0	25
Ninh Thuan	4.05	5.5	0	.74	0	1	76
Phong Dinh	3.87	8.3	10	.42	1	0	28
Phuoc Tuy	6.64	5.1	0	.69	1	0	52
Phu Yen	2.92	3.1	0	.59	0	1	13
Quang Nam	2.83	1.5	0	.40	0	1	18
Quang Ngai	2.22	2.4	0	.45	0	1	18
Quang Tri	3.32	1.5	0	.45	0	1	12
Tay Ninh	3.32	5.7	0	.41	1	0	22
Thua Thien	3.90	2.7	0	.50	0	1	33
Vinh Binh	4.53	9.3	0	.45	1	0	19
Vinh Long	5.96	5.9	20	.44	1	0	64
Regional province averages							
Southern	4.74	8.34	9.5	.53	—	—	34
Central	3.09	3.09	0	.53	—	—	28

[a] Robert H., Stroup, "Rural Income and Expenditure Sample Survey: Preliminary Report," United States Agency for International Development, 1965.

[b] g and L/Ls were calculated from data given in "Report on the Agricultural Census of Vietnam," Department of Rural Affairs, Republic of Vietnam, 1961.

[c] Estimates of Hoa Hao population were taken from "The Religions of Vietnam in Faith and Fact," Southeast Asia Religious Project, Fleet Marine Force Pacific/IMAC (Forward), FPO San Francisco, 96602.

[d] Control Data are those used by Mitchell, *op. cit.*

Hoa Hao and Cao Dai sects are strong in the Southern Region, whereas there are no Hoa Hao and very few Cao Dai in the Central Region.

We investigated the following hypotheses:

1. Saigon Government control increases (or decreases) in direct proportion to increases (or decreases) in measures of rural welfare.

2. Saigon Government control is greater in provinces with substantial percentages of Hoa Hao population and increases proportionately as the Hoa Hao population increases.

3. Relationships between control and welfare differ in the Southern and

Central Regions, the relationship being stronger in the Central Region.

The multiple regression model used to test these hypotheses is as follows[3]:

$$\hat{C} = -11.9 + 8.5I + 16.4D_cI \quad (1)$$
$$\phantom{\hat{C} = }(2.82) \quad (2.50)$$
$$-37D_c + .75HH$$
$$(-1.55) \quad (5.43)$$
$$\bar{R}^2 = .66 \quad F = 13.0 \quad N = 26$$

where: $C =$ percentage of hamlets under Saigon control (data are taken from the Mitchell study);

$I =$ estimates of per capita income, 1000's piastres (VN$) per person;

$HH =$ estimated percentage of province population in the Hoa Hao religion;

$D_c = 1$ for Central Region; and $= 0$ for Southern Region.

Dummy variables are employed to test the hypothesis that the relationship between control (C) and income (I) is stronger in the Central Regon.[4]

For the Central Region $(D_c = 1)$, equation (1) becomes:

$$\hat{C} = -48.9 + 24.9I \quad (2)$$

For the Southern Region $(D_c = 0)$ equation (1) becomes:

$$C = -11.9 + 8.5I + .75HH \quad (3)$$

The Hoa Hao term is dropped in equation (2) because there are no Hoa Hao in the Central Region (see Table 2). In other words, in the Central Region the percentage of hamlets under Saigon

[3] The values shown in parentheses beneath the regression coefficients are t values (the ratio of the regression coefficient to its standard error). The higher the t value the more statistically significant is the regression coefficient.
[4] A good explanation of the use of dummy variables in this fashion is given in J. Johnston, *Econometric Methods* (New York: McGraw-Hill Book Company, 1963), pp. 221–28.

Table 2

CORRELATION MATRIX FOR PROVINCE DATA

	C	I	L/L_s	HH	g
C	1	.40	.28	.60	.45
I		1	.35	.08	.19
L/L_s			1	.39	.05
HH				1	.10
g					1

control increases 24.9 percent for each increase in rural per capita income of 1,000 piastres (5 to 10 U.S. dollars, depending upon which exchange rates are used). In the Southern Region, Saigon control increases 8.5 percent for each increase in per capita income of 1,000 piastres and .75 percent for each 1 percent increase in Hoa Hao population.

The three hypotheses stated above are strongly supported by the statistical analysis thus far. Data from only one year (1965) have been used, but control patterns have not changed markedly over the course of the war. Areas of strong Viet Cong influence in the early years of the war remain strongly pro-Viet Cong. Also, as will be shown below in the hamlet analysis, 1967 control data indicate much the same relationship with income.

$\bar{R}^2$ is the multiple correlation coefficient squared; its numerical value is equivalent to the percentage of variance in the dependent variable that is said to be "explained." In the regression model shown in equation (1), 66 percent of the variance is explained. The remaining 34 percent of the variance which is unexplained may be attributable to error in the data or variables which have not been included in the model.

There are other measures of rural welfare besides per capita income. One variable which provides additional explanatory power in a model similar to equation (1) is the ratio of the mean size of a landholding ($\bar{L}$) to a "minimum subsistence" landholding (L_s). $L_s =$ the amount of land required to provide an average Vietnamese family (5.3 persons) with a daily rice ration of 250 grams per person for one year; it reflects variations in rice yields across South Vietnam and ranges from .17 hectares in some provinces in the Mekong Delta to .40 hectares in Quang Tri—the northernmost province. $\bar{L}/L_s$ reflects the extent to which farmers are securely above the minimum subsistence level. When $\bar{L}/L_s$ is added to the mix of independent variables shown in equation (1) it is found to be highly significant in the Central Region and to have no effect in the Southern Region. We might expect this because $\bar{L}$ is "contaminated" to a certain extent in the Southern Region by the presence of very large holdings; this makes interpretation of $\bar{L}$ uncertain because it is not clear how it reflects the sizes of family farms. In the Central Region, however, $\bar{L}$ is a clear reflection of sizes of family farms because there are virtually no large holdings.

The results of the regression analysis including L/L_s are as follows[5]:

$$\hat{C} = -33.9 + 9.0I + .76HH$$
$$\quad\quad\quad (4.51)\quad (7.18)$$
$$+ 10.9\frac{\bar{L}}{L_s} - 10.9\frac{\bar{L}}{L_s}D_s + 17.3D_s$$
$$\quad (5.43)\quad\quad (-5.13)\quad\quad (1.68)$$
$$\tag{4}$$

$$\bar{R}^2 = .82 \quad F = 22.5 \quad N = 26$$

For the Central Region ($D_s = 0$), equation (4) becomes:

$$\hat{C} = -33.9 + 9.0I + 10.9\frac{\bar{L}}{L_s} \tag{5}$$

For the Southern Region ($D_c = 1$), equation (4) becomes:

[5] D_s is used instead of D_c because it shows in a more straightforward fashion how the $\bar{L}/L_s$ term drops out completely for the Southern Region.

$$\hat{C} = -16.6 + 9.0I + .76HH \tag{6}$$

Equation (4) is a significantly better predictor than equation (1) since 82 percent of the variance is explained (compared to 66 percent in the first model), and the t values as well as the overall F value are much stronger. The difference between the two models is apparent almost entirely in the equations for the Central Region. Note how equations (3) and (6) for the Southern Region are virtually the same, whereas equations (2) and (5) for the Central Region show that when L/L_s is included it provides a degree of explanatory power previously provided by income alone, but it does a more precise job because a higher multiple correlation is achieved.

It would make sense to add a land variable to an income welfare index in the Central Region because land there is more of an issue than in the Southern Region: there are relatively more farmers, their holdings are much smaller and less fertile, and their aspirations for land, naturally, are much greater. The Stroup Survey of rural income and expenditure gives an occupational breakdown for rural heads of household.[6] In addition to the farmer category there are merchants, peddlers, fishermen, clerical workers, laborers (skilled, semi-skilled, and unskilled), etc. In the Central Region 65 percent were listed as farmers compared to 53 percent in the Southern Region. Also, in the Central Region, the average holding is .67 hectares compared to 1.71 hectares in the Southern Region. The Stroup Survey also showed that when rural people were asked what they would buy with a hypothetical increase in income of 10,000 piastres per year, 37 percent in the Central Region replied

[6] Robert H. Stroup, "Rural Income and Expenditure Sample Survey: Preliminary Report," United States Agency for International Development, 1965.

that they would "buy land," compared to 22 percent in the Southern Region.

Since we have seen empirical support for our hypothesis that Saigon control is correlated with higher income and, in the Central Region, larger family farms, we must next ask how this finding can be reconciled with Mitchell's finding of a positive correlation between his measure of inequality and control and his subsequent conclusion that the poor support Saigon more than the rich. Briefly, the answer is that income and inequality are positively correlated, not negatively, as Mitchell assumed. In examining this question I have used a more conventional measure of inequality: the Gini index (see Table 1).[7] I find that the Gini index (g) is indeed correlated ($r = .45$, $N = 26$) with control (C), but that the strength of the correlation lies in the Central Region. In the Southern Region ($N = 17$) the correlation between C and g is .17, which is not statistically significant; in the Central Region ($N = 9$) the correlation is .80, which is highly significant. Thus, although there is a significant overall association between the two variables, we can be misled if we do not examine the two regions separately. The relationship is strong only in the Central Region, where g is highly correlated with income ($r = .57$) and $\bar{L}/L_s$ ($r = .94$).

I also found that the Gini inequality index contributes nothing when added to the regression model shown in equation (4). The Gini index and the coefficient of variation were both tried in equation (4) and each turned out to be insignificant, whereas coefficients and t values of the other variables remained essentially unchanged.

The analysis up to this point has been based upon provincial data. In the next phase of this study we will look at the situation at the hamlet level; as will be seen, the results from the hamlet analysis are very similar to the provincial analysis: income is a strong explanatory variable, and when it is combined with the regional dummy variable it shows very similar patterns.

Hamlet Analysis[8]

In this phase of the analysis we will investigate the relationship between the degree of Saigon government control and per capita income at the hamlet level for a random sample of 94 hamlets. Hamlet data came from two sources: (1) the extent of Saigon control is represented by indices from the U.S. Government Hamlet Evaluation System (HES) reports of December 1967, and (2) per capita income data are taken from information gathered in an income and expenditure survey conducted in the rural areas in 1964.[9] The HES data are subjective security ratings, supplied by local American advisors, on a scale which varies from 0 to 5 (0 = total uncontested Viet Cong control and 5 = total uncontested Saigon control); the data are compiled monthly for virtually all hamlets (approximately 13,000) in South Vietnam. We are not concerned with the absolute levels of the hamlet ratings but rather with their variation from hamlet to hamlet. Therefore, any bias in the ratings (positive or negative) is not likely to have substantial effects on the relationships uncovered so long as it is consistently

[7] For an explanation of the Gini index, see Bruce M. Russett, *Trends in World Politics* (New York: The Macmillan Company, 1965), pp. 117–21.

[8] Hamlets are the smallest jurisdictional areas in South Vietnam. Usually several hamlets make up one village and several villages make up one district. Provinces are composed of three to five districts.

[9] Stroup, *op. cit.* The author is indebted to Professor Stroup for making available the entire set of raw data gathered in the survey (a total of 2,910 quite detailed household interviews).

high (or low); random errors in the security indices will simply make the relationships appear to be a little less strong (in a probabilistic sense) than they actually are.

The set of hamlets sampled for the economic survey in 1964 are a biased sample because interviewers were unable to gather data in areas under strong Viet Cong control. Strictly speaking, then, the relationships we uncover in the hamlet analysis apply to that hamlet population not strongly controlled by the Viet Cong in 1964. This is a meaningful population about which one can draw inferences, but the more interesting question is, To what extent is it possible to generalize the findings to all hamlets, i.e., the population of hamlets that would have been represented by a sample not biased by security conditions in 1964? As far as I can determine, there are no statistical tools that can provide an unequivocal answer. However, I believe that the security bias in the sample does not seriously affect the relationships we find between Saigon Government control and per capita income; in fact, it is likely that the security bias weakens the relationships much the same as the correlation between two variables with a bivariate normal distribution tends to be diminished when the sample points with the highest (or lowest) values of one of the variables are eliminated.

Unfortunately, specific data were not available on hamlet religion or land fertility, so it was not possible to use all the variables used in the province analysis. The first regression model is comparable to equation (1) in the province analysis, leaving out the Hoa Hao term for which we have no data. The results are as follows:

$$\hat{S} = 1.62 + .23X + .49XD_c \quad (7)$$
$$(3.25) \quad (2.41)$$
$$- 1.44D_c$$
$$(-1.98)$$
$$\bar{R}^2 = .25 \quad F = 10.1 \quad N = 94$$

where: $S =$ hamlet security rating (December 1967), and
$X =$ 1964 hamlet per capita income, 1000's piastres per person.

For the Central Region $(D_c = 1)$:

$$\hat{S} = .18 + .72X \quad (8)$$

For the Southern Region $(D_c = 0)$:

$$\hat{S} = 1.62 + .23X \quad (9)$$

In the Central Region the hamlet security rating increases by .72 for each increase of 1,000 piastres in per capita income. In the Southern Region the relationship is weaker; the hamlet security rating increases by .23 for each increase of 1,000 piastres in per capita income.

The important thing to note here is the similarity between equations (7) and (1); in both the province model and the hamlet model the income effect (in terms of the magnitudes of the regression coefficients) in the Central Region is about three times what it is in the Southern Region. This is illustrated more vividly by showing both equations (1) and (7) in nondimensional form (i.e., expressing each variable in terms of its standard deviation):

Province model
$$\hat{U}_c = -.66 + .54U_I + 1.05U_ID_c \quad (10)$$
$$- 2.05D_c + .68U_{HH}$$

Hamlet model
$$\hat{U}_S = 1.35 + .38U_X + .80U_XD_c \quad (11)$$
$$-1.2D_c$$

The two models show a fair degree of similarity. The coefficients in the hamlet model are slightly weaker than in the province model and the fixed term is positive, whereas in the province model it is negative. It is possible, and likely, that the security bias, discussed above, is responsible for the difference. A weakening of the relationship would tend to make the fixed term have a higher value, and in this case it does.

General Comments and a Discussion of the Findings

The main conclusion of this study is that economic and social factors have been predominantly important in the struggle in South Vietnam. The variance in control patterns is explained extraordinarily well without taking into account military or strategic considerations, and the basic relationship between control and income holds up whether we look at the situation in 1965 (as in the province analysis) or in 1967 (as in the hamlet analysis).[10] Certainly there is error in the data, and much of the unexplained variance has to be attributed to this error. That leaves little variance unaccounted for and does not say much for the effectiveness of the vast amount of military resources that have been expended over the years.

Thus far we have not considered the underlying causes of the conflict in Vietnam, nor the specific factors which precipitated hostilities; we have, rather, concentrated on the question of which areas are relatively weaker or stronger in support for the Saigon Government or the Viet Cong, and the factors which explain the variance in intensity of support. There is little doubt that opposition to the various Saigon regimes manifests strong "class" overtones; class is placed in quotation marks because we do not see homogeneous groups either wholly for or against

[10] Actually, there has been little change in the geographical pattern of Viet Cong control throughout the course of the war, although there have been small local fluctuations, and also variations in overall intensity such as the period immediately after the overthrow of the Diem regime in 1963, and after the 1968 Tet offensive. In both cases, the level of Viet Cong control seemed to rise uniformly throughout the country.

the Saigon Government, but a continuous spectrum ranging from poorer to richer areas.

The empirical relationships developed in this study probably also reflect the "cultural distance" between the urban, western-oriented Saigon regime and the rural, agricultural, more traditional peasant. In contrast, however, it is difficult to find much "distance" between the Viet Cong and the peasants —which does not necessarily mean that the Viet Cong are loved. However, the lack of cultural distance between the Viet Cong cadre and the peasants can mean that the cadre has the same rough peasant features and wears the same faded, worn-out clothes as the peasants. When he talks to them, whether they like what he says or not, they understand him, and they also understand what their role is with regard to the system he represents. They know how their behavior relates to the powers of rewards and punishments he possesses; he is capable of "honeyed talk," as it is often described by the peasants, or ruthless terrorism, and he usually has specific reasons for the use of both. However, the cadre who represents the Saigon Government in the hamlet presents an entirely different image: his clean, store-bought clothes and his smooth facial features betray his class origins and often he is noticeably uncomfortable in his surroundings, for he simply does not like being in the hamlet. Just as the peasant does not necessarily love the Viet Cong cadre, he does not necessarily hate the city boy who represents Saigon. He may envy him, admire his status, and wish that he could be like him, but the peasant cannot relate to him on an emotional level, nor can he see how his behavior relates to the authority pattern represented by the city boy: Consequently, the peasant sees no role for himself in the system represented by the Saigon Government. The Allies may dispense artillery and napalm—or economic aid and medical care—but the peasant sees no correlation between either form of assistance and his behavior. His choices are limited: the Viet Cong at least provide a role for him, but all too often the Saigon Government merely provides indifference and uncertainty.

Since my statistical results and conclusions are in conflict with Mitchell's findings, it is useful to examine his work more closely. One of his most prominent mistakes was that he equates his measure of inequality with poverty.[11] This illustrates a very important point: measures of inequality such as the one Mitchell used (and the Gini coefficient, too, for that matter) may be very useful if we are examining one group and want an index to summarize its internal degree of inequality. If we are comparing groups, however, we have to be careful. One group might have a low inequality index, but everyone could be equally poor. Another group might have a high degree of inequality, but the least well off in this group could still have an adequate living standard. For this reason comparisons require absolute measures of welfare such as per capita income (which also has its shortcomings, although they are less important than what we are discussing here). This is precisely the trap into which Mitchell falls. Provinces where inequality (as measured by a single index) is highest are often the richest. We have shown in this study that the strength of Mitchell's relationship between Saigon control and inequality is positively correlated with per capita income, and that when per capita income and the Gini index (as well as the coefficient of variation) are put into the same regression equation, with Saigon con-

trol as the dependent variable, inequality is not significant.

In discussing his findings which suggest that the richer peasants—not the poorer—have provided the resistance in Vietnam, Mitchell asks: "In terms of human behavior, how is one to explain these findings? Part of the explanation may lie in the frequently mentioned docility and low aspirations of poorer peasants."[12] There is no doubt some truth in the hypothesis that poorer peasants tend to be conservative and have low aspirations; however, analysis must go much farther or we shall fail to understand much about the dynamics of Third World revolutions. The important point is that Mitchell stopped short of consideration of changes in aspirations brought on by agit/prop activities by the revolutionaries. When poverty exists in a society it eventually becomes an issue among certain elements of the elite, at which time members of this elite become revolutionaries and agitation and the spreading of propaganda begin. The business of the revolutionary agit/prop is to change aspirations in the poverty sector in order to recruit support for change. The revolutionary elite, often from the middle and upper economic classes, are well aware of the docility of poorer peasants, and see this docility as one of the major barriers to be overcome in the initial stages of a movement. Thus, it is misleading if we consider the poor peasant to be isolated and ignore his interaction with the elite. When there is no tradition of revolutionary agitation, the gap between aspirations and income, i.e., relative economic deprivation, may increase as we consider higher and higher income levels. But this is only one kind of relative deprivation, in which aspirations are a function of standard of living. The aspirational component due

[11] There are other errors in his paper also; a major one is that the regression model he reports contains terms which are not statistically significant, although he reports them as being highly significant.

[12] Op. cit., pp. 422–23.

to agit/prop activities is quite different and we eventually have to consider the combination of both. And there is still the question of which side in a revolutionary situation the individual sees as being most likely to fulfill his aspirations. Overall aspirations are more likely to be solely a function of standard of living in cases wherein there is either tradition of revolutionary agitation, or that agitation has not yet grown to any significant proportions.

In Vietnam it is well known that the Viet Cong appeal particularly to the poor for support and have long had a near monopoly on access to the peasant. The Saigon regimes, by contrast, have been patronizing and contemptuous toward peasants, precluding the formation of a working mass–elite relationship, with the consequence that the authority structure is ill-defined: a functional role for rural elements does not really exist. Saigon policy reflects the westernized elite's attitudes toward peasants; an ex-Viet Cong who had been a Party member in Kien Giang Province and had worked for years as an NLF political cadre stated that[13]:

It would be hard to work for the government as a political worker because it requires degrees and diplomas. I think I am capable of doing psychological warfare, but I don't have the required educational background.

In the various forms it has taken since the departure of the French, the Saigon Government has been more responsive to elite desires than to pressures from below. There is very little viable contact between the masses and the elite. The Vietnamese peasant can perceive little relationship (other than a random one) between his behavior and the pattern of rewards and punishments meted

[13] RAND Corporation Interview AD-543. The Rand Corporation series of interviews with ex-Viet Cong has been made available for general use by scholars.

out by representatives of the central government. By contrast, the Viet Cong maintain a highly organized and consistent pattern of persuasion and coercion with the peasant in which the peasant has no problem comprehending his role. In many ways the Viet Cong's exercise of power can be said to be more congruent with peasant modes of behavior than that of the Saigon Government. The western orientation of the governmental elite and the presence of Americans makes the development of an authority pattern congruent with traditional ones difficult. The central authority is thus caught in a situation in which it is unable to compete with the Viet Cong for the resources of its citizens, nor can it interdict the flow of resources from the villagers to the Viet Cong through political action.

There are thus two factors which influence the overall extent of aspirations among the peasants: their *level of aspirations* is increased by revolutionary agit/prop activities, whereas the *intensity* of those aspirations is roughly a function of the peasants' positions on the standard-of-living scale. The process of aspirational change is a dynamic one in which the respective magnitudes of these two components change with time. It is reasonable to speculate that the comparative magnitudes of the two aspirations components will determine which side the peasant sees as fulfilling his aspirations. For poor peasants with high aspirations, the major component is likely to be the result of agit/prop activity, and they are likely to believe that their aspirations will be realized by support and cooperation with the revolutionaries. Where the other aspirations component predominates it is likely that the *status quo* is the preferable alternative.

In summary, the results of this study are in conflict with earlier work on the same subject which supported an antireform position as being the best strategy for the Saigon government. This study finds that, in the Southern Region of South Vietnam, Saigon control is highest in areas where rural income is highest and where local autonomy, as in the Hoa Hao areas, is greatest. In the Central Region, Saigon control is highest where income is highest, where the size of the average peasant's farm is greatest, and where land is most fertile. Analyses at two levels of aggregation (province and hamlet) were found to give similar results, and, in the province analysis, the socioeconomic variables employed left unexplained so little variance in control that one wonders whether the military efforts of the past decade have had any effect. The roots of the conflict and the reasons for its persistence appear to have been overwhelmingly political and socioeconomic in nature.

Editor's Note: Mr. Russo has asked that the reader be told something about the curious history of this chapter. The author made the study described here while employed by the RAND Corporation. The related study by E. J. Mitchell, whose results are shown by Mr. Russo to be in serious error, also originated as a RAND study and was published as both a classified and unclassified paper by RAND, and later by the journal *World Politics*. It is said to have been influential among policy makers dealing with the American intervention in South Vietnam. RAND chose not to circulate or publish Mr. Russo's revision, though it did grant permission for this commercial publication.

Another reanalysis and critique of Mitchell's study is Jeffery M. Paige, "Inequality and Insurgency in Vietnam: A Re-Analysis," *World Politics*, XXIII (October 1970), 24-37. Professor Paige's conclusion parallels Mr. Russo's: "Mitchell's analysis is based on questionable history, vague theory, and inaccurate observation. To his credit, he published the data on which his conclusions were based, considerably simplifying the job of rebuttal" (p. 37). But of course any policy actions based on Dr. Mitchell's faulty analysis cannot be reversed by academic rebuttals.

THE SCOTTISH NATIONAL PARTY: NONVIOLENT SEPARATISM AND THEORIES OF VIOLENCE

John E. Schwarz*

There is a sizeable number of separatist movements in contemporary political life.[1] Some of them have attracted widespread support, others have not; some are surrounded by violence, others are not. It is the combination of the size and tactics of separatist movements that we wish to examine. Our purpose is to inquire into the conditions that enable regional separatism to attract widespread support without also eliciting violence. Our conclusions will be based on one separatist movement that managed to accomplish this feat, the Scottish National Party.[2]

The Scottish National Party is dedicated to the withdrawal of Scotland from the United Kingdom and the simultaneous establishment of a sovereign Scottish state. It is manned by local (constituency) leaders who are fairly

* The author wishes to acknowledge a grant received from the Office of International Programs, University of Minnesota, enabling him to carry out the research embodied in this study.

[1] Many of the contemporary separatist movements are covered in Walker Connor, "Self-Determination: The New Phase," *World Politics*, XX (October 1967), 39–54; more detailed descriptions of separatist movements in Wales, Brittany, and Quebec may be found in E. Hudson Davies, "Welsh Nationalism," *Political Quarterly*, XXXIX (July-September 1968), 322–32; J. E. S. Hayward, "From Functional Regionalism to Functional Representation in France: The Battle of Brittany," *Political Studies*, XVII (March 1969), 48–75; and Frank L. Wilson, "French-Canadian Separatism," *Western Political Quarterly*, XX (March 1967), 116–32.

[2] A history of Scottish nationalism may be found in Sir R. Coupland, *Welsh and Scottish Nationalism* (London 1954). This is brought up to date in James G. Kellas, *Modern Scotland: The Nation Since 1870* (New York 1968), 201–206.

young[3] and who have had little prior experience in the practice of politics. Few were at all active either in other political parties or in the S.N.P. before they assumed leadership positions.[4]

Moreover, conditions have been such as to stimulate a rapid surge of support for the Party in the mid-1960's. Table I, for example, indicates the Party's rapid membership and organizational growth from 1962 through 1968.

Table I

THE GROWTH OF THE ORGANIZATION AND MEMBERSHIP OF THE S.N.P., 1962–1968

	Numbers of Organized Constituencies	Numbers of Organized Branches	Membership
1962	0	21	2,000
1966	16	110	42,000
1967	33	263	55,000
1968	62	472	120,000

The S.N.P. has also been able recently to attract larger percentages of the regional vote. It has approximately doubled its vote in each national election since 1959, reaching 128,000 votes in the most recent election, in 1966. Although its vote in 1966 still represented only 5 percent of the total Scottish vote, there is every indication that the Party has gained considerably since that time. This is implied, of course, in the Party's rapid increase in membership since 1966. It is also indicated by the 1968 municipal elections held in Scotland. In these elections the S.N.P. became the largest of five electoral parties in Scotland, with approximately 35 percent of the vote. Public-opinion polls carried out in the spring of 1968 indicated that the Party could count on the support of approximately 20 percent of the Scottish electorate in a parliamentary fight.[5] By 1968, then, the S.N.P. had become a formidable separatist movement.

The S.N.P. local leaders were youthful and were newcomers to the political game; they were devoted to regional withdrawal from the established political system; and they were operating under a set of conditions that were apparently wearing even to the wider public. In the light of these facts, it would not have been surprising had the development of this movement been accompanied by a rather high incidence of violence. But the Party was not one that advocated violence to achieve its goal. Its leaders used democratic methods in regard to both the internal organization of the Party and the use of the ballot box as the sole focus for their struggle.[6] Very few of

---

[3] Whereas 79 percent of the local Labour and Conservative leaders interviewed in this study were above the age of 37, only 43 percent of the S.N.P. leaders were above this age.

[4] Only 10 percent of the local S.N.P. leaders had previously been members of other political parties and an additional 7 percent had done limited door-step work. Forty percent of the S.N.P. local leaders had been members of the Party for less than 3 years and 68 percent had been members for less than 5 years. In addition, information sheets handed in to the Party headquarters by 122 S.N.P. candidates for council office indicate that only 8 percent of these candidates recalled any previous political activity, that approximately 62 percent had been members of the S.N.P. for 3 years or less, and that 78 percent had been members for 5 years or less.

[5] BBC-1, "The Disunited Kingdom? An Enquiry into the Forces of Nationalism in Scotland and Wales," transmitted on June 12, 1968, reported a public opinion poll in which 17 percent of the Scottish sample desired complete Scottish independence and an additional 46 percent wanted a regional Scottish government. The figures can be found on BBC-1, 5318/5610, Section h, p.ii. Polls carried out in both Glasgow and Dundee in the spring of 1968 indicated that from 20 to 30 percent of the public intended to vote S.N.P. in general elections. See, for example, *The Scotsman*, July 8, 1968.

[6] The importance S.N.P. local leaders attach to democratic methods is indicated by their answers to the following question: "Is there anything essentially different about the S.N.P.

the local Party leaders either advocated or condoned the use of violence; most felt that any member who did use violence ought to be expelled from the Party.[7] Although there have been a few unsponsored acts of violence by individual members, even these have been atypical.[8]

If conditions were such as to engender the rapid growth of a separatist movement, why did they not also elicit violence? We shall attempt to answer this question by the use of theories of violence. We based our decision to use these theories on the notion that many of the independent variables they employ are potentially continuous ones. Their continuous nature opens the possibility that they could be present at moderate levels sufficient to produce growing support of a nonviolent kind for Scottish separatism but not present at levels sufficiently extreme to elicit violence. In this way, theories of violence might help to account for *both* the rapid surge of the movement and its nonviolent character. We shall therefore focus our attention on the levels at which variables included in theories of violence were present in the Scottish case and, in effect, use these theories not only as theories of violence but also as theories pertaining to nonviolent political change.

I

Theories of violence often focus on psychological factors as instigators of violence.[9] The psychological variables central to these theories may be grouped into the following categories (there is, to be sure, some overlap): (1) intra-personal tension; (2) feelings of isolation or separation from the body politic; (3) feelings of deprivation; and (4) participation in a prospering culture perceived to be distinct from the dominant culture.

We have made certain assumptions in dealing with these variables. First, we have assumed that these variables, if taken together, would account for a high percentage of cases of violent movements. Thus, the likelihood of violence is reduced to the extent that any of these variables is not present to a high degree and becomes minimal if none of these variables is present to a high degree. This assumption is plausible in the light of recent findings.[10] A second assumption was also required. Upon occasion it was possible to apply a variable or an aspect of a variable solely to the local leadership, without benefit of aggregate or interview data for other Party members or for the wider public. Therefore, it was necessary to assume that in such a case observation of the local leadership constituted an adequate test of the variable in question.

---

from the other parties to which you attach great importance besides the policy of Scottish independence?" Although it is an open-ended question, 63 percent of the respondents said the S.N.P. was more democratically organized and more responsive to local demands and pressures. A second indication of the importance most S.N.P. local leaders attach to democratic methods is that 83 percent of them said that no political party (not even a unionist party) should be outlawed if Scotland becomes independent.

[7] Of 40 S.N.P. local leaders interviewed, 36 said that any member who used violence ought to be immediately expelled from the Party, regardless of circumstances.

[8] "Now's the Day, Now's the Hour," *The Economist* (May 11, 1968), 9.

[9] The centrality of psychological variables to most theories of violence is argued in Ted Gurr, "Psychological Factors in Civil Violence," *World Politics*, XX (January 1968), 245–79 [reading 2 in this volume].

[10] Ted Gurr, in "A Causal Model of Civil Strife: A Comparative Analysis Using New Indices," *American Political Science Review*, LXII (December 1968) [reading 10 in this volume], found that "relative deprivation is a necessary precondition for strife" (1122) and that, as a necessary precondition, relative deprivation accounted for 47 percent of the total magnitude of civil strife (1120–21). These findings pertain to only two of the four major psychological variables used in this study.

Most of the psychological variables employed in the study are difficult to measure. Their use in theories of violence is rarely accompanied by precise guidelines by which we may select the appropriate indicators or judge the values that indicators must reach in order to be considered sufficiently critical to produce either violent or nonviolent support. A case study cannot be expected to resolve this kind of problem; moreover, a case study tends to require some indicators that may not have been considered in the theories.[11] In the areas for which this was a problem, therefore, we have utilized indicators or sets of indicators that we thought appropriate to the concepts involved. We made judgments regarding the level of the variable—i.e., critical values—solely on the basis of data forthcoming from these indicators. We shall defend the appropriateness of such judgments in the study.

Theories of violence have been developed on the basis of both aggregate and interview data and we shall also make use of both kinds of data. Very helpful sources for obtaining aggregate data were *The Annual Abstract of Statistics*[12] and secondary sources such as *Why Growth Rates Differ*.[13]

Interview data were forthcoming from a random sample of approximately 20 percent of the most active S.N.P., Conservative, and Labour local party leaders.[14] We interviewed 40 S.N.P.

constituency chairmen or secretaries and 46 constituency secretaries or agents of the Conservative and Labour parties at their places of business or in their homes, at prearranged times. Each interview was approximately three hours long and allowed for a great deal of probing. We made a check for interview error by re-interviewing 14 respondents after a lapse of two months, under completely different conditions. Instead of making a personal appointment at his home or office, we questioned each respondent without notice over the telephone. Out of the approximately fifty original questions, we selected seven for which we felt there lay the greatest likelihood of error (superficial answers, coding errors due to misinterpretation or fatigue on the interviewer's part, etc.). The error discovered was not high (12 percent) and it was random. The results of the study thus seem largely unaffected by error in the interviewing or coding procedures.

We have supplemented our data on local leadership with some data pertaining to the wider population, about both public behavior and public attitudes. Public behavior was indicated by documented surges of public activity on behalf of Scottish nationalism since 1945 (1948–52, 1966–68). It was possible to obtain indicators regarding public attitudes for some of the psychological variables by use of public-opinion polls.

---

11 This is the case especially because regional data for some indicators is not available, so that the researcher is forced to turn to other indicators.

12 Central Statistical Office, *Annual Abstract of Statistics*, HMSO, No. 105, 1968.

13 Edward F. Denison, *Why Growth Rates Differ: Post-War Experience in Nine Western Countries* (Washington 1967).

14 The population of local party officials was calculated on the basis of two active local (constituency) officials per party per constituency. Given 71 Scottish constituencies, this produces a total of 436 active local party

officials for the Conservative, Labour, and Scottish National parties. A random order of 55 constituencies was taken. One S.N.P. local official, who the central party thought was very active, and either one Conservative or one Labourite, was interviewed in 40 constituencies. Again, the central party provided information on the officials it thought were very active. If either the S.N.P. or Conservative or Labour Party local leader could not be interviewed (vacations, no time, etc.), the next constituency on the list of 55 was taken. The total sample of 86 represents approximately 20 percent of the population of 436.

We wish now to place the Scottish movement within the context of existing theories of violence. We shall find that these theories help explain the nonviolent character of the S.N.P. None of the conditions they specify appears to have been present at levels sufficiently critical to elicit violence. On the other hand, we shall attempt to demonstrate that some of the variables, while not present to an extreme degree, were present at levels adequate to help motivate support of a nonviolent nature for the movement. Both aggregate and interview data will indicate the presence of these variables in moderate degrees and suggest the importance of their presence to the development of nonviolent support for Scottish separatism on the part of both the S.N.P. local leaders and the wider public. We shall pay particular attention in the end to the combination of regional and extraregional perceptions that provided the underpinning for the movement.

A first set of theories of violence focuses on intra-personal tension and strain as a significant instigator of violence.[15] We shall use Eckstein's theory as an example. Eckstein postulates that persons who are acutely anomic are susceptible to mass movements of a highly fanatic and presumably violent character. Acute anomie occurs when incongruent social authority patterns obtain. Congruence can be defined as a situation in which "(1) social authority patterns are identical with the governmental pattern, or (2) they constitute a gradual pattern in

a proper segmentation of society, or (3) a high degree of resemblance exists in patterns adjacent to government (parties, interest groups) and one finds throughout the more distant segments (schools, families) a marked departure from functionally appropriate patterns for the sake of imitating the governmental pattern."[16]

By definition, incongruent social authority patterns are present if none of these three conditions exists. Such incongruency requires "the coexistence of different, perhaps even contradictory, norms of conduct in regard to a particular set of actions or an individual's actions in general."[17] That is, incongruency leads to intra-personal strain that, in turn, produces anomie. An example Eckstein provides is that of the incongruent political and social systems of Weimar Germany, which, by giving rise to a fanatical and violent movement, disintegrated only fifteen years after its inception. He compares this to the political and social systems of Britain, which, he argues, have been essentially congruent and free from fanatical or violent movements.

The immediate determining variable for Eckstein is intra-personal strain. Therefore, movements that do not exhibit fanaticism or violence are not likely to include a high percentage of persons suffering from strain. That is, we should not expect such persons to characterize the local leadership of the S.N.P., since the S.N.P. has not been an essentially violent movement.

Eckstein and others who use the same variable give us few guidelines by which we can test this prediction.[18]

[15] See, for example, "A Theory of Stable Democracy," in Harry Eckstein, *Division and Cohesion in Democracy: A Study of Norway* (Princeton 1966); Neil J. Smelser, *Theory of Collective Behavior* (New York 1963); and Chalmers Johnson, *Revolutionary Change* (Boston 1966).

[16] Eckstein, 239–40 (parentheses added).
[17] *Ibid.*, 255.
[18] This is not meant to be critical of Eckstein, for his test focuses on the structural variables rather than on the more immediate psychological variable. Nevertheless, since it is the psychological variable common to these theories, our test focuses on this variable.

Our decision was to use the "Sixteen Personality Factor Test" of the Institute for Personality and Ability Testing,[19] which we administered to each of the eighty-six respondents. One of the factors, Factor C, covered personality characteristics that would appear to be relevant to the matter at hand. Those scoring high on Factor C are considered to be emotionally stable, calm, mature, and realistic about life, with an absence of neurotic fatigue. An opposite decription is of course appropriate for those scoring low on Factor C.[20] The six questions involved in the factor were accompanied by a number of other questions in order to disguise them. The questions of the factor admit a total maximum score of 12 and a total minimum score of 0.

Table II

SCORES OBTAINED BY LOCAL LEADERS OF THE SCOTTISH NATIONAL, CONSERVATIVE, AND LABOUR PARTIES ON FACTOR C OF THE "16 P.F. TEST" (N)

Total Score on Factor C	S.N.P.	Conservative	Labour
11–12	1	3	0
9–10	3	1	4
7– 8	19	10	8
5– 6	15	8	7
3– 4	2	0	5
1– 2	0	0	0
0	0	0	0

[19] Institute for Personality and Ability Testing, *Handbook for the Sixteen Personality Factor Questionnaire* (Champaign, Illinois 1962), 12, by permission of the Institute for Personality and Ability Testing. It is, of course, impossible to know how much the S.N.P. local leaders have changed since they became members of the Party. But there is no significant correlation between the scores and the length of membership in the Party. The distribution of those who have been in the Party less than 2 years is the same as of those who have been in the Party longer than 2 years.

[20] *Ibid.*, 12.

We can see from . . . Table [II] that the distribution of scores is similar, although not exactly identical, for the three parties. It is of particular importance that only two of the forty S.N.P. local leaders are found at the lower end of the scale.

A second factor, Factor Q4, was also utilized. Those scoring high on Factor Q4 are considered to be "tense, irritable, anxious, and in turmoil"; those scoring low are phlegmatic and composed[21] [Table III].

Table III

SCORES OBTAINED BY LOCAL LEADERS OF THE SCOTTISH NATIONAL, CONSERVATIVE, AND LABOUR PARTIES ON FACTOR Q4 OF THE "16 P.F. TEST" (N)

Total Score on Factor Q4	S.N.P.	Conservative	Labour
12–11	0	0	0
10– 9	0	0	1
8– 7	4	3	4
6– 5	5	8	5
4– 3	19	5	9
2– 1	12	6	5
0	0	0	0

The similarity in distribution is less for this factor than it was for Factor C. Yet it is the S.N.P. local leaders who fall lower on the scale—i.e., in the direction away from turmoil and anxiety. No S.N.P. local leader placed at the upper extreme of the scale.

While tests in science can corroborate, they cannot prove, for the next test may always yield disconfirming evidence. The two tests employed in this study do corroborate our expectation that abnormally high levels of intrapersonal strain would not characterize the local leaders of the S.N.P. The tests yield no data to indicate the existence of high degrees of this vari-

[21] *Ibid.*, 19.

able, either on an absolute scale or on a scale relative to the other political parties.

But there are other psychological conditions that also might give rise to violence. A second set of theories focuses on forms of isolation as prominent instigators of violence. Kornhauser, for example, suggests that violence is rooted in mass behavior (direct response to remote objects), which, in turn, is rooted in atomization.[22] Atomization may result from a variety of conditions. One condition is the relation between the individuals and the political system: must individuals make their demands to the political system directly or can they mediate their interests through intermediary groups? A second is the relation between individuals and the wider society: are they integrated with the "opposition" by belonging to and participating in intermediary groups, including the "opposition"? A third is the relation between individuals and the economy: do they perceive their personal economic positions to be deteriorating? A fourth condition is the relation between a region and the wider economy: is the regional economy declining in relationship to the wider economy and, in this sense, becoming isolated from the wider economic system?

Since the S.N.P. is a movement in which violence is neither advocated nor condoned, we must expect that none of these conditions operated at high levels. This appears to have been the case.

The first two conditions leading to individual isolation focus on the intermediary group structure. The British system is one in which strong and effective intermediary groups are present.[23] Scotland is little different along this line,[24] and many of the Scottish intermediary groups are inclusive (in the sense that they have combined with English and Welsh groups to form peak organizations).[25] In addition, most of the local S.N.P. leaders had participated actively in the intermediary group structure before membership in the Party. To be more precise, 84 percent of the local leaders were members of intermediary groups before joining the Party, 58 percent had held either appointive or elective offices in these groups, and 61 percent of the S.N.P. candidates for town-council offices were members of professional, trade, or technical associations.[26] Thus, it would not appear to be the case that intermediary group structures and participation were deficient.

Deteriorating economic positions may also produce feelings of isolation and thereby contribute to mass behavior. Presumably this will be to some extent checked if the intermediary group structure is favorable. Nevertheless, we should note that the type of persons who were drawn into the Poujadist movement, including the leaders, "were tired, discouraged, without hope, without anything . . . who worked harder and longer than before the war and than their parents did but

[22] William Kornhauser, *The Politics of Mass Society* (Glencoe 1963). Allied sociological and political theories are noted, 21–25. The close relationship between mass behavior and violence is made clear by Kornhauser when he quotes Selznick: "Mass behavior is associated . . . with increasing reliance on force to resolve social conflict," 45.

[23] For the variety of groups, see Allen Potter, *Organized Groups in British National Politics* (London 1961); for a case study of their influence, see Harry Eckstein, *Pressure Group Politics: The Case of The British Medical Association* (Stanford 1960).

[24] Kellas, 206–209.

[25] *Ibid.*, 207–208.

[26] The figure pertaining to council candidates is based on the information sheets that 122 S.N.P. council candidates filed at the Party's central headquarters.

who lost ground rather than advanced."[27]

It is apparent from interview data that the local leaders of the S.N.P. were considerably more positive in their outlooks regarding their personal economic positions. Asked whether or not they felt their jobs were secure and their present income and future prospects reasonably satisfying, only 28 percent of the S.N.P. local leaders answered negatively to either part. That is, 72 percent found both their jobs secure and their present income and future prospects reasonably satisfying.

Finally, feelings of isolation may result from perceptions of community discontinuity—in the case of the Scots, perceptions of regional discontinuity. We shall present here only the aggregate data relating to this point, waiting until Section III to present attitudinal data.

The question we are addressing is whether and to what extent the Scottish economy was declining in relation to the British economy. An indicator that might be most suggestive of community discontinuity is the rate of net emigration. During the 1950's and the 1960's, the rate of net emigration from Scotland was about 28,000 persons per year. Although this may appear to be substantial for a population of just over five million, this degree of emigration is not unusual for Scotland. Indeed, the 1950's and 1960's cannot be distinguished from earlier periods in the twentieth century on this basis, for the rate of net emigration from Scotland between 1900 and 1940 was about the same.[28]

Nor could it be argued that the Scottish economy was particularly backward or that it was losing strength in comparison to the English economy.

27 Stanley Hoffmann, *Le mouvement Poujade*, quoted in Kornhauser, 204–205.
28 Figures on net emigration from Scotland are found in Central Statistical Office, 16.

Those industries thought to be relatively weak (agriculture, mining, shipbuilding, and textiles) accounted for less than 15 percent of the Scottish male working population in 1966, including those who were unemployed.[29] Somewhat more than 33 percent of the Scottish male working population, on the other hand, worked in the relatively prosperous fields of engineering and electrical goods, vehicles, construction, and professional and scientific services.[30] This would not appear to be the picture of a stagnant regional economy. It is, in any case, little different from the English-Welsh economies.[31] Indeed, per capita income rose more rapidly from 1960 to 1966 in Scotland than it did in the United Kingdom as a whole. Table [IV] appeared in *The Scotsman*, a newspaper that associates itself with devolution of power to regional centers.

Table IV

PER CAPITA INCOME FOR THE UNITED KINGDOM AND SCOTLAND, 1960 AND 1966 (1958 PRICES IN £)*

	1960	1966	Percent Rise
United Kingdom	425	465	09
Scotland (estimate)	385	445	15

* *The Scotsman*, July 4, 1968. Percent Rise added by author.

29 Figures for 1966 may be found in *The Scotsman's Diary*. 1968, frontispiece; figures for 1961 may be found in the 1961 *Census*, Occupation and Industry, and are reported in Kellas, 244–45.
30 *The Scotsman's Diary*, 1968, frontispiece; figures for 1961 are found in the 1961 *Census*, and are reported in Kellas, 244–45.
31 Figures found in Kellas, 244–45, show that the Scottish and English-Welsh economies were fairly similar in 1961. At that time, the somewhat outmoded industries accounted for 12.4 percent of the English and Welsh working populations and 17 percent of the Scottish working population. The prosperous industries accounted for 30.2 percent of the English and Welsh working populations and 25.4 percent of the Scottish working populations.

These results reveal that there were few detectable problems of deficient intermediary group participation or declining economic positions in regard to the local S.N.P. leaders. Moreover, aggregate data indicate that regional discontinuity was not present at a high level. The growth of the Scottish economy was higher on a per capita basis than that of the United Kingdom, and at the base of the Scottish economy were quite prosperous industries rather than outmoded industries. Still, the rate of net emigration from Scotland leaves little doubt that regional discontinuity, of this sort at least, could be perceived and that it might have entered into calculations of whether to give the Party active support. This suggests the possibility that regional discontinuity provided one basis for the development of a separatist movement but that its level was not sufficiently critical to elicit violence.

A third approach to political instability focuses on feelings of deprivation. The empirical research done by Gurr is representative of this approach.[32] He found that a necessary condition for regional violence was a relatively high degree of persisting regional deprivation and that next in importance was short-term regional deprivation.[33] The existence of certain institutional factors may help to deter civil violence when fairly high degrees of deprivation prevail. But, without deprivation, violence tended not to occur.

Gurr deals with a variety of forms of persistent and short-term deprivation. An analysis of the Scottish situation indicates that the most important of these, persistent deprivation, did not

exist. Short-term forms of deprivation did exist, although it is particularly important to note that some of them were not solely regional in character but extended throughout the United Kingdom.

Let us take up some of the persistent forms of deprivation. The first of these is what Gurr terms "economic discrimination." By this he means that higher or medium economic positions or specific classes of economic activity are closed to the deprived group. In our research, we did not find any indication of discrimination of this kind or that the S.N.P. local leaders felt that either they or the Scottish people were discriminated against in this way. A second factor, "political discrimination," refers to the closure of the political elite to the deprived group. Again, there is little indication that this kind of discrimination existed or that the S.N.P. local leaders felt that it existed. Since 1900, for example, four of the fifteen British Prime Ministers have been Scottish and a fifth (Churchill) sat for a Scottish seat for fourteen years.

A third kind of persistent deprivation involves the way in which a separatist region was unionized. Mutual agreement is accorded the lowest degree of deprivation; force is accorded the highest degree of deprivation. In a formal sense, the Scottish state underwent union with England by mutual consent. Ninety-eight percent of the local Labour and Conservative leaders surveyed believed that mutual agreement in every sense of the term was the method by which union was accomplished. Forty-six percent of the local S.N.P. leaders agreed with this view. The remaining 54 percent thought that mutual agreement was the formal method of accomplishing union but that many of the Scots who consented to union did so out of private interest rather than out of national interest. The importance of bribery was accented by the respondents

[32] Ted Gurr, "A Causal Model." The relation between his approach and other frustration-aggression approaches is found in Gurr, "Psychological Factors."

[33] Although Gurr does not direct his argument to regional movements, its application to them may be deduced from the argument.

who gave this answer. Yet only two respondents felt that their questioning of the propriety of the agreement was at all instrumental in their joining the S.N.P. We can thus conclude that persistent deprivation due to the method of political unification was only a weakly operative factor in the rise of the S.N.P.

A fourth kind of persistent deprivation is relative lack of educational opportunities for a regional population. As we shall see, central government expenditure on education was considerably higher per capita in Scotland in 1966 than it was in England and Wales (Table VII). Moreover, in the academic year 1966–1967, the number of Scottish students "entering British universities was 8.3 percent of the total population of 18-year-olds in Scotland. The corresponding figure for England and Wales was 5.3 percent."[34] Under this circumstance, a case that substantial educational deprivation existed is understandably difficult to make. In fact, Scottish educational backgrounds have produced approximately 9 percent of the British Prime Ministers, Chancellors of the Exchequer, and Foreign Secretaries since 1900.[35]

Factors relevant to short-term deprivation include new restrictions on political participation and representation and trends in international trade, inflation, and gross national products (G.N.P.). No new restrictions have been placed on Scottish political participation or representation. It is well known, however, that the British have faced substantial problems in international trade during the past decade. The balance of trade, favorable through-

out much of the 1950's, slumped to deficits totaling £1,694,000,000 in the 1959–1967 period.[36] This slump was accompanied by a rather sharp increase in inflation. During the years 1963–1967, the rate of inflation was approximately 4.7 percent annually, compared to approximately 2.6 percent during the preceding eight years.[37] Moreover, there were also growing restrictions on consumer expenditure of other sorts. General taxes and luxury taxes have been increased almost yearly since 1961 and limitations have been placed on credit purchase. The government has also sought and received statutory powers to negate certain pay raises. Finally, although rising, the growth of the British economy was perceptibly slower than that of any of the other Western European economies during the 1950's and 1960's. This comparison can be seen in Tables V and VI.

These short-term trends were apparently perceptible to the entire British population. Gallup polls show that neither Heath nor Wilson was able to

Table V

GROWTH RATES OF REAL NATIONAL INCOME, 1955–1964, AND REAL GROSS NATIONAL PRODUCT, 1950–1964*

	1955–1964 Rate	1950–1964 Rate
Germany	5.6	7.1
Italy	5.4	5.6
France	5.0	4.9
Denmark	4.8	3.6
Netherlands	4.3	4.9
Norway	3.9	3.8
Belgium	3.5	3.4
United Kingdom	2.8	2.6

* Edward F. Denison, *Why Growth Rates Differ: Postwar Experience in Nine Western Countries*, Washington, D.C.: The Brookings Institution, 1967, p. 17.

[34] S.N.P., *Scotland v. Whitehall*, No. 1, 14, from a Parliamentary answer by Mrs. Shirley Williams.

[35] David Butler and Jennie Freeman, *British Political Facts 1900–1967* (London 1968), 59–65.

[36] Central Statistical Office, 247.

[37] *Ibid.*, 336.

Table VI

GROWTH RATES OF REAL NATIONAL INCOME PER CAPITA, 1950–1964*

	1950–1964	1955–1964
N. W. Europe	3.9	3.3
Germany	5.9	4.3
France	3.8	3.7
Netherlands	3.5	2.9
Denmark	2.9	4.1
Norway	2.9	3.0
Belgium	2.8	2.9
United Kingdom	2.2	2.1

* [*Ibid.*, Table V], p. 18.

inspire the confidence of 30 percent of the British public in mid-1968, whereas each gained the confidence of more than 50 percent of the public in mid-1965.[38]

Yet we should not overestimate the degree of economic deprivation produced in the 1960's. After all, the British G.N.P. was growing and not declining; the increase in inflation, while sharp, was not extraordinary; and consumer expenditure, even after taxes and inflation, was rising slightly and not falling. We could not accurately describe this as a period of severe deprivation. It was, at most, a period of moderate deprivation.

Moreover, these short-term economic deprivations were, as suggested by the Gallup polls, general to the nation as a whole. They were not particularly regional and did not require a regional framework to inspire protest. Of course, this does not exclude the possibility that regional economic deprivations were also present. Did such deprivations exist and, if so, what was their degree and what was their cause?

It is apparent that regional economic deprivations were present during and even before the period under considera-

[38] *The Times*, July 22, 1968.

tion.[39] Per capita income in Scotland, about 10 percent lower than for the United Kingdom as a whole in 1960, has historically been lower in Scotland than in the United Kingdom.[40] Unemployment has also been of somewhat greater significance in Scotland than in the rest of Great Britain. The unemployed in Great Britain averaged 1.8 percent between 1965–1967 as compared to 3.2 percent in Scotland.[41] It is little different for comparisons for the 1920–1960 period.[42]

Although regional economic deprivation was perceptible during the 1960's, these indicators also reveal that it was relatively mild in degree.[43] Nor is it easy to interpret the causes of even this degree of deprivation as having been the result of contemporary decisions made in Westminster or Whitehall.

Those who believe that regional deprivation was the result of decisions taken in London cite a number of contemporary cases. Favorite examples are toll charges applied on certain Scottish bridges, naming the new British liner "Queen Elizabeth II," and putting anti-inflationary restrictions on the British economy before the Scottish economy had a full opportunity to

[39] Although these economic deprivations have been present for some time and are in this sense persistent, they do not involve discrimination in the sense implied in our discussion of persistent deprivation.

[40] See Table IV. See also Kellas, 246.

[41] Kellas, 243.

[42] *Ibid.*

[43] It should be noted that income per head in Scotland is higher than it is in either Wales or Northern Ireland. See *Report of the Commissioners of H. M. Inland Revenue*, 109, Cmnd. 3200. Moreover, per capita family income (based on median) is about 20 percent lower in the American south than it is in the northeast and 23 percent less than it is in the west. See *Encyclopaedia Britannica, Book of the Year, 1969*, "Developments in the States, 1968." 24. These figures can be compared to the figure of 10 percent for Scotland in relation to the United Kingdom.

expand (there are few data to corroborate or refute the last point).[44]

An opposing view can also find support. Take, for example, the only figures available on contemporary central governmental budgetary expenditure in Scotland, Brought forth as a result of an S.N.P. parliamentary question, the figures are found in a handbook published by the S.N.P. under the heading, "Fiddling Scotland's Money."

Table VII shows that Scotland received more central government expenditure per capita in 1966 than did England and Wales.[45] In addition, it suggests that central governmental expenditure on matters relating to the placement of industry was probably higher per capita in Scotland than in England and Wales. It was also higher on matters relating to education.

However, it is important to note that these figures are not conclusive. They exclude defense expenditures, which, some believe, highly overrepresented England. They also exclude major nonbudgetary policies such as those

Table VII

CENTRAL GOVERNMENT EXPENDITURE PER HEAD OF POPULATION, 1966–1967*

	Scotland £ s. d.	England and Wales £ s. d.
Roads	6 6 0	4 8 2
Agricultural Support	6 6 0	4 0 7
Promotion of Local Employment	3 12 1	9 3
Housing	4 12 1	1 18 4
Education	10 13 6	5 2 5
Health and Welfare	27 3 3	23 2 0
Children's Services	6 6 0	5 11 5
Benefits and Assistance	47 13 11	44 14 6

* The Scottish National Party, *Scotland v. Whitehall*, No. 1, p. 9.

[44] These people believe that deprivation occurs because Scottish parliamentarians can be easily outvoted. In any case, the loyalty of Scottish parliamentarians tends to be more to party than to Scotland. Since the major parties are based in London, and since the British economy depends so heavily on the health of the English economy, party policies are defined by English interests. Perceptions of party discipline helped elicit this view. Also of importance may be the quite low degree of regularized contact many MP's have with their constituencies. See Robert E. Dowse, "The MP and his Surgery," *Political Studies*, XI (October 1963), 333–41 and *The Times*, July 6, 1968.

[45] It is reasonable to assume, on the basis of incremental budgeting processes, that Scotland has been favored for some time. On incrementalism, see Aaron Wildavsky, *The Politics of the Budgetary Process* (Boston 1964). The incremental process is based on pragmatic bargaining. An analysis of pragmatism in British politics may be found in James Christoph, "Consensus and Cleavage in British Political Ideology," *American Political Science Review*, LIX (September 1965), 629–43.

dealing with anti-inflation, which could have prematurely depressed regional economies but for which few regional data are available. It thus remains quite possible that contemporary policies of the central political institutions have contributed to the regional deprivations that face Scotland, but at least some conjecture is required to defend this case. Thus, we must speculate about where defense expenditures were placed, or the regional effects of British anti-inflationary policies, in order to overcome concrete data that known governmental expenditures favored Scotland.

Our examination of deprivation has indicated the presence of both regional and extra-regional forms of economic deprivation. But those regional deprivations that were present (higher rates of unemployment and lower per capita income) were moderate in degree and were unaccompanied by the most significant forms of deprivation related to violence (discriminations such as closure of political elites, economic elites, and of education; forced union). Furthermore, the causes of this regional deprivation were uncertain. Given these findings, we can hypothesize that regional economic deprivation was sufficiently present to provide one basis for development of a separatist movement, but that its level was not sufficient to produce violence.

Finally, violence might be the product of emotion engendered by a prosperous and distinct regional culture. We will see below that feelings of Scottish identity were widespread in Scotland. The question raised here, however, is whether these feelings could have been heightened and made more vehement by the coexistence of a prosperous regional culture.

Scholars have argued that the Scottish culture over the past 200 years has been largely assimilated into the English culture and that a separate and distinct Scottish culture has not prospered for some time.[46] This view is consistent with our findings regarding linguistic differentiation. Only 10 percent of the S.N.P. local leaders responded that either their parents or grandparents spoke Gaelic. Only 7 percent of the local leaders themselves said they spoke Gaelic, and only an additional 14 percent said they even intended to learn Gaelic.

In the absence of cultural distinctiveness or prosperity, Scottish identity was not vehemently felt by most of the S.N.P. local leaders (see Table VIII). The fact that Scottish identity was not strongly felt suggests that it was unlikely, in itself, to inspire S.N.P. local leaders to advocate violence. Yet Table VIII also shows that feelings of regional identity were clearly present. Their presence opens the possibility that they could have served as motivating forces, especially for persons who were not already politically engaged. This condition appears to have held for the local S.N.P. leaders. We noted previously that 83 percent of these leaders had never been members of other parties or done work on their behalf before joining the S.N.P. Indeed, 70 percent of the local S.N.P. leaders either had abstained from voting in at least one-third of the general elections or had not consistently voted for the same party before they joined the S.N.P.

III

Of the many psychological variables theorists have found related to violence, the preceding analysis discovered only four that were operating at a detectable level in the Scottish case. Three of these were regional in nature—regional discontinuity, regional economic deprivation, and regional identity. The fourth was extra-regional economic deprivation.

But the levels of the regional variables were far from being excessive or severe. Aggregate data indicated that regional discontinuity and deprivation were present only to a moderate degree, and interview data indicated that regional identities were not felt vehemently. Indeed, the levels of these regional variables, even taken together, were low enough that they were generally insufficient by themselves to motivate the S.N.P. local leaders to undertake action.

On the basis of answers as to why they joined the S.N.P., we attempted to distinguish those respondents for

Table VIII

FEELING OF SCOTTISH IDENTITY AMONG SCOTTISH NATIONAL, CONSERVATIVE, AND LABOUR LOCAL PARTY LEADERS (IN PERCENT)

	Vehement	Strong	Moderate	Mild, Not at All
S.N.P.	17	83	0	0
Conservative	5	95	0	0
Labour	0	79	17	4

[46] Walker Connor, 39.

whom regional considerations or perceptions were sufficient reasons from those for whom they were insufficient. Solely regional considerations were defined as (a) perceptions of regional deprivation or discontinuity as a sufficient reason; (b) affective commitment to nationhood as a sufficient reason; or (c) a combination of instrumental and affective regional perceptions as sufficient reasons. Considerations other than solely regional were defined as (a) perceptions of extra-regional deprivation (i.e., inflation, higher taxes, loss of empire, and the like) or other extra-regional considerations as a sufficient reason, or (b) perceptions of extra-regional considerations as a necessary condition for joining the Party. Whatever feelings these recruits held toward regional nationhood, deprivation, or discontinuity, the point is that they were not sufficiently intense, by themselves, to act as motivating forces. One S.N.P. local leader said that he felt that Scotland was a nation and had a right to nationhood "just like the ex-colonial countries. But I joined mainly out of protest. The British economy was sick and we seemed to be going no place." Another respondent said, "I joined the Party out of dissatisfaction with things in general—higher taxes, a higher cost of living."

Table IX reveals that feelings of regional discontinuity, deprivation, and nation were not unimportant as motivating forces. They played a part in the decisions to join the Party of 76 percent of the local S.N.P. leaders. Still, only 38 percent of the leadership found such regional considerations alone *sufficient* to motivate them to join the Party. For the remaining 62 percent, perceptions of regional factors were not sufficiently strong that, by themselves, they were able to inspire action.

It thus appears to be the case that without perceptions of regional discontinuity, deprivation, and nation the

Table IX

REGIONAL AND EXTRA-REGIONAL
CONSIDERATIONS AS REASONS
FOR WHICH LOCAL S.N.P. LEADERS
JOINED THE PARTY

	Percent	*Total Percent*
Regional Considerations Sufficient:		
Regional deprivation or discontinuity	0	
Affective commitment to nationhood	10	
Both instrumental and affective regional perceptions	28	
		38
Regional Considerations Insufficient:		
Extra-regional deprivation (or other extra-regional considerations) sufficient	24	
Extra-regional deprivation not sufficient, but necessary (along with regional considerations)	38	
		62
Total		100

S.N.P. would not have been able to recruit most of its local leaders. On the other hand, the fact that these perceptions, even if taken together, were generally insufficient to produce motivation lends credibility to the notion that they were not sufficient to inspire violence. Instead, such motivations had to be sparked by perception of deprivations that were also affecting the English.

It is probably the case that regionally focused perceptions were important to the wider public, as well. For example, public opinion polls revealed that 66 percent of the Scottish public believed that there would be less unemployment if Scotland were responsible for its own internal affairs; and 52 percent thought that the standard of living would improve under Scottish control.[47] Re-

[47] BBC-1, Section *Ic, iii* and *v*.

sponses such as these indicate that the wider public perceived the presence of regional economic deprivation.

Moreover, widespread feelings of regional (national) identity existed in Scotland even without the coexistence of a prosperous regional culture. A study of public attitudes in two Scottish constituencies (Craigton and Govanhill) found that 92 percent of the respondents spontaneously thought of themselves as belonging to the Scottish national group. Over a majority in Woodside and Kelvingrove answered similarly. In addition, the Craigton-Govanhill surveys found that regional identity was almost as important as class identity.[48]

It is possible to argue, along with Leonard Doob,[49] that widespread support for a separatist movement cannot develop in the absence of widespread perceptions of regional identity. Nevertheless, we should note that feelings of Scottish identity within the wider public were probably not intense. This is indicated by the Craigton-Govanhill findings that region had to vie with class as important sources of identity.[50]

Although regional factors were obviously present, an additional input of extra-regional economic deprivation was apparently also required to spark widespread public support. Since World War II, at least, public activity on behalf of Scottish nationalism has tended to surge and decline depending on the state of the British economy. During the 1945–1950 period, for example, British economic problems were such that informal prices and wages rules were established by the government and the pound was devalued by over 25 percent. During the same period Scottish nationalism surged, reaching its zenith in the 1950's. The culminating event was the presentation of the Scottish covenant to Parliament, a petition that had received over two million signatures. Thereafter, however, the British economy gained strength. International trade balances were generally favorable; inflation was relatively low. This improvement was accompanied by a rapid decline in nationalist fervor. The strength of Scottish nationalism, as we have seen, reappeared only in the mid-1960's. But by that time the British economy was once again facing difficult problems, with a relatively sharp rise in inflation, rises in taxes, and unfavorable balances in international trade. Thus, since Wold War II, the appearance and disappearance of widespread nationalist support has consistently followed upon the changing state of the British economy.

[48] Ian Budge and Derek W. Urwin, *Scottish Political Behaviour* (London 1966), 112–20. The significance of class perceptions in British and Scottish politics may be found in Robert Alford, *Party and Society: The Anglo-American Democracies* (Chicago 1963), 123–71.

[49] Leonard Doob, *Patriotism and Nationalism: Their Psychological Foundations* (New Haven 1964).

[50] It is possible that regionalism became politically salient as an identity not only because of its own strength but also because the competing source of identity (class) was declining. Considering the recent changes in British class structure, this possibility is not out of the question. A good assessment of the tenor of class change is found in Ralf Dahrendorf, "Recent Changes in the Class Structure of European Societies," *Daedalus*, XCIII (Winter 1964), 225–70.

IV

Results from our local S.N.P. leadership interviews and from data pertaining to the wider public suggest similar conclusions. This is especially the case when these results are combined with the results of aggregate and interview data presented in Section II. All these data converge in a remarkably consistent fashion.[51]

[51] This leads us to the notion that, when we are dealing with certain variables in studies of violence, we may find that aggregate data are appropriate substitutes for attitudinal data.

Two salient features in the Scottish case were that relatively long-term regional factors were at play and that these regional factors were not operating at high levels. Regional identities in Scotland have surely existed for quite some time. We have seen that regional discontinuity, in the form of net emigration, has operated at least since the beginning of this century. Regional economic deprivations, such as higher unemployment and lower per capita income, also have historical roots. These regional conditions have been continuously present, generally lying dormant, but with the potential to provide the underpinning for a separatist movement.

They have been generally dormant because they were not sufficiently strong to motivate action by themselves. The fact is that feelings of Scottish identity did not exist within the context of a prospering and distinct Scottish culture. According to both interview and public-opinion data, feelings of Scottish identity were not held vehemently by either the local S.N.P. leaders or the wider public. Nor, on the basis of aggregate data, were either regional discontinuity or regional economic deprivation more than moderate in degree. There was, in particular, little political, economic, or educational discrimination applied against the region.

Thus, while present to provide the underpinning for a separatist movement, these regional deprivations were not present in sufficient degree to elicit violence. In order to be activated at all, they required additional inputs. We might presume that had the additional inputs been substantially of a regional nature (i.e., increased regional deprivation, discontinuity, or cultural prosperity), the likelihood of violence would have increased. But both interview data regarding the local S.N.P. leaders and an analysis of wider public support indicated that the additional inputs

in the Scottish case were deprivations of an extra-regional sort. The difference between this type of input and a regional input in the context of a separatist movement should be obvious. It is a type of input from which the opposing actor is also suffering. Therefore, it did not enable Scottish nationalists to focus on the English with the degree of intensity that additional regional inputs might have caused.[52]

Even so, one other consideration was probably also salient. The extra-regional inputs were moderate and not severe in the Scottish case. This was demonstrated earlier on the basis of aggregate data. Because they were present, they were able to spark support for a separatist movement in combination with the underlying and more permanent regional conditions. But because they were only moderate in degree, they were unlikely to inspire violence.

Our purpose in this study was to discover how a separatist movement could flourish without eliciting violence. Such a study, we hoped, would not only lead to a deeper understanding of conditions underlying the Scottish movement; it was also to provide suggestions for approaching the analysis of other separatist movements. The findings of the Scottish case point out in particular the relevance of theories of violence to the study of separatist movements. It should be recalled that these theories not only accounted for the nonviolent character of Scottish separatism during the 1960's; in addition, they offered variables whose presence at moderate levels also helped account for the growth and size of the Scottish movement, thus suggesting

[52] Indeed, approximately half of the S.N.P. local leaders spontaneously asserted that they did not dislike the English. According to *The Economist*, moreover, "Mrs. Ewing is careful to stress the natural friendship of the Scots and English, on and off the platform." *The Economist*, May 11, 1968, 9.

that theories of violence can be pertinent even to the study of nonviolent forms of separatist dissent and protest.

On the basis of these theories, the study prompts us to raise the following general questions in analyses of the size and violent tendencies of separatist movements. (1) Can the movement draw upon widespread regional perceptions that are the result of fairly persistent regional conditions (i.e., regional identity, discontinuity, deprivation)? (2) Are these perceptions of such a moderate degree that they are insufficient to motivate political action? (3) If additional motivational forces are required, are they present? (4) If they are present, are they both extra-regional in kind and moderate in degree? The Scottish case indicates that positive findings for each of these questions will produce a situation in which a separatist movement will burgeon without leading to violence.

COLLECTIVE VIOLENCE IN EUROPEAN PERSPECTIVE

Charles Tilly

As comforting as it is for civilized people to think of barbarians as violent and of violence as barbarian, Western civilization and various forms of collective violence have always been close partners. We do not need a stifled universal instinct of aggression to account for outbreaks of violent conflicts in our past, or in our present. Nor need we go to the opposite extreme and search for pathological moments and sick men in order to explain collective acts of protest and destruction. Historically, collective violence has flowed regularly out of the central political processes of Western countries. Men seeking to seize, hold, or realign the levers of power have continually engaged in collective violence as part of their struggles. The oppressed have struck in the name of justice, the privileged in the name of order, those in between in the name of fear. Great shifts in the arrangements of power have ordinarily produced—and have often depended on—exceptional movements of collective violence.

Yet the basic forms of collective violence vary according to who is involved and what is at issue. They have changed profoundly in Western countries over the last few centuries, and those countries have built big cities and modern industries. For these reasons, the character of collective violence at a given time is one of the best signs we have of what is going on in a country's political life. The nature of violence and the nature of the society are intimately related.

· · ·

Excerpted from Hugh Davis Graham and Ted Robert Gurr, eds., *Violence in America: Historical and Comparative Perspectives*, A Report to the National Commission on the Causes and Prevention of Violence (Washington, D.C.: U.S. Government Printing Office, 1969), Vol. 1, Chap. 1, pp. 5–34, by permission of the author. Footnotes have been renumbered.

... Far from being mere side effects of urbanization, industrialization, and other large structural changes, violent protests seem to grow most directly from the struggle for established places in the structure of power. Even presumably nonpolitical forms of collective violence like the antitax revolt are normally directed against the authorities, accompanied by a critique of the authorities' failure to meet their responsibilities, and informed by a sense of justice denied to the participants in the protest. Furthermore, instead of constituting a sharp break from "normal" political life, violent protests tend to accompany, complement, and extend organized, peaceful attempts by the same people to accomplish their objectives.

Over the long run, the processes most regularly producing collective violence are those by which groups acquire or lose membership in the political community. The form and locus of collective violence therefore vary greatly depending on whether the major ongoing political change is a group's acquisition of the prerequisites of membership, its loss of those prerequisites, or a shift in the organization of the entire political system.

The impact of large structural changes such as urbanization, industrialization, and population growth, it seems to me, comes through their creation or destruction of groups contending for power and through their shaping of the available means of coercion. In the short run, the growth of large cities and rapid migration from rural to urban areas in Western Europe probably acted as a damper on violent protest, rather than a spur to it. That is so for two reasons:

1. The process withdrew discontented men from communities in which they already had the means for collective action and placed them in communities where they had neither the collective identity nor the means necessary to strike together.
2. It took considerable time and effort both for the individual migrant to assimilate to the large city, and thus to join the political strivings of his fellows, and for new forms of organization for collective action to grow up in the cities.

If so, the European experience resembles the American experience. In the United States, despite enduring myths to the contrary, poor, uprooted newcomers to big cities generally take a long time to get involved in anything—crime, delinquency, politics, associations, protest, rioting—requiring contacts and experiences outside a small world of friends and relatives. These things are at least as true of European cities.

In the long run, however, urbanization deeply shaped the conditions under which new groups fought for political membership, and urbanization's secondary effects in the countryside stirred a variety of protests. The move to the city helped transform the character of collective violence in at least three ways:

1. It grouped men in larger homogeneous blocs (especially via the factory and the working-class neighborhood) than ever before.
2. It facilitated the formation of special-interest associations (notably the union and the party) incorporating many people and capable of informing, mobilizing, and deploying them relatively fast and efficiently.
3. It massed the people posing the greatest threat to the authorities near the urban seats of power, and thus encouraged the authorities to adopt new strategies and tactics for controlling dissidence.

For the people who remained in the country, the rise of the cities meant increasingly insistent demands for crops and taxes to support the urban establishment, increasingly visible impact on individual farmers of tariff and pricing policies set in the cities, and increasingly efficient means of exacting obedience from the countryman. All of these, in their time, incited violent protests throughout Europe.

Of course, definitive evidence on such large and tangled questions is terribly hard to come by. Until very recent times few historians have taken the study of collective violence as such very seriously. As Antonio Gramsci, the Italian socialist philosopher-historian, put it:

This is the cutsom of our time: instead of studying the origins of a collective event, and the reasons for its spread . . . they isolate the protagonist and limit themselves to doing a biography of pathology, too often concerning themselves with unascertained motives, or interpreting them in the wrong way; for a social elite the features of subordinate groups always display something barbaric and pathological.[1]

Since World War II, however, a considerable number of French and English historians, and a much smaller number of Americans, have begun to study and write history "from below"— actually trying to trace the experiences and actions of large numbers of ordinary men from their own point of view. This approach has had a special impact on the study of protests and rebellions. As a result, we are beginning to get a richer, rearranged picture of the political life of plain people in France and England (and, to a lesser extent, other European countries) over the last few centuries.

The new variety of evidence makes it possible to identify some major shifts in the predominant forms of collective violence in those countries over the modern period. Without too much difficulty we can place the forms of collective violence which have prevailed during that long period in three broad categories: primitive, reactionary, and modern.[2] . . .

Primitive varieties of collective violence include the feud, the brawl among members of rival guilds or communes, and the mutual attacks of hostile religious groups. (Banditry, as E. J. Hobsbawm has said, stands at the edge of this category by virtue of its frequent direction against the existing distribution of power and wealth, and its frequent origin in the state's creation of outlaws as part of the attempt to extend legal authority to formerly ungoverned areas.) Primitive forms of collective violence share several features: small-scale, local scope, participation by members of communal groups as such, inexplicit and unpolitical objectives. Primitive varieties of violence once predominated, until centralized states began dragging Europeans into political life on a larger than local scale. That transformation accelerated through much of Western Europe after 1600. Since then, the primitive forms of collective violence have dwindled very slowly, but very steadily. Now they occur only rarely, only at the margins of organized politics.

The reactionary forms, by contrast, burgeoned as the national state began to grow. Reactionary disturbances are also usually small in scale, but they pit either communal groups or loosely organized members of the general population against representatives of those who hold power, and tend to include a critique of the way power is being wielded. The forcible occupation of fields and forests by the landless, the revolt against the tax collector, the anticonscription rebellion, the food riot, and the attack on machines were

---

distinction (if not the precise formulation or the exact wording) from E. J. Hobsbawm, *Primitive Rebels* (Manchester: Manchester University Press, 1959). It also underlies much of the argument of George Rudé, *The Crowd in History* (New York: Wiley, 1964). These are the two best general books on the subject of this essay.

[1] Antonio Gramsci, *Il Risorgimento* (Torino: Einaudi, 1950, 3d ed.), pp. 199–200.
[2] I have borrowed the general logic of this

Western Europe's most frequent forms of reactionary collective violence. The somewhat risky term "reactionary" applies to these forms of collective violence because their participants were commonly reacting to some change that they regarded as depriving them of rights they had once enjoyed; they were backward looking.

But the state won the contest; in most countries of Western Europe the reactionary forms of collective violence peaked and then faded away in their turn during the 19th century. They gave way to modern forms of collective violence. The modern varieties of political disturbance (to use another tendentious term) involve specialized associations with relatively well-defined objectives, organized for political or economic action. Such disturbances can easily reach a large scale. Even more clearly than in the case of reactionary collective violence, they have a tendency to develop from collective actions that offer a show of force but are not intrinsically violent. The demonstration and the violent strike are the two clearest examples, but the coup and most forms of guerrilla warfare also qualify. These forms deserve to the called "modern" not only because of their organizational complexity but also because the participants commonly regard themselves as striking for rights due them, but not yet enjoyed. They are, that is, forward looking.

The Transition to Modern Collective Violence

The nature, timing, and causes of these shifts from one major type of collective violence to another are complicated, controversial, and variable from one country to another. They are just as complicated, controversial, and variable, in fact, as the political histories of European nations. The transformations of collective violence depended on transformations of nonviolent political life. Rather different political systems emerged in different corners of Europe: communist, socialist, liberal-democratic, corporatist. Each had a somewhat different experience with collective violence. Yet everywhere two things happened and profoundly affected the character of violent protest.

The first was the victory of the national state over rival powers in towns, provinces, and estates; politics was nationalized. The second was the proliferation and rise to political prominence of complex special-purpose associations like parties, firms, unions, clubs, and criminal syndicates. The two trends generally reinforced each other. In some countries, however, the state gained power faster and earlier than the organizational changes occurred; Russia and France are cases in point. In others, the organizational revolution came much closer to the nationalization of politics; Germany and Italy fit that pattern. In either case, the times of overlap of the two trends produced the most dramatic changes in the character of collective violence.

Some of the contrast appears in crude tabulations of disturbances occurring in France during the three decades from 1830 to 1860 and three later decades between 1930 and 1960.[3]

[3] Our sampling procedure consisted of reading through two national newspapers for each day of the 60 years and pulling out each reported event involving some violence (wounding, property damage, or seizure of persons or property over resistance) in which at least one participating formation had 50 members or more. As well as we can determine, a sample thus assembled overweights events in cities, and especially in Paris, but in a relatively constant fashion. The descriptions of the events coded come not only from the newspaper accounts but also from historical works and French archival material. The data presented here are preliminary and probably contain minor errors. None of the errors I have in mind, however, would substantially affect the conclusions drawn from the data in this essay.

Period	Number of Disturbances	Number of Formations	Formations per Disturbance	Estimated Total of Participants (in Thousands)
1830–39	259	565	2.2	293
1840–49	292	736	2.5	511
1850–60	114	258	2.3	106
1930–39	333	808	2.4	737
1940–49	93	246	2.6	223
1950–60	302	637	2.1	664

This fairly representative set of disturbances includes 1,393 events, involving 3,250 formations (distinct groups taking part in the collective violence). The distribution over time is as above.

The figures show that France by no means became a peaceable nation as urbanization and industrialization transformed her between 1830 and 1960. The two decades from 1850 to 1860 and from 1940 to 1950 produced the fewest disturbances; what actually happened is that during two extremely repressive regimes (following Louis Napoleon's 1851 coup and during the German occupation and Vichy government of the 1940's) there was almost no open large-scale violence. The large numbers for the 1930's include the huge sitdown strikes of 1936 and 1937. Even without them the depressed thirties would look like troubled times. So would the prosperous fifties. In boom and bust, Frenchmen continue to fight.

We can look at the distribution of formations taking part in the disturbances in the second table. The figures show a decided decline in the participation of the ordinary, mixed crowd without any well-defined political or economic identity, and a compensating rise in the participation of crowds labeled as supporters of particular creeds and programs. We find no marked change in the involvement of repressive forces in collective violence, but see an important shift of the task of repression from military forces to police. "Natural" groups like users of the same market (who were typical participants in food riots, invasions of fields, and other small reactionary disturbances) disappeared completely over the 130-year span.

Altogether, the figures show the rise of specialization and organization in collective violence. Just as industry shifted its weight from the small shop to the large factory and population rushed

Type of Formation	1830–39	1840–49	1850–60	1930–39	1940–49	1950–60
Simple crowd	16.5	17.2	8.9	1.5	3.3	1.5
Ideological crowd, activists	17.5	10.4	32.3	48.3	21.5	35.2
Military	20.5	16.2	15.2	3.0	8.5	1.9
Police	10.9	16.9	24.5	24.6	26.4	31.8
Public officials	3.5	6.0	4.3	1.0	3.7	1.5
Occupational group	17.0	17.3	4.7	14.6	24.4	17.7
Users of same market, fields, woods or water	2.5	4.4	1.9	.7	.0	.0
Others	11.7	11.7	8.2	6.3	12.2	10.5
Total	100.1	100.1	100.0	100.0	100.0	100.1

from little town to big city, collective violence moved from the normal congregations of communal groups within which people used to live most of their lives toward the deliberate confrontations of special-purpose associations. Collective violence, like so many other features of social life, changed from a communal basis to an associational one.

As one consequence the average size of incidents went up. Here are some measures of magnitude for the 1,393 disturbances in the sample:

The figures decribe the average dis-

tries, however, the transition from predominantly reactionary to predominantly modern forms of collective violence occurred with striking rapidity. In England, the reactionary forms were already well on their way to oblivion by the time of the last great agrarian rising, in 1830, although they had prevailed 30 years before. In Germany, demonstrations and strikes seem to have established themselves as the usual settings for collective violence during the two decades after the Revolution of 1848.

	1830–39	1840–49	1850–60	1930–39	1940–49	1950–60
Mean number participating	1,130	1,750	925	2,215	2,405	2,200
Mean man-days expended	1,785	3,295	1,525	2,240	2,415	2,200
Man-day per participant	1.6	1.9	1.6	1.0	1.0	1.0
Percent lasting more than 1 day	18	18	25	4	4	5
Mean killed and wounded	25	22	30	19	34	23
Mean arrests	20	53	327	24	22	43

turbance, of course, not the total amount of violence in a decade. They show a distinct rise in the average number of people taking part in a disturbance, despite a strong tendency for disturbances to narrow down to a single day. As the burden of repression shifted from the army to the police, interestingly enough, the use of widespread arrests declined while the number of people hurt stayed about the same. Relative to the number of participants, that meant some decline in the average demonstrator's chance of being killed or wounded. The main message, once again, is that, although the predominant forms of collective violence changed in fundamental ways, collective violence persisted as France became an advanced industrial nation.

The 20th-century figures from France include almost no primitive violence. By the beginning of the century the primitive forms had been fading slowly through most of Western Europe for three centuries or more. In some coun-

The situation was a bit more complicated in Italy, because of the deep division between north and south. The transition to modern forms of collective violence appears to have been close to completion in the north at unification. By the time of Milan's infamous *fatti di Maggio* of 1898, in which at least two policemen and 80 demonstrators died, the newer organizational forms unquestionably dominated the scene. In the south, mixed forms of the food riot and tax rebellion still occurred at the end of the century. Within 10 years, however, even in rural areas the agricultural strike and the organized partisan meeting or demonstration had become the most regular sources of violence on the larger scale.

. . .

The precise timing and extent of the shift from reactionary to modern forms of collective violence in these countries remains to be established. For France, it is fairly clear that the shift was barely started by 1840, but close to complete by 1860. Furthermore, France experienced great, and nearly simultaneous, outbreaks of both forms of collective violence in the years from 1846 through 1851. The well-known events we customarily lump together as the Revolution of 1848 and the less-known but enormous insurrection of 1851 stand out both for their magnitude and for their mixture of reactionary and modern disturbances, but they came in the company of such notable outbreaks as the widespread food riots of 1846–47, the Forty-Five Centime Revolt of 1848–49, and the unsuccessful coup of 1849.

If this account of the transition from reactionary to modern collective violence in Western Europe is correct, it has some intriguing features. First, the timing of the transition corresponds roughly to the timing of industrialization and urbanization—England early, Italy late, and so on. Furthermore, the most rapid phase of the transition seems to occur together with a great acceleration of industrial and urban growth, early in the process: England at the beginning of the century, France of the 1850's, Germany of the 1850's and 1870's, Italy of the 1890's.

Second, there is some connection between the timing of the transition and the overall level of collective violence in a country. Over the last 150 years, if we think in terms of the frequency and scale of disturbances rather than the turnover of regimes, we can probably place Spain ahead of France, France ahead of Italy, Italy ahead of Germany, and Germany ahead of England. France is in the wrong position, and the contrast much less than the differences in the countries' reputations for stability or instability, but there is some tendency for the latecomers (or noncomers) to experience greater violence. If we took into account challenges to national integration posed by such peoples as the Catalans, and

differences in the apparatus of repression, the connection would very likely appear even closer.

The information we have on hand, then, suggests that the processes of urbanization and industrialization themselves transform the character of collective violence. But how? We have a conventional notion concerning the life cycle of protest during the course of industrialization and urbanization: an early stage consisting of chaotic responses to the displacements and disruptions caused by the initial development of urban industry, a middle stage consisting of the growth of a militant and often violent working class, a late stage consisting of the peaceful integration of that working class into economic and political life. This scheme has many faults, as we have seen. Certainly we must correct and expand it to take account both of other groups than industrial workers and of the connections between industrialization and urbanization as such and changes in the political system as such. For the information concerning the character of collective violence we have already reviewed raises grave doubts whether the underlying process producing and transforming protest was one of disintegration followed by reintegration, and whether the earlier forms of protest were so chaotic as the scheme implies.

The experience of France challenges the plausible presumption that rapid urbanization produces disruptions of social life that in turn generate protest. There is, if anything, a negative correlation over time and space between the pace of urban growth and the intensity of collective violence. The extreme example is the contrast between the 1840's, with slow urban growth plus enormous violence, and the decade after 1851, with very fast growth and extensive peace. Cities like St. Etienne or Roubaix that received and formed large numbers of new industrial workers tended to remain quiet while centers of the old traditional crafts, like Lyon and Rouen, raged with rebellion. When we can identify the participants in political disturbances, they tend to grossly underrepresent newcomers to the city and draw especially from the "little people" most firmly integrated into the local political life of the city's working-class neighborhoods. The geography of the disturbances itself suggests as much. It was not the urban neighborhoods of extreme deprivation, crime, or vice, George Rudé reports, "not the newly settled towns or quarters that proved the most fertile breeding-ground for social and political protest, but the old areas of settlement with established customs, such as Westminster, the City of London, Old Paris, Rouen, or Lyons."[4] The information available points to a slow, collective process of organization and political education— what we may loosely call a development of class consciousness—within the city rather than a process of disruption leading directly to personal malaise and protest.

As a consequence of this process, the great new cities eventually became the principal settings of collective violence in France. Furthermore, collective violence moved to the city faster than the population did. Even at the beginning of the 19th century, the towns and cities of France produced a disproportionate share of the nation's collective violence. Yet tax rebellions, food riots, and movements against conscription did occur with fair regularity in France's small towns and villages. After these forms of disturbance disappeared, the countryside remained virtually silent for decades. When rural

[4] George Rudé, "The Growth of Cities and Popular Revolt, 1850–1950, with Particular Reference to Paris" (unpublished draft, 1967), p. 26. I am grateful to Mr. Rudé for permission to quote the paper, of which a later version is to be published.

collective violence renewed, it was in the highly organized form of farmers' strikes and marches on Government buildings. This sequence of events was, to some extent, a result of urbanization.

Early in the 19th century, the expansion of cities incited frequent rural protests—obviously in the case of the food riot, more subtly in the case of other forms of collective violence. We have some reason to believe that groups of people who were still solidly established within rural communities, but were losing their livelihoods through the concentration of property and the urbanization of industry, regularly spearheaded such protests. The most important group was probably the workers in cottage industry. Their numbers declined catastrophically as various industries—especially textiles— moved to the city during the first half of the century. Large numbers of them hung on in the countryside, doing what weaving, spinning, or forging they could, seeking out livings as handymen, day laborers, and farmhands, and railing against their fate. Within their communities they were able to act collectively against power looms, farm machines, tax collectors, and presumed profiteers.

Slowly before midcentury, rapidly thereafter, the increasing desperation of the French countryside and the expanding opportunities for work in the new industrial cities drew such men away from their rural communities into town. That move cut them off from the personal, day-to-day contacts that had given them the incentive and the means for collective action against their enemies. It rearranged their immediate interests, placed them in vast, unfamiliar communities, and gave them relatively weak and unreliable relations with those who shared common interests with them.

The initial fragmentation of the work force into small groups of diverse origins, the slow development of mutual awareness and confidence, the lack of organizational experience among the new workers, and the obstacles thrown up by employers and governments all combined to make the development of the means and the will for collective action a faltering, time-consuming process. Collective violence did not begin in earnest until the new industrial workers began forming or joining associations—trade unions, mutual-aid societies, political clubs, conspiratorial groups—devoted to the collective pursuit of their interests. In this sense, the short-run effect of the urbanization of the French labor force was actually to damp collective violence. Its long-run effect, however, was to promote new forms of collective action that frequently led to violent conflicts, and thus to change the form of collective violence itself.

This happened in part through the grouping together of large numbers of men sharing a common fate in factories, urban working-class neighborhoods, and construction gangs. Something like the class-conscious proletariat of which Marx wrote began to form in the industrial cities. This new scale of congregation combined with new, pressing grievances, improving communication, the diffusion of new organizational models from Government and industry, and grudging concessions by the authorities to the right of association. The combination facilitated the formation of special-interest associations. At first workers experimented with cramped, antique, exclusive associations resembling (or even continuing) the old guilds; gradually they formed mutual-aid societies, labor exchanges, unions, and national and international federations.

The new associations further extended the scale and flexibility of communication among workers; they made it possible to inform, mobilize, and deploy large numbers of men fast and efficiently in strikes, demonstrations, and other common action. These potentially rebellious populations and their demanding associations proliferated in the big cities, in the shadows of regional and national capitals. They therefore posed a greater (or at least more visible) threat to the authorities than had their smalltown predecessors. The authorities responded to the threat by organizing police forces, crowd-control tactics, and commissions of inquiry. The associations, in their turn, achieved greater sophistication and control in their show of strength. The process took time—perhaps a generation for any particular group of workers. In that longer run the urbanization of the labor force produced a whole new style of collective violence.

The experience of the industrial workers has one more important lesson for us. In both reactionary and modern forms of collective violence, men commonly express their feeling that they have been unjustly denied their rights. Reactionary disturbances, however, center on rights once enjoyed but now threatened, while modern disturbances center on rights not yet enjoyed but now within reach. The reactionary forms are especially the work of groups of men who are losing their collective positions within the system of power, while the modern forms attract groups of men who are striving to acquire or enhance such positions. The reactionary forms, finally, challenge the basic claims of a national state and a national economy, while the modern forms rest on the assumption that the state and the economy have a durable existence—if not necessarily under present management. In modern disturbances, men contend over the control and organization of the State and the economy.

What links these features together historically? The coordinate construction of the nation-state and the national economy simultaneously weakened local systems of power, with the rights and positions which depended on them, and established new, much larger arenas in which to contend for power. In Western European countries, as locally based groups of men definitively lost their struggle against the claims of the central power, reactionary disturbances dwindled and modern disturbances swelled. The rapid transition from one to the other occurred where and when the central power was able to improve rapidly or expand its enforcement of its claims. Accelerating urbanization and industrialization facilitated such an expansion by providing superior means of communication and control to the agents of the central power, by drawing men more fully into national markets, and by spreading awareness of, and involvement in, national politics. In the process, special-purpose associations like parties and labor unions grew more and more important as the vehicles in the struggle for power, whether violent or nonviolent. Thus urbanization and industrialization affected the character and the incidence of collective violence profoundly, but indirectly.

PUBLIC PROTEST IN INDONESIA

Ann Ruth Willner

The concept of public protest is a rather broad one if we assume it refers to the social or group expression of discontent with one or more aspects of a prevailing public state of affairs. A typology of forms of public protest might include: petitions in the name of a group, demonstrations, deliberately illegal acts, riots, and revolutions. Public protest can also incorporate the phenomenon of mass *abstention* or *withdrawal* from participation in a normal or institutionalized process of political activity in a society, as exemplified by boycotts and refusals to pay taxes, to vote, to salute a flag, or to be drafted into the armed services.

Public protest can also be categorized in terms of *scope*, for protest may be directed toward a specific objective, such as the dismissal of an incumbent from public office, or systemic change. It may initially be generated with respect to a single issue or individual and may subsequently grow to encompass the overthrow of a system, either purposively or as an unintended and unanticipated consequence. Public protest can be characterized in terms of degrees of violence, ranging from non-violent through limited violent to uncontrolably violent.

Within a particular political system, public protest may be sporadic and somewhat deviant, i.e., a recourse embarked upon when institutionalized means of expressing dissent are perceived to be inadequate. Organized public protest may also be an institutionalized aspect of the process of politics within a political system.

This article is a slightly revised version of a paper prepared for the Twentieth Annual Meeting of the Association of Asian Studies, Philadelphia, March 22, 1968. Copyright © 1968 by the Center for International Studies, Ohio University, which published the paper in *Papers in International Studies*, Southeast Asia Series, No. 2 (1968). Reprinted by permission of the author and the Center for International Studies.

We might also consider the distinction between semi-spontaneous public protest and semi-stage-managed protest. The term "semi-spontaneous" is used because, by and large, a group in action, even if the action is initially unplanned and undirected, tends to develop some leadership and direction or is taken over by leaders and directed. Conversely, group protest which is instigated, planned, and organized by a leader or group of leaders frequently cannot remain as controlled and disciplined as was intended but develops its own momentum. The tight scenario can become a "happening."

Public protest may also be seen as serving a number of functions related to the political system as a whole, political leaders (which can include the leaders who instigate and organize protest), and the mass of participants.

Finally, although the concept of protest denotes a condition of being *against* something, it also includes, if only implicitly, being *for* something else. This may seem rather obvious, but in some societies or under some conditions the preferred alternative may not be explicitly spelled out by the protesting group. Manifestations of opposition to X may only be a mode or, of necessity, the only mode of expressing support for Y, as has sometimes been the case in countries such as Indonesia.

The following discussion of nonviolent forms of public protest in Indonesia will be confined to protest directed at or with reference to governmental authority; we exclude such categories as interethnic conflict, protests directed against foreign minorities, and protests concerned with policies and actions of other governments.

In suggesting some generalizations concerning public protest in Indonesia, we will emphasize three types of protest: (1) withdrawal or noncompliance, (2) demonstration, and (3) remedial extra-legal action. Our discussion will also be applicable to other types of protests as well. Our examples will not be limited to instances of protest by mass groups against public authorities but will also include instances in which groups of public office-holders undertook protest action against their superordinates.

One characteristic of incidents of protest in Indonesia has been that they initially appeared to be or were presented as being limited in scope, that is, dealing with only a single issue. However, the specific issues that occasioned the overt act of protest have generally been manifest expressions of deeper, broader, latent dissatisfactions. It might well be argued that the issues and the actions served as pretexts and symbols for broader issues of concern to the protesters. And the objectives of some of the protesters were more far-reaching than was readily apparent. Members of five parties in Parliament and a number of nonparty members, for example, boycotted a session on March 20, 1951 which had been scheduled in order to discuss a controversial government regulation on the election of regional legislative councils.[1] Ostensibly, the boycott was called in order to protest and preclude further discussion of this measure after a motion to revoke it (spearheaded by the opposition *Partai Nasional Indonesia*, PNI) had been passed. However, the move expressed dissatisfaction by the PNI and some smaller parties with the Masjumi-dominated Natsir Cabinet and a desire to cause the downfall of the cabinet—which actually occurred as a consequence of the boycott.

A similar instance of noncompliance occurred on June 27, 1955, when army officers, acting on orders of Acting Chief of Staff Zulkifli Lubis, boycotted

[1] See Herbert Feith, *The Decline of Constitutional Democracy in Indonesia* (Ithaca, N. Y., 1962), p. 168.

the formal installation of their newly appointed Chief of Staff, General Bambang Utojo, who had been selected by the cabinet despite opposition by territorial army commanders.[2] The overt issue was that his appointment violated seniority; underlying this grievance, however, was the concerted and long-sustained anger of the officers' corps toward what they deemed to be civilian political interference in army affairs. This boycott contributed to the downfall of the (first) Ali Sastroamidjojo cabinet on July 24, 1955.

The so-called "October 17th Affair" of 1952 featured a major mass demonstration in Djakarta that accompanied a protest action by one faction of the military. The precipitating factor had been parliamentary action with respect to the military and the immediate target of both groups was Parliament, which President Sukarno was urged to dissolve. More fundamentally, some of the organizers had also been dissatisfied with the structure of government and wanted to reorganize it.

The student demonstrators in 1966 initially demanded the removal of Foreign Minister Subandrio, the banning of the Communist Party and the newly reconstituted cabinet, and the lowering of prices. Underlying these demands, however, was dissatisfaction with Sukarno and his regime, its policies, and their consequences. Eventually the activities of university and high school students were instrumental in the removal of Sukarno from office. Similarly, student demonstrators in late 1967 and early 1968 overtly protested the rising prices of rice and other essential commodities, expressing a growing disillusionment with the meager economic accomplishments of the "New Order."

Extralegal action, in contravention of a policy objected to, is the third type of protest with which we will deal.

Such action as smuggling and barter activities of regional military leaders in Sulawesi and Sumatra in 1956 is a good example. These activities were undertaken to obtain commodities in short supply in these areas and to remedy what was considered to be the inequitable allocation of government revenues between Java and the exporting outer islands. These actions also expressed the hostile feelings of ethnic groups in the outer islands to what was perceived to be the domination of the Javanese and Java-favored policies in the central government.

The tendency for protests to be focused on a single issue that symbolizes a more basic source of dissatisfaction in preference to the underlying cause itself may be explained in many ways. Basically, this tendency can be attributed to two aspects of the political culture. The first is the reluctance of governments to permit discord to become too overt. This reluctance, which is frequently referred to by students of Indonesian culture as a preference for the maintenance of or at least the appearance of harmony and consensus,[3] stems from a traditional theory of conflict-control based upon a recognition of the difficulties of confining the potentially destructive powers of discord. The greater the areas of cleavage and potential conflict, the greater are the efforts to minimize and cover them up, or at least to delay broad confrontation.

Second, protesters are reluctant to challenge authority too openly or drastically. Dissent is frequently expressed indirectly or tentatively, for example, to test the responses of authority figures, to permit such figures to make concessions in an appropriate manner, or to minimize the risks entailed by open defiance.

[3] An example of this behavior at the village level is given in Clifford Geertz, *Social History of an Indonesian Town* (Cambridge, Mass., 1965), pp. 176–83.

[2] *Ibid.*, p. 399.

The reluctance to challenge authority may also explain in part another characteristic of protest in Indonesia, particularly notable in the case of demonstrations. In form and style, the implicit or explicit demand is directed less *against* the authority figure and more *to* the authority figure which is ultimately held responsible. The demand is more in the nature of an appeal than a challenge or an ultimatum. The legitimacy of formal authority therefore remains recognized. In the October 17th Affair mentioned above President Sukarno was appealed to both by the military group and the mass demonstrators. In fact, several of the participants among the former appealed to him quite emotionally. This style also characterized the initial phase of the 1966 student demonstrations when the "guidance" of President Sukarno was asked and it was not until considerably after the time that he transferred authority to General Suharto that he himself became the direct object of protest. Similarly, the demonstrators of the winter of 1967–1968 appealed to rather than criticized Acting President Suharto.

A third characteristic of protest in Indonesia, perhaps related to reluctance to take risks, is that acts of protest are rarely organized by the leaders of a protesting group without tacit allies, or silent partners or sympathizers, among those in equally strong or stronger power positions than they. During the boycott of 1951, the PNI and allied parties had the tacit support of President Sukarno; the student demonstrators of 1966 were both protected and aided by a number of army generals; the regional military leaders in 1956 could count on the sympathy or leaders of the powerful Masjumi Party. This generally minimized the possibility of punitive or retributive measures against the protesters.

Incidents of public protest in Indonesia by and large do not fall into the category of spontaneous or semi-spontaneous outbreaks of mass popular sentiment. On the contrary, they tend to be instigated, provoked, and planned by one or several members of a political elite. These organizers organize their immediate followers, each member of which organizes his followers for concerted action at a stipulated time, which frequently is left unspecified during the initial stages of the mobilization. That many of these incidents may frequently seem to be somewhat spontaneous appears to be a consequence of inadequate planning, uncoordinated organization, or failure of communications. In short, public protest in Indonesia is largely stage-managed in its initial inception.

In the course of the complicated maneuvers within the military leadersip preceding the October 17th Affair of 1952, the Armed Forces Chief of Staff, Colonel (later Major General) T. B. Simatupang pointed out to his associates the need for accompanying any action of theirs with a *demonstrasi rakjat*—a popular demonstration. Lower-ranking military officers, including the head of the Army Dental Services, as well as cadres of sympathizing political parties, proceeded to round up their followers. Some of the demonstrators were brought into Djakarta by trucks; others already in the city were paid to participate. Part of the mob that had been incited to demostrate against Parliament broke into the building of the Ministry of Foreign Affairs, apparently misinformed as to which building housed the Parliament. In 1955 the officers' boycott took place on the order of Acting Chief of Staff Zulkifli Lubis, one of the contenders for the post of Chief of Staff. And one of the smuggling episodes in Sulawesi had been reportedly instigated by the area commander and ordered by the local commander.[4] Although there

---

[4] Feith, *op. cit.*, pp. 495–96.

certainly appears to have been a greater element of spontaneity in the initiation of the student demonstrations of 1966 than in other instances cited, shortly after 1966 the planning and direction for much of this activity appears to have been taken over by senior military and political leaders. The January 1968 protests against rising prices by high school students seems to have been organized in great part by their teachers.

From my admittedly impressionistic observations and cursory questioning of a few mass participants in several demonstrations, I would divide these participants into the following categories: (1) those who are lower-level leaders and are somewhat sophisticated concerning the issue at hand; (2) their followers, who reiterate slogans with little understanding of their meaning; (3) hired participants; (4) those who participate "for the fun of it"; and (5) coerced or semi-coerced participants. The last three categories may require some explanation. Food and/or a few *rupiahs* and transport offered to poor Indonesians who might otherwise have little incentive to participate can swell the ranks of demonstrators. For some, taking part in demonstrations constitutes a form of recreation. If many members of a residential unit, a school, or a labor union are committed to participate in a protest, other members of that group can either be directly intimidated into joining or will feel the pressure of group solidarity.

The above is not meant to suggest that there are not sufficient sources of frustration and dissatisfaction among the Indonesian masses. In fact, it can be argued that there are so many reasons for frustration that it would be difficult for mass sentiments to coalesce around any single one without the focus and direction given by leaders. Thus, it is not difficult for leaders to select a particular issue of personal or political concern to them around which they can channel diffuse resentments.

Protest, therefore, can be seen largely as a political tactic employed by leaders in their internecine struggles for power. It is, in fact, recognized as such and becomes a standard ploy in the game of politics. One might almost discern the protest prologue. Newspaper editorials suggest that certain groups are strongly opposed to a certain situation or that "the people" are becoming impatient and, unless something is done, may take matters into their own hands. Rumors begin to circulate that something in the nature of a demonstration or an attempted coup is in the offing and speculation becomes rife in politically informed circles as to whether and when a coup will take place.

That protests are premeditated and frequently anticipated does not necessarily detract from their effectiveness as political weapons. As has been mentioned earlier, such outbreaks, however much they may be stage-managed initially, can get out of control and have unforeseen and, at times, undesired consequences. Therefore, mere hints by a political actor that he or his group can barely restrain his supporters from public and perhaps violent demonstrations is often sufficient for him to wring concessions from his opponents in a bargaining situation.

Several characteristics of the game of politics in Indonesia lend added utility to protest as a political tactic. Political contests have generally been multi-actor rather than two-actor games. This has encouraged the formation and dissolution of political alliances, counteralliances and coalitions, often of a temporary nature. There is frequently some discrepancy between the presumed and actual power of any political figure or group, who runs the risk that the radius of his or its support in a showdown does not extend as far as he anticipates; moreover, the support of his opponent might extend further than his. And the looseness of intra-group discipline and cohesion may be such that one cannot necessarily depend upon one's assumed adherents.

The instigation and execution of an act of protest, therefore, can serve several functions for a political leader. It can test the degree and radius of his support and following. If successful, it can bring into his camp the waverers, those waiting to join what is likely to be the winning side, and the group or groups who may hold the balance between him and his opponents. At least it may immobilize them or inhibit the uncommitted from joining the opposition. Finally, insofar as it is a challenge to higher authority, protest can serve as a probe to test the responses of the authority and estimate whether increased pressures toward one's objective are likely to result in repression, compromise, or capitulation.

If an attempt to arouse a public demonstration is unsuccessful, it may save a political figure or group, who was under a misapprehension of his or its relative strength, from overcommitment and risk. Thus, in 1962 when former Vice-President Hatta was urged by some political leaders to take public issue with President Sukarno in the hope of persuading the latter to abdicate, he asked them first to organize their followers to give an indication of mass support.

The instigation of acts of protest in Indonesia can thus be seen as an institutionalized and even ritualized tactic of the game of politics. This may help to explain in part why protest in Indonesia has rarely involved large-scale violence and in most cases has not gone beyond property damage and some personal injury.

It is not difficult to understand why leaders feel the necessity to organize and manifest mass support or protest, however tenuous the commitment of the masses may be. In the tenor of our times, mass support, or the appearance of it, lends legitimacy to one's claims. However much they may recognize and privately admit what they call the "feudal" nature of the basis of their following, many Indonesian leaders are committed to modernization, and apart from the necessity for mobilizing mass support or its appearance as a means of forwarding political objectives, they believe that a modernized polity, as western social scientists have emphasized, involves a high degree of popular participation. For those who are ideologically comitted to building some form of democracy, protest is also viewed as an education device; it builds group cohesion and solidarity and encourages people to "make their voices felt."

In the above, I have briefly touched upon some of the functions of public protest for political leaders and for mass followers. I might add two functions which seem relevant in the current Indonesian context of a period of economic deprivation and the absence of a charismatic figure at the peak of the political pyramid: (1) the function of protest as a mechanism of psychic release of tension, and (2) the function of popular protest as a means of inhibiting elite violations of behavioral norms. These may also explain why a military regime does not strongly repress protest and, indeed, to a limited degree encourages it. Protest releases tensions and serves as an outlet for frustration and thus can inhibit the likelihood of spontaneous and extended violence. It also serves as a control mechanism by the group in power over some of its own members. If internal cohesion is not strong—as is the case with the military elite when there is not a single powerful opponent to serve as a unifying factor—it is not easy for leaders to exert strong disciplinary pressures from above without increasing factionalism and threatening an already precarious unity. One of the modes of curbing the excesses of subordinates with respect to corruption, for example, or in cases of failures or delays in implementing policies, is to permit and even encourage criticism from other sources.

Finally, it can be argued that not only in Indonesia but in many other former colonies, public protest is an institutionalized mode of political behavior. This may, in part, be attributable to the colonial experience, during which the colonized are afforded few, if any, formal political channels through which to present their demands and grievances to formal power-holders. In the absence of such channels or in cases where they are extremely limited, protest becomes the dominant means by which politicized publics can articulate discontent and desire for change. Protest can then become incorporated into the political culture as a legitimate mode of political expression. If a post-colonial political system similarly affords few institutionalized means of registering disapproval of government leaders or their performance, or if existing channels for doing so are perceived as inadequate and ineffectual, protest is the most likely recourse.

PERU:
THE POLITICS
OF STRUCTURED
VIOLENCE*

James Payne

At first glance, Peruvian politics presents a chaotic scene to the political analyst. Demonstrations, riots, rebellions, electoral irregularities, *coups* and dictatorships: the political panorama unfolds so rapidly that there seems to be nothing permanent on which to base an analysis.

The recent political history of Peru has been kaleidoscopic. From 1939 to 1945 the country experienced a repressive government under Manuel Prado. In 1945 elections were held and a period of free government under Jose Luis Bustamante y Rivero ensued. In 1948 Bustamante was removed through a military *coup* and General Manuel Odria headed a dictatorship which lasted until 1956. Elections were held and Manuel Prado took office as President of a free regime once again. In 1962 his term was ended a few days short of the constitutional six-year period by another military *coup* which grew out of the election crisis. A military government—which observed political freedoms—ruled for one year, elections were held again, and Fernando Belaunde Terry emerged as President of a free regime in 1963.

It might seem, after gazing at this record, that the pattern of Peruvian politics is simply incoherent, that there are no regularities. The problem lies, however, in defining the system to be

* This paper was prepared from a full-length study of labor and politics in Peru. Research was conducted in Peru during the entire year of 1961. Most of the information on which this study is based has come from over one hundred interviews with labor leaders, party politicians and government officials, supplemented by personal observation of meetings, assemblies, demonstrations and strikes. The writer is grateful to Drs. Aaron Wildavsky and Robert Anderson of the University of California (Berkeley) for their assistance in the preparation of this article.

Reprinted from *Journal of Politics*, XXVII (May 1965), 362-74, by permission of the author and publisher.

analyzed. An American, familiar with the regular constitutional procedures of the United States, tends to look at the same insitutions in Peru. Finding these practices atrophied or abused, he would become discouraged, concluding lamely that the *system* is "unstable" or "perverted." But his discouragement and his lame conclusions are simply the result of adopting an inadequate theoretical perspective.

Analytically it is impractical to view Peruvian politics in a constitutional framework, for constitutionalism is not the modal pattern of interaction. To treat violence and the military *coup* as aberrations places one in the awkward position of insisting that practically all significant political events of the past half-century are deviations. Demonstrations, clashes with the police, military takeovers: these are *normal* in a purely descriptive sense. They happen frequently and they are significant.

Consequently, we must identify as a system for analysis the pattern of interaction characterized by violence and other extraconstitutional practices. In the same way that elections are central components of a constitutional democracy the military *coup* is considered essential to the functioning of the system in Peru. Riots are fully a part of the Peruvian pattern, not merely distasteful, peripheral incidents—as they are considered in the United States. When we make violence the focal point of analysis the behavior of the participants becomes understandable and— over a certain range—predictable.

In treating Peruvian politics in a short essay we must narrow down our scope of concern. Two explicit restrictions are placed on our analysis. First we shall deal with patterns of decision-making in which violence plays an immediate, critical role. Such issues include: most labor disputes, both specific wage demands and many general laws on such subjects as discharge and length of the working day; some university student-administration (or faculty) conflicts; numerous specific agrarian conflicts (land occupation by peasants, strikes of plantation workers); occasional conflicts over the cost-of-living in general or over prices of specific commodities (cement, meat, gasoline); and certain positions involving foreign policy which organizations of journalists and lawyers as well as workers and students might seek to defend violently in a particular case.

Deciding such violence-connected issues is a substantial part of the activity of government, and as such these cases merit study. In addition, an understanding of these cases is extremely useful in analyzing most of the other decisions of government, since decisions on most non-violent issues are made with the possibility of future violence in mind. For example, the decision made in late 1961 to raise the export tax on fishmeal—opposed by both the producers and the longshoremen's union—was not accompanied by violence. But decision-makers were influenced by the knowledge that to disappoint the longshoremen would engender their animosity and make future violence more probable. By analyzing the decision-making process on issues of violence we thereby gain insights into many other decisions as well. However, we make no attempt to give a complete account of all patterns of conflict resolution.

We shall further limit our analysis to a discussion of interaction during a free regime. A "free regime" may be defined as characterized by the actual freedom of all major political parties and interest groups to exist and operate, and the actual observance of freedoms of speech, press and public protest. Naturally, as in the United States, these freedoms are not absolute; nevertheless there is a wide difference in the degree to which these freedoms are observed in a free regime and in what may be termed a "dictatorship." It should be pointed out that our conception of a "free regime" does not include the idea of permanence. It is simply one phase of a global pattern.

Under a free regime groups may organize and communicate. They may mobilize opinion and gain adherents. Under a free regime groups are able to develop and stage violent attacks upon the government.

The violence to which we refer is not random or isolated; it is politically-structured violence, violence which is meaningful in the political context. In the Peruvian context politically significant violence must have the following characteristics: (1) it must be directed against significant political leaders and/or parties. In nearly all cases the object of the attack will be the President; (2) it must involve a prominent political issue on which there is wide disagreement. A simple murder, for example, does not have these properties and consequently it is not politically relevant.

In its ultimate form structured violence involves a physical attack upon agents of the government over some issue of political concern. An illustration is provided by the assault of the Congressional building in October, 1961 which occurred during the strike of the public school teachers. A group of about 300 demonstrators rushed at the entrance, the guards fired, the demonstrators fled, but one lay behind, killed by a bullet. Were this event isolated it would have been generally condemned as either silly or repugnant. But because it was structured within the political context it had highly significant repercussions.

The teachers' strike—during which this episode occurred—had become a national issue. Opposition parties and newspapers, along with the left-extremists (Communists, Trotskyites, and others) had condemned the government for its stinginess. When the demonstrator was killed it was taken as proof of the cruelty of the government. In spite of the decree suspending Constitutional guarantees (which formally prohibited all public gatherings) a gigantic funeral demonstration was held. Striking teachers joined opposition forces and gathered in the Parque Universitario. The situation was explosive. The slightest incident would have led to a massacre of serious proportions. The army troops carefully kept their distance, waiting in side streets away from the crowd. On this occasion the demonstration ended peacefully. But it could easily have been otherwise.

Uncertainty, as the reader can see from this example, is a feature of this structured violence. No one knows exactly when violence will take place. But all the participants are acutely aware of the relative probabilities of violence occurring at any particular moment. In this sense the violence is structured. Each event bears a relationship to the next so that we must speak of a pattern and not of isolated events. The congressional attack had serious overtones because it led to an even more explosive situation. But the attack in turn had its antecedents in earlier demonstrations, in newspaper invective, in opposition party meetings, in extremist activity on the issue, in the hunger strikes of some teachers, and so on. Structured violence, then, is an entire pattern of interaction, the end product of which is significant physical violence directed against the government.

Why does this pattern exist? How does violence fit into the processes of decision-making and leadership change? These are the questions which we shall attempt to answer. Our discussion will center around five propositions about political interaction during a period of free government:

1. The conflict for control of the Presidency is intense.
2. Opposition forces are disposed to employ extreme methods to destroy an incumbent President—including the use of physical violence.
3. The armed forces will remove a President when widespread "dissatisfaction" exists and incidents of violence become frequent.
4. The President, when his tenure is threatened by the use of violence, will attempt to prevent violence by making concessions to those groups which threaten its use.
5. Therefore politically structured violence is a highly effective weapon for those groups which can employ it.

The underlying drive for the Peruvian system—the mainspring, as it were—is the intensity of the conflict between the opposition and the President. Opposition forces do not view politics as a gentleman's game played for moderate stakes in an atmosphere of restraint. They see it as a struggle of overwhelming significance. The intensity of conflict explains, in large part, the frequent use of violence. Opposition forces see the outcome of this struggle against the executive as *more significant* than constitutional norms, moral injunctions or physical safety. We have in American history occasional examples of conflict so intense that it transcended the usual moral and constitutional norms—the Civil War, for example. But in Peru such intense conflict is not occasional; it is the permanent condition of political society.

We may briefly suggest certain conditions which produce this high level of conflict intensity between opposition forces and the President.

1. The Peruvian government is, and has been since colonial times, highly centralized. At the apex of the system is the President. State and municipal governments, Congress and the courts are, in practice, subordinate to him. The chief executive can and does issue authoritative decrees on almost every conceivable subject. As a consequence of this centralization the President is considered omnicompetent and hence, omni-responsible. From the price of meat to the backwardness of agriculture; from holes in streets of a provincial town to the profit rate in the mining industry: when anything goes wrong the executive is considered to have committed a sin of commission or omission.

Needless to say things do go wrong, many things. And the affected groups hold the incumbent President responsible. In a free environment the dissatisfied sectors will organize and concentrate their opposition on a single point: the executive. Whereas in most of the established Western democracies opposition is directed at diverse points in the various decision-making matrices, in Peru the President and his immediate subordinates, being the only decision-makers of consequence, receive its full impact.[1]

---

[1] It is interesting to note that Alexis de Tocqueville, in discussing the causes of the French Revolution, noted a similar centralization under the *ancien regime:* "In times of dearth—and these were frequent in the eighteenth century—everyone expected the Intendant to come to the rescue as a matter of course. For the government was held responsible for all the misfortunes befalling the community; even when these were 'acts of God' such as floods or droughts, the powers-that-be were blamed for them." *The Old Regime and the French Revolution* (Doubleday, 1955), p. 71. In discussing the stability of the American system, de Tocqueville praised the federal arrangement which insured that "political passion, instead of spreading over the land like a fire on the prairies, spends its strength against the interests and individual passions of every State." *Democracy in America* (Mentor, 1956), p. 85.

In addition to broadening the responsibility for policies, a dispersal of the decision-making processes also serves in countries like the United States to mitigate the opposition to the existing regime. Because opposition forces have, in one way or another, a foothold in the existing system, because they are contained within the government, their hostility to it is never total. In the United States a Southerner may be disappointed with the incumbent President, but he knows that he can make his views felt in the Senate as well as in local decision-making and administration. But in Peru a group excluded from the executive has no other arena in which to exercise influence. Consequently such a group finds its only practicable alternative is that of attempting to unseat the President.

Groups which formed a permanent opposition during the Prado government (1956–62) included the Popular Action Party of Belaunde, the Odria Party, the Christian Democratic Party, seven left-extremist groups—Communists, two Trotskyite factions, the APRA Rebelde, the Progressive Socialists, the Leninist Committee and the Socialists—as well as interest groups in which these parties had a controlling position: the Federation of Students of San Marcos University, the Federation of Bank Clerks, the Lima Union of Construction Workers and a number of others. Consistent with their position of isolation these groups maintained a posture of total opposition to the President.

2. The large amount of patronage which the President dispenses is another factor contributing to the isolation and intensity of the opposition. Whereas in a country like Sweden or Switzerland few posts go to political appointees, in Peru the civil service is based largely on the spoils system. Job hunters (and their friends and relatives) are numerous. In the above-named countries a change of government leaves public employees practically unaffected; in Peru it creates a horde of angered ex-office holders who see the new President as directly responsible for their loss of employment.

3. Another condition which contributes to the intense conflict found in Peruvian society is the existence of exclusive, partisan communication patterns. Holders of different political views tend to locate themselves in the communication channel which reinforces their position. This phenomenon is most clearly seen in the case of the Aprista party organization. The Apristas have their own cafeteria and barber shop, their own medical assistance staff, soccer teams, and party newspaper, *La Tribuna*. In addition there are numerous secondary groups within the party: university students, workers, high school students, artists, lawyers, and so on. Hence an Aprista may live within the party's world and never have his party loyalty weakened by contradictory communications. The other parties, to varying degrees, tend to provide their adherents with similar unified opinion environments.[2]

Two of the three major Lima newspapers, *La Prensa* and *El Comercio*, are part of the partisan channels of communication. The former supported the government in the period 1959–1962, the latter attacked it with skill and venom. Those individuals who sided with the opposition found in *El Comercio* a copious supply of criticism and invective which served to reinforce their dissatisfaction with the Prado government.[3]

[2] The analysis here draws upon the general theory of cross-pressures and attitude formation. For specific reference to the problem of political conflict see: David B. Truman, *The Governmental Process* (New York, 1960), pp. 157 ff., 507 ff.; Sigmund Neumann, *Modern Political Parties* (Chicago, 1956), p. 404; Seymour Martin Lipset, *Political Man*, (Anchor, 1963), pp. 74–79.

[3] The third Lima daily, *La Cronica*, was

Political conflict in Peru, then, is intense and bi-polar: between the In's and the Out's. Those groups which are excluded from the executive become intensely opposed to the incumbent President and are willing to take extreme measures to depose him. Centralization places in the hands of the President practically all formal decision-making power; consequently he is a significant target. Excluded from this pin-point of power opposition forces have no alternative but to work for his downfall. Deprived of patronage and reinforced in their animosity by partisan channels of communication, opposition groups see the destruction of the President as a noble and necessary task.

The visitor to Peru does not pass many days in the country before grasping the polarized nature of political conflict and the intensity of the opposition to the executive. A chat with a taxi driver, a newspaper headline: the American soon realizes that politics is a serious, even deadly, business. The desire to destroy the incumbent President is of paramount significance. The intensity with which this objective is pursued results not only in the use of violence, as we have suggested, but also in the formation of seemingly incongruent alliances. The Christian Democratic Party (in the opposition in 1961) had a peasant affairs bureau which worked closely with members of

the Trotskyite and Rebel APRA parties who were attempting to foment a revolution through rural violence. That the Pope's sworn enemies should walk hand-in-hand with his disciples testifies to the overwhelming importance of the struggle against the executive in the eyes of these participants.

The picture, as far as we have presented it, leaves out an important component: the armed forces. They maintain the chief executive in office; they protect him from the enraged opposition. The guards one finds outside the homes of most high officials are mute testimony to the military's role. And when demonstrations and riots reach excessive proportions, it is the Army which contains and disperses the mobs.

Although the armed forces tend to establish broad limits to the actions of the executive, they are characteristically uninterested in details of policy. What they are interested in is peace. It is incorrect to suppose that the military is the enemy of peaceful free government. Direct military intervention in politics has taken place only in times of acute crisis, in times when civilian political conflict threatened to lead to dangerous extremes. The military *coup* of July, 1962, is a case in point. None of the three major presidential candidates—Odria, Haya de la Torre, and Belaunde—obtained the requisite one-third of the ballots for election. Belaunde, seeing his position was weakest, agitated for annulment of the elections on the grounds of fraud. He was joined by the extremists and *El Comercio*. The other two candidates could not agree—until it was too late—on a coalition. After civilian politicians had struggled for nearly a month and produced only greater uncertainty, the armed forces stepped in and put an end to the chaotic scene.

The logic of the situation dictates that intervention should occur at such times of crisis. The armed forces,

more mass consumption-oriented and tended to avoid partisan political issues. The television stations were also relatively nonpolitical, again apparently because they were attempting to reach the largest possible audience and thus realize the greatest return on their investment. One might expect that *El Comercio* and *La Prensa* may also be forced by economic necessity to "tone down" partisan politics. For a discussion of the relationship between political cleavage, economic variables and the mass media the reader should consult Otto Kirchheimer, "The Waning of Opposition in Parliamentary Regimes," *Social Research*, Vol. 24, No. 2 (1956), pp. 149–150.

composed of different factions holding conflicting ideological and political sympathies, can act unanimously only if the civilian government has demonstrated its inability to keep order. When things are going along smoothly an attempted *coup* by one faction would be opposed by other factions of the armed forces which sympathized with the incumbent regime. A *coup* attempted in times of peace, when the armed forces are divided in their opinions, would be very dangerous. At best it could mean a court martial for the losers; at worth, internecine war.

Consequently, as long as the executive manages to keep unrest at a minimum the military tends to support the incumbent regime. But if the armed forces are repeatedly engaged in clashes with agitated mobs and armed demonstrators, they will come to believe that the wisest course is to depose the object of civilian dissatisfaction, the President. When civil war threatens, the armed forces become united in their disapproval of the existing government and a bloodless *coup* can be quickly executed.

The President of a free regime, then, while all-responsible, is by no means all-powerful. He is situated between a ravenous opposition on one side and an ambivalent military on the other. As the political temperature rises—strikes, solidarity strikes, demonstrations, clashes, deaths, protest demonstrations—the tenure of the chief executive becomes increasingly uncertain. Since the first object of the chief executive is to stay in office, the manner in which he must behave is quite clear: he must attempt to pacify, undermine or at least contain the groups employing violence against him. The most obvious manner in which he can forestall violence is to give those who threaten it a part of what they want.

This leads us to consideration of the dynamic impulse given to the system by interest groups. We have identified three actors with interrelated roles: the opposition, the President, and the military. But what sets these participants in motion? We have shown how violence cannot be random if it is to be politically effective. A group of political party members cannot simply rush out onto the street and attack a policeman. Successful violence must be structured; it must be meaningful. The opposition political parties require substantive issues of conflict on which to construct their attack upon the government.

Interest groups, particularly labor unions, provide these issues. These organizations, through their specific, substantive demands, provide opposition forces with a cause around which violence may be structured—as well as an additional supply of agitators. Once a conflict has been initated by worker organizations—or less frequently by groups of students or peasants—the opposition forces may swing into action. It follows therefore that if these interest groups are relatively quiet or if the President meets their demands rapidly with adequate concessions, violence has little opportunity to build. The crucial, "violence-initiating" position of interest groups under a free regime explains why, first of all, they are successful if they are able to initiate violence and, secondly, why control of these organizations is so important to political parties.

Opposition forces wish to control these groups in order to initiate and extend violence. In the case of labor unions opposition party (or left-extremist) control results in exorbitant demands, prolonged strikes and the frequent use of the solidarity strike for a wide range of political issues. Government-supporting parties (e.g., the APRA party during the Prado regime) wish to control interest groups to prevent their use against the executive. Worker organizations influenced by these forces tend to make their demands moderate, to avoid or curtail strikes whenever possible and to refrain from solidarity strikes except when such strikes clearly involve limited worker objectives.

In practically all major political crises worker organizations play a key role. The June 1961 strike of the construction workers provides a typical example. Called by the Communist-controlled Federation of Construction Workers, the strike was immediately given full and sympathetic coverage by *El Comercio*. The issue began to build. One worker was killed when a group of strikers attacked two policemen guarding workers. In the Chamber of Deputies members of the Popular Action and Progressive Socialist parties presented a motion to censure the Minister of Interior. The opposition-extremist Federation of Bank clerks held a one-day sympathy strike. The extremist-led regional federations of workers in Callao and Arequipa threatened to strike. University students, under the leadership of a member of the Christian Democratic Party, staged a 48-hour protest strike.

In view of the agitated political atmosphere the Ministry of Labor issued a decree granting a 12 to 15 percent (depending on the category) wage increase for construction workers. Interest waned. The construction workers had received substantial gains and were uninclined to remain on strike. Extremist leaders of other unions, although they might have wished to add to the tension, realized that rank and file workers would not obey a solidarity strike order in support of the already successful construction workers. So opposition forces withdrew to wait for the next opportunity which a worker organization conflict would provoke.

The support of political parties which have strength in the labor movement is an important asset for a President since these parties will attempt to moderate the violence which worker organizations will use. One of the major reasons for the 1948 *coup* against Jose Luis Bustamante y Rivero (President from 1945 to 1948) was the 1947 shift of the APRA party, and the many labor organizations it controlled, from support to opposition of Bustamante. The repeated use of violence-oriented strikes and demonstrations by these APRA-led unions greatly added to the political tension which finally resulted in a military *coup*. The support of the APRA party and its labor leaders provides one explanation for the relatively long term of Manuel Prado (1956–1962). This is not to say that APRA labor leaders did not threaten or use violence. But they were careful to circumscribe overt union activity so that their threatened crises seldom materialized.

Through his control over the timing and content of conflict-resolving decrees, the President has another important asset. As we pointed out above, the limits on presidential action are broad. He is not bound by constitutional constraints or similar legal trappings. He (or his ministers with his authority) may issue any decree, which has the force of law, on almost every conceivable subject. By carefully adjusting each decree to a series of variables—preference intensity of the interest groups involved, cohesiveness of these organizations, the possibility of solidarity strikes, the popularity of the cause, and the general political temperature—he can carefully circumscribe violence while not making extravagant, and eventually dangerous, concessions.

In dealing with labor conflicts, the executive has a highly institutionalized procedure to accomplish this dual objective of low violence and sound economics. When a local union voices a demand, it bargains first with management. When it fails to receive satisfactory concessions from the employer it appeals to the Ministry of Labor for a decree and, at about the same time, begins a strike. The Ministry allows time to elapse (3–10 days) in order to gauge the severity of the threat. If violence seems unlikely, the Ministry issues a modest sub-directoral resolution which awards the workers about as much as, perhaps slightly more than, the employer was willing to grant. If violence becomes imminent—solidarity strikes, newspaper agitation, opposition party rallies, university student parades —then a second (directoral) resolution is issued, usually on the eve of a solidarity strike or proposed mass demonstration.

This two-step process makes it possible to allow the assaulting union to expend most of its resources so that it might be disposed to accept a relatively low offer. At the same time the executive has a second, more generous resolution ready which may be used if the situation moves to the brink of full-scale agitation.

In order to absolve itself of the enormous responsibility inherent in "dictating" employer-employee relations throughout the country, the Ministry attempts to maintain that it employs objective criteria for its decisions: cost of living index, comparable wages, "subsistence level." But of course this is mere verbiage. Wage increases are each carved out to fit particular conflict situations, generosity being proportional to the violence potential.

For example, a tiny group of workers for the small shop Ciurlizza Maurer struck in December 1961 for higher wages. The Ministry of Labor granted a 4.26 present increase (the rise in the cost of living index for that year). The workers were not satisfied and continued striking. After nearly thirty days of strike the Ministry made a second offer of 6 percent which the workers eventually accepted. Although

there were minor instances of local violence (fist fights, for example), there was no major incident. The group of workers was very small, they belonged to no higher organization which would carry out a solidarity strike and the issue was virtually unknown to the public.

In the case of the strike of the San Miguel factory textile workers the situation was quite different. This relatively large union belonged to the Federation of Textile Workers which can muster nearly 20,000 workers into the streets in a solidarity strike in support of a member union. And behind the Federation stood the Confederation of Peruvian Workers, the national labor center. The general secretary of the Confederation was a past officer of the Federation and ties between the two organizations were quite close. When the San Miguel workers went on strike in August 1961 the Ministry of Labor granted an 11 percent wage increase, which the workers would not accept. Then, two and one-half weeks after the strike began, during a meeting of the Federation of Textile Workers where a solidarity strike was being discussed, a messenger arrived from the Ministry with a decree granting a 14 percent increase. This the workers accepted. Only by taking into account the political environment can we explain the difference between the outcomes in the case of these two unions.

Violence which is structured into the political context, then, is an eminently successful political weapon in the Peruvian free regime. A President threatened by its use will make generous concessions to the assaulting groups. And it must be thus. Many Americans fail to understand the role of the executive. They complain about his supposedly "unconstitutional," "unnatural" intervention in such affairs as labor disputes. But he must intervene to survive. It is suicidal for a President (and his Labor Minister) to "stand aloof" from such conflicts for the ever-widening circles of violence would quickly engulf him. He could, of course, attempt repression, but the road to and through dictatorship also has its dangers, not the least of which is the problem of military disunity.

The President acts as he must, as do the workers in employing violence. For them violence is a highly successful weapon. The alternative of collective bargaining, a tactic of economic coercion, offers little promise. Successful use of collective bargaining requires that numerous economic variables be favorable, particularly that the supply of unemployed labor be small. In Peru where migration has created severe unemployment, economic strikes would, in most cases, be undermined by replacements. To ask Peruvian unionists to use collective bargaining and refrain from violence is tantamount to urging dissolution of the labor movement.

The leverage of these interest groups comes, in turn, from the intense, bipolar conflict between the opposition and the President. The role which the military plays as arbitrator must also be interpreted in light of this conflict. Were Peruvian political society characterized by friendship and tranquility, the military would not find itself encouraged, even forced, to effect *coups*.

The intense conflict between the President and his opponents, then, we identify as the force which structures the entire pattern of interaction. We have briefly discussed some of the institutional and social variables which contribute to this conflict, but the problem is clearly one which invites further analysis.

APPENDIX: INVITATION TO FURTHER RESEARCH— DESIGNS, DATA, AND METHODS

Rosalind L. Feierabend
Ivo K. Feierabend

The accumulation of knowledge is always an unfinished task and the case of political violence is no exception. Although the works collected in this volume supply considerable insight into the problem, the storehouse of knowledge in the social sciences is still comparatively empty. Research on violence will continue, amending existing theories and developing new ones. More refined analyses will be pursued in the empirical sphere, and the unfolding of social and political realities will alter many established relationships.

This Appendix is intended as an open invitation to join in further inquiry. The invitation comes easily, since the works introduced in this volume are rife with suggestions and insights that need additional thought, elaboration, and testing. Furthermore, many of the empirical analyses can be replicated or carried one step further, and perhaps new analyses can be initiated. We propose that the interested student can study this complex problem on his own, without necessarily resorting to materials beyond those presented in this volume.

The Appendix stands in place of a Conclusion to signify the open-ended nature of all the studies presented in this volume. It should not be mistaken for a comprehensive essay on research design, methods, and data, nor as a substitute for a course in statistical analysis. It is intended as a simple guide for those who otherwise would not try their own "analytical trips," and as an aid for those with little or no background in statistics. The Appendix explains and elaborates a few techniques that can serve the student as quick and easy ways to test his insights and hypotheses.

Let us be specific about the explorations we have in mind. We will start with the simplest: *replication* of the studies.

1. A replication does not necessarily mean an exact duplication of an existing

study. For example, different measures may be used for the same variables that were studied by the original authors. Bwy, the Feierabends, Gurr, Midlarsky and Tanter, as well as Russett, use very much the same notion of political aggression, whether they call it political instability or total magnitude of civil strife. Furthermore, these writers use overlapping cross-national samples for their analyses and devise their own empirical measures. They also claim findings of interest and significance. The obvious question must occur to the thoughtful reader: Will the findings of these authors be supported, or will they have to be modified, if their various measures of violence are interchanged? For example, will Russett's generalizations be sustained by using all of his data, with the exception that his instability profiles are replaced by the strife measures devised by Gurr? If such exchanges yield substantially similar findings, additional confidence in the studies is provided. If similar findings are not yielded, we have to admit ambiguity and perhaps think of better explanations, hypotheses, or measures to put to the test. This sort of replication is essential to the growth of knowledge in general, as well as to our understanding of the underlying conditions of political strife, violence and revolution. The more we can test the same theoretical relationships with different measures and different data—derived from different sources and collected and interpreted by different researchers—the more certain we can be of their validity.

It is surprising how little replication occurs in social science, and this might be one of the reasons for its relative underdevelopment. We urge t ˙ ɛ student to engage in this type of analysis. The suggestion that Russett's study be redone in reference to Gurr's data is only one of many possibilities for replication that exist within the materials presented in this volume. In a similar type of replication, statistical techniques or measures can be varied. Also, the student can perhaps think of evolving his own measures for some variables.

2. The merits of replication must not be underestimated, and neither should the surprises that such replication may yield. The curiosity of the authors counsels this task. However, the careful reader can do more than replicate. He will notice that some very explicit hypotheses, as well as others which are only mentioned in passing or which are entirely implict, go untested in the present volume. The student must exercise his own ingenuity and imagination to explore them. Let us merely offer a sample of what may be done.

2a. Galtung's structural theory of aggression will serve as our example. In Galtung's estimation, the deprived and weak underdog and the privileged topdog should both engage in the fewest acts of aggression. It is the strata in between, as Galtung suggests, that are the perpetrators of violence. Those who in some respects share the fate of the underdog, and in some other respects the privileges of the topdog, feel the pinch of social injustice and relative deprivation. Could you apply Galtung's theory to the international arena? A status discrepancy index could be constructed for a sample of independent nations in reference to such values as modernity and population. Neither modernity level nor size is equally distributed among nations. Are these discrepancies related to the hostile stance different nations exhibit in international relations? Profiles assessing these value discrepancies could be compared to the profiles of international hostility reported in the Feierabend's research or in this Appendix. Also, the student will find an effort to apply Galtung's theory to the internal conflicts of Latin American nations in the article by Egil Fossum, listed in the Suggested Readings for Part II.

2b. Myriad suggestions regarding the sources of violence still need to be elaborated from raw insight to formal hypothesis. We might suppose, for example, that at certain points frustration and discontent may also find expression in individual violence, not only in political acts. National statistics on rates of homicide, accidents, alcoholism, suicide, mental illness, and other such social phenomena could be used as measures of individual aggressiveness (this Appendix includes a table of cross-national rates of homicide and suicide— see Table 12, p. 399). These profiles can then be compared to the instability or turmoil profiles reported in Part II of this book, which is devoted to cross-national research. Again, for a study which uses this approach, see the book by Robert Winslow cited in the Suggested Readings for Part II.

3. Indeed, more is possible that just a comparison of profiles. The relationship between frustration and both collective and individual violence, as well as the relationship between these two forms of aggression, deserve more theoretical attention. Could some meaningful propositions concerning these behaviors be formulated, beyond the suggestions that appear in the first theoretical portion of this book? Theoretical excursions may also be taken in a different direction. For example, does any theoretical insight fit one's personal image of the causes of student violence or the Black Revolution? Could the theoretical wisdom of some of the authors, or of all of them, be extended to include these contemporary phenomena? Which theory fits the best? Is it the relative deprivation model, the J-curve model, or psychological conflict theory? Do all fit, or are they all equally unsatisfactory? Similar questions perhaps can best be resolved through testing, and this would certainly require an independent base of data beyond what is presented here.

As an example of a design clearly beyond the boundaries of the present essays in the empirical sense, and yet inspired by them, one could devise a cross-city violence index, perhaps counting the occurrence of riots in major United States cities. Some studies of this type have been performed and may be found in the literature. Through longitudinal or cross-sectional analyses, one could ask the same type of questions as in the cross-national analyses and case studies presented in Parts II and III of this volume. Does sudden deterioration in conditions, following the Davies J-curve, trigger outbursts of violence in the United States? Or is relative deprivation—the discrepant improvement over time between whites and blacks—responsible? The same analytical approach may be applied to student riots, to determine whether the use of force, as suggested in the theoretical sections, quells or incites further violence.

The preceding discussion could be by far more elaborate regarding the details of specific research designs and could also suggest additional designs to the reader. However, this would largely defeat our purpose, for we offer the student the initiative to further research. Let us now turn to the basic techniques of analysis and retrace some of the statistical procedures that are used in various selections and that might prove useful to the student who wishes to continue with designs and data analysis.

In the following pages we show the step-by-step computations that are involved in a number of correlational techniques (product-moment correlation, rank-order correlation, scatter diagram, Phi coefficient, contingency coefficient, partial correlation, and multiple correlation); contingency techniques (Chi square); and assessments of the difference between two groups (*t*-test, Mann-Whitney *U*-test). For illustrative purposes, we have deliberately used the same two variables in all examples, with the exception of the multiple and partial correlations, for which three variables are needed. The two variables were selected primarily for ease of computation: there are only 18 cases and each variable is scored in extremely small numbers. We use the 18 Latin American countries considered by Midlarsky and Tanter, and carry out a replication of the type suggested above. The level of coerciveness of regime characterizing these countries from 1948–1960 (as scored by Feierabend and Feierabend, Table 11, p. 160) is related to the incidence of revolution between 1958 and 1960 (as determined by Midlarsky and Tanter, Table 2, p. 248).

Exploring this relationship does have theoretical import. It will be recalled from Part II that many authors hypothesize a curvilinear relationship between coerciveness and violence. Therefore, countries scoring very low and very high in coerciveness should experience fewer revolutions than countries scoring at mid-levels of coerciveness. In the following pages, the results obtained with each separate statistical technique show that although there is a linear relationship between coercion and revolution in this sample of countries, there is also some support for the curvilinear hypothesis. If we use these scores for both linear and curvilinear analyses we can see the patterning which is alternately revealed and obscured by different treatments of the data. The student should thus be sensitized to the importance of understanding his data in detail, rather than relying on a final statistical value. The same correlation coefficient can hide a variety of patterns of relationship; only a scatter diagram will show the researcher the actual patterning within the data.

Linear Relationships

CORRELATIONAL TECHNIQUES

Product-Moment Correlation (Pearson r)
The product-moment correlation may be calculated by hand (or with the aid of a desk calculator) from the scores of each country on the two variables of interest. In our example, calculation of the correlation involves matching the coerciveness score and the revolution score for each country. This information in provided in Table 1, which shows all values needed for the computation.

Table 1

PRODUCT-MOMENT CORRELATION

(1)	(2)	(3)	(4)	(5)	(6)
	Coercive-ness		Revolu-tion		
	X	X^2	Y	Y^2	XY
Argentina	5	25	4	16	20
Brazil	3	9	1	1	3
Chile	3	9	0	0	0
Colombia	4	16	2	4	8
Costa Rica	2	4	0	0	0
Cuba	5	25	4	16	20
Dominican Republic	6	36	1	1	6
Ecuador	4	16	0	0	0
El Salvador	4	16	1	1	4
Guatemala	4	16	2	4	8
Haiti	5	25	2	4	10
Honduras	4	16	2	4	8
Mexico	2	4	0	0	0
Nicaragua	5	25	2	4	10
Panama	3	9	3	9	9
Uruguay	2	4	0	0	0
Venezuela	5	25	6	36	30
Totals	70	296	31	101	140

Computation: The formula we will use for the product-moment correlation makes use of the actual score assigned to each country on each dimension: number of revolutions and the rating of coerciveness. These actual scores are called "raw" scores, in contrast to scores which have been converted to some other form, such as a rank or percentile score. Since we have deliberately picked raw data which are reported in very small numbers in order to keep the calculations simple, the raw score formula is easy to use. When the student is dealing with large scores (such as GNP/capita), he will either want to use a desk calculator or convert these scores to some form that is easier to handle.

The raw score formula for the product-moment correlation is:

$$r = \frac{N\Sigma XY - (\Sigma X)(\Sigma Y)}{\sqrt{N\Sigma X^2 - (\Sigma X)^2}\sqrt{N\Sigma Y^2 - (\Sigma Y)^2}}$$

where: $X =$ a country's score on the coerciveness dimension,

$Y =$ a country's score on number of revolutions,

$N =$ the number of countries, and

$\Sigma =$ the sum of (sigma).

The correlation is calculated as follows:

1. $N =$ the number of countries $= 18$.
2. $\Sigma XY =$ each country's coerciveness score $\times$ its revolution score. These products are then summed for all countries. (Column 6 in Table 1 shows these cross-products.) $\Sigma XY = 140$.
3. ΣX may be obtained by summing the revolution scores for all countries (column 2 in Table 1). $\Sigma X = 70$.
4. ΣY is obtained by summing the revolution scores for all countries (column 4 in Table 1). $\Sigma Y = 31$.
5. The numerator of the correlation formula may now be calculated since all required values are known:
   a. Multiply $N (= 18)$ by ΣXY $(= 140)$. $N\Sigma XY = 2520$.
   b. Multiply $\Sigma X (= 70)$ times ΣY $(= 31)$. $\Sigma X\Sigma Y = 2170$.
   c. Subtract 5(b) from 5(a). $2520 - 2170 = 350$.

This is the value of the numerator.

6. ΣX^2 is obtained by squaring each country's coerciveness score and then summing these squared values (column 3 in Table 1). $\Sigma X^2 = 296$.
7. ΣY^2 is obtained by squaring each country's revolution score and then summing these squared values for all countries (column 5 in Table 1). $\Sigma Y^2 = 101$.
8. $(\Sigma X)^2$ is found by squaring the value obtained in step 3, above. It is the square of the sum of all coerciveness scores. $(\Sigma X)^2 = (70)^2 = 4900$.
9. $(\Sigma Y)^2$ is found by squaring the value obtained in step 4 above. It is the square of the sum of all revolution scores. $(\Sigma Y)^2 = (31)^2 = 961$.
10. The denominator of the correlation coefficient may now be calculated:
    a. Multiply $N (= 18)$ times ΣX^2 (step 6 $= 296$). $(18)(296) = 5328$.
    b. Subtract $(\Sigma X)^2$ (step 8 $= 4900$) from the product obtained in 10(a). $5328 - 4900 = 428$.
    c. Find the square root of 428. $\sqrt{428} = 20.69$.
    d. Multiply $N (= 18)$ times ΣY^2 (step 7 $= 101$). $(18)(101) = 1818$.
    e. Subtract $(\Sigma Y)^2$ (step 9 $= 961$) from the product obtained in 10(d). $1818 - 961 = 857$.
    f. Find the square root of 857. $\sqrt{857} = 29.27$.
    g. Multiply the square root value obtained in Step 10(c) times the square root value obtained in Step 10(f). $(20.69)(29.27) = 605.6$. *This is the value of the denominator.*
11. The correlation may now be determined, since the numerator and denominator of the formula are both known:

$$\frac{350.0}{605.6} = .58$$

We now know that for this sample of 18 Latin American countries, the product-moment correlation between the coerciveness level of regime, as measured by Feierabend and Feierabend, and the incidence of revolution, as determined by Midlarsky and Tanter, is $r = .58$. How should we interpret this statistic? The maximum value which may be attained by a correlation is 1.00 (either $+1.00$ or -1.00) and the minimum value is 0. A correlation of $+1.00$ between two variables indicates perfect positive linear relationship, so that an increment in one variable is accompanied by an increment in the other. A perfect negative, or inverse, correlation (-1.00) implies the same degree of association, with the difference that an increment in one variable is now accompanied by a decrement in the other. A correlation value of 0 shows complete lack of relationship. Thus, somewhere between 0 and 1.00 lie all of the possible values which the correlation coefficient may assume. The closer the coefficient is to 1.00, the higher the degree of relationship (e.g., .91 or .85). The closer the coefficient is to 0 (e.g., .15 or .21), the less the relationship between two variables. One way to interpret the size of the correlation coefficient depends upon understanding that the square of the coefficient is equal to the percent of variation in one variable which is explainable in terms of the other. With a correlation coefficient of .58, 34 percent $(.58^2)$ of the variation in occurrence of revolution among the sample of countries studied may be explained from a knowledge of their level of coerciveness of regime.

Why is the correlation coefficient less than perfect (1.00)? There are three possibilities: (1) There may be other factors which are associated with revolution. If coerciveness of regime is only one of a set of conditions related to the incidence of revolution, one would not expect the two to covary perfectly. (2) The actual degree of relationship

between coerciveness and revolution may be greater than indicated. Measurement error is very much involved in this type of research. Definitions of revolution may differ and a country's coerciveness score may be in error because it is based on a gross judgmental rating. In this way, certain nations may have been misvalued on either or both of these dimensions. This type of random error reduces the measured size of the relationship. Systematic error, however, may increase the size of the relationship (see Feierabend and Feierabend, p. 175, n13). (3) The relationship may actually be curvilinear and this statistic measures degree of linear association. We shall discuss methods of determining curvilinearity later in this Appendix.

Rank-Order Correlation (*Spearman Rho*)
A simpler computational method of estimating degree of relationship is through the use of the rank-order correlation. Each country's actual score on a dimension is converted to a rank-order position, and the rank-order positions on the two dimensions are then compared. This method has the obvious advantage of computational simplicity, for once the rank-orders are determined (which may be tedious, but only if the number of countries is very large), the calculations involve the use of small numbers. The savings are especially noticeable when the scores are large numbers, rather than single digits, as in our above example.

One aspect of the rank-order correlation to bear in mind is that it reduces all distances between scores to unit intervals. Thus, extreme scores, or "outliers," are brought into line with other scores in the distribution. This may or may not be considered an advantage. Let us explain how an extreme score may increase (or decrease) the size of a correlation. In our example, we have two countries with extreme scores, although they are not really "outliers" since there is no large interval between their scores and the next highest ones. One of our extreme scorers is Venezuela, with the highest number of revolutions (the only country scoring 6). The Dominican Republic is the other high scorer, with the highest coerciveness rating (again the only country scoring 6). Venezuela contributes heavily to the positive linear relationship between coercion and revolution, since it also scores fairly high in coerciveness (level 5). The Dominican Republic, however, reduces the size of the correlation, because it is the highest in coerciveness but among the lowest in revolutions.

To understand the effect of outliers, let us imagine that the Dominican Republic scored 25 in coerciveness (an impossibility, of course, since coerciveness is measured on a 6-point scale, thus forcing the countries into a unit-interval range). Or suppose that Venezuela were found to have 25 revolutions, whereas no other country had more than 5. In the former case, were it possible, the Dominican Republic would work strongly to nullify the positive relationship between coerciveness and revolution shown by the remaining 17 countries. In the latter case, the positive correlation coefficient would be very much higher (inflated) than when calculated without Venezuela, using only the remaining 17 countries.

A caution regarding Spearman *Rho* is that it should not be used when there are too many ties among scores. There is another rank-order method, Kendall's *tau*, which is not affected by ties, but it is more complicated to compute. In deciding whether to use a Spearman *Rho*, perhaps the best rule for the purposes of this Appendix is to suggest that it is a quick and easy way to estimate the degree of relationship between two variables. If the student discovers a relationship of interest using this technique, he may then explore the relationship further using different statistical methods. Also, as will be seen when we complete the computations, the value obtained from this method is not apt to vary markedly from the value yielded by the product-moment correlation.

Computation: To calculate the rank-order correlation between coerciveness of regime and frequency of revolution, let us look at these two variables in Table 1. We must first order the scores on both dimensions from lowest to highest (or vice versa). The scores may then be assigned rank-order numbers.

1. Assign rank-order positions to the scores on both distributions, as in Table 2. Where there are ties among raw scores, the rank position is averaged among them. For example, in Table 2, three countries fall at coer-

Table 2

RANK-ORDERING

Coerciveness		Revolution	
Score	Rank	Score	Rank
2	2	0	3
2	2	0	3
2	2	0	3
3	5	0	3
3	5	0	3
3	5	1	7.5
4	9.5	1	7.5
4	9.5	1	7.5
4	9.5	1	7.5
4	9.5	2	12.
4	9.5	2	12.
4	9.5	2	12.
5	15	2	12.
5	15	2	12.
5	15	3	15.
5	15	4	16.5
5	15	4	16.5
6	18	6	18

civeness level 2. If they had each scored at a different coerciveness level (e.g., levels 1, 2, and 3), they would have received rank-order positions 1, 2, and 3. As it is, the three rank positions must be averaged, with the result that each country is at rank position 2. The same averaging is necessary for the next three countries, all of which fall at coerciveness level 3. Instead of being assigned rank positions 4, 5, and 6, these three positions are averaged and each country is assigned rank position 5.

There are really too many ties among both sets of scores for the rank-order correlation to be an optimum statistic. However, we will carry out the computation for illustrative purposes and also to show that it provides a reasonable estimate of the degree of relationship.

2. The 18 countries must now be arranged to indicate their rank-order position on both variables. To do this, the country's raw score on each dimension must be located in Table 1 and the rank-order position for this raw score found in Table 2. Country names and rank-order positions are given in Table 3. We now have the basic information necessary for computing the rank-order correlation.

The formula for *Rho* is:

$$\rho = 1 - \frac{6(\Sigma D^2)}{N(N^2 - 1)}$$

where: D = the difference between each country's rank-order position on one variable and its rank-order position on the other,

N = the number of countries, and

Σ = the sum of.

Table 3

RANK-ORDER CORRELATION

(1)	(2) Coerciveness Rank	(3) Revolution Rank	(4) D (Col 2 — Col 3)	(5) D²
Argentina	15	16.5	−1.5	2.25
Brazil	5	7.5	−2.5	6.25
Chile	5	3	2	4.
Colombia	9.5	12.	−2.5	6.25
Costa Rica	2	3.	−1	1.
Cuba	15	16.5	−1.5	2.25
Dominican Republic	18	7.5	10.5	110.25
Ecuador	9.5	3.	6.5	42.25
El Salvador	9.5	7.5	2.	4.
Guatemala	9.5	12.	−2.5	6.25
Haiti	15.	12.	3.	9.
Honduras	9.5	12.	−2.5	6.25
Mexico	2.	3.	−1.	1.
Nicaragua	15.	12.	3.	9.
Panama	5.	15.	−10.	100.
Peru	9.5	7.5	2.	4.
Uruguay	2.	3.	−1.	1.
Venezuela	15.	18.	−3.	9.
Total				324.00

It is apparent from the formula that the value of the rank-order correlation depends upon the size of the difference between each country's rank-order position on the two variables. If the correlation is to be high, the differences must be small. This is only logical within the meaning of a correlation: if coerciveness is associated with the occurrence of revolution, then a country should have approximately the same rank-order position on both variables.

We can see by inspection of Table 3 that two countries stand out as exceptions to the hypothesis. The Dominican Republic ranks highest in coerciveness among the 18 countries, but among the lowest in incidence of revolution. However, Panama ranks among the less coercive countries, but has experienced more revolutions than most. It is an advantage of the rank-order method that these exceptions to the hypothesis may easily be located by inspection, because of the rank-ordering. Those cases which fit the hypothesis are also readily found. We may locate a number of cases which support the hypothesis very well, especially Costa Rica, Mexico, and Uruguay. Only by pursuing the calculation of the rank-order correlation, however, will we be able to determine the degree of relationship for all countries.

3. Subtract the rank-order positions in columns 2 and 3 of Table 3. The direction of difference is unimportant to the calculation (except for the interest value it provides the student), since the differences will be squared. The differences are entered in column 4 of Table 3.
4. Square the differences. The squared values are given in column 5 of Table 3.
5. Sum these squared differences. The total is entered at the bottom of column 5. $\Sigma D^2 = 324$.

We may now solve the formula for *Rho* (ρ) since all required values are known.

6. Multiply 6 times ΣD^2. This is 6 times 324. The numerator of the formula, $6(\Sigma D^2) = 1944$.

To arrive at the value for the denominator of the formula, we must solve for $N(N^2 - 1)$.

7. Multiply N ($= 18$) times $N^2 (= 18^2 = 324)$. $(18)(324) = 5832$.
8. Subtract N ($= 18$) from the value obtained in step 7. $5832 - 18 = 5814$.
9. The ratio for the formula is:

$$\frac{1944}{5814} = .34$$

10. Subtract:

$$1 - .34 = .66$$

The value obtained by the rank-order correlation method is .66, as compared with a product-moment correlation of .58. The rank-order coefficient is slightly higher than the Pearson *r*, but it represents a good estimate of the degree of relationship. Without so many ties among rank-order position, the *Rho* value would be even closer to the value of *r*.

Chi Square (X^2) *Contingency:* A different approach to the positioning of countries on two or more variables lies in the use of a contingency table and the calculation of Chi square. This method is the simplest to calculate but yields somewhat different information than a correlation. It tells you the number of countries which score high (low) on one variable and high (low) on the other. The numbers entered into the contingency table and used in calculating the Chi square are frequencies, not scores.

For example, let us return to the association between coerciveness of regime and the occurrence of revolution. To explore this association through contingency techniques and Chi square, we must ask the question: How many countries show both a high (low) level of coercion and a high (low) frequency of revolution? To answer this question, we must first determine what is a high level and what is a low level of each variable. This may be done by asking: Which score separates the distribution of 18 countries so that half the countries fall below that score and half fall above it? This is known as dichotomizing the distribution at the median, or 50th percentile.

Computation:
1. Order the raw scores on each variable from lowest to highest. This has already been done in Table 2. Since there are 18 countries, we wish to divide them approximately in half, with 9 countries counted as low scorers and 9 countries counted as high scorers. We find that because of the large number of ties, we are not able to cut the distribution of coerciveness scores exactly in half. There are 6 countries scoring at level 4 on coerciveness and we must decide to place them either in the low or the high coerciveness category. Either way, we will be left with one category including 12 countries and the other including 6 countries, rather than the desired equal dichotomy. In this particular case it makes no difference where we decide to place the countries with level 4 coerciveness ratings, since half of these 6 countries are high in frequency of revolution and half are low in revolution. As a result, no matter how we classify them on coercion, half will fit the hypothesis and half will contradict it. So we will simply decide to cut the distribution between coerciveness

ratings 4 and 5; countries scoring 4 and below are counted low in coerciveness and countries scoring 5 and above are counted high. If the student wishes to see for himself that it makes no difference into which coerciveness category the countries at level 4 are placed, he may try including them within the high coercive group. The resultant table will show the following cell frequencies:

| Revolution | Coerciveness | | |
	Low	High	Totals
Low	5	4	9
High	1	8	9
Totals	6	12	18

The Chi square value will be the same as the one calculated from Table 4.

Looking at the ordered revolution scores in Table 2, we see that it is possible to cut this distribution exactly in half. Nine countries score 0 to 1 and 9 score between 2 and 6. This time we have established our cutting point at the median (50th percentile) of the distribution.

2. Form a contingency table as illustrated in Table 4. In this table, countries have been entered into the cells corresponding to their position on both coerciveness and revolution. From simple inspection of the table, it can be seen that more than twice as many cases fit the hypothesis as contradict it (13:5). Also, one of the key advantages of this technique is that the individual countries which fit the hypothesis, and those which are exceptions to it, may easily be identified.

It should be remembered, however, that dichotomizing a distribution into high and low scorers is a very unrefined technique that categorizes together

Table 4

2 × 2 CONTINGENCY TABLE

	Coerciveness		
Revolution	*Low (2–4)*	*High (5–6)*	*Totals*
Low (0–1)	Brazil Chile Costa Rica Ecuador El Salvador Mexico Peru Uruguay 8	Dominican Republic 1	9
High (2–6)	Colombia Guatemala Honduras Panama 4	Argentina Cuba Haiti Nicaragua Venezuela 5	9
Totals	12	6	18

countries which can be quite far apart in score value. For example, on the frequency of revolution index, Guatemala and Venezuela are both considered high scorers and are treated as equivalent, although one country had two revolutions and the other had 6. By the same token Guatemala and the Dominican Republic are placed in different categories, although there is only one score difference between them.

Despite this gross measure of "high" and "low," we do see in Table 4 that the combinations high–high and low–low are more than twice as frequent as the two intercombinations. The question which we must answer by completing the Chi square calculation is whether the degree of association observed is significantly different from chance.

The formula for a 2 × 2 Chi square (X^2) is the following. This formula includes $N/2$ in the numerator, which is a correction for small cell frequencies.

$$X^2 = \frac{N\left[(AD - BC) - \left(\frac{N}{2}\right)\right]^2}{(A + B)(C + D)(A + C)(B + D)}$$

where: N = the number of cases (countries), and
A, B, C, D = the frequencies in the cells of the 2 × 2 table, as follows:

			Totals
	A	B	$A + B$
	C	D	$C + D$
Totals	$A + C$	$B + D$	N

3. To solve for the numerator of Chi square, complete the following steps:
   a. Multiply A (= 8) times D (= 5). (8)(5) = 40 = AD.
   b. Multiply B (= 1) times C (= 4). (1)(4) = 4 = BC.
   c. Subtract BC from AD. $AD - BC$ = 40 − 4 = 36.
   d. Subtract $\frac{1}{2}N$ (9) from the result of 3(c). $(AD - BC) - \frac{1}{2}N$ = 36 − 9 = 27.
   e. Square the value obtained in 3(d). 27^2 = 729.
   f. Multiply N (= 18) times the result of 3(e). (18)(729) = 13122.

4. To obtain the denominator of the Chi square formula, multiply all marginal totals together. $A + B$ ($= 9$) times $C + D$ ($= 9$) times $A + C$ ($= 12$) times $B + D$ ($= 6$). $(9)(9)(12)(6) = 5832$.
5. Solve the formula:

$$\frac{13122}{5832} = 2.25$$

Chi square (X^2) $= 2.25$. What does this number tell us? It cannot be interpreted in the same way as a correlation. It tells us whether or not the distribution of cases in the cells of the table differs significantly from what was to be expected. We determine the expected cell frequencies in terms of proportions. Given the proportion of the total number of cases which is represented by the row total and column total corresponding to a cell, what proportion of cases should fall into that cell? For our example, the calculation is as follows:

		Totals
A?	B?	9
C?	D?	9
Totals 12	6	18

For cells A and C, the row totals are 9 and 9, and the column total is 12. The calculation of expected cell frequencies is the following:

Multiply $\frac{9}{18}$ times $\frac{12}{18}$ times 18. This equals:

$$\frac{1}{2} \cdot \frac{2}{3} \cdot 18 = \frac{2}{6} \cdot 18 = \frac{1}{3} \cdot 18 = 6.$$

For cells B and D, the row totals are 9 and 9, and the column total is 6. The expected cell frequencies are calculated as follows:

Multiply $\frac{9}{18}$ times $\frac{6}{18}$ times 18. This equals:

$$\frac{1}{2} \cdot \frac{1}{3} \cdot 18 = \frac{1}{6} \cdot 18 = 3.$$

Therefore, we find the expected cell frequencies to be the following:

		Totals
6	3	9
6	3	9
Totals 12	6	18

But the obtained, or actual, frequencies as shown in Table 4 differ considerably from the expected, indicating an interaction or association between coerciveness and revolution. The crucial question is: What is the probability that this obtained patterning differs from the expected one to a degree that would not occur by chance alone? Much of statistics, and all of inferential as contrasted to descriptive statistics, consists of making exactly these kinds of probability estimates. Unfortunately, perhaps, in the opinion of the authors, it is neither possible nor advisable to embark on a discussion of statistical inference in these few pages. The student is referred to other works on statistics in the list of Suggested Readings.

We will simply say that it is possible to make these estimates of non-chance ("true") versus chance findings and, in fact, that is what the Chi square calculation accomplishes. The estimates depend, in general, on the following considerations: the method for selecting the sample, the size of the sample, the shape of the distribution of scores, the amount of variation in individual scores (variance), and the degrees of freedom in the distribution of scores.

The concept of "degrees of freedom" refers to the leeway for variation available in a set of scores, once the totals (overall and marginal) are fixed. In a 2×2 table such as we are analyzing, there is only one degree of freedom. This is the case because, given the row and column totals, once the first cell entry is made, the values of all other cell entries are fixed. In general, the degrees of freedom available to a set of scores is always one less than the total number of scores. For example, if we say that a set of five numbers equals 20, and that the values of the first four numbers are 4, 6, 2, and 1, the value of the fifth number has to equal 7. In a contingency table, the number series and their totals are calculated in terms of the rows and columns of the table. Thus, the degrees of freedom of the table correspond to:

(number of rows − 1)
$\times$ (number of columns − 1).

In a 2 $\times$ 2 table, there is always one degree of freedom:

$$(2 - 1)(2 - 1) = (1)(1) = 1.$$

To determine the probability estimate that the obtained Chi square value of 2.25 is likely to occur by chance alone, we must look at a table of Chi square values. This table will be found in any book of statistics. The table is entered in terms of degrees of freedom. For a contingency table with one degree of freedom (that is, a 2 $\times$ 2 table), we find that a Chi square of 3.8 would be likely to occur by chance less than 5 times in 100. This is the customary level for regarding an association as significantly different from chance. Since the obtained Chi square value of 2.25 is less than 3.8, we may say that the degree of association between coerciveness and revolution does not meet the standard test of a significant association.

The student may wonder why 5 times in 100 is selected as the acceptable chance level. A lower chance value than this is obviously even more reassuring. In some studies it is shown that the results could have occurred by chance only one time in 100 or only one time in 1,000. For a 2 $\times$ 2 table, a Chi square value of 6.6 would occur by chance only one time in 100, and a value of 10.8 only one time in 1,000. Note that in many research studies, the obtained Chi square value far exceeds 10.8, indicating an extremely low probability of chance findings (see the values reported by Feierabend and Feierabend in their cross-national research, pp. 146–174). The 5/100 possibility of a chance occurrence is conventionally assumed to be the largest risk which an experimenter is willing to take in claiming that his data show "true" relationship. Probability levels are reported in the following way:

$$p\ .05, \quad \text{or} \quad p\ .01, \quad \text{or} \quad p.\,001.$$

Sometimes they are written:

$$p > .05 \ (> = \text{greater than}), \text{ or}$$
$$p < .05 \ (< = \text{less than}).$$

It is perplexing that the Chi square test does not reveal a significant degree of association, whereas the correlation values are about .6, indicating considerable relationship between these two variables. Also, looking ahead, the other tests of this relationship, the t-test and the Mann-Whitney U-test, do reveal a significant degree of association. There are two possible explanations: First, the correlation value may depend upon the range of revolution scores, which we have classified together into one category and treated as equivalent. It may be the high revolution (and coerciveness) scores of Cuba, Argentina and, especially, Venezuela which contribute a great deal of weight to the correlation. This pattern is apparent in the scatter diagram in Table 5, below. We have lost this weighting of high scores by using the contingency method.

Second, there is a probelm created for all statistical analyses by using very small samples. According to the rules of Chi square, it is not an appropriate statistic where fewer than 5 cases are expected to occur in any cell. This is a rule which we have obviously violated (3 cases were expected to occur in cells *B* and *D*). We did include a correction factor (dividing by N/2) for small cell frequencies. It is interesting to note that with the correction factor omitted, the resultant Chi square value is 4.0, indicating a significant degree of association.

CONTINGENCY:

DEGREE OF RELATIONSHIP

Various techniques are available to test the degree of relationship between two variables from a 2 × 2 contingency table. It is important for the student to remember that Chi square itself is not a correlation. However, from the Chi square, or contingency table, either a *Phi* Coefficient or a contingency coefficient (*C*) may be calculated. These two statistics are, in fact, types of correlations, and range in value from −1.00 through 0 to +1.00. The *Phi* Coefficient is designed to be calculated from a 2 × 2 table and the contingency coefficient may be used with tables having more than two rows and/or more than two columns. These are called complex contingency tables and are discussed in the next section. The contingency coefficient may be used with a 2 × 2 table, however, provided a correction factor is applied.

The calculation of these two statistics is presented now, with the contingency techniques rather than with the correlational methods, because they are calculated directly from a knowledge either of the Chi square value or of the cell frequencies. It is easier for the student to understand the calculations if they are presented here.

Phi Coefficient The formula for calculating the *Phi* Coefficient of degree of relationship is:

$$\frac{AD - BC}{\sqrt{(A + B)(C + D)(A + C)(B + D)}}$$

1. It is clear that we already know the value of $AD - BC$ from the calculation of Chi square. $AD - BC = 36$.
2. We also know the value of the term under the square root sign, which was calculated in (4) of the Chi square computation, above.

$$(A + B)(C + D)(A + C)(B + D) = 5832.$$

3. Take the square root of the result of (2). $\sqrt{5832} = 76.37$.
4. Solve the formula:

$$\frac{36}{76.37} = .47$$

The value of the *Phi* Coefficient is .47, which is lower than the Pearson *r* of .58 and the Spearman *Rho* of .66.

Contingency Coefficient (C) The formula for the contingency coefficient is:

$$C = \sqrt{\frac{X^2}{X^2 + N}}$$

It is obvious that, once the value of Chi square is known, the contingency coefficient may readily be calculated:

1. $X^2 = 2.25$
2. $X^2 + N = 2.25 + 18 = 20.25$
3. $2.25/20.25 = .111$
4. Take the square root of .111 = .333.

This value of .33 is even lower than the value of .47 yielded by the *Phi* Coefficient. It was mentioned above, however, that if the contingency coefficient is calculated from a 2 × 2 table, it must be adjusted by a correction factor. The correction factor derives from the fact that *C* cannot exceed .707 (that is, it cannot achieve the full value of +1.00) when calculated from a 2 × 2 table. So the final step is the application of the correction factor, as follows:

$$\frac{.333}{.707} = .47$$

The student will see that, with this correction, the contingency and *Phi* coefficients are identical in value. Both are lower, however, than the Pearson and Spearman correlation values. If we remember that the value of Chi square did not turn out to be significantly different from chance, using the accepted criterion of a probability level of 5/100, some of the same explanations may be offered. The loss of the range of scores, a loss which occurs when scores are classified into groups, may weaken the association between coerciveness and revolution. Both the *Phi* and the contingency coefficient use the same grouped values as does the Chi square.

Nonlinear Relationships

All the statistical techniques discussed so far assume a linear relationship between two variables. What about the case in which the direction of relationship reverses itself after a certain critical or threshold value? These are nonlinear, or curvilinear, relationships. Within the cross-national studies of violence reported in this volume, a certain number of authors (Bwy, Feierabend and Feierabend, and Gurr) have found a curvilinear relationship between the use of coercion, or repressive force exercised by a government, and the occurrence of political instability, anomic violence, or civil violence. The shape of a curvilinear relationship is as follows:

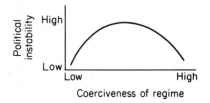

If the relationship between two variables is in fact curvilinear, linear methods will yield very low values. This is inevitable since scores on one dimension will begin to decrease just when they should be increasing (in the case of a positive linear relationship). How, then, may we assess degree of curvilinearity of relationship? A statistic, *eta*, is available for this purpose. However, it is suggested that the student may use two methods which will yield evidence of curvilinearity by simple inspection. One of these is a scatter diagram, or plot of the relationship; the other is a complex contingency table. If, after inspection, there is strong evidence of curvilinearity, the student may pursue more complicated calculations, if he wishes.

Scatter Diagram It is always advisable to plot the relationship between two variables, even where curvilinearity is not suspected, since the same correlation value can be yielded by a variety of scatter plots. If the student really wishes to see the pattern of a relationship, he can only do so by plotting it.

Computation:

1. To diagram the relationship between two variables, it is necessary to determine a set of scale intervals for each variable. Our task is simplified in plotting the relationship of coercion against revolution, since both of these have already been ordered from highest to lowest in previous

And the shape of a linear relationship is, of course:

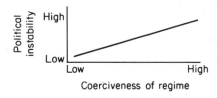

Table 5

SCATTER DIAGRAM

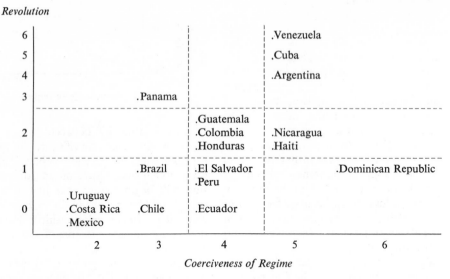

Revolution

6				.Venezuela		
5				.Cuba		
4				.Argentina		
3		.Panama				
2			.Guatemala .Colombia .Honduras	.Nicaragua .Haiti		
1		.Brazil	.El Salvador .Peru			.Dominican Republic
0	.Uruguay .Costa Rica .Mexico	.Chile	.Ecuador			

| 2 | 3 | 4 | 5 | 6 |

Coerciveness of Regime

exercises (Table 2). If this had not been done, it would be the first step for the student to follow.

2. Divide the ordered dimensions into a reasonable number of intervals. The larger the number of intervals, the more information is preserved, but for practical purposes and ease of handling the data, the student may wish to group the data into grosser intervals. Our task is again simplified by the fact that the two dimensions consist of a small range of scores. Hence, they may be plotted as scores, without being grouped into scale intervals.

3. Plot each country's position on both dimensions, as in Table 5. By writing country names into the scatter plot, we can retain more useful information.

Looking at the scatter diagram, we see a strong linear relationship between coerciveness and revolution, from coerciveness levels 2 through 5. A reversal of direction is apparent, however, with the Dominican Republic, the one country at coerciveness level 6. Although

the sample is too small to make this a strong tendency, it is in corroboration of the findings using 84 nations, in which coerciveness level 5 is the threshold value between instability and a reversed trend towards stability (Feierabend and Feierabend).

Complex Contingency Table A related method of determining nonlinearity by inspection is through the use of a complex contingency table, as illustrated in Feierabend and Feierabend (Tables 12, 14, and 15, pp. 161, 164, and 166). The complex contingency table groups countries into larger intervals than does the scatter diagram, and then tallies the number of countries falling into each cell. For example, complex contingency tables tend to divide countries into 3, 4, 5, 6 or more different groups on a dimension. It is not customary to use too many groups; the number which may sensibly be used, of course, depends on the number of cases. A Chi square value may be calculated from complex contingency tables. If the student intends to do so, then too many groups are a disadvantage for two reasons: First, unless there is a very large total number of cases, when the cases are divided into too many subgroups, the expected frequencies for any one cell will be less than 5. This violates the rule for the calculation of Chi square. Second, it is almost impossible to interpret a significant degree of association based on too many intersecting subgroups.

For these reasons, the student will note that Chi square values were not calculated by Feierabend and Feierabend for their expanded contingency tables. The tables do have interest value for simple inspection, however, and may reveal considerable patterning in the data—which is why we present the method here. The actual calculation of Chi square based on complex contingency tables is not given, but may be found in books on statistics (see Suggested Readings).

In the example we are considering in this Appendix, grouping into even a 3×3 contingency table will obscure rather than reveal the very slight tendency toward curvilinearity shown in the scatter diagram. For example, if the countries are divided into 3 equal-sized groups on the dimension of coerciveness, there will be 6 countries at levels 2 and 3, 6 countries at level 4, and 6 countries at levels 5 and 6. It is impossible to trichotomize the revolution dimension into equal groups. Choices are between grouping revolution scores 0–1, 2, and 3–6; 0, 1–2, and 3–6; or, alternatively, 0, 1, and 2–6. A further possibility is to dichotomize this dimension, yielding a 3×2 contingency table.

All these groupings are shown in Table 6, and one is indicated by dotted lines on the scatter diagram (Table 5). This shows the student that a complex contingency table and a scatter diagram are essentially the same, except that the contingency table uses broader groupings. The contingency tables in Table 6 —especially Tables C and D—bring out the linearity in the data. The single

Table 6

COMPLEX CONTINGENCY TABLES

		Coerciveness		
Revolution	2–3	4	5–6	Totals
A.				
3–6	1	0	3	4
2	0	3	2	5
0–1	5	3	1	9
Totals	6	6	6	18
B.				
3–6	1	0	3	4
1–2	1	5	3	9
0	4	1	0	5
Totals	6	6	6	18
C.				
2–6	1	3	5	9
1	1	2	1	4
0	4	1	0	5
Totals	6	6	6	18
D.				
2–6	1	3	5	9
0–1	5	3	1	9
Totals	6	6	6	18

case of the Dominican Republic is lost by being grouped with countries at coerciveness level 5. Where the sample is larger, however, including more countries at each coerciveness level, curvilinear tendencies reveal themselves in complex contingency tables.

Differences between Groups

A different approach to determining the relationship between two variables is to ask whether there is a difference in average score on one dimension between countries grouped into high and low scorers on the other dimension. This question is very close to the one asked in a contingency table, except that it is the average *scores* of the two groups which will now be compared. In our example, the question would be the following: What is the average (mean) number of revolutions experienced by low coercive and high coercive countries? There are two methods which may be used to answer this question. One method, a *t*-test, uses scores; the other method, the Mann-Whitney *U*-Test, uses ranks. We will discuss both of these.

t-test The first step is to divide the sample of countries into low coercive and high coercive groups. We have already performed this step in Table 4 and will maintain the same groupings, with 12 low coercive countries and 6 high coercive ones. We must now calculate the average (mean) number of revolutions experienced by countries in each group. This is done in Table 7.

Table 7

t-TEST

Number of Revolutions			
Group 1: Low Coercive		Group 2: High Coercive	
(1)	(2)	(3)	(4)
X_1	X_1^2	X_2	X_2^2
0	0	1	1
0	0	2	4
0	0	2	4
0	0	4	16
0	0	4	16
1	1	6	36
1	1	19	77
1	1	$\bar{X}_2 = 19 \div 6 = 3.17$	
2	4		
2	4		
2	4		
3	9		
12	24		
$\bar{X}_1 = 12 \div 12 = 1$			

We see in this table that there is an average of one revolution per country among low coercive states, and an average of 3.17 revolutions per country among high coercive states. Is this a statistically significant difference? The *t*-test is a means of determining the significance of a difference in mean score between two groups.

The formula for the *t*-test is:

$$t = \frac{\bar{X}_1 - \bar{X}_2}{\sqrt{s^2\left(\frac{1}{N_1} + \frac{1}{N_2}\right)}}$$

where: $\bar{X}_1$ = the mean (average) score on revolutions for group 1 (low coercive);

$\bar{X}_2$ = the mean (average) score on revolutions for group 2 (high coercive);

N_1 = the number of cases (countries) in group 1 (low coercive);

N_2 = the number of cases (countries) in group 2 (high coercive); and

s^2 = the variance, which may be computed by the following formula:

$$s^2 = \frac{\Sigma X_1^2 - \frac{(\Sigma X_1)^2}{N_1} + \Sigma X_2^2 - \frac{(\Sigma X_2)^2}{N_2}}{N_1 + N_2 - 2}$$

X_1 = the revolution scores for group 1;

X_1^2 = the revolution scores for group 1, squared;

X_2 = the revolution scores for group 2;

X_2^2 = the revolution scores for group 2, squared; and

Σ = the sum of.

Computation:

1. $\bar{X}_1 - \bar{X}_2$ = the difference between the mean revolution scores of the two groups. It is equal to $1 - 3.17 = -2.17$. This is the numerator of the formula.

2. For the denominator of the formula, we must first calculate s^2.

   a. ΣX_1 = the sum of the revolution scores for group 1. It is entered at the bottom of column 1 in Table 7. $\Sigma X_1 = 12$.

   b. ΣX_1^2 = the sum of the squared revolution scores for group 1. The squared scores are given in column 2. The sum is entered at the bottom of the column. $\Sigma X_1^2 = 24$.

c. $N_1 =$ the number of countries in group 1. $N_1 = 12$.

d. $\Sigma X_2 =$ the sum of the revolution scores for group 2. It is entered at the bottom of column 3. $\Sigma X_2 = 19$.

e. $\Sigma X_2^2 =$ the sum of the squared revolution scores for group 2. These squared scores are entered in column 4 and the sum is at the bottom of the column. $\Sigma X_2^2 = 77$.

f. $N_2 =$ the number of countries in group 2. $N_2 = 6$.

g. $(\Sigma X_1)^2 =$ the square of the sum of the revolution scores for group 1. $(\Sigma X_1)^2 = (12)^2 = 144$.

h. $\dfrac{(\Sigma X_1)^2}{N_1} = \dfrac{144}{12} = 12$.

i. $\Sigma X_1^2 - \dfrac{(\Sigma X_1)^2}{N_1} = 24 - 12 = 12$.

j. $(\Sigma X_2)^2 =$ the square of the sum of the revolution scores for group 2. $(\Sigma X_2)^2 = (19)^2 = 361$.

k. $\dfrac{(\Sigma X_2)^2}{N_2} = \dfrac{361}{6} = 60.17$.

l. $\Sigma X_2^2 - \dfrac{(\Sigma X_2)^2}{N_2} = 77 - 60.17 = 16.83$

m. Add the results of 2(i) and 2(l). $12 + 16.83 = 28.83$.

n. Add $N_1 + N_2$. $12 + 6 = 18$.

o. Subtract 2 from the result of 2(n). $18 - 2 = 16$.

p. Divide the result of 2(m) by the result of 2(o). $\dfrac{28.83}{16} = 1.8$.

This is the value of s^2.

3. Multiply the result of 2(p) by $\dfrac{1}{12} + \dfrac{1}{6} = \dfrac{3}{12}$ $(1.8)(.25) = .45$.

4. Take the square root of the result of (3). $\sqrt{.45} = .67$.

This is the denominator of the formula.

5. We may now solve for t. $\dfrac{-2.17}{.67} = -3.24$.

This value of 3.24 may be found in a table of t-values to determine whether or not it is statistically significant. The question is: What is the probability that this difference would occur by chance? For $N_1 + N_2 - 2$ degrees of freedom (16 d.f.), a t value of 3.24 would occur by chance less than one time in 100. It thus meets the test of a significant difference.

The Mann-Whitney U-Test There are methods for discovering the difference between two groups using rank-orders rather than raw scores. One of these is the Mann-Whitney U-Test. It is especially applicable to a case such as ours, where the distribution of scores is skewed and the two groups are of unequal size.

Skewness is a description of the shape of a distribution of scores and may be contrasted to a "normal" or bell-shaped distribution. The normal frequency distribution peaks at the middle score in a range of scores and slopes off symmetrically on either side of the middle toward the extreme high and extreme low scores. Thus, if revolutions had been found by Midlarsky and Tanter to be normally distributed in Latin America in the time period studied, the shape of the curve would look like this:

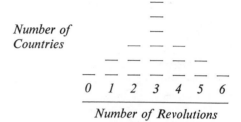

Number of Countries

0 1 2 3 4 5 6

Number of Revolutions

Three revolutions would be the most frequent occurrence, with let us say, 6 countries showing this pattern. Then half as many countries (3) would show one less or one more revolution than the norm. Thus, two-thirds of all countries (12) would exhibit 2 to 4 revolutions. The extreme low scorers and high scorers would also be symmetrical (two countries having 1, and two having 5 revolutions; one country having none, and one having 6 revolutions).

The actual occurrence of revolution in this sample of countries does not show this symmetry. Rather, the distribution is skewed—that is, it peaks to one side or the other. In this case, 14 countries score between 0 and 2 revolutions; only 4 countries score between 3 and 6 revolutions. Let us draw the shape of this distribution as it actually occurs.

Number of Revolutions

Given this skewness, as well as the unequal size of the two coerciveness groups, the Mann-Whitney U-test is a more applicable statistic than the t-test. (The t-test may also be used, however, with groups of unequal size.)

The first step in calculating U is to rank-order the revolution scores for all 18 countries. This has already been done for the rank-order correlation and is shown in Tables 2 and 3. The rank-orders are now listed separately for low coercive and high coercive groups of countries, as in Table 8.

The formula for this statistic is:

$$U = n_1 n_2 + \frac{n_1(n_1 + 1)}{2} - R_1$$

Table 8

MANN-WHITNEY *U*-TEST

Revolution Frequency: Rank-Order

Group 1: Low Coercive		Group 2: High Coercive	
Chile	3	Dominican Republic	7.5
Costa Rica	3	Haiti	12
Ecuador	3	Nicaragua	12
Mexico	3	Argentina	16.5
Uruguay	3	Cuba	16.5
Brazil	7.5	Venezuela	18
El Salvador	7.5	*Total*	82.5
Peru	7.5		
Colombia	12		
Guatemala	12		
Honduras	12		
Panama	15		
Total	88.5		

and

$$U' = n_1 n_2 + \frac{n_2(n_2 + 1)}{2} - R_2$$

where: n_1 = the number of countries in group 1;

n_2 = the number of countries in group 2;

R_1 = the sum of the rank-orders of countries in group 1; and

R_2 = the sum of the rank-orders of countries in group 2.

Computation:

1. Multiply n_1 times n_2. (12)(6) = 72.
2. Multiply n_1 times $n_1 + 1$. (12)(13) = 156.
3. Divide 2 into the result of (2). $\frac{156}{2} = 78$.
4. Add the result of (1) to the result of (3). 72 + 78 = 150.
5. Subtract the sum of the ranks for group 1 from the result of (4). 150 − R_1 = 150 − 88.5 = 61.5.
6. U' may be determined by subtraction. Subtract the result of (5) from the result of (1). 72 − 61.5 = 10.5

The value 10.5, which represents U for the smaller size sample, may be found in a table of U values in a statistics text. Because there are fewer than 8 cases in the smaller sample, the value can be found directly in the table. We find that a U of 10.5 is likely to occur by chance only 2 times in 100. It meets the test of a statistically significant difference.

Multivariate Methods

The methods which we have discussed so far compare two variables at a time. Dealing with large numbers of variables simultaneously is laborious, and the student would be well advised to see that he has recourse to modern electronic computing equipment. But three variables may be handled simultaneously with little effort, using correlational techniques or contingency techniques in a somewhat different manner than previously described.

Two different questions may be asked in a 3-variable analysis. First: How well may the dependent variable be predicted from two independent variables taken in combination? This is multiple correlation and is used in most of the cross-national studies in Part II.

Multiple Correlation (R) For illustrative purposes, we will abandon the relationship between coerciveness and frequency of revolution and deal instead with the intercorrelation matrix in Feierabend and Feierabend (Table 21, p. 175). Here we see that the relationship between coerciveness of regime and external conflict is .27. The relationship between systemic frustration and the same measure of external conflict is .33. The question is: What is the relationship to external conflict of these two variables taken in combination?

The formula for a multiple correlation is:

$$r_{1 \cdot 23} = \sqrt{\frac{r_{12}^2 + r_{13}^2 - 2r_{12}r_{13}r_{23}}{1 - r_{23}^2}}$$

If: 1 = external conflict,
2 = coercion, and
3 = systemic frustration,

then: $r_{12} = .27$,
$r_{13} = .33$, and
$r_{23} = .58$.

Computation:

1. Square r_{12}. $(.27)^2 = .07$.
2. Square r_{13}. $(.33)^2 = .11$.
3. Add the results of (1) and (2). $(.07) + (.11) = .18$
4. Multiply 2 times r_{12}. $(2)(.27) = .54$.
5. Multiply r_{13} times r_{23}. $(.33)(.58) = .19$.
6. Multiply the result of (5) times the result of (4). $(.54)(.19) = .103$.
7. Subtract the result of (6) from the result of (3). $(.18) - (.103) = .077$.
8. Square r_{23}. $(.58)^2 = .34$.
9. Subtract the result of (8) from 1.00. $(1.00) - (.34) = .66$.
10. Divide the result of (7) by the result of (9). $\frac{.077}{.66} = .12$.
11. Take the square root of the result of (10). $\sqrt{.12} = .346$.

The multiple correlation value is .35. This indicates that if we combine country scores on both coercion and systemic frustration, we only very slightly increase our probability of predicting the external conflict level of these countries. We are in a better position than when we use coercion alone, but there is only a very slight improvement over our use of systemic frustration.

Partial Correlation A second, quite different question may be asked of the interrelationship among three variables:

Can the apparent relationship between two of the variables in fact be due to their common relationship to the third variable? For example, we know that coerciveness and systemic frustration are both slightly related to external conflict and also show considerable relationship to each other. We then may ask: How much of the relationship between coercion and external conflict is due to the effect of systemic frustration? Another way of asking the same question is: How much of a relationship will be left between coercion and external conflict if we remove (partial) the influence of systemic frustration?

The formula for a partial correlation is:

$$r_{12 \cdot 3} = \frac{r_{12} - r_{13}r_{23}}{\sqrt{1 - r_{13}^2}\sqrt{1 - r_{23}^2}}$$

Let us use the same notations and correlation values as in calculating the multiple correlation.

Computation:

1. Multiply r_{13} times r_{23}. (.33)(.58) = .19.
2. Subtract the result of (1) from the value of r_{12}. .27 − .19 = .08.
3. Subtract r_{13}^2 from 1. 1.00 − .11 = .89.
4. Find the square root of the result of (3). $\sqrt{.89}$ = .94.
5. Subtract r_{23}^2 from 1. 1.00 − .34 = .66.
6. Take the square root of the result of (5). $\sqrt{.66}$ = .81.
7. Multiply the result of (4) times the result of (6). (.94)(.81) = .76.
8. Divide the result of (2) by the result of (7). $\frac{.08}{.76}$ = .11.

The partial correlation is .11. This tells us that the apparent relationship between coerciveness and external conflict which, admittedly, was small to begin with, is due in large part to the influence of systemic frustration. Very little relationship between coerciveness and external conflict remains when the influence of systemic frustration is removed (partialled) from the equation.

Chi Square Chi square may also be used to explore the relationship between two variables, when the influence of a third variable is controlled. This method answers the same question as does a partial correlation. The cases are first divided into groups on one dimension. The sample may be split in half, forming a high and a low group, or may be subdivided into as many subgroups as seem meaningful to the analysis (e.g., high, medium, and low groups, etc.). The degree of association between the two variables of interest to the researcher will now be explored separately for each subgroup.

For our example, let us return to the country scores with which we are by now familiar. We may hypothesize that the relationship between coerciveness of regime and incidence of revolution in Latin American countries will be different for high GNP per capita and low GNP per capita societies. We might provide theoretical underpinning for this hypothesis by saying that until GNP per capita reaches some threshold value in a society, the inhabitants will not engage in political violence. This is one way (although not necessarily a good way) of measuring the concept of "participant society."

We must return to Table 2 in Midlarsky and Tanter's selection (p. 248) and divide the 18 countries into a high GNP per capita and a low GNP per capita group. We find that GNP per capita ranges from $105 in Haiti to $648 in Venezuela. The sample may be divided exactly in half, 9 countries falling between $105 and $262, and 9 between $263 and $648. We will now construct two separate contingency tables, each relating level of coerciveness to incidence of revolution (see Table 9). One contingency table is for the high GNP per capita group of countries, the other is for the low GNP per capita countries.

Upon inspection of Table 9, we find that in fact GNP per capita does not seem to bear on the relationship between coerciveness and revolution. The patterning of countries in the cells is very much the same in each contingency table. We find the same tendency for a low level of coerciveness to be associated with a low level of revolution, whether the countries are high or low in GNP per capita. Similarly, the occurrence of revolution among high coercive countries is almost the same, whether the countries are high or low in GNP per capita. The only different pattern is shown by the Dominican Republic, a low GNP per capita country. However, from our previous analyses, we can say that the Dominican Republic's

Table 9

CONTINGENCY TECHNIQUE: THREE-VARIABLE ANALYSIS

Low GNP per capita ($105–$262)

Coerciveness

Revolution	Low (2–4)	High (5–6)	Totals
Low (0–1)	Ecuador El Salvador Mexico Peru 4	Dominican Republic 1	5
High (2–6)	Guatemala Honduras 2	Haiti Nicaragua 2	4
Totals	6	3	9

High GNP per capita ($263–$648)

	Low (2–4)	High (5–6)	Totals
Low (0–1)	Brazil Chile Costa Rica Uruguay 4	 0	4
High (2–6)	Panama Colombia 2	Argentina Cuba Venezuela 3	5
Totals	6	3	9

extremely high level of coerciveness (level 6), rather than its low GNP per capita, is apt to be responsible for its low revolution score.

Some observations are in order regarding the relative merits of the partial correlation and the contingency technique, for the student might wonder which method to use. Much depends on the technique which is used to explore the basic relationship of interest in the research. The partial correlation technique is easy to calculate, but only after all the necessary product-moment coefficients are known. If the researcher has all the correlation values at his disposal, then he may readily calculate the partial correlation, but if he has been using a contingency analysis, it will be more convenient to continue with this latter method.

These are purely practical considerations. An equally practical point of a different order is that controlling for a third variable using the contingency technique drastically cuts the size of the sample available for the Chi square analysis. In our example, we are down to 9 cases in each table, which makes it virtually impossible to carry out a meaningful test of significance. So there must be a large number of cases in the total sample if the contingency method is used.

Another more general point should also be made regarding the tactic of controlling for a third variable. This approach can be very fruitful, but only if there is some good theoretical reason for predicting the influence of a third variable upon the relationship. The two selections in Part II which make the most use of partial correlations (Gurr, and Midlarsky and Tanter) rely on theory and prediction of the path of relationship, without which, calculating partial correlations can become something of a game. For example, should we predict a relationship between GNP per capita and revolution, and control for level of coerciveness? Or should we predict a relationship between GNP per capita and coerciveness, and control for number of revolutions? We can go in circles unless sufficient thought has been given to the theoretical basis for analysis.

Conclusion

This completes the brief survey of statistical techniques. All of them can be performed by hand and will allow the student to explore hypotheses and relationships before turning to more complex designs for which an electronic computer is required. The student who has had a course in statistics may find this computational Appendix unnecessary, and for the reader who has never been exposed to data analysis, we repeat our warning that this Appendix cannot serve as a substitute for a more comprehensive course. We have made no effort to provide the theoretical basis for any of the techniques described, and consequently, we have imparted no genuine understanding of statistics. Rather, it is hoped that the reader has gained some practical perspective of a do-it-yourself nature which will enable him to test some of his hunches. Inevitably, some ideas and concepts, especially the meaning of tests of significance, were given short shrift in these few pages. A list of Suggested Readings on statistics is given below.

As a final inducement to the student to explore this field, we are including six additional sets of data in this Appendix (Tables 10, 11, 12, 13, 14, and 15). The first (Table 10) is the set of political instability scores from Feierabend and Feierabend, representing the completed collection drawn from *Deadline Data on World Affairs*, 1948–1965. Countries were profiled for three 6-year periods within the 18 years, and these grouped profiles were then summed. In this way,

countries which experienced a high level of internal violence in one subperiod, but not in the other two, have their final scores tempered by the two periods of quiescence. This distribution is not too markedly skewed. No countries are at the 0 position, but two are at position 1 and only one country, Indonesia, is at scale position 6, indicating a civil war during each of the three 6-year periods. This profiling technique, and other profiles based on the same data, are described in the full text of the article by I. K. Feierabend, R. L. Feierabend, and B. A. Nesvold, "Social Change and Political Violence: Cross-National Patterns," a portion of which is reproduced in this volume (see pp. 107–118).

The second set of data (Table 11) is a frequency count of assassinations drawn from *The New York Times Index*, covering 20 years, 1948–1967. These data were gathered for the National Commission on the Causes and Prevention of Violence. For a description of this data collection and the definitions of *assassination, plot* (including alleged plot), *top government official*, etc., see I. K. Feierabend, R. L. Feierabend, B. A. Nesvold, and F. M. Jaggar "Political Violence and Assassination: Cross-National Patterns," in W. J. Crotty, ed., *Assassination and the Political Order* (New York: Harper & Row, 1971); or J. F. Kirkham, S. G. Levy, and W. J. Crotty, *Assassination and Political Violence*, Vol. 8, A Report to the National Commission on the Causes and Prevention of Violence (Washington, D.C.: U.S. Government Printing Office, 1969).

A somewhat different type of data is provided in Table 12, which gives cross-national rates of homicide and suicide, drawn from the *Demographic Yearbook*, 1965. For some interesting relationships between these scores and political violence, see Robert W. Winslow, *Society in Transition: A Social*

Approach to Democracy (New York: The Free Press, 1970). These scores are also used in relation to frequency of assassination in the two sources on assassination cited above.

Table 13 presents a set of internal and external conflict scores for 86 nations for the time period 1955–1960. Twelve acts of external conflict and nine types of internal conflict are distinguished. These data were collected for 1955–1957 by Rudolph J. Rummel, and for 1958–1960 by Raymond Tanter. They are available from the Inter-University Consortium for Political Research, University of Michigan, Ann Arbor, Michigan. For a more comprehesive description of these data collections, see Rudolph J. Rummel, "Dimensions of Conflict Behavior Within and Between Nations," *General Systems Yearbook*, 8 (1963), 1–50; and Raymond Tanter, "Dimensions of Conflict Behavior Within and Between Nations, 1958–60," *Journal of Conflict Resolution*, X, No. 1 (March, 1966), 41–64.

Two additional sources of cross-national data should be brought to the reader's attention, since both offer a wealth of measured demographic, social, economic, and political dimensions for a large sample of nations of the world. These are: Arthur S. Banks and Robert B. Textor, *A Cross-Polity Survey* (Cambridge, Mass.: The M.I.T. Press, 1963); and B. M. Russett, H. R. Alker, Jr., K. W. Deutsch, and H. D. Lasswell, *World Handbook of Political and Social Indicators* (New Haven: Yale University Press, 1964).

The last two tables (Tables 14 and 15) present country scores on two of the ecological indicators devised by Feierabend and Feierabend. The Satisfaction Index (Table 14) represents 62 countries for the time period 1948-1955. Each country's combined coded score on GNP/capita in U.S. dollars, caloric intake per day, number of newspapers, radios, telephones, and persons per physician is divided by the country's coded literacy or urbanization score, whichever is higher (see the discussion on page 144). The Modernity Index (Table 15) scores 84 countries for the same 1948-1955 time period. Country scores on the eight ecological indicators were converted to standard scores and a mean (average) standard score calculated for each country (see page 145).

Suggested Readings

Amos, J. R., F. L. Brown, and O. G. Mink, *Statistical Concepts*. New York: Harper & Row, Publishers, 1965.

Benson, Oliver. *Political Science Laboratory*. Columbus: Charles E. Merrill, 1969.

Blalock, Hubert M., Jr. *Social Statistics*. New York: McGraw-Hill Book Company, 1960.

Bruning, J. L., and B. L. Kintz. *Computational Handbook of Statistics*. Glenview, Ill.: Scott, Foresman & Company, 1968.

Buchanan, William. *Understanding Political Variables*. New York: Charles Scribner's Sons, 1969.

Garson, G. David. *Handbook of Political Science Methods*. Boston: Holbrook Press, 1971.

Gurr, Ted R. *Polimetrics: An Introduction to Aggregate Political Research*. Englewood Cliffs, N. J.: Prentice-Hall, Inc., 1973.

Tables of
Cross National Data

Table 10

POLITICAL INSTABILITY PROFILES OF 84 COUNTRIES (1948–1965)
(STABILITY SCORE SHOWN FOR EACH COUNTRY IS GROUPED SCORE, AVERAGED)

1	2	3	4	5	6
Netherlands 04021	U.K. 07112	Belgium 10162	France 13435	Argentina 16445	Indonesia 18416
Luxembg. 03012	Ghana 07106	Chile 10156	U. of So. Africa 13422	Bolivia 16318	
	Austria 07057	Mexico 10111	Brazil 13209	Cuba 16283	
	Denmark 07030	Uruguay 10100	Morocco 13194	Iraq 16274	
	Iceland 07026	Israel 10064	Portugal 13190	Colombia 16244	
	W. Germany 06087	Liberia 10036	Turkey 13189	Burma 16213	
	Finland 06056	Ethiopia 10034	Poland 13179	Venezuela 15429	
	Taiwan 06039	Italy 09192	Thailand 13152	Syria 15329	
	Australia 06026	Libya 09069	Jordan 13145	Korea 15291	
	Sweden 06020	Romania 09060	Cyprus 13123	Haiti 15205	
	Ireland 05031	Costa Rica 09058	Hungary 13113	Peru 15196	
	S. Arabia 05018	Afghan. 09029	Philipp. 13105	Greece 14236	
	N. Zealand 05015	Canada 08084	Czech. 13100	Guatem. 14234	
		Switzer. 08042	China (M) 13086	Lebanon 14212	
		Norway 08034	Cambodia 13071	Egypt 14152	
			India 12360	Paraguay 14141	
			Iran 12237	E. Germany 14138	
			Pakistan 12231	Laos 14129	
			Sudan 12189	Tunisia 14126	
			U.S.S.R. 12165	Honduras 14105	
			Ecuador 12117	Panama 14101	
			Nicaragua 12096	El Salvador 14079	
			U.S.A. 11318		
			Spain 11284		
			Dom. Rep. 11195		
			Ceylon 11152		
			Japan 11123		
			Malaya 11108		
			Yugosl. 11077		
			Bulgaria 11071		
			Albania 11067		
Stability					Instability

Table 11

FREQUENCY OF ASSASSINATIONS FOR 84 NATIONS, 1948–1967[a]

	All Persons				Top Government Officials Only				Chiefs of State Only			
	Total Events	Attempts		Plots	Total Events	Attempts		Plots	Total Events	Attempts		Plots
		Suc-cessful	Unsuc-cessful			Suc-cessful	Unsuc-cessful			Suc-cessful	Unsuc-cessful	
Cuba	28	10	6	12	12	1	1	10	11	—	1	10
Korea	20	5	5	10	11	1	3	7	8	—	1	7
Iran	19	8	6	5	12	2	6	4	7	—	3	4
Morocco	17	7	7	3	5	—	4	1	3	—	2	1
United States	16	5	9	2	3	1	1	1	3	1	1	1
Tunisia	16	9	4	3	5	—	3	2	3	—	1	2
Philippines	15	5	2	8	8	—	1	7	5	—	—	5
France	14	1	6	7	11	—	4	7	9	—	3	6
Egypt	14	2	5	7	9	1	3	5	8	1	2	5
Venezuela	12	1	6	5	6	1	2	3	4	1	2	1
Lebanon	12	6	6	—	9	3	6	—	5	—	5	—
Guatemala	12	9	1	2	4	3	—	1	2	1	—	1
Brazil	12	3	3	6	3	—	2	1	1	—	—	1
Laos	10	8	2	—	4	3	1	—	—	—	—	—
Japan	9	2	3	4	5	1	2	2	3	—	2	1
Bolivia	9	1	6	2	4	—	2	2	2	—	—	2
Argentina	9	—	3	6	8	—	2	6	5	—	1	4
India	8	3	4	1	6	1	4	1	4	—	3	1
Syria	7	4	2	1	1	1	—	—	—	—	—	—
Ghana	7	—	4	3	6	—	4	2	6	—	4	2
Dom. Republic	7	3	2	2	5	1	2	2	4	1	1	2
Colombia	7	4	2	1	3	1	1	1	1	—	—	1
Malaya	6	4	1	1	3	1	1	1	1	—	—	1
Jordan	6	2	—	4	4	1	—	3	4	1	—	3
Cambodia	6	2	2	2	5	1	2	2	4	—	2	2
Panama	5	2	1	2	2	1	—	1	2	2	—	1
Pakistan	5	3	—	2	2	2	—	—	2	2	—	—

Country	1	2	3	4	5	6	7	8	9	10	11	12
Nicaragua	3	1	1	5	3	1	1	5	3	1	1	5
Iraq	1	3	—	4	1	3	—	4	1	3	1	5
Indonesia	2	3	—	5	2	3	—	5	2	3	—	5
Haiti	1	1	—	2	1	1	—	2	1	3	1	5
Greece	1	—	—	1	1	1	—	2	2	1	2	5
Czechoslovakia	1	2	—	3	1	3	—	4	1	3	1	5
Cyprus	—	—	—	—	—	2	1	3	—	2	2	5
Burma	—	2	1	3	1	—	1	—	1	—	5	5
Turkey	1	1	—	2	1	3	—	4	—	3	—	4
South Africa	—	—	—	1	—	1	1	2	2	2	2	3
Thailand	1	—	—	1	1	—	—	1	3	—	—	3
Paraguay	1	—	—	—	2	—	—	2	—	—	3	3
Mexico	—	—	—	—	—	—	—	—	—	1	2	3
Italy	—	1	—	1	—	1	—	2	1	1	1	3
Israel	1	—	—	2	1	1	—	2	1	2	—	3
Ecuador	1	1	—	2	1	1	—	3	2	1	2	3
China-Mainland	2	—	—	2	2	—	—	2	1	1	—	3
Yugoslavia	1	—	—	—	1	—	—	—	—	—	2	2
W. Germany	—	—	—	—	—	1	1	1	1	—	1	2
Spain	—	—	—	1	—	1	—	1	1	1	1	2
Saudi Arabia	1	1	—	1	1	1	1	2	1	1	—	2
Portugal	1	—	1	2	1	1	—	2	—	2	—	2
Liberia	1	—	—	1	1	2	—	2	1	—	—	2
Ethiopia	—	1	1	1	1	—	1	1	1	2	1	2
El Salvador	1	—	—	1	1	—	—	1	—	—	—	2
Costa Rica	—	—	—	—	—	—	—	—	1	1	2	2
Ceylon	—	—	1	—	1	—	1	1	—	1	—	2
Australia	—	—	—	1	—	—	—	2	—	—	2	2
Albania	1	1	—	1	—	—	1	1	1	—	—	2
Afghanistan	—	—	—	1	—	—	—	1	—	1	1	2
Sudan	1	—	—	—	1	—	—	1	1	1	1	2
New Zealand	—	—	—	—	—	—	1	—	—	—	1	1
Libya	—	—	—	—	1	—	—	—	1	—	—	1
Hungary	—	1	—	—	—	—	—	—	—	1	—	1
Canada	—	1	—	—	—	—	—	—	—	1	1	1

Table 11 (cont.)

	All Persons				Top Government Officials Only				Chiefs of State Only			
	Total Events	Attempts		Plots	Total Events	Attempts		Plots	Total Events	Attempts		Plots
		Successful	Unsuccessful			Successful	Unsuccessful			Successful	Unsuccessful	
Belgium	1	1	—	—	—	—	—	—	—	—	—	—
Austria	1	1	—	—	—	—	—	—	—	—	—	—
U.S.S.R.	—	—	—	—	—	—	—	—	—	—	—	—
Uruguay	—	—	—	—	—	—	—	—	—	—	—	—
United Kingdom	—	—	—	—	—	—	—	—	—	—	—	—
Switzerland	—	—	—	—	—	—	—	—	—	—	—	—
Sweden	—	—	—	—	—	—	—	—	—	—	—	—
Romania	—	—	—	—	—	—	—	—	—	—	—	—
Poland	—	—	—	—	—	—	—	—	—	—	—	—
Peru	—	—	—	—	—	—	—	—	—	—	—	—
Norway	—	—	—	—	—	—	—	—	—	—	—	—
Netherlands	—	—	—	—	—	—	—	—	—	—	—	—
Luxembourg	—	—	—	—	—	—	—	—	—	—	—	—
Ireland	—	—	—	—	—	—	—	—	—	—	—	—
Iceland	—	—	—	—	—	—	—	—	—	—	—	—
Honduras	—	—	—	—	—	—	—	—	—	—	—	—
Finland	—	—	—	—	—	—	—	—	—	—	—	—
E. Germany	—	—	—	—	—	—	—	—	—	—	—	—
Denmark	—	—	—	—	—	—	—	—	—	—	—	—
China-Taiwan	—	—	—	—	—	—	—	—	—	—	—	—
Chile	—	—	—	—	—	—	—	—	—	—	—	—
Bulgaria	—	—	—	—	—	—	—	—	—	—	—	—
Number of Countries = 84												
Totals =	409	143	134	132	216	34	85	97	152	12	52	88
Means =	4.87	1.70	1.60	1.57	2.57	.40	1.01	1.54	1.81	.14	.62	1.05

ªCountries are rank-ordered on the basis of the total frequency of assassinations.

Table 12

HOMICIDE AND SUICIDE RATES, 1965

Country	Suicide	Homicide
Australia	14.5	1.6
Austria	22.8	1.0
Belgium	14.0	0.7
Brazil	14.2	10.8
Bulgaria	8.7	2.1
Burma	2.9	16.7
Canada	8.2	1.3
Ceylon	11.6	3.2
Chile	3.0	2.3
China, Rep. of (Taiwan)	19.1	1.4
Colombia	4.8	25.5
Costa Rica	3.0	3.5
Czechoslovakia	21.3	1.1
Denmark	19.1	0.8
Dominican Rep.	1.0	2.1
Ecuador	0.6	5.2
Finland	19.8	2.2
France	14.9	0.8
Germany Fed. Rep. of (W)	19.3	1.2
Greece	3.2	1.2
Guatemala	3.0	14.0
Hungary	28.6	1.7
Iceland	9.0	0.5
Ireland	2.0	0.6
India	0.5	2.2
Israel	5.0	—
Italy	5.3	1.1
Japan	14.9	1.5
Jordan	0.3	2.4
Luxembourg	9.4	0.6
Mexico	1.8	22.0
Netherlands	6.5	0.4
New Zealand	8.0	1.4
Nicaragua	1.0	26.0
Norway	8.0	0.7
Panama	5.3	7.3
Peru	1.4	2.1
Philippines	0.6	2.3
Poland	8.4	1.0
Portugal	9.5	1.2
Spain	4.9	0.1
Sweden	18.5	0.8
Switzerland	16.8	0.7
U.A.R.	0.1	4.1
U. Kingdom	11.7	0.6
United States	10.8	5.1
Uruguay	12.2	4.8

Table 13

DOMESTIC AND FOREIGN CONFLICT DATA 1955-1960[a]
(RUDOLPH J. RUMMEL AND RAYMOND TANTER)

A. Domestic Conflict: I

Nations	Assassinations		General Strikes		Guerrilla Wars		Major Government Crises		Purges	
	55–57	58–60	55–57	58–60	55–57	58–60	55–57	58–60	55–57	58–60
Afghanistan										
Albania										
Argentina	3		10	12	2	2	3	4	6	
Australia										
Austria	n.s.[b]		n.s.		n.s.		n.s.	1	n.s.	
Belgium				5			1	1		
Bolivia	1			1		1	2	2		
Brazil	1	1		1					1	
Bulgaria										
Burma					3	3	1	1		
Cambodia		1				1		1		
Canada										
Ceylon				4				3	1	
Chile		1	1	2			2	1	2	2
China						1				
Rep. of China								1		
Colombia	1		3		1	3		1	1	
Costa Rica					1	1				
Cuba	5	2	1	3	3	3		5		5
Czechoslovakia										
Denmark										
Dom. Republic		4				2		3	1	1
Ecuador								1		
Egypt	1	n.s.		n.s.		n.s.		n.s.	2	n.s.
El Salvador		1						1		
Ethiopia										

Country								
Finland	5							
France	2				1	2	2	4
E. Germany								
W. Germany								
Greece						2	2	
Guatemala	1	4			1	2	2	2
Haiti		12			2	2	3	
Honduras	2				1	3	2	
Hungary	1						3	
India	3	2		3	3			
Indonesia	1	6		3	3	3	2	
Iran	1			2	1	1	1	
Iraq	5			2	2	2		4
Irish Republic	1							
Israel	1			1		2	2	
Italy	4		2	1	2	2	2	
Japan	3	3	3			3	3	
Jordan	3	1		1	2	1	1	1
N. Korea								
S. Korea	2			3	3	2		1
Laos	n.s.	n.s.	n.s.	3	3	2		
Lebanon	10		1	3		6	n.s.	
Liberia	1					2		
Libya	n.s.	n.s.	n.s.	3			n.s.	
Mexico	4		3	3		4		
Morocco	n.s.	n.s.	n.s.	2	3	1	n.s.	
Nepal	4				3	4		
Netherlands						1		
New Zealand						3		
Nicaragua	1	2		1	3		2	
Norway						2		
O. Mongolia								

[a] Only values greater than 0 are given.
[b] Not scored.

Table 13 (cont.)

A. Domestic Conflict: I

Nations	Assassinations		General Strikes		Guerrilla Wars		Major Government Crises		Purges	
	55–57	58–60	55–57	58–60	55–57	58–60	55–57	58–60	55–57	58–60
Pakistan	1	1					4	1	1	1
Panama				1		1		2	1	1
Paraguay						2		3		
Peru	1		1						1	
Philippines	1	1	1		3	3				
Poland										
Portugal										
Romania									1	
Saudi Arabia								1		
South Africa		3	2	3		2		2	1	
Spain			1	1		1		1		
Sudan	n.s.		n.s.		n.s.		n.s.		n.s.	1
Sweden							1			
Switzerland										
Syria	2	n.s.		n.s.		n.s.	1	n.s.	2	n.s.
Thailand		n.s.	1			1	1	1		
Tunisia	n.s.		n.s.	1	n.s.		n.s.	1	n.s.	
Turkey							1	1		1
UAR	n.s.		n.s.		n.s.		n.s.		n.s.	
U.S.S.R.									1	
UK										
U.S.A.										
Uruguay				1						
Venezuela	n.s.	1	n.s.	4	n.s.	3	n.s.	3	n.s.	2
N. Vietnam	n.s.		n.s.		n.s.		n.s.		n.s.	
S. Vietnam	n.s.	2	n.s.		n.s.	3	n.s.		n.s.	
Yemen										
Yugoslavia		n.s.		n.s.		n.s.		n.s.		n.s.

A. Domestic Conflict: II

Nations	Riots 55–57	Riots 58–60	Demonstrations 55–57	Demonstrations 58–60	Revolutions 55–57	Revolutions 58–60	No. Killed in Domestic Violence 55–57	No. Killed in Domestic Violence 58–60
Afghanistan	1	2		1		1		143
Albania							5	
Argentina	25	4	8	3	4	4	4,370	41
Australia								
Austria	n.s.ᵃ		n.s.		n.s.		n.s.	
Belgium	2	6	1	9				1
Bolivia	5	7	1		1	6	4	261
Brazil	3	7	1		3	1	15	8
Bulgaria			1					
Burma					3	3	268	934
Cambodia		1						1
Canada	6	7						
Ceylon	5	4		1			10	845
Chile	1	3	1					5
China	2	1			3	4	2,000	4,562
Rep. of China	11	5	3		1	2	566	203
Colombia					1			
Costa Rica							20	
Cuba	8	7	15	3		4	555	4,873
Czechoslovakia	1		5				4	
Denmark								
Dom. Republic		3		1	1	1		144
Ecuador	4	9	1	2			1	50
Egypt	1	n.s.	1	n.s.		n.s.	5	n.s.
El Salvador		2		1		1		1
Ethiopia		1				1		2,225

ᵃ Not scored.

Table 13 (cont.)

A. Domestic Conflict: II

Nations	Riots		Demonstrations		Revolutions		No. Killed in Domestic Violence	
	55–57	58–60	55–57	58–60	55–57	58–60	55–57	58–60
Finland	9	14	12	1				39
France				33				
E. Germany								
W. Germany				1				
Greece		1						1
Guatemala	6	6	6	2	2	2	20	
Haiti	5	1	4	2	4	2	53	42
Honduras	4	2			3	2	38	193
Hungary	15		1		1		13,389	
India	39	41	20	10	3	2	1,672	1,492
Indonesia	1	4	2	4	3	1	4,177	13,641
Iran	1	4		1			127	3
Iraq	15	16	7	3		5	55	2,401
Irish Republic								
Israel	2	3	1					7
Italy	2	12	4	2				1
Japan	4	15		19				
Jordan	3	2	4		1	1		10
N. Korea			1	8				
S. Korea	3	20	n.s.	2	n.s.	4	n.s.	293
Laos	n.s.				n.s.	4	n.s.	
Lebanon	4	30		2		1	23	199
Liberia			n.s.		n.s.		n.s.	183
Libya	n.s.	1		6			n.s.	
Mexico	3	18	n.s.	1	n.s.		28	21
Morocco	n.s.	5			n.s.	2	n.s.	3
Nepal	1		1			2	28	7
Netherlands		1						

Country	1	2	3	4	5	6	7
New Zealand							214
Nicaragua	3	3	1			3	
Norway	2	1	1		2		
O. Mongolia							
Pakistan	1	3		1	3		7
Panama	7			3	3		12
Paraguay					4	10	60
Peru				1	1		2
Philippines	6		9		1	5	66
Poland		8			1	140	
Portugal							2
Romania							
Saudi Arabia							
South Africa	17	11	20		4	69	353
Spain	2	3	1				7
Sudan	n.s.	n.s.		n.s.	n.s.	n.s.	
Sweden							
Switzerland	3	2	n.s.	1			n.s.
Syria	1	1		1	1	13	5
Thailand	n.s.	n.s.					
Tunisia	2	2	13			n.s.	
Turkey	n.s.	n.s.	1		1		15
UAR	3	4	5		6	n.s.	
U.S.S.R.	1	5					
UK	4	2					
U.S.A.	5	2	3		3	50	1
Uruguay							
Venezuela	n.s.	n.s.				22	475
N. Vietnam	n.s.	n.s.		n.s.		n.s.	
S. Vietnam	n.s.			n.s.		n.s.	
Yemen				2			1,545
Yugoslavia			n.s.		n.s.		n.s.

Table 13 (cont.)

B. Foreign Conflict: I

Nations	Antiforeign Demonstrations		Negative Sanctions		Protests		Severance of Diplomatic Relations		Expulsion or Recall of Ambassador		Expulsion or Recall of Lesser Officials		Threats	
	55–57	58–60	55–57	58–60	55–57	58–60	55–57	58–60	55–57	58–60	55–57	58–60	55–57	58–60
Afghanistan	3	1			4	2	1								
Albania					1	1				1	1				
Argentina	8	7				3		2	2	1	1	3			
Australia	1	1				1									1
Austria	n.s.[a]	2	n.s.		n.s.	6	n.s.		n.s.	1	n.s.	1	n.s.		
Belgium		4				2				2		1			
Bolivia		2				1				1					1
Brazil				2		2				1					3
Bulgaria		1			1										
Burma		4				1									
Cambodia	1	1	1		1	2	1								
Canada		2	1					1		1	1	1	1	2
Ceylon					1	1									
Chile		4		2	2	2	1								
China		6		1	2	9	1			1			3	16
Rep. of China	2				2	1		2							1
Colombia		4				1		1							
Costa Rica		1				3		1	1						
Cuba		8		4		3		1	1	2		2			1
Czechoslovakia	1				7	4					2	1			
Denmark		1				1					3				
Dom. Republic		2		1					3			4			
Ecuador		3						1	1						
Egypt	16	n.s.	2	n.s.	4	n.s.	2	n.s.		n.s.	3	n.s.	19	n.s.
El Salvador	1	3			1						1				n.s.
Ethiopia												1			
Finland						1									

Country												
France	15		4	12	18				5		3	5
E. Germany	2	3		3	4							18
W. Germany	1	1		12	1	1						2
Greece	4		3	3	3	1						
Guatemala				3		3	1				1	1
Haiti	3	6	2	2	1	1	2					1
Honduras	3	3	5	3	3	1						
Hungary		8		4			4		2		3	
India	27		1	4	15	10	1	1		3	3	11
Indonesia	2		2	3	3	1	1	2	1	1	1	8
Iran				4	1	1	1	1		1	1	2
Iraq	7		3	2	1	1	1		1		2	1
Irish Republic	41	25			1						13	3
Israel	2			11	1		1	1			1	1
Italy	2	10		1	2			1		2	1	1
Japan	13	9		4	4							1
Jordan	22	1	2	2	1	2		1	1		5	2
N. Korea		1		1								1
S. Korea	7	7	1	3	3	1		1				4
Laos	n.s.		n.s.	n.s.	1		n.s.	n.s.	n.s.		n.s.	1
Lebanon	5	8	2	3	2	1	2		1	1	1	1
Liberia				1								
Libya	n.s.	1		n.s.	n.s.	3	n.s.				n.s.	1
Mexico	1	5	1	1	1		3					1
Morocco	n.s.	1	8	n.s.	12	1	n.s.	1	2	2	n.s.	2
Nepal	1	2		3	3							
Netherlands				2	4		1		1			
New Zealand				2	2		1					
Nicaragua		4		3	2	1		1	1	1	2	
Norway		2		1	3			1				
O. Mongolia												
Pakistan	3	2	1	10	5	2	2				3	2
Panama		4		2	2							1
Paraguay			1		2	1		1				

Table 13 (cont.)

B. Foreign Conflict: I

Nations	Antiforeign Demonstrations		Negative Sanctions		Protests		Severance of Diplomatic Relations		Expulsion or Recall of Ambassador		Expulsion or Recall of Lesser Officials		Threats	
	55-57	58-60	55-57	58-60	55-57	58-60	55-57	58-60	55-57	58-60	55-57	58-60	55-57	58-60
Peru		1		1			1	1						1
Philippines		1		1						1	1		1	
Poland	14				5	3				1		8	1	
Portugal					2	1					1			1
Romania					2	2						4		1
Saudi Arabia		1	1	3	4	3							2	
South Africa		1		1	1	2		1			1			
Spain	1												1	
Sudan	n.s.	1	n.s.	2	n.s.	1	n.s.		n.s.		n.s.	1	n.s.	
Sweden	1	2			6	1					5			
Switzerland	1	1				2					1	4		
Syria	2	n.s.	2	n.s.	5	n.s.	1	n.s.	n.s.	n.s.	2	n.s.	8	n.s.
Thailand		1		3	2	1						1		1
Tunisia	n.s.	5	n.s.	5	n.s.	3	n.s.	1	n.s.	2	n.s.	1	n.s.	5
Turkey	3	3		1	3	2					2		2	
UAR	n.s.	9	n.s.	10	n.s.	13	n.s.	1	n.s.	4	n.s.	1	n.s.	7
U.S.S.R.	6	12		4	26	25			2	2	6	5	25	72
UK	1	5	1		30	10					2		9	2
U.S.A.	23	8	8	8	33	51		1	1	4	7	6	19	35
Uruguay		2			1	2		1						
Venezuela		5			n.s.	1		1	2		1	1		1
N. Vietnam	n.s.	1	n.s.	3	n.s.	2	n.s.		n.s.		n.s.	1	n.s.	
S. Vietnam	n.s.		n.s.		n.s.	n.s.	n.s.		n.s.		n.s.		n.s.	
Yemen		n.s.		n.s.	3	n.s.		n.s.	1	2	1	n.s.	1	n.s.
Yugoslavia	n.s.	1		2	5	13				2		1		1

B. Foreign Conflict: II

Nations	Military Actions 55–57	58–60	Wars 55–57	58–60	Troop Movements 55–57	58–60	Mobilizations 55–57	58–60	Accusations 55–57	58–60	No. Killed in Foreign Violence 55–57	58–60
Afghanistan	1				1		1		1	2		
Albania		1				1			4	4		1
Argentina		2							2	1		1
Australia	1								1	5		
Austria	n.s.ª		n.s.		n.s.		n.s.		n.s.		n.s.	
Belgium										1		
Bolivia									2	1		
Brazil												101
Bulgaria									1	2		2
Burma		1							2	2	83	53
Cambodia	1	1							1	3	1	36
Canada								1	1	3		
Ceylon												
Chile		1							2			
China	3	3		3	3	3		3	45	47	2,385	91
Rep. of China	3	3		3	1				8	6	2,385	29
Colombia										1		
Costa Rica	1								4	1		1
Cuba								2	2	36		4
Czechoslovakia		1							9	3		
Denmark												
Dom. Republic						1			1	13		5
Ecuador									1			
Egypt	3	n.s.	1	n.s.	1	n.s.	1	n.s.	79	n.s.	4,875	
El Salvador		n.s.		n.s.		n.s.		n.s.		1	n.s.	n.s.
Ethiopia		1							1			
Finland		1							1	1		20

ª Not scored.

Table 13 (cont.)

B. Foreign Conflict: II

Nations	Military Actions 55–57	58–60	Wars 55–57	58–60	Troop Movements 55–57	58–60	Mobilizations 55–57	58–60	Accusations 55–57	58–60	No. Killed in Foreign Violence 55–57	58–60
France	1	3	1	3	1	2	1	1	21	13	4,486	68
E. Germany		1							2	10		
W. Germany									2	12		
Greece									2	4		1
Guatemala		1								17		7
Haiti									1	3		
Honduras	1			1					1	3	35	9
Hungary		2	1						10	13	13,350	
India	2	1			1	2			28	22	16	57
Indonesia		1							2	7		2
Iran					1	4			1	2		41
Iraq						1		1	8	8		
Irish Republic						1						
Israel	3	3	1	3			1		141	23	5,228	64
Italy									2	7		
Japan										8		
Jordan	3	2				1			44	21	263	17
N. Korea		3							6	3		15
S. Korea		2				1			21	7		19
Laos	n.s.	1	n.s.		n.s.	1	n.s.		n.s.	11	n.s.	35
Lebanon		1				1			1	3		12
Liberia										1		
Libya	n.s.		n.s.		n.s.		n.s.		n.s.		n.s.	
Mexico						1				2		
Morocco	n.s.		n.s.		n.s.	1	n.s.		n.s.	6	n.s.	7
Nepal						1				1		
Netherlands						3			6	3		1

Country												
New Zealand									1			
Nicaragua	2						1		10	4	35	10
Norway									1	1		
O. Mongolia										2		3
Pakistan	2								21	13	20	
Panama										5		
Paraguay			1							7		1
Peru									1	2		
Philippines										3		
Poland							1		4	9		
Portugal									1	1		
Romania										3		
Saudi Arabia							1		14	6		
South Africa									3	4		
Spain	1	1							2			20
Sudan	n.s.			n.s.	n.s.	n.s.			n.s.		n.s.	
Sweden									2	2		
Switzerland			n.s.									
Syria	3	n.s.		2	2	2			60	n.s.	56	n.s.
Thailand		1	n.s.						3	1		18
Tunisia	n.s.	3		n.s.	1	n.s.			n.s.	10	n.s.	68
Turkey	1			1	1				7	3		41
UAR	n.s.	3	3	n.s.	2	n.s.			n.s.	60		84
U.S.S.R.		2	3	3		1			142	125	n.s.	1
UK	3	1		2	6	1			25	13	13,350	8
U.S.A.		1		3	20				63	77	4,509	133
Uruguay												
Venezuela					2					12		
N. Vietnam	n.s.	2	1	n.s.		n.s.			n.s.	13	n.s.	35
S. Vietnam	n.s.	1	2	n.s.	1	n.s.			n.s.	12	n.s.	39
Yemen	1	n.s.	n.s.						18	n.s.	23	
Yugoslavia				1	n.s.				15	39	23	n.s.

a Not scored.

Table 13 (cont.)

DEFINITIONS OF CONFLICT BEHAVIOR MEASURES

Domestic Conflict Behavior

1. *Assassination:* The politically motivated murder or attempted murder of a high governmental official or politician. Among high governmental officials are included the governors of states or provinces, the mayors of large cities, members of the cabinet, and members of the national legislature. Among high politicians are included members of the inner core of the ruling party or group and leaders of the opposition. An example of an assassination is the "politically motivated" murder of the Governor of Eva Péron Province, Argentina, February 1, 1955.

2. *General Strike:* Any strike of industrial or service workers which involves more than one employer and that is aimed against national governmental policies or authority. A strike is not considered general unless at least 1,000 workers are involved. General strikes do not include those strikes whose nature is to force the government or private industry to grant wage or working concessions. An example of a general strike is the strike of 14,500 African clothing workers in Johannesburg, Union of South Africa, November 19, 1957, in protest against a law requiring certain jobs be held by whites.

3. *Guerrilla War:* Armed activity on the part of bands of citizens or irregular forces aimed at the overthrow of the existing government. Such activity may take the form of sporadic attacks on police posts, small villages, government patrols, or military barracks. A country is also considered to have guerrilla war when sporadic bombing, sabotage, or terrorism occurs. As defined here, guerrilla warfare was present in Cuba during the three years, 1955–1957, of interest.

4. *Major Government Crisis:* Any rapidly developing situation which threatens (excluding revolution) to bring the immediate downfall of the present government. Such situations are usually evidenced by the declaration of military law, state of siege, or the suspension or abrogation of the constitution. A vote of no confidence by a parliamentary majority, or the forced resignation or impeachment of top officials are also considered major government crises. A new major government crisis is not counted unless at least three months of stability have intervened since the previous crisis. A major government crisis is exemplified by the situation leading up to the abdication of the King of Cambodia, March 2, 1955, in protest against Nationalist "politicians" who were trying to alter his policies.

5. *Purge:* The systematic elimination by the political elite either of opposition within their ranks or of opposition within the country by jailing or execution. "Elimination of opposition" refers to the arrest, jailing, exiling, or execution of the opposition leaders. The arrest or execution of non-leader members of opposition groups does not constitute a purge. If the elimination of opposition continues over a period of time without a relaxation of more than three months, then it is one purge. An elimination of opposition incident upon the take over of the government by a new political elite, regardless of whether a purge had been carried on by the old elite up to the take over, is to be considered a new purge only if the opposition purged includes elite politically and/or ideologically associated with the previous regime—if the elite taking over continues to eliminate the same leaders without adding a new category of opposition (e.g. Catholic leaders who were untouched during previous regime) then it is not a new purge as here defined. "Arrest" is considered synonymous with "jailing" and carries no idea of time detained—the fact of arrest *per se* is sufficient to indicate a purge. An example of a purge is the arrest by Jordanian police of more than fifty "leftist" leaders, civil employees, government members, and army officers thought to be hostile to the regime, April–May, 1957.

6. *Riot:* Any violent demonstration or clash of a large group of citizens. The term "violence" refers to the use of physical force, and "large" means at least one hundred people involved. The existence of a riot is generally evidenced by the destruction of property, people being wounded or killed, or by the use of the police of riot control equipment such as clubs, guns, or water cannons. Arrests *per se* do not indicate a riot. Riots of a distinct anti-foreign nature are categorized as anti-foreign demonstrations. A riot as here defined occurred in Turkey, October 24, 1957, when five hundred university students clashed with police as anti-foreign demonstrations. A riot as here defined occurred in Turkey, October 24, 1957, when five hundred university students clashed with police in support of ex-president Inonu.

7. *Anti-government Demonstration:* Any unorganized peaceful, public gathering of at least one hundred people for the primary purpose of displaying or voicing their opposition to governmental policies or authority. This does not include political party rallies or general strikes. Student strikes aimed at the

government are considered anti-government demonstrations. A demonstration which involves the use of force is categorized as a riot. An illustration of a demonstration is the gathering of 100,000 Belgians to protest against a proposed cut in governmental subsidies to Roman Catholic schools, Belgium, March 26, 1955.

8. *Revolution*: Any armed successful or unsuccessful attempt on the part of a group of citizenry to form an independent government (not including colonial rebellions), or any illegal or forced change in the top governmental elites or any attempt at such a change. This may be in the nature of a coup d'état, or an attempted takeover on a grand scale, involving pitched battles between opposing forces. When an attempt to overthrow the government, however, involves only scattered and irregular forces who attack from hiding, it is categorized as a guerrilla war. A revolution occurred in Ecuador, August 1–8, 1956, when a two-hundred man army led by a Lt. Colonel and a Senator attempted to overthrow the government.

9. *Number Killed in Domestic Violence*: This is a summation of the number killed as a direct consequence of any domestic inter-group violence in the nature of riots, strikes, revolutions, guerrilla war, banditry, and tribal warfare. This does not include murders, executions, and suicides. The number of killed for Indonesia in 1955, for example, is 4,176 and is the result of guerrilla war and revolution.

Foreign Conflict Behavior

1. *Antiforeign Demonstration*: Any demonstration or riot by more than 100 people directed at a particular foreign country (or group of countries) or its policies. This includes attacking an embassy, legation, or information office of another country, or attacking for political reasons either foreign nationals on the street or their property (e.g., plantations). This also includes the gathering of more than one hundred people to hear speeches and to march in protest against the policy of another country. Demonstrations and riots against the foreign occupying authority in the occupied part of a country are considered antiforeign demonstrations. Also included in this category are strikes against the goods of another nation, either by dock workers or consumers, and attacks on border posts by unofficial irregular groups (e.g., the Irish Republican Army). An instance of a demonstration is the gathering of 2,000 Warsaw students to publicly protest against the U.S.S.R. and to accuse her of the World War II massacre of Polish officers, Poland, October 25, 1956.

2. *Negative Sanction*: Any act on the part of a government which has as its purpose the punishment of another country for its behavior. This includes such acts as boycotts, withdrawal of military or economic aid, freezing of assets, embargo, or limitation of movement of the other's nationals within the country. Negative sanctions do not include expulsion or recall of diplomats, severance of diplomatic relations, military action and war. An example of a negative sanction is the stopping of all oil shipments to France and England by Saudi Arabia, November 8, 1956, in protest against their actions in the Mid-East War.

3. *Protest*: Any official diplomatic communication or governmental statement by the executive leaders of a country which has as its primary purpose to protest against the actions of another nation. Diplomatic notes of protest are counted as are editorials of protest appearing in a leading government newspaper of totalitarian countries. For example, Bulgaria protested to the U.S. on February 4, 1956, over propaganda balloons being sent over her territory.

4. *Severance of Diplomatic Relations*: The complete withdrawal from all formal diplomatic relations with another country. Such was the case with the Republic of China, for example, when she severed relations with Egypt when the latter recognized the mainland Chinese government.

5. *Expulsion or Recall of Ambassador*: Any expulsion of an ambassador from another country, or any recalling for other than administrative reasons an ambassador to another country. This does not include any expulsion or recall involved during the severance of diplomatic relations. An instance of this measure is Venezuela's recall of her ambassador to Argentina in a dispute over rules of asylum, July 6, 1957.

6. *Expulsion or Recall of Lesser Officials*: Any expulsion of diplomatic officials from another country of lesser than diplomatic rank, or any recalling for other than administrative reasons, such officials. This does not include any expulsion or recall involved in the severance of diplomatic relations. Each act of expulsion or recall is counted rather than the number of officials expelled or recalled. For example, if three diplomats from the same country are expelled or recall at the same time for spying, this is counted as one act. An expulsion of a lesser official was made by the Netherlands, for example, on January 22, 1957, when she expelled a U.S.S.R. Embassy official and charged him with spying.

413

Table 13 (cont.)

7. *Threat*: Any official diplomatic communication or governmental statement by the executive leaders of a country which states or implies that a particular country (or group of countries) will incur certain negative sanctions if it acts in a certain way. Such negative sanctions may not only include those mentioned under "negative sanctions" above, but also severance of diplomatic relations or the use of force. Editorials containing such threats appearing in the leading government newspapers of totalitarian countries are counted. An example of a threat is the statement made by the American Secretary of State, October 17, 1957, when he warned the U.S.S.R. that an attack by her on the territory of Turkey "will bring U.S. retaliation against the territory of the U.S.S.R."

8. *Military Action*: Any action by members of the regular forces of a nation which are directed against the property or citizens of another country and in which fire power is used. When the number of soldiers of a nation involved in the action equals or exceeds in number .02 per cent of the population of the country, then that action is categorized as a war for that country. Military action includes any attack on coastal shipping by gunboats, any attack on a foreign plane by one's own planes or anti-aircraft batteries, shelling of another's territory, or exchange of gunfire between border patrols. Such military action in terms of border clashes, for example, occurred between Afghanistan and Pakistan, 1956.

9. *War*: Any military action for a particular country in which the number of its soldiers involved equal or exceed .02 per cent of its population. This number need not be actually involved in the shooting, but must be involved at the front logistically or as reserves. With respect to this definition, the Mid-East War was a war for France, England, Egypt, and Israel.

10. *Troop Movement*: Any rapid movement to or massing of large bodies of troops, naval units, or air squadrons in a particular area for the purpose of deterring the military action of another nation, gaining concessions, or as a show of strength. Such movement may take place within a nation, or to or between overseas bases or positions. A troop movement occurred during October 19–24, 1956, when Soviet armored units moved into Poland, Soviet troops moved to the East German border with Poland, and two Soviet cruisers stationed themselves off Danzig harbor.

11. *Mobilization*: Any rapid increase in military strength through the calling up of reserves, the activation of additional military units, or the demothballing of military equipment, which is directed at another country (or group of countries). A rapid increase which is due to a change in policy consequent on the change of governments is not counted. The declaration of a state of emergency with respect to another country is categorized as mobilization. An example of mobilization is the general activation of the Nicaraguan reserves by presidential order on May 1, 1957, with respect to a dispute with Honduras.

12. *Accusation*: Any official diplomatic or governmental statement by the executive leaders of a country which makes a charge or allegation against another country (or group of countries). Denunciations are included as are derogatory statements about the character of another nation, its people, or leaders. Editorials containing such accusations appearing in the leading government newspapers of totalitarian countries are counted. An example of an accusation is Yemen's September 17, 1957 charge against England that she had attacked several Yemen towns.

13. *Number Killed in Foreign Violence*: This is the total number of persons killed as a direct consequence of any foreign violence in which the country is involved. If Yemen and the United Kingdom, for example, are involved in military action against each other, and the total number killed in the action is 1,000, then the value on the number of killed in foreign violence for each country is 1,000. Deaths resulting from colonial violence are not counted.

Table 14

SATISFACTION INDEX

Country	Score	Country	Score	Country	Score
Australia	4.75	Uruguay	4.00	Panama	3.00
Belgium	4.75	Austria	3.75	Turkey	3.00
Canada	4.75	Israel	3.75	Venezuela	3.00
Denmark	4.75	Costa Rica	3.67	Greece	2.75
Iceland	4.75	Lebanon	3.67	Egypt	2.67
Netherlands	4.75	Indonesia	3.50	El Salvador	2.67
New Zealand	4.75	Iran	3.50	Guatemala	2.67
Norway	4.75	Pakistan	3.50	Korea	2.67
Sweden	4.75	Tunisia	3.50	Nicaragua	2.67
Switzerland	4.75	Brazil	3.33	Peru	2.67
United States	4.75	Colombia	3.33	Yugoslavia	2.50
Morocco	4.50	Mexico	3.33	Bolivia	2.33
United Kingdom	4.50	Bulgaria	3.25	Ceylon	2.33
Portugal	4.33	Cuba	3.25	Dominican Republic	2.33
Union of S. Africa	4.33	Cyprus	3.25	Ecuador	2.33
Finland	4.25	Italy	3.25	Iraq	2.33
Argentina	4.00	Spain	3.25	Syria	2.33
Czechoslovakia	4.00	Chile	3.00	Thailand	2.33
France	4.00	Haiti	3.00	Paraguay	2.25
W. Germany	4.00	India	3.00	Philippines	1.50
Ireland	4.00	Japan	3.00		

Table 15

MODERNITY INDEX

	Country	Score	Country	Score	
	United States	2.54	Colombia	−.20	
	New Zealand	1.91	Lebanon	−.21	
	Switzerland	1.83	Mexico	−.21	
	Australia	1.71	Brazil	−.23	
	Sweden	1.70	Paraguay	−.26	
	Denmark	1.54	Peru	−.30	
	United Kingdom	1.51	Turkey	−.36	
High	Canada	1.49	Ecuador	−.37	Mid-
modern	Norway	1.41	El Salvador	−.40	modern
	Iceland	1.26	Nicaragua	−.40	
	Luxembourg	1.07	Ceylon	−.41	
	Belgium	.94	Guatemala	−.41	
	Ireland	.93	Dominican Repub.	−.46	
	Netherlands	.89	Honduras	−.46	
	Finland	.81	Egypt	−.47	
	France	.80	Korea	−.49	
	Austria	.61	Syria	−.49	
	W. Germany	.59	Thailand	−.49	
	Argentina	.57	Tunisia	−.49	
	E. Germany	.50	Morocco	−.50	
	Uruguay	.47	Philippines	−.50	
	Israel	.46	Burma	−.53	
	U.S.S.R.	.40	Taiwan	−.53	
	Czechoslovakia	.34	Jordan	−.54	
	Hungary	.24	Bolivia	−.56	
	Japan	.20	Iraq	−.57	
	Bulgaria	.19	Ethiopia	−.60	
	Poland	.19	Iran	−.62	
	Romania	.12	China	−.65	
Mid-	Italy	.11	Ghana	−.67	Low
modern	Cuba	.10	India	−.70	modern
	Chile	.07	Malaya	−.73	
	Costa Rica	.03	Haiti	−.74	
	Panama	.01	Libya	−.77	
	Spain	.00	Pakistan	−.87	
	Union of S. Africa	−.04	Afghanistan	−.97	
	Cyprus	−.05	Saudi Arabia	−.98	
	Greece	−.06	Indonesia	−1.13	
	Yugoslavia	−.09	Laos	−1.25	
	Albania	−.10	Sudan	−1.37	
	Venezuela	−.10	Cambodia	−1.46	
	Portugal	−.16	Liberia	−1.62	

INDEX

Abel, T., 261, 262, 294n
Aberle, D. F., 38
Abney, F. G., 50n
Adams, S., 38n
Africa, independence in, 113
Aggression, psychological theories of, 33–46; social sources of, 85–97; structural theory of, 370 (*Also see* Discontent, Frustration-aggression theory)
Alexander II, 75, 76, 77, 83
Alexander III, 75
Alexander, R. H., 243n
Alford, R., 339n
Algeria, 27
Alienation, 2, 3, 4; as a cause of civil violence, 56–66; stages of, 62–66 (*Also see* Anomie)
Alker, H. R., Jr., 127n, 205n, 246n, 247n, 252n, 393
Allen, W. E. D., 25n
Almond, G. A., 62n, 132n, 144, 157, 159, 165, 181n, 225, 229, 240, 242n
Amos, J. R., 393n
Anabaptists, 69
Anderson, C. W., 267n
Andrews, W. G., 267n
Anomic violence, 229–41 *passim* (*Also see* Turmoil)
Anomie, 22, 329; and political stability, 103–4 (*Also see* Alienation)
Apartheid, 48
Appley, M. H., 59n
Apter, D. E., 116n, 242n
Aptheker, H., 61n
Arendt, H., 10
Argentina, 236; coup d'etat against Peron, 40
Aristotle, 1, 58

Aspirations, 109, 117–18 (*See also* Expectations)
Assassinations, cross-national data on, 396–98; in Mexican politics, 269–82
Atomization, as a cause of Scottish separatism, 331–33
Australia, 134
Austria, 71, 128–29, 159
Authoritarianism, 100n
Authority, patterns of, 4, 5, 98–106 *passim* (*Also see* Congruence theory)

Baggaley, A. B., 252n
Banks, A. S., 123n, 181n, 182n, 197n, 222n, 393
Barringer, H. R., 244
Bay, C., 157, 181n
Beals, R., 278n
Beer, S. H., 99, 106n
Behavioral variables, 2, 18–21
Belaunde Terry, Fernando, 359, 363, 364
Bendix, R., 73n
Bennet, W. T., 297
Benson, O., 393n
Berkowitz, L., 31n, 33n, 34n, 35, 38n, 44, 49n, 50n, 54n, 85, 108n, 136, 181n, 185n, 187n, 305n, 309
Beyle, T., 252n
Black Revolution, 4
Blalock, H. M., Jr., 188, 205n, 253n, 393
Blanksten, G., 244n
Bolivia, 128, 129, 234
Bolsheviks, 77 (*Also see* Communism)
Bonnet, G., 26n
Bosch, Juan, 299, 301–2, 304, 306, 308
Boston Tea Party, 79
Boulding, K. E., 6n, 209n, 249
Bowman, M. J., 128n
Boxer Rebellion of 1900, 71

417

Brazil, 92; 1964 coup d'etat, 261, 262, 264, 265, 295–313
Brennan, J., 71n
Breul, H., 181n
Brinton, C., 6n, 10, 14, 16n, 17, 24, 32n, 59, 60n, 83, 245
Broch, T., 92n
Brogan, D. W., 45
Brown, F. L., 393n
Brown, J. S., 59n, 63n
Brown, R., 59n
Brozek, J., 69n
Bruning, J. L., 393n
Brutzkus, B., 73n
Buchanan, W., 82, 393n
Budge, I., 339n
Bullard, R., 78n
Burke, E., 11, 24
Buss, A. H., 108n, 136, 156, 181n, 225
Bustamante y Rivero, J. L., 359, 366
Butler, D., 334n
Bwy, D., 47, 119–22, 186n, 370, 383

Campbell, A., 134n
Campbell, D. T., 231
Cantril, H., 39n, 82, 83n, 121, 124n, 144, 181n, 296
Carr, E. H., 84n
Carrasco, P., 280n
Cartwright, D., 52n
Case studies, limitations of, 12
Caso, A., 278n
Castro, Fidel, 93n
Cattell, R., 181n
Causal models, of civil strife, 185, 204–9; of political instability, 252–56
Chanderli, M., 27n
Chateaubriand, F. R., 24
Child, I. L., 137, 183n
Chile, 94n
China, 71, 93n; Communist Revolution in, 12
Christoph, J., 336n
Civil strife, causes of, 184–211; cross-national data on, 213–15; magnitude of, 56 (Also see Civil violence, Conflict, Political instability, Political violence)
Civil violence, defined, 33n, 188; forms of, 54–57 (Also see Civil strife, Conflict, Political instability, Political violence)
Cnudde, C. F., 253n
Coercion, 137; and civil strife, 185–86, 195–97, 200–11 passim; cross-national data on, 219–22; effects of, 123; measures of, 122; and modernity, 163–68; and political instability, 154–68, 174–78; and political instability in Latin America, 225–26, 234–41; and political violence, 23–24, 306–7
Coerciveness (See Coercion)

Cofer, C. N., 59n
Cohen, A. R., 48n, 70n
Cohn, N. R. C., 45n, 50n, 52
Coleman, J. S., 132n, 157, 159, 165, 181n, 229, 242n
Communism, 298–99; in Germany, 287
Conflict, and frustration, 110; and modernization, 114–18 (Also see Civil strife, Civil violence, Political instability, Political violence)
Conflict theory, 3
Congo, 42, 48
Congruence theory, 4, 5, 98–106, 263, 329
Connor, W., 325n, 337n
Conroe, W., 149, 181n
Conspiracy, as a cause of political violence, 13–14; causes of, 202–4; cross-national data on, 213–15; defined, 188
Constitutionalism, 100n
Contingency tables, statistical tests for, 377–83, 384–85, 390–92
Correlation techniques: contingency coefficient, 382–83; Phi coefficient, 382–83; product-moment correlation, 372–74; rank-order correlation, 374–77
Coser, L., 6n, 209n
Coules, J., 48n
Coupland, R., 325n
Coups d'état, 32; in Brazil, 1964, 297–313; in Germany, 285; in Latin America, 244, 252; in Peru, 359–68 passim
Crotty, W. J., 124n, 392
Crowe, B. L., 71n
Crozier, B., 11n
Cuba, 94, 235, 238; revolution in, 93n; and U.S. economic presence, 244–45
Cutright, P., 124n, 132n, 143, 165, 181, 224
Cuzzort, R. P., 248n
Czechoslovakia, 242–43

Dahl, R. A., 60
Dahlke, H. O., 46n
Dahrendorf, R., 339n
Davies, E. H., 325n
Davies, J. C., 2, 4, 15, 36, 52n, 59n, 94, 110, 111, 112, 181n, 244n, 371
Davis, H., 232n
de Grazia, A., 16n, 31n
de Grazia, S., 106n
de Hoyos, R., 41n
Democracy, 98–106; in Latin America, 224–25
Demonstration effect, 245, 250
Demonstrations, in Indonesia, 353–58 (Also see Turmoil)
Denison, E. F., 328n, 334n
Denton, F. H., 171, 181n
Depression of the 1930's, 71, 80–81
de Schweinitz, K., 165, 181n, 245n
de Sismondi, J. C. L. S., 9n
de Sola Pool, I., 222n